# RED DAW

# THE ULTIMATE BIOGRAPHY

# SIR LEWIS HAMILTON

DAN LYNCH

A catalogue record for this book is available at the British Library

ISBN: 978-1-0684254-1-7



Published by Dan Lynch Publications

# Table of Contents

# Over The Hill

## 6.26pm local time, Abu Dhabi, 8 December 2024

Lap 58 of 58.

Lewis Hamilton, having started from 16th on the grid in his Mercedes, and teammate George Russell, having started from sixth, entered the final lap at the Yas Marina Circuit.

Hamilton's final-ever lap for Mercedes in Formula One.

As they approached Turn 5, Russell was still running fourth, but Hamilton—now on medium tyres after his last pitstop—was relentlessly closing in.

Surely Hamilton, a man who some had dismissed as 'over the hill,' 'past his best,' 'too old,' and 'not giving 100%" couldn't catch him —let alone beat him.

*"Do your talking on the track."*

Hamilton placed the Mercedes right on the edge, pushing the car to its absolute limit. Ahead, beyond view, another battle was being decided. Norris appeared to be holding his nerve at the front. His teammate, Piastri, had clawed his way to tenth—the final points-paying position. If McLaren held on for just half a lap more, they would reclaim the Constructors' World Championship for the first time in 27 years.

Entering the final half-lap, Hamilton was right on Russell's gearbox. Surely, he couldn't find a way past. Hamilton had a 'shelf life,' Toto Wolff had said. *A shelf life.* Maybe, but *not yet.*

*"Rise above it, son."*

Norris crossed the line, clinching victory, and McLaren were crowned Constructors' Champions. Zak Brown leapt in delight, shouting, cheering, and hugging everyone within reach. The McLaren garage erupted. Two battles were decided simultaneously: McLaren had ended a 27-year drought to reclaim the Constructors' title, and Norris secured second place in the World Drivers' Championship.

Only one fight remained—Hamilton versus Russell.

Out of Turn 5, Hamilton got a superb exit and hammered down the straight. The Mercedes strained every sinew. As Hamilton closed on Russell at 200mph, the car began to bounce—a harsh reminder of three years of physical and emotional suffering. *"We don't need to change the car; we know what we're doing."*

Hamilton rapidly closed in the DRS zone as they approached Turn 6. Russell knew exactly where Hamilton was and moved slightly to the inside, revealing his hand. The unspoken message was clear: *"I know you're here, Lewis, but you won't do it—there are only nine corners left."*

Hamilton rolled off the brakes, letting the Mercedes breathe to the outside of Turn 6 to get maximum traction on the exit, which would set him up for the long back straight. Russell, though not overly defensive through Turn 6, had still compromised his exit slightly. The golden rule of motor racing — or rule number one — has always been 'carry as much speed down the next straight as possible,' and Russell had just broken it.

As Norris crossed the line, fireworks erupted, but Hamilton still had one final rocket to launch.

Heading into Turn 9, the long left-hand hairpin, Russell made his customary defensive move when under pressure. He moved to the middle of the track to block the inside line. A rookie error. Hamilton braked as late as his car would allow on the outside. As they entered the last fifty metres before the corner, sparks flew off Russell's Mercedes as his car bottomed out. Bottoming out—losing braking effectiveness—another mistake.

For Hamilton, it all slowed down. Time went into slow motion, going backwards.

His karting titles wheeled into focus: *1995 Cadet Kart, 1996 MSA Kartmasters, 1997 Super One Yamaha, 1999 Italian and European, and the 2000 World Cup.*

Hamilton came off the brakes, turned in, fed in more throttle, easing the Mercedes wider towards the wall and the marbles. Could a driver with a 'shelf life' pass around the outside, on marbles?

*Formula Renault Champion, 2003. Formula 3 Champion, 2005. GP2 Champion, 2006.*

As both Mercedes clipped the left-hand apex, Hamilton was inches from Russell, both cars starting to drift wide. A collision seemed inevitable.

*Seven Formula One World Championships.*

Hamilton pinned the throttle, the car breathed, just like it had on pole in Hungary, just like it had on every lap of every circuit for 29 years. He corrected a minor bit of oversteer and shot past Russell.

*"Do your talking on the track."*

Not bad for someone over the hill, past his best, not giving 100% and no longer good enough.

Frédéric Vasseur clearly knew what he was doing when he signed Hamilton to Ferrari, that was for certain.

Hamilton crossed the finish line in fourth place. He guided the Mercedes towards the pit wall, acknowledging the team that had been his family for 12 unforgettable years. Russell rolled home behind him. In fifth.

Twenty-nine years of dedication distilled into fifty breathtaking seconds of racing. But where did it all begin?

# Red Dawn: The Beginning

From the humble streets of Stevenage, with its cycle paths weaving through green spaces, to the roaring circuits of Formula One, Lewis Hamilton's journey is a tribute to passion, determination, and extraordinary talent. This biography chronicles the evolution of a boy whose fascination with radio-controlled cars grew into a relentless pursuit of racing glory, culminating in a career that not only redefined motorsport but also reshaped its culture.

Born into modest beginnings, Lewis stood out early on for his innate talent. His insatiable hunger for speed drove him forward, eventually catching the attention of Ron Dennis at McLaren, who gave him the opportunity to rise through the ranks. Later, Mercedes would play a significant role in Hamilton's career, solidifying his path to Formula One stardom. Through these pages, you'll follow Hamilton's meteoric rise from karting to the pinnacle of Formula One, exploring key milestones and influential figures, including Frédéric Vasseur, a mentor and confidant who recognised his brilliance in the junior ranks and helped lay the foundation for his rise to stardom.

Yet Hamilton's path was not paved solely with opportunity; it was also forged in adversity. From facing bullying and racism in his formative years to overcoming the pressures of a sport steeped in tradition, every challenge shaped his character and strengthened his resolve. Central to this journey was his family's unwavering support, particularly from his father, who not only invested in Lewis's career but also instilled the values of hard work and resilience.

Each chapter will immerse you in Hamilton's triumphs and trials, offering a closer look at the brilliance and determination that have defined his career. Relive the electrifying moments: his debut season at McLaren and the extraordinary battle with

Fernando Alonso, his partnership with Jenson Button and his Championship success, through to his move to Mercedes and the subsequent era of dominance, along with rivalries with Nico Rosberg and Max Verstappen. The story also explores his advocacy for safety and equality in Formula One—a fight as enduring as his battles on the track.

The narrative also delves into Hamilton's resilience during the pandemic, his struggles with ever-evolving regulations, and the frustrations of wrestling with machines that constantly tested both his patience and skills. Yet, as his journey unfolds, his destiny comes full circle. In 2025, Hamilton reunites with Frédéric Vasseur, the mentor who once guided his early career, this time under the iconic banner of Ferrari. This new alliance, fusing Hamilton's seasoned expertise with Ferrari's illustrious legacy, marks the dawn of an exciting new chapter.

This book not only revisits these unforgettable events but also celebrates the life and legacy of Lewis Hamilton, a driver who has transcended motorsport to become a global icon. Through his skill and determination, his behaviour as a role model, and his advocacy for diversity and inclusion, Hamilton has inspired millions. This is more than a story of trophies and titles; it is a story of resilience, vision, and courage. We uncover what it means to join Ferrari—the legend, the history, and the people who have influenced and shaped the most iconic brand in motorsport.

Join me as we explore the extraordinary life of a man who continues to push boundaries both on and off the track, rewriting what it means to be a champion. From the shadows of his past to the heights of his influence today, Hamilton's journey isn't just about shaping his own future but driving the evolution of motorsport itself. As a new chapter at Ferrari begins in his story, the dawn of a new era in Formula One is on the horizon—a Red Dawn.

# Born to Race

Lewis Hamilton grew up in an industrial town 30 miles north of London during the 1980s and '90s. He was part of a hard-working, mixed-race, blended family. He spent his formative years honing his love of speed and developing the driving skills that would later form the foundation of his outstanding career as a Formula One driver. For forty years, he has been supported by a loving family who have helped him every step of the way, from humble beginnings to achieving global stardom as a seven-time Formula One World Champion. Let's explore the early influences that shaped the young boy who was born to race.

In the heart of Hertfordshire, England, lies Stevenage, a town that blends post-war optimism with the modern vibrancy of a thriving community. After World War II, the expansion of Stevenage was meticulously planned with a vision of modernity and innovation, aimed at attracting London's growing population away from the capital. The town planners sought to create a self-contained community with residential areas, industrial zones, and ample green spaces. One of the pioneering features of this design was the introduction of dedicated cycle paths, something Lewis Hamilton would make great use of in his childhood. These paths were segregated from the main roads, providing Hamilton with a safe environment to revel in his love of speed.

Stevenage in the 1980s was characterised by its diverse, predominantly working-class population. Many residents were employed in manufacturing, engineering, and service industries. The town's proximity to London made it an attractive location for commuters seeking affordable housing outside the capital.

The demographic composition included a mix of families who had relocated from London, as well as immigrants from various parts of the Commonwealth. This diversity contributed to a multicultural community, though it also presented challenges in terms of social integration and economic disparities. It was here, in this ambitious, growing town, that Lewis Carl Davidson Hamilton was born on January 7, 1985.

By the time Hamilton was born, Stevenage had grown significantly from its humble beginnings. Geographically, the town covered an area of approximately 10 square miles. The population in 1985 was around 70,000 residents, reflecting a steady increase due to ongoing development and urban migration.

For a young Lewis Hamilton, this environment offered both opportunities and challenges. The availability of recreational facilities and open spaces provided avenues to explore his interests. However, the economic limitations and social issues typical of a working-class town also meant that resources for pursuing specialised activities, like motorsports, were scarce.

Growing up in Stevenage, Hamilton was immersed in a community that embodied both the legacy of the past and the promise of the future. The town's emphasis on innovation, evident in its aerospace industry and urban planning, may have subtly influenced his fascination with speed and technology.

**The Role of Family Support**

Hamilton's love for speed and competition began long before he ever sat in a race car. As a child in Stevenage, he spent hours riding his bike around his neighbourhood, imagining he was on a racetrack. These early years marked the beginning of his passion for racing, where the thrill of competition first took root, even if it was just racing against himself. At the age of five, during a holiday, Hamilton encountered a go-kart for the first time. It was here that his fascination with things that had engines and wheels truly began, setting the stage for his eventual career in motorsport.

These memories, combined with the support of his father, Anthony, who worked multiple jobs to fund Hamilton's karting career, laid the groundwork for his eventual rise to motorsport greatness. Hamilton's father gave everything to support his son's dream, but it all began with simple things like bike rides around the park and driving go-karts on holiday.

While the support from his family gave him the tools to succeed in racing, the world outside posed challenges that were less forgiving. As a mixed-race child, Hamilton had to navigate both his personal dreams and the societal difficulties that came with his background. From a young age, he faced racial discrimination and bullying at school. This experience, although painful, helped shape his character, instilling a deep sense of resilience and a drive to prove himself in ways that extended beyond the racetrack.

In addition to facing racial discrimination, Hamilton struggled with dyslexia, a condition diagnosed when he was 17. This learning difficulty led to challenges in reading and writing, often resulting in misunderstandings about his academic abilities. Despite these obstacles, Hamilton excelled in subjects like mathematics and physical education. Dyslexia, though a challenge, was something Hamilton shared with other legends in motorsport. It helped shape his resilience, sharpening his focus and memory—traits that would later prove invaluable in high-pressure situations on the racetrack.

School was often a source of frustration for Hamilton. Misunderstood by teachers and classmates, he found solace and confidence on the racetrack. As Sir Jackie Stewart later reflected, overcoming personal struggles, like dyslexia, makes a person more resilient and sharper in other areas. Eddie Jordan and Mario Andretti have also spoken about how their struggles with dyslexia shaped their ability to think outside the box and problem-solve—skills that would later define their success. For Hamilton, his experiences with dyslexia did not hinder him but instead strengthened his tenacity, helping him develop the mental toughness required to succeed in motorsport.

During his school years and early development, Hamilton began immersing himself in the world of motor racing. Among his earliest and most profound influences was Ayrton Senna, the legendary Brazilian Formula One driver. Renowned for his extraordinary prowess in wet conditions and his deeply philosophical approach to racing, Senna's style left an indelible mark on the young Hamilton. Reflecting on his admiration, Hamilton spoke about how Senna was his greatest inspiration, admiring not just his racing style but his passion for life and the sport. It was the way Senna faced adversity and a system that wasn't always kind to him that particularly resonated with Hamilton, and he often reflects on how Senna's legacy continues to inspire him today.

Hamilton's fascination with speed began at a tender age. An often-overlooked aspect of his early years was his success in radio-controlled (RC) car racing and the influence it had on his formative development. At the age of six, Hamilton received a radio-controlled car from his father, sparking his early fascination with racing. Demonstrating exceptional hand-eye coordination, he quickly began competing in local RC car races against adults.

Recognising his son's keen interest and natural aptitude, Anthony Hamilton started taking Lewis to local RC car racing clubs. Despite his young age, Lewis quickly made a name for himself, even competing against grown men. In 1991, at just six years old, he entered the British Radio Car Association (BRCA) National Championship. Remarkably, Lewis finished second, showing his exceptional talent early on—beating adults and proving he had a special gift.

The most formative period for the mind is up to the age of eight, so Hamilton had another two years to develop his skills in vehicle control, mechanics, strategy, and tactics. In modern motorsport, drivers use advanced simulators to prepare for races, simulating both the physical and strategic aspects of competition. Hamilton's early experience with RC car racing acted as a rudimentary version of this technology. It also provided Hamilton with an early education in fundamental racing principles. Controlling an RC car requires precise timing when applying the brakes to navigate corners effectively. He learned to judge distances and anticipate when to slow down—skills that would prove directly transferable to real-world racing.

Although not physically in the vehicle, Hamilton gained an understanding of how weight distribution and speed affect a car's handling. He observed how entering a corner too fast could cause understeer, making the car push wide, while sudden steering inputs could lead to oversteer, causing the rear to step out. He also learned that if he accelerated too hard on exit, he could oversteer and lose control of the rear of the car. By controlling the vehicle from a third-person perspective, Hamilton analysed optimal racing lines—the most efficient path around the track—and how to maintain momentum. This perspective allowed him to visualise the geometry of corners and the importance of smooth trajectories.

Competing against experienced racers, Hamilton developed tactics for overtaking, such as pressuring opponents into mistakes or finding alternative lines to carry more speed. By controlling the car externally, he engaged in a form of simulation that combined fine motor control, timing, and reflexes—all essential for operating a car effectively. He also developed strategic planning, decision-making, and adaptability skills, akin to the responsibilities of a team principal. He learned when to push, where to push, and for how long. For Hamilton, RC car racing was more than a hobby; it was training on multiple levels. In many ways, racing RC cars was like being in a simulator—learning about vehicle behaviour and race strategy simultaneously.

Controlling an RC car requires dissociating oneself from the vehicle and relying solely on visual cues. This external perspective can enhance cognitive abilities related to spatial reasoning and problem-solving. Psychologists suggest that such activities improve the capacity to mentally simulate different scenarios—skills that are highly beneficial in high-speed decision-making environments like motorsport. Hamilton has mentioned that he doesn't consciously engage in 'visualisation' during his Formula One career, possibly because these skills were ingrained at such an early age and developed to a subconscious level through his extensive early training.

Hamilton's early immersion in RC car racing provided him with a unique perspective on motorsport dynamics. Engaging in RC car competitions from a young age, he developed a keen sense of anticipating competitors' moves and adapting to dynamic conditions. Controlling the car remotely forced him to think differently about racing, requiring him not only to anticipate his own actions but also to predict what others might do. This experience honed his ability to make real-time decisions.

By combining this third-person perspective with the first-person experience of karting, Hamilton developed a holistic approach to racing. He could simultaneously focus on his immediate actions while considering the broader context of the race.

A prominent figure in British karting who later mentored Hamilton observed that novice racers, unfamiliar with racing and race strategy, typically displayed a black number plate for their first six races, meaning they started at the back of the grid. Yet Hamilton, even with this black plate, often found himself battling at the front. His performances stood out dramatically, and it quickly became evident to experienced observers that Hamilton had something truly special.

As Hamilton progressed in his career, he embraced the use of professional racing simulators—a standard tool in modern motorsport for driver development and race preparation. His comfort with simulated environments can be traced back to his RC racing days, where he first developed the ability to anticipate and react in a virtual setting.

At eight years old, Lewis Hamilton's journey from RC car racing into the world of karting began when his father, Anthony Hamilton, bought him his first go-kart as a Christmas gift in 1993. This was no small feat for the Hamilton family, given their financial constraints. Anthony invested £1,000—a significant amount for the family at the time—to purchase a second-hand kart. Despite the tough financial situation, Anthony recognised the passion in Lewis's eyes and knew he had to support his son's dream. He took drastic measures to make it happen, even remortgaging their house and working multiple jobs to afford the kart. His belief in Lewis's talent drove him to make whatever sacrifices were necessary to support his son's journey.

The go-kart Hamilton began with was not brand new but a carefully maintained second-hand machine. Anthony Hamilton modified it himself, ensuring it was both safe and competitive. This hands-on approach not only saved money but also strengthened the bond between father and son through their shared passion for racing mechanics. Working together on the kart provided Hamilton with a foundational understanding of engineering and a deep appreciation for the machinery and teamwork essential to success in motorsport. The go-kart was not simply a toy—it was Hamilton's gateway to competitive racing. He began practising at Rye House Kart Circuit in Hoddesdon, Hertfordshire, which became his training ground, a place where he honed his skills and developed a profound connection with the sport.

### Racing at Rye House Kart Circuit

The renowned Rye House Kart Circuit, established in 1961, is one of the UK's oldest and most respected karting venues.

With a history of nurturing British racing talent, the circuit has become a proving ground for future Formula One drivers, including Jenson Button. Spanning 1,030 metres, the track features a blend of tight hairpins, sweeping corners, and fast straights. Its technical layout demands precision, control, and strategic thinking. Drivers must master braking points, acceleration zones, and racing lines—skills that make the circuit an ideal environment for refining driving techniques.

Rye House's reputation as a breeding ground for talent stems from its ability to challenge drivers in multiple aspects of racing. The circuit's varied corner sequences and the need for smooth handling help develop both technical proficiency and a keen understanding of 'momentum'—a fundamental element of motor racing. The close racing conditions at Rye House also teach valuable racecraft, as drivers learn how to read competitors' on-track behaviour and make quick, strategic decisions.

Racing in the UK's unpredictable weather conditions—dry, wet, or mixed—helped Hamilton, renowned for his wet-weather prowess, adapt his driving style and car set-up to excel under challenging circumstances. His aggressive yet smooth driving style enables him to find grip where others struggle. While many drivers become cautious in the rain, Hamilton has repeatedly delivered remarkable performances in wet conditions. His ability to adapt and thrive in these situations has solidified his reputation as one of motorsport's most versatile and skilled competitors.

For Lewis Hamilton, Rye House wasn't merely a racetrack—it was a formative environment where he cultivated his passion and honed his abilities. Right from his first kart race, Hamilton impressed Martin Hines, former triple World Superkart Champion and creator of the famous ZIP chassis. At Rye House, Hines watched Hamilton battle for the top positions, finishing third in the Cadets' Final. After the race, Hines congratulated Hamilton and his father. Upon learning this was

Lewis's maiden race, Hines suggested they meet again. From that moment onward, Hamilton competed using a ZIP chassis.

Reflecting on his early experiences at Rye House, Hamilton described it as a place run by great people who supported him throughout his career. For many young racers, it was where their careers began, just as his did. The supportive environment at Rye House, along with the camaraderie of fellow racers and the guidance of experienced coaches, was crucial in Hamilton's progression through the karting ranks. These formative experiences not only honed his driving skills but also instilled in him the values of sportsmanship and endurance.

**Karting Success and the Road to Formula One**

Hamilton's skills continued to sharpen, culminating in his landmark victory in the British Cadet Karting Championship at just ten years old. This victory was a significant milestone and a clear demonstration of his growing talent and determination. The win, marked by calculated driving and remarkable composure, caught the attention of the motorsport community.

That same year, Hamilton attended the prestigious Autosport Awards in London, often referred to as the "Oscars of motorsport." This event celebrated outstanding achievements in racing, and attending it was a major honour for the young karter. Reflecting on the experience, Hamilton recalled how he had to borrow a suit from the previous year's winner because his family couldn't afford one. This anecdote underscores the humble beginnings from which he rose. At the ceremony, Hamilton introduced himself to Ron Dennis, then McLaren's Team Principal, and shared his dream of racing for McLaren and becoming a Formula One World Champion. Dennis, recognising Hamilton's determination, advised him to reach out again in nine years. This encounter would later plant the seed for a future partnership. Dennis spoke highly of Hamilton's drive, noting his remarkable determination even at that young age.

This meeting wasn't just a chance encounter; it set in motion a relationship that would shape Hamilton's future. McLaren began closely following Hamilton's progress, and Hamilton has often expressed gratitude for the early recognition, acknowledging that without that support, his journey to Formula One might never have begun.

The financial challenges Hamilton and his family faced during his early karting career were significant. As Hamilton advanced through the ranks, the costs associated with equipment, entry fees, travel, and maintenance grew considerably, placing a heavy financial strain on the family. Anthony Hamilton made tremendous sacrifices to support his son's racing ambitions, including working long hours and forgoing personal luxuries. Hamilton has frequently expressed deep gratitude for his father's unwavering dedication. Anthony Hamilton was proactive in networking within the motorsport community, building connections that were instrumental in Lewis's development. His determination and personable nature played a crucial role in advancing Lewis's career.

The victory in the British Cadet Kart Championship and the recognition at the Autosport Awards marked defining moments in Hamilton's young career. The triumph was more than just about age; it was a testament to the many obstacles he and his family had overcome to reach that point. The victory attracted media attention, and soon, Hamilton was featured in national newspapers and TV programmes. Reflecting on this period, Hamilton described the experience as surreal—one moment, he was a kid racing for fun, and the next, he was being hailed as a prodigy. This early recognition marked the beginning of his rise into the public eye, foreshadowing the remarkable journey that lay ahead.

In 1996, Hamilton secured the Kartmasters British Grand Prix title, further cementing his reputation as a rising star. A year later, he dominated the Super One Formula Yamaha series, showcasing a rare combination of consistency and speed.

Hamilton's success continued. In 1998, during a Formula Junior Intercontinental A (JICA) karting race at Buckmore Park, he started from the back of the grid and executed a sensational drive, overtaking the entire field to claim victory. He often credits Buckmore Park as a pivotal location in his development, where he refined his racing skills.

Hamilton's exceptional performances caught the attention of McLaren and Mercedes, and in 1998, Ron Dennis signed him to the McLaren-Mercedes Young Driver Support Programme, making him the youngest driver to join. This partnership provided Hamilton with invaluable resources and guidance, propelling him even closer to Formula One.

Hamilton's success continued as he advanced through karting, competing in the Intercontinental A (1999), Formula A (2000), and Formula Super A (2001) categories. In 2000, he won the European Championship in Formula A, dominating the sport with maximum points. During this period, Hamilton also competed alongside future Formula One rival Nico Rosberg. Their rivalry, forged in karting, would lay the foundation for their future rivalry in Formula One. Hamilton has often emphasised the importance of excelling in karting to progress in his career, highlighting its significance in shaping his journey.

Hamilton's karting career also saw him race against established names in motorsport. In 2001, he competed in a karting event where he faced off against Formula One legend Michael Schumacher. Although Hamilton finished seventh in the final, behind Schumacher, the event was a significant milestone in his development. His skills behind the wheel didn't go unnoticed, with Schumacher recognising Hamilton's speed and mental strength, predicting that if he continued on his current path, he would undoubtedly make it to Formula One.

Karting remained a formative part of Hamilton's development. It was in karting that he learned the essential skills of combative racing, discipline, and racecraft, understanding that without these foundational experiences, he wouldn't have achieved his success in motorsport.

**The Path to Formula One: Struggles and Triumphs**

While refining his skills on track, Hamilton also began developing the physical and mental toughness that would see him become one of the world's most recognisable icons. His upbringing was shaped by a strong emphasis on education and discipline, instilled by his parents, and has since become ingrained in his psyche. His father was particularly insistent that Lewis maintain good grades and uphold his responsibilities at home. Hamilton continues to advocate for this approach for young drivers today, advising them that education is crucial for their future careers in motorsport, as it lays the foundation for well-rounded development.

In addition to his academic discipline, Hamilton turned to martial arts to defend himself against bullies at school. He began practicing karate, a decision that profoundly influenced his personal growth. He recalled how, as a small and lonely child, he felt like an easy target for bullies and asked his father if he could join a karate class. Karate taught him discipline, respect, and humility, and gave him the confidence to stand up to those bullies, as well as to defend others who were being bullied. These lessons in self-control and stamina complemented his racing career, helping to shape the focused and determined competitor he would become.

Navigating his identity as a mixed-race individual in the competitive world of motorsport added complexity to Hamilton's early experiences. Often the only black child at racing events, Hamilton felt the need to excel to overcome stereotypes and biases. This challenge motivated him to break barriers, pushing him to succeed at the highest levels of motorsport. The desire for acceptance was a driving force, with the belief that winning races would lead to recognition in a world that often did not embrace inclusivity. These formative experiences would later shape his activism and advocacy for diversity in motorsport.

Anthony Hamilton's efforts laid the foundation for Lewis's future success. His willingness to leverage the opportunities presented to him, while overcoming physical, financial, and prejudicial challenges, exemplified the determination needed to succeed in a competitive sport like Formula One. Hamilton frequently reflects on the profound influence his father had on his journey to success. Anthony's relentless support and sacrifices were essential in shaping his early development as a driver. From a young age, Hamilton absorbed the values his father instilled—hard work, discipline, and unwavering dedication—qualities that became the bedrock of his tenacity and determination.

Beyond Anthony's principled and nurturing approach, the unconditional love and support from his mother, Carmen, his stepmother, Linda, and his brother, Nicolas, also played a crucial role in fostering his ambition. Together, their encouragement gave Hamilton the confidence to take bold risks, enabling him to achieve greatness at the highest levels of motorsport.

Hamilton's path to success was anything but smooth. During the late 1990s, he faced numerous challenging races and disappointing results, which only deepened his resolve to learn and improve. Reflecting on these setbacks, Hamilton often emphasises how they helped forge the relentless drive that defines him. He notes that the growth he experienced through those struggles—learning to assert himself, stand up to challenges, and resist being pushed around—was profoundly empowering.

The road to Formula One was marked by tough races and hard-earned lessons in overcoming defeat, forging the mental strength that underpins Hamilton's extraordinary achievements. His recent challenges with Mercedes mirror those earlier struggles, not as insurmountable barriers but as opportunities for growth. Just as his early hardships shaped his determination to succeed, the disappointments he has faced recently with Mercedes will undoubtedly drive his continued evolution as a champion.

Reflecting on his strength, Hamilton once mentioned that he discovered a resilience within himself that he hadn't realised before. This resilience, built through adversity in his formative years, highlights how his experiences in karting and junior racing categories—along with the challenges of facing bullies and racism—were instrumental in shaping the character and perseverance that propelled him to the top of motorsport. These trials gave him immense resolve, which continues to define his career and legacy.

# Building a Champion: Hamilton's Formative Years

As Lewis Hamilton progressed through the ranks of karting and junior formulas, his driving style evolved significantly in response to new challenges, different vehicles, and changing regulations. His adaptability became one of his greatest strengths, enabling him to extract maximum performance from any car he drove. Hamilton's development as a racing driver was built on a multi-faceted foundation, refining his approach to driving while strengthening key areas such as teamwork, effective support networks, physical fitness, and mental resilience.

Hamilton's early experiences, including his time with radio-controlled car racing and the challenges faced at Rye House Kart Circuit, as well as other national and international tracks, helped shape an approach that combined natural talent with learned techniques. This approach became a defining feature of his racing identity, characterised by aggressive precision, adaptability, and an unwavering drive to succeed.

Hamilton demonstrated an exceptional ability to adjust his driving style to suit different cars, regulations, and track conditions. Each year, as he moved through various categories and faced changes in vehicle performance, he adapted his approach to maintain a competitive edge. Two consistent preferences, however, were his affinity for a car with an aggressive front end, enabling him to attack the corner entry with limited understeer, and a stable rear end on exit, so he could get the power down without losing momentum.

Hamilton excelled when he could trust the front of the car to bite on turn-in, while the rear remained planted, allowing him to carry more speed into and through corners. However, to stay competitive, these preferences are not always a given, and he is able to adapt to the vehicle characteristics as much as possible. This adaptability was clear when Hamilton discussed how his driving evolves with each season and car update. Reflecting on the subtle changes in technique required, he knows that the need to adapt is part of the game, especially with a new car and evolving tyres. It's this willingness to adapt his approach that has been key to his continued success in Formula One.

Hamilton's adaptability has been tested and proven repeatedly throughout his career. He has faced significant regulation shifts that impacted car performance, including aerodynamic changes, tyre specifications, and power unit updates. In each instance, he worked closely with his engineers to understand the nuances and adjust his driving accordingly. The key for Hamilton has been flexibility—getting to a place where, if he cannot get the car to adjust to his preferred style, he will alter his approach to suit the car. From karting to Formula Renault, Formula 3, GP2, and ultimately Formula One, Hamilton encountered a variety of vehicle dynamics. He adapted to differences in power, weight distribution, downforce, and braking performance. Even within Formula One, changes in team philosophies and car designs have required adjustments. His move from McLaren to Mercedes in 2013 presented new challenges, but Hamilton's ability to continually adapt ensured continued success.

Hamilton became known for his aggressive yet precise driving style. He possessed an innate ability to push the limits of his kart or car while maintaining control—a balance that many drivers found challenging to achieve. His aggression wasn't reckless; it was calculated. He knew when to take risks and when to conserve, a skill that distinguished him from his peers. Racecraft, which encompasses the strategic and tactical aspects of racing—such as managing tyre wear, fuel consumption, and track positioning—became an integral part of Hamilton's approach. He paid close attention to the technical aspects of his vehicle. Through hands-on experience with his father, Hamilton gained insights into vehicle setup and mechanics. This knowledge allowed him to communicate effectively with his team, helping to make adjustments that enhanced his car's performance. For Hamilton, the experience gained from setting up his RC cars and later his karts proved invaluable, teaching him that even small adjustments could have a significant impact on track performance.

Early in his career, Hamilton demonstrated exceptional adaptability to varying track conditions. Whether racing in dry or wet conditions, he adjusted his driving style to extract maximum performance. His prowess in the rain became particularly notable. While many drivers dreaded wet races due to reduced grip and visibility, Hamilton saw them as opportunities to hone his skill. His ability to find grip where others struggled was largely due to his sensitive throttle control and smooth steering inputs. He modulated his speed and maintained momentum through corners, minimising wheelspin and sliding. This proficiency in adverse conditions earned him significant recognition and respect within the racing community.

Hamilton's talent in wet and changeable conditions became evident early in his career. He often excelled when others struggled, leveraging his skill to gain advantages in difficult races. He later remarked how rain acted as a great leveller, where driver skill outweighed pure car performance. Hamilton drew inspiration from the legendary Ayrton Senna, particularly Senna's iconic opening lap at the 1993 European Grand Prix at Donington Park, where Senna surged from fifth to first amid challenging conditions. Hamilton frequently cited Senna's control and precision in the wet as a major influence, adopting a similar focus and determination when racing in comparable conditions. Like Senna, Hamilton approached wet races confidently, balancing aggression with finesse. Later, as he progressed through the feeder series, he worked closely with his engineers to optimise car setup for rain, considering factors like tyre pressures, aerodynamics, and suspension settings. This dedication paid dividends, notably in the GP2 Series at Silverstone in 2006, where in mixed wet-dry conditions, he crushed the opposition, grabbing everyone's attention. This race proved to be a turning point, reinforcing his confidence in adapting to inclement weather.

Hamilton, like many of his contemporaries, began his journey toward Formula One in the world of karting. The rigours of karting, often underestimated as mere child's play, are actually foundational to building the physical and mental resilience required at motorsport's highest levels. Kart racing is incredibly physically demanding. Recognising the physical demands of racing, Hamilton emphasised fitness from an early age. He has often highlighted the importance of having a robust cardiovascular system as a driver. During a typical two-hour race, drivers can experience average heart rates of 160-170 bpm, peaking as high as 190 bpm during qualifying.

His training regimen focused on cardiovascular endurance, strength training, and flexibility. Running and cycling helped him build stamina for long races and cope with the G-forces experienced in high-speed corners. Weightlifting and bodyweight exercises built muscular strength, particularly in the neck, shoulders, and core—areas critical for handling the physical stresses of racing. Practices like yoga and stretching improved his flexibility, reducing the risk of injury and aiding recovery. Hamilton also understood the importance of maintaining the right balance in muscle mass, acknowledging that while lifting weights was important, Formula One drivers need to avoid excessive muscle gain. Too much muscle can add unnecessary weight, and a low centre of gravity is key to optimising performance in the car.

From 2014 onwards, Formula One cars underwent significant changes, including increases in minimum weight due to the introduction of hybrid power units and enhanced safety features. These shifts allowed drivers to adjust their physiques without compromising performance. Hamilton embraced these changes, developing a more muscular build that complemented the demands of the new cars. As the minimum weight of the cars increased, so did Hamilton's own. He worked with personal trainers to tailor his fitness program, focusing on functional strength with exercises that mimicked the movements and stresses of driving, such as resistance training with bands and weighted neck exercises. High-Intensity Interval Training (HIIT) improved cardiovascular fitness and simulated the bursts of effort required during races. A balanced diet, rich in plant-based foods, proteins, healthy fats, and complex carbohydrates, supported his training and recovery.

Hamilton's commitment to fitness yielded tangible benefits. Enhanced endurance allowed him to maintain peak performance throughout races, reducing fatigue-related errors, vital at tracks like Singapore with high heat and humidity. Strength and flexibility minimised the risk of strains and injuries, contributing to his longevity in the sport. Physical health supported mental well-being, aiding concentration and decision-making under pressure. His influence extended beyond Formula One, inspiring fans and fellow athletes to prioritise their own health and wellness. Quick decision-making is paramount in racing, where reaction times can determine victory or defeat. From an early age, many racers hone their reflexes through various reactivity drills and games designed to improve hand-eye coordination and processing speed. Some drivers develop this from the intensity of racing, while others use methods such as tennis ball drops or light or light sensor reactivity drills. This early training lays the foundation for the split-second decisions required at higher racing levels.

Through kart racing, drivers like Hamilton develop a blend of physical robustness, endurance, quick reflexes, and psychological resilience—all critical for ascending the ranks of motorsport. The early years in karting are not just about learning to race; they are about building the comprehensive athlete capable of handling the demands of Formula One racing. Core, muscular, aerobic, and mental fitness must be maintained at Olympic levels to compete at the highest levels of the sport.

A Formula One driver can experience up to 5G during certain corners or under braking, and this force is sustained for nearly two hours. On top of this, they must contend with wearing fireproof undergarments, a racing suit, boots, balaclava, gloves, and helmet, all while being cramped into a carbon fibre cockpit. With additional challenges like extreme heat from the car and the physical strain of twisting, turning, and bracing, it's no surprise that the average driver loses up to 3kg in fluid during a race. As Hamilton progressed through his career, he placed increased emphasis on flexibility, nutrition, hydration, and mental fitness. Managing his energy levels became paramount, with the use of meditation, mindfulness, and proper recovery becoming integral parts of his routine.

In addition to the physical demands Hamilton needed the mental resilience to compete at the highest levels. He developed a focused mindset, learning to block out distractions and pressures. His ability to centre himself before races, calming his nerves and building confidence, became crucial to his success. Setbacks and failures were inevitable in his journey. Mechanical failures, accidents, and losses tested his resolve, but rather than becoming disheartened, he viewed these moments as opportunities to learn. After each race, regardless of the outcome, he and his father would debrief thoroughly, analysing what went well and identifying areas for improvement. His father would instil in him an unshakable resolve by telling him to rise above these challenges. These lessons would prove vital, as in 2011 Hamilton would face a turning point—a moment where he stood at a crossroads. He could have allowed the challenges and pressures to overwhelm him, veering down a destructive path, but instead, using all the skills he had honed, he chose to adapt and mature, taking a path to greater success and becoming a better person. The lessons from his earlier years, combined with the self-reflection he had cultivated, allowed him to become not only a better driver but also a more measured, resilient, and rounded individual.

Hamilton's curiosity about the inner workings of racing extended beyond just driving the car. He developed a keen interest in the engineering principles behind vehicle dynamics, aerodynamics, and mechanical systems. This fascination led him to ask insightful questions and seek a deeper understanding from the mechanics and engineers around him. His growing technical knowledge enabled him to provide precise feedback on the car's performance, articulating how the vehicle behaved under specific conditions. This ability to communicate effectively with his team played a key role in making successful adjustments to the car. The collaborative relationship between driver and engineer became a crucial element of his success. To Hamilton no detail was too small to consider.

From a young age, Hamilton approached racing with a level of professionalism that set him apart. He was punctual, disciplined, and respectful towards both his team and competitors. His mature attitude earned him respect within the motorsport community, opening doors for valuable mentorship and support. Team managers and sponsors quickly recognised his maturity, a trait that distinguished him from many of his peers. Hamilton and his father took a strategic approach to his career trajectory, carefully selecting racing series and teams that would offer the best development opportunities. Their decisions were driven by long-term goals, rather than immediate rewards, ensuring Hamilton was always pushed to progress. For instance, moving from national to European karting circuits exposed him to higher levels of competition, requiring him to adapt to new environments and learn from a variety of racing styles. These experiences broadened his skill set and prepared him for the global stage.

Another key aspect of Hamilton's development was his ability to build relationships within the racing community. He connected with fellow drivers, team personnel, and industry professionals, creating a network that provided valuable support, advice, and opportunities. Mentors played a significant role in shaping his career, offering guidance at critical points. Additionally, his participation in community events and exhibitions helped raise his profile, introducing him to sponsors and fans and building his confidence in speaking and dealing with large numbers of people. Through these interactions, Hamilton honed his communication skills and gained confidence in public settings.

As one of the few black drivers in motorsport, Hamilton became increasingly aware of the significance of his cultural identity. He recognised the opportunity to represent diversity within racing and fully embraced it. This awareness drove him not only to succeed for his own benefit but also to act as a symbol of progress. When facing challenges related to discrimination, Hamilton chose to address them constructively. By excelling on the track, and behaving with integrity, he defied stereotypes and paved the way for future generations. These early experiences would later influence his advocacy for inclusion and equality in motorsport. If he encountered adversity, on or off the circuit, that seemed out of place in racing, Hamilton's father instilled in him the importance of letting his actions speak louder than words. He was taught to rise above challenges and do his talking on the track, and this mantra became central to his development, helping him build a core of resilience that would serve him throughout his career.

Hamilton's development as a driver was the result of a deliberate and multifaceted approach. As he prepared to enter the world of professional car racing, Hamilton carried with him the lessons and experiences that would propel him to the pinnacle of motorsport.

# The Road to Formula One

## Ron Dennis and the McLaren Legacy

Lewis Hamilton's progress from karting into Formula One was overseen and supported by two charismatic mentors, Ron Dennis and Frédéric Vasseur. Both were instrumental in helping Hamilton develop his driving skills and his technical understanding of racing cars, whilst honing the mental fortitude essential for a successful Formula One driver. Dennis and Vasseur were both inspiring leaders, and they worked together with Anthony Hamilton to nurture Lewis and help him develop his natural talent for racing. It was these influential and dedicated men who created an environment where Hamilton could thrive.

To understand the significance of Hamilton's meeting with Ron Dennis, it is essential to delve into the background of the man who transformed McLaren into a Formula One powerhouse. Ron Dennis was not merely a Team Principal; he was a visionary who reshaped the landscape of motorsport through innovation, meticulous attention to detail, and an unwavering pursuit of perfection.

Born on 1 June 1947 in Woking, Surrey, Dennis developed an early interest in engineering and automobiles. He attended Guildford Technical College, where he studied motor vehicle engineering, equipping himself with both theoretical knowledge and practical skills. This educational foundation dispels the misconception that Dennis was "just" a mechanic; he possessed a deep understanding of engineering principles that would later influence his approach to racing.

Dennis began his career in motorsport as an 18-year-old mechanic for the Cooper Formula One team in 1966. He later joined Brabham, working under the legendary designer Gordon Murray and team owner Bernie Ecclestone. These experiences provided Dennis with insights into team management and the technical aspects of racing at the highest level.

In 1971, leveraging his experience and ambition, Ron Dennis co-founded Rondel Racing with Neil Trundle. The team competed in Formula Two, showcasing Dennis's ability to manage and develop racing operations. Rondel Racing quickly gained a reputation for professionalism and competitiveness, setting the stage for Dennis's future endeavours. The experience provided him with valuable insights into managing a racing team and honed his skills in overseeing racing operations. This phase of his career was crucial in setting the foundation for his future successes, particularly his leadership role at McLaren.

After Rondel Racing dissolved due to the oil crisis in 1973, Dennis established Project Four Racing in 1976. The team's success in Formula Two and the Procar series caught the attention of sponsors and industry leaders. In 1980, with backing from French-Saudi businessman Mansour Ojjeh, Dennis orchestrated a merger between Project Four Racing and the struggling McLaren team, forming McLaren International. The naming philosophy for McLaren's cars stems from this merger. The chassis designation "MP4" stands for "McLaren Project 4," symbolising the unification of the two entities. This nomenclature continued until 2017, reflecting the legacy of Dennis's influence.

On taking control, Ron Dennis set out to revolutionise McLaren both on and off the track. He instilled a culture of excellence and innovation. The team's facilities were upgraded, and a new emphasis was placed on cutting-edge technology and engineering. Ron Dennis's quest for perfection became the stuff of legend within the motorsport community. Known for his meticulous attention to detail, Dennis's standards were exacting, influencing every facet of team operations. From the spotless workshop floors at McLaren to the immaculate presentation of the team and its equipment, his commitment to excellence was omnipresent. Dennis often espoused a philosophy that mirrored the sentiments of early 20th-century American professional football coach Vince Lombardi, believing, "Perfection is unattainable, but if we chase perfection, we can catch excellence." This ethos permeated McLaren under his leadership, driving the team to strive for continuous improvement and setting new benchmarks in Formula One.

A pivotal figure in McLaren's resurgence was Mansour Ojjeh, an entrepreneur and the owner of Techniques d'Avant Garde (TAG). Initially involved with Williams, Ojjeh was persuaded by Dennis to invest in McLaren, a move that proved transformative for the team. This partnership led to the development of the TAG-Porsche engine, a turbocharged powerhouse that propelled McLaren's cars through a highly successful period in the mid-1980s. Ojjeh's substantial financial support provided the stability and resources necessary for Dennis to fully implement his visionary leadership. Together, they formed a formidable duo, under which McLaren soared to new heights, rewriting the annals of Formula One history with their combined strategic and technical prowess.

In a key move to boost McLaren's competitiveness, Dennis successfully persuaded Niki Lauda, a two-time World Champion who had retired in 1979, to return to Formula One in 1982. Lauda's vast experience and technical insight proved to be invaluable assets to the team. Lauda's influence was immediately felt. He played a significant role in car development and offered mentorship to younger drivers. His collaboration with the engineering team drove significant advancements in the car's performance. In 1984, just months before Lewis Hamilton was born, Lauda clinched his third World Championship by a narrow margin of half a point over his teammate, Alain Prost. This victory not only underscored McLaren's resurgence but also highlighted Dennis's adeptness in leveraging top-tier talent to achieve stellar results.

Building on this momentum, Dennis masterfully continued to assemble stellar driver lineups at McLaren. Alain Prost, known as "The Professor" for his meticulous and careful racing style, clinched the World Championship in 1985 and 1986 with the team. In a calculated move in 1988, Dennis signed Ayrton Senna to partner Prost, igniting one of the most iconic rivalries in Formula One history.

The Prost-Senna partnership dramatically redefined the sport. Under Dennis's astute management, McLaren reached an unprecedented peak in 1988, dominating the season with 15 victories out of 16 races, in an era when Formula One cars were not the bastions of reliability they are today. However, the fierce rivalry between the two drivers posed significant challenges. Dennis skilfully navigated the complexities of managing two of the sport's most competitive personalities, striving to maintain team harmony while maximising their performance on the track.

Dennis's relentless drive to lift team performance at McLaren included forming strong technical partnerships. One of the most significant was with Honda, whose engines were celebrated for their power and reliability. From 1988 to 1992, the McLaren-Honda alliance dominated Formula One, securing multiple Constructors' and Drivers' Championships and establishing the team as a benchmark in the sport.

Dennis was a strong proponent of innovation, consistently pushing the boundaries in aerodynamics, materials science, and electronics. Under his leadership, McLaren became synonymous with cutting-edge technology. This reputation not only led to race wins but also attracted a slew of sponsors and some of the best engineering talent in the world, further cementing McLaren's status at the top of motorsport.

The early 1990s brought new challenges as rival teams caught up technologically. Despite this, McLaren remained competitive, with Senna winning the World Championship in 1990 and 1991. Dennis and Senna developed a close relationship based on a shared commitment to perfection. Senna's departure to Williams in 1994 and his subsequent tragic death at the San Marino Grand Prix deeply affected Dennis and the entire McLaren organisation. The loss underscored the risks inherent in the sport and reinforced Dennis's dedication to safety and driver support.

Undeterred by challenges, Dennis focused on rebuilding McLaren. He signed promising drivers like Mika Häkkinen, who joined the team in 1993 and whose trajectory mirrored McLaren's own resurgence. In 1995, as Hamilton was making his initial connections with Dennis, Häkkinen faced a critical moment at the Australian Grand Prix in Adelaide that nearly ended his career.

During the qualifying session on 10 November 1995, Häkkinen's car suffered a sudden and catastrophic failure of the left rear tyre going into a corner at around 155mph (250km/h), leading to a loss of control. The car slammed backwards into the barriers at high speed, resulting in a massive impact that caused Häkkinen to sustain serious head injuries. Emergency medical teams rushed to the scene, performing a trackside tracheotomy to help him breathe, a procedure that was crucial in saving his life.

This harrowing incident, just a year after the sad loss of Senna, not only highlighted the inherent dangers of Formula One racing but also emphasised the importance of spirit and the human element within the sport. Dennis was deeply affected by the accident. Known for his close relationships with his drivers, Dennis visited Häkkinen regularly during his hospitalisation and supported him throughout the recovery process. His commitment to his drivers and the sport's safety advancements became even more pronounced following the accident.

Whilst Häkkinen continued to recover, Dennis fought to give his drivers the best car possible. In 1997, in a masterstroke, he recruited Adrian Newey, one of the most brilliant and innovative Formula One car designers of all time. Newey, known for his groundbreaking work with Williams, brought a fresh and highly technical approach to McLaren's design philosophy.

The impact of Newey's arrival was profound. He was instrumental in the design of the McLaren MP4-13, the car used in the 1998 Formula One season. This car is widely regarded as one of the most successful in the history of the sport, balancing power, agility, and reliability. Under Newey's technical guidance, the team achieved a new level of aerodynamic efficiency and performance.

Häkkinen, now rehabilitated and back to health, and driving the Newey-designed MP4-13, capitalised on this technical superiority to win the World Championship in both 1998 and 1999. These victories were not just triumphs of driving skill but also of engineering wisdom, highlighting the synergy between driver and machine. Dennis's decision to bring Newey on board and work with Häkkinen on his recovery was a reflection of his vision for McLaren's dominance in Formula One, his understanding of engineering, and his empathy, care, and understanding of his drivers. It underscored his belief in integrating cutting-edge engineering with top-tier driving talent to achieve remarkable results.

Ron Dennis's leadership at McLaren has a lot of parallels to Sir Alex Ferguson's management of Manchester United. Both transformed their respective organisations from the 1980s through the 1990s with a clear focus on youth development, discipline, and an unyielding pursuit of excellence. They shared several leadership traits: investing in young talent and nurturing them into world-class performers; implementing long-term strategies that prioritised sustainable success over immediate victories; demanding the highest standards across all aspects of their organisations; continually evolving their strategies to stay competitive in changing environments; and caring for the drivers or players under them.

These comparisons highlight the profound impact visionary leadership can have in achieving sustained excellence and success. Under Dennis, McLaren became a dominant force in Formula One, mirroring Manchester United's rise to prominence under Ferguson. Both leaders left indelible marks on their sports, demonstrating that with the right leadership and strategy, enduring success is achievable.

## The Early Encounter at the 1995 Autosport Awards

Against this backdrop, the 1995 Autosport Awards provided the setting for a fateful encounter. At this prestigious event, attended by the luminaries of motorsport, Dennis, the esteemed Team Principal and CEO of McLaren Racing, was one of the distinguished attendees. At just ten years old, Lewis Hamilton attended the event with his father. It was an opportunity for the young aspiring driver to immerse himself in the world he dreamed of joining. During the evening, Lewis, clutching an autograph book, approached Dennis. According to Hamilton's later accounts, he told Dennis about his aspirations to race for McLaren. Amused and impressed, Dennis wrote humorously, encouraging the young racer to keep in touch.

This encounter marked the beginning of a relationship that would eventually see Hamilton become a McLaren driver. Anthony Hamilton later reflected on the significance of this moment in interviews with major publications, noting his son's confidence and the doors it opened.

Following their initial meeting at the Autosport Awards, Hamilton continued to excel in karting, amassing championships and steadily garnering attention within the motorsport community. Aware of the importance of maintaining a connection with influential figures in Formula One, Anthony Hamilton encouraged his son to periodically update Ron Dennis on his racing progress.

Over the years, Hamilton took the initiative to send updates to Dennis, detailing his achievements and affirming his ambition to drive for McLaren. This proactive approach helped

Hamilton stay on the radar of McLaren's leadership, demonstrating his persistence and dedication to reaching the peak of motorsport. Dennis has noted in various public discussions the positive impression young drivers like Hamilton made on him through their dedication and communication—such attributes being vital for young athletes aspiring to break into highly competitive environments.

Dennis's thoughtfulness about his drivers, such as Häkkinen, was evident in his reflections on Hamilton's development. He often spoke of how Hamilton's character was shaped by his family values, with McLaren merely supplementing those foundational principles. According to Dennis, Hamilton was a well-rounded individual who appreciated not just what McLaren-Mercedes had done for him but also the immense support his family had provided throughout his journey.

Between 1996 and 2000, Hamilton was a formidable force in the karting world, clinching multiple national and international championships. His impressive achievements included triumphs at prestigious competitions such as the Sky TV KartMasters and the Five Nations Championship in 1996, the Junior Yamaha National Kart Championship in 1997, and the European Karting Championship in the Junior Intercontinental A (JICA) class in 1999. In 2000, he continued his exceptional form by becoming the runner-up in the Formula A World Championship, setting a record as the youngest driver to achieve such a feat at the time. His performances drew widespread acclaim, with his achievements in karting and junior racing still remembered as some of the most brilliant in the sport's history. After winning eight championships in just six years of kart racing, Hamilton transitioned to the single-seater ranks, where he went on to claim three major titles.

In 1998, at just 13 years old, Lewis Hamilton's persistence and racing success led to a pivotal opportunity. Dennis, in partnership with Mercedes-Benz, offered Hamilton a place in McLaren's Young Driver Support Programme. This made him one of the youngest drivers to secure a contract that included a potential pathway to a Formula One seat. The programme provided extensive financial support, covering essential racing expenses, equipment, and travel, which significantly eased the financial pressures faced by the Hamilton family. It also offered access to McLaren's state-of-the-art training facilities, engineering staff, and mentorship from seasoned drivers, ensuring that Hamilton's development was both comprehensive and balanced, with an emphasis on sustaining his academic performance alongside his racing commitments.

Dennis and the McLaren team recognised Hamilton's potential early on. His exceptional talent and steadfast determination made a compelling case for his inclusion in the programme. The decision to bring him into the McLaren family was driven by a belief in his ability to grow into a top-tier racing driver. Joining the McLaren programme marked a crucial shift in Hamilton's career, introducing him to a new level of professional expectations. As he began representing a prestigious organisation with a rich history in Formula One, Hamilton was acutely aware of the significant responsibility and the intense scrutiny that came with it. This move was not just a dream come true; it placed a substantial weight of expectation on his young shoulders.

Many of Hamilton's critics noted that being part of such a renowned team meant that there was a widespread expectation for him to win, not just compete. The racing community and fans alike were keen to see if he could live up to the potential that McLaren had seen in him. This perceived need to justify the team's faith brought an additional layer of pressure, driving Hamilton to push his limits further and prove his worth on the racing circuits. He felt a profound obligation to demonstrate that the team's investment in him was justified, which motivated him to excel and meet the high standards expected of a McLaren driver.

As Hamilton's involvement with McLaren deepened, so did the pressure to perform. Media attention and high expectations from one of the most prestigious teams in Formula One brought a new level of scrutiny. Balancing his education with an increasingly demanding racing schedule was no easy task, and Hamilton had to adapt to structured training regimes, rigorous performance evaluations, and the professional expectations of the McLaren programme.

Anthony Hamilton played a vital role in this period, continuing to act as Lewis's manager and mentor. His guidance helped Lewis navigate the challenges of balancing his growing career with the need to remain grounded and focused. Together, they worked to ensure that Lewis met the expectations placed upon him while staying true to the discipline and values that had shaped his early success.

### Transitioning to Single-Seaters

Hamilton's first significant step into single-seaters came in 2001 with Manor Motorsport in the Formula Renault UK Winter Series. This short series was Hamilton's baptism into car racing, and it provided him with his first taste of the challenges beyond karting. Transitioning to cars, Hamilton grappled with the complexities of aerodynamics, mechanical grip, and more strategic racecraft. In 2002, in his first full season in Formula Renault UK, he finished third overall—a remarkable achievement that hinted at his potential but also highlighted the steep learning curve he faced.

By 2003, Hamilton had refined his skills and returned to the Formula Renault UK Championship with a vengeance. Dominating the series, he won 10 out of 15 races. This season was significant not just for the victories, but for Hamilton's deepening understanding of car setup and race strategy, facilitated by a nurturing environment at Manor Motorsport. His success demonstrated a key trait—his ability to learn and adapt swiftly, a characteristic that would define his career. It also put him on the radar of key people in the higher formulas.

After clinching the Formula Renault UK Championship in 2003, Hamilton advanced to the Formula 3 Euro Series in 2004, continuing his collaboration with Manor Motorsport. This team was instrumental in his early career, and their ongoing partnership provided continuity during this period of progression. His rookie season was challenging; Hamilton faced the realities of a steeper competition curve, managing only one win. However, the year was crucial for building toughness and honing his overtaking skills, which were becoming a trademark of his racing style. The series also gave him a taste of some of the international tracks, such as Nürburgring and Hockenheim.

**Frédéric Vasseur**

Hamilton's impressive performance in the Formula Renault campaign and his ability to bounce back in his first season in Formula 3 caught the attention of Frédéric Vasseur, the manager of ASM (Automobiles Sportives et Mécaniques) Formule 3, a leading team in the Formula 3 Euro Series. Born on 28 May 1968 in Draveil, France, Frédéric Vasseur graduated from ESTACA, a prestigious French engineering school specialising in aeronautics and automotive technology. Leveraging his technical expertise and passion for motorsport, Vasseur established ASM in 1996. The team quickly became a notable force in Formula 3, focusing on promoting young drivers and achieving significant success in junior motorsport categories.

Under Vasseur's leadership, ASM was a dominant force in the Formula 3 series, having won the championship in 2004 with Jamie Green. Recognising Hamilton's extraordinary talent, Vasseur offered him a seat for the 2005 season, marking the next step in his climb toward Formula One.

The move to Formula 3 introduced Hamilton to even more complex machinery and higher-calibre competitors, including future Formula One stars like Nico Rosberg. F3 cars are designed with advanced aerodynamics, featuring front and rear wings that generate significant downforce to press the car onto the track, enhancing grip and handling through corners. These cars are powered by 2.0-litre engines that produce approximately 210 horsepower, or around 430bhp per tonne, offering a dramatic increase in power compared to the engines used in karting, which were around 35bhp or approximately 200bhp per tonne in the Formula A category. Additionally, F3 cars are equipped with adjustable suspension and aerodynamic settings, allowing drivers to fine-tune their vehicles based on specific track conditions. The inclusion of more sophisticated data acquisition systems further elevates the level of technical engagement, enabling drivers to analyse and optimise their performance with precision.

Transitioning from karting to racing in more complex vehicles, Hamilton faced the significant challenge of mastering the nuances between mechanical and aerodynamic grip. The dynamics of racing changed dramatically, as the faster the vehicle travelled, the more downforce it generated, allowing for higher speeds in corners but also requiring more precise driving inputs. Understanding the transition from relying primarily on mechanical grip in karts to both mechanical and aerodynamic grip in cars was crucial.

Frédéric Vasseur, recognising the importance of this technical understanding, emphasised education in his management approach. At ASM, he ensured that drivers spent ample time with engineers to grasp the principles of aerodynamics and vehicle dynamics thoroughly. This educational focus aimed to empower drivers like Hamilton to provide effective feedback and continuously improve their performance, thereby enhancing their ability to fully harness the car's potential on the track.

Frédéric Vasseur's leadership style seamlessly blends technical rigour with personalised mentorship. He places a strong emphasis on the technical comprehension of racing vehicles, encouraging drivers to actively engage with their engineering teams. Vasseur advocates for a hands-on approach, where drivers are expected to dissect telemetry data and participate in discussions about setup adjustments. This philosophy not only enhances the drivers' understanding of their cars but also fosters an environment conducive to focused skill development. Under Vasseur's guidance, drivers find themselves supported by a team that values their input and nurtures their growth, preparing them effectively for the demands of competitive racing.

Vasseur is renowned for his holistic approach to team management, which not only emphasises physical preparedness but also takes into account the mental well-being of his team. He is known for fostering a supportive environment that encourages open communication, where drivers and team members are able to freely express concerns and seek guidance. This approach helps manage the immense pressures of racing, enabling drivers to maintain focus and perform at their peak. Vasseur promotes a team-oriented culture, viewing success as a collective effort and encouraging camaraderie among all team members. These values align with Hamilton's own principles, and he would go on to champion them throughout his career in Formula One.

In his interactions with drivers, Frédéric Vasseur consistently emphasises the importance of continual learning and improvement. Vasseur believes that a driver's willingness to engage, ask questions, and seek constant improvement is crucial for their development and success in the demanding world of motorsport. This philosophy of nurturing young talent by encouraging proactive learning and curiosity has been a hallmark of his leadership.

Hamilton's ability to quickly adapt to the aerodynamic demands of F3 cars played a crucial role in his performance throughout the season. The move to Formula 3 was a significant step in Hamilton's career, providing a shop window for his talent and demonstrating his ability to adjust effectively to more complex racing conditions. The partnership between Hamilton and Vasseur played a critical role in his success that year. Under Vasseur's guidance,

Hamilton developed a refined understanding of car setup, allowing him to extract the full potential of his machine.

The 2005 Formula 3 season marked a turning point in Hamilton's career, as he dominated the championship with an extraordinary display of skill and consistency. Driving the Mercedes-powered Dallara F305, Hamilton notched up 15 wins and 13 pole positions out of 20 races—a record that underscored his dominance and adaptability.

One of the season's highlights was the Nürburgring race weekend, a significant event in the Formula 3 championship. Known for its tricky layout and unpredictable weather, the Nürburgring provided the perfect stage for Hamilton to show the qualities that would later define his Formula One career: precision, adaptability, and the will to win. Although Hamilton faced challenges in the first race of the weekend, he bounced back with a decisive victory in the second race, demonstrating his resilience under pressure.

Hamilton’s performance at the Nürburgring, along with his consistent results throughout the season, laid the groundwork for his ascension to Formula One. The trust and expertise he shared with Vasseur foreshadowed the teamwork that would later define his relationships with engineers and strategists. It was a season of record-breaking wins, setting the stage and offering a glimpse of the greatness that was yet to come. This period solidified his reputation and paved the way for his future success, further catching the attention of key figures in higher racing categories.

The lessons learned and relationships built during this time would resonate throughout Hamilton's career. The trust and rapport developed with Vasseur helped establish a network that would benefit him in the years to come. The technical and strategic insights gained during this period enriched his skill set, preparing him for the complexities of higher-level motorsport. Success in such a critical formula reinforced his self-belief, which would prove essential in tackling future challenges. He had a supportive environment in which to experiment with car setup, racecraft, strategy, and when to offer his technical insights—essential elements for building a driver's confidence. Vasseur embraced Hamilton's input.

In the 2005 Formula 3 Euro Series, Hamilton's performance quickly signalled his readiness to compete at a high level. At the iconic Spa-Francorchamps circuit in Belgium, he blew the opposition away in wet conditions, securing a commanding victory that impressed both his team manager, Vasseur, and other competitors. At the Norisring street circuit in Germany, Hamilton demonstrated exceptional control, winning both races of the weekend. Also in this race was none other than Sebastian Vettel, who finished fourth.

Another highlight for Hamilton was his dominant victory from pole position at the prestigious Masters of Formula 3 at Zandvoort in the Netherlands, further proving his growing confidence and mastery under Vasseur's guidance. Throughout the season, Hamilton's performances reflected his exceptional talent and the supportive environment at ASM, culminating in a championship win that set the stage for his future success.

**A Strategic Move for McLaren's Future**

The decision to place Hamilton under Frédéric Vasseur's guidance was a calculated move that aligned perfectly with McLaren's long-term objectives to develop him into a top-tier Formula One driver. This placement was undoubtedly a deliberate strategy by McLaren, reflecting their deep commitment to nurturing Hamilton's potential and steering his career trajectory toward success in Formula One.

Following his success in Formula 3, Hamilton advanced to the GP2 Series in 2006. The GP2 Series, then widely regarded as the final stepping stone to Formula One, provided Hamilton with the opportunity to further hone his skills in a significantly more competitive environment. Recognising Hamilton's exceptional talent and readiness for the challenge, Vasseur guided him through a successful season, which culminated in

Hamilton winning the GP2 championship and securing his path to Formula One.

GP2 cars of 2006 featured advanced aerodynamics, with sophisticated front and rear wings and underbody designs that generated substantial downforce, allowing for greater cornering speeds and stability. Powered by 4.0-litre V8 engines producing approximately 580 to 600 horsepower, these cars delivered a dramatic increase in power compared to their Formula 3 counterparts. Carbon-ceramic brakes, semi-automatic gearboxes, and more complex suspension added layers of technicality, requiring drivers to develop a deeper understanding of vehicle dynamics and control.

For Hamilton, the move to GP2 was a significant challenge. The cars' increased speed and weight demanded greater physical stamina and mental focus, along with a refined driving style to handle the added power and aerodynamic grip. The technical demands of GP2 also introduced Hamilton to the importance of providing high-quality feedback to engineers, a skill that would become crucial in Formula One. Under the guidance of Vasseur and the ART Grand Prix team, Hamilton was able to make this transition successfully. The team's expertise and support helped him adjust to the demands of GP2, preparing him for the challenges ahead.

The move into GP2 meant physical fitness would become an integral part of Hamilton's success. Hamilton had always kept fit, and recognising the physical demands of racing, he committed to fitness from an early age. Karting had required strength, endurance, and agility. Hamilton engaged in activities that enhanced his physical capabilities, such as running, cycling, and playing other sports like football. These activities improved his cardiovascular health, reflexes, and coordination. Physical fitness also contributed to his mental sharpness. A healthy body supported a healthy mind, and much like Senna and Schumacher before him, it would enable him to maintain focus during long races and tough competition.

In 2006, Hamilton stormed into the GP2 Series with the confidence of a champion in the making. What followed was a season that would etch his name into motorsport history and confirm his status as a future Formula One star. The first glimpse of Hamilton's brilliance came at the iconic Silverstone circuit, his home turf. Starting eighth on the grid in the sprint race due to the reversed grid format, Hamilton delivered an inspiring performance. In a brilliant display of racecraft, he carved through the field, trouncing his competition, and crossed the finish line first, arms raised in triumph. It was clear that this young driver was destined for greatness.

Then came Istanbul Park in Turkey, a defining moment of his career. A spin early in the race dropped him to 18th place—a crushing blow for most drivers. But for Hamilton, it was an invitation to show his unparalleled skill and determination. Lap after lap, he hunted down his rivals, passing one after another with a mix of calculated aggression and raw talent. By the chequered flag, he had climbed to second place, leaving fans and commentators in awe.

Hamilton's season was peppered with moments of genius like these, from podium finishes at iconic circuits to breathtaking drives that defied expectations, as well as more light-hearted moments. During the race weekend in Turkey, Hamilton was having dinner with his father when he noticed Fernando Alonso, the reigning Formula One World Champion, dining at a nearby table. After finishing his meal, Alonso came over to introduce himself, which left Hamilton surprised and impressed. The interaction highlighted Alonso's down-to-earth, relaxed, and seemingly calm demeanour, making a lasting impression on the young driver.

By the time the season ended, he had clinched the GP2 championship with an air of inevitability, firmly stamping his authority on the series. Under Vasseur's mentorship, he not only honed his skills but also demonstrated an unrelenting hunger to win, a trait that would define his career. Hamilton's GP2 triumph was not just about trophies; it was about heart, grit, and dogged determination. It was a season that didn't just prepare him for Formula One—it announced to the world that a generational talent had arrived, ready to take on motorsport's grandest stage.

It was also about building relationships. Hamilton and Vasseur developed a strong rapport based on trust and open communication. Vasseur's approachable demeanour made it easy for him to express his thoughts and seek guidance. They frequently engaged in deep discussions about racing strategies, technical feedback, personal goals, and future aspirations like racing for Ferrari. Vasseur provided advice on handling the pressures of fame and expectations, preparing for the spotlight of Formula One.

Their relationship was grounded in mutual respect. Hamilton appreciated Vasseur's honesty and dedication, while Vasseur admired Hamilton's work ethic and humility. Their time together not only honed Hamilton's skills but also shaped his character. The values instilled during this period influenced how he approached challenges and interacted with others. It also embedded in him an ability to galvanise teams around him, an essential skill for any elite racing driver.

Hamilton's success in GP2 solidified his reputation as a future Formula One star, with many in the motorsport community recognising his extraordinary ascent and potential for greatness in the premier racing series. An indication of Vasseur's and ART's brilliance can be found in reviewing past winners of the championships in GP3, F3, GP2 and F2 ART cars; the list includes Nico Rosberg, Romain Grosjean, Nico Hülkenberg, Valtteri Bottas, and George Russell.

### A Critical Partnership: McLaren and ART Grand Prix

The relationship between Ron Dennis, McLaren, and Frédéric Vasseur at ART Grand Prix was instrumental in Hamilton's development during his transition to Formula One. Both Dennis and Vasseur recognised the importance of preparing Hamilton for the challenges of the sport's highest level.

Frédéric Vasseur's leadership was key as Hamilton advanced in his career, competing in Formula 3 and transitioning to GP2. These steps, while a natural progression in his motorsport development, received full support from McLaren. Vasseur's mentorship during this period was instrumental in refining Hamilton's skills, setting him up for success. It was clear from early on, even as he prepared to step into Formula 3 with Vasseur in 2005, that Hamilton was a natural talent—dedicated, singularly focused on achieving his goals. While many drivers claim that their ambition is to become World Champion, few show the relentless focus required to make it a reality; Vasseur felt that Hamilton was one of the rare few who truly exemplified that desire.

Ron Dennis, who had supported Hamilton since his early karting days, entrusted Vasseur with this critical phase, knowing that the experience at ART Grand Prix would be invaluable. The partnership between McLaren and ART Grand Prix ensured Hamilton was equipped with the tools, both technical and psychological, to excel in Formula One. By the end of 2006, Hamilton's GP2 championship win was the result of these efforts coming together—a well-integrated and harmonious approach that paved the way for his record-breaking career.

By the end of the 2006 season, Hamilton had firmly established himself as one of the most exciting young talents in motorsport. His GP2 championship victory justified the trust Ron Dennis and McLaren had placed in him. The next step in Hamilton's journey was the ultimate challenge—Formula One.

Hamilton had had a brief taste of Formula One almost two years earlier when, on 1 December 2004, he tested his first Formula One car with McLaren at Silverstone in an unofficial, untimed test. Two years later, in late 2006, McLaren gave

Hamilton his first official Formula One test at Silverstone, the spiritual home of British motorsport. This was the moment Hamilton had dreamed of since his childhood, when he first approached Ron Dennis at the Autosport Awards and declared his desire to race for McLaren.

**A New Challenge: Formula One**

The test itself was a significant milestone, allowing Hamilton to show his ability to handle the power and complexity of a Formula One car. With the then 2.4-litre V8 engines capable of producing over 700 horsepower, Formula One cars were a significant leap from the GP2 machinery Hamilton had mastered. Yet, Hamilton approached the challenge with the same determination and meticulous preparation that had defined his career thus far.

During the test, Hamilton impressed McLaren's engineers with his adaptability and feedback, a trait honed during his time with ART Grand Prix under Vasseur. His performance validated McLaren's decision to invest in his development and put him in the frame for the 2007 Formula One season.

Hamilton's first Formula One test was more than just a technical evaluation—it was the realisation of a lifelong dream and the first step into what would become a historic career. It marked the beginning of a new chapter, one that would see him rise to become one of the sport's most iconic figures.

Hamilton's impressive performance in the GP2 Series, and his successful Formula One test, coincided with vacancies at McLaren following Juan Pablo Montoya's departure and Kimi Räikkönen's move to Ferrari. After careful consideration, McLaren announced that Hamilton would partner with reigning World Champion Fernando Alonso for the 2007 Formula One season. McLaren's Team Principal, Martin Whitmarsh, expressed confidence in the decision, stating that Hamilton had earned his chance and deserved the opportunity. Reflecting on this milestone, Hamilton acknowledged that to be racing in Formula One with McLaren had been the ultimate goal for him since he was very young.

Stepping into Formula One from GP2 would present new challenges for Hamilton. He would be competing at the highest level, racing against the world's best drivers, including his new teammate, reigning—and double—World Champion Fernando Alonso. This transition would bring increased attention and expectations from the global press, requiring Hamilton to navigate complex relationships within a top-tier team with championship aspirations.

Going into this period, Anthony Hamilton would continue to support his son as his manager, guiding him through the sport's complexities. Recognising that their journey was about to enter a new phase, Anthony emphasised the importance of staying focused on their goals and adhering to the principles that had propelled them to this point.

**The Wheels Come Full Circle**

The bond forged with Vasseur would remain a cornerstone of Hamilton's career, influencing his future decisions and the way he approached challenges and triumphs on and off the track. While their paths diverged after 2006, Hamilton's career continued to flourish, driven by the values instilled in him by Vasseur. Over the years, Hamilton found himself reflecting on the lessons learned during his time with ART Grand Prix, particularly as he built relationships within the Formula One paddock.

It became clear that Vasseur's mentorship—his belief in hard work, resilience, and trust in talent—had shaped Hamilton into the champion he was becoming. This relationship would come full circle when, in 2024, the motorsport world was electrified by the announcement that Hamilton would join Ferrari, now under the stewardship of none other than Vasseur.

The reunion was not just a chance to re-establish old ties; it was the fulfilment of a shared dream. Their partnership—once instrumental in Hamilton's rise to greatness—was now poised to write a new chapter. For Vasseur, it was the return of a driver whose brilliance he had always believed in; for Hamilton, it was an opportunity to complete the journey with the mentor who had first shown him the way.

But before their reunion at Ferrari, Hamilton had 18 years to demonstrate everything he had learned during his formative years in karts, Formula 3, and GP2. From the moment he stepped into a Formula One car in 2007, Hamilton brought the resolve and racecraft that had been honed under the guidance of mentors like his father, Dennis, and Vasseur. Over nearly two decades, he carved out a legacy that would rewrite the history books—amassing victories, championships, and records that showed not only the depth of his talent but also the indomitable spirit forged in his early racing days.

As Hamilton prepared to make his Formula One debut, he carried with him not only the lessons learned and relationships forged but also a staunch determination to succeed. The stage was set for the next chapter in a career destined to redefine the boundaries of Formula One.

# The Season That Changed It All

In 2007, Lewis Hamilton made his much-anticipated debut in Formula One with the McLaren-Mercedes team. At 22 years old, he was stepping into one of the most prestigious teams in motorsport, fulfilling the promise he made to Ron Dennis over a decade earlier. Paired with reigning double World Champion Fernando Alonso, Hamilton faced immense pressure and expectations.

As the 2007 Formula One season unfolded, the world witnessed an unexpected and electrifying rivalry between the seasoned champion Alonso and the sensational rookie Hamilton. Alonso, hailing from Spain, had secured back-to-back World Championships in 2005 and 2006 with Renault, ending Michael Schumacher's reign and establishing himself as the sport's new benchmark. His move to McLaren-Mercedes was heralded as a masterstroke by Team Principal Ron Dennis, who believed that Alonso's experience would spearhead McLaren's return to championship glory. However, the emergence of Hamilton as a formidable contender disrupted the anticipated narrative. The young Briton's performances defied expectations, and his rapid rise set the stage for one of Formula One's most intense rivalries.

Leading up to the season, Hamilton participated in extensive testing sessions to acclimate to the complex and powerful Formula One machinery. The McLaren MP4-22 was a state-of-the-art car, featuring advanced aerodynamics, a 2.4-litre V8 engine with 810bhp, weighing just 605kg, and equipped with cutting-edge electronics.

To put the power of Hamilton's new car into perspective, it is worth noting the power-to-weight ratio, which is used by automotive experts as a comparative indicator of accelerative performance. The MP4-22 had a power-to-weight ratio of around 1,250bhp per tonne. A 2007 Ferrari F430 road car, considered to be a 'supercar' with incredible performance, could manage 333bhp per tonne.

However, one thing that many Formula One drivers talk about is braking power. To put this in context, the Ferrari F430 road car of 2007 could stop from 124mph (200km/h) in 134 metres, or 441 feet. A Formula One car would stop from 124mph in around 60 metres (210 feet)—half the distance. Formula One brakes were literally eye-popping, and drivers would need to withstand 5-6G, or five to six times the force of gravity. In addition, the brake discs of a Formula One car would generate around 1,000°C, further adding to the general discomfort drivers faced.

Stepping into a Formula One car for the first time was a transformative experience for Hamilton. The leap from GP2 to Formula One was monumental, introducing him to unparalleled speed, immense braking and cornering forces, and cutting-edge technology that redefined his understanding of motorsport. The challenges were significant, but the McLaren team worked tirelessly to ensure Hamilton's smooth adjustment to the demands of the sport.

Reflecting on this transition, Hamilton often spoke of the awe and excitement he felt during those early days, as well as the steep learning curve that shaped him into a driver capable of competing at the highest level. The most striking difference for Hamilton was the intensity of understanding the car's technical aspects, which seemed significantly more complex than in the GP2 series, and the physical demands of competing at the highest level. While some drivers initially feel the step up from GP2 is manageable based on a Formula One test, the reality of full race distances revealed a far greater challenge.

Preparing for this meant increased training, dedicating several hours a day to fitness, as well as studying race strategies, pit stops, and the intricate technical details of the car. The differences in aerodynamics, engine characteristics, and overall vehicle geometry required constant adaptation.

With so much information to absorb, the learning curve was steep, but the approach was clear—embrace the challenge, learn as much as possible from the team and experienced figures around him, and ultimately aim for victory.

During this crucial period, Anthony Hamilton remained a driving force behind his son's preparation and discipline. While talent was undeniable, success in Formula One demanded relentless dedication and a methodical approach to mastering the sport's complexities. The McLaren team, known for their meticulous attention to detail under Dennis's leadership, worked closely with Anthony to ensure every aspect of his son's development was covered. The combined effort left little to chance, equipping him with the physical and mental tools needed to make an impact in his rookie season.

However, the challenge extended beyond mastering the car, the team dynamics, and the relentless media attention—there was also his new teammate, Fernando Alonso. When Dennis informed Alonso ahead of the season that Hamilton would be joining the team, the response was pointed. Alonso questioned whether this decision aligned with the goal of winning the Constructors' Championship, suggesting some doubt over Hamilton's ability to contribute significantly to the team's points tally. This hinted at a potential expectation of clear number-one status within the team. It would not take long for Alonso to realise just how serious a competitor Hamilton would be.

### The Dawn of a New Era

On Friday, 16 March, the city of Melbourne vibrated with anticipation as the Formula One season roared to life at Albert Park. Known for its cultural vitality, thriving arts scene, and deep love of sports, Melbourne was the perfect host for motorsport's grandest spectacle. The Albert Park Circuit, a temporary street track that weaves around a serene lake and through lush parklands, combined high-speed straights with tight, technical corners. It was a circuit designed to challenge even the most experienced drivers, let alone a 'rookie' stepping into Formula One for the first time.

Amid the cheers of fans and the thunderous roar of engines, a 22-year-old Hamilton prepared to take his first official laps as a Formula One driver during the opening practice sessions. For many in the paddock, he was just another rookie trying to find his footing in the unforgiving world of Grand Prix racing. But for those who knew his journey—the countless karting victories, the dominance in junior formulas, and the years of meticulous preparation—this moment was the culmination of over a decade of relentless effort and unwavering belief. It wasn't just the start of a race weekend; it was the beginning of a career that would redefine the boundaries of the sport.

From his early days racing radio-controlled cars, where he sharpened his reflexes and strategic thinking, to dominating karting circuits against older and more seasoned competitors, Hamilton had demonstrated an extraordinary ability to stay ahead of the curve from an early age. His triumphs in Formula 3 and GP2 further showed his adaptability, resilience, and unrelenting drive to succeed. Beyond mastering the technical aspects of racecraft, Hamilton learned to navigate the intricate world of professional motorsport in the lower formulas—balancing media obligations, managing team dynamics, and contributing to technical development.

By the time he arrived in Melbourne for his Formula One debut in 2007, Hamilton was not just a promising rookie coming from nowhere; he was a driver whose exceptional talent had been honed through years of meticulous preparation, ready to take his place on motorsport's grandest stage.

Behind Hamilton's extraordinary journey was a steadfast support system that shaped him into the driver and individual he was. His father, Anthony, had worked tirelessly, juggling multiple jobs to fund his son's early racing career and instilling in him the values of hard work and perseverance. Ron Dennis had taken Hamilton under his wing at the age of thirteen, providing the mentorship, resources, and opportunities to nurture his prodigious talent. Frédéric Vasseur, his mentor in the junior formulas, had further refined his skills, imparting a deep understanding of vehicle dynamics and race strategy—tools that would be crucial on Formula One's grand stage.

As he stood on the brink of his Formula One debut, Hamilton carried the weight of their sacrifices and belief in his abilities. His focus was razor-sharp, honed by years of preparation and unwavering determination. The stakes were immense. The paddock had its fair share of scepticism, many expecting him to be outshone by his teammate, Alonso. But for Hamilton, this was not just about proving the doubters wrong; it was about honouring the journey and those who had helped bring him to this moment, and seizing the opportunity to etch his name into motorsport history.

Damon Hill, the 1996 Formula One World Champion, spoke of Hamilton's debut and made it clear that Hamilton had got there on merit, showing determination to rise to the top. Hill said the opportunity had not simply been handed to Hamilton but that he had earned it.

In the lead-up to the Australian Grand Prix, the paddock was rife with speculation. The dominant narrative centred on Alonso's quest for a third consecutive title and how he would lead McLaren back to championship glory. Few anticipated that Hamilton would pose any significant challenge to the established order, certainly in the first few months of the season.

In Formula One, the first rival a driver faces is often his teammate—the only other person with the same equipment. Hamilton was keenly aware of this dynamic. Beating or matching Alonso, the man regarded as one of the fastest on the grid and the current World Champion, would not only establish his credibility but also signal his arrival as a formidable competitor.

**Setting the Stage: Albert Park Circuit**

The Albert Park Circuit is a 5.303 km track that winds around the Albert Park Lake, featuring 16 turns that challenge drivers with a mix of high-speed sections and tight chicanes. The track's temporary nature means that grip levels evolve significantly over the weekend, adding an extra layer of complexity. The weather forecast predicted clear skies and warm temperatures, setting the stage for an intense battle.

The favourites to win were the Ferraris, with Kimi Räikkönen making his debut for the team and Felipe Massa eager to assert himself. McLaren was seen as the main challenger, but many doubted whether they could match Ferrari's pace.

On Saturday, 17 March, qualifying unfolded under the bright Australian sun. Hamilton approached the session with quiet confidence. In the previous practice sessions, he had impressed the team with his speed and feedback, working closely with his engineers to fine-tune the car's setup.

Hamilton showed impressive speed and composure. He comfortably advanced through the three practice sessions, remaining in the top four for each one, building his confidence as he progressed. In the decisive qualifying session, he pushed the limits of the McLaren MP4-22, ultimately securing fourth place on the grid. In front of him on the grid were Räikkönen in pole position for Ferrari, with Hamilton's teammate Alonso in second, and Nick Heidfeld in his BMW Sauber in third. Massa, suffering from mechanical issues, qualified poorly and was relegated to the back of the grid.

After qualifying, Hamilton was seen deep in discussion with his race engineer, analysing telemetry data and discussing strategies for the race. His dedication to understanding every aspect of performance exemplified the work ethic that had brought him this far. He had a calm, relaxed, and focused manner about everything he did, showing maturity well beyond his years.

Pundits were quick to assess Hamilton's early impact following the qualifying session, with former Formula One driver Mark Blundell suggesting Hamilton's qualifying performance was even better than Michael Schumacher's debut with Jordan in 1991. Few rookies had made such an immediate impression. Throughout the paddock, Hamilton's name was on everyone's lips, reinforcing the sense that something special was unfolding.

**The Race: Rising to the Occasion**

Sunday, 18 March, dawned over Albert Park with warm, clear skies—ideal conditions for the season's opening race. Anticipation filled the air as the drivers took their places on the grid, each bracing for the unknowns of a new campaign. Hamilton, making his Formula One race debut, performed his pre-race rituals in quiet concentration, chatting to his mechanics and remaining focused.

When the five red lights went out, Hamilton surged forward, carefully positioning his McLaren near teammate Alonso into the first corner, overtaking him around the outside of Turn 1. In one corner, Hamilton had set his stall out for the rest of the season. By Turn 1's exit, Hamilton settled into third behind Heidfeld's BMW Sauber and Räikkönen's leading Ferrari.

Over the opening laps, Hamilton displayed a maturity beyond his years, maintaining his position and fending off Alonso's attempts to reclaim the spot. His first pit stop went flawlessly, including taking on fuel, allowing him to stay ahead of the two-time World Champion. However, on a different pit strategy, Alonso ultimately found an opportunity to move in front after the second round of stops.

Hamilton's composure under pressure was astonishing to some, but those who had seen all the hard work over the last ten years were not at all surprised. Despite being a rookie in Formula One, he had been racing for over ten years and handled the complexities of race strategy, tyre management, refuelling, and traffic with the aplomb of a veteran. He demonstrated consistent lap times, managing both tyre wear and fuel consumption effectively.

As the race progressed, the order settled with Räikkönen leading for Ferrari, Alonso second, and Hamilton third. When the chequered flag waved, Hamilton crossed the line, securing a third-place podium finish on his debut—a feat not achieved since Jacques Villeneuve in 1996.

On the podium, Hamilton stood alongside Räikkönen and Alonso, his face lit up with a broad smile. As champagne sprayed and the crowd roared, it was a moment he had long envisioned—a fitting reward for years of dedication. After the race, Hamilton was ecstatic, describing the result as an incredible start both for himself and for the team. The excitement surrounding his debut was shared by Alonso, who acknowledged Hamilton's talent and potential, suggesting that their in-team rivalry could prove beneficial in securing valuable points over the season.

Räikkönen, meanwhile, gave little away, remarking that he hadn't needed to push to the limit—a statement that sent an ominous warning to the rest of the paddock about the outright pace of the Ferrari.

Hamilton again praised the efforts of the team. This wasn't just marketing; it was heartfelt, and something he had learned from his father and Vasseur. He had learned that to be the fastest, you needed the best car, and to have the best car, you needed to galvanise the team around you—something they tended not to do if they didn't get the recognition they quite rightly deserved.

Hamilton's remarkable debut prompted a shift in expectations for the season. The assumption that Alonso would dominate within the team was now under scrutiny, as the rookie's speed and composure made it clear that the battle would be far closer than anticipated. His level of preparation and physical conditioning also became a talking point, with Alonso looking tired and sweaty after the race, whilst Hamilton looked fresh as a daisy, highlighting the intense training that had gone into his debut.

There was also growing recognition of his natural talent, with seasoned figures in the sport acknowledging that he was more than just a promising newcomer—he had all the makings of a true contender, with Eddie Jordan remarking that Hamilton was 'the real deal'.

Post-race, the relative performance of the cars became a hot topic. The Ferrari of Räikkönen had shown superior pace, but the McLarens were close behind. The BMW Sauber team also displayed strong form, indicating that the season could be more competitive than anticipated. Within McLaren, the dynamic between Hamilton and Alonso was set to become a focal point. With both drivers demonstrating the capability to challenge at the front, internal competition was inevitable.

Following the 2007 Australian Grand Prix, Ron Dennis expressed satisfaction with both Alonso's and Hamilton's performances, noting Hamilton's impressive debut and acknowledging Alonso's value as a double World Champion. He consistently maintained that McLaren's policy was to treat both drivers equally, giving them the same opportunities to succeed. Dennis emphasised that this approach would strengthen the team's competitiveness over the season.

Hamilton's debut not only marked the arrival of a new star but also set the tone for one of the most thrilling seasons, which would go down to the wire. The battle lines were drawn—not just between McLaren and Ferrari but also within the McLaren garage.

As the teams prepared to head to the next race in Malaysia, a track Hamilton had never raced at before, the world watched with anticipation. Would Hamilton continue to challenge Alonso? How would the team manage this emerging rivalry? Could McLaren overtake Ferrari in the development race? One thing was certain: Lewis Hamilton had arrived, and Formula One would never be the same again.

The initial races of the season saw Hamilton consistently matching or exceeding Alonso's performances, and this unexpected challenge from a rookie began to unsettle the two-time World Champion. The 2007 season's story was shaped by the unexpected and increasingly fierce competition between Hamilton and Alonso. What began as a mentorship opportunity evolved into a battle of equals, with both drivers pushing each other to the limits.

Hamilton's ability to challenge and often outperform Alonso disrupted the established hierarchy. His youth and fresh approach contrasted with Alonso's experience and intensity, creating a captivating dynamic that gripped fans and analysts alike.

One of the remarkable aspects of Hamilton's rookie season was his ability to adapt quickly to circuits he had never raced on before. Unlike Alonso, who had years of experience on these tracks, Hamilton was often learning them during the practice sessions leading up to the race weekend. His hard work paid off, with four podiums in a row, and by the time they left Spain, Hamilton was leading the World Championship from Alonso by two points.

Then they went to Monaco.

**Monaco Grand Prix: The Jewel in the Crown**

The Monaco Grand Prix, held on 27 May, marked a turning point in the simmering tension between Hamilton and Alonso. No venue better underscores a driver's mastery—or tests their nerve—than the famous streets of Monte Carlo. Hemmed in by steel barriers and ancient stone walls, the circuit threads through a glamorous maze of narrow lanes and vertiginous corners, demanding unflinching precision and unshakable confidence. The slightest error can mean instant disaster.

Securing victory at Monaco is akin to engraving your name into motorsport legend. The glittering harbour, teeming with luxury yachts, and the hillside terraces spilling over with global celebrities form the backdrop to this high-stakes drama. As the howl of V8 engines ricocheted through the city's canyons of concrete and glass during free practice, the 2007 race promised not just a triumph on track, but also a defining chapter in one of Formula One's most compelling rivalries. It would shatter the illusion that all was well within McLaren.

Hamilton, racing at Monaco for the first time in a Formula One car, approached the weekend with a mix of excitement and respect for the challenge ahead. He quickly demonstrated his aptitude, navigating the treacherous circuit with skill. In the final qualifying session, Alonso secured pole position with a lap time of 1:15.726. Hamilton was a close second, just 0.179 seconds behind, clocking in at 1:15.905. The narrow gap underscored Hamilton's rapid adaptation to one of the most demanding tracks on the calendar. Both Hamilton and Alonso felt impeded on their fast runs by slower cars, so the positions could well have been reversed.

At the start of the race, both McLaren drivers held their positions, with Alonso leading into Turn 1. Given the tight nature of the circuit, overtaking opportunities were scarce, making strategy and consistency the key factors in determining the race outcome. Throughout the early stages, Hamilton remained close behind Alonso, carefully managing his pace and waiting for the right moment to attack.

As the race progressed, Hamilton began closing the gap, raising speculation about whether he might challenge for the lead. This piled pressure on Alonso, who was already managing concerns over brake wear. Alonso had to increase his pace as a result and became very annoyed over the situation. McLaren eventually instructed both drivers to manage their engines and tyres, ensuring a controlled run to the finish and securing a dominant one-two result for the team.

At the chequered flag, Alonso stepped out of his car in victory and was greeted by Ron Dennis, who made it clear that the race had been carefully managed from the pit wall, with instructions given to Hamilton to ease off. This led Alonso to believe that his win had not been entirely his own, but rather the result of team intervention. Frustration quickly set in, as the implication that Hamilton had been deliberately restrained only fuelled tensions within the team. Hamilton came home in second. The McLarens were so quick that they had lapped everyone up to third place.

After the race finished, the atmosphere within McLaren grew tense. Hamilton, who believed he had the pace to challenge for victory, openly expressed frustration at having been asked to hold position. In post-race interviews, he acknowledged that achieving a one-two finish was beneficial for the team but made it clear he would have preferred the freedom to fight for the win. His remarks, implying that he felt constrained by the team's caution, sparked media speculation that McLaren might be favouring Alonso. The team, however, consistently denied any bias, insisting that the decision to maintain positions was purely strategic—intended to secure maximum points and avoid the inherent risks of racing wheel-to-wheel on Monaco's unforgiving streets.

Only five races into his role as Lewis's Formula One manager, Anthony Hamilton was already showing incredible diplomacy and tact. Reflecting on the race, he acknowledged that Lewis had felt he was quicker at points but had to cool off during the first stint, and that towards the end, it looked like he could have challenged, but with McLaren running first and second, there was little sense in fighting unless absolutely necessary. In the end, second place in a first Monaco Grand Prix was a good result.

Hamilton's performance also drew praise from the paddock. His ability to handle the immense pressure—both from the media and the expectations placed on him—was widely recognised. He had been very sensible throughout the race, showing maturity beyond his years and once again delivering when it mattered, keeping up his brilliant record of podium finishes in every race so far in the season.

After the 2007 Monaco Grand Prix, McLaren faced criticism over their handling of the race, as they were believed to have instructed both drivers to back off and preserve their equipment. At the time, this practice was controversial due to an FIA ban on team orders introduced in 2003. The rule was implemented following the infamous 2002 Austrian Grand Prix, where Ferrari ordered Rubens Barrichello to surrender victory to Michael Schumacher. By 2007, the ban prohibited teams from issuing directives aimed at manipulating race outcomes for strategic gain. This regulation remained in place until the end of the 2010 season, when it was officially lifted.

Following scrutiny by the FIA and media speculation, Ron Dennis acknowledged after the race that they had effectively "brought the car home" to ensure a safe one-two result. Although this was not termed as a direct "team order" to freeze positions, it was widely interpreted as an instruction that prevented Hamilton from making a concerted effort to overtake Alonso.

This decision sparked some controversy and led the FIA to review the team's actions, though no serious penalties were imposed. Ron Dennis was firm in defending the team's approach, making it clear that McLaren operated with complete fairness. Addressing speculation over potential favouritism, he emphasised that both drivers were treated equally, with no preference given to either. Maintaining a level playing field had always been the team's philosophy, and that principle remained unchanged.

As the McLaren team left Monaco, Alonso and Hamilton stood at the top of the Championship with 38 points each. The atmosphere had shifted. Where there had once been mutual respect and calm, a new tension took hold.

Alonso, widely regarded as the preeminent driver in 2007, now faced a formidable challenge from the teammate who refused to bow to seniority. Even more unsettling, from

Alonso's perspective, was the growing sense that McLaren and Ron Dennis might not fully support him. Before long, these suspicions would surface in a dramatic and unforgettable way.

**Canadian Grand Prix: The Wall of Champions**

The next critical chapter unfolded on 10 June at the Canadian Grand Prix, held at the Circuit Gilles Villeneuve in Montreal. The track is renowned for its challenging layout, combining long straights with tight chicanes, and the infamous "Wall of Champions" at the exit of the final chicane—a spot that has claimed several World Champions over the years, including Damon Hill, Michael Schumacher, and Jacques Villeneuve.

Hamilton demonstrated his immense one-lap pace by claiming his first Formula One pole position with a time of 1:15.707. Alonso secured second on the grid, 0.456 seconds adrift, with a lap of 1:16.163.

Following the session, Hamilton remained composed, showing maturity beyond his years, and acknowledged the importance of enjoying the moment, staying focused on keeping relaxed and preparing for the challenge ahead. His preparation for the race was to spend a quiet evening with his father and trainer, get a good night's rest, and return ready to deliver the same level of performance on race day.

On Sunday, the five lights went out, and Hamilton maintained his lead, while Alonso made an uncharacteristic mistake, running wide at the first corner and rejoining in third place. Throughout the race, Hamilton demonstrated exceptional composure, managing several Safety Car periods due to accidents on the tricky circuit. Alonso, meanwhile, struggled with additional errors, going wide and across the grass multiple times at the first corner.

Just one-third into the race, a horrific accident shattered the rhythm of the afternoon. Robert Kubica, in his Sauber BMW, was right on the tail of Jarno Trulli's Toyota as they exited the tight chicane of Turns 8 and 9. Kubica, carrying more speed, swung alongside his rival, the pair now hurtling towards the sweeping left-hand kink before L'Épingle at a staggering 180mph (290km/h).

Sensing the threat, Trulli steered right in a desperate attempt to defend. That single, instinctive movement clipped the Sauber's front wing and forced Kubica's Sauber BMW off the asphalt and onto the grass at close to 170mph. As the car streaked over a small tarmac runoff, its nose suddenly lifted, and in the blink of an eye, the Sauber BMW was airborne.

With sickening force, it slammed head-on into a concrete wall, fragments of carbon fibre bursting outwards like shrapnel from an explosion. Three wheels tore free from their tethers, and both front and rear wings disintegrated as the wrecked chassis ricocheted back onto the track. The car flipped and rolled wildly over the grass, only to crash again into the opposite barrier before finally skidding to a halt on its side.

Inside the cockpit, Kubica's helmeted head lurched uncontrollably, his body frighteningly still—a grim reminder that Formula One's thrills come shadowed by unforgiving dangers. Then he started to move his fingers.

Before stray pieces had even settled, a lone marshal sprinted through a gap in the fence, fire extinguisher in hand, rushing headlong towards what remained of Kubica's machine. Within seconds, the medical team arrived, doctors and medics already kneeling amid the wreckage, committed to salvaging whatever hope remained in this sudden, harrowing silence. The race carried on under waved yellow flags before the Safety Car was deployed, allowing medics to attend to Kubica while marshals worked to clear the debris.

Initially, a standard road-going Honda led the field, with Hamilton at the front, weaving aggressively to maintain temperature in his grooved tyres. Before long, the official Mercedes-AMG Safety Car was brought out, with the rest of the grid forming up behind it.

Kubica's crash was shocking, with many in the paddock remarking on how unusual it was and how severe it seemed. Hamilton, having known and raced against Kubica in the junior categories, had to put aside any emotional distraction and stay focused. Maintaining his rhythm, he continued to warm up his brakes and tyres, keeping his mind on the task ahead.

Despite the chaos, including four separate Safety Car periods, Hamilton remained composed and in control. Managing the race brilliantly, he steered clear of trouble and crossed the line to take a dominant victory.

The 2007 Canadian Grand Prix marked a decisive moment in Formula One history as Hamilton secured his first-ever victory in just his sixth race, a feat that left fans and pundits in awe. The rookie's performance not only established him as a formidable talent but also intensified the spotlight on Alonso. Speculation about Alonso feeling the pressure of being outperformed by his young teammate grew, fuelled by the Spaniard's uncharacteristic errors during the race, such as running wide at Turn 1, which allowed Heidfeld to overtake him.

Hamilton's performance was widely hailed as extraordinary, with many experts believing that he was pushing the boundaries of what was once thought possible in Formula One. His rapid rise redefined expectations for a rookie, as he continued to deliver results that few had anticipated.

Meanwhile, Alonso's difficulties did not go unnoticed. Pushing hard in an effort to keep up, small errors began to creep into his driving—mistakes that were rarely seen from him in the past. The pressure within the team was building, and as the season progressed, the dynamic between the two McLaren drivers was becoming increasingly tense.

Adding to the intrigue, Alonso reportedly did not congratulate Hamilton after the race, a notable omission that only heightened speculation about the growing rivalry between the two drivers and the pressure Alonso faced. The media latched onto these moments, interpreting them as cracks in the armour of the seasoned Champion. The dynamics at McLaren were clearly shifting, with Hamilton's rapid ascent unsettling the team's established hierarchy and setting the stage for an electrifying season of internal competition.

Following the 2007 Canadian Grand Prix, Alonso's post-race demeanour attracted media attention. Reports indicated that he did not participate in the customary post-race celebrations, including the post-podium ceremony team celebrations. This absence was noted by various media outlets, suggesting that Alonso's frustration stemmed from being outperformed by his rookie teammate.

The incident fuelled speculation about internal tensions within the McLaren team, as Alonso's decision to forgo the celebrations was seen as a sign of the mounting pressure he felt due to Hamilton's rapid ascent. As they left Montreal, Hamilton was on 48 points, with Alonso second on 40 points.

**United States Grand Prix: A New Battleground**

One week later, the Formula One circus moved to the United States Grand Prix at the Indianapolis Motor Speedway. The circuit, incorporating part of the famous oval, was unfamiliar territory for Hamilton, but he once again adapted quickly.

Hamilton secured his second consecutive pole position with a time of 1:12.331. Alonso was nearly two-tenths behind, qualifying second with 1:12.500. The Ferraris were third and fourth.

In the race, both Hamilton and Alonso got away well at the start. Over the first lap, Alonso, renowned for his first-lap speed, was all over the back of Hamilton's car, trying to force a way past. Hamilton kept his cool and took some slightly narrower lines to block any overtaking attempts.

The race was marked by a lengthy fight between the McLaren teammates. Alonso applied relentless pressure on Hamilton, attempting overtakes and shadowing his every move. All the cars went through their pit stops, trying to outfox each other with different fuel loads and tyres.

Halfway through the race, Alonso had great drive off the final banked corner onto the home straight and slipstreamed Hamilton at close to 200mph. Hamilton spotted the danger and moved towards the inside, forcing Alonso wide. He then pulled out alongside Hamilton, both cars side by side, Alonso weaving gently towards Hamilton, trying to intimidate him. Hamilton kept his cool and retained his lead into Turn 1.

As had been shown in the junior formulas, there was no way Hamilton would be intimidated by anyone. On the next lap, at full racing speed, Alonso weaved violently across the track towards the pit wall, where the team were holding out his 'board'. It seemed like a strange thing to do, and it looked more and more like Alonso was becoming flustered.

The race finished with Hamilton taking the victory and Alonso in second. In a straight fight, the 'rookie' had beaten the current two-time World Champion.

Hamilton's second victory was praised, especially for his composure under pressure. Reflecting on the achievement, Hamilton acknowledged the significance of winning at two unfamiliar circuits back-to-back. The rapid progress being made, both personally and as a team, made the result even more rewarding, reinforcing the sense that he was establishing himself as a genuine title contender.

The Formula One family moved back to Europe, where Räikkönen would seal back-to-back victories in the Ferrari at France, then Great Britain. Next would be the European Grand Prix.

**The European Grand Prix**

The European Grand Prix, held at the Nürburgring in Germany on 22 July, began under ominous grey skies. The front runners started the race on grooved slick tyres, but before the cars completed the first lap, rain began to fall. The slippery conditions quickly caught drivers off guard, leading to a flurry of pit stops for intermediate tyres.

By Lap 3, the weather escalated dramatically as torrential rain saturated the track almost instantly. At Turn 1, chaos unfolded. Jenson Button in the BAR Honda was the first to lose control and slide off, followed shortly by Hamilton, who, unable to brake, steer, or effectively even see where he was going, aquaplaned straight off and into the gravel trap. Adrian Sutil, in similar fashion, joined the others.

As the conditions worsened, safety teams began deploying recovery vehicles to clear the stricken cars. However, before they could reach Button's car, Nico Rosberg in the Williams came hurtling into Turn 1 backwards at over 50mph, completely at the mercy of aquaplaning. Scott Speed, driving for STR Ferrari, then joined the growing pile-up in what quickly became the most expensive gravel trap in Germany. In just twenty chaotic seconds, five cars had been eliminated at the same corner, all victims of the treacherous conditions.

But the drama was far from over. Worse was yet to come.

The Safety Car was deployed immediately after Scott Speed's dramatic exit, its bright yellow lights flashing atop the sleek Mercedes-AMG. Driven by the highly experienced former DTM racer Bernd Mayländer, the Safety Car exited the pits and approached the first corner to pick up the leading Formula One car. As Mayländer slowed at the end of the straight before the tight first corner, his racing instincts and incredible awareness kicked in. Realising there was imminent danger from behind, he suddenly accelerated hard to clear the corner.

Moments later, Vitantonio Liuzzi, in the second STR Ferrari, came flying down the pit straight—backwards—at nearly

100mph, completely out of control. The car bounced over the inside kerb before skidding across the track and into the gravel run-off. Had the Safety Car still been in place, the consequences could have been catastrophic. Liuzzi's car continued its wild trajectory, eventually crossing to the outside of the circuit, where the rear end clipped a bright yellow recovery truck. Fortunately, no marshals were in its path as they worked frantically to clear stranded cars, and the impact with the truck was minor.

The incident served as a chilling reminder of the dangers posed by recovery vehicles on a live track, particularly in wet conditions. It acted as a forewarning about the risks of deploying them before a race was fully neutralised—concerns that would, tragically, prove prophetic in Japan several years later. The officials responded by red-flagging the race, bringing the chaotic proceedings to a temporary halt.

Unlike several other drivers who had gone off, Hamilton managed to restart when the race resumed, albeit from the back of the field. In the closing laps, Alonso engaged in a tussle with Massa's Ferrari, ultimately making a decisive overtake to secure victory.

As the teams departed Germany, the Championship fight had tightened significantly. Hamilton led the standings with 70 points, closely followed by Alonso on 68. Meanwhile, Räikkönen remained a more distant contender in fourth with 52 points—though his role in the title fight would become critical as the season unfolded.

Next on the calendar was Hungary, where tensions within McLaren would erupt and push the team dynamics to their breaking point. The contrast between circuits like Canada and Hungary highlighted the adaptability required in Formula One. While Canada demanded precision at high speeds with its fast straights and tight chicanes, the Hungaroring in Hungary was a twisty, high-downforce track requiring exceptional aerodynamic grip, confidence in the car, and smooth inputs from the driver.

**Hungarian Grand Prix: The Breaking Point**

The 2007 Hungarian Grand Prix qualifying session was marred by a significant intra-team controversy at McLaren. During the final phase of qualifying, an incident unfolded that had lasting repercussions for both drivers and the team.

The sequence began when Hamilton did not adhere to a pre-arranged plan to allow Alonso to pass during their out-lap, disrupting the team's strategy. In response, during a critical pit stop with less than two minutes remaining in the session, Alonso remained stationary for an additional 10 seconds in the McLaren pit box, directly impeding Hamilton, who was queued behind. This deliberate delay prevented Hamilton from completing his final flying lap. Consequently, Alonso secured pole position with a time of 1:19.674, while Hamilton was relegated to second with a time of 1:19.781.

The race stewards took action, handing Alonso a five-place grid penalty for impeding another driver. In addition, McLaren was later stripped of the right to earn Constructors' Championship points for the race. Ron Dennis was asked if Alonso had acted deliberately in holding Hamilton up in qualifying, and Dennis curtly explained that the matter would be handled internally within the team, offering no further insight into the situation.

This incident not only affected the immediate race outcomes but also intensified the internal tensions within McLaren, shaping the dynamics between their two leading drivers for the remainder of the season. The atmosphere in the post-qualifying press conference was charged with tension. Hamilton was physically bubbling, his body vibrating. It was clear that harmony within the McLaren camp was fractured.

Despite the underlying strife, Hamilton maintained a composed demeanour, choosing to focus on the positives. He praised the team’s efforts in developing the car, highlighting the advancements they had brought to Hungary. His measured responses contrasted with the evident strain between the two drivers, underscoring the mounting tension behind the scenes.

As race day dawned, tension lingered like a storm cloud over the McLaren garage. Hamilton, unfazed by the drama, launched into the lead at the start and never looked back. Alonso, starting sixth due to his penalty, fought hard to claw his way back up the order. The Hungaroring's unforgiving nature, especially in the days before DRS, limited his progress, however. Despite his undeniable skill, Alonso could only manage fourth place, unable to challenge the rookie who had already established himself as a formidable competitor.

Hamilton's flawless drive underlined his poise and maturity, a performance that was described as remarkable given the off-track turmoil. Hamilton had risen above all the controversy and distractions and had not allowed them to get to him.

Dennis reflected on the victory while also addressing the controversy from qualifying, making it clear that what had transpired was unacceptable. Acknowledging the emotional toll, he remained firm that the team would move forward and continue competing with professionalism. He reiterated McLaren's long-standing principle of equal treatment, stating that under no circumstances would one driver be favoured over the other.

Meanwhile, Alonso's frustrations were evident in his post-race interviews. When asked about his future with McLaren, he remained evasive, offering little clarity on what lay ahead, hinting at growing uncertainty within the team.

The result of the Hungarian Grand Prix tightened the Championship standings further. Hamilton extended his lead to 80 points, with Alonso still close behind at 73. The race marked a key moment in the season. The Hungarian Grand Prix epitomised the growing storm within McLaren. It was a race of triumph for Hamilton, who continued to defy expectations in his rookie season, and a race of frustration for Alonso, whose Championship hopes were increasingly clouded by the emerging brilliance of his teammate.

### The Turkish Grand Prix

The Turkish Grand Prix on 26 August became significant not just for the racing but for the growing tensions within McLaren, highlighted by Alonso's blunt remarks. His dissatisfaction with the team was becoming increasingly evident, and when questioned about whether he was receiving equal treatment or felt entitled to preferential status over Hamilton, he responded by saying he was bringing 'six-tenths of a second' to the car with his driving but suggested he was getting nothing in return. The remark carried an air of entitlement, offering insight into his mindset at the time.

Hamilton, by contrast, remained composed and humble, choosing to focus on the collective effort behind McLaren's success. When asked about Alonso's comments, he was quick to credit the entire team, emphasising that any improvements came as a result of a shared effort between engineers, test drivers, and the factory. Rather than engaging in the growing tensions, he reinforced the importance of teamwork over individual contributions.

The contrasting attitudes between the two drivers further underscored the growing divide within McLaren, with Hamilton's humility resonating with the team's ethos and Alonso's comments only deepening the rift.

### The Spygate Scandal Unfolds

At the same time, McLaren found itself at the centre of the explosive "Spygate" scandal, which would cast a long shadow over the 2007 season. In June, Ferrari uncovered that one of their senior engineers, Nigel Stepney, had leaked confidential technical information to McLaren. By July, the FIA had summoned McLaren to answer allegations of possessing Ferrari's proprietary data. The initial hearing took place on 26

July 2007, where McLaren was found to have been in possession of the information. However, the team escaped punishment due to insufficient evidence that the data had been used to gain a competitive advantage.

As investigations continued, new evidence emerged. Emails between Alonso and McLaren's test driver, Pedro de la Rosa, surfaced, revealing discussions about Ferrari's technical data. This revelation led to a second FIA hearing on 13 September 2007. The outcome was a seismic moment in Formula One history: McLaren was fined an unprecedented $100 million and stripped of all their Constructors' Championship points for the 2007 season. In an effort to keep the Championship battle alive, the FIA allowed the team's drivers, Hamilton and Alonso, to retain their points.

The scandal not only tarnished McLaren's reputation but also intensified the already strained dynamics within the team, adding another layer of complexity to an already unforgettable season. It further exacerbated tensions within McLaren and externally between Team Principal Ron Dennis and FIA President Max Mosley. Their strained relationship was evident throughout the proceedings, with Mosley later commenting on the challenges of managing such a high-profile controversy.

"Spygate" not only resulted in unprecedented penalties but also cast a lasting shadow over McLaren's reputation and their 2007 campaign, leaving an indelible mark on Formula One history.

Throughout the tumultuous 2007 Formula One season, Hamilton, in his rookie year, managed to maintain exceptional focus despite the "Spygate" scandal and internal tensions at McLaren. During this period, Hamilton often spoke about the importance of focusing on what he could control—his performance on the track. His public comments frequently emphasised a professional approach, centred on racing excellence, personal accountability, and crediting others who helped him perform.

There were mixed results over the next few races, with Massa winning in Turkey in the Ferrari, Alonso winning in Italy, and Räikkönen winning at Spa in Belgium in the Ferrari. As the teams left Belgium, the points had shifted: Hamilton was now on 97, Alonso on 95, and Räikkönen was chipping away at them both, now on 84 points. If Räikkönen could maintain his trajectory and should one or both McLaren drivers have a misstep or DNF, he was in with a chance.

**Japanese Grand Prix: Mastery in the Rain**

At the Japanese Grand Prix at the end of September, held at the Fuji Speedway, Hamilton faced one of the most challenging races of the season. Fuji Speedway features a mix of high-speed corners and one of the longest straights in Formula One. The race was marked by torrential rain, leading to poor visibility and treacherous conditions, so it started behind the Safety Car. The weather was so bad that the cars had to run behind the Safety Car for nearly 20 laps.

Both Ferraris started on intermediate tyres, despite there being torrential rain and rivers across the track. It wasn't long before Räikkönen slid off backwards, thankfully into a tarmac runoff area, allowing him to rejoin and pit for full wets. Massa also pitted.

On Lap 23, Takuma Sato in the Super Aguri Honda pitted for fuel and tyres. As he left the pit lane, the right side of the car caught fire, the flames seeming incredibly vivid amidst the wet greyness. The rain was so heavy that by the time he had reached the end of the pits, the fire was out. The conditions were borderline, and by mid-race, both Hamilton and Alonso were spun out within a lap of each other after being hit by other cars. Thankfully, both could rejoin without much damage or losing too much time, but Hamilton dropped to fourth.

With 26 laps to go, Alonso had a significant accident, his McLaren aquaplaning off into the wall, tearing a wheel off and putting debris all over the track. The Safety Car was again deployed, and in the changes following pit stops, Hamilton was back in first place. He followed the Safety Car, weaving to get a feel for the conditions and warm the tyres and brakes.

As the Safety Car continued to lead the field, the race took an unexpected turn with a bizarre incident. Sebastian Vettel, driving for the junior Red Bull team, STR Ferrari, was running in third when he misjudged the situation and collided with Mark Webber in the senior Red Bull Renault, who was in second. The impact put both cars out of the race, ending what had been a strong showing for the team.

Back in the pits, Webber was visibly frustrated when asked for his thoughts on the incident. His response was blunt, reflecting his disappointment at losing a potential podium due to what he saw as inexperience, and he lamented about "kids racing in Formula One".

Drawing on the wet-weather racing skills developed during his karting days in the UK, Hamilton remained composed under pressure to secure a commanding victory. As he crossed the finish line, the spray from his McLaren's diffuser and rear wing rose high above the pit wall, creating a striking visual in the soaked conditions. In a moment of pure elation, he pumped his fist in celebration, fully aware of the significance of the win.

Hamilton, quite rightly, was ecstatic. Post-race, he showed some of his emotions, saying that on the last lap he had been thinking about Senna and Prost and how that made him feel, in that he might be on the way to achieving something similar to them. It was a poignant reflection from someone starting out in his career. But little did Hamilton know he would go on to exceed their combined number of race wins and match their total number of Drivers' titles.

**Chinese Grand Prix (7 October 2007 – Shanghai, China)**

The penultimate race of the 2007 season unfolded at the expansive Shanghai International Circuit, under the looming threat of rain. With cool, overcast skies casting a shadow over the track, Hamilton knew that a solid result could secure the Championship. All he needed was to finish ahead of his closest rivals—Alonso and Räikkönen. The weekend had been dry up until this point. In practice and qualifying, Hamilton had shown his pace, claiming pole position with a flawless lap. Räikkönen lined up beside him in second, while Massa secured third for Ferrari, with Alonso in fourth.

As the cars lined up on the grid, the track remained damp from overnight rain, marking the first moisture of the weekend. The teams opted for intermediate tyres, knowing that the tricky conditions would make the start far from straightforward. When the lights went out, Hamilton made the perfect getaway. He pulled away cleanly from Räikkönen, holding his position as the field charged towards Turn 1. The race was on, and with every passing lap, Hamilton's resolve grew stronger—his focus fixed on the elusive title that could be his.

Hamilton made his first pit stop on Lap 15, where McLaren refuelled the car but chose not to change the tyres. The front tyres had worn down by over 70%, leaving them vulnerable if the rain returned. If the track continued to dry, however, it could work in his favour. As he exited the pit lane, a cloud of spray billowed from the track, a reminder that conditions were still unpredictable.

Meanwhile, in the Red Bull pit, David Coulthard kept his strategy straightforward when discussing his next stop with his engineers. His instruction was clear—if rain arrived before the stop, the tyres would be changed accordingly; if not, they would remain the same. His approach echoed Hamilton's, carefully monitoring the shifting conditions and staying flexible to make the right call at the crucial moment. Massa followed suit, pitting for fuel on Lap 17 without changing his tyres.

By the time Lap 24 arrived, the rain had held off, and a dry racing line began to form, though off the line, the track remained slippery and unpredictable. Just as the first cars began to switch to grooved slick tyres on Lap 25, the rain returned, adding yet another layer of uncertainty to the race. A lap later, Ralf Schumacher, on slick tyres, lost grip at the final corner and spun onto the pit straight. A few seconds later, one of the Spyker cars crashed in the same area, signalling that the track was becoming increasingly treacherous. Alonso arrived on the scene moments later, running wide onto the grass but managing to regain control and stay on the circuit. It was clear: the track was slipping out of control for drivers still on slicks.

Räikkönen, on intermediate tyres with better grip, closed rapidly on Hamilton, setting up a tense battle. As they approached the final corner, marshals waved double yellow flags, signalling caution, as well as a yellow flag with red vertical stripes—warning drivers of slippery conditions ahead. Despite the warnings, Hamilton, struggling on his worn intermediates, understeered off the track and onto the astroturf. He was able to recover, still maintaining the lead, but the slippery surface was clearly taking its toll, and more cars began to spin off in the challenging conditions. Half a lap later, Räikkönen took advantage of Hamilton's lack of grip, passing him at Turn 8 as Hamilton drifted wide.

On Lap 31, Hamilton made his way to the pits, but the entry proved treacherous. As he approached the sharp left-hander leading into the pit lane, his worn intermediate tyres lost all grip. The McLaren understeered off the racing line and into the gravel at a near crawl. Despite his efforts to keep the car moving, it became stranded, unable to make it back to the pit lane. With that, his race was over. In the McLaren garage, mechanics could only watch in disbelief, hands on their heads, as the Championship battle took an unexpected turn.

Räikkönen capitalised on the moment, going on to take the victory, while Alonso secured second place.

Reflecting on the Chinese Grand Prix in an interview the following season, Hamilton acknowledged the experience as a learning moment. The challenges of those final races had been tough, but they had shaped him, strengthening his mindset for the future. When asked about the decision to leave Hamilton out on heavily worn tyres, which had been worn down to the canvas, Ron Dennis was pressed on where the responsibility lay. His response was measured, offering little in the way of blame but recognising the fine margins that had defined the race, and he questioned whether stopping him earlier would have made a difference. He rightly pointed out that the circuit was considerably drier than the pit lane entrance, and it was that which made the difference. This moment was a turning point. Where Hamilton once seemed on the verge of making history as a rookie champion, fortune had now forced the title fight down to the final race.

**Brazilian Grand Prix (21 October 2007 – Interlagos, São Paulo)**

Two weeks later, on 21 October, the Championship battle reached its climax at Interlagos, the iconic circuit nestled in the hills of São Paulo. Under clear skies and in front of an electric crowd, Hamilton lined up on the grid knowing that a strong finish would secure the title. However, the race did not go as planned. An early off-track moment, followed by a gearbox issue, saw him drop down the order. Despite a determined recovery drive, seventh place at the chequered flag left him just one point short, as Räikkönen claimed the Championship.

In the immediate aftermath, Hamilton balanced disappointment with perspective. Reflecting on the season as a whole, he acknowledged the scale of his achievements—finishing second in the Championship and outperforming his teammate, a two-time World Champion, in his rookie year. While falling short of the title was a bitter pill to swallow, he was quick to recognise Räikkönen's efforts, conceding that the Finn had delivered a strong and well-deserved campaign.

Looking ahead to 2008, Hamilton's focus was already shifting to the next challenge. Determined to come back stronger, he vowed to use the experience gained over the season to his advantage. With months of preparation ahead before the next race in Melbourne, he was confident that both he and the team would return even better prepared for the fight to come.

The trials of the 2007 season forged Hamilton into a stronger, more resilient competitor. Beating a two-time World Champion in his rookie season, and amidst the turbulence of the "Spygate" scandal, established Hamilton as a legitimate contender, and his ability to deliver under pressure earned respect throughout the paddock. For Alonso, the season had a profound effect on his career trajectory. The intense rivalry and internal team conflicts led to visible frustration. Alonso's difficulties in coping with not being the clear number-one driver highlighted challenges in his approach.

The 2007 season remains one of the most dramatic in Formula One history. It marked the arrival of a new superstar and highlighted the challenges of managing elite talent within a team—a dynamic seen before with the greats: Villeneuve and Pironi, Senna and Prost, Mansell and Piquet. And it would not be the last time, as Hamilton himself would come to learn.

Despite not securing the Championship, Hamilton's rookie season was one of the most remarkable in Formula One history at that time. He achieved the most wins in a debut season, with four, the most pole positions in a debut season with six, and his total of 109 points was the most in a debut season. He was named BBC Sports Personality of the Year runner-up, and also received the Autosport International Racing Driver Award. The motorsport community recognised his extraordinary talent and the impact he had made in such a short time.

The strained relationship with Alonso led to significant changes within McLaren. At the end of the season, Alonso left McLaren by mutual consent and returned to Renault. McLaren focused on building around Hamilton, promoting Heikki Kovalainen as his new teammate for 2008. Alonso's later stints at Renault, Ferrari, and his return to McLaren saw both success and frustration, often reflecting his high expectations and the challenges of competing in an ever-evolving sport.

Hamilton's debut season in Formula One was nothing short of sensational. His ability to compete with and challenge seasoned champions spoke volumes about his talent and determination. The experiences of 2007 laid a strong foundation for his future successes and taught him critical lessons about racing at the highest level. Throughout his debut season, Hamilton leaned on the support of his family and mentors, with his father's guidance remaining a cornerstone of his career. Despite all he had been through, he continued to stay grounded.

As Hamilton set his sights on the 2008 season, his determination to become World Champion was stronger than ever. The coming year would prove pivotal, with challenges ahead, records to break, and the potential for new alliances and opportunities.

# The Road to the First World Championship

The dawn of the 2008 Formula One season brought with it a wave of anticipation and speculation. The previous year's dramatic finale had left fans eager to see how the rivalry between McLaren-Mercedes and Ferrari would unfold. Pre-season testing suggested that both teams would once again be at the forefront, with Ferrari's Kimi Räikkönen and Felipe Massa poised to defend the Scuderia's honour, and McLaren's Lewis Hamilton determined to claim the title that had narrowly slipped from his grasp.

Other teams, like BMW Sauber, showed promising pace, with drivers Robert Kubica and Nick Heidfeld aiming to challenge the frontrunners. Meanwhile, Renault was keen to regain competitiveness, especially with the return of Fernando Alonso.

After a turbulent season with McLaren, Alonso and the team parted ways. While the split appeared amicable, the underlying tensions that had surfaced throughout the year made continuing the partnership impossible. Alonso opted for a return to Renault, the team where he had won his two World Championships.

In outlining his reasons for rejoining Renault, he spoke of a strong connection with the team that had played a crucial role in his development. Confident in their ability to recover from a challenging 2007 season, he looked ahead to a new chapter, believing that together they could return to the front of the grid.

The departure of Fernando Alonso at the end of the 2007 season left McLaren-Mercedes with a crucial decision: who would partner Lewis Hamilton in 2008? The team sought someone who could complement Hamilton's burgeoning talent without reigniting the internal strife that had characterised the previous year. Enter Heikki Kovalainen, a Finnish driver known for his calm demeanour and consistent performances.

Heikki Kovalainen made his Formula One debut with Renault in 2007, delivering a solid rookie season that included an impressive second-place finish at the Japanese Grand Prix. McLaren saw in him a dependable driver who could contribute valuable points to the Constructors' Championship while maintaining a balanced and cohesive team dynamic.

Hamilton welcomed his new teammate with optimism, looking forward to the season ahead and hoping Kovalainen would enjoy his first year at McLaren as much as he had. Likewise, Kovalainen was eager to embrace the opportunity, confident that he and Hamilton would work well together in pursuit of success for the team.

**Technical Rule Changes: Emphasis on Driver Skill**

The 2008 season introduced significant technical regulations that would impact the dynamics of racing. One of the most notable changes for the season was the ban on traction control, a system that had previously helped drivers manage wheel spin under acceleration, especially in wet or slippery conditions. Its removal placed a greater emphasis on driver skill, requiring more precise throttle control and finesse behind the wheel. Additionally, the introduction of a standardised Electronic Control Unit (ECU) for all teams aimed to reduce electronic driver aids and create a more level playing field.

Hamilton welcomed these changes, particularly the traction control ban, seeing it as an exciting challenge. Having previously raced in junior categories without the aid, he was eager to adapt his driving style to suit the new demands. As the season progressed, the rule change further highlighted his natural ability, particularly in mixed conditions, where his exceptional car control allowed him to extract performance purely through skill.

The 2008 season brought fresh challenges, with McLaren determined to reclaim both the Drivers' and Constructors' Championships after being excluded from the latter in 2007 due to the Spygate controversy. Development of the MP4-23 was a key focus, with the team aiming to enhance both reliability and performance. Powering the car was the Mercedes-Benz FO 108V, a 2.4-litre V8 capable of revving to an astonishing 19,000rpm, paired with a seven-speed gearbox designed in-house by McLaren.

Hamilton approached the new season with renewed confidence and determination. The lessons learned from his rookie campaign had sharpened both his skills and mental fortitude. As pre-season testing began, he spoke about his excitement for the year ahead, looking forward to getting to grips with the new car. He also reflected on the importance of taking time to recharge with his family, ensuring he was fully prepared for the challenges to come.

**Season Opener: Victory in Australia**

The 2008 Australian Grand Prix on 16 March set the tone for the season. Under the autumnal Australian sun, the atmosphere at Albert Park was energetic as fans flocked to see the renewed battle between Hamilton and Ferrari. From the outset, Hamilton made his intentions clear, securing pole position with a lap time of 1:26.714, highlighting McLaren's strong pace. Lining up alongside him was a familiar rival, Robert Kubica in the BMW Sauber, a car that had shown impressive straight-line speed. Meanwhile, Heikki Kovalainen, Hamilton's new teammate, started third, ensuring McLaren had a strong presence at the front. Hamilton was delighted with the result, noting the contrast in his approach compared to his debut season. Whereas the previous year had been about proving himself, this time, he arrived in Melbourne determined to start the campaign on pole—and he had done exactly that.

The race itself was chaotic, with multiple retirements drastically reducing the field. Hamilton controlled proceedings from the front, managing his pace and preserving his tyres in the first race under the new traction control ban. Despite the carnage behind, he remained composed, taking a commanding victory ahead of Heidfeld in the BMW Sauber and Nico Rosberg in the Williams Toyota. Kovalainen crossed the line in fifth, adding valuable points to McLaren's tally. The race was marred by incidents and retirements, but Hamilton navigated the chaos. It was a statement win that signalled his intent to challenge for the Championship. Reflecting on the team's performance after the race, Hamilton was full of praise, describing the car as a joy to drive.

The early part of the season tested drivers' adaptability to the new regulations. At the Malaysian Grand Prix, Hamilton qualified fourth but was handed a grid penalty for impeding other drivers, dropping him to ninth on the starting grid. Despite the setback, he fought his way through the field to finish fifth, salvaging valuable points.

The Bahrain Grand Prix in early April proved to be one of Hamilton's toughest weekends, testing his composure and ability to bounce back from adversity. During the second free practice session Hamilton suffered a heavy crash at Turn 7 at around 125mph, the McLaren not riding the kerb as expected and snapping sideways, before suddenly veering across the track. The car slid at high speed through the gravel trap before slamming into the barriers with enough force to trigger the G-force warning system. The impact left most of the right-hand side of the car in ruins, though Hamilton emerged unscathed. Reflecting on the incident later, he acknowledged that pushing the limits sometimes led to mistakes, describing Bahrain as a circuit where the sense of speed felt deceptive due to the open surroundings.

Race day brought further frustration. At the start, the anti-stall system unexpectedly activated, costing Hamilton crucial momentum as much of the field streamed past before he had even reached Turn 1. Alonso capitalised on the opportunity, using the extra speed to overtake Hamilton under braking into the tight first corner. By Lap 2, Hamilton remained close behind Alonso as they navigated the left-right chicane of Turns 2 and 3, leading onto the long straight. As they exited Turn 3, Alonso made an unexpected move—rather than drifting left onto the racing line and accelerating fully, he veered right and appeared to lift off slightly. This sudden change forced Hamilton, who was attempting to pass, into the back of the Renault. The contact briefly sent Hamilton's McLaren into the air, damaging the front wing.

The incident drew criticism, with some questioning Alonso's actions. Observers noted a clear speed differential between the two cars, raising concerns about whether Alonso had backed off deliberately. McLaren later assessed the situation, with Chief Operating Officer Martin Whitmarsh suggesting that the collision appeared to be a racing incident. He also indicated that Hamilton's McLaren had sustained front wing damage prior to the contact. The race continued, with Hamilton finishing outside the points after the collision. Hamilton acknowledged that the weekend had been a disaster for him and said he would come back stronger in the upcoming races.

As the teams left Bahrain, Räikkönen led the Championship with 19 points. Hamilton was playing catch-up with 14 points. The Ferraris of Räikkönen and Massa looked like a more complete package, while Kubica, in the BMW Sauber, also looked threatening.

### The Crown Jewel: Lewis Hamilton's 2008 Monaco Triumph

The 2008 Monaco Grand Prix, held on 25 May, marked one of the most iconic moments in Hamilton's burgeoning Formula

One career. On a day defined by treacherous weather and unrelenting pressure, Hamilton kept a cool head, showing the tenacity that would go on to define his career.

Race day dawned with unpredictable skies, and rain before the start left the streets of Monte Carlo slick and treacherous. The erratic weather patterns kept teams on edge, knowing that split-second decisions on tyres and strategy could decide the race. With the Ferraris locking out the front row, Hamilton started in third. However, by Turn 1, after a good getaway, he had slotted into second behind Massa, who was starting to gain the upper hand in the intra-team Ferrari battle. By Lap 5, the rain had started to really come down, and the cars were struggling on their intermediate tyres.

Hamilton's race took a dramatic turn on Lap 6 when, while navigating the tricky Tabac corner, he brushed the barriers, puncturing his right rear tyre. The incident forced him into an early pit stop, costing valuable track positions and dropping him to fifth. Despite the setback, he remained composed, later admitting that while the mistake was frustrating, Monaco had a way of presenting unexpected opportunities.

Just two laps later, Alonso, running in fourth, also clipped the barriers, sustaining a puncture that left him limping back to the pits. The chaotic nature of the race continued, as a lap later, David Coulthard crashed heavily, tearing off his right front wheel and triggering a Safety Car period. On Lap 14, Alonso—running on the extreme wet weather compound while most of the field was on different tyres—began making aggressive moves through the pack. Attempting a pass on Heidfeld's BMW Sauber at the Grand Hotel hairpin, he misjudged the gap and collided with Heidfeld, creating a nose-to-tail traffic jam. As the rain continued to fall, incidents unfolded across the treacherous circuit.

McLaren turned Hamilton's unscheduled stop to their advantage, refuelling him for a longer stint—a strategic call that would prove decisive. As the rain eased and the track dried, his well-timed switch to dry-weather tyres allowed him to make up lost ground while others struggled on deteriorating wet rubber. In conditions that caught out even the most experienced drivers, Hamilton's calm and calculated approach stood out, positioning him for a remarkable comeback.

On Lap 62, Rosberg suffered a heavy crash in the Swimming Pool complex, first striking the barriers on the right before rebounding into the opposite wall, tearing apart both sides of his Williams. The incident brought out the Safety Car, adding yet another twist to an already unpredictable race.

Hamilton had steadily worked his way to the front, combining clean laps with a well-timed strategy and capitalising on the misfortunes of others. The race's chaotic nature was epitomised by Räikkönen's late collision with Adrian Sutil, but through it all, Hamilton remained unflappable. Leading 40 of the 76 laps, he crossed the line to claim his first Monaco Grand Prix victory, further solidifying his reputation as one of the sport's rising stars. The achievement was quickly recognised by three-time World Champion Jackie Stewart, who saw Hamilton's potential to dominate in Monaco for years to come, placing him alongside the ranks of Formula One's greatest drivers.

The win not only propelled Hamilton to the top of the Drivers' Championship standings but also demonstrated his ability to thrive under pressure. Reflecting on the challenge, he acknowledged just how treacherous the conditions had been, emphasising that simply keeping the car on the track had been a monumental task.

### A Test of Resilience: The 2008 Hungarian Grand Prix

On 3 August, at the Hungaroring near Budapest, the Hungarian Grand Prix unfolded under clear skies, with air temperatures reaching up to 31°C and track temperatures exceeding 40°C, creating a challenging environment that demanded exceptional tyre management.

Hamilton's weekend began on a high note, as he secured pole position with a lap time of 1:20.899, narrowly edging out his McLaren teammate, Kovalainen, who qualified second. However, the race's start saw Massa make a remarkable move from third on the grid, overtaking both McLarens to claim the lead by the first corner. In the opening stages, Hamilton held second place, staying close behind Massa. The race took a dramatic turn on Lap 41 when Hamilton suffered a front-left puncture, forcing an unscheduled pit stop that dropped him down the order. Undeterred, he mounted a determined recovery drive, eventually finishing fifth—a result that kept him at the top of the Drivers' Championship standings.

The race's closing laps saw further unexpected drama as Massa's engine failed just three laps from the finish, cruelly denying him victory. This misfortune handed the lead to Kovalainen, who went on to claim his first Formula One win, becoming the 100th different driver to take victory in a World Championship race. With the title fight intensifying, Hamilton remained narrowly ahead in the standings with 62 points to Räikkönen's 57, while Massa was close behind on 54. For Räikkönen, it would prove to be the closest he would get to the Championship lead for the rest of the season.

**Mid-Season Races**

As the racing calendar progressed, Hamilton faced significant challenges mid-season. At the Canadian Grand Prix in June, he secured pole position, but during a pit stop under Safety Car conditions, Hamilton failed to notice a red light at the pit exit and collided with Räikkönen, ending the race for both. Accepting responsibility, Hamilton apologised to Räikkönen. Robert Kubica, Hamilton's old karting sparring partner, who had suffered a massive accident at the Grand Prix the previous year, won the race from the front row, claiming his first career victory in Formula One.

At the French Grand Prix later that month, Hamilton struggled after receiving a grid penalty due to an infraction at the previous race in Canada. These challenges, combined with finishing outside the points in France, continued to test his resilience. Hamilton remained determined, reflecting a mindset focused on overcoming adversity—crucial for Championship success.

The 2008 Italian Grand Prix at Monza marked a significant moment for Sebastian Vettel, who was in his first full season with Scuderia Toro Rosso. In wet conditions, Vettel secured pole position, becoming the youngest driver at that time to do so, aged 21 years and 72 days. He led from start to finish, managing the race with remarkable composure, claiming his maiden victory, and signalling his potential as a future star. Hamilton, who had raced against Vettel in the Formula Three Euro Series in 2005, recognised Vettel's performance, commenting that he had been fantastic all weekend and had grown stronger throughout the year, with the win showing just how good he was.

Vettel's performance caught the attention of Red Bull Racing, and he would be promoted to their team for the 2009 season. Red Bull, under the technical leadership of Adrian Newey, had been steadily improving since his arrival in 2006. His innovative designs were beginning to pay dividends, setting the stage for Red Bull's rise to prominence.

The 2008 British Grand Prix at Silverstone is often remembered as one of the defining moments of Hamilton's career. Driving for McLaren, Hamilton delivered a masterclass in wet-weather racing, conquering treacherous conditions to claim an emphatic victory, with a dominance of the conditions reminiscent of Senna at Donington in 1993. Hamilton's performance not only showed his immense talent but also established him as one of Formula One's most skilled drivers in changing conditions. After the race Hamilton said the 2008 win at Silverstone would likely be his most special Grand Prix, especially due to the challenging rain.

Pundits were effusive in their praise, with one outlet describing the performance as a "faultless display," noting

Hamilton's exceptional ability to adapt to the conditions and extend his lead with each passing lap. Another outlet called it a "tour de force," highlighting his dominance in what was considered one of the most challenging races of the season.

Hamilton himself was overwhelmed by the support of the home crowd, expressing that it was by far the best victory he had ever achieved. He described winning in front of he British fans as the highlight of his career, he hoped to replicate that feeling many more times in the future.

This victory was not only a highlight of Hamilton's 2008 season but also a critical step in his journey to becoming a global sporting icon. The win at Silverstone solidified his reputation as a driver capable of excelling under the most demanding conditions and marked a pivotal moment in his quest for his first World Championship.

**The Race in the Stewards' Room - Spa**

At the iconic Spa-Francorchamps circuit, Hamilton showed exceptional skill in typically mixed Ardennes weather conditions. At the race's end, he crossed the finish line first after a dramatic duel with Räikkönen— or so he thought.

During the race, as the rain started to fall, Hamilton attempted to overtake Räikkönen around the outside of the final chicane. Räikkönen knew that Hamilton was there but didn't leave any room, so Hamilton was forced to go off track to avoid a collision and came out ahead. Hamilton recognised that he would likely be asked to give the place back, so he immediately backed off to allow Räikkönen to repass on the start-finish straight. As they braked into the first corner of the La Source hairpin, Hamilton went down the inside of Räikkönen and into the lead. The rain continued to fall, and with just three laps to go, many cars were still on grooved slick tyres. Some of the cars lower down the order pitted for intermediates, even though there were just two laps remaining.

Räikkönen went past Hamilton into the right-hander of Les Fagnes (Fagnes Chicane) while Hamilton was trying to avoid a collision with a recovering Rosberg in the BMW Williams. Almost immediately, Räikkönen spun coming out of the left-hand section of Fagnes Chicane. He had the lead but threw it away. He managed to recover from the spin and set off after Hamilton up the hill as the cars came out of Curve Paul Frère towards the super-fast double left-hander of Blanchimont. The track was now noticeably wetter, and as Hamilton came round Blanchimont, his McLaren had a sudden snap of oversteer, which he managed to catch, before letting the car drift wide onto the very limit of the kerbing to maintain control. Räikkönen arrived at the same left-hander moments later but ran wide in his Ferrari. As he attempted to rejoin the track, a sudden snap of oversteer sent him off into the barriers, destroying his front wing and flattening both left-side tyres. He was out of the race, and Massa moved up to second, around ten seconds behind Hamilton.

Hamilton's McLaren was sliding as it powered through Eau Rouge, but Hamilton retained control and crossed the finish line to take what seemed like a superb victory.

After the race, the Stewards imposed a 25-second penalty on Hamilton, ruling that he had gained an advantage by cutting a chicane during his earlier battle with Räikkönen, even though Hamilton had allowed Räikkönen to retake the position before overtaking him again later. The penalty dropped Hamilton to third, handing the win to Massa. At the time, Hamilton remained focused, but years later, he reflected on the decision with frustration, believing he had been unfairly treated by the FIA.

### Japanese Grand Prix (Fuji Speedway)

The race at Fuji Speedway on 12 October proved to be a turbulent affair for both Championship contenders. Hamilton started from pole position but endured a difficult race, with an aggressive move at the start resulting in a penalty for forcing another driver off track. Later, a collision with Massa led to another penalty, compounding his struggles and ultimately leaving him to finish a disappointing 12th.

Massa, meanwhile, managed to recover to seventh place, cutting Hamilton's lead in the Championship standings. The chaotic nature of the race drew criticism, with analysts questioning the composure of both drivers under pressure. Observers noted that their performances reflected the weight of the title fight, with mistakes proving costly on a day when neither emerged unscathed.

**Singapore Grand Prix (Marina Bay Street Circuit)**

A historic moment arrived with the inaugural Singapore Grand Prix on 28 September. It was Formula One's first night race, held under lights on the Marina Bay Street Circuit, a 5.073 km street circuit with 23 corners, demanding high concentration. The illuminated skyline provided a stunning backdrop. High humidity and temperatures around 30°C (86°F), even at night, challenged drivers physically, with the artificial lighting and the city's vibrancy creating a unique spectacle. However, beneath the dazzling lights, a clandestine scheme unfolded, which wouldn't reveal itself for several months.

Alonso, driving for Renault, began the race from a modest 15th position on the grid. An unusually early refuelling strategy saw him pit on Lap 12, rejoining the race at the back of the pack. Just two laps later, his teammate, Nelson Piquet Jr., crashed into the wall at Turn 17, prompting the deployment of the Safety Car. This incident proved advantageous for Alonso, as several drivers pitted under Safety Car conditions, allowing him to climb the order and ultimately secure a very unexpected victory. Piquet's accident appeared unusual, and in time, it would soon be understood why. At the end of the season, Renault did not renew Piquet's contract.

Felipe Massa, who had been comfortably leading the race until this incident, pitted under the Safety Car along with everyone else. This meant Ferrari had to double-stack their cars and rush. Massa was released before the fuel hose was removed, and he set off down the pit lane with the hose still attached to his car. Thankfully, the mechanic who was bowled over was uninjured, and showing remarkable character, he immediately jumped up and manned the spare pump for Räikkönen, who was seconds behind. Massa had to wait an eternity at the end of the pit lane until the mechanics could remove the fuel hose, wrecking his race and leaving him to finish 13th. This would have serious ramifications for his World Championship bid.

## The Brazilian Grand Prix: Title decider on Massa's Home Turf

The season culminated in one of the most dramatic races in Formula One history, the Brazilian Grand Prix on 2 November, held at the revered Interlagos Circuit. A challenging 4.309 km track known for its undulating terrain and anticlockwise layout, the circuit had a carnival atmosphere as passionate Brazilian fans rallied behind Massa, hoping to see their local hero triumph on home soil. Felipe Massa was born in São Paulo and had a deep connection with the circuit. In various interviews, Massa expressed his determination, describing winning at home and fighting for the Championship as a dream—a sentiment that all drivers share.

The Championship standings before the race were Hamilton on 94 points and Massa, just 7 points behind on 87. Hamilton needed to finish at least fifth to secure the title, regardless of Massa's result, but with intermittent rain, the race turned into an exciting battle. Massa led from pole position, whilst Hamilton maintained a careful approach, running in fourth and fifth positions. There was late race tension as rain began to fall with a few laps remaining and teams scrambled to switch to intermediate tyres. With five laps to go, Hamilton pitted for intermediate tyres. Toyota's Timo Glock stayed on dry tyres, moving ahead of Hamilton.

With four laps to go, it looked like a strategic blunder by McLaren, as it was not raining enough to justify moving to intermediate tyres and losing the positions. Ron Dennis on the pit wall looked worried. The intermediate tyres were quicker than the dry, but not by much. With three laps to go, Hamilton had Sebastian Vettel right on his tail, pressuring him to overtake. Glock was over eight seconds ahead. Half a lap later, Vettel overtook Hamilton, putting him out of contention for the World Championship. The Ferrari garage erupted into euphoria, with everyone jumping around. Hamilton kept his cool and let Vettel go ahead. Hamilton's target was to get past Glock.

It started to rain harder, and approaching the final corners, Glock was struggling on his dry tyres. Going into the last lap, Massa led, with Alonso second. Hamilton was running sixth, behind Vettel, and some distance back from Glock, who was fourth; finishing sixth would not be enough to win the Championship.

Massa crossed the finish line first, believing he had done enough to clinch the title. In the Ferrari garage everyone celebrated—his team cheered, his father embraced his brother and family, and the pit crew rejoiced, convinced the title was theirs.

Unnoticed at first amid the celebrations, Hamilton was still on the charge. In the final three corners, he rapidly closed in on Glock, whose dry-weather tyres were struggling in the damp conditions. In a dramatic final twist, Hamilton made the crucial overtake, securing the fifth-place finish he needed to win the World Championship by a single point. The mood in the Ferrari garage shifted instantly from euphoria to devastation as the realisation set in.

Now it was the turn of the McLaren team to go wild and they erupted in celebration. Overwhelmed by the achievement, Hamilton dedicated the moment to his team and family, thanking those who had supported him throughout the season. In Parc Fermé, he embraced his brother Nicolas before making his way back to the McLaren garage, where his father Anthony was waiting. As Hamilton walked in, still processing the enormity of what had just happened, Anthony hugged him tightly. Head down, overcome with emotion, Hamilton broke into tears—a powerful, poignant moment that captured the significance of his triumph. Massa was also in tears on the warm-down lap and again in the pits—utterly inconsolable after coming so agonisingly close to the title.

Hamilton's victory carried immense historical significance. At 23 years and 301 days old, he became the youngest World Champion at the time (a record later broken by Sebastian Vettel in 2010). He was also the first black driver to win the Formula One World Championship, marking an important moment for the sport and inspiring a new generation of drivers from diverse backgrounds.

Speaking after the race, Hamilton struggled to put the achievement into words. Overwhelmed by the magnitude of the moment, he reflected on the long journey that had brought him to this point—the sacrifices, the challenges, and the unwavering support from his family and the McLaren team.

When asked to describe his emotions, he admitted it was almost impossible. The intensity of the title fight had taken its toll, and the strain was still sinking in. He had shed tears, as had many others, but above all, he was filled with pride—pride in his team, in his family, and in what they had achieved together.

### Reflections on the Season

Hamilton's path to the Championship was marked by resilience, growth, and perseverance. He overcame adversity, facing penalties and setbacks with determination. He maintained focus under immense pressure, especially in the final races, and worked effectively with Kovalainen and the team to achieve their collective goals. The ban on traction control highlighted Hamilton's natural abilities and adaptability. He demonstrated that talent, hard work, and perseverance could overcome obstacles, and he began building a legacy that would see him become one of the most successful drivers in Formula One history.

The dramatic finale in Brazil captured global attention, exemplifying the unpredictability and excitement of Formula One. Kovalainen finished the season seventh in the standings, contributing to McLaren's efforts in the Constructors' Championship, where they finished second behind Ferrari. He spoke positively about his teammate's success and recognised that Hamilton was a deserving Champion.

As the season ended, the legendary Murray Walker—by then in his mid-eighties—was asked about Hamilton's impact on Formula One and what the future might hold for him. As always, his insights were thoughtful, and in one instance, eerily prophetic. Reflecting on Hamilton's influence, Walker noted how the young Champion had captured the imagination of a wider audience, sparking interest in the sport among those who had previously paid little attention to it. He believed Hamilton's ability to connect with people, even beyond the traditional fanbase, was something unique.

What Walker said next carried the weight of over fifty years of motorsport commentary. He acknowledged that, given the right circumstances, Hamilton had the potential to become one of the greatest racing drivers, and that missing the title by a single point in his rookie season and winning four races in his debut year were unprecedented achievements, but he was still only at the beginning of his journey. Walker believed that if Hamilton could maintain a competitive seat with the right infrastructure, he could one day surpass even Michael Schumacher's towering records—a prediction that, years later, would prove astonishingly accurate.

Walker, a true gentleman and the voice of Formula One for generations, passed away in March 2021 at the age of 97, leaving behind an unrivalled legacy in motorsport broadcasting

## The Global Financial Crisis and Honda's Departure

While the 2008 season finale delivered high drama on track, Formula One was also beginning to feel the effects of a turbulent global economy. The onset of the Global Financial Crisis forced sponsors to cut back, putting financial strain on teams across the grid. One of the biggest casualties was Honda, which announced its withdrawal from the sport at the end of 2008, leaving Jenson Button and Rubens Barrichello without a drive. The decision reflected the wider uncertainty gripping motorsport, with teams facing increasing pressure to secure funding in a shifting financial landscape. Honda's departure, however, set the stage for one of Formula One's most remarkable success stories. The team's assets were taken over by Ross Brawn, leading to the creation of Brawn GP—a move that would change the course of Formula One history in the season that followed.

# A Champion Tested

The 2009 Formula One season began with a sense of uncertainty that permeated every team. Sweeping technical changes were set to reshape the grid and elevate driver skill in a way not seen in recent years. For Formula One, these changes, coupled with the shocks of the Global Financial Crisis, would bring unexpected victories, new heroes, and powerful shifts among rivals. But no story that year would rival the meteoric rise of Brawn GP—a team that seemed destined to make history even as it teetered on the edge of collapse.

Formula One in 2009 was a sport transformed. Key changes to the regulations promised a season where innovative engineering and raw talent would matter as much as horsepower. Slick tyres, absent from the grid since 1998, returned to deliver grip levels reminiscent of a bygone era, challenging drivers to manage tyre wear while pressing on. For drivers like Hamilton, who had honed his skills in the world of slick-shod karting, this was an opportunity to draw on that instinctive control in search of the tenths and hundredths of seconds that made the difference.

The Kinetic Energy Recovery System (KERS) was another revolutionary addition, designed to store energy under braking and deliver a short burst of additional power at the press of a button. This feature became a tactical advantage on certain circuits, allowing overtakes and defences that might have been impossible otherwise. Yet, not all teams chose to use KERS, a decision that underscored its complexity and, for many, its unreliability.

In response to calls for safer and more competitive racing, the FIA mandated simplified aerodynamic designs, eliminating some of the elaborate winglets and bodywork of previous years. Front wings were also enlarged. These changes were intended to level the playing field, encourage overtaking, and increase the focus on mechanical grip. The new regulations made the 2009 season a proving ground not only for the world's best drivers but also for the ingenuity of Formula One's most innovative engineers.

### The Emergence of Brawn GP

No story from the 2009 season was as improbable or as inspiring as that of Brawn GP. A mere three months before the season opener, Honda, struggling in the face of the global recession, announced its immediate departure from Formula One, abandoning what would soon become one of the most dominant cars on the grid. Amid financial ruin and an uncertain future, Ross Brawn took a leap of faith, purchasing the team with a last-ditch investment and transforming Honda Racing into Brawn GP.

The Brawn team inherited a car, the BGP 001, that was a marvel of forward-thinking design. Originally created with the full backing of Honda, the car had been designed with the 2009 regulations in mind. Central to its success was the innovative double diffuser, a device that skirted the edge of the rules but provided a downforce advantage that the competition simply couldn't match. With the Mercedes engine newly fitted, Brawn GP's machine was now powered by one of the most reliable and powerful engines in the sport, instantly turning this underdog into a contender.

### First Half of the Season

At the season's first race in Australia, the Formula One world witnessed a stunning debut. The white, yellow, and black-liveried Brawn led from the front, with Jenson Button taking a commanding victory, his teammate Rubens Barrichello close behind. Ross Brawn's intuition and technical prowess had paid off; in a matter of months, Brawn GP had gone from near extinction to championship favourite.

Jenson Button, a driver who had long possessed undeniable talent but had yet to find his place at the top, embraced his role as the leader in the team. This was Button's moment, a chance to silence the doubters and prove his skill on the grandest stage. His smooth, measured driving style and exceptional tyre management made him the ideal candidate to exploit the unique qualities of the BGP 001.

Button's performances throughout the season were nothing short of exceptional. Race after race, he maximised the potential of the Brawn GP car, securing six wins in the opening seven rounds and firmly establishing himself as the championship frontrunner. His most commanding victories came at circuits like Monaco, where his precision was on full display. By the halfway point of the season, it was clear that Button was the title favourite, and the entire Formula One paddock had to acknowledge Brawn GP as a serious contender.

Looking back on that extraordinary period, Button reflected on the emotions that ran through the season. The journey from uncertainty and job insecurity to fighting for the championship was almost surreal, and the sense of disbelief carried on throughout the year. His rise from consistent midfield runner to title challenger was a reward for all his hard work.

Meanwhile, for Lewis Hamilton and McLaren, things were less rosy; the 2009 season was a stark contrast to their triumphant 2008 campaign. The team struggled to adapt to the new regulations and the complexities of KERS. Despite their best efforts, the MP4-24 car fell short of expectations, leaving Hamilton and his teammate Heikki Kovalainen battling in the midfield for much of the season.

The season also marked a major turning point for Sebastian Vettel, who had emerged as one of Formula One's rising stars with Toro Rosso. The young German, known initially for his calm demeanour and raw speed, was promoted to Red Bull's main team alongside Mark Webber. Vettel's talent—benefiting from the Adrian Newey-designed Red Bull—was undeniable, and by mid-season, he had already proven his worth, claiming pole positions and podiums that cemented his reputation as a future contender.

David Coulthard, the veteran driver and long-time Red Bull competitor, had retired at the end of 2008, making room for Vettel to join Red Bull Racing. This passing of the torch signalled a new era, with Vettel positioned to become a primary rival to Lewis Hamilton in the years to come. Vettel's performances throughout 2009 offered a glimpse of his potential, and his rivalry with Hamilton would soon become one of the defining narratives in Formula One.

The first seven races of the season were all about Jenson Button in the Brawn. He won in Australia, Malaysia, Bahrain, Spain, Monaco, and Turkey. Only China, on 19 April, eluded him, and Vettel took the win there.

Hamilton and McLaren looked lost. He was disqualified in Australia, seventh in Malaysia, sixth in China, fourth in Bahrain, ninth in Spain, twelfth in Monaco, and thirteenth in Turkey. The McLaren was just not delivering. It was a dreadful start to the season, and with Brawn dominating the first half and Red Bull looking increasingly strong and set to dominate the second half, there seemed to be little that Hamilton could do. That was until the teams went to Hungary.

## Tragedy and Success at the Hungarian Grand Prix

The teams arrived in Hungary and set about their qualifying session. It became the scene of a life-altering accident for Felipe Massa as a loose spring from Rubens Barrichello's car flew into Massa's path, striking his helmet with devastating force. Massa, one of Ferrari's brightest talents and a beloved figure in the paddock, suffered a serious head injury that required emergency surgery and forced him to sit out the remainder of the season.

Massa's accident rocked the Formula One community, reigniting discussions on driver safety. Ferrari, reeling from the loss of one of its key drivers, worked to remain competitive, though their championship hopes had already faded. After spending two days in an induced coma, Massa began his recovery, with the team optimistic about his progress. His rehabilitation would take several months, as he had suffered a fractured skull and concussion. Though he would eventually return to racing, the incident was a stark reminder of the dangers that still existed in the sport. The impact of the injury was profound, and while Massa remained a strong competitor, he would never add another victory to his tally.

Hamilton, speaking on behalf of the grid, expressed the collective concern felt throughout the paddock. The severity of the incident cast a shadow over the race weekend, with everyone wishing Massa a full and swift recovery.

Massa's accident would go on to spark significant safety innovations, particularly in helmet design and head protection. This accident underscored the risks drivers face, and the FIA soon introduced new regulations and protocols to minimise the likelihood of similar incidents in the future.

After a difficult start to the season, the Hungarian Grand Prix marked Hamilton's breakthrough victory of 2009. Held at the Hungaroring, the narrow and twisty circuit was known for being tough on overtaking, particularly in the days before DRS, but Hamilton approached it with his usual tenacity. Coming off a string of disappointing results, he was eager to prove that McLaren still had potential. Qualifying had been decent, with Hamilton starting from the second row, and expectations were cautiously optimistic.

The race itself was a masterclass in timing and skill. By the first round of pit stops, Hamilton had climbed through the field and positioned himself within striking distance of the leaders. Crucially, his tyre management allowed him to take the fight to the Brawn and Red Bull cars that had dominated the season so far. After a flawless performance, Hamilton crossed the finish line in first place, securing McLaren's first win of the season.

The result was met with widespread acclaim, with many viewing it as a turning point. It signalled that Hamilton was once again a force to be reckoned with.

After the race, Hamilton was overjoyed and described the victory as an incredible feeling after what had felt like a long wait. He was proud of the McLaren team and thanked them for their perseverance and refusal to give up, which in his view had made the win possible, even when success had seemed unlikely. Hamilton discussed how the car now felt fantastic, and returning to the top step of the podium was a special and emotional moment for both him and McLaren.

**European Grand Prix (Valencia) – August 23, 2009**

The next race on the calendar where Hamilton would make his mark was the European Grand Prix in Valencia in August. The event took place on a street circuit renowned for its unforgiving layout, where accuracy in placing the car and control were paramount. Hamilton managed a solid qualifying session, securing an incredible pole position to start the race from the front row alongside his teammate Kovalainen. Rubens Barrichello in the Brawn GP qualified third.

Hamilton's race was a picture of consistency, and he looked comfortable. However, at his second pit stop, the team were not ready, the new tyres still in their blankets, which cost him time in the pits. Barrichello waited as long as he could before making his second stop and, in doing so, made up a lot of time, ultimately coming out ahead of Hamilton. The two traded fastest laps, but the damage had been done in the slow pit stop, which prevented Hamilton from being able to challenge Barrichello for the win. Nevertheless, he secured a strong second place—showing his ability to extract the most from the McLaren, even on circuits where it was difficult to challenge Brawn's powerful car.

After the race, Hamilton reflected positively on the team's performance, despite them having dropped the ball, emphasising the progress made. Damon Hill, the 1996 World Champion, was asked his thoughts after the race, and he praised Hamilton's impressive patience despite the setback in the pit stop. Hill felt it would not be long before Hamilton won again.

**Singapore Grand Prix – September 27, 2009**

In September, under the city lights of Singapore, Hamilton achieved his second victory of the season. The Marina Bay Circuit, a street track with challenging corners and high humidity, had proven difficult for drivers in the past. Starting from pole position after an excellent qualifying performance, Hamilton knew he had a strong chance of capitalising on his front-row start.

Hamilton controlled the race from start to finish, fending off pressure from both Sebastian Vettel and Nico Rosberg. His use of KERS allowed him to maintain his lead on the straights, while his precision through the tight, technical sections made him almost untouchable. He managed his tyres carefully, ensuring he could push when needed without risking unnecessary wear. Rosberg's challenge faded away, and Vettel picked up a drive-through penalty for speeding in the pit lane, leaving Timo Glock in the Toyota in second place.

After securing his second win of the season, Hamilton reiterated how difficult the conditions at the Singapore Grand Prix could be, talking of the high heat and humidity, but said he was delighted at how everything had come together on the night. He again emphasised the hard work that had gone into reaching this point and talked about his immense pride in the team's efforts.

His commanding performance earned widespread praise, being labelled as a 'force to be reckoned with'. Winning from pole on such a demanding street circuit was no small achievement, and it demonstrated that despite McLaren's challenges that season, Hamilton remained a formidable competitor.

Hamilton had shown composure under pressure, particularly when dealing with the challenge from Vettel and an issue with the KERS system. It was a performance that reinforced exactly why he was a world champion.

**Japanese Grand Prix – October 4, 2009**

Just a week after his Singapore triumph, Hamilton put in another commendable performance at the Japanese Grand Prix in Suzuka. Known for its high-speed corners and complex layout, Suzuka demands the utmost skill and concentration from drivers. Hamilton qualified third on the grid, just behind Jarno Trulli, with Sebastian Vettel, who had been a dominant force all weekend, on pole.

In the race, Hamilton held his position for much of the opening laps, keeping Vettel within sight. Despite the power disadvantage compared to the Red Bull, he managed to stay in contention, displaying his tenacity and control over the McLaren. However, his car's rear tyres degraded more quickly than anticipated, forcing him to preserve his position rather than push for an overtake. He ultimately finished third, securing a valuable podium and adding to his points tally.

**Brazilian Grand Prix – October 18, 2009**

Interlagos and the penultimate event of the season was one of those races in Hamilton's career that endeared him deeply to the Brazilian fans, as they watched him put in a drive of sheer grit, fighting his way through the field.

The race was dramatic from start to finish. Hamilton had a difficult qualifying session, which left him starting from 17th. Given the chaos that would unfold ahead of him, it was probably a safer place to start.

On Lap 1, Jarno Trulli in the Toyota was battling with Adrian Sutil in the Force India, negotiating the double left-hand turns of Descida do Lago. On the exit, Sutil was slightly compromised and had to lift off for Kimi Räikkönen in the Ferrari, who was slow off the turn due to a broken front wing. Sensing an opportunity, Trulli attempted to go around the outside of Sutil and steered the Toyota onto the sawtooth kerbs as they entered the straight. Without grip, the Toyota snapped sideways and collided with the Force India in an instant. Trulli veered off to the left and into the wall, knocking a wheel off and sliding hundreds of metres off the track, down to the right-hander of Ferradura.

Meanwhile, the hapless Sutil, out of control, veered off the inside of the circuit, skidding at high speed across the grass. As Sutil's car came back onto the track, still sideways, it collided with the Renault of Fernando Alonso. The two cars came to rest on the outside of the turn, not far from Trulli's stricken Toyota.

Despite Trulli being the obvious cause of the accident, he leapt from his car and ran over to Sutil, gesturing wildly, arms flailing and pointing fingers as if Sutil were at fault.

Not long after, Heikki Kovalainen pitted in the McLaren, stopping for fuel and tyres. Before the fuel hose had been released, he accelerated away from the pit box, knocking two of his mechanics over in the process. Räikkönen, who had just pitted, followed closely behind Kovalainen down the pit lane. Fuel began spilling out of the hose and onto Räikkönen's red-hot Ferrari. In an instant, there was a huge fireball. Räikkönen, known as 'The Ice Man' for good reason, wiped his visor and continued on his way, unfazed.

As things settled down, Hamilton wasted no time carving his way through the field. A combination of well-executed overtakes and effective use of KERS saw him steadily climb the order. By the closing stages, he had fought his way to third—an impressive result given his starting position and the car's struggles during the season.

Hamilton spoke about the challenge of racing at Interlagos, praising the incredible atmosphere afterwards. His performance drew admiration, with McLaren's team principal, Martin Whitmarsh, highlighting Hamilton's resilience—no matter where he started on the grid, he was always pushing forward.

Jenson Button finished fifth in the Brawn, which was enough to secure him the Formula One World Championship. Ross Brawn described Button as a fantastic racer who knew exactly what he needed to do and deserved to win the championship. John Button, Jenson's father, embraced his son after the race, and both of them 'cried like babies.' It was a fitting and deserving moment for Button, who had worked hard at BAR and Honda, experiencing both ups and downs over the years but had stuck with it and given his all.

**Abu Dhabi Joins the Calendar**

In November, Formula One witnessed another historic moment with the debut of the Abu Dhabi Grand Prix at the stunning Yas Marina Circuit. As the season's final race, Abu Dhabi offered a unique twilight setting, with drivers starting in daylight and finishing under the floodlights, casting a dramatic glow over the futuristic cityscape. The state-of-the-art facilities, along with Abu Dhabi's luxurious setting, attracted fans from around the world and marked Formula One's continued expansion in the Middle East.

The circuit itself was a technical masterpiece, blending long straights with tight corners, offering drivers the chance to test their skills in a race that promised to become one of Formula One's most glamorous events. Yas Marina quickly became a favourite among drivers and fans alike, adding another iconic venue to the sport's ever-expanding calendar. Vettel won the race, with Mark Webber taking second and Jenson Button finishing third.

In what had been a largely dismal season for Hamilton, it ended much the same way when, on Lap 20, he was forced to retire the car due to brake trouble.

**Crashgate and the Downfall of Flavio Briatore**

The season's controversies extended beyond the track in 2009. As the season wore on a new story emerged regarding the accident that Nelson Piquet Jr. had at the 2008 Singapore Grand Prix, where his 'accident' had benefited Alonso, who went on to win the race.

Nelson Piquet Jr. disclosed to the FIA that he had been ordered by the Renault team—led by Team Principal Flavio Briatore and Director of Engineering Pat Symonds—to crash on purpose at the 2008 Singapore race, a revelation that rocked the sport. This led to the expulsion of Briatore, Renault's flamboyant team principal and a longtime associate of both Michael Schumacher and Alonso. Briatore faced a lifetime ban from FIA-sanctioned events, a penalty that was overturned in 2010. His downfall was swift and public, a fitting end for a figure who had long blurred the lines between strategy and deception. Symonds resigned from his role as a result and was given a five-year ban.

Nick Heidfeld of BMW further fuelled speculation when he told reporters that, after the race, everyone present in the briefing room believed Piquet's crash looked deliberate.

Despite the actions of Briatore and Symonds, Renault as a team was cleared of wrongdoing in the inquiry, with Max Mosley going so far as to describe their cooperation as "impeccable." The Crashgate controversy had long-term consequences, with debates resurfacing years later about its potential impact on the championship and whether the events of that night in Singapore ultimately influenced the title fight.

Crashgate cast a shadow over the sport, raising questions about team ethics and the lengths some were willing to go to achieve success. The scandal prompted renewed scrutiny of team orders and manipulation, leading the FIA to implement stricter regulations to ensure fair play in future races.

Throughout the season, Hamilton praised Button's performances with Brawn GP. He frequently acknowledged Button's composed driving style and his ability to maximise the car's strengths, recognising that Brawn had developed a machine that was significantly ahead of much of the field, but Button still delivered when it mattered. Hamilton spoke about the positive impact on the sport of a new team shaking up the established order, which had created an exciting dynamic in the championship.

Hamilton's reflections on Button's consistency and Brawn's technical advantage were both an appreciation of his rival's achievements and a source of quiet motivation. For McLaren and Hamilton, watching Brawn's success only fuelled their determination to fight back in 2010—a challenge they would take on with Button as part of the team.

Though the 2009 season was tough, Hamilton's victories in Hungary and Singapore, along with podium finishes in Valencia, Japan, and Brazil, underscored his will to fight and his ability to maximise the performance of the car—a car that clearly lagged behind Brawn and Red Bull. His determination showed that even in a season when his car was not competitive, he could make the difference. This doggedness during 2009 paid dividends and put him on the radar of some very influential people, especially a certain Niki Lauda.

Niki Lauda, a three-time World Champion and now a successful businessman running his own airline, remained an influential voice in Formula One. Lauda had watched the races in 2009 and taken note of Hamilton's performances. He spoke openly about Hamilton showing the traits of a true champion in that he would never give up, even when his car was off the pace. He labelled Hamilton a fighter and a driver who had earned every point. Hamilton had earned the respect of Lauda and firmly put himself on Lauda's radar. Lauda's interest in Hamilton would remain high, and it was the performances in 2009 that would bring about change in the years to come.

As McLaren bid farewell to a tumultuous season, they, like Hamilton, were already looking ahead to 2010, determined to build a car that could bring them back to the front.

# British Duo

The 2010 Formula One season marked a new era for McLaren and for Lewis Hamilton. After a challenging 2009 season, Hamilton was eager to return to the front and reclaim his status as a championship contender. His partner in this quest was Jenson Button, who joined McLaren as the reigning World Champion, fresh off his remarkable title with Brawn GP. The pairing of two British champions at the pinnacle of motorsport was a boon for the fans, but it also raised questions about how two competitive talents would co-exist in one of the most prestigious teams in Formula One.

Button's decision to move to McLaren caught many by surprise. After achieving World Championship success with Brawn GP—a team that emerged from Honda's departure—he opted for a new challenge rather than remaining with the outfit that had taken him to the title. Explaining his decision, he spoke about his desire to push himself further, believing that McLaren, with its rich history of champions, offered the perfect opportunity. Hamilton welcomed Button's arrival, describing the driver line-up as both strong and exciting. He expressed confidence that they would work well together and was looking forward to the challenge of having another World Champion as a teammate.

Each with their own legions of fans, they couldn't have been more different in perceived personality and style. Button was known for his smooth driving and calm demeanour, contrasting with Hamilton's perceived aggressive, on-the-edge approach that had won him many races. While Hamilton was already established as McLaren's rising star, Button's arrival as the reigning champion created a delicate dynamic in the team. Button was fully aware of the challenges that came with joining McLaren, approaching the season with his usual humility and professionalism. Acknowledging Hamilton's rapid success and exceptional talent, he recognised the opportunity for both of them to learn from each other, believing that their combined experience could help drive the team forward. His confidence, coupled with the momentum of his championship victory the previous year, added an element of unpredictability to the partnership. How McLaren would manage the ambitions of two World Champions remained an open question, and the dynamic between them was set to be one of the key storylines of the seasons ahead.

## McLaren's Technical Innovations and the 2010 Car

McLaren started the 2010 season with high hopes and an array of new technical updates. After struggling with the MP4-24 in 2009, the team had poured resources into developing a more competitive car for 2010, the MP4-25. Central to the design was the innovative F-Duct system, a device that allowed drivers to adjust airflow over the rear wing to reduce drag on straights, effectively giving them a speed boost without compromising cornering performance. Both Hamilton and Button were quick to recognise the potential of this feature, and Hamilton adapted quickly, exploiting the F-Duct to his advantage in qualifying sessions and on fast circuits. The introduction of a ban on refuelling and the mandatory use of Kinetic Energy Recovery Systems (KERS) added new strategic dimensions to the sport.

Meanwhile, Red Bull Racing had risen to prominence, largely due to Adrian Newey's technical brilliance. Newey, widely regarded as an aerodynamic and engineering genius, had joined Red Bull in 2006 and was now delivering cars with superior aerodynamics. This year, Red Bull would again enter the championship with Sebastian Vettel partnering Mark Webber on the main team. Many still saw Vettel as a rising star, and Red Bull was poised to challenge Ferrari and McLaren at the front of the grid.

Hamilton acknowledged Red Bull's rise, recognising that they had done something special with their car. It was obvious to him and Button that Vettel and Webber were going to be hard to beat. The consensus was that Red Bull, having finished 2009 with the strongest car, had now become the favourites, and McLaren's success would be influenced not only by their car's speed but also by how well Hamilton and Button could balance rivalry with teamwork.

Button's arrival brought a fresh dynamic to McLaren. Unlike in recent seasons, where Hamilton had been the clear number one driver, the team made it clear that both champions would be treated equally. Martin Whitmarsh, who had stepped into the role of team principal following Ron Dennis's departure to the Group CEO, reinforced McLaren's long-standing philosophy of pairing the best drivers available to push the team forward. He made it clear that while they were free to race each other, the only expectation was mutual respect on track.

The contrast in their driving styles was widely discussed. Button's smooth approach, strong tyre management, and strategic thinking differed from Hamilton's aggressive, instinctive racing style, which combined raw speed with a sharp ability to overtake; but Hamilton could do smooth. The general perception was that he was an aggressive racer, which was broadly correct, but he was intelligent, and on tracks where smoothness was the fastest way around, he would adapt his style accordingly.

Despite the public perception that the two had fundamentally different techniques, McLaren's Managing Director, Jonathan Neale, saw it differently. He believed that both had relatively neutral driving styles, suggesting that car development would not be compromised by the partnership. Their collaboration aimed to enhance car development and race strategies. The different skill sets Button and Hamilton brought had the potential to benefit the team by offering different perspectives on car setup and race strategies, while the team's strategies had to accommodate the strengths and preferences of both drivers.

**Pre-Season Preparations**

The 2010 pre-season testing sessions showed the strengths of several teams, particularly Red Bull Racing, with Vettel and Webber displaying impressive pace. Hamilton was optimistic about the season ahead, expressing confidence in McLaren's new car. Having closely followed the development of the MP4-25, he believed it would be a state-of-the-art machine capable of delivering consistent victories for both him and Button.

Amidst the team and technical changes, Hamilton also made a significant personal decision. His father, Anthony Hamilton, had been instrumental in guiding his career from karting through to Formula One, managing him every step of the way. However, in 2010, Hamilton chose to part ways with his father as his manager, aiming to maintain a healthier personal relationship. He later acknowledged that the decision had been his own, recognising that while his father would miss being involved at that level, it was a necessary step for both of them.

Following the split, Anthony Hamilton stepped back from managing his son's career, allowing their father-son relationship to reset. Over time, their bond strengthened, with Anthony returning to races in a purely supportive role rather than as a manager. This renewed dynamic proved important in maintaining Hamilton's emotional and mental balance, ensuring he had the personal support he needed during key moments in his career. As far as decisions went, Hamilton's choice to make this change was key to his personal and professional growth.

With his father no longer managing his affairs, Hamilton would sign with Simon Fuller's XIX Entertainment in March 2011. Fuller, known for working with high-profile figures such as David Beckham, introduced a brand-focused approach, aiming to expand Hamilton's profile beyond motorsport into areas like fashion and entertainment. Discussing the decision, Hamilton welcomed the fresh direction, appreciating the opportunity to work with someone who understood both his racing ambitions and his interests outside the sport. Anthony, too, was pleased with how things had evolved, recognising the maturity in his son's decision and acknowledging that he had taken the time to find the right person to guide the next phase of his career.

**Early Season Races**

The opening races of the season highlighted both the strengths and differences within the new Hamilton-Button partnership. Both drivers brought their A-game, delivering strong performances and pushing each other hard while maintaining respect.

The season began in Bahrain on the extended Sakhir Circuit, offering an early glimpse of what was to come. Vettel took pole position for Red Bull, while Hamilton lined up fourth. True to form, Hamilton attacked the race with intensity, making key passes and capitalising on opportunities to secure a third-place finish and an important podium. Button, starting eighth, took a more measured approach, focusing on tyre management and the timing of his pit stops to finish seventh. It was a strong foundation for the season ahead. With a competitive car and solid points on the board, the focus was on building momentum. Early signs suggested a well-balanced dynamic between the two McLaren drivers, a noticeable contrast to the tensions that had surfaced during Alonso's time at the team, where internal competition had often overshadowed harmony.

At the Australian Grand Prix two weeks later, on 28 March, the rain-affected race in Melbourne brought tyre choice and timing to the forefront. Hamilton's drive at the Australian Grand Prix was emblematic of his fighting spirit. Starting in eleventh place due to a disappointing qualifying session, he fought his way through the field, taking measured risks. The race was dicey, with changing weather conditions that tested every driver's ability to adapt. Hamilton finished sixth after a late-race collision and a controversial pit stop initiated by the team on the pit wall. His charge through the pack to finish sixth earned him widespread praise, but Hamilton made it clear that he was frustrated with McLaren for calling him in.

Button claimed victory in Australia, making the most of the changing conditions and an early pit stop to secure his first win for McLaren. His decision-making under pressure, combined with his trademark smooth driving, proved crucial in a race where strategy was everything. It was a performance that highlighted the different strengths within McLaren's driver line-up—Button's measured, tactical approach contrasting with Hamilton's more aggressive, instinctive racing style.

Hamilton felt that the additional stop had compromised one of his strongest drives. The strategy left him on the back foot, and he believed he deserved a better result. While most of his rivals managed the race with just one stop, his two-stop strategy ultimately cost him the chance to fight for the podium.

Button credited the team but made it clear that the decisive pit stop had been his call. Initially, he feared he had made a mistake as he entered the pit lane to find it still wet but soon realised the decision had been the right one as he built up speed on the drier parts of the track. His ability to read the conditions from inside the car had given him the edge when it mattered most.

At the Chinese Grand Prix in April, both McLaren drivers excelled in variable weather conditions, engaging in a good fight with the Red Bulls and Ferraris. Button secured another victory, with Hamilton finishing second, completing a McLaren one-two. The podium celebration reflected continued mutual respect between the two McLaren drivers, with Hamilton praising Button for making the right strategic call.

While his own race had been eventful, he recognised the hard work of the entire team, crediting their efforts in delivering a competitive car. Hamilton was beginning to realise that, in the last two races, Button had made the difference—by calling the shots himself on pit stops, as opposed to just accepting the team's directives. This would lock itself into Hamilton's psyche and become another weapon in his arsenal.

As the season progressed, the rivalry between Hamilton and Button grew fiercer, but their professional relationship remained intact. McLaren, mindful of the need to maintain harmony within the team, allowed them to race freely, trusting in their experience and maturity. This approach led to some close calls, with both drivers constantly pushing each other to raise their performance levels.

After leaving China, the teams headed to Spain, where Hamilton had been running comfortably in second behind a dominant Webber. However, with just one lap remaining, a mechanical failure in the front-left suspension forced him out of the race. It was a bitter blow, robbing him of what would have been a valuable podium finish. Meanwhile, Michael Schumacher, who had come out of retirement and returned to Formula One with Mercedes following their takeover of the Brawn team, found himself under scrutiny. Button was particularly vocal, criticising Schumacher for excessive weaving during their battle and expressing disappointment that a driver of his experience had resorted to such tactics.

The Monaco Grand Prix, one of the most prestigious races on the calendar, posed a significant challenge for both Hamilton and Button. Navigating the tight, twisting streets of Monte Carlo demands absolute precision and a lot of patience, something Hamilton had always embraced. He secured fifth in qualifying, a few places behind Red Bull's dominant front-row lockout, while Button started from eighth.

Held on 16 May, the race proved to be a gruelling affair. Hamilton found himself caught in the midfield battle, struggling to make progress on a circuit where overtaking is notoriously difficult. A series of incidents led to four separate Safety Car deployments, further complicating strategies. Button's race ended early due to a technical issue, while Hamilton focused on securing points rather than taking unnecessary risks. Understanding the limitations of overtaking, he adopted a long-term approach, ensuring he looked after the car and tyres to maximise his championship chances, finishing where he started, in fifth place.

**Turkish Grand Prix – Red Bulls Lock Horns**

The 2010 Turkish Grand Prix, held on 30 May at Istanbul Park, was unforgettable. The circuit, renowned for its challenging Turn 8, provided a formidable test for drivers. Qualifying saw Red Bull's Mark Webber secure pole position, edging out Hamilton, who started alongside him on the front row, just over a tenth adrift. While there appeared to be harmony between Hamilton and Button, cracks were beginning to show at Red Bull between their drivers.

As the race commenced under cloudy skies, Webber maintained his lead, closely followed by Vettel and then Hamilton. The early stages were processional as teams and drivers conserved their tyres and fuel, expecting rain that never materialised.

The key moment of the race came on Lap 40. Webber was still in the lead, with Vettel closing on the uphill section between Turn 10 and Turn 11. Hamilton was 50 metres behind the pair, applying pressure, followed closely by Button.

Webber crested the rise on the long straight after Turn 10, and, sensing Vettel would attack, placed his car a third of the way across the track, forcing Vettel to go outside of him. Vettel, however, had other ideas and went for a small gap up the inside. Webber had to ease out slightly, recognising that Vettel might go off the track. Vettel had better momentum and slowly started to pass Webber. As he got barely half a car length in front, Vettel moved hard to his right, probably to intimidate

Webber, but with only a foot separating them, Webber had no time to react, and Vettel hit Webber instantly.

The impact damaged Vettel's right rear wheel, and he slid off the track. Webber's car was largely undamaged, but he was forced to run wide as Vettel's car slid wildly out of control. It was a brilliant piece of awareness and skill from the plucky Aussie, but it cost Webber positions, as Hamilton, who could hardly believe his luck, shot through, his bright yellow helmet gleaming in the hazy afternoon. Button also went through, the McLarens nose to tail.

In an incident reminiscent of Massa's accident in Hungary, Hamilton was fortunate to escape a head injury when a large piece of debris, which had flown off one of the Red Bulls, struck his McLaren close to his head at well over 100mph. The impact was so severe that it was audible on the onboard camera, even over the deafening roar of the V8 engine. A few seconds behind, Button ran over the same debris that had just hit Hamilton's car. Concerned, Button immediately radioed the team in the pits to report it, only to be reassured by his engineer that everything appeared fine. Also in the pits was Adrian Newey, who lurched forward in front of the Red Bull monitors, his head in his hands in disbelief. Christian Horner shook his head slowly.

As the two McLarens and Webber drove off into the distance, the drama was far from over. Vettel had a complete meltdown over the radio, asking the team what the hell they were doing, firing off multiple expletives, and shouting that he was going home. He wouldn't be able to go home in the three-wheeled Red Bull, that was for sure.

The McLaren duo then had their own fight out front, with Hamilton eventually coming out on top to secure victory. At one stage, the pair were side by side through various corners until Hamilton stamped his authority on proceedings. It was hard but fair, with both drivers aware of the need to balance team loyalty with personal ambition, particularly after seeing the Red Bulls go off.

Following the race, Hamilton revelled in the thrill of the battle, saying he felt at ease out in front, mainly focused on looking after the car, managing the systems, fuel load, and tyres. Button told a similar story, reinforcing the sense of teamwork despite the intensity of the race. He described the battle as hard but fair and talked about his attack alongside Hamilton into Turn 12, saying he had to at least attempt the move, the two having run wheel to wheel for several corners. It later transpired that both of them had been told to manage their fuel levels once it was clear they could bring the cars home, which was likely code for 'don't crash'.

Hamilton and Button were full of praise for each other, and it was reflective of their relationship: they had fought hard and avoided any serious contact.

Away from McLaren's win, there was lingering tension in the Red Bull camp. Vettel's blame of Webber could have been put down to immaturity, as he was only 22 years of age at the time, but Vettel would repeat this behaviour in the future as he got older, always blaming the other driver. He seemed to deflect, never wanting to take responsibility for his mistakes. This was in complete contrast to Hamilton, who would own up and apologise if he had made an error.

The clash sparked intense debate. Some believed Webber had simply held his position and saw no reason for Vettel to make such an aggressive move. Others were much more direct, placing the blame 100% with Vettel, arguing that he had turned into Webber before he was fully alongside. It was obvious to those who were objective observers that Vettel had deliberately driven into Webber. The incident cost a potential one-two finish and deepened tensions within the team. It marked an early sign of Vettel's growing belief in his own priority within Red Bull.

Christian Horner was understandably irate afterward and described it as unnecessary, stressing the importance of team discipline. Pundits and fans debated the wider implications, recognising the growing pressure within the Red Bull camp. When asked for his view, Webber stated that he had never had an issue with a teammate before and hoped the situation would be resolved by the end of the season. Helmut Marko, Red Bull's motorsport advisor, was interviewed after the race and, despite the overwhelming evidence pointing to Vettel's mistake, firmly defended him. His stance deepened the divide between Vettel and Webber, reinforcing the perception that Vettel had the full backing of senior figures within the team, with a growing indication that Webber was on his own.

Hamilton's victory in Turkey marked his first win of the 2010 season, revitalising his championship campaign and proving McLaren's front-running pace. The race underscored the fine margins in Formula One, where team dynamics and split-second decisions can dramatically alter the course of the championship. The incident at Red Bull caused observers to wonder how long the cosy relationship between Button and Hamilton would last. While McLaren appeared to be operating with a strong sense of unity, Formula One drivers were the elite of the elite, and for them, winning was what mattered. Post-race, Hamilton made it clear that he felt there was trust between him and Button and that neither would take unnecessary risks or endanger the other. Their rivalry was competitive, but it was underpinned by professionalism and respect, ensuring that, while they pushed each other to the limit, the team's overall success remained a priority.

**Canadian Grand Prix**

The Canadian Grand Prix in June proved to be a race that suited both McLaren drivers, with tyre degradation playing a crucial role. McLaren's approach to pit stops was key, allowing them to capitalise on their strengths.

Hamilton was in top form, securing his second victory of the season at a circuit that played perfectly to McLaren's characteristics. The Circuit Gilles Villeneuve, with its long straights and demanding chicanes, provided the ideal stage for him to demonstrate his raw pace. He took pole position with a blistering lap of 1:15.105, delivering a final qualifying effort that drew comparisons to some of the sport's greats. Moments after securing pole, Hamilton was instructed by his engineer to stop the car on track to ensure there was enough fuel left for a sample. This led to an unusual scene as he coasted down the final straight before jumping out and pushing the car along the circuit.

On race day, Hamilton executed a near-perfect drive, controlling the race from the front and managing both tyres and fuel carefully. While he was typically known for an aggressive style, his ability to adapt and preserve his tyres was noted by pundits, with many highlighting how he had approached this race in a way more commonly associated with Button's smooth, measured driving. Button's approach to looking after his tyres saw him leap several rivals, ultimately securing second place behind Hamilton, giving McLaren a one-two finish and a major boost in the Constructors' Championship.

During the post-race celebrations, Hamilton praised the team, acknowledging the crucial role everyone had played in securing another one-two finish for McLaren. He also recognised Button's strong performance. Button, in turn, was equally complimentary about Hamilton's weekend. While admitting—tongue-in-cheek—that he would have preferred the positions to be reversed, he acknowledged that Hamilton's pole lap had been outstanding and beyond reach. Despite this, securing another double podium for the team was a cause for celebration. For Hamilton, the victory was particularly significant, with the two back-to-back wins marking a return to form after a challenging start to the season. The result also moved him into the lead of the World Championship, edging ahead by three points and reinforcing his position as a title contender.

As the season progressed, Red Bull's advantage became increasingly evident, due to their superior aerodynamics. This put McLaren on the back foot, forcing Hamilton and Button to maximise every bit of performance from the MP4-25 to stay in contention. Despite the mounting challenge, tensions at Red Bull were becoming more apparent, with Webber growing frustrated over what he saw as the team's preference for Vettel. Vettel and Webber's RB6 was consistently fast, and Adrian Newey's design innovations, particularly in aerodynamics, gave them an edge in qualifying and race pace. McLaren's F-Duct provided a tactical advantage on high-speed circuits, but it wasn't enough to consistently close the gap to Red Bull's superior downforce at other circuits.

Hamilton and Button continued to battle hard, securing podium finishes in key races such as the British Grand Prix, where Hamilton delighted the home crowd with a strong second-place finish. Silverstone, with its high-speed corners and rich history, holds special significance for British drivers, and Hamilton's performance was a proud moment for both him and his supporters. After the race, he made sure to acknowledge the incredible support from the fans. While Mark Webber took a commanding victory, tensions within Red Bull were impossible to ignore. During the cool-down lap, Team Principal Christian Horner congratulated Webber over the radio, praising his performance. However, Webber's response was pointed, as he quipped, "Not bad for a number 2 driver, cheers," making his frustration over the perceived favouritism towards Vettel abundantly clear. His sharp remark served as a reminder that, despite their success on track, Red Bull's internal rivalry was far from settled.

McLaren found itself fighting with Red Bull for the Constructors' Championship, briefly leading the standings at various points thanks to consistent podium finishes. However, with both Vettel and Webber delivering strong performances, Red Bull kept the pressure on. Meanwhile, Alonso, now driving for Ferrari, remained firmly in the mix, adding another dimension to an already intense title fight. Whitmarsh highlighted the importance of teamwork, stressing that cooperation between the drivers was crucial in the battle for the championship. With such strong competition, he saw unity within McLaren as a key advantage in their pursuit of the title.

As the season neared its conclusion, the Drivers' Championship remained wide open, with Hamilton, Button, Vettel, Webber, and Alonso all still in contention. The South Korean Grand Prix in October brought treacherous wet conditions, leading to a chaotic race filled with incidents. Vettel's race ended in disappointment with an engine failure, while Hamilton capitalised to secure second place, keeping his title hopes alive. Button, however, struggled with tyre temperatures and finished outside the points, dealing a blow to his championship chances.

**Season Finale**

The 2010 season reached its dramatic conclusion at the Yas Marina Circuit in Abu Dhabi on 14 November. With its day-to-night transition, the venue provided a fitting stage for the championship decider, with warm and dry conditions. In qualifying, Vettel secured pole position with a time of 1:39.394, with Hamilton lining up alongside him on the front row. Button started fourth, ensuring McLaren remained in the mix for a strong finish. During the race, Hamilton applied pressure on Vettel but couldn't find a way past, ultimately finishing second behind the German. Button completed the podium in third, securing a solid finish for McLaren. Alonso, who had been leading the championship, pitted in response to Mark Webber's stop during the race. This strategy call proved costly, as Alonso rejoined the track behind Vitaly Petrov's Renault and was unable to find a way past. With overtaking proving impossible, he could only manage seventh place, falling out of title contention. With Alonso stuck in traffic and Vettel leading the race, the Red Bull driver went on to secure victory and, in doing so, claimed his first World Championship.

Button acknowledged the unpredictability of the title fight, recognising Vettel's talent and his deserved success. Hamilton, meanwhile, was pleased with how McLaren had finished the year, highlighting the double podium in Abu Dhabi and their second place in the Constructors' Championship as important achievements for the team. Hamilton was pleased with how he and Button had pushed hard throughout the season and expressed confidence that the team would come back stronger the following year; Button echoed the sentiment.

By the end of the season, Hamilton finished fourth in the Drivers' Championship, with Button 26 points behind in fifth. While the ultimate goal of winning the title had eluded them, both had delivered strong performances, reinforcing McLaren's status as one of the top teams and securing second place in the Constructors' Championship. Hamilton's victories in Turkey and Canada were standout moments, while Button's well-judged wins in Australia and China highlighted his racecraft. Together, they had formed an effective partnership, but in equal cars, Hamilton had just beaten the current World Champion, as he had done with Alonso in 2007.

The experiences of these years played a key role in shaping Hamilton's approach to teamwork, competition, and personal growth. As he looked ahead to the next phase of his career, the lessons learned at McLaren would influence his future decisions and successes. Many noted how he had become increasingly adept at balancing the demands of qualifying and the race itself, showing an ability to adapt his style to the circumstances—one moment attacking like Senna, the next conserving like Prost. This ability to think strategically and adjust in the moment would prove invaluable as he continued to evolve as a driver.

### The Influence of the F-Duct and Its Ban

McLaren's innovative F-Duct not only provided a crucial advantage early in the season but also prompted a wave of development across the paddock, with teams like Sauber quickly producing their own versions in an attempt to match McLaren's straight-line speed. However, despite its effectiveness, the system raised concerns about safety and driver distraction, as it required drivers to adjust their positioning in the cockpit to activate it. By the end of the season, the FIA had ruled to ban the F-Duct for 2011, aiming for a simpler and safer approach to improving straight-line performance.

Although outlawed, the concept behind the F-Duct influenced the sport's direction. The FIA introduced the Drag Reduction System (DRS), a new overtaking aid that allowed drivers to adjust the rear wing to reduce drag and increase speed in designated zones. Unlike the F-Duct, DRS was activated via a button and was subject to strict regulations to ensure fairness. It remains a fundamental part of Formula One's overtaking strategy, a testament to McLaren's influence on the sport's technical evolution.

As the sport evolved, so too did Hamilton's ambitions. The next phase of his career would bring new challenges, pushing him to make a bold move that was widely questioned at the time—one that would ultimately redefine his legacy in Formula One.

# The Crossroads

The 2011 Formula One season was a transformative chapter in Lewis Hamilton's career. Entering his fifth year with McLaren, Hamilton faced an immensely competitive grid dominated by Red Bull Racing, led by Sebastian Vettel. The season was marked by Hamilton's incredible highs and deep personal and professional challenges, creating a tapestry of triumphs, controversies, and lessons that shaped his evolution as a driver and individual. It was a formative year, both in terms of dealing with adversity on the track and off it in the Stewards' rooms.

Hamilton entered the 2011 season with a mix of optimism and realism, fully aware of Red Bull Racing's growing dominance. Adrian Newey had once again produced a formidable machine in the RB7, and with the momentum from their 2010 success, Red Bull carried increasing confidence into the new campaign.

McLaren's response came in the form of the MP4-26, a car designed to challenge Red Bull's technical advantage. While it showed promise in testing, its performance proved inconsistent across different conditions. The team dynamic was also shifting. In their first season together, Hamilton and Button had established a respectful working relationship, but now, in their second year as teammates, the honeymoon period was over. Both were World Champions, both wanted to lead the team, and while their mutual respect remained, it was inevitable that more friction would emerge as they fought for supremacy within McLaren.

Ahead of the first race, Hamilton spoke openly about the challenges in front of him. While excited to get behind the wheel of the new car, he recognised the difficulty of the task ahead, given the regulation changes and the fresh competitive landscape. The teams were still adjusting to the new technical landscape, grappling with the complexities of the Drag

Reduction System (DRS), Kinetic Energy Recovery System (KERS), and the latest tyre compounds. These changes played to the strengths of some teams while exposing weaknesses in others. However, one thing remained constant—Red Bull, with Adrian Newey shaping the design philosophy, continued to set the benchmark for aerodynamic excellence, demonstrating the value of having a world-class engineer at the heart of car development.

Amid the ongoing battle between Red Bull and McLaren, Mercedes GP Petronas entered their second season as a re-established works team, following their full return to Formula One in 2010. Under the leadership of Ross Brawn, a figure renowned for his technical expertise and past successes with Ferrari and Brawn GP, the team aimed to take a step forward. Their driver lineup combined experience and proven talent, with seven-time World Champion Michael Schumacher alongside Nico Rosberg, a highly regarded driver who had been one of Hamilton's key rivals in junior categories. With both drivers bringing skill and insight, Mercedes hoped to edge closer to the frontrunners.

Mercedes' technical department underwent significant strengthening in 2011, with key personnel joining to enhance the team's engineering expertise. Bob Bell, who had previously enjoyed success at Renault, took on the role of Technical Director, bringing with him a wealth of experience. Aldo Costa, formerly of Ferrari, joined as Engineering Director, adding further insight into car development, while Geoff Willis, who had worked with Red Bull Racing, was appointed Technology Director. These high-profile additions signalled Mercedes' long-term ambitions—while not yet among the frontrunners, the team was clearly laying the foundations for future success.

Mercedes entered the 2011 season with the MGP W02 chassis, powered by the Mercedes FO 108Y 2.4L V8 engine. Despite hopes of closing the gap to the leaders, the car struggled to match the pace of Red Bull and McLaren. Aerodynamic efficiency proved to be a weakness, and tyre management became a persistent challenge under the 2011 regulations, which placed greater emphasis on the new Pirelli tyres and DRS. While the W02 showed glimpses of promise, it was clear that more development was needed before Mercedes could consistently challenge at the front.

From the outside, Mercedes still appeared to be in the early stages of rebuilding, but within the paddock, their intent was obvious. For a driver like Hamilton, it would have been hard not to take notice. With key personnel arriving and the team positioning itself for long-term success, the groundwork was being laid for something bigger—something that, in time, could become an enticing prospect.

McLaren, with its driver lineup of Lewis Hamilton and Jenson Button, entered the 2011 season as one of the strongest teams on the grid. Having finished as runners-up in the Constructors' Championship the previous year, they were expected to be Red Bull's closest challengers. The MP4-26, despite some inconsistencies in testing, was a well-developed package, capable of fighting at the front.

In contrast, Mercedes, still in the process of re-establishing itself as a top contender, was not yet able to challenge McLaren on a regular basis. While the Silver Arrows had strong backing and a growing technical team, they remained a step behind the frontrunners in terms of outright performance. Red Bull, having dominated the previous season, remained the benchmark.

### A Promising Start in Melbourne

The Australian Grand Prix at Melbourne's Albert Park Circuit on 27 March marked the season opener. Hamilton qualified second, behind Sebastian Vettel, who was nearly eight-tenths of a second ahead on pole, setting the tone for a year where Red Bull's qualifying dominance would often frustrate McLaren. Webber in the other Red Bull started in third, just ahead of Button. Despite damage to his undertray early in the race, Hamilton delivered a gritty performance to finish second, securing a strong start to the campaign. Vettel's win, however, underscored the uphill battle McLaren faced in matching Red Bull's pace. Webber came in some 16 seconds behind Hamilton in fifth place and Button was over thirty seconds down on Hamilton, finishing sixth.

**Early Highs: Victory in Shanghai**

After a challenging outing in Malaysia, where Hamilton's tyre strategy faltered, the Chinese Grand Prix in Shanghai provided an early highlight for him. Vettel was again on pole, seven-tenths in front of Button, who had qualified second. Hamilton was a mere four one-hundredths of a second behind his teammate in the sister McLaren. Webber, having had a torrid qualifying, was down in 18th position. Starting third on the grid, Hamilton executed the perfect getaway and led into Turn 1. Christian Horner, Red Bull's boss, could be seen on the pit wall with his head bowed, scratching his temple in frustration at Vettel's poor start. Once the race settled, Hamilton delivered a demonstration in racecraft and strategy, biding his time when necessary with the help of his team and picking the best tactical options for pit stops.

Having had an indifferent start to their season, Mercedes gave a glimpse of what might be to come as Rosberg led the race for 14 laps. When he emerged from the pits mid-race, Rosberg was instructed by the team to keep Hamilton behind over the radio. Rejoining the track, Rosberg defended hard, cutting across Hamilton's path before making a late move under braking to cover the outside line. At the next series of double right-hand bends Rosberg stayed right after the first corner to ensure Hamilton could not come down the inside. Hamilton went to go around the outside and Rosberg jinked violently to his left to block Hamilton. Hamilton was on the radio immediately, complaining that Rosberg's driving was dangerous.

Hamilton maintained his composure and, less than a lap later, went past Rosberg, slightly locking up his right front wheel in the process. Hamilton's engineer, demonstrating the importance of teamwork and the bigger picture, told him that the best time to attack the drivers ahead would be towards the end of the race, as their tyres would be very old relative to Hamilton's. Hamilton continued his charge through the field, overtaking Massa on the start-finish straight, which was met with celebrations in the McLaren garage, before passing Button soon after and setting off in pursuit of Vettel.

As the race neared its conclusion, Hamilton closed in on Vettel and eventually made his move, taking the lead in the closing laps. The McLaren team, fully engaged in the battle, kept him informed on the gaps behind, ensuring he had everything he needed to maintain his position. In the garage, the mechanics erupted in celebration, clapping and giving thumbs up as their driver edged closer to victory. Meanwhile, Webber, taking advantage of fresher tyres, demonstrated Red Bull's underlying strength by carving through the field from near the back of the grid. In the final laps, he caught and passed Button, securing a strong finish.

Hamilton crossed the line to claim his first victory of the season, bringing an end—at least temporarily—to Red Bull's early dominance. Elated, he expressed his gratitude to the team over the radio on the cooldown lap, acknowledging their efforts in the pit stops and urging them to keep pushing for more success. Vettel secured second place, but one of the standout performances came from Webber, who finished just seven seconds behind Hamilton after charging through the field. His strong recovery underlined Red Bull's pace, proving that even from the back, the car remained a formidable contender. Webber was applauded by his team, and in reply, he quipped, 'There's life in me yet, boys!'

Mercedes also showed encouraging signs, with Rosberg finishing fifth, demonstrating the car's potential. Schumacher crossed the line in eighth, adding more valuable points to the team's tally.

After the race, Hamilton talked about the dedication of the team, both at the circuit and back at the factory. The result reflected the effort behind the scenes, with every development, strategy call, and pit stop contributing to the success. It was a sentiment he would go on to express time and again throughout his career—always sincere, always appreciative of the people working tirelessly to give him a competitive car.

However, there were some wobbles in the mid-season, and controversy was looming. The Monaco Grand Prix would be a turning point in Hamilton's season, and not for the better. In a McLaren that lacked the outright pace of the Red Bull, Hamilton was constantly pushing to the limit—and sometimes beyond it. This was an era before the one-move rule under braking was introduced, meaning drivers had more freedom to defend aggressively, often making late moves on the straights and under braking. As a result, wheel-to-wheel battles were intense, and at times, controversial.

By the time Formula One arrived in Monaco, Hamilton had already been summoned to the Stewards on multiple occasions that season. His driving—and his growing frustration with officiating—was becoming a focal point of discussion within the paddock. The Monaco Grand Prix, held from 26–29 May, proved to be another flashpoint. A series of incidents, including collisions with Felipe Massa and Pastor Maldonado, resulted in multiple penalties and a sixth-place finish. After the race, Hamilton voiced his frustration, openly criticising the frequency of his trips to the stewards and suggesting that his aggressive style was being unfairly penalised. When asked if he felt he was being targeted, he attempted to defuse the situation with humour, quoting Ali G's famous line: *"Is it because I'm black?"* The remark was met with widespread criticism, leading to an apology in the aftermath. The incident only amplified the scrutiny surrounding Hamilton at the time, with his words making headlines far beyond the world of Formula One.

Hamilton's behaviour during this period reflected the immense pressure he had placed on himself to succeed. The high expectations he set at the start of the season, combined with frustrations both inside and outside the car, were beginning to take their toll. His emotions were becoming more visible, and it was clear he was at a crossroads—not just as a driver, but as a person. This was a defining moment. He could either step back, reflect, and grow from the experience, or let the frustration consume him. He chose the former. While criticism came thick and fast, many within the paddock—especially those who had faced similar challenges—recognised these as growing pains. Experienced voices offered guidance and support when he needed it most. Ultimately, however, his future would be shaped by the choices he made in the months that followed. The way he responded to adversity during this period would prove to be a crucial step in his evolution, both on and off the track.

The Canadian Grand Prix on 13 June brought yet another dramatic twist to Hamilton's season. In one of the most chaotic and rain-affected races in Formula One history, incidents unfolded one after another. At Turn 1 on the opening lap, Hamilton made a move down the inside of Webber. As they exited the corner, slight contact sent Webber spinning at the pit lane exit. Hamilton managed to continue largely unaffected, while Webber dropped down the order, losing over a dozen positions. By lap 8, the Stewards confirmed that both drivers were under investigation for the incident.

By this stage, Hamilton had closed in on Button in the sister McLaren. Exiting the final chicane, he took a tighter line, getting a stronger run onto the start-finish straight. Button, leading, glanced in his left mirror before moving across towards the pit wall, unaware of how quickly Hamilton had gained ground behind him. At over 160mph, Hamilton pulled out of the dense spray being thrown up in Button's slipstream, attempting to pass between Button and the wall. Button, following his usual racing line, continued to drift left, unaware that Hamilton was now alongside. With nowhere to go,

Hamilton's front wing clipped Button's left rear wheel, sending Hamilton's car into the pit wall. Button's McLaren snapped sideways but remained on track, narrowly avoiding disaster. The right side of Hamilton's front wing shattered on impact, sending pieces of endplate spiralling across the track. As he rejoined, it became clear that his left rear tyre—damaged from striking the pit wall—was rapidly deflating. With the spray causing difficult conditions, Button would probably have had limited visibility in his mirrors, making it impossible to spot Hamilton's move.

By Lap 19, the rain had become relentless, forcing the race to be red-flagged. After the restart, the action briefly settled before tensions flared once again on lap 37. While battling Alonso in the Ferrari, Button attempted a move into the second chicane but clipped Alonso's right rear wheel, sending the Ferrari into a spin and leaving it beached on the kerb. Button sustained a puncture in the contact and was forced to pit for the fourth time, adding to an already eventful race that had also included a drive-through penalty.

As conditions improved and the racing line began to dry, Schumacher used his vast wet-weather experience to pass Massa and move into second. However, by lap 64, Webber had caught the seven-time Champion, with Button closing in behind them. With impressive momentum, Button swept past Webber coming off the Wall of Champions and set his sights on Schumacher. A lap later, he made the move, taking second place and beginning his chase of Vettel. Under pressure on the final lap as Button closed in, Vettel made a rare unforced error, running slightly wide and opening the door for Button to seize victory in dramatic fashion. It was a remarkable comeback in a race filled with setbacks, multiple pit stops, and a drive-through penalty.

Beyond the celebrations, the result had wider implications within McLaren. Button's win reinforced his status as a genuine title contender, proving he could match Hamilton not just in strategy and consistency, but also in raw racecraft. It added another layer to their intra-team rivalry, with both drivers now firmly established as equal challengers.

**A Resurgent Hamilton: Redemption in Germany**

After a series of underwhelming performances, Hamilton had a reset and found redemption at the German Grand Prix. Held at the Nürburgring, the race saw Hamilton qualify second, less than a tenth of a second behind Webber, who was on pole in the Red Bull. Vettel qualified third, with Alonso in the Ferrari in fourth. Hamilton made a good start, taking the lead into Turn 1. Behind him, Webber, Vettel, Alonso, and now Massa in the second Ferrari were nearly four abreast as they jostled for position.

Ten laps into the race, and following yellow flags for an accident, Webber had gone into the lead. On Lap 12, Webber got a poor exit with oversteer coming out of the final corner onto the start-finish straight. Hamilton went down the pit lane side of the track and nearly hit the wall as Webber forced him as far across as he dared. Red Bull realised they couldn't pass Hamilton on the track, so they went for the undercut, calling Webber in early.

As the pit stops cycled through, Hamilton found himself in second place behind Webber, with Alonso close behind. Another round of stops followed, and after a series of rapid laps, Hamilton rejoined just ahead of Webber. The two engaged in a fierce battle for position, pushing each other to the limit around the lap. The fight took an unexpected turn when Alonso emerged from the pits ahead of them both, having gained track position through an alternative strategy. Hamilton, however, wasted no time in responding. At Turn 2, he swept around the outside of the Ferrari, reclaiming the lead with a bold and decisive move. From there, he controlled the race to secure a spectacular victory.

On the podium, Hamilton's delight was unmistakable. His performance had been a reminder of his ability to dominate a race when everything clicked. Pundits hailed his drive as one of his finest, with some describing him as untouchable—a performance that reinforced exactly why he was a World Champion.

Hamilton's victory also reignited McLaren's hopes of taking the fight to Red Bull in the Constructors' Championship, though consistency remained a challenge. While the team had the pace to compete, maintaining that level across a full season was proving difficult.

In a post-race interview with the BBC following his triumph in Germany, Hamilton appeared noticeably different from the frustrated figure who had left the Stewards' office in Monaco just weeks earlier. He seemed to have grown immeasurably in a short space of time. After a turbulent spell—dealing with a car that often fell short of Red Bull, intense media scrutiny over his personal life, and frequent clashes with race officials—it was as if a reset had taken place. There was a newfound calmness about him. He spoke with clarity, maturity, and a renewed sense of purpose. The aggression remained on track, but off it, his composure and humility had returned. It marked a shift in both his season and his career—a moment where he appeared to have rediscovered the balance he needed to move forward.

However, the season still had more challenges in store. The Belgian Grand Prix proved to be another difficult moment in a campaign filled with highs and lows. Hamilton's race ended abruptly following a collision with Kamui Kobayashi, sending him heavily into the barriers. What stood out, however, was his reaction. Reflecting his growing sense of perspective, Hamilton later took full responsibility for the incident, acknowledging that he had misjudged the space available. It was an example of the self-awareness that had been developing throughout the season—recognising where the limits were, both in racing and in his approach to setbacks. The crash was another reminder of the fine margins at play in a year where moments of brilliance had too often been accompanied by costly miscalculations.

The 2011 Abu Dhabi Grand Prix, held at the Yas Marina Circuit on 13 November, provided an opportunity for Hamilton to regain momentum. In qualifying, he secured a front-row start, narrowly missing out on pole to Sebastian Vettel, who equalled Nigel Mansell's record of 14 poles in a single season. The stage was set for a strong performance as Hamilton looked to end the season on a high.

The race commenced under the circuit's signature twilight conditions, with temperatures cooling as the evening progressed. There was an immediate twist on the first lap when Vettel suffered a puncture, forcing his retirement and opening the door for Hamilton to seize the lead. Demonstrating exceptional control and pace, Hamilton maintained his position at the front, fending off challenges from Alonso in the Ferrari, who finished second, and his McLaren teammate Jenson Button, who secured third place. After the race Hamilton spoke with a renewed sense of confidence: an absolute aura of calm flowed from him. A person at peace. The victory in Abu Dhabi was more than just another race win—it symbolised his ability to weather adversity and emerge stronger.

Within McLaren, there was a belief that this triumph could be a turning point. Team Principal Martin Whitmarsh acknowledged the challenges Hamilton had faced during the season and the progress he had made both as a driver and as an individual, observing that this was a sign of him moving beyond the difficulties of the past few months. There was a sense that this shift in dynamic was not just a return to form, but a foundation for even greater success.

Hamilton's third victory of the season was a show of perseverance. In a year marked by moments of sheer brilliance, there had been some frustrating setbacks. The win reinforced his position as one of Formula One's elite drivers—capable of delivering at the highest level, even in challenging circumstances. It was a fitting reminder of his determination to close out the season on a high and build momentum for what lay ahead.

In what would later prove to be a telling sign for Hamilton's future, Nico Rosberg talked openly about Mercedes' position and his growing frustration with the team's inability to challenge Red Bull, McLaren, or Ferrari. Despite occasional flashes of promise, Mercedes remained a step behind the frontrunners, and Rosberg was eager to see progress. Team Principal Ross Brawn sought to reassure him, stressing that the team was fully committed to long-term success. He urged patience, emphasising that the foundations were being laid for future victories. The message was clear—Mercedes was playing the long game, and those willing to stick with the project would eventually reap the rewards.

These discussions would not have gone unnoticed by Hamilton. While fully focused on his own challenges at McLaren, the developments at Mercedes hinted at a team quietly preparing for a more competitive future—something that, in time, would become an important factor in his own career decisions.

Off the track, Hamilton faced personal struggles that inevitably had an impact on his performances. His high-profile relationship with Nicole Scherzinger, combined with the relentless pressures of competing at the highest level, created a challenging environment. Looking back, Hamilton later admitted that 2011 had been the toughest year of his life, both professionally and personally. Years later, Jenson Button reflected on the mental and emotional toll that season had taken on Hamilton. He spoke about the importance of having a strong support system—something he credited as essential in his own career—and suggested that Hamilton had struggled without that same level of guidance. Button highlighted how elite athletes often battle in silence, with the demands of

Formula One pushing them to their limits, both mentally and physically.

The 2011 season had tested the 26-year-old Hamilton in ways he had never experienced before. On track, he battled through inconsistency, penalties, and intense competition. Off it, personal struggles, the pressure of being in the public eye, and the challenges of competing at the highest level had all taken a toll. However, another layer to his journey was beginning to emerge—one that would later define his role beyond racing.

His *"Is it because I'm black?"* remark in Monaco, though meant as a joke, was an unguarded moment of frustration that hinted at something deeper. It reflected the difficulty of navigating a sport where he was the only black driver in a historically white-dominated space. While the comment was widely criticised at the time and later required an apology, it was an early indication that Hamilton was beginning to engage with the realities of how he was perceived and treated in Formula One.

At that stage of his career, he was still finding his voice—both in dealing with personal struggles and in negotiating his place in a sport where he often felt like an outsider. It was a year of lessons, where he was forced to confront setbacks, criticism, and his own expectations. The resilience he developed during this period would serve him well in the years to come, not just as a driver, but as someone who would go on to reshape the conversation around diversity and inclusion in Formula One.

Despite the turmoil, the flashes of brilliance remained. His victories reminded the world of his extraordinary talent, and by the end of the year, he had rediscovered some of the balance he had lost. The season had been punishing, but it had also been formative—a year that shaped not just the competitor, but the man.

# Transition

The 2012 Formula One season began with a level of unpredictability that both delighted fans and challenged teams alike. Seven different drivers won the first seven races—a record that underscored the sheer competitiveness of the grid. For Lewis Hamilton and McLaren, the season held immense promise, but it would also become one of the most turbulent years of his career—filled with highs, frustrations, and the beginning of a new chapter that would change the course of Formula One history.

McLaren's car for the 2012 season, the MP4-27, was an evolution of the previous year's design, incorporating subtle improvements aimed at enhancing both performance and reliability. The car's sleek, low-drag design provided impressive pace on high-speed circuits, and McLaren's engineering team, led by Paddy Lowe, was confident in their ability to challenge for both the Drivers' and Constructors' Championships.

Red Bull's initial dominance in the DRS and KERS era began to wane as other teams gained a better understanding of the regulations. While they still had the best car, the gap was closing as their competitors made significant strides.

In the off-season, Ferrari worked tirelessly to develop the F2012, their 58th Formula One car, designed to comply with the latest technical regulations. Led by Technical Director Pat Fry and Chief Designer Nikolas Tombazis, the design team introduced several bold innovations. Among the most notable was a stepped nose—an aesthetic consequence of new FIA safety regulations—and a pull-rod front suspension, marking a significant departure from the conventional push-rod setup. These changes were aimed at improving aerodynamic efficiency and lowering the car's centre of gravity. The design choices, especially the unconventional nose, sparked much discussion within the paddock. Tombazis acknowledged its unusual appearance but defended its effectiveness, explaining that the regulations required a lower nose, while aerodynamic priorities favoured a higher chassis. Although not visually appealing, the design was deemed the most aerodynamically efficient solution available.

Pre-season testing produced mixed results for Ferrari. While the F2012 proved reliable, its outright pace was inconsistent, raising concerns about how it would fare against its rivals. The drivers, Fernando Alonso and Felipe Massa, remained cautiously optimistic, understanding that early performance in testing didn't always reflect race-day competitiveness. Alonso tempered expectations, noting that there were still several weeks before the true pecking order would be revealed in Melbourne. Pundits shared the uncertainty surrounding Ferrari's new design, with many questioning whether the team's bold approach would yield results. There was widespread recognition that, while the F2012 featured innovative solutions, there was no clear indication it would be competitive from the outset. The general sentiment was that Ferrari had taken a calculated gamble—one that could either bring them back to the front or leave them struggling to match their rivals. As the season opener approached, speculation remained over whether their aggressive technical choices would translate into success on track.

Mercedes AMG Petronas Formula One Team unveiled the F1 W03, their third car since returning as a works outfit. The design was led by Technical Director Bob Bell, with input from Engineering Director Aldo Costa and Technology Director Geoff Willis. The car featured several innovative aspects, including a stepped nose—similar to Ferrari's—to comply with new FIA regulations, and a unique double DRS system, designed to enhance straight-line speed by reducing aerodynamic drag.

Pre-season testing suggested potential, but also revealed a few issues with the F1 W03. Nico Rosberg and Michael

Schumacher set competitive lap times, indicating promising pace, but reliability concerns emerged, particularly regarding the complexity of the double DRS system. Despite these issues, confidence within the team remained high, with leadership emphasising that the focus was on race-day performance rather than just qualifying speed. The belief was that podiums had now become a realistic target. As the season opener approached, Mercedes was no longer considered a midfield team—they were edging closer to challenging Red Bull, Ferrari, and McLaren. The F1 W03 had the ingredients to compete at the front, but whether it could do so consistently remained the key question. The season opener would be an important test to confirm the optimism surrounding the car.

**Season Opener**

The 2012 Australian Grand Prix, held on 18 March at Melbourne's Albert Park Circuit, marked the beginning of the Formula One season. Hamilton secured pole position with a time of 1:24.922, narrowly edging out his teammate Button by a tenth of a second. At the start of the race, Hamilton faced immediate pressure. Button made a cleaner getaway, overtaking Hamilton into the first corner. Hamilton held onto second place, closely trailing his teammate. The McLaren duo appeared poised for a strong finish

The race changed when the Safety Car was deployed after Vitaly Petrov's Caterham stopped on the main straight. The intervention bunched up the field, erasing the gaps that had been built earlier. Vettel took full advantage, using the pit stop phase to move ahead of Hamilton, dropping him to third. The positions remained unchanged as they crossed the line, with Button taking victory. While Hamilton was visibly frustrated, many saw the result as a solid starting point for the season. With a long campaign ahead, securing a podium in the first race provided a strong foundation to build upon.

As Jenson Button drove the cool-down lap, his father, John Button, stood draped in the Union Flag in the pit lane, waiting to share in his son's success. John tapped his chest and said, "My heart!" joking about the stress, his trademark huge smile spread across his face.

After the race, Hamilton acknowledged his disappointment but remained focused on the bigger picture. He admitted that his start had cost him and recognised that he needed to reset his approach for the races ahead. A week later, at the Malaysian Grand Prix, Hamilton finished third behind Pérez, with Alonso winning the race. After Malaysia, the teams moved on to China.

**China**

The 2012 Chinese Grand Prix, held on 15 April at the Shanghai International Circuit, marked a milestone for Nico Rosberg and the Mercedes team. Rosberg claimed pole position for Mercedes, delivering a statement performance with a lap half a second clear of Hamilton, who had been quick but unable to match the outright pace of the Silver Arrows. A late gearbox change for Hamilton resulted in a grid penalty, promoting Schumacher to second and securing a Mercedes front-row lockout. As the mechanics cleared the grid for the formation lap, the two silver cars sat motionless at the front, poised for the start. Rosberg, his bright yellow helmet standing out, took a moment with his visor open and eyes closed, gathering his thoughts. Beside him, Schumacher, head slightly tilted forward in his distinctive red helmet, appeared deep in concentration. On the Mercedes pit wall, anticipation reached its peak.

Both Mercedes drivers launched well when the lights went out, leading into Turn 1 as the race got underway. What followed was a tactical battle, with pit stops and tyre choices playing a crucial role as teams tried to outmanoeuvre each other. It was looking good until the first pit stop.

Schumacher pitted and as he left the pit box the team immediately knew there was a problem, his car not having the right front wheel fitted correctly. He was forced to retire on the spot. True to his team spirit, Schumacher changed into casual clothes and a black Mercedes fleece, before rejoining the engineers in the garage and donning a pair of team headphones to watch the race unfold.

Meanwhile, Hamilton worked his way through the field, benefiting from McLaren's well-timed pit stops and his own overtaking skills. He had a few close encounters with Webber and Alonso but maintained excellent race pace throughout, securing a solid third-place finish and marking his third consecutive podium of the season.

The race was historic for both Mercedes and Nico Rosberg. Rosberg secured his maiden Formula One victory, leading from pole position and delivering a dominant performance. This win marked Mercedes' first as a works team since 1955, a significant milestone in their racing history. The Mercedes team went wild. Norbert Haug, Chief of the Mercedes operation, was seen walking along the pit lane, waving his arms in the air, absolutely elated. He came face to face with Charlie Whiting, the FIA Technical Director, who was standing alone at the Parc Fermé entrance, waiting for the winning cars to arrive. Haug walked up to Whiting and went to give him two high-fives but changed his mind, and instead, they embraced in a big hug. It was a reminder of how high the stakes are and the passion that is the lifeblood of motorsport.

After the race, Hamilton congratulated Rosberg and Mercedes, praising Rosberg for his outstanding drive and well-deserved victory. Talking of his own race, Hamilton said he had enjoyed the battles with Alonso and Webber, pointing out it was one of the best races of the season. Pundits lauded Rosberg's achievement, emphasising the significance of his win. Rosberg finished 20 seconds ahead of Button and Hamilton, underscoring the dominant nature of his performance and hinting that it was an early sign of Mercedes' potential in Formula One,

Hamilton's determination paid off in the first half of the season, with a series of impressive performances. His victory at the Canadian Grand Prix stood out as one of his best drives. Starting from second on the grid, Hamilton carefully coaxed the McLaren, conserving his tyres when necessary and pushing flat out when needed. His ability to manage the pace—switching between conservation and all-out speed—was outstanding in Canada. It was all worth the effort as he secured his first win of the season. He celebrated by acknowledging the fans in Canada, a circuit that was becoming one of his most successful. He dedicated the victory to them for their constant support and positivity throughout the year. Hamilton spoke to the crowd about the significance of winning at a circuit where he had claimed his first-ever Grand Prix victory, expressing how much it meant to him to win there again.

However, despite moments of brilliance, Hamilton's season was marred by a series of setbacks. Reliability issues with the MP4-27 cost him crucial points, while several team-driven miscalculations left him feeling frustrated.

The 2012 European Grand Prix at Valencia's street circuit on 24 June was a defining moment in Hamilton's season. It was marked by a strong qualifying performance and clouded by controversy. Hamilton was rapid during qualifying, securing second place on the grid with a time of 1:38.410, just behind pole-sitter Sebastian Vettel. He was pleased with starting on the front row, especially since other teams had made significant improvements to their cars that weekend.

The race unfolded with numerous tussles across the field. In the closing stages, Hamilton found himself defending third place against Williams driver Pastor Maldonado. On the penultimate lap, Maldonado attempted an overtake, resulting in a collision that sent Hamilton into the barriers and out of the race. Though frustrated, Hamilton acknowledged that setbacks were part of racing, and it was sometimes hard to take the knocks, especially as he had put his heart and soul into the race. He reflected on the inevitable ups and downs of motorsport. While speaking about the nature of racing, he emphasised that he was now looking forward to the

Silverstone Grand Prix. This marked another sign of Hamilton's growing maturity, as he began to approach incidents with a more objective mindset, balancing his passion for racing with the lessons learned along the way. Maldonado would later become synonymous with a reputation for crashing, earning the nickname 'Crashtor' Maldonado, retiring in 30% of his races, and receiving FIA penalties in nearly every other race. His incident in Europe would be no different and drew significant attention from the racing community.

While Hamilton fought his own battles, Alonso and Vettel were locked in a scrap that would define much of the season. Alonso, now in his third year at Ferrari, was under immense pressure to deliver a Championship for the iconic team. The expectations were sky-high, and despite the Ferrari F2012 being less competitive at the start of the season, Alonso's driving was nothing short of extraordinary. He squeezed every ounce of performance from the car, securing surprise victories in Malaysia and Valencia, and demonstrating his ability to capitalise on every opportunity.

Many fans felt that Alonso was carrying an uncompetitive car, a sentiment reflected in the stark gap between him and his teammate, Massa. Maybe Alonso did bring six tenths after all? Massa struggled throughout the season, consistently outpaced by Alonso, and his underperformance drew criticism from both fans and the media. However, critics perhaps overlooked the fact that Massa had not long ago suffered a serious traumatic brain injury in Hungary. The imbalance within the Ferrari camp was clear, with Alonso single-handedly keeping Ferrari in the Championship fight.

Sebastian Vettel and Red Bull remained a formidable force throughout the season. The RB8, designed by Adrian Newey, continued to evolve, and Vettel's consistency in the latter half of the year proved crucial in his title bid. The rivalry between Vettel and Alonso intensified, with both drivers exchanging blows in key races. At the Italian Grand Prix in Monza, tensions boiled over when Vettel was penalised for forcing Alonso off the track—a moment that encapsulated the intensity of their struggle. Vettel, feeling the pressure from Alonso, recognised that every point would be crucial. Around this time, rumours began circulating that Ferrari was interested in signing Vettel, further fuelling the already intense rivalry between the pair.

One of the season's most thrilling races came at the Hungarian Grand Prix at the end of July, where Hamilton delivered a stunning drive to secure his second victory of the year. Starting from pole, he expertly managed tyre degradation and resisted pressure from Kimi Räikkönen's Lotus to take the win. It was a display of defensive brilliance, marked by composure. Some began to recognise that Hamilton's ability on tracks requiring smooth inputs was in contrast to the preconceived notion of him having an aggressive driving style.

However, just as quickly as the highs came, so did the lows. The Singapore Grand Prix on 23 September brought heartbreak, as Hamilton was leading comfortably when a gearbox failure forced him to retire. His frustration was evident, but he maintained his resolve, acknowledging the challenge of closing the gap. Vettel, Alonso, and Räikkönen were consistently finishing races. The McLaren was quick but fragile, breaking down too often. Post-race, Hamilton remained hopeful that this would mark the end of the team's bad luck. However, it wasn't what he said that was interesting, it was how he seemed. Hamilton was often optimistic in his outlook, but even after the gearbox failure had robbed him of the win, he seemed even more upbeat than usual. It would only take a few days to work out why.

### Hamilton's Decision: A Leap of Faith

As the 2012 season progressed, Hamilton found himself at a crossroads. The MP4-27 was fast but fragile, and McLaren's inability to deliver consistent results had begun to wear on him. At the same time, Mercedes was showing signs of progress. Michael Schumacher and Nico Rosberg were making incremental gains, and the team had secured its first victory since returning to the sport as a works team in 2010, with Rosberg winning the Chinese Grand Prix. Mercedes seemed to be on the rise, while McLaren appeared to be on the decline.

Professionally and personally, Hamilton was beginning to carve out his own path. He had parted ways with his father as his manager, opting instead for representation by XIX Entertainment. His longstanding relationship with Ron Dennis and their day-to-day contact had effectively ended when Dennis handed the operational reins of McLaren to Martin Whitmarsh in 2009. On a personal level, Hamilton had moved overseas—first to Switzerland and later to Monaco—symbolising a detachment from his roots and a deliberate focus on shaping his own future. He was no longer the young protégé; he had grown into a man defining his own destiny.

At McLaren, a combination of internal changes and the car's recurring reliability issues only added to Hamilton's frustration. Meanwhile, he observed the structural and managerial evolution taking place at Mercedes. The team, under new leadership and bolstered by key hires, was showing signs of transformative ambition. In September 2012, Niki Lauda, a legendary Formula One Champion, was appointed as the non-executive chairman of the Mercedes AMG Petronas Formula One Team. This move, orchestrated by Daimler AG, Mercedes' parent company, aimed to strengthen the team's leadership. Lauda's vast experience and insight, particularly his collaborations with Team Principal Ross Brawn and Executive Director Toto Wolff, played a crucial role in shaping the team's direction. Lauda was not only a brilliant sportsman but also a successful businessman. His direct, no-nonsense approach, combined with genuine care for his team, was exactly what Hamilton needed at this stage of his career.

Lauda recognised Hamilton's talent and the opportunity to build a Championship-winning team around him. Discussions between Hamilton and Lauda intensified during the 2012 season, with Lauda emphasising Mercedes' long-term vision and its determination to become a dominant force in Formula One. Lauda was eager to bring Hamilton on board as the driver to lead Mercedes into a new era of success, and encouraged Hamilton to talk to Brawn about plans for the team.

On September 28, 2012, it was officially announced that Hamilton would be leaving McLaren to join Mercedes for the 2013 season. The timing felt right—it was time to move on. The announcement of Hamilton's move to Mercedes sent tremors through the Formula One world.

Hamilton was gracious towards McLaren, acknowledging the team's significant role in his career, but he made it clear early on that his focus was now on the future with Mercedes. He spoke passionately about the opportunity to join Mercedes, highlighting their incredible heritage in motorsport and their shared passion for winning. Hamilton believed that, together, he and Mercedes could rise to the challenge and achieve their ambitious goal of World Championships.

Ross Brawn, Mercedes' Team Principal, sent a strong signal of intent to the rest of the grid, expressing confidence in the team's potential. He believed that the pairing of Hamilton and Nico Rosberg would be the most dynamic and exciting on the grid. Brawn spoke about the foundation the team had been building over the past few years, positioning Mercedes to compete regularly for the World Championship, with the potential to match any team on the grid. Brawn, a key member of the Ferrari-Schumacher-Todt dream team of the early 2000s and the genius behind Brawn GP's success, was a seasoned operator. If he believed the team had potential, it was a worrying message for the others.

Hamilton's decision to join Mercedes was anything but straightforward. It was a bold gamble—one that carried significant risks but also great opportunities. Despite the optimism from Lauda and Mercedes, many in the paddock questioned Hamilton's decision. Some, including McLaren's CEO Martin Whitmarsh, publicly stated that Hamilton had made a mistake in leaving McLaren for Mercedes. There were concerns that Mercedes would struggle to produce a competitive car in 2013. The car's potential for 2014 was also under scrutiny, with many suggesting that Hamilton faced a tough challenge ahead. A number of people believed Hamilton was taking a huge risk in leaving a team with a proven record.

Despite the scepticism, there were those who believed in Hamilton's ability to make the move work. Some acknowledged that, while it was a risk, Hamilton's speed and talent could bring Mercedes closer to the front of the grid. It was clear that, if the team could harness his raw pace, he could extract more performance from the car, potentially leading to a race victory in 2013. For those who recognised Hamilton's driving ability, there was little doubt that he had what it took to succeed, even in uncertain circumstances.

Hamilton's decision was bold and risky, but he was excited about the new challenge. He finished the 2012 season in fourth place, securing three victories, but couldn't help reminiscing about what might have been. Button, in the sister McLaren, finished the season in fifth. Hamilton's time at McLaren had been marked by incredible highs and bitter lows—on the track, in the Stewards' room, and in the public domain, where his personal life had been dissected to the point of destruction. Instead of letting all of this pressure, negativity, and criticism define him, he embraced it and used it as fuel—fuel to drive him forward. It had made him one of the sport's most formidable competitors, and as the other teams and drivers were about to find out, he now had everything he needed: the car, the skills, the maturity, and the wisdom. As he prepared to embark on a new journey with Mercedes, the stage was set for a new era—one that would redefine his career and the landscape of Formula One.

## Michael Schumacher's Final Goodbye

The end of the 2012 season also marked the retirement of a true legend. In October 2012, Michael Schumacher announced his retirement from Formula One, closing the chapter on an illustrious career. Ross Brawn, Team Principal of Mercedes AMG Petronas and long-time collaborator with Schumacher, expressed deep appreciation for his contributions. Brawn spoke of the many experiences they had shared together at Benetton, Ferrari, and Mercedes, praising Schumacher as the greatest Formula One driver and highlighting the significance of his record-breaking achievements. Brawn had been instrumental in helping Schumacher become a seven-time world champion, and he was now being instrumental in helping Hamilton do the same.

The transition from one era to another was complete, with Hamilton poised to lead Mercedes into the future and carry forward the legacy that Schumacher had helped establish. As the Formula One world looked to 2013, the winds of change were undeniable. The retirement of a giant like Schumacher and the arrival of a new star in Hamilton set the stage for a thrilling new era—one that would redefine the sport and its champions.

As the season came to a close, there was a glimmer of hope for McLaren, despite the knowledge that Hamilton was about to step out of the door. At the American Grand Prix, the penultimate race of the year, Hamilton won, narrowly beating Vettel.

The teams then moved on to Brazil, where, in Hamilton's final race for McLaren, he again led, only to be hit by Nico Hülkenberg and forced to retire. Button, in the sister McLaren, won. As the teams packed up from Brazil, and Hamilton left the McLaren garage for the final time, it would have been understandable to pause and think, 'Two wins back-to-back—am I doing the right thing leaving McLaren?'. But this was Lewis Hamilton. He pushed all of that negativity deep down into his mental reserves, fuelling himself and preparing for 2013 and a new start with Mercedes.

Vettel won the Driver's Championship with 281 points. Alonso, having fought valiantly all year, came in second, just three points behind—a bitter pill to swallow.

Adrian Newey had once again provided Red Bull with a dominant car, and they secured the Constructors' Championship with 460 points, followed by Ferrari in second on 400, and McLaren in third on 378. Mercedes, Hamilton's new home, finished fifth in the table with 142 points.

# Red Bull Dominate

The 2013 Formula One season marked a period of change for Lewis Hamilton. After spending his entire career with McLaren, his decision to move to Mercedes was a leap into the unknown. Many had questioned the wisdom of leaving one of the most storied teams in Formula One history for a manufacturer that had yet to prove itself as a consistent front-runner. Yet, for Hamilton, the move represented an opportunity to build something new and be part of a long-term project with immense potential.

The 2013 grid introduced several new dynamics and familiar rivalries. Valtteri Bottas was promoted to a race seat at Williams, marking his Formula One debut.

Red Bull Racing unveiled the RB9, designed by Adrian Newey, with the aim of continuing their dominance. The car featured an evolutionary design, with refined aerodynamics and a purple livery to promote a new title sponsor. It was described as "an evolutionary car with the devil very much in the detail" during its testing phase, which demonstrated strong performance, reinforcing its status as a title contender. Sebastian Vettel expressed confidence, showing excitement about racing the new car. Meanwhile, Mark Webber was seen as increasingly determined, gaining a better understanding of the cars and tyres, with many feeling it was set to be his year.

At Mercedes, the new F1 W04 was introduced, developed under the guidance of Technical Director Bob Bell. The car featured a more refined aerodynamic package and a new front wing design. Pre-season testing showed promising pace. Hamilton said the car felt good, and he flagged some areas for improvement once testing was complete. Ross Brawn appreciated Hamilton’s detailed feedback, saying he was straightforward in his nature and showed an interest in all aspects of the car, even in minor details like sticker placement.

Brawn praised Hamilton's keen eye for detail and felt Hamilton would become a real asset to the team given the qualities he brought with him.

The Mercedes W04 was a work in progress. While it showed flashes of brilliance, the car struggled with tyre degradation and lacked the consistent pace to challenge the likes of Red Bull and Ferrari over a full race distance. However, its impressive straight-line speed and one-lap performance made it a threat in qualifying, where Hamilton's raw pace often shone through.

Ferrari aimed to provide Alonso with a competitive car with the introduction of the F138, designed by Technical Director Pat Fry. This model sought to address the shortcomings of its predecessor, featuring a more conventional nose design and enhanced aerodynamics. During testing the car showed consistent performance, with Alonso expressing satisfaction with its predictable behaviour. Team Principal Stefano Domenicali remained cautiously optimistic, suggesting that while the F138 might not be the fastest at the start of the season, the close competition could make anything possible over the course of the year.

Meanwhile, McLaren, Hamilton's former team, introduced the MP4-28, a bold design shift under the guidance of Technical Director Paddy Lowe. The new model featured a higher nose and pull-rod front suspension, both intended to improve aerodynamics. However, the car's performance during testing was problematic, with Jenson Button noting significant inconsistencies in its handling and a lack of sufficient running to fully understand its potential.

For Lewis Hamilton, the early stages of his tenure at Mercedes provided some validation for his decision to move, especially as his former teammate, Jenson Button, faced challenges with the new McLaren. Button was now joined by Sergio Perez, who had made the move from Sauber.

## Season Openers

## Australia

The season commenced at Melbourne's Albert Park Circuit. Hamilton qualified third, the Mercedes W04 looking quick over a single lap. During the race, he maintained a strong pace, finishing fifth. Afterwards he talked about how he had a good start to the race, but the performance seemed to drop off as it wore on. On balance though he felt the car and team had done better than expected, although they needed to analyse where time was being lost to competitors. Nevertheless, he praised the team for delivering a car with potential.

Red Bull's Sebastian Vettel secured pole position but finished third, while Lotus Renault's Kimi Räikkönen clinched victory. His teammate, Romain Grosjean, ended up in tenth, nearly a full lap behind—highlighting Räikkönen's dominance in the sport. McLaren, struggling with their radical new car, saw Jenson Button finish ninth, while Sergio Pérez placed eleventh. Despite Nico Rosberg failing to finish, Mercedes' strong performance indicated they had the pace to compete at the front.

## Malaysian Grand Prix

The Malaysian Grand Prix was one for the history books and would be remembered by millions of Formula One fans worldwide, with major controversy overshadowing the event.

Held at the Sepang International Circuit on 24 March 2013, the race was defined by in-fighting, particularly within the Red Bull and Mercedes teams.

The Red Bull pair locked out the front row, with Vettel on pole and Webber starting alongside him.

The race began under damp conditions, prompting teams to start on intermediate tyres. As the track dried, drivers transitioned to slicks, leading to a variety of pit stops that shuffled the order. By the midpoint, Webber had taken the lead, followed closely by Vettel.

In the closing stages, Red Bull issued a team order—internally referred to as "Multi-21"—instructing their drivers to hold positions, with Webber in first and Vettel in second, in order to conserve the cars and secure a 1-2 finish. Despite this directive, Vettel aggressively pursued Webber, leading to a tense wheel-to-wheel battle. Ignoring repeated calls from the pit wall, Vettel overtook Webber on lap 46 to take the lead.

In the post-race cooldown room, Webber was understandably unhappy and made his feelings known, gesturing at Vettel and referring to 'Multi-21'. The atmosphere was electric. After the podium celebrations Webber was still seething at having had to follow team orders, while Vettel disregarded them. Known for his direct manner, Webber remarked pointedly that Vettel had made his decision and, as usual, 'would be protected'.

Vettel later admitted it was not a victory he could take much pride in, acknowledging that it should have been Webber's. It was a moment that laid bare the fragile alliances within a championship-winning team.

Mercedes faced their own team orders dilemma in Malaysia. Lewis Hamilton and Nico Rosberg were running third and fourth, respectively. Rosberg, demonstrating superior pace, requested permission to overtake Hamilton. However, the team instructed both drivers to hold positions to ensure a safe finish. Rosberg complied, ultimately crossing the line in fourth. After the race, Hamilton candidly admitted that, in reality, his teammate had deserved the podium spot.

Mercedes Team Principal Ross Brawn defended the decision, stating that issuing team orders was not in his sporting nature, but under the circumstances, it was necessary. He pointed out that, in the past, the team had often allowed their drivers to race freely.

The race concluded with Vettel taking victory, followed by Webber and Hamilton. The fans were captivated, not just by the team-on-team battles, but also by the underhanded dealings within the teams themselves. Perfect Formula One.

**China**

Hamilton's first major highlight with Mercedes came at the Chinese Grand Prix on 14 April, where he secured his first pole position for the team. It was a moment that silenced some critics and proved that Mercedes had the potential to compete at the sharp end of the grid. Although he finished third in the race, the result was a promising sign of things to come. Alonso won in the Ferrari, with Räikkönen second in the Lotus Renault. This marked the beginning of a strong run for Alonso, who would go on to win again a month later at his home race in Spain.

**Monaco Grand Prix**

The prestigious Monaco Grand Prix, held on 26 May, saw Mercedes lock out the front row, with Rosberg on pole and Hamilton second. It was an incident-filled race.

As the race settled into its rhythm, Felipe Massa crashed his Ferrari in an incident strikingly similar to one he had suffered in final practice. The crash was later attributed to a front-left suspension failure. Massa was able to exit the car unaided, but doctors placed him in a surgical neck brace as a precaution before transporting him to the hospital for further checks. He was later released without serious injury.

During the ensuing safety car period, Hamilton lost positions during the pit stops. Over the radio, he questioned how he had been passed by two cars, to which his engineer, Peter Bonnington, responded with frustration, admitting that losing positions to both Red Bulls had been unexpected.

Shortly after the race resumed, 'Crashtor' Maldonado was involved in a high-speed incident that launched his Williams into the air, sending it into the TecPro barriers at approximately 150 mph. The impact was so severe that the barrier wrapped around the car, which, along with the now severely damaged Williams, slid across the track, blocking a significant portion of the circuit. The track near the swimming pool section was also blocked from all the debris that had cascaded along the tarmac. The race was red-flagged.

As the remaining cars returned to the grid to await the restart, tension filled the air. Over the radio, Bono provided a calm update, informing Hamilton that there were 33 laps remaining and that he could step out of the car if he wished, as they would receive a ten-minute warning before the restart.

The extended red-flag delay tested each driver's mental resilience, and in Monaco's cramped pit lane, each handled the pause in their own way. Rosberg, aiming to block out the surrounding chaos, kept his earplugs in, walking slowly in circles beside his Mercedes, sipping an isotonic drink while appearing lost in deep thought. Alonso, in contrast, leaned casually against the barriers, alternating his gaze between the cars ahead and the ground beneath him, seemingly reflecting on the race so far. Hamilton, meanwhile, sought solitude. Sitting cross-legged on the floor between the front-left wheel and the side pod of his car, with his back to the cockpit. His golden crash helmet rested on the nose cone as he lowered his head, deep in concentration. Like Rosberg, he kept his earplugs in, shutting out the noise of the grid and the world around him. Monaco's unique setup offered an intimate glimpse into how drivers managed the psychological demands of racing, each displaying their own approach to focus and composure amid uncertainty.

While attention was drawn to the glamour of Monaco—the luxury yachts filled with sunbathers, movie stars mingling in the paddock, and the multimillion-dollar cars on the grid—a different scene unfolded along the barriers. Track marshals, the unsung heroes of every Grand Prix, worked tirelessly in their distinctive orange overalls and white helmets to repair the damaged TecPro barriers. Armed with nothing more than hard-bristled brooms, they meticulously cleared debris, their efforts standing in stark contrast to the opulence around them. Yet, without their dedication, the spectacle of Formula One would not be possible.

Drivers and commentators alike often recognise the crucial role marshals play in the sport, acknowledging their commitment and the sacrifices they make. Hamilton has frequently described them as the unsung heroes who make racing possible. In Monaco, where glamour meets grit, the marshals' relentless efforts quietly ensured that the show could go on.

When racing resumed, Rosberg faced pressure from both Red Bulls, while Hamilton, now in fourth, pushed hard behind them. Another incident at the exit of the tunnel brought out the Safety Car once again, requiring further intervention from the marshals.

Rosberg ultimately secured victory, delivering a major win for Mercedes at one of Formula One's most prestigious events. As he began his cooldown lap, Ross Brawn congratulated him over the radio, acknowledging the outstanding drive. Red Bull's Vettel and Webber completed the podium, while Hamilton finished fourth. Alonso crossed the line in seventh.

While Mercedes had demonstrated impressive one-lap speed throughout the season, their race pace – though masked in Monaco – remained a concern at other circuits. Analysts noted that, despite their dominance in qualifying, sustaining competitive performance over a full race distance continued to be their biggest challenge.

**British Grand Prix**

At Silverstone at the end of June, Hamilton secured pole position, thrilling the home crowd. However, during the race, he suffered a tyre failure, dropping him to the back of the field. Undeterred and roared on by thousands of fans, Hamilton gave the Mercedes a good workout and fought back to finish fourth. Afterwards, he admitted that while he had been pushing hard, he still felt nervous for the rest of the race, fearing another tyre issue.

The race was chaotic, with multiple tyre failures affecting several drivers. Rosberg capitalised on the situation, securing victory. Red Bull's Vettel retired due to a gearbox failure, while Ferrari's Alonso finished third. The spate of tyre failures prompted Pirelli to review their tyres, with commentators noting that the incidents overshadowed what had been an otherwise exciting race. Webber, who had previously voiced concerns about Pirelli's tyres but had tempered his views for commercial reasons, finished second.

Meanwhile, tensions were beginning to mount within Mercedes. Rosberg had claimed two wins in three races, while Hamilton—despite being consistently competitive—had yet to secure a victory. However, it wouldn't be long before his turn came.

**Hungarian Grand Prix**

In the sweltering heat of late July 2013, Formula One arrived at the Hungaroring for the Hungarian Grand Prix. Track temperatures soared above 50 degrees Celsius, presenting a formidable challenge for both drivers and their machines. Pirelli had introduced new, more durable tyres for the race.

Hamilton, in his debut season with Mercedes, had shown promise but was still in search of his first victory with the team. During qualifying, he stunned the paddock by securing pole position with a lap time of 1:19.388, edging out championship leader Sebastian Vettel. Despite the achievement, Hamilton remained cautious, remarking that a win would require a "miracle," given the team's previous struggles with tyre degradation in the high temperatures.

Race day dawned with clear skies and unrelenting heat, intensifying the tactical demands on teams. At lights out, Hamilton made a clean start, maintaining his lead into the first corner. Behind him, the pack jostled for position, with Räikkönen making notable progress from sixth on the grid.

After Hamilton's first pit stop, he rejoined the track near Jenson Button, whose McLaren was running on worn tyres and had yet to pit. Button's slower pace threatened to disrupt Hamilton's rhythm and strategy, potentially allowing rivals like Vettel and Räikkönen to close the gap. Recognising the danger, Hamilton made an assertive pass, ensuring his race remained under control. This aggressive yet calculated move proved crucial in maintaining his lead.

Throughout the race, Hamilton received guidance from his race engineer, Bono. In one exchange, Bono relayed the gap to Vettel, emphasising the importance of managing tyre wear while maintaining a competitive pace. Hamilton's ability to strike this balance showed his growing synergy with the Mercedes team. As the laps dwindled, his lead remained unchallenged, and he crossed the finish line to secure his first victory for Mercedes—a win that had seemed improbable, given the team's earlier tyre issues in hot conditions.

Post-race, Hamilton reflected on the significance of the moment, expressing optimism that if they could perform well under such extreme conditions, they could be competitive on all types of circuits. He described the victory as one of the most important of his career, relishing the privilege of winning for Mercedes. Analysts noted that while there was nothing supernatural about the win, it was the result of the perfect combination of factors—the car, the strategy, and Hamilton's execution under challenging conditions, along with the potential impact of the new, harder Pirelli tyres.

The 2013 Hungarian Grand Prix not only marked Hamilton's 22nd career win but also signalled Mercedes' emergence as a genuine contender in Formula One. It laid the foundation for the team's future dominance and reinforced Hamilton's standing as one of the sport's elite drivers. However, Mercedes' optimism would soon face a significant challenge. Adrian Newey and Red Bull were preparing to introduce a series of mid-season upgrades that would set a new benchmark for all the teams.

**Belgian Grand Prix**

Nestled in the Ardennes Forest of Belgium, the Spa-Francorchamps circuit is one of Formula One's most iconic and revered tracks. Known for its sweeping corners, dramatic elevation changes, and unpredictable weather, Spa has long been a favourite among drivers and fans alike. At just over 7 kilometres (4.35 miles), Spa is the longest circuit on the Formula One calendar, offering a unique blend of fast straights and challenging corners that demand good aerodynamic grip and a dose of bravery. Its high-speed nature rewards those willing to push their cars to the limit, but it also punishes mistakes, with little room for error at such high speeds.

The track's most famous feature is Eau Rouge and Raidillon, a daunting sequence of corners that begins with a downhill plunge followed by a sharp ascent. Drivers approach Eau Rouge at nearly 300 km/h (186 mph), navigating the blind crest at Raidillon while managing significant g-forces. Successfully mastering this section is considered a hallmark of skill and courage. Many have come unstuck here—most notably in 1999, when Jacques Villeneuve and Ricardo Zonta both destroyed their BARs in separate but identical crashes while attempting to take Eau Rouge flat out.

Spa is also notorious for its rapidly changing weather. The circuit's vast layout means that it can be raining at one end while remaining dry at another, often leading to dramatic and unpredictable racing. This duality adds to its mystique and makes it a stage for legendary performances. Beyond its physical characteristics, Spa is steeped in history. First opened in 1921, the circuit has evolved over the decades but retained its essence as a true test of driver ability. Its blend of tradition, technical challenge, and natural beauty cements Spa-Francorchamps as a cornerstone of Formula One.

At Spa, Hamilton secured his fourth consecutive pole position on one of Formula One's most challenging 'drivers' tracks'. However, his lead was short-lived. At the start, Vettel, starting alongside him, capitalised on the slipstream, overtaking Hamilton on the opening lap and holding the lead for the remainder of the race.

Fernando Alonso had a strong weekend in the Ferrari, but his race nearly ended in disaster at the iconic Eau Rouge. Pushing hard in traffic while chasing down Vettel, he was determined to make up for a disappointing qualifying session.

Approaching Eau Rouge at 300 km/h (186 mph), Alonso found himself trailing two cars, with the disturbed air from their slipstreams adding to the challenge. Committing fully to the sequence, he kept the throttle pinned through the left-hander. As he crested the rise at Raidillon, the turbulent airflow caused his Ferrari to snap sideways at 290 km/h.

What followed was a stunning display of reflexes and car control. Alonso's lightning-fast reactions prevented what could have been a catastrophic crash. Data showed only the slightest lift of the accelerator as he fought the car, applying full opposite lock at one point to regain control. Remarkably, he quickly got back to full throttle, losing minimal time in the process.

It was a paragon of skill and bravery, demonstrating the razor-thin margins at which the best drivers operate—a vivid reminder of the risks they take at every corner, and their ability to quickly compartmentalise near misses. Alonso recovered to finish second behind Vettel.

After standing on the top step of the podium, Vettel described the race as fantastic, giving credit to his team for their strong tactics and excellent start. He also mentioned that the tow from Hamilton through Eau Rouge helped him accelerate past into the lead.

Hamilton, who finished third, acknowledged the difficulties he faced, noting that the Mercedes package wasn't yet on the same level as the Red Bulls and Ferraris. He emphasised the need for improvements ahead of the next round at Monza.

The 2013 Belgian Grand Prix reinforced Red Bull's competitive advantage, with Vettel extending his championship lead. Meanwhile, Ferrari's strong performance with Alonso signalled their continued competitiveness. Red Bull had benefitted the most from the summer break, and the updates on their car served as a wake-up call for the other teams at Spa.

**Italian Grand Prix**

Early September brought the Italian Grand Prix at Monza, a circuit that posed challenges for Hamilton. His impressive streak of 67 consecutive Q3 appearances came to an end after being impeded by Adrian Sutil during a crucial lap, leaving him 12th on the grid.

At the front, Vettel dominated the race, securing victory and extending his championship lead. Alonso finished second, much to the delight of the passionate Tifosi, while Webber completed the podium in third.

**Singapore Grand Prix**

The Formula One circus then moved to Singapore for the night race at the Marina Bay Circuit. Hamilton qualified fifth and finished in the same position in a race defined by Vettel's staggering dominance. The Red Bull driver led every lap and finished over 50 seconds ahead of Hamilton's Mercedes, underlining the design supremacy of Red Bull.

Mercedes adopted a different strategy from their rivals, keeping Rosberg and Hamilton out longer. However, this approach backfired as tyre degradation became a major issue in the latter stages. Hamilton battled fiercely to get past Massa's Ferrari but struggled as his worn tyres left him with little grip. After the race, he expressed a mix of frustration and determination, acknowledging the team's efforts while recognising the need for improvements to close the gap to the frontrunners.

Team Principal Ross Brawn praised Hamilton's consistent performance, highlighting the importance of strategy in such a demanding race. Meanwhile, Red Bull's speed further cemented their dominance, while Alonso's second-place finish reinforced his standing in the championship. Although Ferrari's car was not the fastest, Alonso's superb race pace ensured he remained a constant threat in the fight for podiums.

Within Mercedes, the dynamic between Hamilton and Rosberg remained a key storyline. Their history stretched back to their karting days, where they had built a strong mutual respect, but the intensity of Formula One inevitably tested their friendship. As the season progressed, tensions occasionally flared, foreshadowing the increasingly fractious relationship that would define the coming years as both drivers fought for supremacy within the team.

While Red Bull, led by the seemingly unstoppable Vettel, dominated the latter half of the season, Mercedes continued to make strides. The technical team worked tirelessly to understand the car's weaknesses and prepare for the upcoming regulation changes. The 2014 season would see the introduction of turbo-hybrid engines, a transition that Mercedes had been planning for years. The foundations laid in 2013 were crucial, and Hamilton's input played a significant role in shaping the team's direction.

After Singapore it was a one-horse race with Vettel winning at the remaining six Grand Prix. Red Bull had utterly destroyed the opposition thanks to Adrian Newey's genius. The 2013 season concluded with Red Bull and Vettel celebrating their fourth consecutive championships. Alonso was second again, but this time he wasn't three points adrift—he was 155 points behind, such was the dominance of the Red Bull.

But change was on the horizon. Mercedes had shown glimpses of what was to come, and Hamilton's first year with the team had laid the groundwork for a new era. As Formula One braced for the seismic shifts of 2014, Hamilton stood ready, eager to embrace the future and continue his journey toward greatness. As the teams left Brazil on 24 November, talk turned to the new era in Formula One.

In media interviews Hamilton stated that Mercedes was constructing something special for the following year: he bubbled with anticipation. His extensive experience and technical knowledge would prove invaluable in developing the Mercedes F1 W05 Hybrid, the team's 2014 challenger. His feedback on car behaviour, balance, and performance in various conditions provided the engineering team with critical insights, guiding design decisions and optimising race setups. The little details Ross Brawn had talked about would all be checked and rechecked by Hamilton.

Hamilton's relationship with Rosberg remained cordial at the end of the season, but the seeds of a fierce rivalry had been sown. The dynamic between the two would go on to define the turbo-hybrid era, but in 2013, the focus remained on growth and mutual respect. As Mercedes' non-executive chairman, Lauda was a strong advocate for Hamilton's role in leading the team to success. In various interviews, he emphasised Hamilton's exceptional talent and the strategic importance of his recruitment in shaping Mercedes' future ambitions in Formula One.

## Mark Webber's Retirement

While many had anticipated it, 2013 saw Mark Webber announce his retirement from Formula One, bringing an end to a distinguished 12-year career that left a lasting impact on the sport. Known for his tenacity and straightforward demeanour, the Australian made his Formula One debut with Minardi in 2002 before racing for Jaguar, Williams, and most notably, Red Bull Racing. Over his career, Webber competed in 215 Grands Prix, securing nine victories, 42 podium finishes, and 13 pole positions.

Webber played a key role in Red Bull Racing's rise to dominance, contributing to their four consecutive Constructors' World Championships. His maiden Formula One victory at the 2009 German Grand Prix was a significant milestone, and he became a double winner of both the Monaco and British Grands Prix—two of the sport's most prestigious races.

Upon announcing his retirement, Webber spoke candidly about his decision, acknowledging that motivation had been a challenge in recent years. He reflected on the demands of Formula One, noting that the fire in his belly was not quite the same as it had been in his early 20s.

His departure was met with widespread respect and admiration from the Formula One community. Red Bull Team Principal Christian Horner acknowledged the difficulty of stepping away from the sport after more than a decade at the top, recognising the magnitude of Webber's contribution to the team and wishing him well for the future.

Webber's retirement marked the end of an era for both Red Bull Racing and Formula One. His influence, both on and off the track, as well as his sharp wit and easy-going nature, left an enduring legacy, inspiring future generations of drivers—including emerging Australian talent. His connection to the sport would not end there; in the years to come, he would return in management and commentary roles, continuing to shape the world of Formula One from a new perspective.

As the teams packed up and prepared for a seismic shift in the regulations, Hamilton dedicated his winter to working with the engineers in the factory and testing the new car. And what a new car it would be.

# Turbo-Hybrid Revolution

In the lead-up to the 2014 season, Mercedes underwent significant management restructuring to strengthen their competitiveness and lay the foundations for success in the new turbo-hybrid era.

Three-time World Champion Niki Lauda was brought in as a non-executive director, offering invaluable experience and insight. Lauda had played a pivotal role in recruiting Lewis Hamilton from McLaren, a move that would prove instrumental in Mercedes' future dominance and had already begun paying dividends in 2013. However, Lauda himself acknowledged that the person who secured Hamilton's signature was Ross Brawn, crediting him for negotiating the contract and bringing the British driver onboard.

Toto Wolff had also joined Mercedes in early 2013, acquiring a 30% stake in Mercedes-Benz Grand Prix Ltd. and assuming the role of Executive Director. His expertise in motorsport management and investment brought a fresh perspective to the team's operations.

These appointments complemented the leadership of Team Principal Ross Brawn, who had been with Mercedes since 2010. Brawn's technical acumen and leadership were critical during this transitional period. However, at the end of 2013, Brawn announced his departure, leaving Wolff and Paddy Lowe—who had joined Mercedes as Executive Director (Technical) in mid-2013—to take on more prominent leadership roles. Lowe would ultimately benefit from the groundwork Brawn had laid.

The 2014 Formula One season marked the dawn of a revolutionary new era. The introduction of turbo-hybrid engines represented one of the most significant transformations in the sport's history. The high-pitched roars of naturally aspirated V8 engines were replaced by 1.6-litre V6 turbo-hybrid power units, incorporating advanced Energy Recovery Systems (ERS). These cutting-edge systems not only altered how cars performed but also redefined the approach to racing.

This seismic shift was driven by regulations designed to emphasise energy efficiency, innovation, and sustainability. Among all teams, Mercedes stood out as the best prepared for this new era. Having implemented extensive organisational changes, the team was primed to capitalise on the opportunity and emerge as a dominant force in Formula One.

Beyond the power units, the regulation overhaul extended to aerodynamics, resulting in cars that looked and performed differently from their predecessors. These changes were introduced not only to improve environmental efficiency but also to promote closer racing.

One of the most noticeable alterations was the redesign of the car noses. Formula One's governing body, the FIA, mandated lower nose heights to improve safety by reducing the risk of cars launching into the air during collisions. The maximum allowable nose tip height was lowered to 185mm above the ground, a significant reduction from previous regulations.

These stringent requirements led teams to develop distinctive and often unconventional nose solutions, balancing regulatory compliance with aerodynamic efficiency. Some, such as Lotus, opted for radical approaches featuring asymmetric or twin-pronged nose structures, sparking debates over their legality and effectiveness.

The diversity of designs during the 2014 season underscored the challenges teams faced in adapting to the new regulations while maintaining aerodynamic optimisation.

The Mercedes W05 Hybrid was a marvel of engineering and quickly established itself as the class of the field. Developed by Mercedes High Performance Powertrains, the PU106A Hybrid power unit delivered an unrivalled blend of power and efficiency. Testing revealed its strong performance and reliability, positioning Mercedes as early favourites for the season ahead.

The aerodynamic package, overseen by Paddy Lowe and Aldo Costa, complemented the engine's strengths, giving Mercedes a distinct advantage. The W05 featured a low, open-nose design and an efficient cooling system, both of which were noted by analysts as key factors in the car's superiority.

Hamilton, was optimistic in pre-season testing at Jerez, highlighting the team's ability to complete its test programme while others were still focusing on single-lap runs. He described the car as feeling strong, especially given how early it was in development. Other teams had gone their own way with design and engineering.

Designed by Adrian Newey, the Red Bull Racing RB10 featured a distinctive nose solution, which the designer referred to as a 'keel nose' to comply with new safety regulations. Pundits, however, dubbed it the 'finger nose.' Powered by Renault's Energy F1-2014 power unit, the RB10 endured a troubled pre-season, with persistent reliability issues. Overheating problems and complications with the energy recovery system severely limited Red Bull's track time during testing.

Team Principal Christian Horner admitted the difficulties, conceding that the team had encountered numerous challenges related to both the Renault power unit and the car's chassis cooling. Despite the setbacks, he remained confident that the issues were solvable before the second test in Bahrain. However, there was an undeniable concern within the team about the comparative weakness of the Renault power unit compared to Mercedes'. Despite these struggles, Red Bull's aerodynamic expertise was expected to keep them competitive. While four-time World Champion Sebastian Vettel remained the team's leading driver, he was now partnered with Australian Daniel Ricciardo, who had impressed during his time with Scuderia Toro Rosso.

Ferrari's F14 T stood out due to its distinctive nose structure. Unlike many rivals that opted for protruding or 'finger' noses, Ferrari took a different approach, adopting a wide, flat nose that tapered down smoothly to meet the new height regulations. This design was intended to balance compliance with aerodynamic performance, particularly by optimising airflow beneath the car. Additionally, Ferrari placed a strong emphasis on cooling solutions, recognising their importance under the new regulations.

The car was powered by Ferrari's 059/3 power unit, which, during testing, demonstrated a balance between performance and reliability. However, the outright pace of the F14 T lagged behind that of its competitors. During testing in Bahrain, Alonso acknowledged that the car was missing something in terms of outright speed but noted the team's strong reliability. He highlighted that Ferrari had completed a significant number of laps without major issues, which was an encouraging sign for the season ahead.

Pundits noted that while Ferrari's reliability was commendable, achieving competitive speed would be essential. While Fernando Alonso remained at Ferrari, he was now partnered with Kimi Räikkönen, who was rejoining the team as its last Formula One Champion, having won the title in 2007. It would not have been lost on Alonso—or others in the paddock—that Alonso had yet to bring the championship back to Maranello.

Hamilton's former team, McLaren, introduced the MP4-29, overseen by Technical Director Tim Goss. The car featured a distinctive "anteater" or "finger" nose, characterised by a narrow protruding section extending from the main body to comply with revised crash test requirements. This design allowed McLaren to meet regulations without lowering the entire front end, thereby preserving optimal airflow beneath the car for aerodynamic performance. While the "anteater" nose divided opinion aesthetically, it reflected the engineering challenges teams faced in balancing regulatory compliance with performance.

Powered by the Mercedes PU106A Hybrid engine, the MP4-29 demonstrated promising pace in testing. However, reliability concerns emerged, particularly with the suspension and brake systems. McLaren retained Jenson Button as its lead driver, now joined by rookie Kevin Magnussen. Button expressed confidence in the car's potential, describing it as having a good feel. Analysts suggested that while McLaren had a solid foundation, addressing reliability issues would be crucial.

Following several seasons of struggling for results, Williams introduced the FW36 for 2014, marking a significant departure in both design philosophy and performance. The FW36 was the first Williams car to be powered by a Mercedes-Benz engine, specifically the PU106A Hybrid 1.6-litre V6 turbocharged unit also used by McLaren. This partnership was expected to provide a competitive advantage in the new hybrid powertrain era. Like McLaren, Williams adopted an "anteater" nose design to comply with the new regulations.

Chief Technical Officer Pat Symonds highlighted the technological advancements, emphasising the complexity of the new hybrid systems. During pre-season testing, the FW36 showed strong performance and reliability, regularly setting competitive lap times. The team's driver lineup featured Valtteri Bottas and Felipe Massa, the latter having joined from Ferrari. Massa noted the car's positive reaction to setup changes and expressed optimism about its potential. The FW36's primary strengths lay in its aerodynamic efficiency and the power of the Mercedes engine, which provided excellent straight-line speed and traction. However, the team faced challenges in adapting to new regulations regarding cooling, weight distribution, and gearbox design. Symonds acknowledged that while the team had completed extensive development work on the gearbox, reliability remained a concern, particularly given the increased torque from the hybrid power units. Weight management was also an issue, with the new power units being significantly heavier than the outgoing V8s.

Commentators viewed Williams' prospects with cautious optimism. The combination of experienced drivers, a strong technical team, and the Mercedes partnership suggested that the team could be on the verge of a competitive resurgence. Observing from McLaren, Button remarked that the Williams had looked quick in pre-season testing. The FW36 represented a major step forward for Williams, combining innovative design with a powerful engine package. While challenges remained, the developments indicated a potential return to form for the historic team.

**The Season Opener: Australia**

The 2014 season began in Melbourne, where Hamilton secured pole position. However, his race was cut short due to a misfiring cylinder, forcing an early retirement. This left the door open for Rosberg, who delivered a commanding performance to take victory for Mercedes.

Daniel Ricciardo, making his debut for Red Bull, initially finished second but was later disqualified for exceeding fuel flow limits. This promoted Magnussen to second and Button to third, giving McLaren a double podium finish. Alonso came home in fourth, while Williams, demonstrating their pre-season form and the strength of the Mercedes power unit, saw Bottas finish in fifth.

After the race, Rosberg expressed his delight, describing it as an amazing day. Hamilton, despite his early exit, remained optimistic, stating that the team would bounce back. It was a strong start for Mercedes', having laid down a clear marker for the season ahead.

**Malaysia: Mercedes' True Pace is Revealed**

In Malaysia, Mercedes reinforced its dominance as Hamilton secured pole position. Vettel demonstrated Red Bull's one-lap pace by qualifying alongside him on the front row, while Rosberg lined up third.

Hamilton led the race from start to finish, securing his first win of the season and delivering a Mercedes one-two, with Rosberg finishing second. Vettel completed the podium in third.

However, the most ominous sign for rival teams came from the fastest laps. At this stage of Formula One, no points were awarded for the fastest lap, meaning the data provided a true representation of overall performance. Hamilton's fastest lap was a 1:43.066, with Rosberg's at 1:43.960. Crucially, Hamilton was over a second faster than the next non-Mercedes car, Alonso's Ferrari. He was over two seconds per lap quicker than the McLarens—proof, if it were needed, of the wisdom of his decision to join Mercedes.

Hamilton described the victory in Malaysia as an incredible moment, noting that it had taken him eight years to finally win at the circuit. Rosberg and Hamilton both acknowledged the team's exceptional strength and the hard work that had gone into developing their dominant package.

After the race, Ajit Devadason from Sify.com asked Hamilton about a detail on the back of his helmet—an insightful question that led to an even more revealing response about what drives him.

*"Lewis, this is to do with your helmet design: the words that you have chosen for this season on the back of your helmet, 'Still I Rise', are you thrilled that it's working your way and matching your belief?"*

Hamilton responded by explaining the personal significance behind the phrase, which he had tattooed on his back and had now incorporated into his helmet design. He described it as a metaphor for perseverance, something his father had instilled in him from a young age. He talked about the challenges they had faced throughout their lives and careers, recalling how his father always encouraged him to rise above difficulties and let his performances on track do the talking. Coming off a tough race previously, he had done exactly that in Malaysia, and he expressed satisfaction with how the weekend had unfolded.

The Mercedes' performance was a hot topic and considered dominant. It was the team's first one-two finish since 1955.

**Bahrain Grand Prix: A Thrilling Duel**

The 2014 Bahrain Grand Prix, held on 6 April at the Bahrain International Circuit, was a classic. The race, marking the 900th Formula One World Championship event, was defined by an intense battle between Mercedes teammates Lewis Hamilton and Nico Rosberg.

Rosberg secured pole position with a time of 1:33.185, while Hamilton qualified second, setting the stage for a front-row Mercedes lockout. At the start, Rosberg initially reacted well, but Hamilton had the stronger second phase of acceleration. As they approached the pit lane exit, Hamilton had drawn alongside Rosberg, executing a crucial move to take the lead into Turn 1. This allowed him to control the race pace from the front.

Further down the grid, Sergio Pérez made an excellent start in the Mercedes-powered Force India, moving up to fifth behind the Williams cars. Bottas, defending aggressively, moved across Pérez's front, unsettling the airflow and causing Pérez to lock up into the first corner, sending tyre smoke billowing behind him. However, Pérez recovered well, managing to get past Massa and maintain his momentum.

The race got interesting on the first lap at Turn 4. Rosberg, with better momentum exiting Turn 3, attempted to go around the outside of Hamilton. However, Hamilton held firm, edging Rosberg to the limits of the track to keep him behind. It was aggressive but fair racing between teammates—setting the tone for the rest of the race.

Throughout the grand prix, Hamilton and Rosberg pushed each other hard, particularly after the first round of pit stops. Rosberg, now on fresher medium tyres, closed the gap to Hamilton, leading to several tense exchanges as they traded places multiple times.

It got a bit fraught on Lap 18 when Rosberg made a bold move up the inside of Turn 1, briefly passing Hamilton. At the exit Hamilton executed a switchback manoeuvre, and, as soon as he was ahead chopped across the front of Rosberg, before using his superior exit speed to reclaim the lead. Rosberg, miffed at being outfoxed, radioed to complain about Hamilton chopping across the front of him, saying "that was not on!." The two continued to duel, running side by side through multiple corners, while behind them, the rest of the field was rapidly falling away. Hamilton pulled away and focused on maintaining his lead, discussing tyre strategy and optimal braking areas: even in the middle of the race Hamilton was examining data real time with Bono to understand how he could eke out every tenth of a second whilst minimising damage to the tyres. It was one of the things that set him apart.

The race took another dramatic turn on Lap 41 when Pastor Maldonado, now driving for Lotus Renault, left the pits and then collided with Esteban Gutiérrez in the Sauber Ferrari. Maldonado's ambitious lunge up the inside launched Gutiérrez into the air, flipping the Sauber upside down before it landed wheels-down. Thankfully, Gutiérrez emerged unhurt, but the crash brought out the Safety Car, eliminating Hamilton's lead over Rosberg and setting up a tense final stint. The Sauber driver, whilst unhurt, clearly had no idea who had hit him, how, or why, exclaiming over the radio, "Whoah, what was that?".

Upon the restart, Mercedes instructed both drivers that they were free to race but must avoid contact. What followed was some of the most thrilling racing of the season. Rosberg, now on the softer medium tyre compound, launched a series of attacks on Hamilton, who was on the harder tyres. However, Hamilton's defensive driving was impeccable, fending off Rosberg's repeated attempts—particularly into Turn 1, where late braking and precise positioning proved decisive.

Hamilton crossed the finish line just 1.085 seconds ahead of Rosberg, securing his second consecutive victory of the season. Toto Wolff, delighted with the result, celebrated with his Mercedes colleagues on the pit wall. Sergio Pérez delivered an outstanding performance for Force India, finishing third and earning the team's first podium since 2009. Daniel Ricciardo, starting 13th due to a grid penalty, drove well to finish fourth, beating Vettel along the way and underlining Red Bull's speed, provided it kept going.

In post-race interviews, Hamilton described the race as an intense and exhilarating battle, saying he had been on the limit throughout. Rosberg, despite finishing second, admitted his frustration at losing out but acknowledged it had been one of the most exciting races of his career.

The Grand Prix was widely regarded as one of the best displays of pure racing in years, with many noting how rare it was to see teammates in equal machinery battling so fiercely yet fairly. The wheel-to-wheel fight between the two Mercedes drivers provided classic edge-of-the-seat excitement from start to finish.

The Bahrain Grand Prix cemented Mercedes' dominance in the 2014 season, with the team securing their second consecutive one-two finish. The growing rivalry between Hamilton and Rosberg became a central storyline, drawing fans in and setting the tone for the season ahead. On the podium, Rosberg appeared in good spirits, playfully spraying champagne at Hamilton, who was also in a celebratory mood. It was the calm before the storm.

### Shanghai: Hamilton Extends His Streak

In Shanghai, Hamilton continued his winning run, securing pole position and leading every lap to claim his third consecutive victory in commanding fashion. Rosberg recovered from a poor start and a lack of telemetry data to finish second, while Fernando Alonso put in a strong drive to take third for Ferrari—his first podium of the season, finishing five seconds behind Rosberg.

Once again, Ricciardo outpaced Vettel, finishing fourth and beginning to assert himself within the Red Bull team. Meanwhile, Räikkönen, in the sister Ferrari, struggled to match Alonso's pace and finished eighth.

Hamilton paid tribute to his team for their hard work. He was also particularly vocal about his appreciation for the Chinese fans, noting how their support had grown each year. He shared how touched he had been by a special video his supporters had compiled for him, presented via a digital photo frame. His victory in China appeared effortless. Given the team's overwhelming advantage, it became clear that only mechanical issues or errors would likely prevent them from winning races. Hamilton's triumph also marked an important milestone, as he matched Jim Clark and Niki Lauda on the all-time winners list—further cementing his status among the sport's greats.

### Spanish Grand Prix: Another Mercedes Battle

The Spanish Grand Prix at Barcelona on 11 May provided another close contest between the Mercedes drivers. Hamilton secured pole position and led the race, but Rosberg closed the gap in the final stages. Despite intense pressure, Hamilton held on to claim his fourth consecutive win, with Rosberg finishing just 0.6 seconds behind.

Ricciardo finished third, marking his first official podium following his disqualification in Australia. Hamilton's victory moved him ahead of Rosberg in the standings, making him the new Championship leader.

In the post-race interviews, former team boss Eddie Jordan (who would sadly pass away on 20 March 2025, aged 76) asked Hamilton to reflect on his move to Mercedes:

*"Lewis, are you surprised by the dominance? A lot of people questioned your decision to leave McLaren for Mercedes 18 months ago. Did you always believe this potential was there?"*

Hamilton responded by recalling his early discussions with Ross Brawn, admitting that while he had believed in Mercedes' vision, even he had not anticipated the sheer scale of their advantage. He expressed gratitude for being part of the team and for contributing to their success, highlighting their fourth one-two finish as a remarkable achievement.

The opening races of the 2014 season firmly established Mercedes as the dominant force in Formula One, while the rivalry between Hamilton and Rosberg became one of the sport's most captivating storylines. Hamilton, with four consecutive victories, had seized early momentum, overtaking Rosberg in the standings and cementing himself as the driver to beat. For Rosberg, the challenge was clear: he needed to fight back.

Lauda and Wolff frequently voiced their satisfaction with both drivers performing at such an exceptional level, emphasising how their internal battle was driving the team forward. However, their message carried an unspoken warning: "Race hard, but don't take each other out."

**Monaco Grand Prix: Controversy and Tension at Mercedes**

The 2014 Monaco Grand Prix, held on 25 May, was overshadowed by a controversial qualifying session that intensified the rivalry between the Mercedes teammates. In the final moments of Q3, Rosberg went off track at Mirabeau, triggering yellow flags that prevented Hamilton from completing his final flying lap. The incident was investigated by the Stewards, but Rosberg was cleared of any wrongdoing.

Hamilton, visibly frustrated, noted that he had been on a strong lap before the yellow flags but said he would move on. When pressed on whether Rosberg's off-track moment had been a mistake or something more, he remained non-committal, hinting that time would reveal the answer.

The incident drew comparisons to Michael Schumacher's controversial 2006 qualifying moment at Rascasse, where he was penalised for obstructing rivals. While Rosberg faced no similar consequences, the situation added fuel to the growing tension between the two drivers. Some within the paddock questioned whether Rosberg's off had been entirely accidental, speculating that it had come at a convenient moment.

When asked if the incident had changed his relationship with Rosberg and whether it now resembled the famous Senna-Prost rivalry, Hamilton said he admired how Senna had handled such situations, implying that he would adopt a similarly uncompromising stance going forward. The intensifying mind games suggested that the fight for the Championship was now as much about mental strength as raw speed on track. Rosberg secured pole position, with Hamilton second and Ricciardo third.

When the lights went out, Rosberg led from the start, with Hamilton closely following. The two Mercedes drivers controlled the race, gradually pulling away from the rest of the field. However, the tight and unforgiving streets of Monaco contributed to multiple incidents and retirements. Defending World Champion Sebastian Vettel retired on Lap 5 due to a power unit failure, continuing his difficult season. A major crash on Lap 24 for Adrian Sutil brought out the Safety Car, temporarily neutralising Mercedes' advantage and bunching up the field.

In the latter stages of the race, Hamilton reported an issue with his vision, later revealed to be dirt in his eye. This allowed Rosberg to extend his lead, though Hamilton managed to hold off a fast-charging Ricciardo in the closing laps.

Rosberg took his second victory of the season, reclaiming the lead in the Drivers' Championship by four points over Hamilton. Mercedes' dominance in the Constructors' Championship remained unchallenged, as their rivals struggled to match their pace. The race also saw a historic moment for Marussia, with Jules Bianchi finishing eighth on the road, earning the team its first-ever points in Formula One. However, a five-second penalty for a Safety Car infringement officially classified him ninth.

**Canadian Grand Prix: Mercedes Falter, Ricciardo Seizes Victory**

The Canadian Grand Prix in early June saw both Mercedes cars lock out the front row in qualifying. The race, held in unusually warm conditions for Montreal, delivered unexpected drama.

At the start, Hamilton got the better getaway, drawing alongside Rosberg into Turn 1. As he attempted to go around the outside, Rosberg braked late, locked up, and ran wide, forcing Hamilton slightly off track and allowing Vettel to slip into second place. It took Hamilton until Lap 10 to pass Vettel and reclaim second.

The race's first major incident occurred on Lap 1 when Jules Bianchi and Max Chilton collided. Attempting to overtake his teammate, Bianchi lost control as both Marussias slid sideways through a chicane. Chilton made contact with the rear of Bianchi's car, tearing off a wheel and sending Bianchi into the barriers. The crash ended the race for both drivers.

As the race progressed, the fight between the Mercedes drivers became the focal point. On Lap 25, Hamilton closed in on Rosberg at the final chicane. Under pressure, Rosberg locked up and missed the corner, cutting across the run-off area and gaining an advantage. The incident was noted but went unpenalised.

By Lap 37, Mercedes' race took a dramatic turn when Hamilton radioed the team reporting a loss of power. A lap later, Rosberg experienced similar issues. Team personnel, including Niki Lauda, could be seen looking on from the pits, clearly concerned. Both cars had suffered simultaneous MGU-K failures, meaning they lost a crucial part of their hybrid power boost.

The problem forced Hamilton to push his braking harder, leading to excessive heat buildup. By Lap 46, he ran deep into the hairpin and was re-passed by Rosberg. Attempting to fight back into the final corner, Hamilton ran straight on. On Lap 47, his right rear brake overheated, causing smoke to pour from the wheel. Moments later, he radioed the team confirming what was already visible—his brakes had failed, forcing him to retire. Despite his own power loss, Rosberg managed to continue, albeit at reduced pace. Red Bull's Daniel Ricciardo, who had been closing in, saw his opportunity. With just two laps remaining, Ricciardo swept past Rosberg to take the lead, securing his maiden Formula One victory. Rosberg salvaged second place, while Vettel completed the podium in third.

Although Mercedes still led the season convincingly, the race highlighted Ricciardo's growing confidence at Red Bull. While the team had struggled against Mercedes, Ricciardo was now consistently outperforming his four-time World Champion teammate, Vettel, and had established himself as a serious contender.

The race nearly ended in disaster for Vettel on the final lap. As he approached Turn 1, Felipe Massa, battling for fourth place in his Williams, collided with Sergio Pérez. The impact sent Massa's car skidding past Vettel's left side at high speed, while Pérez spun off on his right. Massa's car hit the barriers heavily, but both drivers fortunately escaped injury. Due to the incident, Ricciardo crossed the finish line under waved yellow flags.

**Austrian Grand Prix: Rosberg Extends His Lead**

The Austrian Grand Prix on 22 June marked the return of Formula One to the Red Bull Ring. Williams stunned the paddock by locking out the front row in qualifying, with Felipe Massa taking pole position and Valtteri Bottas securing second.

However, in the race, Mercedes once again demonstrated superior race pace. Rosberg took the lead after the first round of pit stops and held on until the chequered flag, securing victory. Hamilton, who had started ninth, made an impressive recovery drive to finish second. Bottas claimed his first career podium in third place, underlining his growing reputation.

Some observers noted that Hamilton appeared to be held for longer than usual during his pit stops compared to Rosberg, fuelling speculation in the media that Mercedes was favouring Rosberg in the Championship fight.

After the race, Rosberg was happy with his win and pleased with the strength of his car. When Hamilton was questioned about the pit stop time loss he played down any controversy, stating that he hadn't initially realised the delay, but would review the details with the team. Despite losing time in the pits, he acknowledged that Mercedes had performed well and had not made any critical mistakes.

For Bottas, third place—finishing ahead of both Ferraris and Red Bulls—was an outstanding achievement. It was a sign of his growing capabilities and professionalism, something that Mercedes would take note of for the future. He expressed his satisfaction with how smoothly the race had gone, reflecting on how much progress Williams had made.

**British Grand Prix: Redemption for Hamilton**

The 2014 British Grand Prix at Silverstone on 6 July was a defining moment in Hamilton's season. It began with disappointment in qualifying but ended with a triumphant home victory.

In Q3, changing track conditions made tyre choices and timing critical. Mercedes advised Hamilton that if he didn't believe he could improve, he should pit. Believing the track wouldn't allow for better lap times, Hamilton aborted his final flying lap, only to see the track improve dramatically, leaving him sixth on the grid while Rosberg secured pole position. Acknowledging his mistake, Hamilton admitted that the decision had been entirely his own and expressed his regret, particularly for the home fans who had turned out in support.

Rosberg, starting from pole, was optimistic, believing that Hamilton would take some time to move through the field come Sunday. Meanwhile, Vettel qualified second, and home favourite Jenson Button, known for excelling in mixed conditions, lined up third.

Race day saw an electrifying atmosphere, with over 122,000 fans in attendance. Hamilton made an aggressive start, swiftly overtaking Vettel, who had lost ground. Button moved into second, while Rosberg began pulling away at the front. Determined to recover, Hamilton immediately pushed hard, setting a blistering pace to close the gap. A major incident brought the race to a halt halfway through the first lap. Räikkönen lost control on one of the straights and crashed heavily, registering an impact of 47G. The race was red flagged as barriers needed repair, allowing the field to reset. At the restart, Hamilton wasted no time. By Lap 4, he had overtaken both McLarens and was up to second, setting off in pursuit of Rosberg.

On Lap 29, Rosberg suffered a gearbox failure, forcing him to retire. With Rosberg out, Hamilton took the lead to the delight of the British crowd. His race engineer, Peter Bonnington, immediately radioed him, advising caution to ensure the car made it to the finish. Hamilton managed his tyres and mechanical components carefully, maintaining a steady pace without taking unnecessary risks. He secured a dominant home victory, much to the jubilation of the Silverstone crowd. Bottas continued his strong form, climbing through the field to finish second, while Ricciardo claimed third for Red Bull.

After the race, Hamilton discussed his emotional comeback, admitting that the previous day had been difficult but that he had channelled the frustration into delivering a strong performance. He paid tribute to the overwhelming support from British fans, emphasising how much their encouragement had meant to him.

### German Grand Prix: A Battle Through the Field

The 2014 German Grand Prix at Hockenheim on 20 July was another dramatic chapter in the season, particularly for Hamilton, who had to fight through adversity.

During qualifying, a right-front brake disc failure sent Hamilton crashing at high speed. The impact was severe enough that he had to be taken to the medical centre for checks on his knees. Despite feeling sore, he was cleared to race, stating that even if something had been broken, he would still have competed the next day.

Rosberg cruised to an easy victory on race day, extending his Championship lead. Bottas once again impressed, securing second place for Williams. By now, he had firmly established himself as the lead driver in the team, holding 91 points to Massa's 30. Starting from 20th on the grid, Hamilton delivered an exceptional drive, carving his way through the field to finish third. His performance was widely praised, with many praising his ability to stay composed and execute critical overtakes under pressure. The result helped him minimise the damage in the Championship standings, keeping him within striking distance of Rosberg.

As the 2014 Formula One season reached its midpoint, the battle between Rosberg and Hamilton had become the defining storyline. As they left Germany, Rosberg led the standings with 190 points, while Hamilton sat second on 176.

Ricciardo was third with 106, while the gap between Mercedes and the rest of the field was evident—Jenson Button, in sixth, was already 120 points adrift of Hamilton.

The intense rivalry between Hamilton and Rosberg had delivered high drama with mechanical failures mixing up things. With nine races remaining, the question loomed: who would emerge victorious?

### Hungarian Grand Prix: A Race of Attrition and Strategy

The Hungarian Grand Prix delivered one of the most unpredictable races of the season. With changing weather conditions set for the weekend, it provided multiple incidents, and strategy played a crucial role in determining the outcome.

Hamilton's weekend took another hit when his car caught fire during qualifying, forcing him to start from the pit lane. He expressed concern about how difficult overtaking would be at the tight and twisty circuit, admitting that even breaking into the top ten would be difficult.

Beyond the immediate race challenge, Hamilton also voiced concern about the potential impact of the fire on his season. With Formula One's strict engine limit of five units per season, he feared that reliability issues could become a factor in the title fight.

The race began in wet conditions. Rosberg made a clean getaway from pole, retaining his lead into Turn 1. Bottas, starting third, had an excellent launch and capitalised on the conditions, overtaking Vettel around the outside to move into second in the Williams. Further back, Hamilton struggled for grip on cold tyres and spun off on the opening lap. However, he quickly recovered and rejoined the race, minimising the time lost.

Early incidents saw the Safety Car deployed twice—first on lap eight and again on Lap 14—shuffling the order as teams adjusted their strategies. As the track dried, drivers transitioned to slick tyres. On Lap 23, Sergio Pérez lost control coming out of the final corner, hitting a damp kerb and oversteering into the pit wall at high speed. The impact destroyed his car, scattering debris across the start-finish straight and triggering another Safety Car, which proved beneficial for Daniel Ricciardo's race strategy.

A near-identical incident occurred on Lap 33 when Vettel lost control on the same kerbing. However, in a remarkable display of skill, he managed to recover from a full 360-degree spin without making contact with the barriers, missing them by mere centimetres. Later in the race, with 20 laps remaining, Mercedes instructed Hamilton to let Rosberg pass, as Rosberg was on a different strategy. Hamilton refused, responding over the radio that Rosberg needed to close the gap himself if he wanted to overtake. The decision further strained the already tense team dynamics, and Rosberg later avoided discussing the matter in post-race interviews.

Ricciardo seized on late opportunities, executing his usual late braking overtakes to take his second victory of the season. Alonso finished second, while Hamilton secured third, holding off Rosberg, who having dropped down the order, finished fourth.

Post-race Ricciardo spoke of his joy, expressing how much the win meant to him. Meanwhile, Hamilton was asked about the team order to let Rosberg through. He explained his reasoning, stating that despite being on different strategies, they were still in the same race. Allowing Rosberg through would have put Hamilton at a disadvantage later when Rosberg pitted, potentially costing him track position.

As Formula One headed to Spa, Rosberg retained an 11-point lead over Hamilton, but the tension within Mercedes continued to build.

**Belgian Grand Prix: A Collision That Shook Mercedes**

The Belgian Grand Prix, held on a lovely summer day on 24 August, was overshadowed by a dramatic clash between the Mercedes teammates.

Hamilton and Rosberg started the race from the front row and as the lights went out, Vettel briefly passed Rosberg for second place. However, Vettel ran wide at Malmedy, dropping back to third, leaving Hamilton and Rosberg to battle for the lead.

On the second lap, Rosberg gained all the way up the long Kemmel Straight and made a move around the outside of the right hander at Les Combes, but as he attempted to pass Hamilton, his front wing clipped Hamilton's left rear tyre. The contact caused an immediate puncture. Hamilton radioed the team, "Nico hit me! That's unbelievable guys, I can't believe he hit me". In a sign that Hamilton was continuing to mature, his voice was very measured and more resigned than angry. Some of the Mercedes mechanics were shaking their heads in disbelief, others had their hands over their face covering their eyes. Toto Wolff was on the pit wall remonstrating with his team, his left hand going backwards and forwards in a chopping motion: he looked angry. Hamilton coaxed the stricken Mercedes back to the pits as slowly as he could, but the flailing tyre damaged his bodywork in the process.

Ricciardo sensed yet another opportunity. When Vettel ran wide, Ricciardo seized the moment to pass his teammate, continuing his impressive form to take a deserved victory. The damage to Hamilton's car was too severe for him to recover, and he was eventually forced to retire.

Despite Rosberg requiring a lengthy pit stop to replace his front wing, he salvaged second place. Bottas delivered another standout performance for Williams, securing third after an impressive overtake on Vettel at Les Combes—the same place where Rosberg had failed to make a move stick earlier in the race.

In the garage, Toto Wolff approached Hamilton to discuss the incident. Hamilton, still wearing his helmet, listened before walking away without appearing to say much. Later, when giving interviews, Hamilton made his frustration clear, stating that he had left enough space and didn't understand why the collision had happened. His disappointment extended beyond his own result, as he believed Mercedes had lost out on an easy one-two finish.

Rosberg was met with boos from the crowd when he stepped onto the podium. Acknowledging the controversy, he later admitted that he had apologised to Hamilton after reviewing the incident. When asked whether the apology was prompted by the team, Rosberg insisted it was his own decision and was not influenced by the feedback he had received. It could, however possibly have had something to do with the booing.

After the podium Wolff was still unhappy. While stopping short of directly blaming Rosberg, he made his feelings clear, criticising the fact that Mercedes had lost a potential race win due to unnecessary contact between their own drivers. To add further pressure on Rosberg—and to a lesser extent, Hamilton—Niki Lauda publicly voiced his frustration over the incident, calling it unacceptable. He emphasised that while such clashes might be excusable in the heat of battle towards the end of a race, losing a likely victory for Mercedes as early as the second lap was unnecessary. His remarks reinforced the growing discontent within the team.

Rosberg had clearly been reprimanded, and the impact on his confidence was evident. This, combined with his defeat in Hungary, where Hamilton had fought through the field from the pit lane while Rosberg had started from pole, added to the psychological strain. Hamilton's ability to stay composed through the controversy earned him increasing support within the team, further intensifying the internal battle. It also helped that morally he had done nothing wrong.

The fallout from Spa was viewed as a defining moment in the title fight, with some within the paddock noting its potential influence on the rest of the season. The pressure was mounting on Rosberg as the Championship battle continued.

**Italian Grand Prix: Hamilton Strikes Back**

The Italian Grand Prix at Monza on 7 September saw Hamilton deliver another strong performance.

A poor getaway at the start dropped him to fourth, forcing him to fight his way back through the field. On Lap 10, he made more progress, passing Massa in a daring move around the outside of Turn 1.

Once Hamilton was clear of Massa, he started to eat into Rosberg's lead. Rosberg, being updated by his engineer, started to feel the pressure and began to overdrive the car, small mistakes beginning to creep in.

A few laps later, Rosberg ran wide at Turn 1 but managed to rejoin without losing the lead. The pressure went up another notch. Hamilton, smelling blood, started to close in.

On Lap 19 Rosberg made another mistake at Turn 1, locking up under braking and running deep into the chicane. Forced to take the escape road, he lost momentum—allowing Hamilton to seize the lead. On the pit wall, Toto Wolff smiled broadly as Hamilton powered ahead, taking control of the race.

As Hamilton crossed the finish line and saw the chequered flag, he weaved across the track in celebration, securing a decisive victory. Rosberg followed three seconds behind in second place, while Felipe Massa claimed his first podium of the season in third for Williams, with Bottas finishing fourth. Both Red Bulls followed in fifth and sixth, highlighting the power difference between the Mercedes-powered cars in the top four and the Renault-powered Red Bulls.

In the immediate aftermath, Hamilton was interviewed by former Ferrari driver Jean Alesi, with swarms of *Tifosi* gathering around to listen. Acknowledging their passionate support, Hamilton expressed his appreciation for the atmosphere at Monza, remarking on how incredible it was to see the main straight completely filled with fans.

The result was a psychological blow to Rosberg: he had cracked and gone to pieces under pressure. Although he still held a 22-point lead in the Championship, helped by Hamilton's no-score in Spa, the defeat in a straight fight was significant. While disappointed about making his mistake, Rosberg remained pragmatic, recognising that second place still meant valuable points.

**Singapore Grand Prix: A Turning Point in the Title Fight**

On 20 September, Hamilton arrived at the Singapore Grand Prix full of confidence and secured pole position with a lap time of 1:45.681, narrowly edging out Rosberg in second place. The close qualifying battle reinforced the fierce intra-team competition that had defined the season.

However, cracks in Rosberg's weekend emerged before the race even began, with his car developing electronic issues during the final warm-up laps. The challenging Marina Bay Street Circuit, with its humid conditions and unforgiving layout, already promised a tough race, but Rosberg's technical woes made it even more difficult.

Struggling to launch off the line, Rosberg quickly fell down the order. As his issues worsened, it became clear that his car was barely drivable, and after just 13 laps, he was forced to retire due to a wiring loom failure. With his main rival out, Hamilton had a golden opportunity to seize control of both the race and the Championship standings.

From the front, Hamilton delivered a commanding performance, leading 58 of the 60 laps. He managed his tyres and fuel even though two Safety Car periods bunched up the field, making things tricky. Midway through the race, the team calculated that he needed to build a significant gap to Vettel, who was running a different strategy, before making his final pit stop. Rising to the challenge, Hamilton responded with a sequence of rapid laps, extending his lead and maintaining full control under pressure.

Crossing the line first, Hamilton secured his seventh win of the season, with Vettel and Ricciardo completing the podium for Red Bull. More significantly, Hamilton's victory propelled him into the lead of the Drivers' Championship, holding a narrow three-point advantage over Rosberg as the title battle entered its final stretch.

The Singapore Grand Prix was more than just another win—it was a defining moment. In the absence of his closest competitor, Hamilton delivered an emphatic statement, showing his ability to maximise opportunities when they arose. The result solidified his position as the favourite for the title, while Rosberg's reliability issues, along with his recent wobbles under pressure, raised concerns about his ability to sustain his challenge in the remaining races.

Following Rosberg's retirement in Singapore, Mercedes Team Principal Toto Wolff was frustrated about reliability, commenting how the team had suffered four failures in a row, and wanted the team to address the reliability issues, emphasising that the Championship should not be decided by mechanical failures. He stressed that the team needed to remain focused, working to minimise the risk of further technical problems for both drivers.

The next race in Japan, however, would put into context what really mattered.

### A Tragic Day at Suzuka: The 2014 Japanese Grand Prix

The 2014 Japanese Grand Prix, held at the Suzuka Circuit on 5 October, will forever be remembered for the tragic accident involving Jules Bianchi, an incident that deeply affected the Formula One community. It also marked the first appearance of a young Max Verstappen, who took part in Free Practice 1 for Scuderia Toro Rosso.

Typhoon Phanfone brought torrential rain to Suzuka, creating treacherous conditions. In qualifying, Rosberg secured pole position, with Hamilton alongside him on the front row. Bottas once again demonstrated strong form for Williams, lining up third.

On race day, as the rain continued to lash down, drivers waited on the grid, many appearing pensive as they observed the weather. Vettel looked skyward with a half-frown, while Rosberg, standing under an umbrella, studied the conditions intently.

Once the race was deemed safe to start, the drivers went through their pre-race preparations and climbed into their cars. As the mechanics cleared the grid, Hamilton sat in his Mercedes, waiting to move off. In the gloomy, rain-soaked conditions, three words stood out on the side of his cockpit: *Keep Fighting Michael*—a tribute to Michael Schumacher, who was still in hospital undergoing rehabilitation following his skiing accident in December 2013. All the drivers had chosen to display similar acknowledgments in support of the seven-time World Champion.

The race started behind the Safety Car, but the conditions were immediately deemed too dangerous. After two slow laps, the red flag was shown, and the race was temporarily halted. When conditions improved slightly, the race resumed, with Rosberg leading the field.

Hamilton, in pursuit of his teammate, initially ran wide at Turn 1 but recovered quickly. After a few relentless laps, he launched a bold move around the outside into Turn 1, taking the lead. The Japanese fans responded with enthusiastic applause.

As the rain intensified, teams monitored the worsening conditions, with mechanics stepping out from under the pit wall covers to assess the rainfall. Hamilton's race engineer, Peter Bonnington, warned him over the radio that the rain was building up, a message that underscored the growing challenge.

On Lap 42, Adrian Sutil lost control of his Sauber and spun off at Turn 7, triggering yellow flags. A recovery vehicle was deployed to remove his car, with the medical car also arriving at the scene. Drivers passing through the sector saw the incident and adjusted accordingly.

A few laps later, with the recovery vehicle still on track, the green flag was waved at the marshal post next to the recovery vehicle, indicating normal racing conditions. In the poor visibility and worsening rain, Bianchi lost control at the same corner where Sutil had gone off. His Marussia left the track and crashed into the rear of the recovery vehicle with severe force, knocking Sutil's car off the crane. Bianchi, just 25 years old, suffered a traumatic brain injury.

Medical teams arrived at the scene immediately. Bianchi was extracted from the car and transported to Mie General Medical Centre in Yokkaichi, where he underwent emergency surgery before being placed in intensive care.

In the aftermath, drivers and team personnel expressed deep concern. Sutil, who had witnessed the accident firsthand, acknowledged the difficulty of making the right decisions in real-time but suggested that the race might have been better stopped earlier given the worsening conditions. Vettel admitted that the conditions had been extremely difficult, especially on worn tyres. He emphasised that discussing the race itself felt secondary, as all thoughts were with Bianchi and his family.

Despite the efforts of the medical team, Bianchi remained in a coma until he passed away on 17 July 2015.

The FIA launched an investigation into the accident, leading to significant safety changes. The Virtual Safety Car (VSC) system would be introduced in 2015 to control the speed of cars during double yellow flag situations, aiming to prevent similar incidents in the future.

The 2014 Japanese Grand Prix served as a painful reminder of the dangers of motorsport and became a catalyst for continued efforts to improve safety standards in Formula One.

**The Russian Grand Prix: A New Era for Formula One**

The 2014 season also saw the return of a race in Russia for the first time in a century. The last event, held in 1914, had been won by Mercedes driver Willy Scholl in St. Petersburg.

This time, the race was staged at the newly built Sochi Autodrom, set against the backdrop of the Olympic Park. The circuit's combination of long straights and technical corners made it a fascinating challenge, one that played to Mercedes' strengths. Hamilton dominated the weekend, securing victory and further strengthening his Championship charge.

**The Title Decider: Abu Dhabi Grand Prix**

The season finale in Abu Dhabi carried even more weight than usual due to the controversial double-points rule introduced for the final race. Hamilton entered the weekend with a 17-point lead over Rosberg, knowing that a mechanical failure or mistake could cost him the title.

When the lights went out, Hamilton made a flawless start, overtaking Rosberg into Turn 1 and pulling ahead immediately, later saying it was one of the best starts of his career. From there, he controlled the race, maintaining his composure as Rosberg's challenge faded due to mechanical issues. With Rosberg struggling, Hamilton cruised to victory, crossing the finish line to become the 2014 Formula One World Champion—his second career title and his first with Mercedes. Overcome with emotion, he thanked his team over the radio, still processing the magnitude of his achievement. It was the culmination of a season-long battle and a demonstration of his ability to come from behind, rising above the adversity thrown his way.

After Hamilton climbed out of his car, he seemed to struggle to find the right words. He expressed his immense gratitude and thanked the fans for their incredible support, his family for being by his side, and his team for their unrelenting efforts throughout the year. He talked about the significance of the moment, admitting this title felt even more special than his first, almost like experiencing it for the first time all over again.

On the podium, an elated Toto Wolff celebrated by pouring champagne over Hamilton, marking the culmination of a dominant season for Mercedes.

After the race, Hamilton revealed an intriguing insight into his mindset leading up to the decisive Grand Prix. He admitted to barely sleeping the night before, going to bed late and waking up early. Instead of resting, he opted for a morning run and a massage, expecting fatigue to hit during the race—but instead, he felt composed and focused. A surprise visit from his family at breakfast had given him a boost, making the moment even more memorable.

Discussing his journey with Mercedes, Hamilton acknowledged that his decision to leave McLaren for the Silver Arrows had been questioned by many at the time. However, he described the progress made since joining the team as "unbelievable," crediting both the technical strides and the unwavering fan support as driving forces behind his success. Overwhelmed by the scale of his achievement, he described the experience as surreal, almost like watching it unfold from outside himself.

The 2014 season firmly established Mercedes as the dominant force in Formula One. Between them, Hamilton and Rosberg claimed victory in 16 of the 19 races, with Hamilton winning 11 to Rosberg's five. Their combined efforts delivered a staggering 701 points for Mercedes, far ahead of Red Bull with 405 and Ferrari with just 216. Meanwhile, McLaren, the team Hamilton had left, found themselves struggling in fifth place.

Mercedes' superiority made Hamilton's move to the team look like a masterstroke, but beyond the numbers, the season was defined by the intense battle between its two drivers. Once childhood friends from their karting days, Hamilton and Rosberg had now become fierce rivals, pushing each other to new limits. Though the tension between them had been undeniable, Hamilton acknowledged the sincerity in Rosberg's congratulations after the title was decided.

While the season had been a career-defining moment for Hamilton, it was also a sobering reminder of the dangers that still existed in motorsport. The tragic accident involving Jules Bianchi at Suzuka cast a long shadow over the year, reinforcing the reality that despite all the advancements in safety, Formula One remained an inherently dangerous sport.

As Hamilton celebrated his triumph and Rosberg retreated to regroup for the next season, the FIA turned its attention to further improving driver safety. The events of 2014 had shaped not only a Championship battle but also the future of Formula One itself.

# Hamilton's Hat-Trick

The 2015 Formula One season began with a sense of expectation. Mercedes had set an incredibly high benchmark in 2014, and the feeling was that the Silver Arrows would remain the team to beat. That prediction proved correct, but the season was far from straightforward. The rivalry between Lewis Hamilton and Nico Rosberg escalated further, while Ferrari mounted a resurgence.

The end of the 2014 season saw significant changes to the driver lineup, with moves involving Fernando Alonso, Sebastian Vettel, and the introduction of exciting young talents Max Verstappen and Carlos Sainz Jr.

Alonso's five-year stint with Ferrari came to an end, a period marked by near-misses but no Championship victories. Frustrated by the team's struggles under the new turbo-hybrid regulations, he felt it was time for a change. Talking about his departure, he said that finishing runner-up repeatedly had taken its toll. His outspoken nature often made him appear more like a disgruntled employee than a team leader, despite his undeniable skill over a race distance.

Returning to McLaren, Alonso reunited with the team he had controversially left years earlier following the infamous 2007 "Spygate" scandal, in which McLaren was found to have obtained confidential Ferrari technical information. The team, however, seemed willing to move past their history, welcoming Alonso back as part of a new project alongside Jenson Button. McLaren had rekindled its partnership with Honda, hoping to recreate the dominance they had enjoyed in the late 1980s and early 1990s with Senna and Prost.

However, McLaren's ambitions quickly met harsh reality. The Honda power unit proved to be slow, underpowered, and plagued by persistent technical issues. The car lacked straight-line speed, and frequent retirements left the team languishing at the back of the grid. Alonso's frustration would boil over during the Japanese Grand Prix when, over the team radio, he compared the car's power unit to that of a *GP2 engine*. While optimistic about the long-term prospects, he admitted that podium finishes, and race wins were still a distant goal.

Meanwhile, Sebastian Vettel made a high-profile move to Ferrari following a disappointing 2014 campaign with Red Bull: having been comprehensively beaten by his younger teammate Daniel Ricciardo, Vettel sought a fresh challenge. His decision to join Ferrari was driven by a desire to rebuild and lead the team back to championship contention, embracing the opportunity to create something new.

The 2015 season also introduced two promising rookies at Scuderia Toro Rosso—Max Verstappen and Carlos Sainz Jr. Verstappen, at just 17 years old, became the youngest driver in Formula One history. His rapid rise through the junior ranks, including a standout season in European Formula 3, made him a driver to watch. Motorsport was in his blood, as his father, Jos Verstappen, had been a well-known figure in Formula One during the 1990s.

Sainz Jr., the son of rally legend Carlos Sainz, also arrived with an impressive résumé, having won the Formula Renault 3.5 Series in 2014 with seven victories. Both drivers came through the Red Bull Junior Team, designed to nurture young talent, and their promotion to Toro Rosso was seen as a key step towards potential future seats at Red Bull Racing. Helmut Marko, the head of Red Bull's driver development program, praised Verstappen's abilities, believing he had the qualities to become a future World Champion. Verstappen's arrival was particularly exciting for the passionate Dutch fans, who had long awaited a driver capable of competing at the highest level.

## Alonso's Head Injury

The excitement surrounding the 2015 season was accompanied by renewed concerns over driver safety. During pre-season testing at the Circuit de Barcelona-Catalunya in February, Fernando Alonso suffered a significant crash in his McLaren MP4-30. His car veered off at Turn 3, striking the inside wall at high speed.

Trackside medical teams responded immediately, and Alonso was airlifted to hospital after showing signs of confusion. Reports later emerged suggesting that, upon regaining consciousness, he had briefly lost memory of the past two decades, allegedly believing he was still a karting driver aspiring to reach Formula One. Fortunately, his memory gradually returned, but the accident raised fresh discussions about the potential long-term effects of head trauma in motorsport.

Alonso remained hospitalised for three days following the crash, undergoing CT and MRI scans to assess his condition. Medical specialists advised him to rest and recover, warning of the dangers of *second impact syndrome*—a potentially life-threatening condition that can occur if a second head injury is sustained before full recovery from an initial one. As a precaution, Alonso was ruled out of the season-opening Australian Grand Prix.

While the physical effects of his concussion seemed to subside relatively quickly, the crash raised questions about potential lingering effects. Throughout the season, Alonso—typically known for his sharp wit and confidence—appeared increasingly irritable and frustrated. Given McLaren's well-documented struggles with their Honda power unit, this was unsurprising, but his head injury could also have been a contributing factor. Studies have shown that approximately 30% of individuals with moderate concussions experience changes in mood or behaviour, though determining the precise impact of Alonso's crash on his season remains speculative.

Comparisons were drawn to Felipe Massa's head injury in 2009, which had more severe immediate consequences but also appeared to influence his later performances and approach to racing. While Alonso's case was far less severe, any potential neurological effects—however subtle—could have played a role in his reactions and mindset during the 2015 season. Fortunately, he had some support within McLaren, led by Ron Dennis, who had experience guiding Mika Häkkinen through his near-fatal crash in Adelaide in 1995.

As Alonso recovered, speculation about the nature of his injuries began circulating. Some reports exaggerated the extent of his memory loss, with rumours suggesting he had woken up believing he was a teenage karting driver in 1995. Keen to put these to rest, Alonso released a video message on 26 February 2015, assuring fans that he was "completely fine." He expressed frustration at the misinformation and clarified that, while he did experience a brief period of memory loss, the more extreme claims were untrue.

In a later interview, Alonso explained that he had no recollection of a four-hour window while in hospital, which he attributed to medication. Medical professionals later identified this as *post-traumatic amnesia (PTA)*, a common symptom of concussions where individuals experience temporary disorientation and difficulty recalling events immediately before or after an impact. The duration of PTA is often used as a marker for the severity of a brain injury, with longer episodes indicating more significant trauma. Alonso's four-hour memory gap fell within the range associated with mild traumatic brain injuries, but for an elite driver, even minor cognitive effects could be relevant.

Formula One requires exceptional cognitive function, with reaction time, spatial awareness, and split-second decision-making being critical to performance. Even minor disruptions to brain processing can have significant consequences in high-speed environments. Some specialists in sports neurology have noted that racing drivers operate under extreme mental demands, where even subtle impairments can affect their ability to perform at the highest level.

Although Alonso's recovery appeared swift, his performance across the season was scrutinised. Some attributed his increasingly outspoken frustrations to McLaren's struggles, while others wondered if his accident had played a role in his demeanour. As the season unfolded, his results compared to those of teammate Jenson Button would offer some insight into whether his challenges were purely car-related or if there were lingering effects from his crash.

After being sidelined for the season-opening Australian Grand Prix as a precautionary measure, he returned to the Malaysian Grand Prix and faced an uphill battle—not only was he recovering from his accident, but he was also at the wheel of a McLaren MP4-30 hindered by an uncompetitive Honda power unit. Despite the setbacks, Alonso remained publicly optimistic, later reflecting on the importance of resilience in sport and the role of proper rehabilitation following a concussion.

As the season progressed, however, his frustration with the car's performance became increasingly evident. McLaren and Honda had entered the year full of optimism, but reality painted a starkly different picture. The team's reliability issues, lack of straight-line speed, and persistent technical failures left both Alonso and Button unable to fight near the front of the grid.

Alonso's accident and its aftermath served as yet another reminder of the risks in Formula One, even for the most experienced drivers. It also highlighted the fine margins of health, safety, and performance that competitors must navigate in one of the world's most demanding sports.

## Season openers

The 2015 Formula One season opened with some cracking races, each adding a new chapter to the unfolding championship story. The season opener in Melbourne on 15 March saw Mercedes assert their dominance. Hamilton secured pole position, a full six-tenths ahead of Rosberg. Felipe Massa had a brilliant qualifying, securing third in the Williams, ahead of Vettel in the Ferrari in fourth. Among the debutants, Carlos Sainz impressed with seventh place on the grid, while his teammate Max Verstappen delivered a strong performance to qualify eleventh. Both Sainz and Verstappen outperformed Daniil Kvyat, who could only manage twelfth in the senior team's supposedly superior Red Bull.

Jenson Button, in the McLaren, could only qualify 16th, with his temporary teammate Kevin Magnussen in 17th. McLaren had already warned that the Australian race would serve as more of a test session than a competitive outing. The stark contrast between Hamilton, on pole in the Mercedes, and his former team at the back of the grid further justified his decision to leave McLaren.

Hamilton led the race from start to finish, with teammate Rosberg completing a dominant one-two for Mercedes. Ferrari's Sebastian Vettel finished third, marking a promising start with his new team. Button finished in eleventh and last place, as many teams struggled with reliability.

## Malaysian Grand Prix – Ferrari Stuns Mercedes

At the Malaysian Grand Prix in Sepang on 29 March, Hamilton once again secured pole, but this time, Vettel was within a tenth of a second in the Ferrari. Rosberg qualified third, some half a second behind Hamilton. For Alonso, having left Ferrari believing they were no longer competitive, qualifying eighteenth in the McLaren would have been hard to accept. His decision to leave was about to come under even sharper scrutiny in the race. Among the newcomers, Sainz put his Toro Rosso in 15th, while Verstappen delivered a standout lap to qualify sixth—just three-hundredths of a second behind Kvyat in the works Red Bull.

The race would prove to be a defining moment in the early season, as Ferrari delivered a performance that few had expected. Having dominated the season opener in Australia, Mercedes arrived in Malaysia as overwhelming favourites. Hamilton made a strong getaway from pole, keeping his lead into the first few corners. Further back, Räikkönen, starting from eleventh in the second Ferrari, picked up a puncture on Lap 2 and limped back to the pits.

On Lap 4, Marcus Ericsson spun his Sauber into the gravel, bringing out an early Safety Car. This moment changed the entire complexion of the race. Both Mercedes cars pitted for fresh tyres, with Rosberg stacking up behind Hamilton in the pit lane. Ferrari, however, opted for a different strategy, keeping Vettel out on track.

By Lap 24, Vettel had the advantage. As Hamilton dived into the pits, Vettel swept past into the lead. Ferrari's alternative strategy, combined with better tyre management in the intense heat, allowed Vettel to keep both Mercedes drivers behind. Meanwhile, frustration was growing in the Mercedes camp. Rosberg was eager for information on Vettel's pace but was given a stock response, as rules at the time prohibited sharing direct competitor data.

Hamilton was equally concerned, questioning the state of his tyres, but was reassured by his team that there was no need to change approach. Despite this, his body language in the cockpit suggested a growing frustration. As the laps ticked down, the gap to Vettel only increased, and it soon became clear that Ferrari had played its hand to perfection.

As the race neared its conclusion, Vettel continued to extend his lead, crossing the finish line to claim Ferrari's first victory since the 2013 Spanish Grand Prix. It was a significant statement of intent from Ferrari, signalling their return as a genuine contender. Hamilton secured second place, with Rosberg completing the podium. On the cool-down lap, Vettel's excitement was clear, celebrating what was an unexpected but well-earned win.

Alonso's day ended in disappointment, forced to retire on Lap 21, adding to McLaren's early-season struggles.

Hamilton, gracious in defeat, acknowledged Ferrari's impressive performance, recognising their strong pace and their canny pit stop strategy. His remarks suggested a degree of concern over the challenge posed by the resurgent Scuderia. Rosberg, echoing a similar sentiment, admitted that Ferrari had simply done a better job on the day and that Mercedes would need to come back stronger at the next race.

For Vettel, the victory was deeply personal. As he embraced the Ferrari team, his emotions were evident—this was a defining moment in restoring Ferrari to its former glory. Post-race, he went over the challenges of the previous season, expressing how much it meant to him to be driving for the team he had idolised since childhood. He described his first day at Maranello as a dream come true, recalling his younger years watching Schumacher from behind the fence and now finding himself behind the wheel of the very same red car. As he spoke, Hamilton listened intently, while Rosberg, seated beside him, looked visibly frustrated.

Commentators were quick to highlight the broader implications of the race. Observers noted that Ferrari's victory had injected a new dynamic into the Championship, and Mercedes would no longer have things entirely their own way. The 2015 Malaysian Grand Prix served as a reminder to Hamilton, and to the sport as a whole, that even amid Mercedes' dominance, the competition remained fierce, and Ferrari was not to be discounted.

**Chinese Grand Prix - Rosberg reaches boiling point**

The 2015 Chinese Grand Prix, held at the Shanghai International Circuit on 12 April, illustrated Mercedes' continued supremacy and the escalating tensions between teammates Hamilton and Rosberg, as each driver sought to assert their authority within the team.

Hamilton secured pole position and led the race from start to finish, claiming his second victory of the season. Rosberg finished second, ensuring another Mercedes one-two, while Vettel completed the podium in third for Ferrari. Despite this outward success, underlying tensions within the Mercedes camp became increasingly apparent during and after the race.

During the race, Rosberg grew frustrated, believing Hamilton was deliberately managing the pace in a way that was compromising his own strategy and allowing Vettel to close in. Over team radio, he voiced his concerns saying that Hamilton was driving very slowly, urging the team to ensure he increased his speed. However, Hamilton remained focused on tyre conservation and overall race strategy, choosing to maintain his approach. The team opted not to intervene, allowing the situation to play out naturally, which only heightened the tension between the two drivers.

Elsewhere on track, the order remained largely unchanged. In the latter stages, Button made contact with Maldonado in a battle for 13th, sending both momentarily off the road, which allowed Alonso to gain a position. Meanwhile, Verstappen suffered a dramatic retirement on Lap 54 when his Toro Rosso came to a halt on the start-finish straight, his rear wheels appearing to lock up—suggesting a terminal mechanical failure.

In the post-race press conference, the tension between Hamilton and Rosberg was electric. When asked about the pit-to-car messages, Rosberg did not hold back, making it clear that he felt Hamilton had only been thinking about his own race rather than the bigger picture for the team. He suggested that the controlled pace had forced him into a defensive position against Vettel, ultimately extending his tyre stint and leaving him vulnerable towards the end of the race. His words carried an edge of frustration, bordering on bitterness, further underlining the growing rift between the two drivers.

When asked about the situation, Hamilton made it clear that his focus was on his own race rather than managing Rosberg's. He emphasised that his responsibility was to bring the car home as quickly and safely as possible, adding that if Rosberg had wanted to get past, he had the opportunity to try. While Hamilton's response was measured, Rosberg's expression made his frustration obvious.

It was evident that Rosberg was running out of answers unless he changed his approach or became more aggressive on track. As the interviews wrapped up, Rosberg's body language suggested a sense of determination—whether that would translate into a stronger challenge in the coming races remained to be seen.

Mercedes' non-executive chairman, Niki Lauda, was asked for his view on the situation. He acknowledged that all top-level drivers are highly competitive and that racing at the highest level requires a degree of selfishness. He dismissed the idea that tensions between the two would escalate further, suggesting that while rivalries might flare up in the heat of the moment, things would settle down before the next race in Bahrain.

The media and commentators were quick to analyse the dynamic between the two Mercedes drivers. Many observed that since mid-2014, Hamilton had consistently outperformed Rosberg, and if Rosberg wanted to keep his Championship hopes alive, he needed to find a way to shift the balance of power—otherwise, he risked falling into a clear number two role within the team.

**Bahrain – Hamilton dominates**

At the Bahrain Grand Prix on 19 April, Hamilton maintained his strong form, taking victory from pole position. Kimi Räikkönen put in an impressive performance for Ferrari, securing second place after overtaking Rosberg in the closing laps. Rosberg finished third, marking another disappointing result in the context of the Championship battle. The weekend showed Ferrari's improving pace—Vettel had qualified second, with Räikkönen third, and in race conditions, both Ferraris kept the Mercedes drivers under pressure.

**Spain – Rosberg turns a corner**

At the Spanish Grand Prix on 10 May, Rosberg made a strong start from pole, while Hamilton, starting second, struggled with wheelspin and dropped to third, allowing a Ferrari through into second place. During his first pit stop on Lap 14, Hamilton lost time due to a slow change on his left-rear tyre, further adding to his challenge.

Later in the race, Alonso ran wide at the first corner and immediately reported a problem with his brakes. McLaren instructed him to pit, and though he sounded composed over the radio, the issue quickly became more serious. As he entered the pit lane, his braking system failed entirely, sending him rolling straight through his pit box. His quick-thinking front jack man managed to jump out of the way just in time, but the car still clipped the jack, dragging it several metres. Alonso was instructed to shut down the engine, and as the McLaren mechanics pushed him back into the garage, dark blue smoke billowed from the front brakes, signalling yet another mechanical failure in a frustrating season.

Rosberg went on to secure his first win of the season and was delighted. Hamilton finished second after a challenging race, with Vettel once again in third. Mercedes stamped their authority, being some 45 seconds ahead of the Ferrari. Rosberg's victory reignited his Championship campaign, narrowing the gap to Hamilton to just 20 points. Vettel, meanwhile, was only 11 points behind Rosberg, the top three drivers comfortably ahead of the rest.

**Monaco – Mercedes drops the ball**

By the time the circus arrived in Monaco later in May, Hamilton seemed secure with his established lead in the Championship. However, the streets of Monte Carlo would provide one of the most controversial moments of the season. Hamilton led comfortably until Lap 64 of 78 laps.

Max Verstappen in the Toro Rosso was closing quickly on Romain Grosjean in the Lotus Mercedes across the start-finish straight. As Grosjean lifted off and started to brake for Turn 1, Verstappen missed his braking point and ran straight into the back of the Lotus at well over 130mph before smashing into the barriers in a heavy impact, the front of his Toro Rosso buried deep in the Tecpro. Verstappen had attempted to dummy Grosjean but misjudged the braking point, leading to the collision. The crash brought out the Safety Car and Mercedes decided to pit Hamilton on Lap 65, believing he had enough gap to maintain the lead. Hamilton was held an extra second or two in his pit box as they waited for a Sauber to go past. However, upon rejoining, he found himself behind Nico Rosberg and Sebastian Vettel, finishing the race in third. Hamilton displayed composure despite the setback, but said he was struggling to put his feelings into words.

Niki Lauda acknowledged the mistake, openly admitting the team had 'screwed it up'. Team Principal Toto Wolff also took responsibility, saying the error was on the team and expressing confidence that Hamilton, as a great leader and driver, would understand that mistakes sometimes happen.

Over the next seven races, Hamilton won four, Rosberg one, and Vettel two. It was looking more and more like another World Championship for Hamilton.

At the Austrian Grand Prix in June, held at the Red Bull Ring, Rosberg overtook pole-sitter Hamilton at the start and maintained his lead to win the race. Hamilton's attempt to regain the lead was thwarted by a five-second penalty for crossing the white line at the pit exit. This victory allowed

Rosberg to close the points gap in the Championship standings to just ten points.

In July, during the British Grand Prix at Silverstone, Hamilton and Rosberg engaged in a duel influenced by changing weather conditions. Hamilton's timely switch to intermediate tyres during a rain shower enabled him to secure victory, while Rosberg, who delayed his tyre change, finished second. The race illustrated Hamilton's sharp decision-making and Rosberg's frustration with the timing of his pit stop.

Later in the month, the Hungarian Grand Prix at the Hungaroring was chaotic, with both Mercedes drivers facing challenges. Hamilton made a poor start and received a drive-through penalty for colliding with Daniel Ricciardo. Rosberg, running second in the closing stages, suffered a puncture after contact with Ricciardo, dropping him to eighth place. Hamilton finished sixth, and both drivers were miffed with their performances.

In August at the Belgian Grand Prix at Spa-Francorchamps, Hamilton secured pole position and led the race to victory. Rosberg had a poor start, recovering to finish second. Post-race, he acknowledged his start issues, stating he had completely messed it up.

At the Italian Grand Prix in early September, held at Monza, Hamilton dominated the race, while Rosberg started from fourth due to an engine change. Rosberg was running third when his engine failed with three laps remaining, resulting in a retirement. This incident widened Hamilton's lead in the Championship and highlighted the reliability challenges faced by Rosberg. After Italy, Hamilton was on 252 points against Rosberg's 199, a seemingly unassailable lead as they headed first to Singapore, and then to Japan in late September.

Hamilton again won at the Japanese Grand Prix on 27 September. However, it will be forever remembered for Fernando Alonso's tactless comments over the radio about the performance of his engine. During the race, as Alonso went across the start-finish straight, his McLaren was passed by Max Verstappen in the Toro Rosso. As Verstappen came past, Alonso got on the radio to the McLaren pits, "This is very embarrassing, GP2 engine, GP2, aargh," showing his frustration with the power deficit in his Honda engine, which reduced the top speed. The Japan race was Honda's home Grand Prix and this criticism was an insult Honda would not forget.

**Russian Grand Prix – Mechanical woes for Rosberg**

Held on the weekend of 9–11 October, the Russian Grand Prix took place at the Sochi Autodrom under near-perfect racing conditions—some cloud cover, but with temperatures hovering around 18 degrees Celsius.

Rosberg, knowing he needed to strike back in the title fight, delivered a stellar qualifying lap, securing pole with a 1:37.113—three tenths ahead of Hamilton, who lined up alongside him in second.

As the lights went out, Rosberg held firm into Turn 1, but Hamilton was relentless through Turns 2, 3, and 4, swarming all over the back of his teammate and primed to attack. Just as the battle was about to ignite, the Safety Car was deployed following a three-car pile-up beyond Turn 1.

At the restart, Bottas, the only Williams inside the top 10, underlined his racecraft by dispatching Räikkönen and moving up to third. Moments later, Rosberg's race unravelled. A technical issue with his throttle left him struggling for control, and Hamilton wasted no time in sweeping past. With no choice but to limp back to the pits, Rosberg was forced into retirement, his title hopes slipping further away.

A second Safety Car was triggered on Lap 14 after Romain Grosjean's Lotus Mercedes was left wrecked against the barriers. When racing resumed, Hamilton was untroubled, dictating the pace with complete authority and cruising to victory.

On the final lap, chaos unfolded between the two Finns. Räikkönen and Bottas tangled, sending Bottas spinning out of contention and into retirement—his hopes of a podium gone in an instant.

Up on the podium, Hamilton, resplendent in a traditional Ushanka hat, revelled in his victory, grinning as he sprayed champagne. The title now felt like a formality. The teams left Russia and headed for the United States, where hats would play another role.

**United States Grand Prix - Capgate**

The United States Grand Prix, held on 25 October at the Circuit of the Americas in Austin, Texas, was set to be the defining moment of the Formula One season, with tensions running high between Mercedes teammates Lewis Hamilton and Nico Rosberg. Heading into the race, Hamilton sat on 302 points, holding a commanding 73-point lead over Rosberg, with the chance to clinch the Championship. Rosberg, meanwhile, had slipped to third in the standings after Russia, trailing Vettel by four points.

The race began under tricky conditions, with a damp but gradually drying track creating a chaotic start. Most drivers opted for intermediate tyres. Hamilton, starting alongside pole-sitter Rosberg, attacked immediately, forcing his teammate wide at the first corner after the slightest of contact. Rosberg rejoined in fifth, yet another poor getaway compounding his season's frustrations—he had converted just two of his nine pole positions into victories.

What followed was an electrifying contest, with both Mercedes drivers duelling for position in a relentless game of cat and mouse. On Lap 18, they fought wheel-to-wheel for over half a lap, trading positions in a sequence of daring overtakes. Just when it seemed inevitable that contact would be made, Hamilton was called into the pits for fresh tyres, with Rosberg following a lap later. Despite the still-damp track, Rosberg emerged with his lead intact.

Further down the order, McLaren showed signs of life. As the season progressed, their car had become more reliable, and on Lap 40, Alonso produced a series of great overtakes to move into sixth place behind his teammate.

On Lap 43, Daniil Kvyat lost control of his Toro Rosso, his right-front wheel snapping violently as he skidded across damp astro turf and into the barriers. The wrecked car, stranded on the track, triggered a Safety Car. Hamilton pitted under the caution and rejoined in second place, poised for an attack. With just seven laps remaining, Rosberg cracked under pressure, running wide at Turn 12 and gifting Hamilton the lead. From there, there was no stopping him. The Briton charged to the chequered flag, securing victory and, with it, his third World Championship title.

Crossing the line, Hamilton placed his hands on his head, overcome. Bono came over the radio to confirm the momentous achievement, but Hamilton, voice thick with emotion, could only manage a few words of gratitude before breaking into quiet sobs between deep breaths. Moments later, he gathered himself and thanked the team, his family, and everyone who had supported him on the journey. Before facing the media, three-time World Champion Sir Jackie Stewart sought Hamilton out to personally congratulate him—a fitting tribute from one champion to another.

In the cooldown room, the tension between Hamilton and Rosberg was impossible to ignore. When Hamilton casually tossed a second-place cap towards his teammate, Rosberg, still simmering from his defeat, threw it straight back. The moment, caught on camera, laid bare the frostiness in their relationship.

In a rare moment during an interview in the paddock, Hamilton turned away from the interviewer and looked straight into the camera, speaking directly to his parents, his brother, and his management. He told them he hoped he had made them proud and thanked them for their unwavering support. Midway through, Helen Stewart—wife of Sir Jackie Stewart and his lifelong partner—interrupted the interview, leaning over the barriers to embrace Hamilton with a heartfelt hug and kiss. The moment was spontaneous and touching, leaving even the interviewer momentarily speechless before continuing.

Mercedes' non-executive chairman, Niki Lauda, reflected on the first-corner incident, acknowledging Rosberg's frustration but making it clear that the German had been in control of the race before making a costly mistake. Team Principal Toto Wolff also weighed in on the intra-team rivalry, reinforcing that while competition was encouraged, it had to remain within the boundaries of the team's objectives.

## Hamilton's Triumph, Rosberg's Reckoning

The 2015 United States Grand Prix not only secured Hamilton's Championship but also delivered another back-to-back Constructors' title for Mercedes.

While Mercedes remained dominant, Ferrari made significant strides in 2015. Sebastian Vettel's arrival injected fresh energy into the team, with three victories reigniting hope among Ferrari fans after a winless 2014. Ferrari's leadership acknowledged the shift in momentum, admitting they were still chasing Mercedes but were steadily closing the gap.

Hamilton, however, remained the benchmark. By season's end, he had taken 10 wins and amassed 381 points, while Rosberg secured six victories and finished with 322. Mercedes' supremacy was undeniable—703 points in the Constructors' Championship, towering over Ferrari's 428.

Vettel, having taken Alonso's seat at Ferrari, finished third in the standings on 278 points. Alonso, now back at McLaren, endured a torrid season, finishing 17th with just 11 points. McLaren was still grappling with its renewed partnership with Honda, but for Alonso, it was another case of moving to the right team at the wrong time.

Hamilton's third World Championship placed him among the sport's elite, and the scale of his achievement was widely recognised. As the curtain fell on the 2015 season, he stood at the pinnacle of his career, but his rivalry with Rosberg was far from settled. The seeds of future battles had been firmly planted, and within Mercedes, the fight for supremacy was only just beginning. Rosberg, bruised but unbowed, went away to reassess what needed to be done.

# The Battle Reaches Fever Pitch

The 2016 Formula One season was another of the greats, with a bitter contest between Lewis Hamilton and Nico Rosberg in their dominant Mercedes. It was a battle that would define their careers. Some new elements added complexity and intrigue to the Formula One world, from the debut of Haas to the determined rise of Max Verstappen and the emergence of new tracks like Baku in Azerbaijan.

The 2016 season welcomed a new team to the Formula One grid: Haas F1 Team. Owned by American businessman Gene Haas, the team entered the sport with ambitions to challenge the midfield using a unique partnership with Ferrari. This arrangement allowed Haas to use Ferrari's power units and other components, setting them apart from typical new entrants. Hamilton expressed enthusiasm about the addition of an American team to the grid and acknowledged that Haas's presence was beneficial for the sport, bringing a fresh dynamic and broadening Formula One's appeal, particularly in the United States. Romain Grosjean and Esteban Gutiérrez became the driver line-up for Haas.

Renault re-entered Formula One as a full constructor after acquiring the Lotus F1 Team, marking their return after a four-year absence. To lead this renewed effort, Renault appointed Frédéric Vasseur as the Team Principal. Vasseur, well known in racing circles and respected by many, brought extensive experience from his successful tenure in junior categories, including leading ART Grand Prix to multiple Championships. His appointment was part of Renault's strategy to rebuild and strengthen their Formula One team, aiming to return to competitive form in the Championship. However, Vasseur's contract would be short-lived, and he left his role within the year after just one season with the team.

Vasseur's exit was attributed to differing views in the team's management, particularly with Cyril Abiteboul, Renault's managing director. Vasseur admitted there were too many differing visions in the team's leadership and acknowledged that success in Formula One required clear direction from a single figure. It was a diplomatic perspective from Vasseur, a person who many felt was affable and easy to get along with. Conversely, Abiteboul was known for his direct and assertive management style, and his approach had led to other public disputes and internal tensions. There were several notable instances involving public disagreements with Red Bull Racing's team principal, Christian Horner, over the early Renault engine performance and reliability issues when Renault supplied engines to Red Bull. Horner criticised Renault's power units, to which Abiteboul responded in kind with some belligerence. Nico Hulkenberg, considered quite diplomatic in Formula One, and at one point a Renault driver, would later publicly criticise Abiteboul for his strategic decision-making.

There were also some minor changes to tyres and regulations. Pirelli introduced a fifth dry-weather compound, the ultrasoft tyre, marked with purple sidewalls, and teams had greater flexibility in tyre selection, choosing three of the five compounds for each race weekend. The FIA imposed stricter limits on radio communications between teams and drivers during races, to place more emphasis on driver skill.

After the spat between Horner and Abiteboul, where Red Bull had publicly criticised the Renault engine for poor performance and reliability, the two parties agreed to continue their partnership under different terms for 2016. Red Bull continued to use Renault power units but rebranded them as "TAG Heuer" engines for the 2016 season. The rebranding was part of a sponsorship deal with the Swiss luxury watch manufacturer TAG Heuer, which became the official naming sponsor of Red Bull's engines.

Renault focused on improving its power unit for 2016, introducing upgrades during the season, and Red Bull's performance improved significantly compared to 2015. This arrangement allowed Red Bull to maintain competitive performance while managing the optics of their relationship with Renault, whose branding was absent from Red Bull's car.

Daniil Kvyat started the season with Red Bull but was replaced by Max Verstappen after just four races.

**Season Openers**

The 2016 Formula One season commenced with a series of races that emphasised Mercedes' dominance. The season opener in Australia at Melbourne's Albert Park on 20 March saw the start of another year-long battle between Hamilton and Rosberg. Hamilton qualified on pole with a lap time of 1:23.837, with Rosberg alongside, just over two-tenths down in second. Vettel qualified third but was half a second adrift—light years in Formula One. Behind Vettel was Räikkönen in the sister Ferrari. The surprise of the qualifying session was a young Max Verstappen in the Toro Rosso Ferrari, who qualified in fifth place, with his teammate Carlos Sainz in seventh. Daniel Ricciardo qualified in eighth place in the Red Bull Racing TAG Heuer, but Ricciardo's teammate Daniil Kvyat was languishing down in 18th after a poor qualifying. On a circuit where good power and straight-line speed were important, the Red Bulls suffered.

The lights went out, and Vettel got a lightning start in his scarlet Ferrari. Rosberg had a poor start and immediately went defensive to try to cover off Räikkönen. Hamilton, whose initial start was good, got significant wheelspin in the second phase of his getaway, and Vettel shot through the gap between the two Mercedes. Rosberg seemed surprised to see Vettel alongside and tried to go defensive, staying on the shallower, dirtier inside line. As the cars approached the 100-metre braking marker board, Vettel had squeezed Rosberg up against the white line but had left just enough room. The front three cars all hit their brakes at the same time at well over 150 mph, and Rosberg was caught out by a significant bump—an area of the track rarely used in racing conditions—and he locked his front wheels heavily. Unable to slow the car down enough, Rosberg ran on at the apex, pushing Hamilton wide and just off the circuit. As Vettel shot off into the lead, closely followed by Rosberg, Hamilton tried to regain the track and, by Turn 5, was down in sixth position.

By Lap 14, Rosberg, having pitted a lap earlier for the yellow medium tyres, charged down the start-finish straight to find Vettel emerging from the pits on fresh red soft tyres. A fierce battle ensued as the two jostled for position. Just three laps later, on Lap 17, the race took a dramatic turn with a horrifying accident involving Fernando Alonso in his McLaren and Esteban Gutiérrez in the Haas. Alonso, travelling at 186 mph, clipped the rear of Gutiérrez's car, sending the McLaren hurtling into the barriers.

The remains of the McLaren came to rest in a crumpled heap, and Alonso slowly climbed out, clearly shaken. Standing gingerly next to the wreckage, he bent forward, hands on his knees, appearing winded but uninjured. The severity of the crash prompted an immediate Safety Car deployment, followed by a red flag to suspend the race while the debris was cleared. Alonso was evaluated at the medical centre and found to have rib fractures and a small pneumothorax (collapsed lung). He was advised to rest and have follow-up scans to monitor his recovery. Afterwards Alonso said how grateful he was for the safety measures in modern Formula One, acknowledging that they may have saved his life.

As the remaining cars returned to the grid, the drivers stepped out, either to chat with their engineers or take a quick break. Hamilton, even with the most dominant car on the track, took the opportunity to wander over to Daniel Ricciardo's Red Bull. Strolling around the back of the car, he closely examined its rear aero package, his curiosity to learn every possible detail from the competition evident.

The race restarted on Lap 19. The running order was largely unchanged, with Vettel in the lead, Rosberg second, and

Räikkönen third. Hamilton was in seventh, still behind the Red Bull and both Toro Rossos. On Lap 23, Räikkönen radioed the pits to say something had gone wrong on the car. He pulled into his pit box, and smoke could be seen coming from the left-hand bank of cylinders, out of his left exhaust. As he pulled up to a stop, flames spouted out of his air intake above his head and licked the top of his helmet. One of the fire marshals was immediately on hand and gave the air intake a quick spurt of his extinguisher, dousing the flames.

Hamilton battled his way through the midfield, and on Lap 42, he passed the local favourite, Ricciardo, to take second place, though Rosberg was far ahead in the lead. Vettel was eager to reclaim second from Hamilton, but on Lap 55, he locked his wheels while attempting a move and ran wide onto the grass, losing time. Hamilton pulled away, securing second place. Vettel had to settle for third on the podium, but it was another strong race for the Scuderia.

HAAS made an impressive debut at the Australian Grand Prix, with Romain Grosjean finishing sixth, a remarkable achievement for a new team. Pundits were surprised and praised the team's performance, saying that scoring points in a debut race was almost unheard of. Sainz in the Toro Rosso beat his teammate Verstappen, the cars finishing ninth and tenth respectively.

In the aftermath of Alonso's dramatic crash, former Formula One driver and commentator Johnny Herbert publicly suggested that Alonso should consider retiring from the sport. He argued that the Spaniard's performance had declined and that his absence from the Bahrain Grand Prix, due to injuries sustained in the crash, suggested a lack of motivation. Herbert said he did not believe Alonso should return to racing, questioning whether the two-time World Champion was still at his best, and suggested that McLaren had not seen the expected dominance from Alonso and Jenson Button had outperformed him. These were strong views, and people wondered what Alonso would think. Well, they would soon know.

At the Bahrain International Circuit on 3 April, Rosberg continued his winning streak, leading from start to finish. Räikkönen secured second for Ferrari, while Hamilton, after a collision at the first corner, recovered to claim third place. Ricciardo finished fourth for Red Bull, while Grosjean achieved a commendable fifth place for Haas. Verstappen finished sixth in the Toro Rosso, ahead of Kvyat in the works Red Bull. Already, mutterings were circulating in the paddock about whether Kvyat would retain his seat, given the pace of Verstappen and Sainz in the junior team.

The race, however, was memorable not just for the on-track action but for the events leading up to it involving Alonso, who was still smarting from Herbert's comments in Australia about his retirement. Alonso, present at the Bahrain circuit but sidelined for the weekend, had been declared 'unfit' to race due to the injuries he sustained in his Australia accident. He had allegedly requested permission to return to the car during Free Practice 2 but was denied by the FIA. Meanwhile, Herbert, once again commentating for Sky, reiterated his belief that Alonso's absence reflected a lack of motivation.

Herbert perhaps spoke with more authority than most, having experienced a catastrophic accident in 1988 that left him with severe injuries to his lower extremities. The crash resulted in multiple fractures to his legs, ankles, and feet, posing a significant threat to his racing career. At one stage, amputation was considered. After multiple surgeries and months of intense physiotherapy, Herbert managed to avoid that outcome. However, his mobility was permanently affected, forcing him to adapt his driving style to accommodate his limitations. Despite these challenges, he went on to win Grand Prix races, proving his mettle. Having lived through the physical and mental toll of a near career-ending crash, Herbert had earned the right to express his views. Alonso, however, saw things differently.

In a tense moment at the Bahrain International Circuit, Alonso confronted Herbert following his latest comments. As Herbert was speaking live on camera, Alonso walked into view, shook his hand, and pointedly remarked that he would not be retiring, before adding that he was a two-time World Champion, whereas Herbert had ended up as a commentator because he was not. It was a sharp exchange that revealed Alonso's mindset following his 2015 accident.

Alonso later denied any intent, insisting he had not actively sought Herbert out, saying it was merely unfortunate timing that he arrived in the paddock while the filming was taking place. Some in the paddock sided with Alonso, while others backed Herbert. Regardless, the incident was another illustration of the intense pressure Formula One drivers faced—not just from themselves, their teams, and sponsors, but also from the public and pundits. The mental strain was relentless, and Alonso, like everyone else, was only human.

Two weeks later, Formula One arrived in China, where the Shanghai International Circuit witnessed Rosberg's third consecutive win. The race was chaotic in the opening laps, with multiple incidents as several cars collided. Hamilton's race had already been compromised by a power unit issue in qualifying, forcing him to start from the back of the grid. In the melee of the first lap, he clipped Felipe Massa's Williams as Massa took evasive action to avoid Räikkönen, who had been forced off at the first corner after being hit by his own teammate.

Hamilton would finish seventh. Red Bull's Kvyat secured third place, while Vettel and Räikkönen finished second and fifth, respectively. Both Räikkönen and Hamilton were helped by a Safety Car early in the race. It was early in the season, but already Rosberg was looking strong. This was also a strong race for Williams, with their powerful Mercedes engines helping them to fourth and fifth place.

At a very warm and sunny Russian Grand Prix in Sochi on 1 May, Rosberg dominated once again, achieving a grand slam by securing pole position, fastest lap, and leading every lap of the race. Hamilton started from tenth due to another power-related issue. At the first corner, Vettel was battling with Ricciardo and went down the inside. Kvyat, in the other Red Bull, despite being well behind Vettel, ran into the back of him, which pushed Vettel into Ricciardo. The incident caused several front runners to concertina outwards. Hamilton, on the outside of the circuit, found himself vulnerable to a collision, but his quick reactions and instinctive thinking saw him keep his foot down and power deep into the runoff area at near full racing speed.

Just one corner later, as the cars powered out of the fast left-hander, Vettel, nursing rear-end damage to his Ferrari from the earlier contact, was running slightly slower than those around him. Kvyat, seemingly undeterred by his mistake at Turn 1, struck again—this time slamming into the back of Vettel's car at high speed. The impact sent Vettel's Ferrari careening into the barriers, ending both his race and any chance of recovery.

Meanwhile, Rosberg controlled the race from the front, taking a commanding victory. Hamilton delivered an impressive comeback after early technical issues and the first-corner chaos to secure second place. Räikkönen produced another strong performance for Ferrari, rounding off the podium in third.

After the race, Vettel was not best pleased, accusing Kvyat of being a madman and coming at the back of his Ferrari 'like a torpedo'. Kvyat was unrepentant, saying he was just racing. His lack of acknowledgement for the mistake was another example of the contrast with Hamilton, who would reflect carefully if he felt he had made an error. However, it wasn't only Vettel that was unhappy; Christian Horner wasn't happy either.

Post-race analysis showed that there was no gap for Kvyat—he had simply run into the back of Vettel twice. Red Bull had seen enough, and their patience had run out. Before the next race in Spain, Kvyat was replaced by Verstappen. The decision to promote Verstappen generated significant discussion in the motorsport community. It was observed that, while the move might have appeared ruthless, it was a pragmatic decision for Red Bull, securing Verstappen for the team's long-term future. Red Bull Team Principal Christian Horner explained that Verstappen had proven to be an exceptional young talent, delivering impressive performances at Toro Rosso, and that the team was pleased to give him the opportunity to step up into the senior Red Bull seat.

Verstappen's promotion may have surprised many, but for some insiders in the paddock, it felt inevitable. Among them were those who had already recognised Verstappen's exceptional talent the previous year, noting his composure and confidence in the car. There was a strong belief that Verstappen would find himself in a Championship-winning team before the age of 20, with comparisons being drawn to past greats. Observers described him as a young driver with the maturity of a seasoned competitor, acknowledging that while he would inevitably make mistakes, his sheer speed and adaptability set him apart. The qualities that would soon make Verstappen one of Formula One's brightest stars had already been evident, long before his headline-making Red Bull promotion. It wouldn't take long for Verstappen to make an impact in the Red Bull.

Heading into the Spanish Grand Prix in the middle of May, Hamilton faced a daunting 43-point deficit to his teammate Rosberg. A combination of technical issues in two races and being forced off track in another had left Hamilton playing catch-up in the Championship battle. To keep his title defence alive, he needed to make a decisive statement in Barcelona—and the weekend promised to deliver plenty of drama for racing fans.

## Collision Course: Hamilton and Rosberg's Rivalry Explodes in Spain

Qualifying at the Circuit de Barcelona-Catalunya on 14 May saw Hamilton rise to the occasion, securing pole position with a commanding lap nearly three-tenths quicker than Rosberg. Ricciardo took third in his Red Bull, while his new teammate Verstappen, making his debut for the team, impressed by qualifying fourth—just four-tenths shy of Ricciardo. Behind them, the two Ferraris of Räikkönen and Vettel locked out the third row in fifth and sixth, setting the stage for a great battle on race day.

15 May dawned warm in Spain. The hours ticked by until the early afternoon, and the cars gathered on the grid. As the lights went out, Rosberg made an excellent start off the line. Hamilton, also quick off the mark, immediately moved to defend his position as they charged down the hill into Turn 1. Sweeping across the track towards the pit exit, Hamilton aimed to block Rosberg from making a move up the inside. Rosberg, however, capitalised on a strong slipstream and, as they approached the braking zone, made an aggressive move to the left, pulling alongside Hamilton on the outside. With limited options and the risk of a collision looming, Hamilton was forced to brake slightly earlier than usual. Rosberg seized the opportunity, sweeping around the outside into the lead and cleanly navigating Turn 2 as the race briefly swung in his favour.

As both Mercedes cars powered through the sweeping right-hander of Turn 3 at over 160 mph, Rosberg took a tighter, shallower line, while Hamilton used the full width of the track to maximise his exit speed. Hamilton's superior traction allowed him to close right up to Rosberg's rear as they entered the straight, setting up a potential overtake. Sensing he was vulnerable after his poor exit, Rosberg moved to the right to defend. Hamilton had already committed to a move down the inside, having made the same adjustment a fraction of a second earlier. Before either car had reached the midpoint of the straight, Rosberg continued edging right, forcing Hamilton onto the grass at around 160 mph. Rosberg's manoeuvre was so aggressive that his own right-side tyres grazed the white line at the track's edge.

For Hamilton, there was no runoff area—just grass. Once on the grass, his car became uncontrollable, bouncing violently on the uneven surface. With the rear stepping out, his Mercedes began to slide sideways at an alarming speed. Rosberg, meanwhile, had started to brake for the Turn 4 hairpin, but Hamilton's car, now almost perpendicular to the track and still travelling at over 100 mph, was beyond saving. Without grip or the ability to brake effectively, Hamilton was a passenger, his car sliding precariously toward disaster.

A split second later, as Rosberg braked for Turn 4, Hamilton's Mercedes, dragging clumps of grass and dried mud onto the track, collided with the rear of Rosberg's car. The impact was severe, tearing off Hamilton's front-right wheel and sending debris flying. Rosberg's car was also heavily damaged, and both Mercedes were out of the race.

Before Hamilton's car had even come to a stop in the gravel trap, he raised his hands to his helmet in disbelief. Commentators captured the moment, with the assessment that both drivers shared responsibility for the collision. As marshals gathered around Hamilton's car, he vented his frustration by hurling his steering wheel towards the barrier. Meanwhile, the race carried on, with the Mercedes collision marking a dramatic turning point that reshaped the Grand Prix.

Verstappen won the race, becoming the youngest-ever winner of a Formula One race. The Red Bull team was jubilant. Christian Horner was full of praise for Verstappen's victory, commending his performance on his debut.

While Red Bull and Verstappen celebrated a historic debut victory, Mercedes was left facing the media, and tensions were running high. Niki Lauda, Mercedes' non-executive chairman, was blunt in his assessment, calling the incident unacceptable and emphasising that the team had lost a race they could have won. Toto Wolff also acknowledged the seriousness of the situation, stating that it was a disaster for the team and that discussions would take place once emotions had settled.

Some of the drivers who were immediately behind the Mercedes collision were asked for their views. Vettel, himself no stranger to inter-team battles and with a ringside seat for the incident, took a measured approach, pointing out that while it was unfortunate to see teammates collide, such things could happen in hard racing. Ricciardo, who had been right behind in his Red Bull, commented on how rare it was to see teammates taking each other out, particularly on the first lap, adding that it reflected just how competitive the situation had become.

The severity of the incident prompted post-race analysis, with commentators debating where the blame lay. The conclusion was that, while it was a racing incident, it was one that should never have happened. Both drivers would have to take responsibility for it. Damon Hill, who had experienced his share of clashes with Michael Schumacher in his career, was critical of the lack of caution, suggesting that both drivers had been too aggressive and that, particularly on the first lap, they should have considered the team's interests.

Both Hamilton and Rosberg were subdued after the race. Hamilton, typically animated, was notably reserved, indicating his disappointment. Rosberg maintained a calm exterior but was evidently concerned about the ramifications of the incident. Their body language suggested a mutual understanding of the gravity of the situation and a shared commitment to addressing it constructively within the team. The incident not only affected their individual standings but also intensified the scrutiny on team dynamics.

In the aftermath, it was revealed that discussions inside the Mercedes motorhome had been frank. There had been immediate debate over who was at fault, with one perspective being that Hamilton had been too aggressive in his move to the right, lost control on the grass, and ultimately collided with Rosberg. The counterargument was that Rosberg's defensive manoeuvre had left Hamilton with nowhere to go, escalating the incident.

It was acknowledged that opinions within the team differed, with Hamilton disagreeing with some assessments that he had been primarily responsible. The key takeaway, however, was that such incidents could not be allowed to happen again. Following Spain, Mercedes put stricter rules in place, including potential penalties for the drivers if a similar situation arose, with even the threat of contract terminations being discussed as a deterrent. For now, there was an uneasy sense that matters had been settled, at least within the team. However, it would not be long before further tensions surfaced.

**Rain on the escarpment**

In late May, the iconic streets of Monte Carlo presented a wet and challenging race. Ricciardo secured pole position for Red Bull Racing. Rosberg qualified in second and Hamilton third. Ricciardo led the initial stages, but a botched pit stop, where his team was unprepared with the correct tyres, cost him the lead. Hamilton seized the advantage, managing his tyres expertly to leapfrog Rosberg and claim his first win of the season. Ricciardo finished second, visibly frustrated by the team's error. Sergio Pérez delivered a commendable performance, securing third place for Force India. Rosberg finished nearly a lap down in seventh. Where engine power was less of a factor, Alonso, in a return to form, finished a commendable fifth in his McLaren.

**Canada**

At Circuit Gilles Villeneuve in June, the two Mercedes teammates resumed battle. Vettel made another incredible getaway and led into Turn 1. Behind him, Rosberg tried to outbrake Hamilton around the outside, but as he ran out of room, both cars touched wheels gently, forcing Rosberg off the track and across the tarmac and grass runoff area. He rejoined well down the order but started working his way back up.

Midway through the race, Rosberg picked up a slow puncture and was forced to pit. Shortly after, while trying to overtake one of the Red Bulls, he lost control of the Mercedes under braking into the final chicane and slid sideways, then backwards across the runoff area before rejoining.

Hamilton, Vettel, and their respective teams engaged in a calculated battle. After Vettel took an early lead, Ferrari's two-stop strategy allowed Hamilton—on a one-stop plan—to overtake and secure victory. Valtteri Bottas, in his number 77 car, achieved a strong third-place finish for Williams, showing both the power of the Mercedes engine and his own ability. It was a performance that did not go unnoticed by Toto Wolff and Niki Lauda.

On the cooldown lap, Hamilton's joy was evident as he referenced one of his greatest sporting heroes, Muhammad Ali, playfully laughing over the radio as he delivered a tribute. It was his 44th career win, and in post-race interviews, he acknowledged the challenge posed by Vettel.

Reflecting on the triumph, Hamilton spoke candidly about the emotional toll of the season so far. He admitted that overcoming setbacks was mentally draining and that staying motivated when things weren't going well was a constant challenge. He recalled words of encouragement from his father, instilled in him from childhood, about never giving up and pushing forward no matter how tough things got. To never give up. It was the thing his father had told him when he was seven years old in the boxing ring, taking punches from an opponent.

The message was simple—never give up, keep pushing, and eventually, success would come. Hamilton reflected that the day's result had once again proved his father right, reinforcing the motto he had carried with him throughout his career.

It was a clear insight into the mental struggles Hamilton faced and how, when times got tough, he leaned on his support network. It also provided an early glimpse into something that would become more public in later years—his battle with mental health.

### European Grand Prix - Baku

A week later, at the inaugural European Grand Prix at Baku City Circuit in Azerbaijan, Rosberg dominated from start to finish, extending his Championship lead to 141 points. Vettel secured second place, while Pérez continued his impressive form with a third-place finish.

Hamilton faced technical issues during qualifying, starting tenth, and finished fifth. Rosberg expressed satisfaction with his performance, describing it as a weekend where everything had gone to plan. As they left Baku, Hamilton was now 24 points adrift of his teammate.

### Red Bull Ring – Rosberg punches below the belt

The Red Bull Ring in Austria hosted a thrilling race in early July. Hamilton qualified on pole by over half a second from Rosberg, who was second. However, due to a technical issue, Rosberg dropped to sixth for the start. Nico Hülkenberg had an impressive qualifying session, achieving third, but with Rosberg's penalty, he started from the front row. Jenson Button in the McLaren also qualified well and started third.

As the lights went out, Hamilton made a clean getaway, holding the lead. Button followed suit and slotted into second, with both British drivers pulling clear of the pack as they exited Turn 1. Behind them, Räikkönen moved into third, using the superior speed of his Ferrari to overtake Button down the hill at Turn 3 on Lap 7. Rosberg pitted early on Lap 11 to leap ahead of the Ferraris. Hamilton stopped on Lap 22 but lost time due to a sticking left-rear wheel, allowing Rosberg to get ahead as Hamilton rejoined the track.

On Lap 27, Vettel suffered a high-speed puncture on the start-finish straight, his tyre exploding and sending him bouncing lightly off the inside barriers before coming to rest just before Turn 1. The Safety Car was deployed, neutralising the race until Lap 37, when racing resumed with Rosberg leading Hamilton.

By the final lap, Lap 71, Hamilton had closed to within a second of Rosberg. His Mercedes looked visibly quicker as they approached Turn 1 for the last time. Rosberg, under pressure, took too much inside kerb and was compromised slightly on exit. Hamilton, carrying significantly more speed, surged through the corner and gained momentum down the long straight towards Turn 2. Sensing the threat, Rosberg, in a repeat of Spain, moved to the inside to defend. Hamilton feinted left and committed to the outside as they approached the tight 130-degree right-hander at Turn 3. Both drivers braked heavily from over 190 mph as they passed the 100-metre board.

As they decelerated past the 50-metre mark, Hamilton was completely over to the left of the track, inches from the white line, and was already half a car length ahead of Rosberg. But rather than committing to the corner, Rosberg delayed his turn-in, rolling off the brakes and drifting from the inside line towards the middle of the track. He made no attempt to take the apex, leaving Hamilton with nowhere to go.

Contact was inevitable. As Hamilton, running out of road, finally turned in, Rosberg's front wing clipped the side of his car. It was a move that bore similarities to past controversial moments in Formula One—reminiscent of clashes between Michael Schumacher and Damon Hill in 1994 and Jacques Villeneuve in 1997. However, just as had been observed when Schumacher collided with Villeneuve at Jerez, Rosberg had struck the wrong part of Hamilton's car, and the move backfired. Sparks flew from Rosberg's front wing as the contact sent fragments scattering across the track. Hamilton, with no choice but to run off the circuit, rejoined over the grass, momentarily dropping behind Rosberg. Inside the

Mercedes garage, emotions boiled over—Toto Wolff slammed his fist on the desk in frustration, while Lauda gave a subtle shake of his head.

Meanwhile, both Mercedes cars dropped down the hill towards Turn 4, with Rosberg in the lead. As they approached nearly 200 mph, the downforce on Rosberg's car reached its maximum load, and the left side of his front wing, weakened by the impact with Hamilton, suddenly failed, showering the circuit and the entire left side of his car in sparks. The right side of Rosberg's wing retained some strength, and as the strong side fought against the weaker, the contest ended—pieces of carbon fibre flew off into the air. Fearing that the remains of the wing might detach completely and lodge under the car, Rosberg slowed significantly, allowing Hamilton, along with some of the lapped backmarkers, to pass. A few corners later, Verstappen in the Red Bull and then Räikkönen in the Ferrari moved through into second and third, respectively. Rosberg limped across the finish line in fourth.

The internal inquiry began immediately. Hamilton's race engineer, Peter Bonnington, offered congratulations over the team radio in a backhanded manner, acknowledging the win but conceding it was not the race they had aimed for. Hamilton, however, was resolute, making it clear that he had been on the outside and had not caused the collision. Rosberg, interviewed after the race, claimed he had been struggling to slow the car. He maintained that being on the inside, he had the right to dictate the corner. His body language, however, told a different story—he looked tense, as though under pressure. His comments implied that he had driven into the side of Hamilton because he believed he had the right to do so. The idea that a driver having 'the line' justified not conceding in a corner would resurface in future clashes.

Hamilton, when questioned after the race, was composed. He insisted he had left plenty of room and had not attempted to squeeze Rosberg, pointing out that he had gone all the way to the white line. He acknowledged that perhaps Rosberg had the corner, but he had made a mistake and caused the contact. Hamilton appeared calm, refreshed, and content—a stark contrast to Rosberg's demeanour. He went on to say that if he was going to win the World Championship, he would have to "dig deep" and had done exactly that, giving everything he had in the race. He left with no regrets, knowing he had not left any stone unturned. Rosberg, in his own post-race interview, was very frustrated, describing himself as "massively disappointed."

Niki Lauda did not hold back regarding the clash. While he had been critical of Hamilton behind closed doors on previous occasions, this time, publicly, he placed the blame firmly on Rosberg, but also stated the team would need to review the incident as Rosberg had experienced some brake issues.

Team Principal Toto Wolff voiced his annoyance, describing the collision as 'brainless' and bemoaned his frustrations, saying he thought Rosberg and Hamilton had learned their lesson from Barcelona. He made it clear he was fed up with these clashes and admitted that after the race, he simply wanted to put his head in a bucket of cold water.

The Stewards investigated the collision and found Rosberg responsible. He was given a 10-second time penalty and a warning for causing the crash and for continuing with a damaged car. The verdict sparked wider debate in the paddock, with some agreeing with the decision while others felt it was a racing incident. Jacques Villeneuve, the former World Champion and now a pundit, described Rosberg's driving as dangerous.

**Albion**

The 2016 British Grand Prix was once again held at the Silverstone Circuit on 10 July. Renowned for its high-speed corners and rich motorsport heritage, the circuit hosted the race under unpredictable weather conditions. A downpour just before the start led to the race beginning behind the Safety Car, with drivers cautiously navigating a wet track that gradually dried as the laps unfolded. The conditions were treacherous—at one stage, Hamilton had to take to the grass partially when following the Safety Car due to aquaplaning.

Once the race got underway properly, Hamilton, starting from pole position, expertly managed the changing conditions, maintaining his lead throughout. The track remained tricky, and on Lap 6, Pascal Wehrlein in the Marussia was a passenger as his car aquaplaned off into the gravel.

Verstappen showed great wet-weather skill, executing a daring overtake on Rosberg around the outside of Becketts—an audacious manoeuvre that drew widespread acclaim. In the heat of battle, Rosberg complained over the radio that Verstappen was moving twice on the straight and under braking. Rosberg managed to pass Verstappen and would end the race crossing the line in second place. However, he received a 10-second penalty for a breach of the radio communication regulations. After experiencing a technical issue, he had been instructed by the team to avoid seventh gear—guidance deemed a violation of the rules. The penalty relegated him to third place and Verstappen was classified second.

Hamilton stamped his authority over both the circuit and the evolving weather, securing his third consecutive victory at Silverstone. The home crowd, a sea of Union Jacks, erupted in celebration as Hamilton crossed the finish line. In stark contrast to the previous race, Niki Lauda clasped Toto Wolff's hand with his hands, and both of them beamed in absolute delight as Hamilton took the win.

After the race, Hamilton conveyed his elation, saying he felt his personal momentum was recovering after the early season dramas. He spoke of his renewed energy, explaining that it was easy to arrive at a race weekend with the wrong mindset, but that he had come into Silverstone feeling fresh, powerful, and confident, delivering exactly what he had set out to do. He described it as his best week of the year so far. With

Hamilton's victory at Silverstone, he had now closed to just one point behind Rosberg in the standings. Pundits widely praised Verstappen's bold overtake on Rosberg, with some calling it one of the best overtakes seen in years. It was further proof that Verstappen was quickly establishing himself as a real talent in the sport.

**Land of the Magyars**

The Hungarian Grand Prix was held in July at the Hungaroring, a circuit characterised by its tight and twisty layout—a stark contrast to Silverstone's high-speed nature. Under clear skies and sweltering temperatures, the track's limited overtaking opportunities placed a premium on qualifying performance and race strategy.

Hamilton capitalised on a strong start, overtaking pole-sitter Rosberg into the first corner. Maintaining his lead throughout the race, he managed his tyres and pace effectively, securing his fifth victory at the Hungaroring—a record at the time. Rosberg finished second, unable to mount a significant challenge to Hamilton's lead. Ricciardo completed the podium for Red Bull Racing, delivering a consistent performance and highlighting the efficiency of Red Bull's aerodynamic package.

After the race Hamilton credited the team's strategy, preparation, and the efforts of those back at the factory, acknowledging their role in delivering a strong result. Analysts discussed the dominance of Hamilton's performance, noting that he always had pace in hand. Having trailed Rosberg since the start of the season, Hamilton left Hungary in the lead of the Championship.

**Germany**

Returning to Hockenheim after a year's absence, the German Grand Prix was held under sunny skies in late July, with enthusiastic local fans eager to support their home drivers. The circuit's mix of long straights and technical sections provided a comprehensive test for teams and drivers. Rosberg secured pole position, much to the delight of the German crowd. However, a poor start, with massive wheelspin, saw him drop to fourth by the first corner. Hamilton seized the opportunity, taking the lead and controlling the race from the front. His composed drive culminated in a dominant victory, extending his lead in the Championship standings.

Rosberg—desperate to regain ground in the title race—was more aggressive than usual, battling fiercely with Ricciardo and even taking to the grass on Lap 1 as Ricciardo defended vigorously. Twenty-eight laps later, Rosberg was engaged in a tense fight with Verstappen. Heading into a tight right-hander, Rosberg forced Verstappen off the track in a move that bore similarities to his clash with Hamilton in Austria. It was clear that Rosberg had made no attempt to turn into the corner. Over the radio, Verstappen, his voice devoid of emotion, stated "he pushed me off the track."

The Stewards reviewed the incident and issued Rosberg a five-second penalty. When informed, Rosberg's response was telling—he asked his engineer to explain to race control that he was at full lock and could not steer more. The irony was that his engineer had not specified what the penalty was for, yet Rosberg had instinctively admitted guilt. This kind of 'pleading by radio' from drivers and teams would become an increasing issue in the years to come, culminating in controversy at Abu Dhabi in 2021.

Hamilton expressed satisfaction with his performance in the post-race press conference. He was then asked about something that happened before the race, as he was seen to stare for a long time at the inside of Turn 1 before he climbed into his car. Hamilton explained that he had been touched by the performance of the German National anthem singer, saying how this had gripped him. He reflected on the challenge of staying composed in the moments before a race, describing how he focused on keeping cool and studying the racing line. He went on to express deep gratitude to his team, acknowledging the struggles and setbacks they had faced throughout the season and how their resilience had inspired him.

The interview provided insight into the intricate emotions that fuelled Hamilton's drive to win—his deep connection to music and the arts, his appreciation for his team's efforts, and the emotional intelligence that set him apart. Unlike Rosberg, whose approach often seemed more self-focused, Hamilton drew strength from a unique blend of influences both inside and outside of racing. His resilience, forged through childhood challenges, his father's wisdom, the love of his family, and his ability to absorb the smallest details and appreciate them, all combined to propel him to extraordinary heights. These qualities formed the foundation of his success.

Going into the mid-season break, Hamilton—who had trailed Rosberg for much of the early part of the year due to technical issues and clashes—was now 19 points ahead in the Championship standings.

In late August, fresh from the summer break, the Formula One circus returned to Belgium and the Circuit de Spa-Francorchamps, nestled in the Ardennes Forest. On race day, the sun shone brightly, providing ideal conditions for both the Mercedes drivers and the passionate fans lining the circuit.

Rosberg, starting from pole position, capitalised on his advantage, leading the race from start to finish. Hamilton faced further reliability issues with his Mercedes which affected his race. He had a daunting task ahead, starting from the back of the grid due to multiple engine component changes.

On Lap 8, Kevin Magnussen, driving for Renault, lost control at the top of Eau Rouge and crashed backwards into the barriers at very high speed. The impact was so severe that the head protection padding from his cockpit flew out onto the circuit. The Renault was destroyed and the red flag was immediately brought out. Magnussen climbed out of the wreckage unaided but was limping as a marshal helped him across the track. At the medical centre, he was diagnosed with an injury to his left ankle and was later sent to hospital to have a cut treated.

Frederic Vasseur, who was still at Renault, was asked about Magnussen's accident and whether he blamed Magnussen for it. Vasseur replied that he would never blame a driver for trying too hard and that he didn't want to talk about it. Whereas some team principals would be quick to criticise their drivers, what Vasseur said spoke greatly about his level of integrity and perhaps illustrated why Hamilton respected him so greatly.

Following the restart, Hamilton demonstrated remarkable skill and determination, carving his way through the field to secure a commendable third-place finish. Ricciardo delivered a solid performance for Red Bull Racing, finishing second.

After the race, Rosberg talked about his win, describing how much it meant to come first at such a legendary circuit. He discussed his challenges of getting the setup right over the weekend. Meanwhile, Hamilton, when asked about his impressive recovery drive, was quick to credit his team and made a note of the hard work of the Mercedes team at Brixworth who were building the engines as well as those who were fitting them.

Hamilton's drive from the back row to the podium was widely praised, with broadsheets calling it a remarkable performance that underlined his ability to fight through adversity.

**Tifosi**

On 4 September, the teams prepared for the Italian Grand Prix at Monza, the Temple of Speed, renowned for its long straights and the passionate Tifosi supporters. Under clear skies, the atmosphere was electric, with fans eager for a strong performance from Ferrari. Hamilton secured pole position but had a sluggish start, allowing Rosberg to seize the lead. Rosberg maintained his advantage throughout the race, securing victory. Hamilton recovered to finish second, while Vettel thrilled the home crowd by taking third place.

Reflecting on his win, Rosberg acknowledged that the start had been the decisive factor, describing it as the key to his victory. Meanwhile, Vettel, clearly elated at being on the podium in a Ferrari in Italy, addressed the Tifosi with a passionate speech in Italian, declaring that Ferrari had the best fans in the world and thanking them for their support.

As the teams departed Monza, Rosberg was on 248 points, just two behind Hamilton on 250—both Mercedes drivers far ahead of third-placed Ricciardo, who was on 161 points.

Damon Hill was asked for his perspective on the Championship battle, as many believed that without reliability issues and collisions, Hamilton would have comfortably beaten Rosberg. Hill, however, emphasised that if Rosberg won the title, it would be well deserved. He noted that since the disappointment of losing in Austin the previous year, Rosberg had shown a transformation, winning all the remaining races of 2015 and delivering a strong campaign in 2016. Some of his drives had been described as impeccable. Hill's view was consistent with his earlier prediction in February that Rosberg would be a serious contender.

**Sepang – More Reliability Woes for Hamilton**

The Sepang International Circuit in Malaysia is known for its unpredictable weather, and this race was no exception. Under sweltering conditions, the race took a dramatic turn when Hamilton, leading comfortably, suffered a catastrophic engine failure, forcing him to retire. As flames licked the back of his stricken Mercedes, Hamilton's frustration was palpable, exclaiming in disbelief as he coasted to a stop.

This incident handed the lead to Red Bull Racing's Ricciardo, who went on to win, with teammate Verstappen finishing second, marking a memorable one-two finish for the team. Rosberg, despite being involved in a first-lap collision, recovered to finish third. An emotional Ricciardo dedicated the win to the late Jules Bianchi, making a heartfelt tribute to Bianchi and his family in his post-race interview.

Hamilton described the moment as surreal, admitting that it was difficult to remain positive. He acknowledged that of all the Mercedes-powered cars on the grid, his had been the only one to suffer repeated failures, something he found hard to accept.

Speaking later, he reflected on how odd it was for a brand-new engine to fail, pointing out that out of all the Mercedes engines in use that season, only his had encountered such issues. Pundits estimated that the five major failures Hamilton had suffered—at China, Russia, the European Grand Prix, Singapore, and now Malaysia—had cost him around 40 points in total. He now trailed Rosberg by 28 points.

**Suzuka**

The Suzuka Circuit, with its figure-eight layout and passionate fans, provided a picturesque setting under clear skies. Rosberg secured pole position and converted it into a dominant victory, extending his lead in the Championship. Hamilton, after a poor start that saw him drop to eighth, fought back to finish third, with Verstappen taking second—another strong result for the Dutchman.

Mercedes, once again head and shoulders above the competition, secured their third consecutive Constructors' Championship. Rosberg was thrilled, describing it as an incredible weekend, with everything going to plan from the outset. He pondered how special it was to win at such a legendary circuit and acknowledged the efforts of the entire team in securing the title. When asked about the performance, Hamilton was quick to shift focus to the team, expressing pride in being part of Mercedes and gratitude to those working behind the scenes at the factory. He emphasised that their collective efforts had made the success possible.

With only four races remaining, Rosberg was firmly in control of the Championship, sitting on 313 points to Hamilton's 280. However, Hamilton was a three-time World Champion for a reason—he never gave up. The teams packed up in Japan and made their way across the northern hemisphere to America.

**Texas**

On 23 October, the United States Grand Prix at the Circuit of the Americas in Austin, Texas, provided a vibrant atmosphere and good weather. The grandstands were busy. Hamilton, having taken some time in the United States to recharge, appeared reinvigorated, carrying an air of laser focus. Starting from pole position, he delivered a commanding performance, leading the race from start to finish. Rosberg, knowing he only needed to minimise his losses, played it safe and secured second place, while Red Bull Racing's Ricciardo completed the podium in third.

This victory marked a significant milestone in Hamilton's career—his fiftieth Grand Prix win. Only Alain Prost and Michael Schumacher had previously achieved this feat. Hamilton, when asked about the achievement, admitted he had completely forgotten that it was his fiftieth win. He reflected on how long the journey had been, acknowledging the ups and downs, the talented individuals he had worked with, and the unwavering support of his family, without whom he said he would not be where he was today.

It was yet another reminder of Hamilton's appreciation for both his team and those closest to him. With his victory, the Championship gap narrowed, intensifying the title race. Asked post-race whether he would take the fight to Rosberg in the remaining rounds, Hamilton's response was simple and direct—he would be going for it.

**Rare Air**

The Autódromo Hermanos Rodríguez presented unique challenges for teams and drivers, largely due to its location at an altitude of over 2,200 metres (7,200 feet) above sea level.

The thin air significantly impacted car performance, with reduced air density affecting engine power and downforce. Teams were forced to make extensive adjustments to optimise performance, as aerodynamic efficiency decreased while cooling systems faced increased strain. For drivers, the high-altitude environment demanded peak physical fitness, as lower oxygen levels added an extra layer of difficulty to an already intense race.

The circuit itself, with its long straights and a mix of high-speed and technical corners, tested both precision and outright speed. One of its most distinctive features was the Foro Sol stadium section, originally a baseball stadium, which transformed into an arena packed with tens of thousands of passionate fans. The steep grandstands amplified the roar of the crowd, creating an all-enveloping atmosphere that drivers described as surreal.

Unlike most circuits, where the podium ceremony takes place in a secluded area, Mexico's top three finishers parked in front of Foro Sol and celebrate on a raised platform in the heart of the fans, making it one of the most immersive podium experiences on the calendar. Heading into the weekend, anticipation was high. Hamilton, coming off his crucial win in Austin, was determined to maintain momentum, while Rosberg aimed for a strong result to edge closer to his first World Championship. The Mexican Grand Prix, with its vibrant atmosphere and challenging conditions, set the stage for another key moment in the 2016 season.

Hamilton continued his strong form, securing pole position and converting it into a race win, despite a dramatic moment into Turn 1 when he locked up his wheels and ran wide over the grass. Behind him, Rosberg clashed with Verstappen in the first corner as the Red Bull ran deep and made wheel-to-wheel contact with the Mercedes. Fortunately, there was no damage, and Rosberg went on to finish second, maintaining his lead in the championship by 19 points.

For Verstappen, however, the drama was far from over. In the closing laps, Vettel was chasing him in the battle for third. On Lap 68, Verstappen locked up under braking and cut across the grass at Turn 1, rejoining the track ahead of Vettel with a slightly bigger gap than before he had gone off. Aware of the potential controversy, Verstappen checked his mirrors and, recognising he had gained some distance, backed off momentarily to allow Vettel to close in, before resuming full speed. His engineer advised him to relinquish the position, but Verstappen ignored the instruction and instead backed Vettel into the pursuing Ricciardo. Vettel was incandescent, saying over the radio, "He has to let me go, he has to let me go," indicating that Verstappen, by retaining an advantage off circuit, should hand him the position. Vettel's engineer acknowledged his transmission and told him to stay calm.

As Vettel defended against Ricciardo, he moved under braking, causing Ricciardo to lock up and resulting in slight contact. After the race, Verstappen was handed a five-second penalty for leaving the track and gaining an advantage, dropping him to fifth. However, as Verstappen had not significantly gained time, the penalty was met with some debate. Vettel, initially classified fourth, was promoted to third—but only briefly. He was later penalised ten seconds for moving under braking, demoting him to fifth and elevating Ricciardo to the podium. It was a busy day for the stewards.

After the celebrations, Hamilton was asked about equalling Alain Prost's 51 career victories and Mercedes securing 17 wins in one season. His moved the focus away from himself and made it all about the team, discussing it was them that made everything possible. Later, when asked about his commanding victory, Hamilton showed his characteristic humour, joking that he had led the race "from grass to finish."

Verstappen was later asked about his five-second penalty, and he was perplexed, saying that when Hamilton and Rosberg had both gone off the track on Lap 1 at Turn 1 and retained their positions, that did not result in a penalty.

## Interlagos

On the weekend of 11–13 November, Formula One moved to Brazil and Interlagos, a circuit renowned for its passionate fans and unpredictable weather. True to form, the race was rain-soaked, creating treacherous conditions that led to multiple incidents and Safety Car periods. Hamilton showcased his wet-weather mastery, leading every lap to secure victory. Rosberg finished second, ensuring that the Championship fight would go down to the final race. Red Bull's Verstappen delivered a standout performance, recovering from a late-race spin to finish third. His remarkable overtaking skills in the wet captured the attention of fans, who voted him Driver of the Day.

Hamilton had always enjoyed a close relationship with the Brazilian fans, given his deep admiration for Ayrton Senna. When asked about his focus for the upcoming title decider, he remained in the moment, reflecting on how special it was to win in Brazil, recalling childhood memories of watching Senna race. As they left Brazil, Rosberg led on 367 points, and Hamilton was second on 355. Secure in third, but a long way back, was Ricciardo on 246 points.

## Abu Dhabi

The Yas Marina Circuit in Abu Dhabi, with its twilight setting, provided a dramatic backdrop for the season finale in late November. Among the many high-profile guests in attendance was Roger Federer, one of the greatest tennis players of all time, there to witness the decisive battle.

Hamilton, needing a win and for Rosberg to finish outside the top three to clinch the title, adopted a strategic approach. He led the race but deliberately slowed the pace to back Rosberg into the chasing pack. Despite the tactic, Rosberg held his nerve, finishing second behind Hamilton and securing his first World Championship. Vettel completed the podium in third.

Hamilton was interviewed after he climbed out of the car, asking him about his emotions. He simply said he had done everything he could in the last four races and that was all he could ask of himself. He spoke about celebrating with the team, accepting that while things had not gone his way, he was still grateful for both the successes and the challenges faced throughout the season. He pointed out that Rosberg had enjoyed a very clean year without major issues, which had ultimately decided the title. He congratulated Rosberg and looked ahead to the prospect of fighting him again the following season.

Rosberg, meanwhile, was thrilled but visibly drained. He described the race as unbelievably tense, admitting that being backed up into the Red Bulls by Hamilton had been extremely stressful, and that one small mistake could have cost him the Championship. In a later interview, Rosberg's exhaustion became more apparent, and he was asked about his mindset before the race. Rosberg, looking almost emotional, admitted that the pressure had been immense, unlike anything he had ever experienced before. He described the race weekend as mentally draining, revealing that his first overwhelming emotion after crossing the line was sheer relief, and that he had been in tears on his in-lap.

At the end of a breathtaking season, Rosberg won the title with 385 points, just five ahead of Hamilton on 380. But for his technical issues, Hamilton would likely have secured his fourth title, but as Ron Dennis, his old mentor, used to say: To finish first, first you have to finish. Ricciardo secured third in the Championship. Mercedes' dominance was unquestionable with Hamilton having won 10 races, Rosberg nine, and Red Bull claimed two victories, one for Ricciardo and one for Verstappen.

Amidst the Championship battle, another poignant moment unfolded. Jenson Button's Formula One career came to an end on Lap 12 when his McLaren suffered a suspension failure. Limping back to the pits in a shower of sparks and smoke, Button climbed out of a Formula One car for the final time.

Despite the disappointment of retiring from his last race, he spoke about the gratitude of his career, describing how he had arrived in Formula One with dreams and was leaving with memories. Button also took the opportunity to thank those who had supported him throughout his journey, making special mention of his late father, expressing his hope that he was looking down with pride.

It was a poignant farewell for the 2009 World Champion, who departed Formula One as not just one of its most respected drivers but also a beloved figure among fans. Tributes poured in, celebrating Jenson Button's immense contributions to the sport. Button's retirement marked the conclusion of an extraordinary 17-year career, during which he competed in 306 Grand Prix races, claimed 15 victories, secured eight pole positions, and stood on the podium 50 times. Most notably, he captured the 2009 World Championship with Brawn GP in a remarkable season. His journey from a promising young talent to a seasoned Champion left a lasting legacy, inspiring future drivers and cementing his place in Formula One history.

As the sun set on the dramatic conclusion of the season and the paddock bid farewell to Jenson Button, everything seemed right in the world. Yet, Formula One was on the verge of being rocked by an announcement no one had anticipated

**The Final Twist**

On 2 December 2016, just five days after securing his maiden Formula One World Championship, Rosberg sent shockwaves through the motorsport world by announcing his immediate retirement. The revelation came during the FIA Prize Giving Ceremony in Vienna, where Rosberg was poised to receive his Championship trophy. His decision marked one of the most unexpected twists in Formula One history, capping a career that had culminated in his hard-fought triumph over Hamilton.

The timing and nature of the announcement left fans and the paddock in stunned disbelief, adding an extraordinary final chapter to the 2016 season's legacy. In his statement, Rosberg explained that he had fulfilled his dream and the 'one thing' he wanted in his 25 years of racing was to become the Formula One World Champion, and that now he had made it he felt it was the right moment to step away. He reflected on the sacrifices and hard work that had led him to this point, saying that his dream had now been fulfilled.

Rosberg's emotional state during his interviews in Abu Dhabi suddenly made sense when he revealed what had really been going through his mind during that weekend. He admitted that on the morning of the race, he knew it could be his last, and that realisation allowed him to enjoy every moment of the experience. After the most intense 55 laps of his life, he made his decision the following day. The first people he told were his wife, Vivian, and his manager, followed by Mercedes-Benz Head of Motorsport, Toto Wolff. Wolff praised Rosberg's decision, recognising the courage it took to retire at the peak of his career. He described Rosberg's choice as unprecedented and acknowledged the significant legacy he was leaving behind.

Former Formula One driver Allan McNish proffered his view on the challenges facing drivers and why Rosberg may have felt the time was right to step away. He highlighted the relentless demands of the sport—the constant travel, physical conditioning, and the strain on family life. Rosberg, who had married a couple of years earlier and recently become a father, had perhaps reached a point where he questioned what he wanted for his future.

For Hamilton, Rosberg's retirement marked the end of an intense rivalry. When asked about his teammate's decision, Hamilton responded diplomatically, acknowledging that while the sport would miss Rosberg, he wished him well. He admitted that while many might have been surprised, he was not, given their long history. Hamilton reflected on the fact that Rosberg had won the title after 18 years of racing and understood why he had chosen to walk away, citing family priorities and the all-consuming nature of Formula One. When asked whether he would miss the rivalry, Hamilton admitted that he would.

Rosberg openly acknowledged the mental toll of competing at the highest level. To gain a competitive edge over Hamilton, he had engaged in extensive mental training, including multiple sessions with a sports psychologist each week. He revealed that the psychological strain extended far beyond the racetrack, affecting his personal life and relationships. He described how Formula One impacted not just the driver but their entire family, with both the suffering and the joy carrying over into everyday life, making it an all-encompassing experience.

Hamilton's ten victories to Rosberg's nine demonstrated just how close the Championship had been. Many believed that, without his reliability issues, Hamilton would have claimed the title. Their rivalry had left an indelible mark on the sport, and the 2016 season would be remembered as one of the most dramatic and emotionally charged in Formula One history, evoking memories of past great battles—Senna and Prost, Mansell and Piquet, Lauda and Hunt. As the year ended, speculation turned to who would take Rosberg's seat alongside Hamilton at Mercedes.

# The Challenge from Ferrari

The 2017 Formula One season ushered in another period of change. The sport saw the departure of its long-time supremo, Bernie Ecclestone, who had been at the helm for over four decades. Under his leadership, Formula One had grown into a global phenomenon, with Ecclestone playing a pivotal role in shaping the modern era of the sport.

Commentator Martin Brundle reflected on his impact, describing him as the ultimate *circus master*—a leader who ran the sport with absolute authority. He acknowledged that while Ecclestone could be feared in the paddock, many had benefited from being part of the empire he built.

McLaren Executive Director Zak Brown recognised Ecclestone's contribution, stating that Formula One would not have become the international powerhouse it was without his influence. 1996 World Champion Damon Hill also highlighted Ecclestone's immense impact, noting that every professional driver over the past 40 years had, to some extent, been shaped by his decisions.

Ecclestone, the son of a fisherman, was the ultimate wheeler-dealer. He disliked emails, preferring to conduct business with a handshake. He openly admitted that he preferred to operate as a dictator, believing that leadership required someone who could make swift, decisive calls. His approach to management was famously uncompromising—he once stated that democracy was not the way to run an organisation, whether a company or a sport, because it required a single, authoritative figure to make the key decisions.

Former driver Mark Webber summed up Ecclestone's style succinctly, describing him as a *brutal negotiator* who thrived on the hustle and loved making deals.

As Ecclestone stepped aside, a new era began under Liberty Media, with Ross Brawn returning to Formula One as the Managing Director of Motorsports. Known for his strategic brilliance, Brawn brought fresh ideas, with a focus on improving racing spectacle and sustainability.

The regulation changes for 2017 introduced a new generation of Formula One cars, featuring wider tyres, increased downforce, and more aggressive aerodynamics. The result was machines that were several seconds faster per lap, demanding more from drivers both physically and mentally.

Lewis Hamilton, however, expressed concerns that the new regulations could negatively impact racing. He feared that the increased emphasis on aerodynamics would make following a car in 'dirty air' more difficult, potentially reducing overtaking opportunities and making the spectacle less exciting for fans.

Speaking about the shift in regulations, Hamilton noted that all teams were essentially starting from scratch. He speculated that Ferrari or Red Bull could emerge as the new frontrunners and highlighted Red Bull's expertise in generating downforce, suggesting they could be particularly strong under the new rules.

The cars of 2017 featured bold engineering and creative interpretations of the new rules, with each team bringing unique designs to the grid. The regulation changes helped level the playing field, with Ferrari emerging as a genuine contender.

The Ferrari SF70H, developed under the leadership of Maurizio Arrivabene and technical director Mattia Binotto, was unveiled, a car designed to maximise the potential of the 2017 regulations. It featured a high-rake design, a concept first popularised by Red Bull, where the rear of the car was elevated higher than the front, creating a downhill stance when stationary. This design improved aerodynamic efficiency by optimising airflow under the car. The SF70H also reintroduced the distinctive shark fin behind the engine cover, a feature last seen on a Ferrari in 2010 when Fernando Alonso narrowly missed out on the Championship. The shark fin helped stabilise airflow to the rear wing, enhancing the car's balance and performance.

The chatter during pre-season testing suggested Ferrari had unlocked something special with the SF70H. Its speed and handling hinted that the team was ready to challenge Mercedes' dominance. The car's name, SF70H, paid homage to Ferrari's 70th anniversary, adding a sense of history to its ambitious 2017 campaign. Sebastian Vettel was particularly optimistic about Ferrari's prospects.

Mercedes, under the technical leadership of James Allison, unveiled the W08—a car that proved both powerful and adaptable. Its longer wheelbase gave it stability and versatility across a variety of circuits, cementing Mercedes' position as the team to beat.

With Adrian Newey at the helm, Red Bull's RB13 pushed aerodynamic innovation to its limits. Another to feature a prominent shark fin and sleek design, the car was expected to shine on high-downforce circuits.

Peter Prodromou's vision brought the striking McLaren MCL32 to life, reintroducing the iconic orange livery. However, its potential was hampered by persistent reliability issues with Honda's power unit, a theme that frustrated both the team and fans alike.

The 2017 Formula One season brought major changes to driver line-ups, starting with the shockwaves of Nico Rosberg's unexpected retirement just days after winning the 2016 World Championship. Mercedes moved quickly, signing Valtteri Bottas from Williams to partner Hamilton. Bottas, known for his consistency and already experienced with Mercedes-powered cars, seemed a natural fit for the reigning Champions.

At Ferrari, the experienced duo of Sebastian Vettel and Kimi Räikkönen remained, with the team viewing the new regulations as a chance to return to title contention. Red Bull Racing also retained their exciting pairing of Daniel Ricciardo and Max Verstappen, banking on their blend of youth and proven skill to challenge their rivals.

Meanwhile, McLaren turned the page on an era, with Stoffel Vandoorne stepping in alongside Fernando Alonso following Jenson Button's retirement. The team hoped the fresh-faced Belgian could inject new energy as they sought to rebuild.

**Barcelona Testing: Reading Between the Lines**

All the teams headed to Barcelona for pre-season testing and as was the norm, assessing true speed from the lap times was difficult, with some teams running higher fuel loads to mask performance. The early signs of competitiveness were hard to judge objectively from outside the teams themselves.

For Mercedes, early indications pointed to another strong year. Toto Wolff discussed the team's evolving structure and the addition of Bottas. He also commented on the margins seen in testing, acknowledging that while the gaps at the front appeared to have shrunk, true performance would only be revealed in Melbourne. Wolff summed it up bluntly, stating that when the racing began, speculation would end.

Wolff also shared insights from discussions with Hamilton and Bottas, both of whom described the new-generation cars as aggressive, violent machines—just as Formula One cars should be.

After the third day of pre-season testing at Barcelona, where Mercedes set the fastest time, Hamilton talked about the car's performance positively, but he still had some reservations. He expressed his excitement, describing the speed of the car as incredible, knowing that only he and his teammate would have the opportunity to drive it.

He talked about how quick the new cars were and likened the experience to being on a rollercoaster, acknowledging that it was the fastest he had ever driven in Formula One. However, he warned that the turbulence from the car ahead was now significantly stronger, raising questions about how overtaking would play out in races.

Bottas, speaking to the BBC during pre-season testing, summarised the changes effectively. He explained that the new regulations aimed to make the cars up to five seconds a lap faster while making them more physically demanding for drivers. He highlighted the increased downforce, stability in high-speed corners, and greater overall grip, adding that he had enjoyed the experience.

Niki Lauda also shared his thoughts on the new cars. He recalled seeing the car in its early development stage and being excited about its broader design and larger tyres, believing that fans would appreciate the more aggressive look.

Observers noted Mercedes' strong performance in pre-season testing, with many suggesting that the team remained the benchmark despite the regulatory changes. However, there were also signs that Ferrari and Red Bull had closed the gap, pointing to a potentially more competitive season ahead. Ferrari, in particular, appeared to have a well-balanced package, and Vettel was in a buoyant mood as the season approached.

**The Opener Down Under**

The season opener on 26 March in Melbourne, Australia, delivered a wake-up call for Mercedes. Hamilton secured pole position with a blistering lap, outpacing second-placed Vettel by seven tenths, reinforcing the perception that Mercedes remained the team to beat. However, the race told a different story.

While Hamilton pitted early to cover Vettel, the Ferrari driver stayed out, capitalising on clean air to leapfrog the Mercedes and take a commanding victory. After the race, Hamilton acknowledged the challenge, offering congratulations to Ferrari and Vettel. He admitted struggling with tyre wear towards the end of his first stint, which forced him to pit earlier than expected and left him unable to mount a challenge.

Mercedes Team Principal Toto Wolff accepted that Ferrari had the stronger race pace, stating that despite pushing flat out, they simply lacked the speed to pull away. He was clear that the loss came down to performance rather than strategy, acknowledging that Vettel was the deserved winner.

For Hamilton, the defeat was another reminder of how quickly momentum could shift in Formula One. Vettel's win signalled Ferrari's intent, and Hamilton knew he would need to respond. Back at the Mercedes factory in Brackley, the team took note and immediately began working on new developments.

Bottas, in the sister Mercedes, secured third place, just a few seconds behind Hamilton, while Räikkönen followed in fourth in the other Ferrari. Verstappen continued to show his ability, finishing fifth, just six seconds adrift of Räikkönen, proving once again that Red Bull would be a factor in the season ahead.

### Shanghai – A Wet and Wild Battle

Race day in China brought a damp track, leading to difficult choices on tyre selection. Starting from pole position, Hamilton controlled the race masterfully, demonstrating exceptional skill in tricky conditions. Vettel, lining up alongside him on the front row, made an early switch to slick tyres during a Virtual Safety Car period. This temporarily dropped him to sixth place, but he fought back to secure second.

Max Verstappen delivered a standout performance, charging through the field from 16th on the grid to claim the final podium position in third, just ahead of his teammate Ricciardo. Ricciardo's afternoon was eventful, engaging in a fierce wheel-banging duel with Vettel, the friction between their cars sending smoke into the air.

The race featured several notable incidents. Lance Stroll in the Williams, and Sergio Pérez in the Force India Mercedes, collided on the opening lap, forcing Stroll to retire: it was a clumsy challenge by Pérez. On Lap 4, Antonio Giovinazzi crashed on the start-finish straight, destroying the front of his Sauber Ferrari and bringing out the Safety Car. Bottas spun whilst warming his tyres behind the Safety Car and dropped several places to 12th before the Safety Car came in. Carlos Sainz Jr. took a bold gamble by starting on slick tyres despite the damp conditions: initially, this seemed like a miscalculation, but the strategy eventually paid off, with Sainz finishing an impressive seventh.

The changing weather conditions shook up the order, leading to some interesting scraps throughout, much to the delight of the 145,000 spectators in attendance.

Still only 19 years old and racing for Red Bull, Verstappen was asked to talk about his remarkable recovery drive. He admitted he hadn't expected such a result after starting so far back and was particularly pleased with making up nine positions on the opening lap alone. His modesty belied the sheer skill and confidence he displayed in the wet-dry conditions, which perfectly suited his bold driving style. Ricciardo, noting Red Bull's success, left Shanghai determined to refocus.

After the race, Hamilton was asked about Verstappen's performance. With a smile, he quipped that having Verstappen alongside him on the podium made him feel younger before praising the Dutchman's impact on the sport, calling him a breath of fresh air. Hamilton then shifted focus to the broader Championship battle, expressing his hope that Red Bull would improve as the season progressed, believing a three-way fight would make the season even more exciting.

Red Bull Team Principal Christian Horner was full of praise for Verstappen's first lap, describing it as remarkable. He said

Verstappen displayed an instinctive ability in wet conditions, showing no intimidation and exploring every inch of the circuit to find grip. One particular move, where Verstappen swept around the outside of several cars into Turn 6 before cutting back, was singled out as especially impressive.

Verstappen's performance in Shanghai was more than just an inspired drive—it was a statement. As Red Bull, backed by Adrian Newey's design brilliance, began to emerge as a more serious threat, it was clear that challenges lay ahead for both Hamilton and Vettel.

Hamilton was asked what he thought about the challenge from Ferrari, and he said that he felt they were generally very strong in warmer weather.

**Bahrain – Desert Darkness**

In mid-April, the teams moved to Bahrain for the desert night race, where Ferrari once again emerged victorious. Bottas started from pole and held the lead into Turn 1, with Vettel slotting in behind and Hamilton in third. Behind them, Verstappen made an excellent getaway, sweeping around the outside of Ricciardo to move ahead of his teammate. This bold move marked the end of Verstappen's learning phase—he was now fighting to establish dominance within Red Bull.

Ricciardo, unwilling to concede, weaved aggressively in an attempt to reclaim the position, but Verstappen held firm. However, his advantage was short-lived. On Lap 12, his race came to an abrupt end when a brake failure sent him into the barriers. Frustrated, he jumped out of his stricken Red Bull and kicked the Tecpro barrier in anger.

Moments later, further drama unfolded as Lance Stroll's Williams and Carlos Sainz's Toro Rosso collided, forcing both cars into retirement and triggering a Safety Car.

Hamilton, poised to attack for the lead, saw his chances compromised as Mercedes opted to double-stack their cars under the Safety Car, with Bottas pitting first. As Hamilton approached the pit lane entry, he deliberately slowed before the pit lane speed limit marker, holding up Ricciardo behind him. This earned him a five-second penalty, further complicating his race.

Afterwards, Hamilton admitted some frustration with how the race unfolded, saying he felt deflated and acknowledged his aim had been to deliver for the team, and he didn't feel he had executed to his full potential.

Vettel secured another victory for Ferrari, propelling him into the lead of the Championship with 68 points, while Hamilton remained just seven points adrift. The battle between Ferrari and Mercedes was now fully ignited, and with momentum shifting, Hamilton and his team knew they had a fight on their hands.

**Russia**

The Russian Grand Prix on 30 April belonged to Valtteri Bottas. In just his fourth race for Mercedes, the quiet Finn delivered a commanding performance, securing his maiden Formula One victory after a lightning start from third on the grid. Bottas led from the opening lap and, in the closing stages, held off a charging Vettel with nerves of steel.

Understandably elated, Bottas reflected on his breakthrough moment, describing it as "amazing" and admitting that, after more than 80 races, the wait had been well worth it.

Niki Lauda, never one to downplay the importance of a first victory, praised Bottas and spoke about the psychological boost that comes with breaking through. He noted that winning a first Grand Prix lifts a huge weight off a driver's shoulders, making every victory that follows easier.

Ferrari had another strong weekend, with Räikkönen following Vettel onto the podium, reinforcing the team's growing challenge to Mercedes.

As the paddock left Sochi, Vettel maintained his Championship lead with 86 points, Hamilton sat second on 73, and Bottas, now firmly in the fight, was third on 63.

### Sunshine in Spain

The 2017 Spanish Grand Prix, held on 14 May at the Circuit de Barcelona-Catalunya, was a turning point in the Formula One season, culminating in a colossal scrap between Hamilton and Vettel. The sun-bathed the circuit, created ideal racing conditions for the fervent crowd of 177,984 spectators.

Qualifying was incredibly tight, with Hamilton securing pole position with a lap time of 1:19.149, just 0.051 seconds ahead of Vettel. At an average lap speed of 200 km/h, and with Formula One cars measuring approximately 5.5 to 5.7 metres in length, this gap translated to Vettel trailing by just 2.8 metres—roughly half a car length. To put this into perspective, the average human blink lasts between 100 and 150 milliseconds (0.1 to 0.15 seconds). The gap between Hamilton and Vettel was shorter than the blink of an eye, highlighting how incredibly fine the margins are in Formula One. Two completely different teams and different drivers, and less than a blink between them.

Starting from pole position, Hamilton faced immediate pressure as Vettel's Ferrari rocketed off the line, seizing the lead into the first corner. The opening moments were chaotic, with cars running wide on the outside of Turn 1 and cutting across the inside of Turn 2 as drivers fought tooth and nail for position. Amidst the scramble, several cars made contact, and Kimi Räikkönen's race took a disastrous turn. His Ferrari suffered severe damage to the front-left suspension, the wheel awkwardly twisted inward. Smoke poured from the tyre as it dragged sideways along the track while Räikkönen attempted to limp back to the pits. A heart-wrenching moment followed as the circuit's giant TV screens captured a young Ferrari fan in tears, dressed in his red Ferrari T-shirt and cap, devastated to see his hero's race unravel. Recognising the futility of continuing, Räikkönen ultimately pulled off the track, parking his wounded car in the gravel, ending his day prematurely.

The early laps were intense with both Vettel and Hamilton driving flat out. By Lap 12, Hamilton was just two seconds behind Vettel when his race engineer encouraged him to push hard, reminding him of the critical phase of the race. Hamilton, fully focused, dismissed the radio call, making it clear he wanted to be left to concentrate.

On Lap 15, Ferrari took the initiative, bringing Vettel in for fresh tyres. Mercedes, in response, urged Hamilton to push to the limit, emphasising that this was the moment to make up ground. Hamilton, however, had already been playing a calculated game, holding back in the opening stint to protect his tyres, ensuring he could extend his run. He stayed out for another seven laps before making his stop, emerging behind Vettel but with fresher tyres—setting up a fierce battle for the remainder of the race.

Bottas played the perfect team role, holding up Vettel as Hamilton worked to close the gap. However, Vettel, with his Ferrari performing flawlessly, wasted no time and overtook Bottas on the following lap.

On Lap 36, chaos unfolded when Stoffel Vandoorne misjudged his move and collided with Felipe Massa at Turn 1. The incident triggered a Virtual Safety Car, sending teams scrambling to adjust strategies. Mercedes reacted instantly, calling Hamilton in for a fresh set of tyres. The pit crew's response was flawless—lightning-fast and precisely timed. Ferrari, unable to react as swiftly, brought Vettel in a lap later, allowing Hamilton to claw back crucial time.

As Vettel exited the pits, Hamilton came charging down the outside into Turn 1. The two rivals went wheel-to-wheel into the braking zone, with Vettel aggressively holding his line, forcing Hamilton wide. Despite the aggressive move, Hamilton kept his momentum, staying in the fight.

It was fitting that on Lap 44—his personal race number—Hamilton made his move, blasting past Vettel on the main straight at over 330 km/h (208 mph). The Mercedes sailed ahead before Turn 1, the sheer speed leaving no chance for a counterattack. In the Mercedes garage, the tension broke as the team celebrated, with Toto Wolff slamming his fist onto the workstation in a rare show of emotion, fully aware of the significance of the overtake.

Hamilton crossed the line first, securing a hard-fought victory, just 3.4 seconds ahead of Vettel. Daniel Ricciardo finished third for Red Bull Racing, but the gap to the leading pair was immense—over a minute behind.

Hamilton was elated, immediately crediting the team's work behind the scenes. He talked about the synergy needed with all the elements needing to work and be flawless to beat Ferrari—the factory upgrades, the pit stop execution, the strategy calls, and the continual push from every person involved. He recognised the collective effort that had gone into making the victory possible, adding that he hoped he had delivered as much as the team had.

Post-race, Hamilton was visibly fatigued as he slumped into a seat near the cool-down room, looking spent. The demands of pushing flat out were clear, but he relished the physical battle, saying how much he had enjoyed the challenge. Unlike many races dictated by strategy and tyre conservation, this had been a pure, relentless fight—one that had pushed him to his limits and delivered a thrilling spectacle for the fans.

### Monaco - Scuderia on Top

In the glitz and glamour of Monte Carlo on 28 May, Ferrari delivered a crushing blow, securing a front-row lockout in qualifying, with Räikkönen clinching pole position—his first in nine years, with Vettel in the sister Ferrari alongside. At the start, Räikkönen maintained his lead, navigating the narrow streets of Monte Carlo deftly. Vettel remained in close pursuit, both drivers executing flawless laps. The pivotal moment unfolded during the pit stop phase: Räikkönen pitted on lap 33, while Vettel stayed out, delivering a series of rapid laps. When Vettel eventually pitted, he emerged ahead of Räikkönen, seizing the lead. This overcut proved decisive, allowing Vettel to control the remainder of the race and secure his third victory of the season.

Vettel and Räikkönen secured a one-two finish, with Vettel extending his Championship lead. Daniel Ricciardo of Red Bull Racing capitalised on a similar strategy, extending his stint and executing swift laps to leapfrog both Valtteri Bottas and Max Verstappen, clinching the final podium spot. It wasn't without incident, as he clipped a wall towards the end of the race, but the Red Bull proved sturdy enough to withstand the impact.

For Hamilton, who qualified a disastrous 14th (but started 13th), the race was about damage limitation. He clawed his way to seventh, salvaging a handful of points. Despite the setback, Hamilton took the positives from the weekend, pointing out that, given the team's expectations before the race, finishing seventh had exceeded their initial projections. He reminded the team that the fight was far from over and that Ferrari could expect strong opposition in Canada. The title battle was well and truly on, and with 14 races remaining, Hamilton knew there was still a long way to go.

As the Championship moved on from Monaco, Vettel held a 25-point lead over Hamilton. The first six races had been packed with drama and intrigue, sending a clear signal: 2017 would not be a repeat of Mercedes' dominance. For Hamilton, the challenge ahead was undeniable, setting the stage for a season that would demand every ounce of his expertise and determination.

### City of A Hundred Steeples

At the Circuit Gilles Villeneuve in Canada on 11 June, Hamilton delivered a devastating performance. Starting from pole position, he dominated the race, leading every lap to claim his sixth Canadian Grand Prix victory. This triumph marked his third win of the season and cut Vettel's Championship lead to just 12 points. After the race Hamilton again discussed his strong connection with the Montreal circuit, describing how he had felt comfortable there from his very first visit.

Mercedes celebrated a one-two finish, with Valtteri Bottas joining Hamilton on the podium in second place, while Daniel Ricciardo claimed third for Red Bull.

Adding to the post-race festivities was actor Patrick Stewart, whose deep voice and legendary film and television career made him a familiar presence. Conducting the podium interviews, Stewart fully embraced the lively celebrations. Ricciardo, known for his now-famous 'Shoey' tradition, removed his right racing boot, filled it with champagne, and drank from it, much to the delight of the crowd. The fans roared as Ricciardo then turned to Stewart and jokingly offered him a sip. With no hesitation, Stewart enthusiastically accepted, prompting Ricciardo to remove his other boot, fill it with champagne, and hand it over.

With a theatrical flourish, Stewart lifted the boot, declared a celebratory toast, and downed its contents to raucous applause from the fans. The light-hearted moment capped off what had been a dominant day for Hamilton and Mercedes.

Hamilton had now cut Vettel's Championship lead in half as the season moved on from Canada. With the title battle finely poised, the pressure was mounting, and both drivers knew the importance of asserting their dominance. As so often in Formula One, the stage was set for tensions to ignite.

**The City of Winds – Vettel blows hot**

The 2017 Azerbaijan Grand Prix, held on the streets of Baku on 25 June, became one of the most controversial races in recent Formula One history due to a dramatic incident between Championship contenders Lewis Hamilton and Sebastian Vettel.

The Mercedes duo had locked out the front row. As the lights went out both made clean starts with Hamilton maintaining first into Turn 1, while Bottas maintained second. Behind them, the Ferraris—starting third and fourth—jostled for position. Vettel attempted to dive down the inside of Räikkönen into Turn 1, his Ferrari fishtailing under braking but narrowly avoiding contact. Räikkönen, carrying good momentum, attempted to pass Bottas around the outside a few corners later. Squeezed on the inside, Bottas hit the kerb hard, his Mercedes briefly leaping into the air before banging into Räikkönen's Ferrari. A chunk of carbon fibre flew into the air. Though Räikkönen continued, he lost momentum and dropped to fourth, allowing Vettel to slip through into second and begin his chase of Hamilton. Bottas suffered a front-right puncture in the contact and was forced to limp back to the pits: Hamilton had just lost his wingman.

As cars scrambled to avoid the chaos, Sergio Pérez in the Force India capitalised and moved up to third, with Verstappen close behind. The opening lap saw much of the field struggling with low grip, as drivers wrestled their cars to avoid the barriers and each other. By Lap 5, Hamilton had built a comfortable three-second lead over Vettel, controlling the race from the front. Meanwhile, Ricciardo, running just inside the top ten and reporting brake issues, pitted early on Lap 6. Red Bull's mechanics discovered debris lodged in one of the brake intakes, quickly removed it while changing tyres, and sent Ricciardo back out. He rejoined in 17th but wasted no time, clawing his way up to 11th by Lap 11.

Drama struck on Lap 11 when Daniil Kvyat's Toro Rosso suffered a technical failure and came to a stop on track, bringing out yellow flags. Moments later, Max Verstappen's Red Bull emitted a puff of grey smoke, signalling an engine failure. Verstappen immediately confirmed the problem over the radio, with Lap 12 marking the end of his race. He did not hide his frustration as he climbed out of the Red Bull—it was his fourth DNF in six races due to mechanical failure.

It took several laps to clear the stranded Toro Rosso, and the race resumed on Lap 16. Hamilton, leading the pack, backed them up early to position himself for a clean restart. Timing it to perfection, he caught Vettel off guard and floored the throttle. The Mercedes squirmed slightly under the force of acceleration, but Hamilton quickly gained a solid gap. As the Safety Car peeled away, Hamilton streaked down the straight, leaving Vettel scrambling to react.

Behind them, the cold tyres caused further chaos as drivers jockeyed for position. Räikkönen was involved in another clash, losing his right barge board. Vettel, slow to respond at the restart, narrowly retained second place under heavy pressure from Sergio Pérez.

The action was short-lived, as the Safety Car was redeployed on Lap 17 following another incident. Teams seized the opportunity to adjust strategies, with Mercedes bringing Hamilton in immediately and Ferrari following suit for Vettel, throwing the race into uncertainty once more.

The field spent a few more laps behind the Safety Car, and by Lap 19, preparations were underway for another restart. Leading the pack, Hamilton adhered to Safety Car protocols, slowing down to maintain control and get heat into his tyres. Vettel, mindful of being caught napping earlier, stayed glued to Hamilton's rear wing. However, as Hamilton weaved to warm his tyres, Vettel, anticipating Hamilton might bolt away, misjudged the pace through one of the turns and drove clean into the back of the Mercedes.

Vettel was livid and immediately accused Hamilton over the radio of brake-testing him, adding "what the **** is going on?!". What followed was one of the most controversial moments of the season. The red mist descended, and in apparent frustration, Vettel pulled alongside Hamilton. A millisecond later Vettel deliberately swerved into the side of the Mercedes, making contact. The tension was palpable over the team radios. Hamilton immediately questioned Vettel's actions, expressing disbelief at what had just happened. Meanwhile, amidst the drama, Daniel Ricciardo capitalised and quietly climbed into fifth place.

As the race resumed, another incident unfolded when Esteban Ocon, in the pink Force India, collided with his teammate Pérez. The resulting debris littered the circuit, but both Force Indias managed to continue. Räikkönen, however, was less fortunate, running over shards of carbon fibre and suffering a puncture, further compounding his woes in an already turbulent race. On Lap 22, the race was red-flagged so the debris could safely be cleared.

The race restarted on Lap 24, with Hamilton again holding firm and pulling away from Vettel. Meanwhile, Ricciardo passed two cars into Turn 1 to slot into third. From Lap 29 to Lap 31, Hamilton battled with a loose head protection unit on his Mercedes. He tried to keep it in place, but not wanting to risk a black flag, he pitted on Lap 31 to get the unit replaced, which compromised his race. At the same time, the Stewards in Race Control announced that Vettel had been given a 10-second stop-and-go penalty for "dangerous driving," one of the most severe in-race penalties short of disqualification. Ricciardo, who had been in 17th only twenty-five laps earlier, was now in the lead. He went on to win the race, with Bottas in second and Stroll, in the Williams Mercedes, finishing third. Vettel finished fourth with Hamilton fifth.

The incident between Vettel and Hamilton ignited widespread debate across the paddock. Hamilton, still seething after the race, made his feelings clear, condemning what had happened and calling the penalty insufficient. The Stewards investigated the telemetry and found that Hamilton had done exactly what he had done on the previous restart—he had simply not accelerated coming out of the corner where the incident took place. There was no evidence of brake-testing. It was not the first time Vettel had caused a collision and blamed others.

Ricciardo, who had the most to gain from the situation and was unaffected by the clash, was asked for his opinion on the incident. He noted that the race leader had the right to dictate the pace, and Vettel had simply misjudged the situation. Ricciardo added his own perspective saying that Turn 15 was way too early anyway to even contemplate the restart, and that Vettel had probably been over-excited. He added with his characteristic Aussie humour and a huge cheeky grin, that tensions were bound to rise as the Championship fight intensified, and now, with the gloves off, the season was well and truly heating up.

The FIA summoned Vettel for a disciplinary hearing, where he issued a formal apology, and the governing body decided to take no further action. The Baku clash became a fissure in Vettel's mental resilience, highlighting the level of stress he was under. From here, his mental strength would be on the wane.

**Austria – Bottas Shines**

Valtteri Bottas once again demonstrated his growing confidence at the Red Bull Ring in Austria in early July, securing his second career victory with a commanding performance. Hamilton, hindered by a five-place grid penalty for a gearbox change, started from eighth but battled through the field to finish fourth. Meanwhile, Vettel's second-place finish extended his Championship lead over Hamilton to 20 points.

Hamilton, experienced in the ebb and flow of a title fight, remained composed, knowing there were still plenty of races ahead. With Silverstone next on the calendar, he had every reason to feel optimistic—Vettel would need to produce something extraordinary to beat him on British soil.

**Silverstone – Five times British Grand Prix winner**

At Silverstone on 16 July, Hamilton put on a demonstration in front of his home crowd, delivering a commanding lights-to-flag victory at the British Grand Prix. It was his fourth consecutive win at the circuit and his fifth British Grand Prix triumph overall, equalling the record held by Jim Clark and Alain Prost. The race proved significant in the Championship battle, as Vettel suffered a late puncture, dropping to seventh and allowing Hamilton to slash the points gap to just a single point.

Overjoyed with the result, Hamilton immersed himself in the celebrations, engaging with the ecstatic fans and even taking the moment to 'crowd surf' in the grandstands. His post-race festivities caused an unintended delay to the official FIA press conference, leaving Bottas and Räikkönen—both typically reserved Finns—waiting patiently. Their expressions, a mix of quiet amusement and mild bewilderment, spoke volumes as they sat in silence, observing the extended celebrations unfold.

**Hungary – Integrity Wins the Race**

Ferrari dominated the Hungaroring on 30 July, securing a one-two finish with Vettel leading Räikkönen home. The tight, twisty circuit played to the Scuderia's strengths, while Mercedes found themselves on the back foot.

Hamilton, running behind teammate Bottas, was given the opportunity to move ahead in an attempt to chase down the Ferraris. Despite pushing hard, he couldn't find a way past Räikkönen, and in the closing stages, he made good on a pre-race agreement—relinquishing the position back to Bottas and settling for fourth place. It was a moment of sportsmanship that left him 14 points adrift of Vettel as the Championship battle headed into the summer break.

After the race, Hamilton pondered the move, making it clear that keeping his word mattered more than any immediate gain. He said he had agreed that if he couldn't pass Räikkönen, he would let Bottas back through, and although there could be a moment later in the season where a few points might make a difference, he wanted to win the right way. He believed it was important to race fairly, and he believed that the right approach would bring its own rewards.

Mercedes Team Principal Toto Wolff was visibly frustrated when Hamilton handed the place back, though the team later played down any suggestion of internal disagreement. Wolff admitted it was a difficult call but stood by the decision, acknowledging that upholding team values sometimes came at a cost.

While Hamilton's sportsmanship was a talking point, Red Bull faced internal controversy. At the very start of the race, Verstappen and Ricciardo tangled, with Verstappen's over-aggressive move ending his teammate's race. Ricciardo's anger was clear, and the incident further strained the dynamic between the two drivers.

With Ferrari extending its lead and tensions rising in the Red Bull garage, Hamilton and Mercedes headed into the summer break knowing that every race from this point forward would be critical.

As they left Hungary Vettel led on 202 points, with Hamilton on 188 points.

**Spa – Café of Europe**

The 2017 Belgian Grand Prix, held on 27 August at the iconic Spa-Francorchamps circuit, marked a significant milestone in Lewis Hamilton's illustrious career. After securing pole position with a superb 1:42.553 on Saturday, Hamilton lined up alongside Vettel for his 200th Formula One start, with less than two-tenths separating the rivals in qualifying. The margins were razor-thin over the longest circuit on the calendar, setting the stage for another dramatic showdown.

Hamilton made a perfect getaway, leading the pack cleanly through the tight right-hand hairpin at Turn 1, known as La Source. Typically, a hotspot for first-lap chaos, the corner remarkably saw all the drivers emerge unscathed. Heading downhill towards Eau Rouge, Esteban Ocon in the trailing Force India Mercedes attempted an ambitious move on his teammate Sergio Pérez. Pérez, preoccupied with a Renault in his sights, was seemingly unaware of Ocon's charge. The two Force Indias made slight contact, with smoke briefly rising from Pérez's right front and Ocon's left front tyres. Disaster was narrowly avoided as Pérez, sensing the danger, backed out of the duel.

Up through Eau Rouge, Vettel's Ferrari was locked onto Hamilton's gearbox and both cars showered hundreds of sparks as they bottomed out on the kerbs at over 180 mph. The heavy fuel loads strained the suspension to the limit as the cars surged through the iconic section. As they hurtled onto the Kemmel Straight, Vettel pulled out of Hamilton's slipstream at over 200 mph, eyeing a move into the Les Combes chicane. However, Hamilton's Mercedes proved incredibly efficient aerodynamically, enabling him to stay ahead. The two rivals braked at the very last moment before the right-hander, showcasing their prowess as they avoided contact. Vettel tucked back in behind Hamilton, continuing his pursuit. Meanwhile, Hamilton settled into a rhythm, managing the race from the front.

On Lap 8, Max Verstappen's race ended in heartbreak as his car suffered another mechanical failure on the run down to Eau Rouge from La Source. His father, Jos Verstappen, stood in the Red Bull garage, stone-faced and shaking his head gently in frustration. Max, also shaking his head in the car, sensibly parked his Red Bull near an escape road just past Raidillon, allowing marshals to quickly remove the Red Bull. As he climbed out, he was met with the cheers of a sea of orange-clad Dutch fans, who had made the journey in droves to support their rising star. It was a bitter end to their hopes of seeing Verstappen fight at the front.

On Lap 29, Pérez, running in ninth place in his bright pink Force India, once again found Ocon right behind him. The two teammates made it through La Source without issue, but a replay of their earlier drama was about to unfold. As they charged downhill toward Eau Rouge, Ocon attempted to squeeze between Pérez and the wall. This time, however, Pérez was ready and closed the door early. Ocon, seemingly unaware of the narrowing gap—or the fact that it was his teammate he was about to collide with—ploughed into the back of Pérez's right rear tyre at around 140 mph. The impact sent a piece of Ocon's left front wing flying into the air. Pérez, showing restraint, yielded slightly as they went into Eau Rouge, but the damage was already done. As he approached the uphill right-hander, his car went into a wild tank-slapper, fishtailing violently. The culprit was quickly revealed—a right rear puncture caused by the earlier contact.

Ocon, meanwhile, was quick to get on the radio, blaming Pérez for the incident. It was another poor display of sportsmanship, reminiscent of the finger-pointing seen from some other drivers when things didn't go their way. The debris from Pérez's car littered the Kemmel Straight, forcing race control to deploy the Safety Car.

The Safety Car prompted a flurry of pit stops as teams took the opportunity to change tyres. Mercedes opted for the yellow side-walled Pirelli tyres, prioritising durability for the remainder of the race. Ferrari, however, took a more aggressive approach, fitting Vettel with the purple side-walled Ultra Softs, theoretically giving him a performance advantage for the restart. As the green flag waved, Hamilton surged ahead, maintaining his lead through La Source.

As the cars thundered into Eau Rouge at over 180 mph Vettel's Ferrari was glued to the back of the Mercedes, almost as if tethered by a tow rope. The Ferrari remained firmly in Hamilton's slipstream, piling on the pressure. As Vettel crested Raidillon, he pulled out of Hamilton's slipstream early to attempt an overtake. However, once again, the Mercedes' superior top-end speed proved decisive. Without the aerodynamic advantage of the slipstream, Vettel's Ferrari hit the full force of the air resistance, causing his speed to plateau. Hamilton held firm, keeping Vettel at bay. Forced to slot back in behind the Mercedes, Vettel could do little as Hamilton, despite being on the theoretically less grippy tyres, began to pull away lap by lap. In the end, Hamilton delivered a flawless performance to take the win.

Hamilton and the Mercedes team delivered a masterclass at one of the most demanding circuits on the calendar—a true "driver's" track. While Ferrari's early-season form had brought them on par with Mercedes in terms of performance, it was the finer details—and the brilliance of Lewis Hamilton—that were tipping the scales. It looked like Mercedes had stemmed the tide. Leaving Spa, Vettel maintained his lead in the Championship with 220 points, but Hamilton was closing in, just seven points behind on 213. Bottas sat in third with 179 points, a considerable gap to the top two.

In the Constructors' Championship, Mercedes extended their advantage, leading with 392 points. Ferrari remained in second with 348 points, while Red Bull, hindered by ongoing reliability issues, held third place with 199 points. Bottas' consistent teamwork proved instrumental in keeping Mercedes ahead in the title fight.

**Monza**

At the 2017 Italian Grand Prix, held at the historic Autodromo Nazionale Monza on 3 September, Hamilton took the Championship lead for the first time in the season with a dominant victory—his 59th career win. In the lead-up to the race, Hamilton made headlines by breaking Michael Schumacher's record for the most pole positions, securing his 69th pole with a lap of 1:35.554. Verstappen delivered an impressive qualifying performance in his Red Bull, taking second, with Ricciardo in the sister car in third. However, both drivers, along with several others, were hit with penalties for MGU-H (Motor Generator Unit – Heat) and engine changes, shuffling the grid significantly. As a result, Verstappen started down in 13th, while Ricciardo lined up 16th.

Starting from pole, Hamilton controlled the race from the front, leading a Mercedes one-two finish, with Bottas in second. Vettel secured third, slipping three points behind

Hamilton in the standings. Hamilton acknowledged the energy of the Ferrari supporters – the tifosi - saying how much he enjoyed the atmosphere and the enthusiasm. Bottas continued to play the perfect support role, securing crucial points and taking them away from Vettel at a key moment in the Championship fight.

Ricciardo stole the show with a storming drive from 16th on the grid to finish fourth, showing the raw pace of the Red Bull when reliability issues didn't appear.

**Singapore – Vettel scores an own goal**

The 2017 Singapore Grand Prix, held on 17 September at the Marina Bay Street Circuit, became the defining moment in the Championship battle between Hamilton and Vettel, as well as Mercedes and Ferrari. Vettel had secured pole position with a time of 1:39.491, narrowly edging out Verstappen, who was quickly establishing himself as a qualifying powerhouse.

The drama unfolded immediately, even before the cars reached the first corner. In wet conditions, both Vettel and Verstappen got decent starts from the front row, but Verstappen had the momentum and was beginning to close in on Vettel as they shifted into second gear. Meanwhile, Räikkönen, starting from fourth in the other Ferrari, made an exceptional getaway and surged down the inside, close to the pit wall, rapidly gaining on Verstappen. Sensing the danger, Verstappen moved to cover Räikkönen but realised the Ferrari was already alongside, forcing him to stay parallel.

Disaster struck as Vettel, having got a poor start from pole position on the right-hand side of the track, aggressively veered to his left, aiming to cut off Verstappen. The move was overly ambitious. Verstappen, now sandwiched between the two Ferraris, attempted to back out and tried to seek refuge in edging closer to Räikkönen, but there was no escape. Vettel clipped Verstappen, sending him into Räikkönen.

The chain reaction was catastrophic. Räikkönen's Ferrari, struck hard, lost its right rear wheel, which remained tethered but flailed violently. The car snapped sideways, colliding with Verstappen's Red Bull before careening into Vettel. Räikkönen's front wing was wedged under his front wheels, rendering the car uncontrollable as it slid towards Turn 1 at over 100 mph. Verstappen, now caught in the chaos, was then shunted into Fernando Alonso by the out-of-control Räikkönen, who was a passenger in his stricken machine. Räikkönen and Verstappen were both out on the spot, while Alonso limped away, only to retire later.

Vettel, having initially escaped the worst of the collision, continued around Turn 1, but his Ferrari had sustained critical damage. Coolant poured from a gaping hole in the car's left side, but the spray from the damp circuit obscured it from Vettel's view. As he charged down the next straight, his rear wheels lost grip on the coolant, causing the car to spin violently. Vettel clipped the wall, losing his front wing, and spun several hundred yards backward before coming to a stop. Although he attempted to rejoin, the car's damage was terminal. Ferrari instructed him to retire due to coolant loss. The Ferrari pit wall was left stunned as their ambitious race weekend turned into a nightmare within seconds of the start. On a circuit where Mercedes had struggled in previous years, this had been Ferrari's prime opportunity to regain control of the Championship. Räikkönen asked his team what had happened, clearly frustrated, and described the incident as "ridiculous." He was sanguine about it afterwards, saying, that the only thing he could have done differently to avoid the incident was to not be there in the first place.

It was another own goal for Vettel, and one that could easily have been avoided. The incident dealt a devastating blow to Ferrari's Championship ambitions, gifting Mercedes and Hamilton a significant advantage as Vettel suffered his first retirement of the season. The Singapore Grand Prix would go down as one of the most chaotic races of 2017. Amid the turmoil, Hamilton remained composed in the sweltering, wet conditions, delivering a commanding victory. Ricciardo, managing to keep his Red Bull intact, secured second place, while Bottas completed the podium in third. As the teams departed Singapore, the Championship pendulum, previously balanced and poised to swing either way, had decisively shifted in Hamilton and Mercedes' favour.

Hamilton's unexpected victory in Singapore was a turning point in the 2017 season. With Vettel's retirement, Hamilton's lead in the Championship standings increased to 28 points, providing him with a significant advantage in the title race. Some observers noted that Vettel had effectively shattered his and Ferrari's Championship hopes in one move.

As the 2017 Formula One season approached its climax, the battle for the World Championship intensified, with Hamilton and Vettel vying for supremacy. The final six races, spanning from Malaysia to Abu Dhabi, would determine the season's outcome.

### Sepang – Farewell to Malaysia

The 2017 Malaysian Grand Prix, held on 1 October at the Sepang International Circuit, marked the final Formula One race at the venue. The weekend was fraught with challenges for Ferrari, despite showing impressive pace during practice sessions.

In qualifying, Vettel faced a significant setback when an air-intake issue prevented him from setting a time, relegating him to the back of the grid. His teammate, Räikkönen, secured a front-row start alongside pole-sitter Hamilton. Räikkönen's qualifying was improving significantly as the season progressed and he was less than a tenth behind Hamilton. Meanwhile, the Red Bulls of Ricciardo and Verstappen locked out the second row, continuing their resurgence as the Adrian Newey-designed car extracted every bit of performance available when the power unit held together.

Race day brought further misfortune for Ferrari. Räikkönen encountered an issue similar to Vettel's with his air-intake while heading to the grid, forcing him to withdraw before the race even began. At lights out, Hamilton held his lead, but Verstappen, celebrating his 20th birthday that weekend, had other ideas. On Lap 4, he made a decisive move to take the lead, pulling away comfortably to secure his second career victory. Hamilton, knowing the Championship was now his to control, settled for second place, extending his lead over Vettel.

Verstappen's commanding win at Sepang underlined his growing stature in the sport. Meanwhile, Vettel, starting from 20th, drove a determined race through the field, climbing to fourth. A late-race battle with Ricciardo for the final podium spot was hard-fought, but the Red Bull driver held firm to take third.

After the race, an unusual incident unfolded during the cooldown lap. As is customary, some drivers slowed significantly to collect "marbles"—small pieces of rubber from the tyres—to help bring their car's weight up to the minimum limit. Others, confident in meeting the weight requirement or following specific cooldown protocols, continued at a faster pace back to the pits.

Sebastian Vettel was driving his cooldown lap relatively quickly and he started to catch Lance Stroll's slow-moving Williams. Stroll, having finished his race after being lapped by Max Verstappen, was cruising near the inside of a long left-hand corner, several meters away from the kerb. Vettel, travelling much faster, began tightening his line through the corner, turning his steering wheel increasingly to the left. His trajectory became noticeably tighter than Stroll's, and the gap between their cars quickly reduced. Despite the looming risk of a collision, Vettel continued to steer toward Stroll. At the last moment, Stroll noticed Vettel's Ferrari drawing dangerously close and tried to turn away. However, it was too late. Vettel's rear-left wheel struck Stroll's front-right, resulting in a significant impact. The force of the collision tore

Vettel's wheel away from its suspension arms and driveshaft, leaving it tethered by safety cables. The wheel flailed violently, flipping over the top of the Ferrari before coming to rest awkwardly on the car's right side.

Vettel seemed agitated, immediately venting over the radio that Stroll wasn't paying attention. It was another instance of Vettel showing unusual aggression for an error of his own making. Stroll, meanwhile, radioed his team, calmly stating that Vettel had driven into him. Stroll's Williams appeared undamaged, a stark contrast to Vettel's three-wheeled Ferrari. This incident added to a series of mistakes for Vettel during a critical phase of the championship, intensifying scrutiny of his decision-making under pressure. Still, there was at least some immediate salvation for Vettel, in the form of Pascal Wehrlein.

In a moment reminiscent of Nigel Mansell giving Ayrton Senna a ride on his Williams at Silverstone in 1991, Pascal Wehrlein pulled up alongside Vettel's damaged Ferrari in his Sauber. Vettel, taking his steering wheel with him to prevent anyone from tampering with it, placed it on Wehrlein's lap before climbing onto the right-side pod of the Sauber. Sitting on the side of the car, he held onto the cockpit and Wehrlein's right mirror for balance as the crowd cheered loudly. It was a spirited and sporting gesture, providing a rare light-hearted moment in what was otherwise a frustrating day for the German driver.

With the sport bidding farewell to Sepang, Hamilton left Malaysia in a dominant position in the Drivers' Championship, leading with 281 points to Vettel's 247. Just three races earlier, he had been trailing by seven points. His consistent, calculated approach—pushing hard when necessary but avoiding unnecessary risks—was proving to be the defining difference. In contrast, Vettel's season was unraveling with costly errors and reliability woes.

Bottas, continuing to perform a strong supporting role for Mercedes, remained third in the standings with 222 points. In the Constructors' Championship, Mercedes extended their advantage, leading with 503 points to Ferrari's 385. Red Bull, despite reliability challenges, had cemented third place with 270 points, showing glimpses of their potential through Verstappen's performances.

With Japan next on the calendar, Hamilton had one hand on the title. Ferrari, needing a dramatic turnaround, had no choice but to take risks if they wanted to keep their Championship hopes alive.

## Japan – Ferrari's Last Stand Falls Apart

The next race in Japan loomed as a critical juncture for Ferrari and Vettel. They needed a flawless weekend, combined with difficulties for Mercedes, to keep their Championship hopes alive. With the clock ticking, the pressure was firmly on as the teams arrived at Suzuka.

The 2017 Japanese Grand Prix on 8 October marked another defining moment for Ferrari's title challenge. Hamilton, who had never before started from pole at Suzuka, delivered a beautiful lap of 1:27.319 to secure his first at the circuit. Vettel lined up alongside him on the front row, the tension between the title rivals unmistakable.

However, before the race had even begun, problems struck Ferrari again. As Vettel completed his lap to the grid, he reported a lack of power. The team scrambled to diagnose the issue, identifying it as a spark plug failure. Despite frantic attempts to resolve it, the problem persisted, leaving Vettel severely compromised at the start.

When the lights went out, Vettel's Ferrari, visibly down on power, was swallowed up by the pack. Within two laps, he had tumbled down the order, his title hopes slipping further with every corner. On Lap 4, Ferrari called him in to retire the car, delivering what was effectively the final, crushing blow to his Championship ambitions.

Hamilton went on to take victory, his first win at Suzuka since 2015. Verstappen, pushing hard in the closing stages, kept the pressure on Hamilton all the way to the flag, but the Mercedes driver held firm. Ricciardo secured third place, ensuring a strong result for Red Bull as they continued their late-season resurgence.

As the race concluded, Ferrari's pit wall was a picture of disappointment. Team Principal Maurizio Arrivabene, usually composed, looked visibly dejected and later laid the blame for Vettel's woes with suppliers. Meanwhile, Mercedes boss Toto Wolff, in a rare display of sympathy for his rivals, walked over to Ferrari's pit wall to console his counterpart. It was a poignant reminder of what sets Formula One apart—fierce competition and the desire to win, but also moments of mutual respect when the battle is lost.

Niki Lauda, always direct, offered his assessment after the race. When asked whether the title was now Hamilton's, he remained cautious but realistic, saying that while Vettel had a big deficit, the title wasn't won or lost, until it was won or lost. Wise words indeed.

**United States Grand Prix – A Champion in Waiting**

The 2017 United States Grand Prix, held on 22 October at the Circuit of The Americas in Austin, Texas, proved to be a decisive moment in the Championship battle. Hamilton and Mercedes delivered a commanding performance, all but securing the Drivers' Championship and further asserting their dominance in the Constructors' standings.

Hamilton started the weekend on a strong footing, securing pole position with a 1:33.108. This marked his 72nd career pole and his second at the Austin circuit, setting the stage for a high-stakes showdown.

At the start, Vettel launched off the line with better traction, diving down the inside into Turn 1. Hamilton, keen to defend, edged him towards the outside but left just enough room to avoid unnecessary risk—a calculated show of patience from a driver with his sights firmly set on the title. Even at speeds nearing 200 mph, Hamilton was thinking strategically, knowing this battle would extend well beyond the opening corner.

On Lap 2, a determined Daniel Ricciardo, running in fourth, launched one of his trademark "late-braking" moves into Turn 1, diving up the inside of Valtteri Bottas seemingly out of nowhere. As they went through the apex side by side, Ricciardo pushed the limits, forcing Bottas off the track and beyond the white lines.

Bottas, often viewed as mild-mannered and a cautious racer by many in the paddock, showed a different side. Rolling up his sleeves, he fought back fiercely. Through the switchbacks of Turns 2, 3, and 4, the two cars raced wheel-to-wheel, neither giving an inch. Bottas, however, muscled his way ahead, firmly reclaiming his position and putting Ricciardo back in his place. It was a display of grit and determination from the usually reserved Finn.

While the opening exchanges provided action for the crowd, Hamilton remained composed. Between laps 2 and 6, he meticulously prepared for his inevitable move on Vettel. He managed his tyres carefully, avoiding unnecessary overheating in the turbulent air behind the Ferrari. Aware that energy management would be key, Hamilton also optimised the complex hybrid power unit, ensuring that the additional boost from the electrical systems would be at full capacity when he launched his attack.

This meticulous approach paid dividends. As they approached Lap 6, Hamilton pounced with clinical precision, sweeping past Vettel with a move that was as inevitable as it was decisive. Vettel attempted to respond, but the contest was already settled—Hamilton had the pace, the composure, and the strategic execution that made all the difference.

On Lap 16, Ricciardo's Red Bull broke down, saying to the team, "engine's gone." Christian Horner didn't look too happy.

From that point forward, Hamilton controlled proceedings with an assured drive. Behind him, Vettel struggled to mount any serious challenge, while the battle for the final podium positions intensified. Ferrari attempted an early pit stop to undercut Mercedes, but the move fell short. Räikkönen, running strongly, eventually overtook Vettel, but team orders dictated that the position be returned, much to the Finn's frustration.

As the laps wound down, attention turned to Verstappen, who had scythed his way through the field after starting 16th due to engine penalties. The Dutchman's aggressive approach was on full display, first in his battle with Bottas and later as he closed in on Räikkönen. On the final lap, he attempted a daring pass for third, but his move took him well inside the white line limits of the corner. It was an audacious effort, but stewards quickly deemed it a case of leaving the track and gaining an advantage, handing him a five-second penalty that dropped him to fourth. Räikkönen, despite having briefly lost the place on track, reclaimed third as a result.

Hamilton's dominant victory at the Circuit of The Americas—his fifth at the Texas venue—extended his lead in the Drivers' Championship to 66 points over Vettel, placing him firmly on the cusp of his fourth World title. The triumph also confirmed Mercedes as the Constructors' Champions for the fourth consecutive season, further cementing their dominance in Formula One's hybrid era.

The race was not without controversy. Verstappen's late penalty reignited debates over track limits and the consistency of stewarding decisions. Many felt that the ruling was too harsh, while others pointed out that the regulations were clear—if a driver left the track and gained an advantage, a penalty was inevitable.

As Hamilton and Vettel sprayed champagne on the podium, Räikkönen enjoyed his first podium in six races. In a rare moment of exuberance, the usually reserved Finn tossed his red Ferrari cap into the crowd, a quiet nod to a performance that had deserved more.

**Mexico – Four-time World Champion**

The 2017 Mexican Grand Prix, held on 29 October at the Autódromo Hermanos Rodríguez, was another belting race. Vettel secured pole position with a lap time of 1:16.488, narrowly edging out Verstappen. Hamilton qualified third, setting the stage for a tense afternoon.

As the lights went out, Verstappen made a strong start, tucking in behind Vettel down the long straight, looking for an opportunity into Turn 1. Hamilton launched well, too, and was soon half alongside. As they approached the braking markers, the three title protagonists—Vettel, Verstappen, and Hamilton—were three-wide into the first turn. Hamilton, always calculating, braked slightly earlier to avoid unnecessary drama.

Vettel and Verstappen remained side by side, with Vettel aggressively squeezing Verstappen towards the edge of the track, hoping to force the Red Bull driver to back out. However, Verstappen, now firmly establishing himself as a force in Formula One, refused to be bullied and held his ground.

At the exit of Turn 1, Vettel's Ferrari drifted wide, nudging Verstappen further towards the track limits. Verstappen, fully aware of the risks of overtaking off-track, kept his car just inside the white lines, but contact was inevitable. A brief puff of tyre smoke signalled the first clash of the race. Into Turn 2, Verstappen had the inside line, using his superior momentum to push through into the lead. Vettel, unwilling to yield, clipped Verstappen's right rear wheel, adding to his troubles.

Compromised on his exit of Turn 2, Vettel was left vulnerable to Hamilton, who swept past him on the short stretch between Turn 2 and Turn 3. Hamilton, mindful of avoiding an incident, gave Vettel plenty of space, riding high over the kerbs at the exit of Turn 3 to stay clear. However, Vettel, seemingly frustrated at losing positions so rapidly, misjudged his braking and allowed his Ferrari to drift wide. In doing so, he struck Hamilton's right rear wheel and tyre with his front wing—Vettel's third contact of the opening lap. Hamilton queried over this team radio as to whether Vettel had hit him deliberately. As Vettel's front wing shattered, pieces of carbon fibre flew into the air, while Hamilton immediately felt the effects of a puncture. Forced to limp around the lap with a deflated rear tyre, Hamilton was at a significant disadvantage. The start had been chaotic, leaving both Championship rivals with a mountain to climb.

Both drivers pitted at the end of the opening lap. Vettel had a new front wing fitted and switched to soft tyres, rejoining in 19th. Hamilton, now dealing with floor and diffuser damage from the contact, rejoined in last place. From there, both began the long task of recovering lost ground. Vettel carved his way through the field with determined overtakes, ultimately finishing fourth. Hamilton, with a compromised car, battled hard to salvage a ninth-place finish.

On Lap 6, Daniel Ricciardo's frustrating race came to an early end. Starting from the back of the grid due to a penalty for a new engine component, the Australian retired with engine troubles. Christian Horner, Red Bull's team principal, glanced back at the stricken car in the pits, his expression sombre. Despite the setback, he found some consolation in Verstappen's strong performance at the front of the field.

While the title contenders struggled, Verstappen took full advantage. The Dutchman controlled the race from the front, extending his lead with every lap. By the chequered flag, he had built an advantage of nearly twenty seconds over Bottas in second. Räikkönen completed the podium, finishing 54 seconds behind—a staggering margin that highlighted Red Bull's raw pace when reliability wasn't an issue.

Recovering after the incident with Vettel, Hamilton managed to work his way back up to ninth, but it was enough. With

Vettel's fourth-place finish, Hamilton was now a four-time World Champion, joining an elite group in Formula One history. Overjoyed with the achievement, he talked about the need to never give up, encouraging others to push through adversity. He talked with great fondness about how he owed so much to his family and team.

Vettel, despite his costly errors in the opening laps, was gracious in defeat. Acknowledging Hamilton's performance over the season, he admitted that his rival had been the strongest across the year and that this was his moment.

Bottas, discussed the season after the race and was clear in his assessment, remarking that Hamilton had simply been the best driver that year. He acknowledged his teammate's relentless work ethic, talent, and consistency, while making it clear that he was aiming to challenge him the following season. The sentiment was echoed by Mercedes, who highlighted how Hamilton had delivered a season without a single moment of weakness.

Elsewhere in the paddock, former Champions weighed in on Hamilton's place among the greats. Felipe Massa, who had battled Hamilton in 2008 for the title, suggested that Hamilton now belonged in the same league as Formula One's most legendary figures, mentioning that it was impossible to separate him from names like Senna and Schumacher. Hamilton, however, always remained grounded when asked about such comparisons, preferring to acknowledge the legacy of those who came before him. He had always spoken highly of Fangio, the five-time Champion from the 1950s, and how his achievements in such a dangerous era of racing would forever be respected.

Hamilton's fourth title placed him alongside Alain Prost and Sebastian Vettel, and ahead of greats such as Senna, Lauda, Stewart, and Piquet. The Championship battle had been fierce, but in the end, it was Hamilton's consistency, speed, and ability to remain unshaken under pressure that had secured him yet another place in the sport's history books.

## The Final Stretch: Brazil and Abu Dhabi

With the Championship already decided, the season concluded with two final races in Brazil and Abu Dhabi.

At Interlagos on 12 November, Vettel delivered a commanding performance, overtaking pole-sitter Bottas at the start to claim victory for Ferrari. Räikkönen secured third, giving the Scuderia a double podium finish. Hamilton, starting from the pit lane due to a crash in qualifying, put on a determined display, carving his way through the field to finish fourth, narrowly missing out on a podium spot.

The season finale at Yas Marina in Abu Dhabi on 26 November was dominated by Bottas. He secured pole position and converted it into a race win, leading a Mercedes one-two finish with Hamilton following in second. Vettel completed the podium in third, cementing his position as runner-up in the Drivers' Championship.

## Hamilton's Fourth World Championship

With the chequered flag in Abu Dhabi, the 2017 season concluded with Hamilton crowned World Champion, finishing with 363 points. Vettel ended the season second with 317 points, while Bottas secured third place with 305 points.

In the Constructors' Championship, Mercedes once again reigned supreme, clinching their fourth consecutive title with 668 points, demonstrating their continued dominance in the hybrid era. Ferrari's resurgence saw them secure second place with 522 points, while Red Bull Racing finished third on 368 points, their performance hampered by reliability issues but still competitive.

As the season ended, Red Bull talked about their challenges with the reliability and performance of their Renault-supplied power units. Team Principal Christian Horner said there had just been too many DNFs (Did Not Finish) due to reliability. He highlighted that the RB13 had 13 podiums and 13 DNFs. This sentiment was not new; tensions between Red Bull and Renault had been escalating over the years due to engine performance issues. In 2014, Horner had criticised the Renault power unit's performance as "unacceptable" following disappointing races. Ever the optimist, Horner said he hoped for better reliability going into 2018. If the reliability could match the aerodynamic performance, then Red Bull would be a serious contender, and Hamilton would have more than just Vettel and Ferrari to worry about.

**Massa Bows Out**

One of the most poignant moments of the post-season was the farewell of Felipe Massa. The Brazilian, who had come within a whisker of winning the 2008 World Championship and amassed 11 career victories, bowed out after his final race with Williams in Abu Dhabi. His professionalism and warmth had earned him deep respect throughout the paddock, and his departure left a noticeable void. Williams reflected publicly on the privilege of working with him, recognising the dedication and leadership he had brought to the team.

Massa's journey had been remarkable—not only for his long and successful career but also for his resilience after the life-threatening head injury he suffered in 2009. His return to the sport and ability to compete at the highest level for another seven years reflected his determination. As the season ended, Formula One continued to evolve its approach to driver safety, introducing further measures to reduce the risks of head injuries in the years ahead.

The post-season also brought celebrations of the year's achievements. At the FIA Prize Giving Ceremony at the Palace of Versailles, Hamilton was officially crowned the 2017 World Champion, while Mercedes AMG Petronas Formula One Team collected their fourth Constructors' Championship trophy.

Hamilton was further recognised for his performances, receiving the International Racing Driver of the Year award at the Autosport Awards—a reflection of the dominance and consistency he had displayed throughout 2017.

As the season drew to a close, teams turned their focus to what lay ahead. With winter testing on the horizon, engineers and strategists worked tirelessly to extract every possible tenth of a second that could define the outcome of 2018.

# Change and Development

As the 2018 Formula One season approached, the sport braced for another chapter in its ever-evolving story. For Lewis Hamilton, the defending World Champion, the year represented an opportunity to build on his legacy, while rivals like Sebastian Vettel in his Ferrari, and the rising Red Bull stars of Max Verstappen and Daniel Ricciardo aimed to unseat him. Valtteri Bottas, Hamilton's teammate, had also made it known he was keen to go toe-to-toe with him this year.

For Mercedes and Hamilton, the 2018 season brought a sense of continuity. Bottas remained alongside as his teammate, and the team maintained a stable foundation, with few changes to its personnel or the overall design philosophy of the car. Elsewhere on the grid, however, significant developments in technical regulations and in other teams were unfolding.

Several key updates to the technical and sporting regulations promised to influence the season. To enhance reliability and reduce costs, drivers were restricted from four internal combustion engines to just three for the entire 21-race calendar. Similarly, teams could only change the turbocharger on a driver's car three times, whereas in 2017 it was four, the same with the Motor Generator Unit – Heat. Some other notable items that could previously be replaced four times in the 2017 season, could now only be replaced twice, or grid penalties would be incurred. These were: Motor Generator Unit – Kinetic (MGU-K), Energy Store (the battery), and Control Electronics.

This was not great news for Christian Horner and the Red Bull team, who had been mired with reliability concerns in 2017 from their Renault-supplied engines. Horner recognised this risk, and the team would alter their usual pre-season rituals as a result, knowing that any additional failures could see them spending much of 2018 starting from the back of the grid.

The reduction in allowable power unit components for the 2018 Formula One season prompted various reactions from teams and drivers, reflecting concerns over the increased emphasis on reliability and the potential for grid penalties. The FIA acknowledged these concerns and revised the power unit penalty system to mitigate confusion and manage the impact of potential penalties. Under the new system, any driver incurring a grid penalty of 15 places or more would start from the back of the grid. If multiple drivers received such penalties, their starting positions at the back would be determined based on the order in which the infringements occurred. This rule had an immediate impact on teams like Red Bull and McLaren, both of whom were frequently caught out by reliability issues.

In terms of aerodynamics, the visually divisive T-wings and shark fins, prominent in 2017, were banned for 2018, streamlining the cars' appearances. The FIA aimed to simplify aerodynamics and improve the aesthetics of the cars.

The more striking visual change, however, was the mandatory introduction of the Halo cockpit protection device. Designed to shield drivers from head injuries caused by flying debris or crashes. The Halo safety device had been in development for several years, its mandatory implementation for the 2018 season reignited debates about aesthetics, performance concerns, and the impact of additional weight higher up in the car.

The Halo was introduced in response to several fatal and serious accidents in motorsport. The deaths of Jules Bianchi in Formula One, Justin Wilson and Dan Wheldon in IndyCar, as well as Henry Surtees in junior racing, had highlighted the risks of head injuries in open-wheel racing. Even in cases where drivers survived, such as Felipe Massa's near-fatal accident in 2009 when a spring struck his helmet, or Mika

Häkkinen's crash in 1995, it was clear that more protection was needed. Hamilton was asked about the Halo and said he didn't argue against it and felt that Formula One needed to move forward. Other drivers and team principals had varying views.

One of the most vocal critics of the Halo in 2017 was Romain Grosjean, who publicly opposed its implementation. However, he would later change his view dramatically after his horrific crash at the 2020 Bahrain Grand Prix, where the Halo played a critical role in saving his life. World Champions Sebastian Vettel and Fernando Alonso were strongly in favour of the Halo, despite any aesthetic concerns, and welcomed it with open arms. Alonso reflected on how the device would have saved drivers over the years.

Christian Horner and Toto Wolff both expressed scepticism about the necessity of the Halo, with Wolff even voicing significant reservations. Meanwhile, three-time World Champion Jackie Stewart drew parallels between the Halo's introduction and earlier safety innovations in Formula One. He talked about being the first driver to wear a seatbelt in a Formula One car, a measure that was initially met with resistance but ultimately became standard practice. Stewart emphasised that the Halo represented a similar step forward for driver safety, noting that, like seatbelts, it would eventually be accepted as a vital part of the sport. The Halo seemed to divide opinion, but several drivers, including Hamilton and Grosjean, would undoubtedly be grateful for it in the years to come.

While the ballistic helmets introduced in the 2010s were designed to stop small debris from hitting a driver's face or skull, they did little to mitigate the risks posed by larger objects, such as a stray wheel, another car, or barriers striking the cockpit.

The Halo was one of the most controversial yet crucial safety advancements in Formula One's history. Over time, its effectiveness would become clear, and by the end of 2018, even its harshest critics had little doubt about its value.

Pirelli introduced a wider range of compounds, including the Hypersoft tyre, identifiable by its pink markings. Teams saw this as an opportunity for more varied strategies. At the opposite end of the spectrum was a new 'orange' sidewall tyre, which was classed as a Superhard. In total, the teams and drivers now had seven types of slick Pirelli tyres to choose from. Going from softest to hardest, these were: Hypersoft (Pink sidewall), Ultrasoft (Purple sidewall), Supersoft (Red sidewall), Soft (Yellow sidewall), Medium (White sidewall), Hard (Blue sidewall), and the Superhard (Orange sidewall). On top of this, if it rained, teams still had the choice of Intermediates or Full Wets, making nine options in total. While Pirelli expanded the range of compounds, only three would be available for each race weekend, simplifying choices for teams and fans.

**Renault woes**

In 2017, Renault's works team struggled with significant power unit reliability issues. Their aggressive approach to engine development—intended to boost performance—ultimately backfired, leading to frequent failures, retirements, and grid penalties. Reflecting on the season, Renault admitted they had been "too aggressive" in their pursuit of performance, acknowledging the fine balance between power and dependability.

Red Bull, as Renault's primary customer team, suffered greatly from these issues. Verstappen, in particular, endured several frustrating retirements, robbing him of potential victories. This struggle set the stage for Red Bull's eventual decision to part ways with Renault and switch to Honda for 2019. While the decision was not taken lightly, the team felt it was necessary to gain greater control over its power unit performance. The 2018 season would be crucial in determining whether Renault could solve its issues or if Red Bull's gamble on Honda was justified.

Renault Sport F1 managing director Cyril Abiteboul remained optimistic that lessons had been learned, stating that the focus for 2018 would shift towards reliability rather than outright power. This was welcome news to Christian Horner, whose Red Bull team had endured a frustrating 2017 campaign plagued by multiple Renault-related failures. However, after years of promises that had failed to materialise, Horner remained wary, knowing all too well the risks of relying on Renault's assurances.

Given Renault's ongoing struggles, McLaren's decision to switch from Honda to Renault power units for 2018 raised eyebrows. Many questioned whether this was a genuine upgrade, given Red Bull's well-documented reliability concerns with the same power unit. However, McLaren viewed the move as an opportunity to benefit from Renault's established infrastructure and recent internal restructuring. Renault had expanded its resources at the end of 2017 in preparation for supplying two top-tier teams alongside their own works outfit. McLaren, after three painful years with Honda, hoped that Renault would provide them with a more competitive and stable platform to return to the sharp end of the grid.

**Honda finds a new home**

As McLaren parted ways with Honda at the end of 2017, the Japanese manufacturer found a new home with Toro Rosso, Red Bull's junior team. The move was met with scepticism in some quarters, given Honda's well-documented struggles over the previous three seasons. McLaren and Honda's partnership had been fraught with reliability issues, underperformance, and mounting frustration, leading many to wonder if Toro Rosso was being used as a testing ground for an eventual full-scale supply deal with Red Bull Racing.

For Honda, the Toro Rosso deal provided a much-needed reset, away from the intense pressure and media scrutiny that had accompanied their time with McLaren. Unlike McLaren, who had publicly criticised Honda's shortcomings, Toro Rosso embraced the manufacturer with a more patient, collaborative approach. The team, operating with lower expectations than McLaren, offered Honda a less pressurised environment in which to refine its power unit in Formula One's increasingly complex hybrid era, without immediate demands for podiums or race wins. From Red Bull's perspective, the move was widely seen as a strategic decision—one that could prove to be a game-changer.

Although Renault had powered Red Bull Racing since 2007, relations between the two had steadily deteriorated due to repeated reliability issues and increasingly public criticism from both sides. With Toro Rosso now running Honda engines, Red Bull had a front-row seat to evaluate Honda's progress and potential. If Honda demonstrated significant improvement, it would give Red Bull a viable alternative should they choose to sever ties with Renault at the end of 2018.

Christian Horner and Helmut Marko played down speculation that this was merely a trial run for Red Bull Racing, but the implications were clear. If Honda could deliver, Red Bull had the flexibility to switch suppliers and secure the works partnership they had long sought but never achieved with Renault. The 2018 season would serve as a crucial test, not just for Toro Rosso, but for Red Bull's long-term engine strategy.

The partnership with Red Bull Technology also marked a shift in Honda's approach to Formula One. Whereas McLaren had largely left Honda to develop the power unit independently, Toro Rosso and Red Bull integrated much more closely with Honda's engineers. Red Bull provided technical expertise, particularly in chassis integration and energy recovery system efficiency, helping Honda optimise how its power unit worked within the car's overall package. The team also adjusted its design approach to better accommodate Honda's evolving power unit—something McLaren had been reluctant to do in the past.

By embedding Honda within Toro Rosso, Red Bull had a first-hand opportunity to evaluate Honda's improvements. If progress was sufficient, it gave them the option to switch to Honda for 2019, securing an exclusive works partnership—something they had long sought but never achieved with Renault. Christian Horner and Helmut Marko were putting in place the final pieces of the jigsaw for long-term stability and success.

After participating in select races in 2017, Pierre Gasly secured a full-time seat for 2018 with Toro Rosso. The Frenchman aimed to capitalise on his prior experience to make a significant impact. He was partnered with Brendon Hartley from New Zealand, a former World Endurance Champion, who continued with Toro Rosso after debuting late in the 2017 season.

For 2018, Red Bull introduced the RB14, aiming to address early-season performance challenges that had plagued them in previous years. The car debuted with a striking 'special edition' blue and black livery, with flashes of white, all in a matt finish, which garnered significant attention. It was a beautifully designed car, but sadly, the livery was only a temporary feature before the season commenced proper.

To mitigate early-season performance issues, Red Bull deviated from their usual compressed timeframe of leaving development to the last minute. Instead, they took a more considered approach, shaking down the RB14 at Silverstone a week before pre-season testing. Christian Horner believed this would allow the team a greater opportunity to identify and resolve any initial issues, ensuring they maximised performance during the official testing sessions.

Alfa Romeo made a long-awaited return to Formula One in 2018, re-entering the sport as Sauber's title sponsor in a move that rebranded the team as Alfa Romeo Sauber. The deal strengthened Sauber's technical ties with Ferrari, providing increased support and a more competitive power unit.

At the helm of this transformation was Frédéric Vasseur, who had taken over as Team Principal in mid-2017 following the departure of Monisha Kaltenborn. Vasseur, a highly respected figure in the paddock, had previously co-founded ART Grand Prix, the junior team that nurtured talents such as Lewis Hamilton and Charles Leclerc. His leadership and experience were seen as crucial in revitalising Sauber's fortunes.

The team's fresh direction was further reinforced by the arrival of highly rated rookie Charles Leclerc, the reigning Formula 2 Champion. Seen as Ferrari's most promising young talent, Leclerc's placement at Alfa Romeo Sauber was widely viewed as a stepping stone to a future Ferrari seat. His debut season would serve as both a proving ground and an extended audition, allowing him to gain experience in Formula One before making the expected leap to Maranello.

Elsewhere, Williams Racing ushered in a new lineup, featuring Sergey Sirotkin alongside Lance Stroll. Sirotkin secured his seat after an extensive evaluation process, bringing significant financial backing to the team.

In 2017, Williams was led by Claire Williams, who served as the Deputy Team Principal. She had taken on the role in 2013, effectively running the team after her father, Sir Frank Williams, stepped back from day-to-day operations. Going into the 2018 season, Claire Williams remained in charge, continuing to oversee the team's operations. However, the team was already showing signs of decline, with financial struggles and performance issues becoming more evident.

The shift towards pay drivers, such as Lance Stroll and Sergey Sirotkin, was seen as a symptom of Williams' increasing reliance on external funding rather than securing top-tier driver talent. Although Claire Williams continued in her leadership role, the 2018 season would be another step in the team's long-term downturn, eventually leading to significant changes in management and ownership in the following years.

McLaren, eager to move on from their troubled Honda era, also saw major internal shake-ups. After years of underperformance and growing frustration, the team's patience with Racing Director Eric Boullier had run out. Boullier, who had been appointed by Ron Dennis in 2014, came under increasing scrutiny as McLaren failed to deliver results. Zak Brown, who had joined the McLaren Technology Group as Executive Director in late 2016, was appointed CEO of McLaren Racing in April 2018. By July, Boullier had 'resigned', and McLaren embarked on yet another restructuring effort, hoping to reclaim its place at the front of the grid.

Brown meant business. Recognising that McLaren, as one of the biggest teams in Formula One with an incredible heritage, had lost its way, he saw that the team lacked a clear identity. The cars had sported corporate-inspired colour schemes that failed to resonate with fans or evoke McLaren's past successes. Determined to bring McLaren back to the top, Brown made a conscious effort to re-establish a strong brand identity. He decided to resurrect the papaya colour scheme originally introduced by team founder Bruce McLaren in the 1960s and 1970s. Naming it 'Papaya Spark'—reflecting McLaren's Papaya Orange Metallic shade used for over fifty years—he aimed to send a clear message: McLaren was back.

All these changes added further intrigue to the start of the 2018 season. With Vasseur leading Alfa Romeo Sauber into a new era, Williams facing growing uncertainty, and McLaren continuing its quest for resurgence under new leadership and a rekindled identity, the landscape of Formula One was shifting. Meanwhile, Hamilton and Mercedes prepared to defend their titles against an increasingly determined Ferrari team, with Red Bull, still one of the top teams in aerodynamic terms, hoping for better results with increased reliability.

## Pre-Season Testing: A First Glimpse at 2018 Performance

Pre-season testing for the 2018 Formula One campaign took place at the Circuit de Barcelona-Catalunya, where teams arrived in late February with everyone unsure about how things would play out. Much of the first week was affected by unusually cold conditions and even snowfall, limiting running and making it difficult to draw firm conclusions about true performance. Still, observers quickly noted that Mercedes, Ferrari, and Red Bull appeared likely to maintain their status as front-runners.

There were days when Daniel Ricciardo and Max Verstappen put Red Bull near the top of the time sheets, yet Sebastian Vettel in the Ferrari also recorded impressive runs. While the raw lap times hinted at Ferrari's potential, many in the paddock believed Mercedes was holding back and focusing on longer runs.

The reigning Champions Mercedes ran their W09, an evolution of their dominant predecessors. Its long-wheelbase design promised stability and adaptability, giving the team confidence that they had maintained their advantage. Mercedes topped the mileage charts during testing, clocking up an astonishing 1,040 laps in total. Ferrari were not far behind in total laps, but they looked incredibly quick in outright pace.

One of the most significant changes Ferrari introduced was an extended wheelbase, bringing the SF71H closer in design philosophy to Mercedes' dominant Silver Arrows. Compared to its predecessor, the SF70H, the new Ferrari was approximately 5 to 6 centimetres (50-60mm) longer. This was a calculated decision, aimed at improving aerodynamic efficiency and high-speed stability, two areas where Mercedes had held an advantage in previous seasons.

The benefits were clear from the outset. A longer wheelbase allowed for a more efficient aerodynamic package, reducing drag and improving straight-line speed—a key weakness Ferrari had struggled with in 2017, where Vettel, even with the benefit of a slipstream, had been unable to overtake Hamilton at high-speed tracks like Spa. Additionally, the extended chassis provided greater stability in high-speed corners, giving the SF71H an edge on circuits with sweeping turns like Silverstone and Suzuka. Ferrari also expected this change to help manage tyre wear, ensuring the car remained competitive over long race stints.

However, extending the wheelbase came with trade-offs. A longer car meant Ferrari risked losing the agility that had made the SF70H so competitive in low-speed corners, particularly on tracks like Monaco and Singapore. It also made the car more sensitive to setup changes, requiring the team to fine-tune their approach to each race weekend.

Despite the risks associated with their new car design, pre-season testing in Barcelona suggested Ferrari had struck the right balance. The SF71H was lightning fast, with Vettel setting the quickest lap of testing, a 1:17.182 on the hypersoft tyres. His teammate, Räikkönen, followed closely behind, further proving Ferrari's pace. Their rivals took notice—Mercedes and Red Bull, though quick, seemed to lack the outright one-lap speed that Ferrari had demonstrated. Some suggested Mercedes had been 'sandbagging', downplaying their outright speed and instead focusing on reliability and overall race pace.

Räikkönen, who had finished the 2017 season 112 points behind Vettel, with no wins to his teammate's five, was already under intense scrutiny before the 2018 campaign had even begun. His future at Ferrari was in serious doubt, and with Charles Leclerc making his debut at Alfa Romeo, the pressure was mounting. Ferrari had made it clear that unless Räikkönen delivered significantly improved performances, his time with the team would come to an end.

Sergio Marchionne, Ferrari's president in 2018, was blunt about Räikkönen's situation, stating that the Finn needed to demonstrate greater consistency if he wanted to keep his seat.

He commented that Räikkönen had shown flashes of brilliance, such as his performance in Monaco, but needed to maintain that level across the season. The message was clear—this was Räikkönen's last chance to prove himself at Ferrari.

At the same time, Marchionne made no secret of Ferrari's interest in Leclerc, hinting that a generational shift was on the horizon. He spoke openly about Leclerc, Verstappen, and Giovinazzi as drivers with immense potential, suggesting that a shake-up in the driver market was inevitable.

Räikkönen remained one of the most beloved figures in the Formula One paddock, admired by fans and fellow drivers for his dry wit, straightforward attitude, and sheer natural talent. But despite his popularity, it was becoming increasingly clear that his time at Ferrari was running out.

**Hamilton's Pre-Season Approach**

For Lewis Hamilton, preparation for the 2018 season followed a familiar yet rigorous routine, with a focus on fitness, mental discipline, and technical refinement. His commitment to physical conditioning remained central to his approach, ensuring he was in peak shape to handle the demands of a gruelling season. Between races, he often shared glimpses of his workouts on social media, highlighting the importance of maintaining both physical and mental resilience. He reflected on the role of exercise in his mindset, noting how it helped him stay positive and work through any challenges.

Hamilton's training regimen included endurance workouts, weight training, and yoga, ensuring he remained flexible, focused, and relaxed. Yoga became an essential part of his preparation, not just for its physical benefits but also as a mindfulness practice to manage stress and maintain composure under pressure. He frequently spoke about how exercise left him feeling more alert, upbeat, and energised.

By 2018, Hamilton had fully committed to a plant-based diet, a shift he had begun experimenting with in 2017. His diet, rich in fruit, vegetables, whole foods, and protein shakes, played a key role in his overall well-being. He credited the change with improving his energy levels and reducing recovery time after workouts, giving him more time to focus on his training and race preparation.

Beyond physical conditioning, time at Mercedes-AMG Petronas Formula One Team's Brackley headquarters was another key component of Hamilton's preparation. During these visits, he engaged in debriefing sessions with engineers, reviewed data, and spent hours in the simulator fine-tuning his understanding of the car.

As one of the most successful and dedicated drivers in Formula One, Hamilton's mastery of cutting-edge technology played a significant role in his race preparation. The Mercedes Formula One simulator became an integral tool in his arsenal, allowing him to refine his skills without stepping onto an actual racetrack. Through simulation, he virtually "drove" each circuit before a race weekend, studying the layout, braking points, and ideal racing lines—critical factors that would shape his race strategy.

However, the simulator was not just about track familiarisation. It also served as a testing ground for car setups, where Hamilton could experiment with different aerodynamic configurations, suspension settings, and tyre compounds. By analysing how the car responded to various adjustments, he and the Mercedes team could fine-tune the setup for optimal performance at each Grand Prix.

The simulator's value extended beyond technical refinement; it was also a key tool for strategic preparation. Hamilton used it to practice tyre management, assess pit stop timing, and evaluate fuel usage, all of which were crucial for executing successful race strategies. The ability to simulate different race scenarios ensured that Hamilton was always one step ahead when he took to the track.

With Formula One's stringent restrictions on real-world testing, the simulator became an indispensable part of Hamilton's routine. In a season where every fraction of a second mattered, the insights gained from virtual testing played a crucial role in keeping him at the top of his game.

As Hamilton set his sights on a fourth consecutive World Championship, his meticulous preparation—both physically and technically—ensured he was ready for any challenge that lay ahead. The simulator, while often overlooked, was one of the unsung heroes of his continued dominance in the sport.

Outside of the racetrack, Hamilton immersed himself in his growing passion for fashion, using it as a way to step away from the relentless pressures of racing and give his mind a much-needed break. In 2018, he attended events in Shanghai and New York to promote his clothing line, created in partnership with Tommy Hilfiger. His venture into fashion wasn't just a casual hobby; it was a means of creative expression, offering him an artistic outlet that complemented his high-intensity career in Formula One.

Despite his demanding schedule, Hamilton ensured that his outside interests complemented rather than distracted from his racing commitments. In many ways, these pursuits became an integral part of his mental well-being, allowing him to be mindful and present, enjoying life beyond Formula One. The ability to disconnect from the sport at times played a crucial role in his ability to return refreshed and focused.

Hamilton's approach—integrating professional discipline with personal creativity—became a defining characteristic during this period, particularly in his battle with Ferrari and Vettel. While other drivers may have solely concentrated on the Championship fight, Hamilton's ability to balance competitive intensity with self-expression allowed him to maintain both his sharp edge on track and his individuality off it. This perspective helped him stay grounded, injecting colour and joy into his life—an essential component for any elite athlete managing immense pressure.

As the 2018 season progressed, this balance contributed to some of Hamilton's most memorable performances, helping to differentiate him from his rivals. His ability to combine elite racing with broader interests not only kept him motivated but also continued to shape his legacy as one of Formula One's most multifaceted and dynamic personalities.

# Showdown with Vettel

For 2018 there were high expectations at Maranello. Ferrari had shown impressive pace in pre-season testing, and pundits speculated that the Scuderia could finally dethrone Mercedes. Hamilton, Mercedes, Lauda, and Wolff had other ideas. The first race in Australia set the tone for the season.

In late March the season got underway in Melbourne, where Hamilton put down an emphatic marker during qualifying, taking pole with a stunning lap nearly 0.7 seconds faster than Ferrari's Räikkönen, with Vettel qualifying in third. It was Hamilton's seventh pole position in Australia. Verstappen was fourth, with his teammate Ricciardo fifth in the sister Red Bull. The margins between the Ferraris and the Red Bulls were paper-thin, with just three-tenths separating the four cars.

Whilst the Mercedes team had undoubtedly provided Hamilton with the tools to do the job, his commitment in the final attempt in Q3 had made all the difference: he had given it his all, throwing his Mercedes into every corner on the absolute limit: it was a brilliant piece of individual skill.

On race day, Hamilton was challenged in the first few corners by Räikkönen, who looked particularly feisty in his Ferrari: the threat of Charles Leclerc coming to replace him looming large in both his mirrors, giving him added motivation. Into Turn 1, Verstappen had to brake slightly earlier to avoid running into the back of Vettel, and the lovable rogue Kevin Magnussen in the Haas drove straight around the outside of Verstappen and into fourth place. A few laps later, on Lap 5, Verstappen spun rapidly into Turn 1 as he tried to get as close as possible to Magnussen for a potential overtake. He recovered and continued in eighth.

Magnussen was having an astonishing run for HAAS. He pitted from fourth on Lap 23. As he left the pits it soon became clear that there was a problem, and he stopped the car in an escape road. His teammate Romain Grosjean now inherited fourth place and he pitted the following lap. However, as soon as he left the pits, he also had a problem and pulled over on the side of the circuit, unable to find an escape area: both cars had failed to have one of their wheels correctly fitted in the stops, with the wheel nuts on each car being cross threaded. It was a disaster for HAAS. The brash Gunther Steiner looked on from the pit wall, ready with a string of expletives. He then slumped forwards onto the monitors in front of him. Elbows on the counter. His head in his hands in despair.

Hamilton had been leading comfortably, but with Romain Grosjean's Haas stopped on track, a Virtual Safety Car (VSC) was deployed. Ferrari seized the moment, pitting Vettel. The timing allowed Vettel to leapfrog Hamilton, emerging ahead as the VSC ended.

Hamilton, clearly frustrated, radioed the team asking what had happened. Bono said they would investigate. There was silence, then Hamilton, always keen to understand if he had made a mistake or whether there was an opportunity to learn, made another call asking if he had made a mistake by not going fast enough under the VSC. He hadn't, but it was a clear reflection of his ability to learn and take responsibility for any issues if he had contributed to them.

The race restarted on Lap 32 and Hamilton tried everything he could to pass Vettel, running wide on occasion as he went past the limits of what his Mercedes could give. He never gave up. Vettel held his nerve and kept his lead to the end, taking Ferrari's first victory of the season.

Ferrari's race win wasn't a case of outright pace but a brilliant tactical call by Ferrari. Vettel acknowledged this over the radio, saying there was still work to do. For Hamilton, it was a reminder that the battle for 2018 would require more than speed—it would need a Mercedes team who could raise their already stratospheric bar even higher. It would also show the importance for the rest of the season that the driver who showed stronger mental resilience to bounce back after adversity and avoid costly mistakes would be the one most likely to succeed. It was set to be a fascinating season. Two four-time world champions going head-to-head in largely equal machinery.

Räikkönen made up the podium places, finishing in third. Behind him, Ricciardo finished in fourth place in his Red Bull, ahead of a resurgent Fernando Alonso in the McLaren, who came in fifth. Verstappen, in the other Red Bull, finished sixth.

Whilst the title fight was playing itself out with Hamilton and Vettel, Verstappen, now in his second full year at Red Bull, would need to assert his dominance over Ricciardo, who thus far had largely beaten all his teammates comfortably: this was a make-or-break year for Verstappen.

**Bahrain – A Desert Duel**

On 7 April, the Bahrain International Circuit provided a spectacle as Vettel put his Ferrari on pole in the desert night. Alongside him and second in qualifying was Räikkönen, reinforcing that Ferrari had indeed built a rapid car for 2018, the long wheelbase helping with overall top speed and balance. Hamilton, penalised five grid places for a gearbox change, started ninth, while Bottas lined up on the second row just behind Vettel and Räikkönen.

Pierre Gasly was the surprise of the field, qualifying his Toro Rosso Honda in sixth and starting fifth after Hamilton's penalty. Verstappen, in the Red Bull, was down in 15th after losing control of his RB14 at Turn 2, spinning into the barriers and damaging his car. The Red Bull had spun in Australia unexpectedly: Red Bull and Verstappen needed to get on top of managing corner-exit snap oversteer when coming off kerbs.

At the race start, Vettel led cleanly. Räikkönen was slipstreamed by Bottas, who went around the outside of his fellow Finn into Turn 1 in a brilliant pass. Into the first few corners, there was mayhem as cars battled for track position, at one point being nearly five abreast.

As they came out of Turn 5, Hamilton could be seen making various adjustments inside his cockpit. At the start of Lap 2, Verstappen got a strong tow from Hamilton's Mercedes. In what would become one of his signature moves in later years, he dived down the inside into Turn 1, running Hamilton wide and forcing him to the edge of the track. Hamilton, unwilling to leave the circuit, was pushed wide, but Verstappen didn't leave enough room, and both cars made slight contact—Hamilton's Mercedes briefly skipping into the air. Verstappen had full steering lock applied, but his refusal to allow Hamilton racing space backfired seconds later as his Red Bull began to weave along the straight—he had a puncture. Hamilton swept past as Verstappen limped back to the pits.

Red Bull's troubles worsened within moments. As Verstappen struggled to return to the pits, he passed a stricken Ricciardo, who had just pulled off the track with a terminal failure. Clearly devastated, Ricciardo later reflected on the sport's unforgiving nature, saying it could rip your heart out.

The VSC ended on Lap 4, and by Lap 5, Alonso, Ocon, and Hülkenberg were engaged in a fierce scrap for sixth place. The three cars roared down the track, going three abreast at 200 mph, sending sparks flying into the night sky. Hamilton had moved up to ninth place before the VSC period and, as it ended, he went on the attack. As Alonso, Ocon, and Hülkenberg battled wheel-to-wheel down the start-finish straight, Hamilton seized the opportunity, diving down the inside of all three towards Turn 1. His Mercedes bottomed out over the bumps, sparks flashing from the floor as he managed to get around the apex comfortably.

As the race unfolded, Bottas closed in on Vettel, his longer-lasting medium tyres giving him the advantage. In the final laps, he was within striking distance, but Vettel, carefully managing his ageing soft tyres, defended with precision. The balance of power between Mercedes and Ferrari was finely poised—though for Ferrari, the evening would take a disastrous turn.

On Lap 36, Räikkönen pitted from third place, just six seconds off the lead. A quick stop was crucial, and the front two wheels and the right rear were changed in seconds. However, the left rear wheel was not removed due to an issue with the wheel gun and nut. Despite this, the car was dropped to the ground by the jack men, and the front pit crew, unaware of the issue, gave the green light for Räikkönen to go. The mechanic at the left rear, with his back to the signal, was caught off guard.

Räikkönen, seeing the green light, accelerated away, his rear wheels spinning. The unsuspecting mechanic, Francesco Cigarini, was sent sprawling to the ground. Realising something had gone wrong, Räikkönen halted his car halfway down the pit lane. Cigarini suffered fractures to his shinbone and fibula and was taken to a Bahraini hospital for surgery. It was a stark reminder of the dangers not just for the drivers, but for everyone involved in the sport, from mechanics to spectators. Ferrari was fined fifty thousand euros by the FIA for the unsafe release.

Despite the incident, Vettel went on to win the race, though his thoughts were with the injured mechanic. After the race, he expressed his concern, saying he was saddened by what had happened and hoped Cigarini would recover quickly.

Bottas crossed the line just a few tenths behind Vettel but never quite got close enough to make a serious attempt at passing. Meanwhile, Hamilton, who had started 12 places behind his teammate, delivered an impressive recovery drive to secure third place. Amidst the focus on the front-runners, Pierre Gasly delivered a stunning result for Scuderia Toro Rosso Honda, bringing his car home in fourth.

After the race, Hamilton was asked about his contact with Verstappen. He acknowledged Verstappen's skill and speed but also recognised that the young driver was still refining his racecraft. He remarked that developing drivers sometimes made the wrong calls and that he hoped Verstappen was learning from the experience. Hamilton noted that he had faced similar situations when he was younger, and it was easy to get ahead of oneself and overlook the need to respect the space of others on track. He pointed out that he had been ahead for some time before backing out, expecting Verstappen to try and run him wide. Hamilton felt there was no need for Verstappen to keep going to the edge of the track.

### A Safety Car Shakes Up Shanghai

The Chinese Grand Prix on 15 April at Shanghai served up a thriller, thanks to a well-timed Safety Car. Ferrari once again locked out the front row in qualifying, with Mercedes on row two and Red Bull occupying the third row. Vettel produced a superb lap to take pole with a 1:31.095, setting a new track record.

Early in the race, Vettel and Bottas traded the lead after pit stops, with Bottas emerging ahead after the undercut. The Ferraris and Mercedes were evenly matched. However, a mid-race Safety Car, triggered by debris from a collision between both Toro Rossos, prompted Red Bull to gamble by pitting both cars, double-stacking them for fresh yellow-walled medium tyres.

Ricciardo, who had started sixth, began a series of sensational overtakes. He swept past Räikkönen, Vettel, and Bottas with clinical precision, including a bold lunge into Turn 6 that left Bottas with no response.

On Lap 42, Hamilton, running on older hard white-walled tyres, was overtaken by Verstappen, who was charging through in an attempt to catch his teammate. Given the disparity in tyre age, it was no contest. Hamilton played the long game, avoiding unnecessary contact and loss of momentum, opting to let Verstappen through rather than defend and further compromise his overall race time.

Verstappen, by contrast, desperate to catch Ricciardo, tangled with Vettel on Lap 43 at the tight right-hand hairpin, spinning both cars and dropping down the order. Vettel recovered to finish eighth, while Verstappen received a ten-second penalty for causing the collision. Vettel radioed the team, his voice devoid of emotion, saying he didn't need to say anything.

Ricciardo's charge ended in a spectacular victory. Summing up his fearless overtaking moves, he quipped that sometimes, you just have to lick the stamp and send it. His performance was widely praised, with some calling it a masterpiece and others describing his drive as sublime. His clean yet assertive overtakes stood in stark contrast to Verstappen's race, where another overzealous move resulted in a penalty. It was perhaps a reflection of Verstappen's youth and his eagerness to establish dominance over Ricciardo, who had decisively beaten him in 2017.

As the teams departed China, Vettel retained the championship lead with 54 points, ahead of Hamilton on 45. Ricciardo sat on 37 points, Räikkönen was on 30, while Verstappen trailed with 18.

### A Dramatic Showdown in Baku

The narrow streets of Baku in Azerbaijan promised unpredictability, and the race on 29 April delivered in bucket loads. The championship protagonists lined up alongside each other on the front row, ready for battle. However, it would not be the only fight of the afternoon. The race would be remembered for one of the most dramatic teammate clashes in recent history, evoking memories of Senna and Prost, or Hamilton and Rosberg.

Vettel, starting from pole, got away cleanly, with Hamilton slotting in behind. No incidents occurred into Turn 1. While Hamilton took a measured approach in his Mercedes, allowing tyre temperatures to stabilise and maintaining a sensible gap to Vettel, Verstappen was anything but patient. The Red Bull driver immediately began pressuring his teammate, Ricciardo, in a bid to seize position.

As they braked for Turn 1, Verstappen attempted a move around the outside, but Ricciardo edged him wide—firm but fair—leaving just enough room. Verstappen's car twitched as he aggressively applied the throttle on exit, forcing him to slot back in behind. Into Turn 2, Verstappen renewed his attack, darting from side to side in Ricciardo's mirrors, hoping to force a mistake. On the exit, he weaved again, trying to unsettle the Australian. It was classic Verstappen—relentless and aggressive, using every trick in the book to apply pressure.

As this Red Bull battle unfolded, the race was already producing drama elsewhere. Esteban Ocon, attempting to turn in on Räikkönen's Ferrari, misjudged the move and was sent into the barriers, ending his race. Räikkönen let out a deep sigh over the radio.

Immediately after the start, Sergey Sirotkin, in the Williams, was pushed into Alonso by an erratic Renault, leaving the Russian with nowhere to go. Alonso limped back to the pits for a new set of tyres and a replacement nose cone, having suffered two punctures. Sirotkin also had to pit for fresh rubber. With debris scattered from the Force India, McLaren, and Williams, the Safety Car was deployed on Lap 2, bunching up the field.

At the restart, it was déjà vu for Ricciardo and Verstappen, who once again went wheel-to-wheel into Turn 1 in a near replay of their first-lap duel. As the cars settled into single file approaching Turn 2, Verstappen jinked out from behind Ricciardo and forced his way down the inside. Moments later, before Turn 3, he made another aggressive move, overtaking Carlos Sainz's Renault in a show of intent. Verstappen was clearly on a mission. Ricciardo, refusing to back down, regrouped and set off in pursuit of his teammate.

The pair fought for position for the next 30 laps, neither giving an inch and both pushing their cars to the limit. Ricciardo was the first to pit on Lap 38, switching to the ultra-soft purple tyres. Verstappen followed soon after and emerged ahead of Ricciardo by a few seconds.

Recognising his driver would have to pass Verstappen again, Simon Rennie, Ricciardo's race engineer since 2014 and someone who understood his driver's mindset better than most, knew it was time to galvanise the Aussie, and he told him over the radio he would have to do it again, and finished by saying, 'let's get him.'

As both Red Bulls powered through Lap 40, the growing tension was palpable. With no team orders in place to reduce their pace, the risk of disaster was becoming increasingly obvious. Christian Horner watched on, his face expressionless. It wouldn't be for long.

Both Red Bulls exited the final corner and surged onto the long straight, crossing the start-finish line. Ricciardo, reaching nearly 340km/h (210mph), closed in as Verstappen began weaving slightly, trying to break the tow.

In a move reminiscent of Nigel Mansell, Ricciardo first darted left towards the pit entry, only for Verstappen to mirror him, shutting the door. Ricciardo, still at full speed, then feigned a move around the outside to the right. Verstappen responded immediately, shifting right to cover. At that moment, Ricciardo switched back left, aiming for the inside. Seeing the attack unfold, Verstappen, already under braking, moved left again. With nowhere to go and a sudden loss of downforce as Verstappen cut across, Ricciardo ploughed into the back of his teammate at 340km/h.

Both Red Bulls, engulfed in tyre smoke and shedding shards of carbon fibre, slid helplessly into the runoff area at Turn 1.

On the pit wall, Adrian Newey, Red Bull Racing's Chief Technical Officer, shook his head in frustration, picked up his red A4 folder, and walked away.

The collision immediately triggered a Safety Car, resetting the race, but the incidents didn't stop just because the Safety Car was out.

Romain Grosjean, running in the train of cars behind the Safety Car, began weaving left and right, accelerating and decelerating to generate heat in his tyres. A routine procedure—until it wasn't. As he flicked the car to the right, he applied too much throttle, causing an abrupt snap of oversteer. In an instant, the Haas speared into the barriers, tearing off its right front wheel. The Safety Car stayed out a bit longer.

The timing played perfectly into Mercedes' hands, and amid the chaos of pit stops, Bottas emerged in the lead ahead of Vettel. Hamilton slotted into third, tucked behind his Ferrari rival.

The race restarted on Lap 47 with Bottas still at the front, Vettel right on his gearbox, and Hamilton looming in third, ready to strike. As they hurtled down the straight, the trio closed up, with both Vettel and Hamilton benefiting from Bottas' slipstream.

Under pressure from Hamilton, Vettel attempted an ambitious lunge down the inside of Bottas into Turn 1. It was a move borne out of desperation, and it backfired—he locked his inside front wheel and ran deep into the corner. Bottas swept back through, and Hamilton followed, the Silver Arrows now running out front. Vettel's misfortune didn't end there. Carrying better momentum out of Turn 1, Räikkönen capitalised, breezing past his teammate into Turn 3.

Early in Lap 49, Bottas ran over debris at 190mph, instantly suffering a puncture on his right rear tyre. He limped around the track briefly before retiring, crushing his hopes of victory. Hamilton, who had spent much of the race in the background but kept his race clean, inherited the lead and claimed his first win of the season. Despite the victory, Hamilton admitted to feeling conflicted given Bottas' misfortune, acknowledging that his teammate had driven exceptionally and deserved the win. He described the race as emotional, admitting that it had been untidy on his part but that he had to take the result.

Over in the Red Bull camp Christian Horner was frustrated by his team's self-inflicted disaster, revealing that both drivers had been told to cool down and avoid unnecessary risks, saying the drivers needed to recognise that their actions were unacceptable. Despite the crash, Horner confirmed that Ricciardo and Verstappen would still be allowed to race freely in the future. Red Bull Motorsport Advisor Helmut Marko echoed Horner's sentiments, placing blame on both drivers and emphasizing that the incident had been entirely avoidable.

**The European Season Begins in Spain**

The European leg of the season kicked off in Spain at the Circuit de Barcelona-Catalunya, where Mercedes introduced significant upgrades to counter Ferrari's strong one-lap and race pace.

At the start, Hamilton got away cleanly from pole, while Vettel surged past Bottas around the outside of Turn 1. The rest of the front-runners largely held position, but the midfield was far more chaotic, with several cars locking wheels and jostling for space through Turns 2 and 3.

The real drama unfolded at Turn 3 when Romain Grosjean lost control of his Haas on the outside of the corner. Oversteering sideways, he made a critical mistake—rather than backing off, he floored the throttle, sending his car spinning across the track in a thick cloud of tyre smoke. Blinded by the haze, Nico Hülkenberg in the Renault and Pierre Gasly in the Toro Rosso had no chance to react, slamming into the out-of-control Haas. The impact was especially violent for Gasly, whose left front wheel was torn from its mountings, though the tethers did their job in keeping it attached. The crash triggered an early Safety Car period, which lasted until Lap 6, allowing marshals to clear the wreckage from the track.

Hamilton was untouchable despite the Safety Car with a dominant lights-to-flag victory. He led every lap and crossed the line a commanding 20 seconds ahead of Bottas. The upgrades had given Mercedes—and Hamilton—a significant boost, perfectly suiting the aerodynamic demands of the Barcelona circuit. For Mercedes, this race signalled a resurgence, with the team securing their first one-two finish of the season.

Ferrari, by contrast, struggled with tyre degradation. Vettel, running second early on, made an extra pit stop that dropped him to fourth. Verstappen, despite a collision with Lance Stroll, rounded off the podium with an impressive third-place finish.

Räikkönen's race ended prematurely due to a power unit issue on Lap 25, marking a disappointing day for Ferrari. Meanwhile, Kevin Magnussen delivered a strong performance for Haas, finishing sixth, and local favourite Fernando Alonso brought his McLaren home in eighth.

Hamilton was in high spirits after the win, praising the team's efforts and describing the synergy he had felt with the car—a feeling he admitted had been missing earlier in the season.

The first five races of the 2018 season highlighted the shifting momentum in the championship battle. Ferrari emerged strong early on, Red Bull seized opportunities to claim victories, and Mercedes showed they were never to be counted out. For Hamilton, the fight was just beginning—a season that would test his resilience, skill, and place in Formula One history.

As the teams departed Spain for Monaco, Hamilton led the championship with 95 points, ahead of Vettel on 78. Bottas sat third with 58 points, delivering strong support for Mercedes, while Räikkönen, now 30 points behind his teammate, had 48. Ricciardo was the leading Red Bull driver with 47 points. For Ferrari and Vettel, it was clear—they needed to halt Mercedes' growing momentum.

**Ricciardo vs Verstappen – The Monaco Battle**

The glitz and glamour of the Monaco Grand Prix at Monte Carlo on 27 May set the stage for Daniel Ricciardo's quest for redemption after his 2016 heartbreak.

Before the race, Ricciardo and Verstappen were locked in a battle in Free Practice 3, each pushing their Red Bull to the limit in preparation for qualifying. The margins were incredibly tight, with Ricciardo setting a 1:11.786 and Verstappen a 1:11.787—just 0.001 seconds behind.

As the session neared its end, with just eight minutes remaining, Verstappen, determined to beat his teammate, pushed too hard and put his Red Bull into the barriers at the exit of the Swimming Pool complex. Attempting to navigate the tight chicane, he clipped the inside barrier, unsettling his RB14 and sending it into the outer wall, causing substantial damage to the front-right suspension. The extent of the damage prevented Red Bull from repairing the car in time for qualifying, forcing Verstappen to start the race from the back of the grid.

This crash was a pivotal moment in Verstappen's 2018 season, marking his sixth incident in as many races and increasing scrutiny over his aggressive driving style. If he could rein in his determination just slightly, he had all the makings of a great. Christian Horner was empathetic, and recognised Verstappen was pushing the boundaries, but he now felt it was time for Verstappen to stop making the errors and learn from them. Verstappen would take note.

For Ricciardo, it was a dominant weekend, securing pole position with a scintillating lap. In the race, Ricciardo faced a significant challenge when his Red Bull suffered an MGU-K failure, costing him 25% of his car's power on Lap 28. Despite this, he managed to fend off Vettel's Ferrari for over 50 laps.

Ricciardo was over the moon with the win, but admitted that when the issue struck, he thought his race was over and wondered what more he had to endure to finally win at Monaco. His drive was described as outstanding by those within the team.

Hamilton, after qualifying a strong third, finished in the same position behind Vettel, who took second. Frustrated by the lack of overtaking opportunities, Hamilton remarked that it didn't feel like real racing, as they had been forced to cruise to the finish rather than push to the limit.

**Vettel Dominates in Canada**

At the Circuit Gilles Villeneuve in Canada on 10 June, Vettel delivered a flawless performance. The cooler temperatures, and Ferrari's better straight-line speed from an improved power unit, gave Vettel the edge.

Starting from pole, the German made a brilliant getaway. Behind him, Bottas—who had lined up second—battled fiercely with Verstappen, starting third. The Mercedes and Red Bull were separated by mere inches as they navigated Turn 1 and headed into Turn 2. In a sign of growing maturity, Verstappen fought hard but was careful to leave enough space, backing out when a collision seemed imminent. It was a smart, measured approach that suggested he was learning from previous incidents.

Hamilton started from fourth and once again relied on his experience and composure to stay out of trouble. With Ricciardo's Red Bull looming in his mirrors, he held position without taking unnecessary risks. Rather than pushing desperately to gain places, he remained focused on the bigger picture.

Just seconds into Lap 1, local favourite Lance Stroll and Toro Rosso's Brendon Hartley were involved in a dramatic crash that sent both drivers into immediate retirement and brought out the Safety Car. Stroll had struggled for traction through the mid-track chicane and, in an attempt to stay ahead of Hartley, applied too much throttle. The resulting oversteer sent his Williams into Hartley, forcing the Toro Rosso into the wall. Both cars were badly damaged and out of the race.

When the race restarted, Vettel maintained his lead, demonstrating Ferrari's impressive pace on the high-speed circuit. Behind him, Bottas and Verstappen battled for podium positions. Vettel romped home for the win, propelling himself back to the top of the Drivers' Championship standings by a single point.

In the post-race interviews, the championship protagonists shared their thoughts. Vettel was thrilled with his weekend, reflecting on Ferrari's heritage and the legendary drivers who had contributed to its iconic status. Aware of the team's passionate supporters, he acknowledged the significance of the victory, noting that it was a special day and remembering past Ferrari wins at the circuit.

Hamilton revealed why he had been conservative in the race, managing performance rather than pushing to the limit. From the start, he had been down on power, with his engine overheating, and had feared it would fail at any moment. Every lap, he expected the power to drop away completely, yet it held on. While fifth place was not an ideal result, he recognised that it could have been far worse.

Hamilton's drive in Canada again showed why winning a championship is about more than just raw speed—it requires intelligence, adaptability, and mechanical empathy. Rather than pushing flat out and risking retirement, he carefully balanced performance with preservation, adjusting braking and throttle inputs while working with his engineers to nurse the car home. It was a demonstration of his ability to think strategically under pressure, understanding that a championship is won over a season, not just a single race. By salvaging valuable points despite his struggles, Hamilton showed that the best drivers don't just drive fast—they drive smart.

**Formula One Returns to France**

Formula One returned to France on 24 June at Circuit Paul Ricard, ending a decade-long absence. Hamilton made the most of his pole position, controlling the race from the front and cruising to victory.

The opening lap saw immediate drama as Vettel collided with Bottas, dropping both drivers to the back of the field. Vettel received a five-second penalty for causing the incident, while Bottas, nursing damage, had little hope of recovering. Vettel's impatience cost him dearly, a stark contrast to Hamilton's measured approach. While Hamilton excelled at thinking long-term, Vettel's tendency for unforced errors continued to undermine his championship challenge year after year.

Hamilton's win put him back on top of the championship standings. Over team radio on the cool-down lap, he celebrated with his team, calling it a great Sunday and acknowledging their effort.

After the race, Hamilton once again praised the relentless work of his Mercedes colleagues, expressing his gratitude for the team's dedication. He reflected on their continued push for performance, both at the track and back at the factory, and described the victory as a great moment, thoroughly enjoying the race.

Max Verstappen, Christian Horner's words ringing in his ears from Monaco no doubt, delivered a very strong drive to finish second, seven seconds behind Hamilton, showing his ability to adapt quickly to a new circuit.

Meanwhile, Fernando Alonso had suffered a miserable race, and on Lap 7 was plum last. His frustration with McLaren's struggles became increasingly clear. Over the radio, he voiced his discontent, stating he had no brakes, no tyres and bemoaned that he was out of the points. He capped off these words of positivity by saying that he didn't care very much. His words reflected a driver who seemed to be losing patience with Formula One.

## Verstappen Capitalises as Mercedes Falters in Austria

The Red Bull Ring in Austria on 1 July witnessed a dramatic race as both Mercedes cars, having locked out the front row in qualifying, retired due to mechanical failures. Mercedes Team Principal Toto Wolff described the double retirement as a dark day for the team and looked visibly dejected. For Mercedes, the Austrian Grand Prix was a historic moment for all the wrong reasons, marking their first double retirement since 1955. Hamilton, who retired on Lap 64 due to a fuel pressure issue, voiced his disappointment and concern over the team's performance. However, he also acknowledged Mercedes' remarkable reliability in recent seasons. Reflecting on the weekend, he described it as one of the worst in recent memory but remained optimistic, expressing confidence that the team would recover.

Max Verstappen seized the opportunity, securing his first win of the season in front of a sea of Dutch fans, known as the Orange Army. He was amazed by the sheer number of supporters who had travelled to Austria, marvelling at their dedication despite the long journey from the Netherlands. Verstappen's teammate, Ricciardo, failed to finish due to technical issues. Räikkönen finished second in the Ferrari, with Vettel in third.

## Hamilton's Recovery Drive at Silverstone

Qualifying for the British Grand Prix on 7 July saw Hamilton claim pole to the delight of the home crowd. At the start of the race, however, he was overtaken by Vettel and Bottas. As the cars approached Turn 3, Räikkönen's Ferrari made contact with Hamilton's Mercedes, causing Hamilton to spin and drop to the back of the field. He immediately radioed the pits, suspecting damage to the car. Reassured by his engineers that there were no significant issues, Hamilton pressed on, delivering one of the sport's most impressive recovery drives.

At the same time, Räikkönen acknowledged his mistake over the radio, apologising to the Ferrari garage. He later received a ten-second penalty for the incident.

The race saw two Safety Car periods following crashes, which closed up the field and provided Hamilton with the opportunity to fight back. Displaying remarkable resilience, he climbed from 18th to second. In the immediate aftermath, he hinted at Ferrari's tactics being questionable but later clarified his comments, stating he had no grudge against Räikkönen and had accepted his apology. The incident sparked debate among pundits and fans, adding to the intensity of the title fight.

With Vettel now leading the championship on 173 points to Hamilton's 163, the battle was heating up. A two-week break followed before the next round in Germany—Vettel's home race.

**Championship Showdown in Germany**

The Hockenheimring set the stage for a pivotal race on 22 July. Vettel, racing on home soil, secured pole position and led comfortably for much of the race.

The opening lap was action-packed. Vettel got away well, retaining his lead in the Ferrari. Meanwhile, Hamilton faced a challenging start from 14th on the grid due to a hydraulic failure in qualifying. Verstappen pressured Räikkönen but refrained from taking unnecessary risks, demonstrating a growing level of patience. Ricciardo, however, was not as fortunate, suffering another reliability issue and being forced to retire.

As the race progressed, Hamilton climbed steadily through the field. By Lap 33, with the pit stops complete, Ferrari held a one-two position, with Räikkönen leading and Vettel just a second behind. Hamilton, now in third, was three seconds adrift of Vettel and beginning to apply pressure. Bottas followed in fourth, while Verstappen, continuing his more measured approach, held fifth.

Dark clouds began forming around the circuit, prompting teams to warn their drivers that rain was expected within ten minutes. Jock Clear, Ferrari's Senior Engineering and Driver Coach, instructed Räikkönen to let Vettel through. The decision was made to aid Vettel's championship campaign, as he was on fresher tyres and expected to have better pace. Though not thrilled, Räikkönen complied a few laps later.

By Lap 40, the first drops of rain started to fall. Despite the looming downpour, Mercedes called Hamilton in for fresh ultrasoft tyres on Lap 42. On Lap 44, rain intensified in certain parts of the circuit, creating an unpredictable surface.

By Lap 51, as drivers struggled for grip, the field began to bunch up. Bottas quickly closed in on Räikkönen and, halfway through the lap, made his move, setting off in pursuit of Vettel, who was seven seconds ahead. Despite the worsening conditions, Vettel appeared to be taking more risks than necessary, seemingly ignoring the cautious wisdom of past champions who understood the art of managing a lead in treacherous conditions.

On Lap 52, an increase in the rain made conditions more treacherous. Struggling for grip, Vettel lost control and skidded into the barriers at the Sachskurve, bringing his race to a dramatic and heartbreaking end. Over the radio, he let out a string of expletives, his frustration evident. Sitting in the cockpit, he pounded his fists against the steering wheel repeatedly in anguish, while an advertising hoarding slumped over his stricken Ferrari—a visual metaphor for his crushing disappointment.

The Safety Car was deployed so marshals could recover the Ferrari safely. Most cars started to head for the pits and Hamilton capitalised on the chaos.

For once, Peter Bonnington's typically calm demeanour gave way to sheer urgency as confusion unfolded. Hamilton entered the pit lane under the Safety Car and was instructed to "keep the gap to Bottas," signalling that Mercedes planned to double-stack both cars. But as he approached the final corner leading into the pit box, he made a bold decision. Realising that Räikkönen was staying out, Hamilton abandoned his pit entry at the last second, cutting across the grass and gravel to rejoin the circuit.

Bonnington, momentarily losing his composure, was virtually screaming over the radio, "in in in in in in," urging Hamilton to pit. Hamilton, unfazed, simply replied that Räikkönen was staying out, so he would follow suit and he continued at Safety Car speeds behind the Ferrari. A moment later, Bonnington, regaining his usual composure, reassured him to keep going. Hamilton had clearly taken onboard the times he had witnessed Jenson Button at McLaren calling his own shots, and had made the brave decision to stay out despite what his team told him.

On the next lap, still under the Safety Car, Räikkönen pitted, promoting Hamilton into the lead with Bottas slotting into second. Räikkönen rejoined in third, while Verstappen, showing an unusual level of patience, remained in fourth.

When the Safety Car came in and racing resumed on Lap 58, Bottas immediately attacked, pushing Hamilton through several corners and momentarily looking like he might challenge for the lead. With tensions rising, Mercedes' Chief Strategist James Vowles quickly intervened over the radio, instructing Bottas to hold position. Bottas, professional as ever, acknowledged the instruction, ensuring Mercedes secured a one-two finish in Germany, their 'home' race. The senior management of the team were elated, celebrating in the garage as Hamilton crossed the line. Rounding out the podium was Räikkönen, while Verstappen finished a strong fourth—an encouraging result for Red Bull.

Vettel's crash in Germany was a pivotal moment in the 2018 season. Former Formula One Champion Nico Rosberg, now a pundit, described it as one of the most damaging moments of Vettel's career, criticising the Ferrari driver's lack of caution in changing conditions. He pointed out that Vettel had done everything perfectly up until that lap, but with such a comfortable advantage, he could have taken a more measured approach rather than pushing too hard and crashing out on his own.

Rosberg, who knew better than most what it meant to go head-to-head with Hamilton, highlighted the stark contrast between Vettel's costly mistakes and Hamilton's relentless, calculated performances. He emphasised that Hamilton always found a way to bounce back, no matter the circumstances, showing remarkable speed, decision-making, and fighting spirit to win the race.

The crash at Hockenheim was more than just a mistake; it was a gut-wrenching moment that seemed to take a toll on Vettel. Up until that point, he had looked every bit a champion, but in the aftermath, doubts began to creep in. The weight of expectation, the pressure of leading Ferrari's title charge—it all seemed to bear down on him. From here, cracks began to show, and Ferrari, once in control of the championship, found themselves slipping away. The psychological toll was undeniable, and though the fight wasn't over on paper, it felt like a turning point from which they would never truly recover.

### Wet and Wild Qualifying in Hungary

The Hungaroring, with its tight, twisting layout, posed a challenge for teams as the championship reached the end of July. Qualifying began in dry conditions, but ominous black clouds loomed on either side of the circuit, threatening rain.

The usual frontrunners from Mercedes, Ferrari, and Red Bull comfortably progressed through Q1, though Ricciardo found himself lower in the order than expected.

Between Q1 and Q2, the skies opened, drenching the track and making the decision between intermediates and full wets a tricky one. Vettel wisely set an early banker lap before the rain intensified, rendering intermediates useless as standing water began to form. Several drivers struggled, with Lance Stroll losing the back end of his Williams and damaging his front wing against the barriers before limping back to the pits.

As conditions worsened, those who had delayed their runs found themselves in trouble. Ricciardo was one of the victims, unable to improve his time and failing to make it into Q3, while Verstappen progressed with ease. Both Ferraris and Mercedes also advanced.

By the time Q3 began, the downpour had turned torrential, forcing all drivers onto full wet tyres. With each passing lap, the spray lifted more water off the racing line, creating narrow grooves of grip. Unlike Q2, where setting a time early had been crucial, the key to Q3 was going as late as possible when conditions were at their best.

The last of the frontrunners to cross the line was Hamilton. As his Mercedes roared through the final corners with no time left on the clock, enormous rooster tails of spray shot twenty metres into the air. The stormy skies and the deep orange glow of the fading light created an almost ominous atmosphere, but Hamilton never wavered. He delivered a breathtaking lap, dethroning his teammate Bottas and clinching pole with a masterful display of control.

Hamilton crossed the line, finishing nearly three-tenths ahead of Bottas and over half a second clear of Räikkönen. On the pit wall, Toto Wolff was ecstatic. Vettel, just fractions behind his Ferrari teammate, had to settle for fourth. On a high-downforce circuit where overtaking was notoriously difficult outside of Turn 1, securing pole position was crucial—and Hamilton had delivered when it mattered most.

One of the standout performances of the session came from Carlos Sainz, who put in a stunning lap to take fifth for Renault. It was an impressive display from the Spaniard, and the Renault team had every reason to be thrilled with their young driver's effort.

Hamilton later spoke about the immense mental pressure he placed on himself to elevate his performance beyond the rest of the field, describing how crucial it was to seize those rare opportunities. He reflected on the weight of expectation in those decisive moments, acknowledging that everything he had worked for came down to executing that one lap to perfection.

Race day on 29 July was picture-perfect, with warm temperatures and soft white clouds drifting lazily over the circuit. The conditions favoured Ferrari, who had looked strong in the warm, dry weather leading up to qualifying. Everything felt calm on the start-finish straight as the cars completed their formation lap, weaving to generate heat in their tyres. But as the last car slotted into position and the lights came on, the tension reached its peak.

Hamilton made the most of pole position with a clean getaway, and both Mercedes drivers executed the start flawlessly. Hamilton and Bottas worked in perfect harmony through the first five corners, defending as a unit and preventing Vettel and Räikkönen from finding a way through. Hamilton led into Turn 6, with Bottas tucked in behind, while Vettel and Räikkönen, starting from fourth and third respectively, set off in pursuit of the Silver Arrows.

Early in the race, on Lap 5, Verstappen's Red Bull suffered an engine failure, forcing him to retire on Lap 6 and triggering a brief Virtual Safety Car. On the pit wall, Christian Horner shook his head in frustration, contemplating yet another setback with Red Bull's Renault power unit. However disappointed Horner appeared, it was nothing compared to Verstappen's fury. After a strong qualifying performance, his race was over in an instant, and his frustration spilled over the radio in a flurry of expletives.

Hamilton pitted on Lap 25, switching to soft tyres, while Vettel extended his stint until Lap 39, aiming to capitalise on fresher tyres in the latter stages. However, Vettel's pit stop was slower than anticipated, causing him to rejoin behind Bottas.

As the race wore on, Vettel, benefiting from fresher tyres, steadily closed in on Bottas. On Lap 65, he launched an attack into Turn 2, but Bottas defended forcefully, resulting in contact that damaged his front wing and allowed Räikkönen to slip through into third.

Shortly after, Daniel Ricciardo, who had carved his way through the field from 12th on the grid, found himself in a fierce battle with Bottas for fourth. The pair made contact, but Ricciardo ultimately forced his way past as Bottas, struggling with damage, conceded the position on the final lap.

For Bottas, these incidents were uncharacteristic. Usually known as a reliable and measured racer, he had found himself at the centre of two costly clashes in the closing stages.

Hamilton secured victory, finishing over 17 seconds ahead of Vettel, with Räikkönen completing the podium. This win extended Hamilton's lead in the Drivers' Championship to 24 points over Vettel. It was Hamilton's sixth victory at the Hungaroring, easily surpassing Michael Schumacher's previous record of four wins.

After the race, Hamilton reflected on how he and Mercedes had once again managed to beat what was ultimately a quicker Ferrari. He acknowledged that Ferrari had the advantage in outright pace, but highlighted that championship success was not just about speed—it was also about making the right strategic calls, minimising mistakes, and managing the bigger picture over the course of the season.

Looking ahead to the second half of the season, Hamilton sent a clear message to his rivals, stating that this was typically the point in the year where he and Mercedes found their strongest form. He emphasised the need to prepare thoroughly and come back even stronger after the summer break.

As the team packed up and left the circuit, an unusual tension lingered between Toto Wolff and Valtteri Bottas. Wolff had described Bottas as a "sensational wingman" and this did not sit well with the Finn, who felt it implied Mercedes were prioritising Hamilton's title bid while casting him in a supporting role. Frustrated by the suggestion, Bottas subtly expressed his discontent on social media, making it clear he was unhappy with how the situation was unfolding. However, in the days that followed, he softened his stance publicly, admitting that his frustration stemmed more from his own performance than any team orders. He acknowledged that his tyre struggles had left him unable to fight for the win but also made it clear that he expected to be treated as Hamilton's equal for the remainder of the season.

The gap between the Hungarian Grand Prix on 29 July and the Belgian Grand Prix on 26 August was the longest break of the season, nearly four weeks in total. However, only two of those weeks were part of Formula One's mandatory summer shutdown, during which teams were required to cease all operations. The factory doors at Brackley and Brixworth were locked, wind tunnels and simulators fell silent, and engineers and mechanics took a rare period of rest before the intense final stretch of the Championship.

For Hamilton, the summer break was never about switching off completely. While he took time to relax, travel, and spend time with close friends and family, his fitness regimen remained a top priority. He trained rigorously, often cycling or running in high temperatures to maintain peak endurance. Strength training and reaction-based exercises were also part of his routine, ensuring he returned to the cockpit as sharp as ever.

Beyond physical preparation, Hamilton often used the break to clear his mind. Music, one of his biggest passions, provided an escape, as did time spent in nature—whether on a beach or out hiking. He had always spoken about the importance of balance, knowing that a refreshed mind was just as crucial as a strong body when fighting for a Championship.

By the time the summer break ended and the paddock reconvened at Spa, Hamilton was ready. The time away had recharged him, and he arrived in Belgium focused, motivated, and prepared to take on the crucial next phase of the season.

### A Crucial Weekend at Spa

The 2018 Belgian Grand Prix at Spa-Francorchamps was another key moment in the Championship fight between Hamilton and Vettel. With momentum shifting towards Mercedes in recent races, the question was whether Vettel could turn the tide.

Saturday's qualifying session was unpredictable, with dry conditions early on before a sudden downpour in Q3 added an extra challenge. Once again Hamilton thrived in the wet, mastering the tricky conditions to take pole, with a lap of 1:58.179. Vettel secured second on the grid but was nearly seven-tenths adrift. Meanwhile, the newly rebranded Racing Point Force India team made a statement, with Esteban Ocon and Sergio Pérez locking out the second row in a stunning performance. Räikkönen, however, struggled, qualifying only seventh and over three and a half seconds behind Vettel. While he had shown flashes of strong form in recent races, this result did little to strengthen his case amid growing speculation that Ferrari would replace him with Charles Leclerc for the following season.

On race day, the weather was clear—ideal for Ferrari. At the start, chaos unfolded at La Source as a major collision involving Hülkenberg, Alonso, and Leclerc resulted in immediate retirements and forced the deployment of the Safety Car. Several other drivers also found themselves caught up in incidents, including Bottas. It was a dangerous incident,

Alonso's McLaren getting airborne and appearing to hit the top of Leclerc's Sauber.

Further back, Ricciardo made contact with the rear of Räikkönen, tearing chunks out of his front wing and scattering carbon fibre debris into Räikkönen's right rear tyre. Before the Safety Car was called, Vettel seized the moment, using the slipstream to power past Hamilton on the Kemmel Straight and take the lead.

As the Safety Car was deployed, Räikkönen limped back to the pits, his punctured right rear tyre flailing helplessly, signalling the rapid unravelling of Ferrari's hopes for a strong team result.

When the race restarted, Vettel controlled the pace at the front, gradually pulling away from Hamilton. Despite Hamilton's best efforts, the Mercedes simply couldn't match Ferrari's speed at Spa.

Vettel took a commanding victory, crossing the line 11 seconds ahead of Hamilton. Verstappen delivered another impressive drive, charging from seventh on the grid to secure third. Bottas, despite his first-lap setback, fought his way through the field to finish fourth, while Racing Point Force India capped off an exceptional weekend with both of their cars in the top six—Sergio Pérez and Esteban Ocon finishing fifth and sixth respectively.

This result narrowed Hamilton's lead in the Championship standings, intensifying the rivalry as the season progressed. The win reignited Vettel's Championship hopes and, as the teams and drivers left Spa, Hamilton led with 231 points, while Vettel was close behind on 214. Räikkönen remained a distant third with 146 points.

As the teams packed up and reflected on the chaotic first-lap incidents, it became clear that, despite initial scepticism from some drivers and team owners, the Halo had already proven its worth. At Turn 1, when Alonso's McLaren was launched into the air after being rear-ended by Hülkenberg's Renault, the impact had sent Alonso flying over the top of Leclerc's Sauber, with his front wheel coming perilously close to Leclerc's head.

Formula One's Sporting Director, Charlie Whiting, later remarked that without the Halo, there would likely have been tyre marks on Leclerc's helmet—a statement that, if anything, understated the severity of the near miss. The right front side of Leclerc's Alfa Romeo nose cone had been scraped down to bare carbon fibre, as had parts of the Halo itself, a chilling indication of the potential consequences had the device not been in place.

Leclerc, who had previously voiced scepticism about the Halo, openly acknowledged his change of heart after the race, admitting that he was very glad to have had it over his head that day. Many within the paddock echoed the sentiment, including former drivers Felipe Massa—who had suffered his head injury in 2009—and Nico Rosberg, both of whom believed the Halo had played a crucial role in protecting Leclerc and may well have saved his life.

**Hamilton vs Ferrari at Monza**

Monza, the Temple of Speed, was awash with red as Ferrari fans anticipated a home victory. It was 2 September 2018, and the Tifosi were about to witness just how determined Hamilton was.

The Ferraris were rapid in qualifying trim, locking out the front row with Räikkönen taking a stunning pole position, putting him in the best place for his first victory since 2013. The Tifosi were buoyed by Ferrari's performance and expected Räikkönen or Vettel to storm to victory on a circuit that suited the Ferrari's top speed and stability under braking. Hamilton, however, had other ideas.

At the start, Räikkönen maintained his lead from pole, while Vettel and Hamilton battled for second into Turn 1 at Prima Variante, with Hamilton narrowly avoiding contact with the rear of the Ferrari. As they exited the long sweeping right-hand corner of the flat-out Turn 2, Curva Biassono, Hamilton got a great exit and into Vettel's slipstream. As soon as the track straightened out, and before Vettel could react, Hamilton darted right to challenge into the Seconda Variante chicane.

Räikkönen sailed through Seconda Variante unchallenged and set off down the road. Right behind, Hamilton braked at the very limit, right up against the outside white line, managing to turn in alongside Vettel. At this point, Vettel should have realised he was beaten—Hamilton had the inside line for the right-hander—but, as had happened before, Vettel misjudged the moment and hit the side of Hamilton. The contact spun the Ferrari 180 degrees.

Just like Grosjean in Spain, Vettel mashed the throttle in frustration, attempting to spin the car back around as smoke poured from the rear tyres. A chunk of red carbon fibre dropped off the Ferrari as Vettel rejoined at the rear of the field.

Hamilton closed in on Räikkönen and, at the end of Lap 3, took the lead. Verstappen, who had been cautious in the opening laps—seemingly a transformed driver from his early-season incidents—moved up to third as they entered Lap 4. However, Räikkönen was not finished. In a carbon copy of Hamilton's move on Vettel, the Finn used DRS and Ferrari's superior straight-line speed to overtake Hamilton into Seconda Variante. Unlike Vettel, Hamilton didn't take unnecessary risks, backing out early and tucking in behind the flying Ferrari. The Tifosi erupted in celebration.

Räikkönen pitted on Lap 21, while Hamilton extended his stint, as did Bottas.

On Lap 25, Ricciardo's Red Bull was forced into retirement after yet another Renault engine failure. Christian Horner, already frustrated with Renault's reliability issues, was likely finalising his decision on the team's future power unit supplier. It was a disappointing moment for motorsport fans as well as Red Bull, given Renault's rich history of producing formidable racing machines.

Hamilton pitted on Lap 29 after a long first stint, temporarily handing the lead to Bottas. When Hamilton rejoined, he was five seconds behind Räikkönen. Meanwhile, Bottas executed his role perfectly, briefly holding up Räikkönen to allow Hamilton to close the gap. After Bottas eventually pitted, Räikkönen regained the lead, and for a moment, it looked as though Ferrari's home crowd, the Tifosi, would have something to celebrate.

On Lap 43, Bottas, now back on fresh tyres, rapidly closed in on Verstappen's Red Bull for third place. Verstappen, who had put together a series of clean and mature performances in recent races, made a critical misjudgement.

As they thundered down the start-finish straight toward Turn 1 at Prima Variante, Verstappen moved right to block Bottas from attempting a dive down the inside. By the 150-metre braking marker, he had positioned himself well past the pit exit line, leaving Bottas no room on that side. Undeterred, Bottas switched to the outside, preparing for a late-braking manoeuvre.

However, as they approached the 50-metre board, Verstappen suddenly swerved left, squeezing Bottas as far wide as possible to gain a better entry into the corner. His head was already turned toward the apex, making it clear he hadn't intended to make contact, but in the tight margins of battle, he clipped Bottas inadvertently. The Mercedes momentarily lifted into the air before skipping across the escape road, losing valuable time.

Verstappen was handed a five-second penalty, with his race engineer breaking the news over the radio. Furious, Verstappen lashed out, arguing that he had left Bottas enough room and accusing the officials of making overly harsh decisions before venting his frustration in a flurry of expletives.

Meanwhile, Hamilton took a measured approach, allowing his Mercedes' systems to cool and the energy unit to recharge over the next two laps as he prepared for a decisive attack on Räikkönen. On Lap 45, with DRS wide open and his car in full "party mode," he launched his move. The battle mirrored the earlier duel between Verstappen and Bottas, with Räikkönen defending the inside line while Hamilton braved the outside. It was a high-risk manoeuvre, but both drivers showed immense skill and respect, navigating the corner cleanly as Hamilton surged into the lead.

From there, Hamilton pushed hard for the remainder of the lap to break Räikkönen's tow before settling into a comfortable rhythm. He ultimately crossed the line nine seconds clear of Räikkönen, securing a crucial victory. Verstappen initially finished third but was demoted to fifth after his penalty, promoting Bottas to the final podium spot and Vettel to fourth after an impressive recovery drive. For Vettel, it was yet another case of "what might have been." Despite setting a strong pace and trading fastest laps with Hamilton throughout the race, his early setback had once again left him playing catch-up.

The Tifosi, though passionately devoted to Ferrari, knew greatness when they saw it. As Hamilton completed his cool-down lap, many in red put their rivalry aside and applauded his tremendous drive. Bottas caught up with Hamilton on the cool-down lap, and the two Mercedes cars cruised side by side all the way back to the pit lane—a silent yet powerful statement.

The pundits were quick to weigh in on the first-lap incident, with one of the most vocal being Nico Rosberg. Summing things up bluntly, he stated that mistakes like Vettel's would ultimately cost him the Championship. Rosberg was critical of Vettel's approach, arguing that he had run too wide, collided with Hamilton, and spun himself out—an entirely avoidable situation.

Hamilton's victory at the 2018 Italian Grand Prix was another step towards his Championship campaign. In the heart of Ferrari territory at Monza, he produced a drive that blended bravery, precision, and passion. Not only did he overcome the intense battle on the circuit with both Ferraris, but he also faced the mental challenge of racing in front of a fiercely partisan crowd. By the end of the race, he had conquered both—the competition on the circuit and, unexpectedly, the respect of the Tifosi.

The mental strain on drivers—especially those fighting at the top—was immense, and once again, Hamilton proved that when the pressure was at its peak, he could rise above mistakes, balancing aggression with control. Over the years, he has spoken openly about the importance of managing stress and maintaining mental resilience, revealing the tools he used to cope with the relentless demands of racing. He credited therapy, meditation, and self-reflection as key elements in his approach. He later reflected that he had worked behind the scenes to develop strategies that helped him deal with challenges, constantly seeking new ways to strengthen his mindset.

These behind-the-scenes strategies appeared to give Hamilton an edge, allowing him to remain composed under pressure—an advantage he would continue to exploit as his battle with Vettel intensified throughout the season.

As the teams left Italy and prepared for the Singapore Grand Prix in mid-September, an important announcement reshaped the grid for 2019. On 11 September, Ferrari confirmed that Charles Leclerc would join the team for the following season, replacing Kimi Räikkönen. Leclerc, who had delivered outstanding performances in his debut season with Sauber, signed a multi-year deal, becoming the first Monegasque driver to race for Ferrari. His promotion was seen as a reward for his impressive rookie campaign.

Räikkönen, despite strong performances in 2018, was moved to Sauber on a two-year deal. It was a fitting finale, as the team had given him his Formula One debut in 2001.

### A Masterclass Under the Lights in Singapore

The Singapore Grand Prix took place on 16 September at the Marina Bay Street Circuit, a track known for its unforgiving tight corners and intense humidity, making it one of the toughest tests on the calendar.

In qualifying, Hamilton produced a breathtaking lap, widely regarded as one of the finest of his career, to secure pole position. His performance left the paddock in awe, with Toto Wolff describing it as one of the most extraordinary laps ever seen at the circuit. Verstappen, in the Red Bull, qualified second, again demonstrating incredible one-lap pace, while Vettel in the Ferrari secured third spot on the grid.

At the start of the race, Hamilton maintained his lead, managing his tyres and pace perfectly, while Vettel overtook Verstappen to move into second place. However, strategy proved decisive. Ferrari opted for an aggressive early pit stop for Vettel, aiming to undercut Hamilton. The plan backfired, as Vettel rejoined behind slower traffic, allowing Verstappen to regain second place after his own stop.

The race was relatively uneventful at the front, with Hamilton controlling the pace and maintaining a comfortable lead. He crossed the finish line first, with Verstappen finishing second, just under nine seconds behind, and Vettel in third, nearly 40 seconds adrift.

Vettel, who had made several costly mistakes throughout the season, was quick to criticise his team after the race, arguing that their race strategy had cost them a better result. He suggested that Ferrari had not maximised their potential and implied that the team had beaten themselves.

It was a harsh assessment, given Ferrari had provided a fast car throughout the season and had given Vettel full support in his title bid. However, too many missed opportunities and unforced errors had undermined their Championship hopes. This was ultimately what set Hamilton apart from Vettel. When things went wrong, Hamilton took responsibility alongside his team, and when things went right, he gave full credit to Mercedes—a trait that defined a true Champion.

As the 2018 Formula One season approached its conclusion with six races to go, Hamilton's journey from the Russian Grand Prix to the Abu Dhabi finale highlighted his brilliance and determination. At a time when he could have cracked under the pressure, he merely shifted into another gear, finding another level, and leaving Vettel behind.

**Dominance in Russia**

The 2018 Russian Grand Prix, held on 30 September at the Sochi Autodrom, was another demonstration event from Mercedes, their car developments moving the team ahead of Ferrari in both qualifying and race pace. In qualifying, Bottas secured pole position with a time of 1:31.387, narrowly edging out Hamilton, who started second. The Ferrari duo followed, with Vettel in third and Räikkönen in fourth. The Red Bulls started towards the back of the grid following various technical setbacks, with Ricciardo starting 18th and Verstappen 19th.

At the start, Bottas maintained his lead, with Hamilton and Vettel slotting in behind. There was some jostling for position in the first few turns, and Vettel made a few lunges at Hamilton, forcing him to defend while also keeping pressure on Bottas. He had an opportunity to make a move on Bottas but opted to play it safe, thinking of the Championship. On Lap 2, Charles Leclerc, seemingly liberated at the prospect of joining Ferrari in 2019, drove his Sauber Ferrari around the outside of Magnussen into fifth place.

The early stages of the race were relatively uneventful, with the top qualifiers holding their positions. Verstappen, however, put on a stunning display of skill and determination, carving his way through the field. By Lap 8, he had moved from 19th to sixth.

On Lap 14, Ferrari made the first move, pitting Vettel in an attempt to undercut Hamilton. Mercedes responded the following lap, bringing Hamilton in. As Hamilton rejoined, he found himself just behind Vettel. Incredibly, Verstappen was now up to second, behind Räikkönen, who was leading. Bottas, running in third, was potentially in a position to slow Vettel and back him into Hamilton.

On Lap 16, Hamilton got a fantastic tow down the long straight after Turn 1, rapidly closing in on Vettel. Sensing the threat, Vettel moved more than halfway across the track toward the pit exit, leaving just a car's width between his Ferrari and the wall. Hamilton spotted the gap and went for it. Amazingly, despite seeing Hamilton jink out, Vettel moved again—this time even closer to the wall—attempting to shut the door at the last possible moment. It was a dangerously late move, but Hamilton's razor-sharp reflexes saved what could have been a massive crash as he stamped on the brakes to avoid contact.

Heading into Turn 3, Hamilton was now committed to one of the most demanding corners on the calendar. The 750-metre-long left-hander, taken at over 255 km/h (158 mph), subjected him to sustained lateral forces of 4 to 5 G. His neck muscles strained to keep his vision steady as his body fought the crushing force compressing his ribcage, making every breath harder. Despite this immense physical load, his mind remained laser-focused, processing every tiny shift in balance as he worked the steering wheel to keep the car right on the edge of adhesion.

At such speeds, Hamilton covered 71 metres per second, constantly adjusting between understeer and oversteer as the car's mechanical and aerodynamic grip fluctuated within split seconds. His arms and shoulders absorbed the relentless strain of the steering load, his hands making countless micro-corrections as he danced the Mercedes through the corner. The car control was masterful—holding the limit without ever exceeding it.

As they approached Turn 4, a sharp right-hander, Hamilton let the Mercedes drift slightly wide at the exit of Turn 3, setting up the perfect line to attack. By now, Vettel was powerless to defend. The sheer force of Turn 3 had drained Vettel's rear tyres, and Hamilton, still in complete control, swept past into the braking zone. It was a breathtaking display of composure, precision, and raw physical endurance—shaking off the danger of the previous incident only seconds before and executing a flawless overtake when it mattered most. Vettel's Ferrari squirmed and slid sideways on the exit of Turn 4 as his rear wheels lost traction.

The race's most controversial moment occurred on Lap 26 when Mercedes issued a team order instructing Bottas to allow Hamilton to pass, aiming to maximise his points advantage in the Championship. Bottas complied, relinquishing second place to Hamilton, but notably did not respond to James Vowles over the radio.

Verstappen led the race but was out of pit stop sequence. This decision by Mercedes, once Verstappen had pitted on Lap 43, ensured a Mercedes one-two finish, with Hamilton taking victory, Bottas in second, and Vettel completing the podium in third. Räikkönen came home fourth, with Verstappen and Ricciardo in fifth and sixth respectively.

On the podium, Bottas did not look entirely delighted, and Hamilton, appearing uncomfortable, placed his right hand on Bottas' left shoulder, offering a silent gesture of empathy and appreciation.

The use of team orders by Mercedes sparked considerable debate within the Formula One community, and many fans were vocal in their disapproval. While some understood the strategic necessity given the Championship context, others criticised the move for compromising the spirit of fair competition.

Hamilton himself expressed mixed feelings about the decision, acknowledging the benefit to his title campaign but empathising with Bottas's disappointment. Bottas later admitted that he found the call so galling that he briefly contemplated retiring from Formula One at the end of 2018.

This victory extended Hamilton's lead over Vettel in the Drivers' Championship to 50 points, solidifying his position as the favourite for the 2018 title. The race underscored Mercedes' calculated approach and highlighted the complexities teams face when balancing individual driver ambitions with collective goals. Toto Wolff faced numerous questions throughout the weekend, but for him and Mercedes, the ends justified the means.

**Suzuka – A Championship on the Line**

The 2018 Japanese Grand Prix, held at Suzuka on 7 October, presented Hamilton with the perfect opportunity to all but seal the Championship against a faltering Vettel.

Under ominous dark skies, Hamilton got his weekend off to the best possible start by taking pole position in Saturday's qualifying. In stark contrast, Vettel endured yet another disastrous session. Pushing too hard in Q3, he ran wide at Spoon Curve, leaving himself without a competitive time on the board.

With just minutes remaining, teams warned their drivers that rain was imminent. As the downpour arrived, Vettel's hopes of salvaging his session disappeared. He ended up nearly four and a half seconds off Hamilton's pole time and was left stranded in eighth place on the grid. It was another costly unforced error, the latest in a series of mistakes that had stripped away what remained of Vettel's once-formidable aura.

On race day, the weather cleared, and Suzuka basked in warm sunshine. At lights out, Hamilton maintained his lead, with teammate Bottas slotting into second, establishing a Mercedes one-two. Vettel, starting from eighth, made rapid progress and was fifth by the end of the first lap, his Ferrari coming alive in the warm conditions.

An early incident unfolded when Verstappen rejoined the track after an off-track excursion, making contact with Räikkönen and pushing him wide. The stewards handed Verstappen a five-second penalty, though the decision was met with mixed reactions. Verstappen had not attempted to gain an advantage—he could have simply cut the chicane—and had been on maximum lock trying to avoid Räikkönen. Told of the penalty over the radio, Verstappen was unfazed, simply stating that he had done the best he could. Räikkönen, however, was unimpressed, believing Verstappen had simply forced him off track.

Shortly after this, Leclerc in the Sauber Ferrari was squaring up to pass Kevin Magnussen's Haas down the start-finish straight. Magnussen moved to block Leclerc, but far too late, and Leclerc was unable to avoid hitting the rear of the Haas at nearly 200 mph. Fortunately, there was no major crash, but Magnussen limped around with a puncture while Leclerc was left with a damaged front wing.

By Lap 7, Hamilton still led, with Bottas right on his tail and Verstappen in third, only a second behind. Vettel, now in fourth, was desperate to make further progress. On Lap 8, in a bold but ill-judged move, he attempted an overtake on Verstappen at Spoon Curve. The attempt resulted in contact, spinning Vettel's Ferrari and dropping him to 19th position.

It was a mistake reminiscent of his spin in Italy—avoidable and entirely down to driver error. The stewards deemed it a racing incident, opting not to take further action. However, for Vettel, it was yet another self-inflicted wound in a season that was slipping away.

As the race progressed, Ricciardo, who had started 15th due to mechanical issues in qualifying, was getting a spurt on. By Lap 14, he had climbed to fifth place, eventually finishing fourth, just behind his teammate Verstappen.

At the front, Hamilton was in complete control. He led every lap, securing victory by 13 seconds over Bottas and clinching his 71st career win. Bottas ensured a Mercedes one-two, while Verstappen completed the podium in third, pressuring Bottas hard all the way to the chequered flag. It was a mature performance from Verstappen, who kept his head despite the penalty.

Hamilton was elated over the radio as he took the chequered flag, expressing his love for the car, the team, and the Suzuka circuit, thanking everyone for their work.

With this win, Hamilton extended his Championship lead over Vettel to 67 points. It was becoming clear that only a catastrophe could prevent him from claiming his fifth world title.

Post-race discussions focused on the collision between Vettel and Verstappen. Frustrated, Vettel was quick to assign blame to Verstappen. It was a familiar pattern—making a mistake and then pointing the finger elsewhere. Some commentators questioned whether Vettel's actions were a sign of desperation in his battle to keep up with Hamilton.

Hamilton's performance at Suzuka underlined his status as the driver to beat. From his sublime pole lap to his dominant race victory, he had complete mastery of a circuit he regularly described as one of his favourites. As the teams left Japan, Hamilton held 331 points, Vettel 264, and Bottas 207. Barring a miracle, the title was all but secured.

**A Title Opportunity in Austin**

Arriving at the Circuit of the Americas in the United States on 21 October, Hamilton had his first opportunity to clinch the Championship. Starting from pole, he faced stiff competition from Räikkönen and Verstappen. Despite a strong performance, he finished third, postponing his title celebration. Vettel came in fourth.

On the podium, as the tickertape flew, Räikkönen celebrated in his customary style, taking a hearty swig from the champagne bottle. In post-race interviews, he spoke with his usual understatement, expressing genuine affection for his family. Joking that his kids had probably fallen asleep during the race, he provided a moment that was both amusing and touching. It was a reminder that beyond being elite athletes, drivers were also partners, fathers, sons—people with lives beyond the track.

Hamilton's next chance to seal the title was only a week away.

### Championship Glory in Mexico

The 2018 Mexican Grand Prix, held at the vibrant Autódromo Hermanos Rodríguez on 28 October, was set to be the stage where Hamilton could clinch his fifth title.

In qualifying, the Red Bulls locked out the front row, the high altitude and thinner air playing to their strengths. Hamilton, who had qualified third, just ahead of Vettel, got a lightning start and passed Ricciardo into Turn 1. He slotted in behind Verstappen and settled into second place.

The lead six cars swapped positions both in the pit stops and on track, but Verstappen looked particularly rapid.

On Lap 39, Vettel overtook Hamilton. Rather than defending aggressively, Hamilton thought about the bigger picture and let him go. On Lap 47, battling Ricciardo, Hamilton ran wide but managed to recover.

By Lap 60, Verstappen led comfortably, 11 seconds clear of his Red Bull teammate Ricciardo, with Vettel and Räikkönen third and fourth in the Ferraris. Hamilton, struggling in the thin air that hampered Mercedes' performance, was holding station in fifth.

A lap later, Ricciardo's Red Bull suffered yet another engine failure—his eighth retirement of the season. He pulled off to the side of the track, wisps of smoke drifting sadly from one of the engine banks.

Verstappen crossed the line first, 16 seconds ahead of second-placed Vettel. It was a dominant victory for the Dutchman, who had won on merit. Räikkönen finished third, followed home by Hamilton and Bottas in fourth and fifth respectively.

As Hamilton crossed the line to take the chequered flag, he became a five-time World Champion. He had now equalled the legendary Juan Manuel Fangio's five titles, placing himself among the sport's greatest, with only Michael Schumacher's record of seven Championships still ahead.

Hamilton's rise to this moment had been nothing short of extraordinary. Since making his Formula One debut with McLaren in 2007, he had rewritten records and established himself as one of the sport's most consistent and dominant forces. By the time he secured his fifth title in Mexico, he had started 227 races, stood on the podium 132 times, and taken 71 Grand Prix victories.

His qualifying prowess was equally remarkable, with 81 pole positions, surpassing Schumacher's once-thought-untouchable record of 68. He had also set 41 fastest laps, further underlining his speed over a race distance.

What made these numbers even more impressive was the relentless nature of his success. In just 12 seasons, Hamilton had built a career many drivers could only dream of—winning races in every single year he competed and consistently challenging for Championships.

Just as crucial as his talent behind the wheel was his bravery beyond it. His move to Mercedes in 2013 was widely questioned—why leave a competitive McLaren team for a midfield outfit that had won only one race in three seasons? But Hamilton saw the potential, took the gamble, and became instrumental in building the team into a powerhouse. He wasn't just a passenger in their success; he was at the heart of it, pushing the team forward, shaping its culture, and driving it to dominance.

With five titles to his name, Hamilton had already achieved more than most drivers in history. But the numbers suggested his journey was far from over.

The celebrations began immediately as Hamilton guided his Mercedes into the infield at the baseball stadium section, thrilling the Mexican crowd with a series of jubilant donuts. The atmosphere was electric as he climbed out of his car—only to be met by Vettel, who sportingly put an arm around him in congratulations.

While Vettel's performances had been inconsistent that season, his sportsmanship never wavered. It was a moment of mutual respect between two Champions, a fitting tribute to a season of fierce competition.

But there was more to the embrace than just a gesture of sportsmanship. Hamilton later revealed the deep respect he had for Vettel, acknowledging the support Vettel had shown him during difficult moments. In return, Hamilton sympathised with Vettel, who had faced criticism from certain sections of the media and fans after high-profile mistakes in 2018. In that moment, it wasn't just about victory or defeat—it was about understanding, respect, and the shared struggles of two of the sport's greatest drivers.

After the race, Hamilton took a moment to reflect on his monumental achievement with humility and gratitude. Standing before the roaring crowd, he was asked to put his fifth title into words. Hamilton paid tribute to his family, acknowledging their sacrifices, unwavering support, and the role they played in his journey. He spoke of how none of it would have been possible without the hard work and dedication of those closest to him, a heartfelt reminder of the commitment behind his success.

As Verstappen celebrated his race win, Hamilton headed off for a debrief with his engineers. When asked how he felt now that he had a moment to process his fifth title, he was quick to credit the collective effort behind his success. Reflecting on the team's dedication, he spoke about how united they had been throughout the season and how each individual had raised their game. He described himself as just one part of the chain, acknowledging that while his contribution was crucial, so too was the work of every single member of the team.

Hamilton was also asked to reflect on the intensity of the season-long battle against Vettel and Ferrari. His response offered a rare insight into the unseen struggles of elite athletes, highlighting the immense preparation and effort required to reach the top. He admitted that, like many fans watching sport from the outside, even he sometimes underestimated the sheer level of work involved.

Addressing his fight with Vettel directly, he was candid about the challenge. He spoke about how difficult the season had been, racing against a four-time world champion and a Ferrari team that had been so fast for much of the year. Despite often having the quicker car, Ferrari had been overhauled, and he made clear that it had been a collective effort that had allowed Mercedes to turn the tide.

His words underscored the magnitude of what Mercedes had achieved—winning against a Ferrari team that, on many weekends, had the faster package. Analysis of the season reinforced Toto Wolff's belief that Hamilton had been the defining factor in the Championship battle. The team principal described Hamilton's performance as the best he had ever seen from him, praising not only his driving but also his approach away from the car. Wolff credited Hamilton's success to a rare combination of talent, work ethic, intellect, and emotional intelligence—four attributes he believed all great champions possessed. And with that, he made one thing clear: there was still more to come.

In Mexico, Hamilton was asked how it felt to be spoken about in the same breath as Fangio. He took a moment to reflect before responding, acknowledging Fangio's place as one of the greats and the respect he had for the legends who had come before him.

Perhaps the most powerful words on Hamilton's achievement came from Fernando Alonso. Having raced against him since his sensational rookie season in 2007, Alonso was asked where he ranked Hamilton among the all-time greats. His response was both gracious and emphatic. He placed Hamilton among the sport's very best, recognising his talent from day one and praising his ability to win races even in years when his car was not the best. Alonso noted that matching Fangio was a remarkable achievement and, if any driver from their generation had to do it, he was pleased it was Hamilton. Coming from a two-time world champion who had shared the track with him since the beginning. It was a nice gesture and showed just how special this moment was.

As the teams left Mexico there were still two races left to run.

**A Controversial Clash in Brazil**

The 2018 Brazilian Grand Prix, held at São Paulo's Interlagos circuit on 11 November, was a spicy affair. Hamilton secured victory, but the race's story was deeply influenced by a significant incident involving Verstappen in the Red Bull and Ocon in the Force India Mercedes.

Starting from pole position, Hamilton maintained his lead initially. However, Verstappen, again showing great speed, quickly climbed from his fifth-place starting position. By Lap 40, he had overtaken Hamilton and appeared set for a commanding win. The race took a dramatic turn on Lap 44 when Ocon, in an attempt to un-lap himself, collided with race leader Verstappen. Both cars spun, with Verstappen sliding backward into the runoff area. Ocon received a 10-second stop-go penalty for causing the incident, but the damage had been done—Verstappen lost the lead, handing the win back to Hamilton.

After the race, tensions flared as Verstappen confronted Ocon during the driver weigh-in, expecting an apology but not receiving one. This led to a physical altercation, with Verstappen losing his temper. When later asked what Ocon had said to provoke him, Verstappen remarked that he had been caught off guard by the response and had expected an apology. He defended his reaction, arguing that drivers are not robots and that emotions run high in such situations. He pointed out that while others might have expected him to shake Ocon's hand, he could not accept finishing second instead of winning. The stewards later handed Verstappen two days of community service for his actions.

Hamilton's win, combined with Bottas finishing fifth, clinched Mercedes' fifth consecutive Constructors' Championship. Räikkönen secured third place for Ferrari, marking his 103rd and final podium finish in Formula One.

### Abu Dhabi – A Season's Farewell

The 2018 Abu Dhabi Grand Prix at Yas Marina Circuit on 25 November marked the conclusion of a remarkable season for Hamilton. Starting from pole position, he secured his 11th victory of the year, bringing his total points to a record-breaking 408.

The race also featured a poignant moment as Hamilton and Vettel joined Fernando Alonso, who was stepping away from Formula One, in performing celebratory donuts on the main straight—a gesture honouring Alonso's illustrious career.

The sight of three champions spinning their cars side by side under the floodlights of Yas Marina was a fitting way to close the season. It was a moment of mutual respect between great rivals, marking not just the end of another Championship fight, but also a farewell to one of the sport's most iconic drivers.

### Fernando Alonso Bids Farewell to Formula One (for now)

Fernando Alonso's departure from Formula One at the end of the 2018 season marked the conclusion of a remarkable 17-year career in the sport. Having announced his decision in August, Alonso commented on his time in Formula One, acknowledging the incredible journey he had experienced.

Alonso's tenure in Formula One was distinguished by two World Championships and 32 Grand Prix victories. However, his final years with McLaren were challenging, characterised by uncompetitive machinery and limited success. Explaining his decision to step away, he remarked that he had other challenges beyond what Formula One could offer him. McLaren's Team Principal, Zak Brown, expressed his admiration for Alonso, praising him as a great ambassador for the sport.

Alonso's departure was met with respect from his peers. Hamilton described him as one of the most talented drivers in the sport's history, noting how difficult it would be to find someone who could match his raw ability. Felipe Massa, who had raced alongside Schumacher in 2006, and Alonso at Ferrari from 2010 to 2013, was particularly enthusiastic about Alonso's capabilities, describing him as one of the most complete drivers he had ever competed against—fast, consistent, aggressive, and possessing an all-round skillset that made him formidable. Massa admitted that of the two, he had struggled more alongside Alonso.

Following the conclusion of the 2018 Formula One season, Hamilton's achievements were recognised through various accolades and public appearances, highlighting his exceptional performance and influence both within and beyond motorsport.

On 7 December 2018, Hamilton was officially presented with the World Drivers' Championship trophy at the FIA Prize-Giving Gala in St. Petersburg, Russia. The ceremony celebrated his fifth title, further cementing his place among Formula One's greatest champions. Grateful for the achievement, Hamilton once again emphasised that he was just a small part of a larger team effort, acknowledging the contributions of every individual within Mercedes.

He talked about his position as one of the more experienced drivers on the grid and discussed the challenge of competing against a new generation of talent. While they brought youth and energy, he believed that experience remained a key advantage. He noted the importance of reviewing his year in detail and taking the time to assess areas for improvement.

In December, Hamilton was nominated for the BBC Sports Personality of the Year Award, recognising his outstanding contributions to British sport. Although he did not win, the nomination underscored his status as one of the nation's premier athletes.

Hamilton's impact extended beyond racing. In 2018, he significantly expanded his presence in the fashion industry, collaborating with renowned designer Tommy Hilfiger to launch the TommyXLewis collection. The collaboration debuted to global acclaim, with Hamilton expressing his belief in fashion as a means of celebrating individuality and breaking conventions. Throughout the year, he attended major fashion events, including the Met Gala and Paris Fashion Week, where his distinctive style made him a prominent figure in the industry.

Hamilton also dedicated time to philanthropic efforts, supporting various charities, including UNICEF, Save the Children, and the Great Ormond Street Hospital. He spoke about the importance of giving back, sharing how grateful he was to be in a position to make a difference.

His post-season activities reflected the breadth of his interests beyond racing, providing him with a sense of balance and keeping him grounded. Whether excelling on the track, making his mark in the fashion world, or using his platform for charitable causes, he continued to shape his legacy both in and out of Formula One.

# Photos (Photo Gallery)

**McLaren – one of Formula One's most storied teams**

This image shows Denny Hulme's McLaren from 1970, the same year **Bruce McLaren** was tragically killed while testing a Can-Am McLaren at Goodwood.

**Photo: Author**

**The iconic McLaren MP4/4 – Ayrton Senna's 1988 race car**

Senna, Hamilton's idol, won the World Championship in this car, beating **Alain Prost** to the title. At this time, McLaren was being run by **Ron Dennis**, another figure who would play a significant role in Hamilton's life.

**Photo: Author**

**Senna's 'office' – the cockpit of the MP4/4**

Note the lack of head protection: no foam sides or Halo. The **MP4/4** was equipped with a six-speed manual gearbox, no power steering, no traction control, and no ABS – a lot of hard work on a street circuit like Monaco. **Photo: Author**

**Michael Schumacher in the Ferrari F2004, designed by Rory Byrne.**

**Location:** Magny-Cours, France, 2004. Three years earlier, Schumacher had raced Hamilton in karts in Kerpen, Germany.

**Photo: Author**

**The beginning. The first lap.**

**Lewis Hamilton** in the **McLaren MP4-22**, Melbourne, Australia, 16 March 2007. Hamilton would go on to overtake his new teammate **Fernando Alonso** around the outside of **Turn 1** on the opening lap of the race.

**Photo: Author**

**McLaren MP4-22**

Note the complexity of the rear suspension and the rear diffuser. Also, observe the grooved tyres, which were eventually phased out in 2009 when slicks were re-introduced.

**Photo: Author**

**Triumph and Tragedy – Suzuka, 2014**

An unbelievable photo. **Lewis Hamilton** in the **W05 Mercedes**. While TV cameras can cut through mist and rain, making conditions appear manageable, this photo truly captures the **atrocity of the conditions** at this race. Hamilton would go on to win, but the victory would be overshadowed. Tragically, **Jules Bianchi** would suffer the fateful accident from which he would never recover.

**Photo: Taka Suzuki**

**Spain, 2017**

**Lewis Hamilton** in the **Mercedes W08** leads **Sebastian Vettel** in his **Ferrari SF70H**. Hamilton drove flat out for the entire race, passing Vettel on Lap 44 after a thrilling duel. This moment marked a turning point in the season, where Hamilton would assert his dominance over Vettel, breaking him mentally. Note the winglets, which would later be banned.

**Photo: Daniele Paglino**

**Spain, 2017**

**Lewis Hamilton** in the **Mercedes W08**. This is an excellent photo, showcasing the complexity of the aerodynamics from this era. Note the sawtooth leading edges on the floor ahead of the cockpit, the barge boards, and the additional sidepod aero elements. The sharkfin tail is particularly noticeable from this angle. Finally, observe the extensive head protection around the cockpit and how confined the space is.

**Photo: Daniele Paglino**

**Spain, 2017**

Lewis Hamilton turns the Mercedes W08 hard left. Note how the right rear tyre begins to deform under load. This would all change with the introduction of the **18-inch wheel and tyre** combination in 2022, which made the cars notably trickier to drive. The lower-profile tyres, combined with ground effect aerodynamics, resulted in more frequent spins and drivers experiencing harsher oscillations due to the reduced tyre compliance.

**Photo: Daniele Paglino**

**Monza 2017**

**Lewis Hamilton** and **Valtteri Bottas** share in the elation of a 1-2 finish on Ferrari's home soil. Races like this would go on to cement Hamilton's legendary status with the **Tifosi**. **Sebastian Vettel** finished third.

**Photo: Daniele Paglino**

**Hamilton leaves the solace of the Mercedes motorhome.**

Behind the scenes, team debriefs, massage, rehydration, food, and relaxation continue. With cap on, shades in place, and earphones firmly in, the message is clear: "I do not want to be disturbed."

**Photo: Daniele Paglino**

**Italian Grand Prix, 2018**

**Hamilton** carves his way around **Monza**, chasing **Kimi Räikkönen** early in the race. The pair would have a thrilling battle, with Hamilton ultimately coming out on top, overtaking Räikkönen around the outside of **Turn 1** near the end of the race.

**Photo: Daniele Paglino**

**Italy, 2018**

Once again, on the **Tifosi's** home soil, **Hamilton** blitzes Ferrari. The euphoria of his win is palpable here. I find this photo incredibly moving. His helmet rests on the barge board, the steering wheel on the nose, while **Kimi Räikkönen** looks on forlornly, still wearing his helmet. His body language speaks volumes. In the background, **Paul Di Resta**, former Formula One driver turned pundit, watches on with the TV crew.

**Photo: Daniele Paglino**

**Italy, 2018**

**Hamilton** goes to share the victory with his team. He would always thank them for their hard work after every race, and this moment was no exception. The sheer joy is evident on every team member's face, a testament to their dedication.

**Photo: Daniele Paglino**

**On the verge of number 5**

**Hamilton** takes victory in Suzuka, leaving **Vettel** with a mountain to climb. He takes a moment to share his elation with the fans, celebrating the win with them.

**Photo: Taka Suzuki**

**Seeing the Light**

**Hamilton** exits the tunnel at Monaco at around **175 mph**, straightening the car and preparing to brake for the incredibly tight **Nouvelle Chicane**.

**Photo: Daniele Paglino**

**Monaco, 26 May 2019**

**Hamilton** leads the pack up the hill through **Beau Rivage**. Just six days earlier, his friend and mentor, **Niki Lauda**, passed away at the age of 70. Hamilton wears a fitting tribute helmet in Lauda's honour, with the **halo** also painted in Lauda's iconic colours.

**Photo: Daniele Paglino**

**Reflection**

**Hamilton**, having won the Monaco race, walks away from his car in deep reflection, head bowed, with his Lauda tribute helmet still donned.

**Hand on Heart – Monaco, 2018**

In front of **Albert II, Prince of Monaco**, and **Charlene, Princess of Monaco**, **Hamilton**, listening to the British National Anthem and standing in front of the Union Flag, places his hand on his heart in tribute to **Niki Lauda**. **Vettel**, who finished second, looks on with a stony expression. **Bottas** stands alongside his teammate, having finished third.

**Photo: Daniele Paglino**

**This one's for Niki**

**Hamilton** looks to the skies, trophy in hand, after winning Monaco 2019.

**Photo: Daniele Paglino**

**Contentment**

One of my favourite photos of **Hamilton**, looking content and relaxed. A miracle in itself, given the stress and clamour surrounding him on a race weekend. It's his ability to stay calm under pressure that sets him apart—not the jewellery he's wearing—earrings, nose piercing, and necklace—a reflection of his love for fashion. The **FIA** would later impose a ban on these items during races, citing 'safety grounds'.

**Photo: Daniele Paglino**

**Feeling the Heat.**

**Hamilton** hits the brakes. The front discs, made from carbon composite materials, glow at around **1,000°C**—the same temperature as molten lava. Cooped up in the cramped cockpit, with fire-retardant undergarments, overalls, balaclava, helmet, and gloves, alongside the heat soak from the car itself, the drivers endure extreme heat. This would become apparent time and again in races like **Singapore** and **Bahrain**.

**Photo: Daniele Paglino**

**Dancing in the Moonlight**

**Hamilton** uses every inch of the circuit, riding the sausage kerbs in the **Mercedes**. He's running the **purple side-walled Ultrasoft tyres**, which were introduced by **Pirelli** in 2016 to expand the range of tyre compounds available to teams.

**Photo: Daniele Paglino**

**Encased**

**Hamilton** during testing in **Barcelona, 2020**. Following **Felipe Massa's** accident and in response to broader safety concerns, the FIA introduced stricter crash helmet safety requirements in 2019. Note the narrow visor aperture, a result of these changes. The cockpit is a cramped space, and this image illustrates the benefits of the **halo**, the device that would go on to save lives, notably protecting **Romain Grosjean** from serious injury at the 2020 Bahrain Grand Prix, and playing a key role in the **Italian Grand Prix 2021** where the Red Bull landed on top of Hamilton's car.

**Photo: Daniele Paglino**

# Domination

The 2019 Formula One season began with a number of changes, with new young talents stepping up and other driver movements reshaping the field. Technical updates further influenced the landscape. For Lewis Hamilton, now a five-time world champion, the year hinted at further opportunities as he sought to cement his legacy.

One of the biggest moves was Daniel Ricciardo's high-profile switch from Red Bull Racing to Renault, marking a new chapter in his career after several successful seasons alongside Max Verstappen. Explaining his decision, Ricciardo stated that he felt the time was right for a fresh start and a new challenge. He acknowledged that Hamilton's success with Mercedes had influenced his thinking, noting that if he could replicate something similar at Renault, it would be a remarkable achievement.

Renault was not expected to be a title contender immediately, making Ricciardo's move a bold gamble—one driven by his desire to step out of Verstappen's shadow at Red Bull. Christian Horner admitted he was surprised by the decision, particularly as Red Bull had begun to strengthen their partnership with Honda after years of reliability struggles with Renault power units.

Ricciardo had outperformed Verstappen in both the 2016 and 2017 seasons and had appeared well-settled at Red Bull, making his departure unexpected to many. While his 2018 season seemed disappointing on paper, much of it was dictated by reliability issues rather than a decline in performance. He suffered eight retirements, many due to mechanical failures, leading him to describe his car as "cursed." Given his strong form when the car was reliable, it was plausible that he could have matched or even outscored Verstappen over the season.

Pierre Gasly was promoted from Toro Rosso to Red Bull Racing, stepping up to fill the seat left vacant by Ricciardo. It was a big opportunity for the French driver, who had impressed in his first full season with Toro Rosso, including a standout fourth-place finish in Bahrain. It would be a case of 'careful what you wish for,' for Gasly.

At Toro Rosso, Daniil Kvyat returned to the grid after a year away, having spent time as a Ferrari development driver. He was partnered with rookie Alexander Albon, who earned his Toro Rosso seat after a strong Formula 2 campaign, finishing third behind George Russell and Norris.

Russell, the 2018 Formula 2 Champion, also made the jump to Formula One, joining Williams. Despite the team's struggles at the back of the grid, Russell was highly rated, having been part of Mercedes' junior driver programme and serving as a test driver for the team. His arrival in Formula One, alongside fellow rookies Norris and Albon, signalled a generational shift, with a new wave of young talent eager to make their mark.

Carlos Sainz Jr. also made a key move, leaving Renault to replace Fernando Alonso at McLaren. With Alonso stepping away from Formula One, Sainz saw McLaren as a long-term project where he could establish himself as a team leader. He was partnered with Lando Norris, who was promoted to a full-time Formula One seat after finishing as runner-up in the 2018 Formula 2 Championship. Their arrival marked a fresh start for McLaren, which was rebuilding with a young and dynamic driver pairing.

Williams provided one of the most emotional comeback stories in Formula One history as Robert Kubica returned to the grid after an eight-year absence following a near-fatal rally crash in 2011. Once regarded as one of the sport's most naturally gifted drivers, Kubica had suffered severe injuries in the accident, including a partially severed right arm, which left him with permanent mobility limitations. His return to

Formula One was a remarkable feat, proving his determination and resilience.

However, his appointment raised some questions. During his previous outings in Williams test sessions, Kubica had been consistently slower than Felipe Massa and Sergey Sirotkin, leading to doubts over whether he could still perform at the highest level. Yet, his extensive experience and technical knowledge made him an asset to a struggling Williams team.

Williams, once a dominant force in Formula One, had endured a steady decline under the leadership of Claire Williams, finishing last in the 2018 Constructors' Championship. With Kubica joining alongside highly-rated rookie George Russell, the team faced an uphill battle to regain competitiveness.

Williams had been using Mercedes power units since 2014, and while customer teams still paid for their engines, some contracts allowed flexibility in negotiations when a top manufacturer like Mercedes was keen to place a junior driver. While Mercedes never publicly confirmed any financial arrangement, it was widely believed that Williams may have received a discount on their engine supply or additional technical support as part of the deal to sign Russell. At the same time, Williams was in a difficult financial position and needed funding. Kubica, in the other Williams seat, brought significant sponsorship backing from Polish oil company PKN Orlen, which provided much-needed financial support.

This meant Williams had one driver with strong financial backing and another with factory-team support, helping them balance funding and talent while struggling at the back of the grid. How Kubica would measure up against Russell, a rising star backed by Mercedes, became one of the most intriguing storylines of the season.

For the 'big three' teams, the competitive landscape was evolving. Mercedes entered the 2019 season as the undisputed benchmark in Formula One, having dominated the turbo-hybrid era since 2014. They had claimed five consecutive Constructors' and Drivers' Championships, with Hamilton securing four of those titles and Nico Rosberg taking one in 2016. The team's technical excellence, strategic execution, and driver consistency had made them the team to beat.

The driver lineup remained unchanged for 2019, with Hamilton partnered once again by Valtteri Bottas. While Hamilton had been the dominant force within the team, Bottas had shown flashes of brilliance and was determined to mount a stronger challenge after a winless 2018 season. His contract extension for 2019 signalled Mercedes' faith in his ability to support their Championship ambitions.

The team's new car, the Mercedes-AMG F1 W10 EQ Power+, was unveiled at Silverstone on 13 February 2019. Under the latest technical regulations, the W10 featured a revised aerodynamic package, including a reshaped front wing, modified bargeboards, and updated sidepods to optimise airflow. The changes were aimed at maintaining their edge in a season where the FIA had introduced rules to improve overtaking by reducing aerodynamic turbulence.

As the season prepared to get underway, the narrative was set—Hamilton would seek to defend his title, Bottas aimed to prove himself as a genuine contender, Ferrari and Red Bull were determined to challenge Mercedes' dominance, and a new generation of drivers were ready to make their mark on Formula One.

Behind the scenes, Mercedes made key personnel adjustments ahead of the new campaign. Aldo Costa, who had played a crucial role in the team's technical dominance, stepped back into a consulting role, handing greater responsibility to Chief Designer John Owen. Performance Director Mark Ellis also took a sabbatical, with Loïc Serra stepping up to take on a more prominent role in vehicle dynamics. These changes were part of Mercedes' long-term strategy to ensure continued success while gradually transitioning leadership within the technical department.

As pre-season testing approached, Mercedes faced growing threats from Ferrari and Red Bull. Ferrari had demonstrated serious pace at times in 2018, while Red Bull's switch to Honda power meant they could be a dark horse—or a dark bull—in the title fight. The question was whether Mercedes could maintain their dominance or whether their rivals had finally closed the gap.

One of the most significant team changes ahead of the 2019 season was Red Bull Racing's decision to switch from Renault to Honda power units. The move followed years of mounting frustration between Red Bull and Renault over reliability and performance issues. Explaining the decision, Christian Horner stated that the team had evaluated all options with one clear objective—to secure a partnership that would allow them to compete at a higher level. After careful consideration, they were confident that Honda was the right direction for the team.

Honda, having spent the previous season supplying Toro Rosso, saw the expansion of their partnership with Red Bull as a natural next step. The manufacturer believed that working with two teams would allow them to gather more data, accelerating development and bringing them closer to their goal of winning races and Championships. Their optimism was well-placed, as the Honda-Red Bull collaboration soon yielded success, paving the way for Verstappen's future title challenges.

Ferrari entered the 2019 season with renewed determination to break Mercedes' stranglehold on Formula One and claim their first Championship since 2008. The team had shown glimpses of title-contending pace in 2017 and 2018, but a combination of strategic misjudgements, operational mistakes, and driver errors had ultimately cost them.

In an effort to turn their fortunes around, Ferrari underwent a significant leadership change, with long-time technical chief Mattia Binotto replacing Maurizio Arrivabene as Team Principal. Binotto, an engineer by background, was widely respected within the team and seen as the right person to bring stability and a more collaborative approach to Ferrari's operations.

Binotto's leadership style was a stark contrast to his predecessor's. Where Arrivabene was fiery, authoritative, and corporate-driven, Binotto was methodical, soft-spoken, and deeply embedded in Ferrari's engineering culture. Having joined the team in 1995, he had steadily climbed the ranks, playing a key role in engine development during Ferrari's dominant Schumacher years and later becoming Chief Technical Officer.

As a leader, Binotto was known for his calm and analytical approach, preferring to defuse tension rather than escalate it. He was not the type to deliver dramatic soundbites or engage in public rivalries; instead, he operated with quiet confidence, trusting in Ferrari's engineering expertise. However, his reluctance to enforce strict team orders would later be scrutinised, particularly as he attempted to manage the growing rivalry between Vettel and Leclerc.

Unlike some previous Ferrari bosses, Binotto was first and foremost an engineer. His strengths lay in car development rather than the political manoeuvring often associated with Ferrari's leadership. His promotion to Team Principal represented a major shift—not just for him personally, but for Ferrari as a whole, as they moved away from a more authoritarian structure towards a collaborative model. The big question was whether this approach could finally deliver the Championship that had eluded them for over a decade.

There was also a change in Ferrari's driver lineup. After five seasons with the team, Kimi Räikkönen departed for Alfa Romeo, making way for Charles Leclerc. The young Monegasque had impressed in his rookie season with Sauber in 2018, demonstrating both raw speed and maturity beyond his years. His arrival at Ferrari set up an intriguing dynamic alongside four-time world champion Sebastian Vettel, who was looking to bounce back from a mistake-ridden 2018 campaign.

The team's new car, the SF90, was unveiled in February, featuring a striking matt red livery—a first for Ferrari, introduced to reduce weight. The car itself was a bold evolution of its predecessor, featuring an aggressive aerodynamic philosophy that included a distinctive low-drag front wing concept. Ferrari's design focused heavily on straight-line speed, a decision that gave them a significant advantage on power-sensitive circuits but raised questions over whether they had sacrificed too much downforce for cornering performance.

**2019 Technical and Safety Changes**

The 2019 Formula One season introduced several technical regulations aimed at enhancing overtaking and improving the overall racing spectacle. The front wings were widened by 200mm, raised by 20mm, and moved 25mm forward, with simplified designs to reduce the turbulent air affecting trailing cars. Rear wings were also widened by 100mm and raised by 20mm, featuring larger DRS openings to increase the system's effectiveness. Additionally, winglets were removed from brake ducts to minimize their aerodynamic influence.

These adjustments were designed to make it easier for cars to follow one another closely, reducing the effects of 'dirty air' and increasing overtaking opportunities. However, the true impact of the changes remained uncertain as teams adapted their designs in pre-season testing.

A significant change for 2019 was the separation of driver weight from the car's minimum weight requirement. Previously, drivers and cars had a combined minimum weight, which disadvantaged taller and heavier drivers. From 2019 onwards, a minimum driver weight of 80kg was introduced. If a driver weighed less than this, teams were required to add ballast to meet the minimum, ensuring fairness across the grid. This was a welcome development, as some drivers had struggled to maintain the previous weight limits. Jenson Button and Mark Webber had both commented in the past on the difficulties of reaching the minimum weight. Webber had even joked on social media that he had "not eaten for the last five years" before later deleting the post.

Hamilton welcomed the change, noting that in previous seasons, he and other drivers had to maintain a lower body weight, which was not always ideal for their health or performance. He appreciated the ability to be at a more natural and comfortable weight. However, Hamilton also pointed out that while drivers could now be heavier, they still had to be mindful of where the weight was distributed. A bulkier upper body could raise the car's centre of gravity, affecting handling and performance. Ahead of the season, Hamilton stated that he now felt "stronger and fitter than ever, all round."

These regulatory adjustments were part of Formula One's ongoing efforts to create a more competitive and engaging racing environment, addressing both technical performance and driver well-being.

The 2019 season also saw a significant advancement in driver safety with the introduction of stricter helmet regulations. The FIA mandated that all helmets conform to the FIA 8860-2018 standard, a design developed over a decade to enhance protection against high-impact crashes and debris strikes.

The most noticeable change was the reduction of the visor opening by 10mm, further shielding drivers from potential projectiles. Helmets now had to pass a series of rigorous tests, including standard impact, low-velocity impact, lateral impact, ballistic protection, crush resistance, and shell and visor penetration tests. The complexity of these assessments underscored the incredible engineering behind modern Formula One safety.

Constructed from advanced composite materials, the updated helmets offered improved resistance to penetration while maintaining lightweight durability. This regulation change was another step in Formula One's continuous efforts to improve driver safety, following the introduction of the Halo device in 2018.

The stricter helmet standards were a direct response to past incidents, including Felipe Massa's serious head injury in 2009 and other accidents involving high-velocity debris. The FIA's Safety Director at the time remarked that while existing helmets were already the safest in the world, these new standards would take protection "to the next level." The move was widely praised across the paddock.

Another key change for 2019 was a revision to the points system. Formula One introduced a new rule awarding an additional Championship point for the fastest lap of the race, provided the driver finished inside the top ten.

This change was designed to add a fresh strategic element, encouraging teams to push for quick laps in the closing stages if they had a gap to the car behind. The rule revived an old system last seen between 1950 and 1959, bringing an extra layer of excitement to the Championship battle.

### Pre-Season Testing

Pre-season testing remained a crucial period for teams to fine-tune their cars and assess performance ahead of the Championship. Over time, testing regulations had been tightened to control costs and maintain competitive balance, limiting the amount of running teams could complete.

By 2019, pre-season testing was restricted to two sessions, each spanning four days, held at the Circuit de Barcelona-Catalunya in Spain. These sessions provided teams with their only opportunity to evaluate their new cars under controlled conditions before the season commenced. Each day was divided into a morning session from 9:00 to 13:00 and an afternoon session from 14:00 to 18:00, giving teams eight hours of track time daily.

However, a key restriction remained—each team was permitted to run only one car at a time. While multiple drivers could take part over the course of testing, teams had to carefully manage track time to ensure both race drivers, and sometimes test or reserve drivers, got sufficient mileage.

Unlike race weekends, where track time is shared among all teams, pre-season testing allowed each team to run as many laps as possible within the allotted time. There were no specific mileage limits, but unforeseen circumstances such as red flags, technical issues, or poor weather could reduce running time.

This structured yet restricted testing environment was a stark contrast to earlier eras when in-season testing was more prevalent. The reduction in testing aimed to curb escalating costs and provide a more level playing field among teams with varying resources. As a result, teams had to maximise efficiency during these sessions, meticulously planning their programmes to gather essential data on aerodynamics, tyre performance, and reliability.

For drivers, pre-season testing was a vital opportunity to get accustomed to new machinery and refine car setups. It also offered an early glimpse of the competitive order, though teams often ran with different fuel loads and engine settings to mask their true performance.

By 2019, Formula One's pre-season testing had evolved into a tightly regulated and strategically crucial part of the sport, balancing cost control with the need for teams to prepare effectively for the season ahead. Pre-season testing at the Circuit de Barcelona-Catalunya provided the first indication of how the teams stacked up under the new regulations.

Ferrari appeared to have the edge in outright pace, with Vettel topping the timesheets on multiple occasions. After the first day of running, he commented, "I couldn't have hoped for a better first day. Unbelievable." Autosport observed that Ferrari's pace and consistency suggested the team was in "good shape." Vettel was quickest overall, with Leclerc third, only a few hundredths behind his teammate. The early signs were promising for Ferrari.

Mercedes, as they had done in previous years, focused on heavier fuel loads and race simulations, making direct comparisons difficult. Their times were not reflective of their full potential, leaving both drivers and pundits unsure of their true standing. Despite this, Hamilton still finished second overall in testing, only a fraction behind Vettel—an ominous sign for the competition. The rivalry with Vettel looked set to reignite.

Red Bull were encouraged by their new Honda power unit and the overall performance of their car. Verstappen noted, "If we look at our longer runs, it all looks pretty promising." The team entered the season with optimism, believing that the Honda partnership had the potential to deliver results.

Williams endured a disastrous start to the 2019 season, with their pre-season preparations thrown into chaos when their FW42 car was not ready in time. The team missed the first two and a half days of testing in Barcelona, severely limiting their ability to gather data and refine their setup.

Deputy Team Principal Claire Williams admitted the situation was "embarrassing," particularly for a team once renowned for its efficiency and professionalism. The delays and setbacks became a defining moment for Williams' season. When the FW42 finally hit the track, it was painfully off the pace, showing little sign of competitiveness.

The fallout from the disastrous start was immediate. Chief Technical Officer Paddy Lowe was placed on gardening leave soon after and ultimately left the team. Despite its striking ROKiT livery, the FW42 was woefully slow, marking another chapter in Williams' ongoing decline from their once-dominant past.

The 2019 season was shaping up to be fiercely contested. Ferrari looked strong, Red Bull was eager to make strides with Honda, and Mercedes remained the benchmark. Everything pointed towards another hard-fought Championship fight.

For Hamilton, the pursuit of a sixth title would demand his trademark blend of skill, determination, and consistency. As the season got underway, it quickly became clear that he and Mercedes were once again setting the standard, stamping their authority early in the campaign.

**The Season Begins – 2019 Australian Grand Prix**

The 2019 season kicked off at Melbourne's Albert Park Circuit on 17 March with anticipation running high. Hamilton secured pole position, maintaining his reputation as a qualifying specialist, but at lights out, it was Bottas who made the stronger start, surging past his teammate into Turn 1.

Ricciardo's home race began in disaster. Running onto the grass near the pit exit on the approach to Turn 1, he hit a dip, tearing off the front wing of his Renault before even reaching the first corner. Pieces of debris were strewn across the track, forcing him to pit at the end of Lap 1.

On Lap 11, Carlos Sainz, driving the Renault-powered McLaren, suffered a failure of the MGU-K component in his power unit. Flames and smoke billowed from the rear of the car, forcing him to retire.

From there, Bottas dominated, building a comfortable lead and taking a commanding victory, while Hamilton settled for second, securing a one-two finish for Mercedes. The win was particularly significant for Bottas, who had endured a winless 2018 despite driving a Championship-winning car. As he drove the cool down lap, the difficult 2018 season and all the negativity that came out of it spilled over in an instant on the team radio as Bottas delivered a blunt message to his critics: "To whom it may concern: **** you!"

Hamilton believed there was still more performance to unlock from his Mercedes and planned to go through the data with his engineers after the race: proof of his relentless attention to detail.

Verstappen secured a solid third-place finish, giving Red Bull and Honda plenty of encouragement. Finishing just a few seconds behind Hamilton on a power-sensitive circuit was a promising sign that Honda had made real progress in their first season supplying Red Bull.

Ferrari's weekend ended in disappointment, with Vettel and Leclerc finishing fourth and fifth. More concerning for Vettel was that Leclerc was right on his tail at the chequered flag, just a second behind. It was clear that the German wouldn't just be fighting Hamilton for supremacy—he now had Leclerc and Verstappen to contend with as well.

Ricciardo recovered to the pits and continued after his early misfortune, but his race ended on Lap 31 due to a mechanical failure in his Renault.

As the teams packed up and left Australia, the true competitive order remained uncertain. Ferrari had underwhelmed, Red Bull had impressed, and Mercedes had begun the season with a dominant one-two finish. The battle for the Championship was just beginning.

**Bahrain**

The 2019 Bahrain Grand Prix, held at the Bahrain International Circuit on 31 March, delivered drama. Leclerc, in only his second race for Ferrari, secured his first career pole position, leading a front-row lockout for the team. Hamilton qualified third, with Bottas alongside him. Verstappen had pushed his Red Bull hard and started in fifth.

At the start, Leclerc lost positions to teammate Vettel and Bottas but quickly regained his composure, overtaking Bottas and then Vettel to reclaim the lead by Lap 6.

On Lap 38, Hamilton, running third, closed up on Vettel, applying pressure into Turn 4, a tight 120km/h right-hander. Hamilton, carrying momentum from the long straight prior, went around the outside of Vettel. Both drivers left each other room, but as they exited the corner, Vettel, in a move reminiscent of several incidents in 2018, spun his Ferrari. Hamilton powered past as Vettel tried to regain control. As Vettel accelerated back up to racing speed, his front wing failed under stress from the tyre vibrations, snapping off at over 250km/h and briefly lifting the Ferrari's nose skywards. It was another unforced error. As Vettel limped back to the pits, Ricciardo and Hülkenberg were squabbling in their Renaults, briefly touching wheels.

Leclerc appeared set for a maiden victory, building a substantial lead. However, on Lap 46, he reported a sudden loss of power due to an engine issue, later diagnosed as a failed cylinder. His pace dropped dramatically, allowing both Hamilton and Bottas to overtake him. A late-race Safety Car, deployed after both Renault cars retired simultaneously due to mechanical failures, preserved Leclerc's third-place position, marking his first Formula One podium.

Hamilton, who inherited the lead following Leclerc's misfortune, acknowledged the young driver's impressive performance, telling him, "You drove great. You've got a great future ahead of you." In a sign of things to come, Hamilton and Leclerc stood with arms around each other during the post-race interviews, mutual respect already established. Verstappen, who had driven well throughout, finished fourth. With Vettel's spin having caused significant tyre vibrations leading to his front wing failure, after an unscheduled pit stop, he finished fifth.

## The 1,000th Grand Prix – 2019 Chinese Grand Prix

The 1,000th World Championship race, held in China at the Shanghai International Circuit on 14 April, carried a sense of history, and Hamilton rose to the occasion. Starting second on the grid behind Bottas, Hamilton took the lead into Turn 1 with a clean and decisive move. Behind them, Leclerc went past Vettel for third. However, on Lap 11, Ferrari instructed Leclerc to let Vettel through, despite the Monegasque driver holding the position comfortably. Leclerc's frustration was evident over the radio, but he obeyed the order.

From Lap 11 onwards, Hamilton controlled the race, leading every lap to secure his 75th career victory. As he crossed the line, Alain Prost waved the chequered flag. Over team radio, Hamilton was jubilant: "Awesome job, guys. What a fantastic result today. I'm so proud of everyone—thank you so much for all the hard work." Bottas secured second place, with Vettel completing the podium in third. Verstappen demonstrated the growing strength of the Honda-powered Red Bull by overtaking Leclerc and finishing ahead of the second Ferrari.

Ferrari, however, seemed to be creating problems of their own. In Australia, they had instructed Leclerc to hold position behind Vettel, a command he followed. In Bahrain, he was once again told to stay behind for two laps but ignored the order, overtaking his teammate on merit. Now, in yet another controversial call, Ferrari had asked Leclerc to let Vettel through. It was a baffling approach to race strategy, particularly so early in the season, and could only have dented Leclerc's confidence. At the same time, it did little to help Vettel's increasingly fragile mindset. He now faced mounting scrutiny from the press, forced to field repeated questions about Ferrari's handling of team orders. The situation was quickly becoming a distraction, and with tensions already simmering just two races into the season, it did not bode well for the months ahead.

**2019 Azerbaijan Grand Prix – Another Mercedes One-Two**

The 2019 Azerbaijan Grand Prix, held on 28 April at the Baku City Circuit, saw Bottas claim victory, leading a Mercedes one-two finish with Hamilton in second place. This result marked Mercedes' fourth consecutive one-two finish of the season, underscoring their dominance in the early stages of the Championship.

Bottas secured pole position during qualifying, narrowly edging out Hamilton. At the race start, Hamilton challenged Bottas into Turn 1 and Turn 2, but Bottas maintained his lead and gradually extended it as the race progressed. Hamilton settled into second, playing the long game.

Vettel finished third for Ferrari, unable to match the pace of the leading Mercedes duo. His teammate, Leclerc, who had started eighth after a crash in qualifying, managed to lead the race for several laps due to an extended first stint on medium tyres. Leclerc eventually finished fifth but secured the fastest lap of the race, earning an additional Championship point. Verstappen continued his consistent performance for Red Bull Racing, finishing fourth and maintaining his record of top-four finishes in every race of the season up to that point.

With Mercedes firmly in control of both Championships, the early stages of 2019 had played out in a way that few had expected. Ferrari had shown flashes of speed but lacked execution. Red Bull looked strong but weren't quite at Mercedes' level yet. For Hamilton, the early rounds had reinforced what he already knew—winning Championships wasn't just about having the fastest car; it was about maximising every opportunity and minimising mistakes. And so far, he was doing just that.

A bizarre incident unfolded between Ricciardo and Kvyat during the race. Ricciardo attempted a move on Kvyat at Turn 3 but misjudged the corner, forcing both cars wide into the escape road. As he tried to rejoin the track, Ricciardo inadvertently reversed straight into Kvyat's car, damaging both and forcing them to retire. Ricciardo admitted afterwards that he had no idea Kvyat was there. It was a moment that highlighted Ricciardo's growing struggles. Once seemingly untouchable at Red Bull—aside from reliability issues—his time at Renault was proving far more challenging, and cracks were beginning to show.

This race further solidified Mercedes' dominance in the 2019 season, with Bottas reclaiming the lead in the Drivers' Championship by a narrow margin over Hamilton. Ferrari's struggles continued, as their decisions and on-track incidents hampered their efforts to challenge Mercedes' supremacy. Following the 2019 Azerbaijan Grand Prix, Hamilton reflected on Mercedes' strong start, stating, "Until Ferrari start performing at the level we are now, this is how it's going to be."

**The 2019 Spanish Grand Prix - Another Mercedes One-Two**

The 2019 Spanish Grand Prix, held on 12 May at the Circuit de Barcelona-Catalunya, saw sunny conditions, with track temperatures exceeding 40°C.

Mercedes had struggled with tyre overheating in previous seasons, but by 2019, they had developed a car that handled warm conditions better. Their W10 chassis and aerodynamics allowed for improved airflow and tyre cooling, reducing wear over long stints. This gave them the flexibility to dictate strategy rather than react to excessive degradation, blistering, or overheating. However, while they had found the sweet spot for high-temperature circuits, extreme conditions – such as those found in Bahrain - still posed challenges.

Ferrari's SF90 was strong in straight-line speed but struggled with downforce and tyre degradation. The car's low-drag philosophy meant it did not generate as much heat into the tyres, and on hotter circuits like Barcelona, this often left them lacking grip over a race distance.

The race saw another dominant display from Mercedes, with Hamilton securing victory ahead of teammate Bottas. The result marked the team's fifth consecutive one-two finish of the season, further solidifying their grip on the Championship.

Bottas had taken pole position with a stunning lap in qualifying, but at the race start, Hamilton reacted quickest. As the lights went out, he gained the better launch and kept the inside line, drawing alongside Bottas, both Mercedes running neck and neck. Behind them, Vettel surged off the line even quicker, and as they approached the 150-metre braking marker, the cars were three abreast at over 250 km/h.

Vettel attempted to pass both Mercedes around the outside, but under braking, his front right tyre locked up heavily, sending a plume of smoke skyward and creating a giant flat spot. Turning in, he found Bottas and Hamilton already there. Bottas had to back out or risk a collision. The lock-up left Vettel wayward into Turn 2, and Leclerc, who had a grandstand view of the incident, attempted to pass him around the outside. Vettel, alert to the move, blocked his teammate, forcing Leclerc to back off and compromising his momentum. Verstappen seized the opportunity and breezed past the Ferrari driver into third place before immediately overtaking Vettel for second. From that point, Hamilton controlled proceedings at the front.

On Lap 12, with Leclerc clearly quicker than Vettel—who was struggling with his badly flat-spotted tyre—Ferrari eventually allowed the Monegasque driver through. However, too much time had already been lost while Ferrari hesitated over the decision. The team later reversed the order on Lap 36 once both cars had new tyres, again forcing Leclerc to concede position to Vettel. The strategy seemed counterproductive and raised further questions about Ferrari's race management.

A mid-race Safety Car, triggered by a collision between Lando Norris and Lance Stroll, briefly bunched up the field but did little to disrupt the order. Hamilton maintained his lead at the restart and secured victory, also taking the fastest lap for an extra Championship point. Bottas followed him home in second, while Verstappen comfortably held off the Ferraris to claim third. Carlos Sainz, the home favourite in the McLaren, finished eighth, earning loud cheers from the Spanish crowd, many waving papaya orange '55' flags.

With the victory, Hamilton regained the lead in the Drivers' Championship, further cementing his position as the title favourite. Meanwhile, Ferrari's struggles persisted, with their lack of pace relative to Mercedes and continued mismanagement of team orders raising doubts. Verstappen, however, had no complaints—Ferrari's inconsistency had allowed him to climb to third in the Championship standings.

### Drive to Survive and the Growth of F1 Social Media

Social media engagement surged in 2019 following the launch of *Drive to Survive* on Netflix, which premiered on 8 March. While Formula One had long been discussed on platforms like Reddit (founded in 2008) and Twitter, the documentary introduced a wave of new fans to the sport. Although Season 1 primarily focused on midfield teams—since Ferrari and Mercedes declined to participate—it significantly boosted Formula One's online presence and attracted a younger audience.

While today, platforms like Twitter (X), Reddit, Discord, and TikTok serve as central hubs for Formula One debates, news, and fan content, in 2019, social media engagement with the sport was just beginning to surge. After the Spanish Grand Prix, Reddit was filled with discussions speculating on why Ferrari continued to struggle against Mercedes. Fans analysed the differences in car design and performance, offering intriguing perspectives on the team's shortcomings. The online debates often mirrored those within the paddock, as social media increasingly became an integral part of how Formula One was consumed and discussed.

The first five races of 2019 highlighted Mercedes' dominance and Hamilton's ability to consistently deliver. While Bottas emerged as a stronger challenger than before, Hamilton's racecraft and tactical brilliance ensured he remained at the forefront of the Championship battle. For Hamilton, it was the perfect platform for another title charge.

**A Tribute to Niki Lauda in Monaco**

The Monaco Grand Prix held special significance as the paddock mourned the passing of Formula One legend Niki Lauda, who had died just six days earlier at the age of 70. Hamilton secured pole position, making it clear over the radio that the pole position was 'for Niki'. For the race, he wore a special tribute helmet in Lauda's iconic red, complete with the two distinct white double "L's" on each side. The halo was also painted red. Many other drivers paid tribute with personalised helmets or Lauda's name painted onto their own. Before the race, all 20 drivers gathered solemnly around a plinth holding one of Lauda's racing helmets. With heads bowed and hands clasped, each driver wore a red baseball cap with 'NIKI' emblazoned across the front. It was a poignant and fitting tribute to a legend, and someone who had been close to Hamilton.

Hamilton got a good start from pole and led throughout, but he faced significant pressure from having a different tyre strategy to the other runners, using the medium tyres while his closest competitors were on harder compounds. Despite tyre degradation and pressure from Vettel, he delivered a defensive masterclass to take the win, later describing it as one of the hardest races he had ever driven. After taking the chequered flag, he was quick to acknowledge Lauda's presence in his mind throughout the race, explaining that he had worn the tribute helmet to honour him and had it made at the last minute as a way to pay tribute. Hamilton thanked Bell Racing for their help in making the helmet so quickly for him.

Hamilton later admitted that while he could compartmentalise emotions in the car, dealing with Lauda's passing outside the cockpit had been far more difficult. He reflected on how athletes had to focus entirely on their performance during a race, but once back in the garage, the emotional toll of the week had been significant. Winning Monaco in those circumstances was a huge achievement, not just in sporting terms but as a tribute to Lauda, a man who had played a pivotal role in his career at Mercedes. Lauda's resilience had been an inspiration to many, and Hamilton's performance that weekend was a fitting way to remember him.

### Controversy in Canada

At the Circuit Gilles Villeneuve in Canada on 8 June, Vettel secured pole position, with Hamilton lining up second. During the race, Vettel controlled the lead until Lap 48, when he ran wide at the Turn 3-4 chicane and rejoined the track, forcing Hamilton to take evasive action. The Stewards deemed the move an unsafe re-entry and issued a five-second penalty. Commentators and pundits were divided on the call, with some feeling it was harsh and that Vettel had no real alternative but to return to the track the way he did.

Although Vettel crossed the finish line first, the penalty meant Hamilton inherited the victory—much to Mercedes' delight and Ferrari's absolute fury. Over team radio, Vettel was livid, repeatedly insisting the Stewards were stealing the race from him. His frustration only intensified on the cool-down lap, where he launched into a furious rant, exclaiming that it was ridiculous to expect a driver to have full control when bouncing over the grass and that he had been lucky not to hit the wall. He made it clear that, in his view, there had been nowhere else to go.

By the time he reached the pits, his anger had not subsided. In protest, Vettel refused to park in parc fermé, leaving Hamilton's car alone in the first-place slot while his own designated number two marker board sat abandoned. Rather than heading to the podium immediately, he stormed into the

Ferrari motorhome. It took some persuasion from the team to get him to return for the podium ceremony, and even then, he made a statement by walking through the pit lane and passing through the Mercedes garage, earning cheers from the crowd.

As he reached the podium area, he took one final opportunity to make his displeasure clear, swapping the first and second place markers in front of the cars—symbolically placing himself back in the position he believed he had earned. The gesture summed up the entire incident: frustration, drama, and defiance in equal measure.

Ferrari initially signalled their intent to appeal Vettel's penalty but later withdrew, knowing that stewards' decisions rarely got overturned. The incident sparked widespread debate in the Formula One world, with opinions split. Hamilton himself sympathised with Vettel, saying it wasn't the way he wanted to win, but he also pointed out that when a driver rejoins the track, they are expected to do so safely and not move straight back onto the racing line.

As the teams packed up and left Canada, the Championship picture became clearer. Hamilton had pulled well ahead with 162 points, Bottas trailed in second on 133, while Vettel, stuck on 100 points, had bigger concerns than just the standings. Ferrari had seemingly lost their momentum, and Vettel, once the dominant force in Formula One, was now battling both his rivals and his own frustrations.

**A Dominant Display in France**

The 2019 French Grand Prix, held on 23 June at Circuit Paul Ricard, was another demonstration of Mercedes' superiority. In blistering heat, with track temperatures peaking at 54 degrees, Hamilton secured pole position and led from start to finish, claiming his sixth victory of the season from eight races. Bottas followed him home, securing yet another one-two finish for Mercedes, while Leclerc rounded out the podium in third after applying some late pressure on Bottas.

The race itself lacked drama at the front, with overtaking opportunities limited among the leading pack. Vettel, starting from seventh on the grid, managed to recover to fifth and secured the fastest lap on the final lap, picking up an extra point. In the midfield, Carlos Sainz impressed for McLaren, finishing sixth. The most excitement came in the closing stages as Ricciardo, Räikkönen, and Hülkenberg fought hard for seventh place. Ricciardo initially finished ahead but was later handed two five-second penalties for exceeding track limits and gaining an advantage, dropping him out of the points entirely.

Despite Mercedes' dominance, Hamilton acknowledged the need for closer racing, hoping Ferrari would develop their car further to improve competitiveness. However, the reality was stark—no one seemed likely to challenge Mercedes. The race was widely criticised as one of the dullest of the season, with ESPN describing it as a 'drab afternoon of racing.' The Championship was beginning to look like a foregone conclusion, with Hamilton leading the standings on 187 points, Bottas on 151, and Vettel down in third with 111. Verstappen was close behind on 100 points, while Leclerc sat on 87.

For Bottas, the path to the title was slipping away. If he had any hope of mounting a challenge, he needed to start winning races quickly and hope for some misfortune on Hamilton's side. At Ferrari, Leclerc trailed Vettel by a significant margin, and if he was to justify Ferrari's decision to promote him over Räikkönen, he needed a strong second half of the season. He would not disappoint. Meanwhile, Verstappen continued to extract everything possible from the Red Bull, averaging fourth-place finishes, while Gasly lagged behind in eighth. It was becoming clear that Red Bull was effectively a one-driver operation, and Gasly's underwhelming performances would only increase pressure on the team to make a change.

**A Thriller in Austria**

The 2019 Austrian Grand Prix, held on 30 June at the Red Bull Ring, provided one of the most exciting races of the season. With high temperatures pushing teams to their limits in terms of cooling and tyre wear, the race delivered a tense and dramatic battle at the front.

Leclerc had been rapid all weekend, securing pole position for Ferrari with a stellar lap of 1:03.003. Hamilton initially qualified second but was handed a three-place grid penalty for impeding Räikkönen in Q1, dropping him to fifth (later fourth after another penalty for Magnussen). This promoted Verstappen to the front row alongside Leclerc, with Bottas and Norris occupying the second row.

As the lights went out, Leclerc made a clean getaway and held onto the lead, while Verstappen suffered from anti-stall, dropping from second to seventh before reaching Turn 1. Bottas and Hamilton capitalised, moving up to second and fourth respectively. While Verstappen began his fightback through the field, Hamilton ran into trouble of his own. Running over a kerb damaged his front wing, forcing him into a longer-than-expected pit stop for repairs, which effectively ended his podium hopes.

Lando Norris continued McLaren's resurgence, running comfortably in the top six for the first half of the race, showing genuine pace in the papaya-coloured car. It was another encouraging sign that McLaren was gradually clawing its way back to competitiveness.

As the race progressed, Verstappen recovered brilliantly, making his way back through the field. By Lap 50, he was up to third and hunting down Bottas. With fresher tyres, he made a decisive move on the Finn and then set his sights on Leclerc. With just a handful of laps remaining, the stage was set for a dramatic showdown.

Verstappen's fresher tyres meant he was the fastest car on track. On Lap 68, he and Leclerc engaged in a breathtaking duel, swapping positions multiple times. Just when it seemed a collision was inevitable, both drivers showed just enough restraint to keep it clean. Leclerc, under immense pressure, displayed remarkable composure, defending with everything he had.

With three laps to go, Verstappen made his decisive move at Turn 3. As he dived up the inside, the two cars made slight contact, forcing Leclerc slightly wide on exit. The move was aggressive, drawing comparisons to past clashes at the same corner, though it was ultimately ruled a racing incident by the stewards. Leclerc, though, was singularly unimpressed, venting over the radio. Verstappen claimed victory, Red Bull's first of the season and the first Honda-powered win since 2006.

Leclerc was frustrated but had to settle for second, while Bottas completed the podium in third. Vettel, who had struggled to match his younger teammate all weekend, came home fourth, with Hamilton in fifth—the first time all season he had finished off the top two steps of the podium.

Verstappen, reflecting on his win, acknowledged he thought the race was lost after his poor start but had been able to recover with strong pace after the pit stop. Leclerc, though disappointed, admitted he struggled more with tyre wear than anticipated in the closing stages. Hamilton, meanwhile, was realistic about his fifth-place finish, conceding that overheating issues had made it impossible to push.

The scorching temperatures in Austria pushed the cars to their absolute limits, but it wasn't just the heat causing problems. The elevated altitude of 2,165 feet meant thinner air, reducing cooling efficiency for engines, brakes, and other key components. For Mercedes, this became a serious problem. Their car, dominant in cooler conditions, struggled in the heat, with overheating becoming a critical issue.

Toto Wolff admitted the problem had been there all season, lurking beneath the surface, and now it had been fully exposed. Mercedes needed to find a solution quickly, with several more hot European races ahead.

Verstappen's win broke Mercedes' unbeaten run in 2019, proving that Red Bull could challenge at certain circuits. More significantly, it marked the first true showdown between Verstappen and Leclerc, setting the stage for a rivalry that would only intensify in the years to come. The difference between the excitement in Austria and the dull race in France a week earlier was stark.

**Hamilton Makes History at Silverstone**

The British Grand Prix at Silverstone saw Hamilton start second behind Bottas. A Safety Car allowed Hamilton to seize the lead, and from there, he controlled the race. He went on to take victory at his home Grand Prix for a record-breaking sixth time, setting the fastest lap on the final tour in the process.

As he crossed the finish line, Hamilton's radio message to his team captured the emotion of the moment. He expressed gratitude to the fans, acknowledging the incredible support he had received throughout the weekend. The podium ceremony was a celebration of British motorsport, with Hamilton taking a moment to embrace his family in a display of pure joy.

Damon Hill, the 1996 World Champion and son of Formula One legend Graham Hill, later wrote a piece for the Jersey Evening Post, offering fascinating insight into Hamilton's career and how it compared to Ayrton Senna's. Hill recalled first meeting Hamilton as a young driver at the Autosport Awards and had followed his career ever since.

He highlighted Hamilton's ability to deliver extraordinary performances under pressure, noting that whenever a special performance was needed, he seemed to have something extra in reserve. On comparisons to Senna, Hill believed Hamilton was the fairer racer, saying he had never seen him do anything spiteful or underhand, whereas Senna was known to use his car aggressively in battle.

Hamilton's generosity and kindness were also key differences, according to Hill. As someone who raced against Senna, Hill knew firsthand how ruthless the Brazilian could be. He concluded his article with a bold prediction: Hamilton might be interested in a move to Ferrari in the future.

With his sixth home victory secured, Hamilton's Championship lead was extended further. The dominance of Mercedes remained intact, but the new generation—Verstappen and Leclerc—was beginning to make its presence felt.

**A Chaotic German Grand Prix**

The Hockenheimring on 28 July hosted a dramatic and rain-affected German Grand Prix. Hamilton secured pole position, with Verstappen alongside him on the front row, but the race quickly turned unpredictable as intermittent rain caused havoc. At his home Grand Prix, Vettel faced an uphill battle after a turbocharger failure in Q1 prevented him from setting a time, forcing him to start from the very back of the grid.

As the lights went out, Hamilton made a strong start, leading Bottas into Turn 1, while Verstappen struggled off the line and dropped several positions. Rather than reacting with his usual aggressive urgency, Verstappen took a more measured approach, calmly picking his way through the field. It was a clear sign of his growth as a driver—after nearly three seasons alongside Ricciardo, he was no longer just a raw talent but someone capable of leading Red Bull. Vettel, meanwhile, wasted no time cutting through the pack, gaining six positions within the first half of the opening lap.

The track gradually began to dry, and Hamilton pitted on Lap 29 for slick tyres. By this point, most cars had switched to slicks, but it was a high-risk strategy with the surface still damp in places. Leclerc, who had also just pitted, lost control at the final corner and crashed out. Seconds later, Hamilton, still adjusting to the grip levels on his new tyres, slid off at the same corner but managed to recover and rejoin the pits, cutting across the entry marker. The team was not ready for him, and while a new nose cone was fitted quickly, the stop dragged on as mechanics scrambled to find the correct tyres. The pit lane error, combined with missing the pit entry bollard, earned him a five-second penalty.

With the Virtual Safety Car deployed, Verstappen now led the race. Hulkenberg, in the bright yellow Renault, was a surprise presence in second, with Bottas in third. Hulkenberg's chance of a podium ended on Lap 41 when he lost control at the same slippery section that had already claimed Hamilton and Leclerc, skidding helplessly into the barriers and retiring on the spot.

On Lap 57, Bottas crashed out at high speed at Turn 1, taking off a wheel and destroying the front of his car in a heavy shunt. Toto Wolff, dressed in traditional German clothing to celebrate Mercedes' 200th race, was seen thumping the desk in frustration as Bottas' car slammed into the barriers. Hamilton's race had already unravelled with a combination of the pit stop delay, a penalty, and a spin, leaving him to finish 11th. He was later promoted to ninth due to post-race penalties for Räikkönen and Giovinazzi, but it remained a weekend to forget for Mercedes.

Verstappen went on to win his second race of the season, while Gasly, running in the points in the other Red Bull, collided with Albon's Toro Rosso late on, causing damage that forced him to retire. It was another blow to Gasly's already fragile standing within the team. Vettel, meanwhile, had produced a strong recovery drive to finish second, while Kvyat secured a remarkable podium for Toro Rosso in third. Hamilton summed up his weekend by calling it a bad day at the office.

## Tactical Brilliance in Hungary

At the Hungaroring on 4 August, Hamilton started third behind Verstappen and Bottas. Into Turn 1, Verstappen held the lead, followed by Bottas and then Hamilton. As the cars dropped into Turn 2, Hamilton went around the outside of Bottas, making a daring move. Bottas, while defending, locked up and drifted wide.

The race continued, and there was an incident involving Vettel and Bottas, dropping them down the order. Meanwhile, Hamilton engaged in a tense battle with Verstappen. On Lap 48, Mercedes made a strategic second pit stop, switching Hamilton to fresh medium tyres—a move that Red Bull did not anticipate, leaving Verstappen out on his worn rubber.

As Hamilton exited the pits, he voiced concerns over the strategy, questioning whether his tyres would last. His engineer, Peter Bonnington, reassured him over the radio, urging him to push. The reaction in the Red Bull garage was one of concern, with team members holding their heads in their hands as they realised the strategic misstep. Verstappen himself saw the writing on the wall, radioing his team on Lap 63 to say his tyres were gone.

The Mercedes strategy paid off as Hamilton rapidly closed the 20-second gap, overtaking Verstappen on Lap 67 of 70 to secure his seventh victory at the Hungaroring. Afterwards, he talked about how the medium tyres were not initially performing well after he rejoined but improved as he got into a rhythm. He spoke of putting any doubts aside and simply going for it, determined to recover from the disappointment in Germany.

As the teams went on their summer break, Pierre Gasly found himself at the centre of a major shake-up. On 12 August, Red Bull announced Gasly would be demoted back to Toro Rosso, with Alexander Albon taking his seat at the senior team. The change took effect from the Belgian Grand Prix on 1 September.

Gasly had struggled to match Verstappen's pace, regularly finishing well behind him. His crash in Germany, where he collided with Albon in the sister Toro Rosso, coupled with his general lack of performance compared to Verstappen, contributed to Red Bull's decision. By the summer break, Gasly had 63 points and was sixth in the standings, with a best finish of fourth at Silverstone and no podiums. In qualifying, Verstappen had outperformed him 11-1. By contrast, Verstappen had five podiums, including two race wins, and was third in the Championship with 181 points.

Albon's promotion was a gamble, given that he was a rookie who had only just stepped up to Formula One at the start of the year. Meanwhile, Gasly handled the demotion professionally, keeping his focus sharp. His determination and Toro Rosso's continued faith in him would be repaid in Brazil later in the season. In hindsight, many of Verstappen's future teammates would come to understand just how high the benchmark was against him.

**Tragedy at Spa**

The Spa-Francorchamps weekend was overshadowed by the tragic passing of Formula 2 driver Anthoine Hubert. During the Formula 2 race on Saturday, a high-speed collision at the top of Eau Rouge resulted in fatal injuries for Hubert, while Juan Manuel Correa, also involved in the accident, suffered fractured legs and a spinal injury. It was a stark and devastating reminder of the risks of motorsport, shaking the Formula One paddock to its core.

At the time of the crash, Hamilton was mid-interview with several media outlets, but his focus shifted as he saw the incident unfold on the large TV screens behind the journalists. He was visibly taken aback, his hand instinctively moving to his head as he muttered how shocking it was. He watched in silence for a moment, shifting on his feet as he took in the seriousness of what had happened, before finally stating that it looked terrifying. Unable to continue, he cut the interview short and walked away. Around him, journalists and team personnel were equally horrified, many covering their mouths in shock.

On Sunday, before the Formula One race, the drivers stood in solemn tribute on the grid. Leclerc, who had raced alongside Hubert in junior categories, stood beside Hamilton as both bowed their heads. The entire circuit—drivers, team members, and fans—observed a minute's silence. Joining them on the grid were Hubert's mother, Nathalie Gabert, and his brother, Victhor Hubert, both showing incredible composure despite their grief. As the silence ended, a quiet but heartfelt applause rippled through the track in tribute.

Despite the heavy hearts in the paddock, the race had to go on. In qualifying, Hamilton secured third place, while Leclerc took pole. The following day, Leclerc secured his maiden Formula One victory, finishing ahead of Hamilton. While realising a lifelong dream, the emotions were bittersweet. Wearing a black armband, he dedicated the win to Hubert, looking up to the sky as he raised the first-place trophy.

Leclerc later admitted that the opening lap had been especially tough, as he tried to push through the grief and focus on the job at hand. He reflected that racing through the same corner where Hubert had lost his life was one of the hardest things he had ever had to do, as the reality of the accident still lingered in his mind.

Hamilton also shared his thoughts after the race, posting a heartfelt message on social media. He described Hubert as someone who had made the ultimate sacrifice in chasing his dreams, reminding everyone that drivers risk their lives every time they step into a car. He called for greater appreciation of that fact, feeling that it was often taken for granted by those watching from the outside.

**Monza: A Victory for Ferrari at Last**

A week later, the 2019 Italian Grand Prix at Monza was a race Ferrari fans had waited nearly a decade for. On 8 September, Leclerc delivered a performance that cemented his status as Ferrari's new golden boy.

In qualifying, he had already shown his skill, taking pole in a chaotic session filled with drivers playing strategic games with slipstreams. With Ferrari's straight-line speed advantage, expectations were high—but he had the two Mercedes of Hamilton and Bottas ready to pounce.

At the start, Leclerc made the perfect getaway, keeping Hamilton at bay into the first chicane. Meanwhile, his teammate Vettel, starting from fourth, was hoping to join the fight at the front. But his race quickly unravelled.

On Lap 6, Vettel lost control of his Ferrari at the Ascari chicane, spinning out on his own. In his desperation to rejoin, he re-entered the track in a way that left Stroll with nowhere to go, causing contact between the two cars. The move was dangerous and earned him a ten-second stop-go penalty—a harsh punishment.

For Vettel, it was another self-inflicted mistake, adding to a growing list of costly errors stretching back to the previous season. His struggles only highlighted the contrast between himself and Leclerc, who was delivering under immense pressure.

Leclerc's real challenge, however, came from Hamilton. The reigning Champion kept relentless pressure on the Ferrari, forcing Leclerc to defend aggressively. At one point, Leclerc edged Hamilton towards the edge of the track in a move that pushed the limits of fair racing. Hamilton was forced to back out, and the stewards noted the incident but did not penalise Leclerc, instead issuing him a black-and-white warning flag—a rare but significant caution in Formula One.

The duel continued for several laps, with Leclerc refusing to surrender his lead. Hamilton tried multiple times to find a way past, but Leclerc's defensive driving was impeccable. Ultimately, Hamilton's tyres began to fade, forcing him to back off. A lock-up later in the race sealed his fate, allowing Bottas to move into second place.

Leclerc held on to take an emotional victory in front of the adoring Tifosi. As he crossed the line, Ferrari's pit wall gushed in celebration, knowing they had finally secured a win at Monza for the first time since 2010. The home crowd roared in approval, waving their red flags and cheering their new hero.

With back-to-back wins in Belgium and Italy, Leclerc had firmly established himself as a future Ferrari leader. Vettel, by contrast, was now under immense pressure. His mistakes were piling up, and the dynamic within the team had clearly shifted.

For Hamilton and Mercedes, it was a reminder that Ferrari could still pose a challenge on the right circuits. However, in the bigger picture of the Championship, Hamilton remained comfortably in control. Bottas finishing second at Monza helped Mercedes maintain a strong lead in the Constructors' standings, and Hamilton, despite finishing off the podium, remained in prime position for a sixth title.

The next race in Singapore would present a very different challenge, one where Ferrari's straight-line speed advantage could make the difference. With the Championship beginning to reach its climax, all eyes turned to how the battle between Hamilton, Leclerc, and Verstappen would unfold in the coming rounds.

### Singapore: A Ferrari One-Two

The 2019 Singapore Grand Prix, held on 22 September at the Marina Bay Street Circuit, was a night race that delivered an unexpected result and marked a significant milestone for

Ferrari. Leclerc continued his impressive run by securing pole position—his third consecutive top spot—with a lap time of 1:36.217. Hamilton lined up second, while Vettel started third. When the lights went out, Leclerc maintained his lead, with Hamilton and Vettel closely behind. The early laps saw the frontrunners carefully managing tyre wear, knowing the real battle would unfold in the second half of the race.

The turning point came during the pit stops. Vettel pitted on Lap 19 in a bid to undercut Leclerc, gaining track position. When Leclerc pitted a lap later, Vettel's earlier stop had worked, allowing him to leapfrog his teammate and take the net lead. It was a decisive move, as overtaking on Singapore's narrow street circuit was notoriously difficult. The race was interrupted by three Safety Car periods, triggered by separate incidents involving George Russell, Sergio Pérez, and Kimi Räikkönen. Each time, Vettel managed the restarts effectively, ensuring he held onto the lead.

After 61 laps under the floodlights, Vettel crossed the line first, taking his first win since the 2018 Belgian Grand Prix—a 392-day wait. Leclerc followed in second, securing Ferrari's first one-two finish since Hungary in 2017. Verstappen completed the podium for Red Bull, while his new teammate Albon finished sixth, signalling solid form.

Vettel's victory made him the most successful driver in Singapore Grand Prix history, with five wins. It also reinforced Ferrari's resurgence, marking their third consecutive victory of the season. Pirelli's Head of Formula One and Car Racing, Mario Isola, offered insight into the strategic element of the race, explaining that managing the tyres in anticipation of Safety Cars had been a crucial factor. The unique demands of the Singapore circuit placed significant strain on the front tyres under braking and turn in, whilst teams had to protect the rears for traction out of the slow corners.

Hamilton debriefed journalists on the race and admitted that, in hindsight, the team should have taken the risk and undercut Leclerc first. He had raised the idea in the morning briefing, but ultimately, the decision had gone against it. However, he reiterated that Mercedes won and lost as a team, and while the missed opportunity was frustrating, they had to take it on the chin and move forward.

As the season entered its final phase, the battles across the grid intensified. From the unpredictable weather at Suzuka to the passionate crowds in Austin and the dazzling spectacle of Abu Dhabi, each race felt like another chapter in a story still unfolding. Before all of that though was Sochi.

**Mercedes' Strategic Masterclass in Russia**

On 29 September at the sprawling Sochi Autodrom in Russia, with its picturesque backdrop of the Black Sea and autumnal hues, the stage was set for a masterclass from Hamilton and Mercedes. Ferrari's Leclerc sat on pole under a crisp blue sky, but tension brewed within the Scuderia as teammate Vettel leaped into the lead at the start. Hamilton, starting second, stayed close to the Ferraris.

On Lap 28, Vettel's car ground to a halt with a hybrid system failure, triggering a Virtual Safety Car (VSC). Mercedes reacted rapidly, pitting Hamilton, who emerged in the lead. The Silver Arrows were untouchable around the Russian circuit. As Hamilton crossed the line for victory, his radio message was filled with energy, describing the effort as exactly what the team needed, emphasising their refusal to give up.

At this stage, Hamilton's lead appeared unassailable, sitting at 322 points compared to Bottas' 249 in second. Leclerc held third place with 215 points, but Verstappen in the Red Bull, already hinting at his future ambitions, was close behind with 212. The battle for third in the standings would be a real test of Verstappen's skill and determination as he sought to outpace Leclerc and Ferrari. Vettel, the four-time World Champion, was now in fifth on 194 points, with Leclerc having firmly stamped his authority over him in the second half of the season. When asked about his title chances now that it seemed all but over, Hamilton remained grounded, explaining that he preferred to take things one step at a time, avoiding complacency.

### Drama in Suzuka: Bottas Leads Mercedes to a Sixth Title

The 2019 Japanese Grand Prix at Suzuka on 13 October was a race weekend packed with drama and a few unexpected twists. Typhoon Hagibis forced qualifying to be postponed until Sunday morning. When the session finally got underway, Vettel claimed pole position, with teammate Leclerc alongside him, securing another Ferrari front-row lockout. Bottas and Hamilton lined up just behind, ready to pounce.

As the lights went out, Vettel had a hesitant start, momentarily creeping forward before stopping and then launching again. This hesitation gave Bottas the perfect opportunity to dart into the lead by Turn 1. Leclerc's getaway wasn't ideal either, and things worsened when he tangled with Verstappen in the opening corners, sending the Dutchman into a spin and dropping him down the order.

With Bottas comfortably leading, the focus shifted to the battle behind. Hamilton, running a different tyre strategy, found himself chasing down Vettel in the latter stages. Despite having fresher tyres, he couldn't find a way past the determined German, who was making up for his earlier error. Mercedes opted for a two-stop strategy for Bottas, ensuring he kept his lead, while Hamilton was left out longer to try and challenge for the win on a one-stop. The plan didn't quite pay off, and Hamilton had to settle for third, finishing behind his teammate and Vettel. The final laps weren't without incident, as Sergio Pérez found the barriers after a tussle, but due to a chequered flag mix-up, his earlier position was reinstated, adding a quirky footnote to the race.

Bottas' victory sealed Mercedes' sixth consecutive Constructors' Championship, an incredible feat that cemented their dominance in the hybrid era. Hamilton's podium meant he edged closer to his sixth drivers' title, though the fight wasn't mathematically over just yet.

Toto Wolff dedicated the sixth straight Constructors' Championship to the late Niki Lauda, describing how instrumental he had been to the team from the very beginning. Wolff talked sadly about how much he missed Lauda, admitting he often asked himself what the three-time Champion would have thought about certain decisions. While the success was deeply satisfying, Wolff made it clear that Lauda's absence was still strongly felt.

**High Altitude and High Drama in Mexico**

The Autódromo Hermanos Rodríguez in Mexico buzzed with excitement on 27 October, as the passionate crowd—draped in vibrant colours and waving flags—cheered for another spectacle. The thin mountain air at 7,342 feet above sea level posed unique challenges for drivers and machinery alike. Saturday's qualifying session was filled with drama. Verstappen initially secured pole position for Red Bull, but a post-session investigation determined that he had failed to slow for yellow flags following Bottas' crash. This led to a three-place grid penalty, promoting Ferrari's Leclerc to pole, with Vettel alongside him, securing another front-row lockout for Ferrari. Hamilton would start third alongside Verstappen.

As the five red lights flickered off, the race began with the usual intensity. Leclerc held his lead into Turn 1, while Verstappen and Hamilton engaged in a fierce battle for position. The two made contact, forcing both to take a detour across the grass, costing them valuable time and positions. Verstappen's misfortune continued when a subsequent attempt to overtake Bottas resulted in a puncture, dropping him to the back of the pack.

The Mexican circuit, notorious for its high altitude and challenging conditions, often turns races into a game of chess. Mercedes, not traditionally dominant at this venue, opted for a bold one-stop strategy. Hamilton pitted early, switching to hard tyres, and managed them masterfully for the remainder of the race. Ferrari, conversely, committed to a two-stop strategy for Leclerc, which ultimately proved less effective.

As the race neared its conclusion, Hamilton found himself leading, with Vettel in hot pursuit. Despite the German's fresher tyres, Hamilton's impeccable tyre management and consistent pace kept him ahead. Behind them, Bottas recovered from his qualifying crash to secure third place, ensuring a double podium for Mercedes. Hamilton crossed the finish line to claim his 10th victory of the season, bringing him tantalisingly close to his sixth World Championship title. Vettel secured second, while Bottas's third-place finish kept his slim Championship hopes alive. Leclerc, despite his pole position start, had to settle for fourth, hindered by a slow pit stop that ended his podium chances.

After the race, Hamilton made a point of acknowledging the absence of his race engineer, Peter Bonnington, who had missed the weekend. Speaking to the team, Hamilton dedicated the win to Bonnington, describing the race as tough and praising the effort from everyone.

**Coronation in Texas**

On 3 November, the sprawling Circuit of the Americas in Austin brought a festival-like atmosphere, filled with cowboy hats, barbecues, and the energy of American motorsport fans. On a warm, clear afternoon, Hamilton started from fifth on the grid. The tension was palpable as the crowd anticipated a potential title celebration. Hamilton worked his way through the field with care, overtaking Ferrari's Leclerc and setting his sights on Bottas. Although Bottas—who had qualified on pole—ultimately claimed victory, Hamilton's second-place finish was enough to seal his sixth World Championship.

After the race, Hamilton was overwhelmed by the achievement, calling it an incredible moment. He recalled the advice his father had given him as a child: to never give up. Despite pushing as hard as possible in the race, he admitted there wasn't enough left in the tyres to challenge for the win. As for his future, he remained uncertain about how many titles he could win but said he still felt as fresh as ever and was ready to keep pushing

While many in his position might have taken a moment to revel in their triumph, Hamilton instead chose reflection—not on his own success, but on the people who had shaped his journey. One absence in particular was deeply felt. Speaking in the post-race interviews, his voice carried the weight of emotion as he paid tribute to Niki Lauda, the man who had been instrumental in bringing him to Mercedes and had become both a mentor and a friend. Hamilton recalled how Lauda's presence had always been a driving force within the team and how much he missed the Austrian's humour and sharp insights. He emphasised the lasting impact Lauda had left, not just on him personally, but on the entire Mercedes operation. This insight would prove prophetic in the years to come.

Lauda had been more than just a symbolic figure; his relentless drive, his honesty, and his deep understanding of what it meant to be a Champion had left an imprint on everyone at Mercedes. In his moment of greatest triumph, Hamilton carried Lauda's legacy forward.

Despite all the success, Hamilton's thoughts weren't far from the darker moments that had defined the season. Among them was the tragic loss of Anthoine Hubert at Spa, a stark and painful reminder of the risks they all faced every time they climbed into the cockpit. Speaking candidly about the impact of that moment, Hamilton admitted that witnessing the crash had made him question the sport and whether he wanted to continue. He acknowledged that moments like those brought doubt, forcing drivers to confront the reality that their careers came with extraordinary risks.

The tributes to Hamilton's achievement poured in, but some also placed his legacy in a wider context. The late Eddie Jordan, speaking on talkSPORT, compared Hamilton to Michael Schumacher, arguing that Hamilton had already surpassed the seven-time Champion. Jordan, who had given Schumacher his first drive in Formula One, believed Hamilton's achievements carried a different weight, particularly in the way Mercedes operated. He pointed out that, unlike Schumacher's time at Ferrari, where contract clauses often favoured the German, Hamilton had never had such protections, always having to fight for his victories on equal footing.

Jordan expanded on his views, stating that Hamilton had placed himself in a different league to Schumacher through sheer talent and determination. He emphasised that Hamilton had done it on his own, without any contractual advantages that protected him from competition within his own team. For Jordan, what Hamilton had achieved was something his family and those who supported him could take great pride in.

Hamilton and Mercedes left America champions and headed for Brazil.

**Drama in Brazil**

Under the hazy skies of São Paulo on 17 November, the undulating Interlagos circuit delivered a thrilling race. Verstappen, starting from pole, underlined Red Bull's growing strength by clinching a comfortable victory. However, the real drama unfolded behind him. Gasly, now back with Toro Rosso, seized a career-defining second place, marking his first-ever podium finish. Carlos Sainz Jr., starting from the back due to a qualifying issue, carved through the field to claim third, securing McLaren's first podium since 2014.

The race was particularly notable for the dramatic collision between Ferrari teammates Vettel and Leclerc on Lap 66, which led to both drivers to retire, triggering a Safety Car. The incident eliminated Ferrari from podium contention and had repercussions for their Championship standings. After the race, both drivers acknowledged their roles in the crash, with Vettel suggesting that he had positioned himself for a pass and believed he had the right to move. Ferrari Team Principal Mattia Binotto was less sympathetic, making it clear the incident was unacceptable. The collision reignited questions about Ferrari's internal dynamics and their approach to race strategy. Ultimately, it was another unnecessary incident, as Vettel's slight move left while alongside Leclerc caused the contact.

Shortly after the restart, Hamilton attempted an overtake on Red Bull's Alexander Albon, resulting in contact that sent Albon into a spin, dropping him out of podium contention. Hamilton crossed the line in third but received a five-second penalty for the incident, demoting him to seventh and elevating Sainz to the podium.

Verstappen's victory in Brazil strengthened his hold on third place in the Drivers' Championship, widening the margin over Leclerc. Heading into the race, the battle between Verstappen, Leclerc, and Vettel had been tight, but Ferrari's double retirement proved costly. The lost points meant Verstappen had a clear advantage, one that would prove decisive as the season concluded.

**The Season Finale in Abu Dhabi**

The Yas Marina Circuit, bathed in twilight and lined with illuminated yachts, provided a fitting backdrop to the season finale on 1 December. Hamilton delivered a flawless weekend, starting from pole and leading every lap. To underline his dominance, he also set the fastest lap, securing his 11th win of the season. In comparison, Bottas had four victories, highlighting just how imperious Hamilton had been throughout 2019.

As Hamilton cruised to victory, his race engineer Peter Bonnington remarked over the radio that it looked as though he hadn't even broken a sweat, having led so comfortably. Hamilton, ever mindful of the team and the fans, responded by thanking everyone and dedicating the win to those who had supported him throughout the year.

When asked about his plans for the winter break, Hamilton's answer was simple and unsurprising—he was looking forward to quality time with his family.

As the 2019 season ended and teams packed up for the winter break, few could have predicted the seismic changes awaiting the world in 2020. Concerns over the COVID-19 virus were growing, and Formula One, like the rest of society, would soon have to adapt in ways it had never faced before. The luxury of spending time with family, something Hamilton valued deeply, would soon become a privilege as the world grappled with the reality of the pandemic.

# Race against the pandemic

The 2020 Formula One season began under extraordinary circumstances. As Lewis Hamilton prepared to defend his sixth World Championship title, the sport faced significant changes, both on the grid and in the wider world.

The off-season saw a few adjustments in the driver line-up. Esteban Ocon returned to the Formula One grid with Renault after a year as Mercedes' reserve driver, partnering Daniel Ricciardo. Ocon expressed pride in becoming a Renault driver, emphasising his long-standing attachment to the team that had launched his motorsport career at Enstone, initially with Lotus in 2010 and then Renault. Nicholas Latifi earned a seat at Williams after finishing second in the Formula 2 Championship, marking the Canadian's debut in Formula One. Latifi expressed excitement at stepping up as a race driver for 2020. Latifi replaced Robert Kubica.

As teams unveiled their new challengers, Mercedes' innovation and Ferrari's challenges dominated the headlines. The reigning champions introduced the Mercedes W11, a car combining speed with groundbreaking technology. Its Dual-Axis Steering (DAS) system allowed drivers to adjust the toe angle of the front wheels on the fly, immediately sparking intrigue. The DAS system worked by the drivers pulling and pushing the steering wheel, altering the toe angle in or out. This created greater or lesser friction on the tyres, enabling drivers to either warm them up more quickly or reduce tyre wear. It was an unusual and groundbreaking innovation.

Ferrari's car, the SF1000, commemorated the team's 1000th Grand Prix and focused on refining aerodynamics. However, early signs suggested the car lacked competitiveness. Vettel admitted the team were not where they wanted to be.

Red Bull's RB16, designed with Adrian Newey's characteristic high-rake philosophy, featured an improved Honda power unit. Verstappen expressed confidence he could challenge Mercedes this year. After bedding in with Honda during 2019, Red Bull looked increasingly promising. Verstappen had clearly established himself as the number one driver, demonstrating maturity and increased consistency.

Pre-season testing at the Circuit de Barcelona-Catalunya in Spain provided the first glimpse of the 2020 pecking order. Mercedes showcased reliability and pace, completing a remarkable 903 laps over two weeks, totalling 2,612 miles. The DAS system remained a focal point. Mercedes, particularly Hamilton, looked unstoppable. Toto Wolff expressed cautious optimism but viewed Red Bull as their biggest threat for 2020.

For 2020, Mercedes changed the colour scheme of their car as part of a statement against racism and to promote diversity and inclusion. The decision was announced before the start of the 2020 season, and the car was revealed in its new black livery at the Silverstone launch event in February 2020. The black livery replaced Mercedes' traditional silver colour as part of broader efforts supporting the #WeRaceAsOne initiative and racial equality, particularly following the resurgence of the Black Lives Matter movement. The team, including drivers Hamilton and Bottas, also wore black race suits in solidarity with the cause.

Ferrari completed 844 laps but lagged behind, raising concerns about their power unit and overall pace. Red Bull Racing showed strong performance with their RB16 car, completing 780 laps and appearing quick in race trim.

**COVID-19 Hits Formula One**

The paddock arrived in Melbourne for the Australian Grand Prix amid growing concerns about the COVID-19 pandemic. In late 2019, reports emerged of a novel coronavirus outbreak in Wuhan, China. The World Health Organisation (WHO) declared the outbreak a Public Health Emergency of International Concern on 30 January 2020 but had not yet classed it as a pandemic. Australia's first confirmed COVID-19 case was reported on 25 January 2020, involving a man who had travelled from Wuhan to Melbourne.

As the virus spread globally, the WHO officially characterised COVID-19 as a pandemic on 11 March 2020, just as all the Formula One teams had arrived or were arriving in Australia. Although organisers initially planned for the race to proceed, the situation deteriorated after a McLaren team member tested positive for the virus. This prompted McLaren to withdraw, sparking crisis talks among teams and the FIA. Amid escalating concerns, the Australian Grand Prix, scheduled for 15 March 2020, was cancelled just days before the event, marking a significant early impact of the pandemic on international sporting events. During pre-race interviews, Hamilton voiced his surprise and shock that the race was still planned to go ahead given the situation.

Ultimately, the race was cancelled just hours before practice was due to begin, marking the first in a series of disruptions that reshaped the 2020 season. Following the abrupt cancellation of the Australian Grand Prix due to the escalating COVID-19 pandemic, Formula One faced unprecedented challenges. The FIA, teams, and stakeholders swiftly collaborated to navigate the crisis, implementing measures to ensure the safety of all involved and to salvage the racing season.

In the wake of the cancellation, the FIA and Formula One established a dedicated COVID-19 Task Force to monitor the situation and develop protocols. This included regular testing, social distancing measures, and the creation of a bio-secure environment at events. Teams were required to operate within isolated 'bubbles' to minimise contact. The traditional summer shutdown was advanced to March and April, extending from 14 to 21 days, allowing teams to pause operations during the peak of the pandemic.

The original 22-race calendar underwent significant revisions. Several Grands Prix were postponed or cancelled, including Monaco, France, and the Netherlands. The FIA and Formula One worked diligently to reschedule events where possible, focusing on European circuits to reduce travel complexities. This led to the inclusion of venues like Mugello and Portimão, which had not been part of the original schedule.

After months of uncertainty, the season was set to commence with the Austrian Grand Prix at the Red Bull Ring on 5 July 2020, mid-summer and a time when RNA-type viruses posed lower risks. Extensive preparations were undertaken to ensure safety, including mandatory COVID-19 testing for all personnel before and during the event, strict hygiene protocols, and the absence of spectators to limit potential exposure. Teams adapted to new operational procedures, such as remote working and reduced on-site staff, to comply with health guidelines.

The lead-up to the first race was fraught with challenges, including logistical hurdles and the constant threat of virus outbreaks. The FIA remained vigilant, ready to adjust plans as needed. The commitment to flexibility and safety allowed Formula One to embark on a season that, while unprecedented, demonstrated resilience and adaptability in the face of global adversity. These concerted efforts culminated in the successful launch of the 2020 season, marking a significant achievement for the sport during a tumultuous period.

On 12 May, Ferrari announced they would not be renewing their contract with Sebastian Vettel for 2021. The news was unsurprising to many, as Charles Leclerc had consistently demonstrated superior outright speed once he became accustomed to the Ferrari. With improved consistency, Leclerc regularly outpaced Vettel, whose performances had become increasingly unpredictable and error-prone.

Mattia Binotto, Ferrari's Managing Director and Team Principal, described the decision as mutual and amicable, emphasising that both the team and Vettel agreed it was best to part ways to achieve their respective goals. Binotto acknowledged it had been a challenging decision due to Vettel's value both as a driver and as a person but insisted there was no specific trigger beyond the shared belief that their paths should diverge.

Vettel himself echoed this sentiment, confirming his relationship with Scuderia Ferrari would end after the 2020 season. He highlighted the necessity of perfect harmony between driver and team to achieve optimal results, acknowledging both parties had realised their mutual desire to remain together beyond 2020 no longer existed. He clarified that financial considerations had played no role in the decision, stressing that money was not and would never be his primary motivation in making such choices.

The leading candidates to replace Vettel were Daniel Ricciardo and Carlos Sainz. It didn't take long for a decision to be made, and on 14 May it was announced that Sainz would join Ferrari on a two-year deal from McLaren for the 2021 season.

### Austrian Grand Prix: Season Opener

The Red Bull Ring, nestled in the lush Styrian hills of Austria, opened the season under brilliant sunshine on 5 July for the Austrian Grand Prix. The silence of empty grandstands created an unnatural stillness, broken only by the roar of the hybrid engines.

Hamilton started fifth after a controversial three-place grid penalty for failing to slow under yellow flags during qualifying. Bottas, starting on pole, launched cleanly into the lead. The race soon descended into chaos, with nine retirements, including Verstappen due to electrical issues and Ricciardo with cooling problems.

Hamilton worked his way up the field but tangled with Albon while fighting for second place on Lap 61. It proved to be one of the race's defining moments. Albon, on fresh tyres, attempted an outside pass at Turn 4 but collided with Hamilton's front-left wheel, sending the Red Bull spinning into the gravel. Albon's chance for victory evaporated, and the Stewards handed Hamilton a five-second penalty. It wasn't the first time they had come together.

Albon expressed frustration over the incident, calling Hamilton a 'sore loser'. Hamilton, however, viewed the incident as a racing event but accepted the penalty handed down by the stewards and aimed to move forward.

Pundits shared their perspectives, some expressed sympathy for Albon, acknowledging he had no choice but to attempt the pass and that both drivers had articulated their positions well and concluded that while unfortunate, the penalty seemed justified.

Bottas claimed victory, with Leclerc second. As the race unfolded Norris climbed steadily through the chaos. On the final lap, Norris set the fastest lap of the race, allowing him to leapfrog Hamilton (due to Hamilton's penalty) and secure third place—his first Formula One podium.

Once Norris's podium was made official, the McLaren team celebrated exuberantly, jumping, hugging, and high-fiving each other. Norris himself was left speechless, reflecting briefly on moments during the race when he believed he'd made mistakes. His decisive overtake on Sergio Perez secured him the podium, and his sheer joy as he celebrated with his team contrasted starkly against the empty grandstands. It was a breakthrough result marking Norris as one of Formula One's rising stars.

**Styrian Grand Prix**

The 2020 Styrian Grand Prix, held a week later on 12 July, unfolded under vastly different conditions compared to the previous weekend's season opener. While qualifying featured torrential rain, the race itself was bathed in sunshine.

The rain-soaked qualifying session became a shop window for driving ability. With rivers of water cascading across the track, visibility was limited, grip was minimal, and aquaplaning was an ever-present risk. Hamilton delivered a remarkable lap, claiming pole position by over a second. After the session he talked about how much he had enjoued the challenge of such difficult weather conditions, despite experiencing huge aquaplaning on his penultimate lap, which left his heart in his mouth.

Verstappen secured second, pushing hard in treacherous conditions, with his Red Bull frequently twitching into snap oversteer around the circuit. Approaching the final corner, Verstappen was distracted by another car off the track and a slower vehicle on the inside, causing him to run wide, catch the kerb, and partially spin. Although initially frustrated over the radio, Verstappen quickly calmed down, demonstrating his growing maturity with measured and encouraging communications to his team.

Under clear skies on Sunday, Hamilton converted his pole position into a clean start, immediately pulling away from the pack, the black Mercedes glinting in the sun. Verstappen slotted into second, while Sainz came under pressure from Bottas, who started fourth. Hamilton's Mercedes, finely tuned and in its element, allowed him to establish a significant gap early on.

Into Turn 3 AMS AG corner, the sharp right-hander after the long straight, both Ferraris - having had a dreadful qualifying and starting 10th and 14th - made contact with each other again. Vettel limped back to the pits to retire, his rear wing hanging off. Leclerc retired a few laps later.

As Hamilton extended his lead, the focus shifted to the intense battle for second between Bottas and Verstappen. By Lap 60, Bottas, armed with fresher tyres, began closing the gap to Verstappen. The Red Bull driver defended aggressively, fending off Bottas's first attempt with a perfectly timed move at Turn 4 on Lap 66. The drivers battled for an entire lap before Bottas managed to get in front. It was brilliant driving from both.

Hamilton's victory was a commanding performance, marking his first win of the season and restoring his momentum after a challenging opener. Bottas's second-place finish cemented another strong result for Mercedes, while Verstappen's third-place effort demonstrated Red Bull's spirit. Right behind Verstappen in fourth was his teammate Albon: a good weekend for Red Bull. The Styrian Grand Prix highlighted Hamilton's ability to dominate, but it also showed the fiery determination of his rivals. The Verstappen-Bottas duel reminded fans and pundits alike of the raw competitiveness that defines Formula One at its best.

**Hungarian Grand Prix**

The 2020 Hungarian Grand Prix, held at the Hungaroring on 19 July, unfolded under unique circumstances due to the ongoing COVID-19 pandemic. The absence of spectators lent an eerie silence to the event, contrasting sharply with the usual fervent atmosphere. The weather was unpredictable, with a wet start that transitioned to partly cloudy conditions as the race progressed.

Hamilton demonstrated his exceptional skill by securing pole position with a time of 1:13.447, stamping his authority over the circuit and taking pole position by more than a tenth from teammate Bottas. The Hungaroring, known for its narrow, winding layout akin to a karting track, suited Hamilton's accuracy and Mercedes' superior grip. It was his 90th Formula One Pole Position and he described it as a solid lap but also acknowledging there were always improvements to make. He said it felt surreal to have achieved 90 pole positions.

The day of the race day began with uncertainty as morning rain had left the track damp, but it was drying quickly. Just before the race, Hamilton and several other drivers wore black t-shirts that read 'End Racism'. Hamilton took a knee in front of a large 'end racism' sign, surrounded by fellow drivers, and then wore a 'Black Lives Matter' t-shirt. It marked the beginning of what would become a regular gesture throughout the season.

35 minutes before the race had started, there was an incident, as Verstappen, who was warming up his intermediate tyres on his way to the grid, slid off at Turn 1, damaging the front-left suspension. He managed to crawl back around the circuit, where the mechanics, working against the clock, pushed the car from the back of the grid—minus the front wing—to its grid spot. In an incredible display of skill, the Red Bull crew managed to repair the damage in under 20 minutes, allowing Verstappen to take his original starting position. Over the team radio, Verstappen praised his mechanics, describing their efforts as incredible, unbelievable work, and expressed sincere thanks.

When the race began, Hamilton executed a flawless start, pulling away as chaos unfolded behind him. The track was already showing signs of starting to dry out. On Lap 4, Hamilton pitted for slick tyres as the track dried, with Mercedes' strategy perfectly timed. He extended his lead lap by lap, lapping everyone up to fifth place by the end of the race. Verstappen made a remarkable start despite his car being repaired, going from seventh to third by the end of the first corner, and ultimately finishing second behind Hamilton. He again thanked his mechanics as he crossed the line, calling them 'legends'. Bottas, starting from second on the grid, had a challenging race. A poor start saw him drop positions, and despite a strong recovery drive, he finished third.

Hamilton expressed his satisfaction with the team's performance, congratulating the team, and in particular Mercedes High Performance Powertrains who developed the engines, and who Hamilton felt had unlocked even more performance. Hamilton's eighth win at the Hungaroring equalled Michael Schumacher's record for the most wins at a single circuit (Schumacher had achieved the feat at Magny-

Cours). Hamilton also set the fastest lap on the final tour, earning an additional point and underlining his dominance.

After the race, Verstappen praised his mechanics for their amazing job fixing the car, remarking that he didn't know how they managed it and described their efforts as incredible. He added he was pleased to repay their hard work with second place. Analysts praised Hamilton's performance, with his drive described as 'supreme'.

**Drama at Silverstone**

The iconic Silverstone Circuit for the British Grand Prix on 2 August seemed muted without the roaring cheers of Hamilton's home crowd. On a beautiful English summer day, Hamilton started from pole and led comfortably for most of the race.

On Lap 13, Daniel Kvyat in the Alpha Tauri had a massive accident, removing one of the wheels entirely, both front and rear wings and generally destroying the car. The accident seemed unusual, and it raised questions as to whether there had been some mechanical failure or a tyre failure. Mercedes double-stacked their cars as the Safety Car came out.

Disaster struck Mercedes on the penultimate lap when Bottas suffered a front-left tyre failure, having had some vibrations for a few laps prior. Red Bull, sensing the danger, pitted Verstappen with just two laps to go, to avoid a puncture of their own and to go for fastest lap. Verstappen was now in second with Bottas having dropped out of contention, was 35 seconds behind Hamilton. The Dutchman set about going for fastest lap on his new soft tyres.

On the last lap, Carlos Sainz had a front-left puncture, in a carbon copy of Bottas' issue. All the teams looked on nervously. Seconds after Sainz's failure, with over a third of a lap left to run to the chequered flag, Hamilton experienced the same fate, his left front tyre delaminating and deflating. With Verstappen rapidly closing the gap, Hamilton skilfully managed his stricken car to cross the line first, with only three functioning tyres. Verstappen finished just five seconds adrift. Leclerc was third in the Ferrari.

In the press conference after the race, each driver was seated, wearing their Covid-19 face protection. The microphones, usually shared amongst the drivers by hand, were all separate and on stands to minimise risk of infection. Hamilton reflected on how, now the adrenaline had subsided, he was grateful that he didn't have the tyre failure in one of the high-speed sections, and he had no inkling it would give way.

The multiple failures raised concerns about the types of compounds being used. Pirelli, always responsive to team feedback, went away to examine the issues.

### 70th Anniversary Grand Prix: Verstappen Ends Mercedes' Dominance

The 2020 70th Anniversary Grand Prix, held at Silverstone on 9 August, was an exciting and unexpected race, marking the second event at the British circuit in as many weeks. With a tyre failure on the previous race's horizon, teams had to be cautious about their tyre choices, especially in the heat. This race also featured an unusual twist, as Mercedes' dominance was broken by Red Bull, who took advantage of Mercedes' struggles with tyre wear.

Verstappen stunned everyone by winning. Driving a flawless race with excellent tyre management, ending Mercedes' run of dominance at Silverstone. Verstappen's win was a significant boost for Red Bull, who had struggled to match Mercedes in previous races, but Silverstone proved to be more suited to their car this time.

Hamilton started the race from the front row and was in a strong position early on, but his chances of victory took a hit when Mercedes struggled with tyre management. Despite making his way back after a late pit stop, Hamilton finished in second place. It was an impressive result given the challenges he faced with his car's tyres. Bottas faced similar struggles with tyre wear and was unable to recover after his early pit stop. He finished third, cementing another strong finish for Mercedes.

Behind the top three, there were some exciting battles throughout the field. Ferrari had a mixed race, with Leclerc finishing in a solid fourth place, while Vettel struggled and couldn't finish in the points. Given Vettel's continued struggles, Ferrari's decision to part ways with him at the end of the season appeared to be a sensible one. Albon, in the second Red Bull, came in fifth, nearly forty seconds down on his teammate. Verstappen had made Albon, who was considered a quick driver, look decidedly ordinary in the last five races: it's something he would continue to do with any teammate he had.

As the teams left Silverstone, Hamilton was first on 107 points, Verstappen second on 77 points, and Bottas third on 73 points. Leclerc in the Ferrari was on 45 points, and Norris in the McLaren in fifth on 38 points. Albon was sixth on 36 points. Even at this early stage in the season, Hamilton looked as if he would dominate, but the battle for second place, unlike previous seasons, looked as if it may go down to the wire between Bottas and Verstappen. Albon would need to up his game if he wanted to stay at Red Bull.

### Spanish Grand Prix: A Test of Endurance

As the 2020 Formula One season progressed, the racing world continued to adapt to its new reality under Covid. The Circuit de Barcelona-Catalunya on 16 August, set against the backdrop of Catalonia's rolling hills, was bathed in relentless sunlight. With air temperatures over 30°C and track temperatures soaring past 50°C, the Spanish Grand Prix became a test of endurance and tyre management.

Hamilton started from pole, controlling the race from the outset. The extreme heat strained both cars and drivers, with the pit crews working in sweltering conditions. Hamilton, however, seemed unfazed and sealed an easy victory from lights to flag. Behind him, Verstappen struggled to match

Mercedes' pace but managed second, while Bottas settled for third after a poor start. Hamilton lapped every driver except the top three, underscoring his dominance. Verstappen was frustrated to be unable to match Mercedes' pace with his rear tyres going off quickly but managed second, while Bottas settled for third after a poor start. Bottas did well in the race, but there was a comical moment as he lamented over the radio just how hot his black Mercedes overalls were in the Spanish heat.

**Belgian Grand Prix: Hamilton's Emotional Tribute**

Spa-Francorchamps on 30 August provided cooler conditions for the Belgian Grand Prix, set amidst long straights and iconic corners like Eau Rouge. Mercedes again locked out the front row with Hamilton over half a second clear of Bottas. Verstappen picked up 'best of the rest' qualifying third just one thousandth of a second behind Bottas.

Hamilton's pole position was marked by an emotional tribute. Sombre and clearly upset by the death of actor Chadwick Boseman earlier that day, Hamilton performed a 'Black Panther' salute—arms crossed across his chest—in honour of Boseman after qualifying. Hamilton dedicated his pole to Boseman, acknowledging the actor's achievements and lasting legacy in an emotional social media tribute.

When the race began, Hamilton executed a flawless start, pulling away as chaos unfolded behind him. Verstappen settled into third, just behind Bottas. Making a welcome return towards the front, having been largely anonymous all year, was the beautiful bright yellow and black Renault with Ricciardo at the helm. Ricciardo slotted directly behind his old teammate Verstappen as the cars plummeted down towards Eau Rouge, adding excitement to the race start.

As the cars reached the top of the Kemmel Straight, Ricciardo pulled out to pass Verstappen up the inside. They went through the Les Combes section right-hander wheel to wheel, and as they came to Turn 6, the left-hander, Verstappen was on the inside. He ran Ricciardo out wide and off the track. Ricciardo maintained his composure and slotted back in behind Verstappen.

On Lap 11 Antonio Giovinazzi lost control of his Alfa Romeo coming out of the 170mph downhill double left-hand bend of Pouhon. He oversteered on the exit, then overcorrected just as the rear tyres suddenly found grip. His car then turned violently right and smashed heavily into the barriers, before spinning aggressively back across the track. The impact was so violent it completely ripped the left rear wheel off the Alfa and worryingly, George Russell, who was following behind and still at full speed, felt the full force of the impact from this loose wheel, as it smashed into his Williams' right front wheel, detaching that. From there, Russell was a passenger as his car then ploughed into the barriers. The Alfa was beached half on and half off the circuit, minus the rear wing with mud and carbon fibre all over the track. The crash brought out the Safety Car and teams pitted their drivers.

The serene Belgian countryside was pierced by the engines' roar at the restart, but the absence of fans seemed at odds against the noise of the cars. Hamilton expertly managed things as they got back to full racing speed, pulling away from Verstappen and Bottas. Hamilton won, with Bottas second for another Mercedes one-two. Verstappen had a strong race, topping off the podium in third. Renault had an outstanding race with Ricciardo fourth and Ocon in fifth.

**Monza: Hamilton's Penalty Costs Victory**

On 6 September, Monza, the "Temple of Speed", in Italy, was bathed in sunshine, with air temperatures hovering around 28°C. Hamilton started from pole and dominated the early stages of the race, pulling out a comfortable lead.

Chaos ensued on Lap 20 when Kevin Magnussen's car stopped near the pit entry, leading to a Safety Car deployment. Unaware that the pit lane was closed, Mercedes called Hamilton in, resulting in a 10-second stop-go penalty a few laps later. However, before Hamilton could take his penalty there was a crash.

On Lap 25, Charles Leclerc had a severe accident at the Parabolica, burying his Ferrari in the safety barrier. This caused the race to be red-flagged. The race restart had Hamilton on the front row with Pierre Gasly alongside in his AlphaTauri. They got away cleanly but on the next lap, Hamilton had to take his ten-second penalty in the pits, leaving Gasly to go into the lead. He went on to claim a shock victory for AlphaTauri, a rare triumph for the midfield teams. Hamilton, having rejoined in 17th after his penalty had fought his way back, finishing seventh.

Hamilton, always gracious, was quick to acknowledge Gasly's win. He talked about Gasly's performance and his journey since being demoted by Red Bull in 2019, and offered huge congratulations to him, calling it a fantastic result. He acknowledged the hardship Gasly had been through being dropped by Red Bull, yet beating them on merit. The AlphaTauri team were understandably triumphant, with all of them hugging each other and many of them in tears of joy. On the podium, Gasly, now covered in green ticker tape, lowered his face mask and took a great gulp of his champagne.

After the race, Hamilton admitted the penalty was gutting, explaining he didn't see the boards and accepted responsibility, but was pleased he "gave it everything" to fight back.

**Historic and Chaotic Tuscan Grand Prix**

The 2020 Tuscan Grand Prix was a race of its time, filled with turmoil. Taking place on 13 September, this inaugural event - held at the Mugello Circuit - also marked Ferrari's 1,000th Formula One race, adding a historic touch to an already thrilling weekend. Ferrari ran their cars in a special 'classic' colour scheme, the cars in a much darker burgundy red, reminiscent of the 125 S Ferrari Formula One car from 1950.

Even the drivers' numbers were in a different font to reflect the 1950s car: they looked stunning.

From the outset, the race was anything but ordinary. Pole-sitter Hamilton didn't get the best launch, allowing his Mercedes teammate Bottas to seize the lead into the first corner. Behind them, chaos ensued. Verstappen, after a power unit issue, found himself entangled in a collision with Gasly and Räikkönen, leading to immediate retirements for both Verstappen and Gasly. This incident brought out the Safety Car, setting the tone for a race that would test drivers' gumption.

As the Safety Car period concluded, the field was preparing to resume racing, but chaos unfolded immediately as the field concertinaed. Antonio Giovinazzi lost control, crashing into Kevin Magnussen, and they also collected Nicholas Latifi and Carlos Sainz Jr. The severity of the crash, with cars and bits strewn across the entire start and finish straight, caused an immediate red flag. After a lengthy delay, the race resumed with a standing start.

Once the race resumed, pole-sitter Hamilton didn't get the best launch, allowing his Mercedes teammate Bottas to seize the lead into the first corner. Behind them, Leclerc initially held position but began slipping down the order as his Ferrari struggled. Ricciardo, driving for Renault, capitalised on this by overtaking Leclerc and moving into podium contention.

Just as strategies were unfolding, drama struck again on Lap 43, when Lance Stroll, who had been running competitively, suffered a high-speed tyre failure at the Arrabbiata corner. His Racing Point crashed heavily, prompting another race stoppage.

Hamilton managed the restart expertly, pulling away from Bottas. Further back, Albon in the Red Bull was on a charge. Determined to secure his first Formula One podium, Albon executed a daring overtake on Ricciardo, clinching third place and becoming the first Thai driver to stand on a Formula One podium, joining Hamilton for the win and Bottas in second.

Hamilton described the day as one of the most challenging of his career, emphasising the intense concentration required at each restart, saying it had felt like 'three races in one day'. His ability to maintain his focus and composure during the disruption and repeated restarts underscored his status as one of the sport's greats.

**Controversy at Sochi**

Sochi, with its mix of long straights and tight corners, posed a different challenge. However, controversy struck before the race had even begun. Hamilton performed two practice starts beyond the usual pit exit area, having received confirmation from his engineer that this was acceptable. Despite this, the stewards penalised Hamilton for conducting his practice starts outside the designated area, handing him two separate five-second penalties. It seemed an incredibly harsh judgement as he was well away from other cars, and had first sought clarification.

Hamilton was frustrated with the decision, describing the penalty as gutting and discussed how he had performed similar starts in previous years without any issues, saying he had done the same things at a million tracks and that it had never been questioned before. Asked if he thought the penalties were excessive, Hamilton responded emphatically, saying that he felt they (the stewards) were trying to stop him (from winning). He seemed resigned about it and said he would just keep his head down and stay focussed.

Mercedes' Team Principal Toto Wolff defended Hamilton's actions, clarifying that in the FIA Director's notes it said, 'you can make practice starts, after the lights [pit exit lights] on the right-hand side', which is what Hamilton had done.

Bottas capitalised on the penalties, finishing first, with Verstappen second and Hamilton third. This wasn't the end of it. Initially, the penalties also included two penalty points on Hamilton's super licence, bringing him closer to a race ban.

However, after reviewing the incident, the FIA rescinded the penalty points, acknowledging that the team had provided erroneous instructions regarding the practice start location. Instead, Mercedes was held responsible for the oversight and given a €25,000 fine.

Michael Masi, the race director, explained the decision to rescind Hamilton's penalty points and instead penalise the team with a fine was due to inappropriate instructions being given to Hamilton. Masi was becoming increasingly involved in poor decision-making, and would become synonymous with poor decisions the following year as his rulings affected the outcome of the title.

**Hamilton Equals Schumacher's Record in Germany**

The Nürburgring returned to the Formula One calendar under cold and cloudy conditions, with temperatures barely above 10°C. The Eifel Grand Prix, run on 11 October, was nestled in Germany's Eifel mountains, and was unforgiving circuit demanding focus.

Hamilton started second behind teammate Bottas. At the start, Bottas defended aggressively into Turn 1 and was forced wide by Hamilton, but Hamilton, recognising he had perhaps been a bit assertive, allowed Bottas by on the inside of Turn 2. The decisive moment came when Bottas ran wide under pressure, allowing Hamilton to take the lead. Ricciardo brought his Renault home in third place, a fitting result for the team who appeared to have buried their reliability gremlins at last.

Crossing the line for his 91st career victory, Hamilton had equalled Michael Schumacher's all-time win record. In a touching gesture after the race, Mick Schumacher, Michael's son, presented Hamilton with one of his father's racing helmets. Hamilton described receiving the helmet as incredibly humbling, expressing gratitude towards his family for honouring him and praising Mick as a great talent and genuine human being. Hamilton added that it felt like a special moment, reflecting on his respect for Michael Schumacher's legacy.

**Hamilton Makes History at Portimão**

The Autódromo Internacional do Algarve in Portugal made its Formula One debut, a striking venue with rollercoaster-like elevation changes and dramatic corners. It provided a visually spectacular backdrop for the Portuguese Grand Prix.

Hamilton started on pole but dropped to third during a chaotic opening lap as it started to rain, with cars sliding and locking wheels, many of them unable to generate heat into the tyres. Hamilton took a conservative approach, bringing his tyres slowly up to temperature. Carlos Sainz in the McLaren was able to fire up the slick tyres in the damp, cool conditions quickly and went into the lead ahead of Bottas briefly, before Bottas retook the position.

Once Hamilton's tyres warmed, he methodically reclaimed positions, overtaking Sainz and then Bottas on Lap 20. Hamilton then drove a commanding race, extending his lead comfortably.

Crossing the finish line first, Hamilton secured his 92nd Formula One victory, surpassing Michael Schumacher's all-time record. His race engineer Peter Bonnington congratulated Hamilton enthusiastically, highlighting how he was rewriting the history books. Hamilton radioed the team on the cool-down lap and credited the achievement to them, thanking them for continuing to believe in him, and saying what an honour it was for him to work with them. Bottas followed Hamilton home in second, with Verstappen rounding off the podium.

After Portugal, Hamilton led the championship convincingly on 282 points, followed by Bottas in second on 197 points, and Verstappen in third with 162 points. Ricciardo had moved up to fourth with 95 points, Leclerc fifth on 85 points, while Vettel languished down in 13th place with just 18 points. Albon faced increasing pressure, having fallen to eighth with 64 points, facing mounting scrutiny over his future at Red Bull.

## Mercedes' Record at Imola

The next race was the Emilia Romagna Grand Prix at the start of November. Returning to the historic Imola circuit in Italy for the first time since 2006, Formula One embraced the challenge of a two-day event format. The cool, crisp autumn air added to the circuit's nostalgic charm, but the race was challenging with the low grip conditions.

Hamilton started second behind Bottas and Mercedes split strategies, with Hamilton extending his first stint longer than his teammate. A perfectly timed Virtual Safety Car allowed Hamilton to pit and emerge in the lead.

Hamilton cruised to victory, helping Mercedes secure their record-breaking seventh consecutive Constructors' Championship. Hamilton, Bottas, and Wolff hailed their colleagues in the Mercedes team. Hamilton described the moment as very overwhelming, emphasising how he thought of everyone back at Brackley and Brixworth, calling them the unsung heroes who grafted away tirelessly, never giving up, and continuing to push, elevate, and innovate. He congratulated the team on a hugely deserved Constructors' title. Bottas also praised the team, emphasising how they kept pushing and raising the bar, and said it was inspiring to work with such a dedicated and driven group.

Toto Wolff reflected on the unusual challenges faced by everyone during the 2020 season due to Covid. He expressed immense pride in achieving the constructors' title, recognising the significant effort and sacrifices made by everyone behind closed doors. Wolff gave massive thanks to everyone in the team, both at the track and back home at Brixworth and Brackley.

## Hamilton Clinches Seventh World Championship in Turkey

Two weeks later, the teams moved onto the Turkish Grand Prix. On 15 November, Istanbul Park presented drivers with one of the most treacherous races in recent memory. Heavy rain, combined with a recently resurfaced track, left the surface like ice. Temperatures hovered around 13°C, adding to the challenge. For Hamilton, it would be a true Champion's drive. He qualified a disappointing sixth, while Racing Point's Lance Stroll claimed a surprise pole.

The opening laps were chaotic, with drivers struggling for traction and multiple position changes. Hamilton cautiously avoided chaos, falling back briefly but recovering as the field struggled for grip. Opting for a long stint on worn intermediate tyres, he defied expectations by extending his lead over the field. He crossed the line 31 seconds ahead of second-placed Sergio Perez, securing his seventh World Championship in dominant style. On the cool down, Hamilton emotionally dedicated his victory to all the kids out there who dream the impossible, emphasising that they could achieve their dreams too.

After the race, Hamilton spoke candidly about those who had helped him achieve so much in his career. Due to Covid, his family could not attend, so that was an odd thing for him to process. He felt it had taken a long time to get to this point, and he talked about how grateful he was—and would forever be—to everyone who had helped him. He thanked his team for believing in him, Ron Dennis for taking him on as a child, and Mercedes for supporting him continuously from when he was 13 years old. Hamilton expressed particular gratitude to his family, emphasising how thankful he was for their support and hoped that they were celebrating at home.

In the post-race press conference, Hamilton was asked if he had spoken to his family and replied that he had not, but he knew he had significant support from them, even though they might not talk regularly. He hoped that they felt fulfilled, and he spoke lovingly about how his parents had sacrificed so much for him to be there—something he never took for granted. Reflecting on the struggles and challenges they faced, including criticism from schools and individuals who doubted his potential, Hamilton hoped that he and his family had earned respect through their perseverance.

Hamilton talked about his emotions later on and again spoke with great love and affection about his family, saying he could not have done it 'without the great man behind me.' He credited his father as the person who had supported him through moments of doubt, always keeping him going whenever he felt inadequate. Hamilton also mentioned his stepmother and brother, who had stood by him through thick and thin. He said he didn't want to lift his visor up at the end of the race, as he had promised himself, having seen other drivers cry, that he would never do it. But he was overwhelmed with emotion, and the tears came out.

**Grosjean's Horrific Crash in Bahrain**

The Bahrain Grand Prix on 29 November was set under the desert's shimmering floodlights and poised to be a relatively straightforward race for Hamilton, who started on pole. However, it will forever be remembered not for the competition on track but for the horrifying and miraculous survival of Romain Grosjean in one of the most shocking accidents in modern Formula One history.

The Bahrain International Circuit provided a stunning night-time spectacle, with its undulating straights illuminated under a cool desert sky. The serene atmosphere belied the intensity on the grid as drivers prepared for the race. Hamilton got away cleanly, holding the lead as the field jostled behind him. But the calm was shattered just seconds into the opening lap.

Heading into Turn 3, Romain Grosjean's Haas clipped the front-left wheel of Daniil Kvyat's AlphaTauri. The contact sent Grosjean's car careening sharply to the right, straight into the metal guardrail at an estimated speed of 192 km/h. The force of the impact was measured at a staggering 67G, splitting the car in two as the fuel tank ruptured, creating an immediate fireball.

Within moments, Grosjean's cockpit was engulfed in flames. The fire raged around him; a towering inferno visible across the track.

The FIA Medical Car, driven by Alan van der Merwe with Dr Ian Roberts on board, was already following the field on the opening lap. Upon arrival at the scene, the crew acted without hesitation. Dr Roberts ran toward the blaze with a fire extinguisher, while marshals worked to contain the inferno. Grosjean, trapped in the cockpit for 27 seconds, wrestled free, finally emerging from the flames like a phoenix rising from the ashes. Van der Merwe later described seeing Grosjean leap out as the most incredible thing he'd witnessed, attributing it as a testament to modern safety. Grosjean was immediately attended to, his hands and ankles showing clear signs of burns, but he walked unaided to the medical car, a miraculous sight that left the paddock in awe.

Grosjean later described the surreal experience, explaining that while he was trapped in the car with flames surrounding him, he thought of Niki Lauda and decided his life couldn't end that way. He recalled feeling that he had to escape for the sake of his children. Grosjean felt at one point his body relax, recognising he was going to die, before again thinking of his three children. He described how he turned his helmet to the left-hand side, pushed upwards, twisted his shoulder, and partially freed himself. Realising his foot was stuck, Grosjean described sitting back down and pulling his left leg as hard as possible, which caused his foot to come out of his shoe. He then tried again, managing to get his shoulders through, and knowing then that he was going to escape.

Hamilton reflected on the event after securing his victory, acknowledging how unsettling the accident had been. He described how people often take for granted the risks that drivers face, emphasising how they constantly operate on the edge and can never predict when incidents like this might occur. He expressed sincere hope that Grosjean was alright, praising the FIA and marshals, highlighting their swift and effective response.

Grosjean's accident highlighted the effectiveness of modern safety equipment. Although Grosjean himself had not been supportive of the halo device initially, he later admitted his perspective had changed entirely, stating that he now believed it was the greatest innovation brought to Formula One and acknowledging that without it, he wouldn't have survived to discuss the accident. The halo deflected the barrier, his helmet protected him from flames and debris, and the Head and Neck Support (HANS) device prevented severe spinal injuries. Every element of safety performed as intended, ultimately saving Grosjean's life.

The accident cast a shadow over the entire race, leaving drivers and teams shaken. Grosjean was treated for burns to his hands and ankles after the race but remarkably escaped without life-threatening injuries. His dramatic emergence from the flames became one of the defining images in modern Formula One, illustrating the sport's non-stop efforts to improve safety. The FIA immediately launched an investigation, resulting in recommendations to improve barrier designs and enhance fireproofing measures further.

**Final Races: Hamilton Sidelined by COVID-19**

The last two races of the 2020 Formula One season proved a mixed bag for Hamilton.

The teams moved on to the Sakhir Grand Prix at the Bahrain circuit, scheduled for 6 December. Hamilton had tested positive for COVID-19 and was forced to miss the race, opening an unexpected opportunity for George Russell, who stepped into Hamilton's Mercedes. Russell, starting second behind teammate Bottas, was eager to impress.

At the start, Russell showed composure, out dragging Bottas into Turn 1 and seizing the lead. Behind them, chaos unfolded as Leclerc collided with Pérez and Verstappen, sending Leclerc and Verstappen into retirement. Pérez was hit incredibly hard and was spun to the back of the pack, but his race was far from over. It was a major blow to Verstappen's hopes of securing second place in the Championship. Pérez was last but one, but not for long.

Russell dominated the early laps, driving with the precision of a seasoned Champion. On Lap 21, Pérez had fought his way into the points and overtook Albon around the outside halfway around the lap. This was a deathblow for Albon, whose seat had been looking more precarious each race: Christian Horner looked on, musing his options for 2021. Pérez, effectively out of a seat now that Vettel was moving to Aston Martin, was driving to stay in Formula One and putting it all on the line.

Mercedes' dominance seemed unassailable in the race until a double-stack pit stop during a Safety Car period unravelled everything. A botched tyre allocation meant Russell and Bottas were sent back out on mixed sets of tyres, forcing both drivers to pit again. Capitalising on the Mercedes chaos, Pérez clawed his way back from last place, overtaking cars with clinical efficiency. By Lap 69, Pérez had taken the lead. With five laps to go, Russell had worked his way back towards the front and was just two seconds from attacking Pérez. However, he suffered a puncture and had to pit for new softs.

Pérez never looked back, securing his maiden victory. Pérez stood on the podium looking understandably emotional. Racing Point teammate Lance Stroll joined him in third, with Esteban Ocon in the Renault splitting them in second.

### Verstappen's Dominance at Abu Dhabi

The 2020 Abu Dhabi Grand Prix, held on 13 December at the Yas Marina Circuit, ended the Formula One season with a race that, while not the most thrilling, saw Verstappen of Red Bull Racing secure a commanding victory. This win marked Red Bull's second triumph of the season and their first at this circuit since 2013 and would be an indicator of the team's rise to prominence.

Verstappen started from pole position, having outpaced the Mercedes duo in qualifying. From the moment the lights went out, he maintained his lead, with impeccable control and pace. The Dutch driver led every lap, finishing comfortably ahead of Bottas and Hamilton, who completed the podium in second and third places, respectively.

The Mercedes team, which had dominated much of the season, found themselves unable to mount a serious challenge to Verstappen's supremacy in Abu Dhabi. Both Bottas and Hamilton acknowledged the superior performance of the Red Bull on the day, with Hamilton, returning after a bout of COVID-19, admitting he wasn't at peak fitness during the race.

Behind the leading trio, Albon finished fourth, closely trailing Hamilton, which added weight to his case for retention at Red Bull for the following season. McLaren's drivers, Norris and Sainz, secured fifth and sixth places, respectively, crucially earning the team enough points to clinch third place in the Constructors' Championship—a significant achievement for the Woking-based outfit, and of great help to them financially in their efforts to rebuild and renew as the third-place finish meant a greater share of the prize money. Zak Brown was understandably pleased, but he was already planning his next steps to lift their performance even further.

Ricciardo, in his final race for Renault, finished seventh and recorded the fastest lap of the race on the final lap. Gasly and Ocon took eighth and ninth places, respectively, with Ocon overtaking Stroll on the last lap to secure his position.

As the season ended, Mercedes won the Constructors' on 573 points. Red Bull, largely kept afloat by Verstappen, finished second on 319 points, with McLaren third. Fourth was Racing Point on 195 points, and fifth Renault on 181 points. Whilst it had been a dream year for Mercedes, and Red Bull were understandably buoyant for 2021, Ferrari, the darling of the sport, languished in sixth on 131 points.

Ferrari's 2020 Formula One season was a disaster by their own high standards, marking their worst performance in 40 years. Having finished second in the Constructors' Championship in 2019, expectations were high, but a combination of technical setbacks, a weak engine, and internal mismanagement saw the Scuderia plummet to sixth place. It was a humbling year for the team, exposing deep flaws that needed urgent attention.

The most significant issue was the engine. In 2019, Ferrari had the most powerful power unit on the grid, raising eyebrows among rivals who suspected something was not entirely legal. The FIA launched an investigation but never revealed its findings. Instead, a confidential agreement was reached between Ferrari and the governing body before the 2020 season began. The details were never disclosed, but following this settlement, Ferrari's power unit lost significant performance. Many in the paddock speculated that Ferrari had been exploiting a loophole in fuel flow regulations and that the FIA's technical directives had effectively shut it down.

McLaren CEO Zak Brown publicly challenged Ferrari to disclose details of the confidential agreement, emphasising the need for transparency within the sport. He suggested it would be beneficial if Ferrari revealed the specifics of the secret settlement reached with the FIA regarding the alleged breach of engine regulations.

Whatever the truth, the impact was clear. Ferrari's engine, once dominant on the straights, became the weakest on the grid. The team found themselves struggling to keep up, not just with Mercedes and Red Bull but with midfield teams like McLaren, Racing Point, and Renault. Ferrari's customer teams, Haas and Alfa Romeo, also suffered, their cars hampered by the same underpowered unit.

The problems didn't stop at the engine. The SF1000 chassis was fundamentally flawed. Ferrari had designed the car assuming they would have the same power advantage as

2019, but when that advantage disappeared, the weaknesses in the design became painfully obvious. The car produced too much drag, making it slow on the straights, and it lacked the downforce needed to compensate in the corners. The rear end was unstable, making the car difficult to control, especially in qualifying.

Even if Ferrari had more engine power, their aerodynamic issues meant they would still have been behind the leading teams. The car was simply not competitive. While Leclerc managed to extract some strong performances, finishing on the podium in Austria and Silverstone, Vettel struggled. The four-time World Champion, in his final season with Ferrari, looked increasingly frustrated as the year went on. Vettel's deteriorating relationship with the team did not help matters, and he later admitted that the team had not even offered him a new deal, saying he felt like an outsider in his own team. He managed just one podium all year, a third-place finish in Turkey, but for much of the season, he was fighting in the midfield, often unable to break into the top ten.

Mattia Binotto, Ferrari's Team Principal, faced heavy criticism throughout the season. Many questioned whether he was the right man to lead the team, given Ferrari's continued decline under his leadership. Some former Ferrari figures, including Luca di Montezemolo, criticised the way the team had been managed. Several pundits called for Binotto to step down, arguing that Ferrari needed a complete reset. The statistics told the full story of how far Ferrari had fallen. They failed to win a single race for the first time since 2014. Their best qualifying result was fourth, achieved only twice. They managed just three podiums, while Vettel regularly struggled to even reach Q3 in qualifying. At Monza, their home race, both cars finished outside the points, with Vettel retiring early. It was an embarrassment for a team with Ferrari's history.

By the end of the season, Ferrari knew they had to change direction. They worked on a completely new power unit for 2021, aiming to claw back some of the lost performance. Binotto also took a step back from attending races to focus on restructuring the team. It was clear that Ferrari's long-term focus had shifted to the new regulations coming in 2022, and they accepted that rebuilding would take time. The 2020 season was a reality check for Ferrari. Their weaknesses had been exposed, their reputation had taken a hit, and they had a long way to go before returning to the front of the grid. But for a team as historically successful as Ferrari, failure was never going to be permanent. The only question was how long it would take to recover, and what pieces would they bring into play in the coming years.

Ferrari's challenging season ended on a subdued note, with Leclerc and Vettel finishing eighth and 13th, respectively. This race marked the end of Vettel's six-year tenure with the Scuderia, as he prepared to move to Aston Martin for the 2021 season.

Having secured his seventh World Championship, and with more victories than any other driver, Hamilton was the most successful Formula One driver in history. As the 2020 Formula One season ended, Hamilton stood at the pinnacle of the sport. Yet, his focus extended beyond mere statistics. The year had been one of immense personal and professional growth, with a commitment to self-improvement and social advocacy, as well as having to come to terms with Covid, not only around the 2020 calendar and his family, but the personal effects of having been infected. To try and counter the various impacts the season and the virus had, he strived to keep his health in shape. He later spoke openly in interviews about his struggles with self-doubt and emphasised the importance of addressing mental health, an area often overlooked in elite sport, especially when Covid struck. The challenges of the 2020 season, including contracting COVID-19 late in the year, had only reinforced his belief in the importance of holistic self-care.

**Hamilton's Rise as an Advocate**

While he had spent much of his career avoiding controversy, 'keeping his head down', and 'doing his talking on the track', 2020 saw Hamilton emerge as one of sport's most influential voices for social justice. The death of George Floyd and the subsequent rise of the Black Lives Matter movement resonated deeply with him, leading him to take an active role in advocating for racial equality. He used his platform to push for greater diversity in motorsport, encouraging the FIA and Formula One to take meaningful action. He also made powerful personal statements, taking a knee before races and wearing a T-shirt calling for the arrest of the police officers involved in the killing of Breonna Taylor. His stance was not universally supported within the paddock, but Hamilton remained steadfast, believing it was his responsibility to use his influence for a greater cause.

His activism did not go unnoticed. Hamilton was recognised as one of TIME's 100 Most Influential People of 2020, and in early 2021, he received the Laureus Athlete Advocate of the Year award for his efforts. His influence extended beyond public statements; he also launched the Hamilton Commission, a research initiative aimed at increasing representation of black talent in motorsport, a project that underscored his commitment to enacting real change.

As he prepared for the 2021 season, Hamilton found himself pausing for thought. He had achieved everything there was to achieve in Formula One, yet he remained motivated to push forward. His contract negotiations with Mercedes stretched into the early months of the year, fuelling speculation about his future. Despite his expressed desire to continue with Mercedes, negotiations were prolonged, partly due to the global economic uncertainties brought about by the COVID-19 pandemic. Hamilton acknowledged the situation, noting he felt uncomfortable negotiating a significant new contract during such challenging global circumstances.

The delay in finalising his contract led to widespread rumours about a possible switch to Ferrari. The allure of driving for the iconic Italian team has tempted many drivers, and Hamilton was no exception. Speculation grew that Hamilton had been in discussions with senior Ferrari figures, including chairman John Elkann, prompting debate within the paddock about a potential move. However, both Hamilton and Ferrari publicly downplayed the significance of these rumours, reiterating their commitments to their respective teams.

While Hamilton was thought to be intrigued by the possibility of driving for Ferrari, conditions within the team—potentially including the future of Team Principal Mattia Binotto—would likely have needed to change significantly for him to seriously consider such a move. Despite ongoing speculation, no formal agreement or substantial progress was ever confirmed.

Ultimately, Hamilton and Mercedes ended speculation by agreeing to a one-year contract extension covering just the 2021 season, rather than a multi-year deal. Both parties recognised that significant changes to Formula One regulations scheduled for 2022 presented uncertainty. Opting for a shorter-term deal allowed Hamilton and Mercedes to reassess their respective futures within a rapidly evolving Formula One landscape. The one-year extension quietened rumours, at least temporarily, allowing both Hamilton and Mercedes breathing space to reconsider their long-term plans amid upcoming regulatory changes.

But for Hamilton, the challenge ahead went beyond mere contract decisions or speculation. The 2020 season had marked the start of a new phase in his life and career—one defined not only by sporting success but also by his commitment to meaningful change. As Hamilton prepared for 2021, he stood not just as a seven-time World Champion but as a prominent advocate for social justice, facing his greatest challenge yet, both on and off the track. He would need all his strength for 2021, where he would be battling against more than just his competitors.

# Clash of the Titans

The build-up to the 2021 Formula One season offered a unique combination of anticipation and adaptation. For Lewis Hamilton—now Sir Lewis Hamilton, after his New Year knighthood—the off-season provided a chance to reflect, recharge, and prepare for what would be a key year in his illustrious career.

Off the track, Hamilton continued to use his influence to drive positive change. He took part in various philanthropic undertakings, including environmental campaigns and diversity initiatives. As part of his ongoing environmental advocacy, Hamilton pushed for better protection of the environment and the planet. In February 2021, he voiced concerns about protecting wildlife, highlighting how the illegal wildlife trade threatened endangered species and how efforts to combat this had been reduced following COVID-19.

Hamilton also made headlines later in the season at the Met Gala, where he sponsored a table featuring emerging black designers to spotlight underrepresented talent in fashion. He explained that the Met Gala was the most significant fashion event of the year, and he had chosen to create something meaningful that would stimulate conversation around diversity and representation.

Despite the limitations imposed by the ongoing COVID-19 pandemic, Hamilton remained closely engaged with the Mercedes-AMG Petronas Formula One Team. He visited the factory in Brackley to work with engineers on refining the new car.

The pandemic continued to cast its shadow over the sport. Travel restrictions and health protocols affected pre-season preparations and the scheduling of races. The FIA implemented stringent measures, including regular testing and restricted paddock access. Formula One's comprehensive "Return to Racing" plan was put in place, aiming to ensure as many races could safely proceed as possible. Amendments had been made to Appendix S of the International Sporting Code by the FIA, effectively meaning that, for Formula One, the FIA would collaborate closely with local health authorities and continually adapt risk mitigation strategies as the pandemic evolved.

The pandemic also forced delays in the introduction of major new technical regulations. Initially planned for 2021, the changes were postponed to 2022 to provide financial relief to teams. As a result, teams were required to use their 2020 chassis for the 2021 season. Hamilton accepted the challenges posed by these disruptions and remained focused on adapting to the evolving circumstances. He stated that everyone in the team had to adjust. The challenges had strengthened their determination and made the team even more resilient.

A new Sprint Qualifying format was also introduced to enhance the spectacle. It added a short race to select events on Saturdays, offering fresh challenges for the teams.

As the 2021 Formula One season loomed, anticipation mounted around Hamilton's pursuit of a record-breaking eighth World title. His knighthood added another layer of recognition to his already illustrious career. However, the delayed technical regulations, the continued impact of COVID-19, and significant team and driver changes meant the new season promised not only personal milestones for Hamilton but also sweeping transformations across the grid. Together with the resurgence of Red Bull Racing, these elements would combine to make 2021 a historic year, concluding in dramatic fashion unlike any season before it.

Even though a major overhaul of the regulations concerning the cars had been put back to 2022, the FIA still tried to curb the speed of the cars by introducing some minor changes for 2021, focusing on brake ducts, diffusers, floors, and weight.

These changes were designed to reduce downforce by around 10%. The teams would manage to recover most of this as the season progressed.

The minimum weight of a car, in its unfuelled state, was now 752kg, including the power unit, having been 746kg in 2020. The minimum weight of the power unit had also increased from 145kg in 2020 to 150kg. These weight increases were primarily introduced for two reasons: safety, and to discourage teams from using exotic materials that would be prohibitively expensive.

As Hamilton and Mercedes prepared for the 2021 Formula One season, their focus shifted to the new W12 car, an evolution of the W11, designed to continue the team's dominance in the hybrid era. After seven consecutive Constructors' Championships, expectations were high. However, with largely stable regulations and limited development due to cost-saving measures, the challenge was more about refining an already formidable package than building something entirely new.

During pre-season testing, the W12 began to show signs of instability, particularly at the rear. Concerns arose that the balance of the car had been compromised by FIA-mandated changes to the rear floor and diffuser. The loss of downforce affected low-rake cars like Mercedes more than their high-rake rivals, such as Red Bull. As a result, Mercedes found themselves on the back foot. Bottas remarked that the W12 felt unusually twitchy and unforgiving compared to its predecessor.

Mercedes engineers worked tirelessly to refine the car's setup, but it was clear from the outset that this season would not be as straightforward as previous years. Mercedes' strategy team openly expressed concerns during early testing, acknowledging that the W12 was noticeably difficult to handle. They observed that, in contrast, the Red Bull appeared exceptionally stable and well-balanced, especially in the more technically demanding sectors of the track.

Despite these challenges, the car retained many of the strengths that had made its predecessor so dominant. The Mercedes power unit was still regarded as the best on the grid, delivering exceptional performance and efficiency. The team also continued to refine their suspension and aerodynamic efficiency, ensuring the W12 remained one of the fastest cars over a race distance.

Hamilton, preparing to defend his title against an increasingly competitive Max Verstappen and Red Bull, acknowledged the difficulties early on. He recognised that the W12 was not as easy to drive as some of its predecessors but remained confident in the team's ability to extract performance from it over the course of the season. Hamilton was well aware that the challenge ahead would differ significantly from previous years, with Red Bull now posing a genuine threat to Mercedes' dominance.

As the season began, the W12's strengths and weaknesses became apparent. It remained a race-winning machine, but it no longer had the outright advantage Mercedes had enjoyed in previous years. Strategy, tyre management, and in-season development would prove crucial in determining whether it could deliver yet another title for Hamilton and the team.

Ferrari, still recovering from a lacklustre 2020 season, focused on improving their power unit, with encouraging signs of progress. However, they continued to grapple with aerodynamic inefficiencies, particularly drag, which hindered their top-speed performance on straights. Team Principal Mattia Binotto stated Ferrari had made significant improvements on the power unit but emphasised that the team still needed to address the issue of aerodynamic drag. Binotto recognised the trade-off between aerodynamic drag and downforce, saying that, based on their data, straight-line speed was no longer the severe disadvantage it had been the previous year. This was promising news for Ferrari.

Red Bull's RB16B, developed under the leadership of Adrian Newey and powered by Honda's much-improved engine, emerged as a formidable contender. The car had effective aerodynamics, impressive straight-line speed, and consistent balance, giving Verstappen a newfound sense of confidence. Verstappen described pre-season testing positively, highlighting the predictability and overall balance of the car. He noted that the testing programme had gone smoothly without any significant issues, leaving the team feeling optimistic.

Verstappen tempered his enthusiasm slightly by acknowledging that testing performance does not always translate directly into race weekends. Nonetheless, the feeling within the team was unquestionably positive. This was worrying news for the other teams.

Christian Horner, the Red Bull Team Principal and Chief Executive Officer, recognised that Honda had made great progress since 2019. However, Horner faced a challenging period as Honda had signalled their intention to withdraw from Formula One at the end of the 2021 season. Horner confirmed that Red Bull would establish a new powertrain operation to continue running the Honda-designed engines from 2022 onwards.

Partnering Verstappen was Sergio Pérez. Pérez was an interesting choice. In the seasons preceding 2020, he had regularly been involved in accidents and had struggled with consistency. In 2020, when the power unit in the Force India was dominant and Ferrari-powered cars struggled, Pérez's performances appeared somewhat flattered. Only time would tell how he would perform alongside Verstappen.

Several other significant driver and team changes reshaped the grid. One of the biggest team developments was the rebranding of Racing Point to Aston Martin. This move brought four-time World Champion Sebastian Vettel into their line-up. Team Principal Otmar Szafnauer expressed confidence in Vettel's experience and ability, highlighting his proven track record in winning races and World Championships.

Carlos Sainz Jr., meanwhile, departed McLaren to fulfil a lifelong dream of driving for Ferrari, replacing Vettel. Reflecting on his new role, Sainz revealed that he had always envisioned himself as a Ferrari driver, a sentiment he had carried throughout his career. His move solidified Ferrari's bid to rebuild after a challenging 2020 campaign.

Ricciardo found a new home at McLaren, taking Sainz's former seat. His switch from Renault to McLaren was viewed as a step towards competing for podiums more consistently.

Another significant comeback graced the 2021 season as two-time World Champion Fernando Alonso returned to Formula One with Alpine, the rebranded Renault team. Replacing Ricciardo, Alonso expressed enthusiasm for the new challenge, appearing refreshed and reinvigorated by his time away from Formula One.

At Haas, an entirely new driver pairing was introduced, featuring rookies Mick Schumacher and Nikita Mazepin. Schumacher, the son of seven-time World Champion Michael Schumacher, entered Formula One as the reigning Formula 2 Champion. AlphaTauri also welcomed fresh talent in the form of Yuki Tsunoda, who replaced Daniil Kvyat. A rising star from Japan, Tsunoda's promotion from Formula 2 was widely anticipated.

The build-up to the 2021 season set the stage for a fiercely contested opener in Bahrain. Red Bull and Mercedes emerged as the teams to beat, each aware of the other's strengths and weaknesses. Behind them, Ferrari and Aston Martin worked to close the gap, knowing that small changes in regulations could create unexpected opportunities.

For Hamilton, this season was about more than just defending his title—it was about making history. As the cars lined up on the grid in Bahrain, the scene was set for what would become one of the most dramatic and controversial seasons Formula One had ever seen.

The anticipation surrounding the new season was unlike anything in recent years. Hamilton, the reigning Champion, faced arguably the toughest challenge of his career in Verstappen and Red Bull Racing. The first three races—Bahrain, Imola, and Portimão—provided an early glimpse of the intensity to come, setting the tone for a battle that would define the season and the sport itself.

**Bahrain: Sparks Fly Immediately**

The season opened on the night of 28 March at the Bahrain International Circuit. The desert sky was clear, and the cool, dry air carried the anticipation of a fresh Championship.

Under the floodlights, Verstappen had qualified on pole, while Hamilton lined up alongside him on the front row. The Red Bull looked formidable, but Hamilton was ready for a fight.

The first twenty seconds of the race set the tone for the remainder of the year.

As the five red lights went out, Verstappen and Hamilton both made good starts. Verstappen moved immediately from the outside of the start-finish straight off the racing line to the inside near the pit wall, crossing the entire width of the track up the pit lane exit and forcing Hamilton to his left. Dust, lifted by the strong aerodynamics and rear diffusers, swirled everywhere as all 20 cars crossed the start-finish straight at well over 100mph. Approaching Turn 1, Verstappen swept left across the circuit, across Hamilton, and towards the racing line, leaving just enough racing room. Verstappen's car, heavy with fuel, showered thousands of sparks from the titanium skid block high into the air as the suspension bottomed out. Hamilton slotted in behind Verstappen, recognising the risk should he attempt a move down the outside.

Two corners later, Mazepin lost control going over the kerbs and smashed his Haas into the barrier, bringing out a Virtual Safety Car. The restart was a rerun of the opening lap as Verstappen again moved off and then back onto the racing line, sparks showering the drivers behind.

Hamilton and Mercedes played a waiting game and went for the undercut on Lap 14, with Hamilton pitting for new hard tyres. Red Bull kept Verstappen out on medium tyres until Lap 18. As Verstappen exited the pits, he saw Hamilton go through into the lead. By Lap 40 of 56, both had pitted again, and Verstappen came out on the fresher tyres, ready to hunt Hamilton down.

In the closing stages, Hamilton was informed by his race engineer, Bono, about the need to manage his tyres to maintain the lead over Verstappen. Hamilton responded, up for the challenge but saying how difficult it would be to keep Verstappen behind. This exchange underscored the tension as Hamilton worked to preserve his tyre performance against Verstappen whilst trying to minimise any losses.

Esteban Ocon, driving for Alpine, was going about his race when Sebastian Vettel misjudged his braking and ran into the back of him at Turn 1. Vettel was quick to shift the blame, questioning why Ocon had moved under braking—despite there being no evidence that he had.

By Lap 53 out of 56, Verstappen was right on Hamilton's tail, challenging for the lead. Hamilton defended at Turn 1, taking the inside line, and Verstappen bided his time on his fresher tyres, dropping back behind, ready for another attack—a sign of Verstappen's increased maturity and patience. Verstappen had a good run out of Turn 3, slipstreaming Hamilton down the long straight and going down the outside before Turn 4, staying to the outside of Hamilton in the right-hand corner. Both cars started to run wide, but while Hamilton's Mercedes remained within track limits, Verstappen passed on the outside, clearly outside track limits, and was deemed to have gained an advantage. He was promptly instructed by Red Bull to give the position back to Hamilton, a decision that proved pivotal to the race's conclusion, with Hamilton winning and Verstappen less than one second behind. Verstappen could be heard venting his frustrations over team radio at having to give the position back.

After the race, Hamilton was elated over team radio, acknowledging that although they weren't the quickest, they had still managed to achieve victory, attributing the success entirely to teamwork. Following the podium celebrations, Hamilton spoke candidly about the intense pressure from Verstappen, describing the race as incredibly challenging. He admitted to barely being able to keep him behind, knowing Verstappen would catch up and thinking holding him off would be nearly impossible. Hamilton shared that it had been one of the toughest races he'd experienced in a long time, adding that he relished the challenge.

Verstappen, though frustrated to finish second, was invigorated by the battle and proud of his ability to go wheel-to-wheel with Hamilton. He was disappointed not to win but chose to focus on the positives, emphasising that Red Bull was genuinely taking the fight to Mercedes—a perfect start to the year, as he put it.

As for the other runners, Bottas finished third, nearly 40 seconds behind Hamilton, underscoring just how much Hamilton had pushed his car to the limit throughout the race. Norris, in the McLaren, had an impressive result, finishing fourth. Pérez, despite encountering technical issues at the start, fought back to finish fifth in the second Red Bull. The drivers were interviewed after the race, and while they were clearly delighted to be back racing, their COVID face protection made it hard to read some of their reactions.

The Bahrain Grand Prix was not only a spectacular start to the season but also a sign of the fierce battle ahead. It highlighted the need for teams to be at their peak in decision-making, with fine margins likely to decide the outcome. It set the tone for the season, where track limits and team calls would continue to play vital roles in the Championship fight.

**The Emilia Romagna Grand Prix – A Test of Skill**

Three weeks later, on 18 April, the teams arrived at the iconic Imola circuit in Italy for the Emilia Romagna Grand Prix. Nestled in the Italian countryside, the Autodromo Enzo e Dino Ferrari greeted the drivers with a damp, treacherous track following a morning downpour. Rain clouds still loomed as the grid lined up, with Hamilton on pole and Verstappen starting third. As a reflection of how wet the conditions were, before the race had even begun, Leclerc spun off into the gravel at Acque Minerali—of all places—but managed to regain the circuit.

The start was chaotic, with Verstappen launching aggressively off the line to muscle past Hamilton into Turn 1. Hamilton, forced to the outside, was edged off the track as Verstappen held his line, sending the Mercedes bouncing over the sausage kerbs and shedding bits of carbon fibre. The slippery conditions claimed several drivers, particularly among the lower and midfield teams, as they spun off under their own steam. Mick Schumacher half-spun into the pit wall while warming his tyres.

Sergio Pérez had a brief off-track excursion behind the Safety Car in the Red Bull and, while rejoining, overtook two cars—an error that earned him a ten-second penalty. The conditions sat in that awkward middle ground where it was too dry for intermediates but too wet for slicks.

Patches of water running across the circuit caught several drivers out, and even Hamilton wasn't immune to mistakes. On Lap 31, while lapping backmarkers, he was forced offline on his slick tyres and lost grip at Tosa, sliding into the gravel and damaging his front wing. Rather than attempting a three-point turn and risking getting stuck, he reversed smoothly over the gravel trap, a quick-thinking move that kept him in the race. Moments later, fortune intervened again, turning what could have been a disaster into a lifeline.

There was then an almighty accident as Russell tried to pass Bottas at high speed, but he misjudged the manoeuvre and lost control of the Williams, hitting the Mercedes and taking both cars out. With such a high-speed accident, debris blocked the track. Russell then went into overdrive on the radio with a multitude of expletives. He leaped out of his car and stormed over to Bottas, who, seated in his car, was still taking in all that had just happened. Russell leaned over Bottas' cockpit and tapped him on the helmet. Bottas returned the favour with a friendly one-fingered wave. Russell's actions were another example of a driver refusing to acknowledge their mistakes, showing that while Russell had raw speed, his maturity was still a work in progress. Due to all the debris and grass littered across the circuit, the Stewards red-flagged the race.

The red flag gave Hamilton a crucial opportunity. The stoppage allowed his car to be repaired, setting the stage for a remarkable recovery. Restarting from eighth, he launched a clinical charge through the field, finishing second behind Verstappen, who delivered a dominant performance to claim his first win of the season.

After the race, Hamilton mused over the challenging conditions, and praised Verstappen's strong performance, and saying how competitive his own pace had been in the rain. He admitted that a moment of impatience with backmarkers had caught him out but emphasised that mistakes were part of being human. He was really happy to get back in the race and recover to second. Verstappen, meanwhile, also talked about just how tricky the conditions had been, admitting he had almost lost control of his Red Bull on the restart after the Safety Car.

Lando Norris claimed a brilliant third place for McLaren. It was a strong result following his fourth place in the previous race, signalling intent from McLaren and delighting fans who were eager to see the team back in contention. Leclerc and Sainz brought their Ferraris home in fourth and fifth on home soil, trailing Norris to the flag. The pair looked strong, with Sainz beginning to find his stride in red.

Verstappen, Leclerc, Sainz, and Norris—Formula One's new generation was well and truly taking shape. But while Hamilton now found himself among the so-called 'old guard,' he wasn't ready to fade just yet.

**The Championship Battle Heads to Portugal**

The Championship battle moved to the sun-drenched Algarve International Circuit in Portugal on 2 May. The rolling hills of Portimão, combined with gusty winds, created a few challenges for the drivers. Bottas started on pole, with Hamilton second and Verstappen third, setting the stage for another showdown. The stands, as in Italy, remained completely empty.

Bottas led the pack into Turn 1, with Hamilton in close pursuit and Verstappen hot on his heels. An early incident saw Räikkönen retire after running into the back of his teammate, Antonio Giovinazzi, at full speed on the start-finish straight, bringing out the Safety Car. Upon the race's resumption, Verstappen briefly overtook Hamilton but exceeded track limits in the process. Hamilton, following the same line, also ran wide, meaning the Stewards did not intervene.

Hamilton regrouped over the next few laps, letting everything settle in. On Lap 11, he sailed up the inside of Verstappen into Turn 1 and set off after Bottas. Hamilton caught Bottas on Lap 20 and shot around the outside of him to claim the lead. He didn't look back, winning by almost thirty seconds from Verstappen. Bottas came in third. Pérez, in the second Red Bull, managed a commendable fourth place, while Norris continued his strong form, finishing fifth for McLaren. Leclerc secured sixth, and the Alpine duo of Ocon and Alonso finished seventh and eighth respectively, marking a positive weekend for the team.

After climbing out of the car, Hamilton discussed the conditions and his start, talking about how the wind had made it very easy to make a mistake. He admitted that he hadn't got quite as good a start as Bottas and had then lost out on the restart, something he was not happy about.

When asked about his plans given the short gap to the next race in Spain, Hamilton shared insights into his routine, saying he would head back home for just a couple of days, where recovery and a lot of physio would be the main focus. Angela Cullen would be with him, ensuring he recovered and got himself turned around as quickly as possible for the next race. He mentioned that there would be a lot of debriefs and a lot to download from the race, with areas for improvement to look at. While the day had not been perfect, he emphasised the importance of going over those areas and trying to turn over every stone.

### Angela Cullen – A Vital Presence in Hamilton's Career

Angela Cullen was at the heart of Hamilton's physical preparation. She was his long-time physiotherapist, performance coach, and one of the most trusted members of his inner circle. Cullen, originally from New Zealand, had been working with Hamilton since 2016. With a background in sports science and physiotherapy, she had previously worked with high-performance athletes at the English Institute of Sport.

Her role with Hamilton went far beyond typical physiotherapy. She was responsible for ensuring he was in peak physical condition, helping him recover from races, managing any injuries or strains, and maintaining his flexibility and endurance.

On race weekends, she was a constant presence in the Mercedes garage, making sure Hamilton was physically and mentally ready for every session. Her duties included everything from warm-up routines, stretching, and hydration management to pre-race meals and travel logistics. Between races, she worked closely with him on strength training, mobility exercises, and recovery protocols, ensuring he remained in optimal condition across a gruelling season.

Their partnership was based on mutual trust and a deep understanding of the demands of elite motorsport. Hamilton often spoke about the vital role she played in his success, describing her as one of the most important people in his life. Cullen's influence extended beyond physical preparation—she also provided emotional support, helping Hamilton stay focused and motivated amid the intense pressures of Formula One.

Cullen was instantly recognisable in the Formula One paddock, always seen by Hamilton's side. Petite and athletic, she had short blonde hair and striking blue eyes, often framed by her ever-present sunglasses. Her dedication to fitness was evident in her lean, toned physique, a reflection of the high-performance lifestyle she advocated.

Her appearance was often practical and understated, dressed in Mercedes team gear and comfortable sportswear, ready to assist Hamilton at a moment's notice. Whether carrying his helmet, preparing his hydration drinks, or overseeing his warm-ups, she exuded a quiet but unmistakable authority. As well as her professional expertise, Cullen had an energy that set her apart. She was known for her calm and positive nature, offering steady reassurance and motivation. Her New Zealand roots and background in elite sports gave her a no-nonsense approach, but she also carried a warmth that made her more than just a trainer—she was a trusted confidante, a key figure in Hamilton's daily routine, and a grounding presence in the high-pressure world of Formula One.

As Hamilton prepared for the Spanish Grand Prix, Cullen's work would be crucial in helping him recover from the physical and mental toll of Algarve and ensuring he was in top form for the next race.

The first three races of the 2021 season encapsulated the contrasting strengths of Hamilton and Verstappen. Bahrain highlighted Hamilton's defensive brilliance, Imola demonstrated his resilience under pressure, and Portimão showed his strategic genius and his patience. Each race carried the promise of more dramatic encounters to come, as the battle for the Championship gained momentum—but it was a momentum that was set to move away from Hamilton and towards Verstappen.

**The Spanish Grand Prix**

The Spanish Grand Prix has long been a track that tests a driver's finesse and their ability to carry high corner speed. It is also a test for the teams and challenges their strategy calls. On 9 May, it lived up to its reputation.

Hamilton started on pole, but Verstappen made an audacious move into Turn 1, going down the inside and letting the Red Bull drift menacingly towards the Mercedes. Hamilton had to back out or there would have been a collision—Verstappen had seized the lead in a bold statement of intent.

Lap 26 of the race was a notable first for Formula One and something that would ultimately sway the outcome of the 2021 Championship, and not in a good way.

In a bid for greater transparency, the FIA, working with Formula One, had agreed to broadcast messages not just between teams and drivers, but between teams and the FIA. Hamilton was pushing to get on terms with Verstappen and was being held up by Nikita Mazepin in the Haas Ferrari. At that moment, Toto Wolff radioed Michael Masi, the FIA Chief Steward, demanding blue flags and stressing that Mazepin was making them lose the position. Günther Steiner later remarked that he felt Wolff wanted to assert authority and show who was in command. While Wolff's transmission was not material in itself, the Team Principals would increasingly attempt to influence race outcomes by pressuring Masi and the Stewards over the radio. This practice would ultimately lead to disaster at the end of the season.

Hamilton got past Mazepin, and from there, the race evolved into a tactical duel. Mercedes opted for a two-stop strategy, pitting Hamilton on Lap 42 for fresh tyres. At the time, he trailed Verstappen by 22 seconds. With a mountain to climb, Hamilton asked Peter Bonnington how far behind he was after the stop and how much he needed to catch up. Bonnington responded with excitement and encouragement, reminding Hamilton that they had done it before.

Red Bull grew increasingly nervous, fearing a repeat of Hungary 2019, where Hamilton had made an additional stop and then overtaken Verstappen towards the end of the race. Their concerns proved justified, as on Lap 60 Verstappen was defenceless when Hamilton drove past him into Turn 1. The race was effectively over, and Verstappen brought the Red Bull home in second, some sixteen seconds behind.

Bottas, largely anonymous in the other Mercedes, rounded off the podium in third, some 26 seconds behind his teammate. Leclerc, in fourth, was nearly a minute down, highlighting Ferrari's struggles on a circuit that required a strong aerodynamic package. Pérez, Verstappen's teammate in the other Red Bull, finished fifth, an embarrassing 47 seconds behind Verstappen.

**The Monaco Grand Prix**

The Monaco Grand Prix, one of Formula One's crown jewels, brought its usual blend of prestige and peril. Held on 23 May under sunny skies, the narrow streets of Monte Carlo presented a remarkable test for the drivers. In qualifying, Leclerc secured a dramatic pole position but crashed in the final minutes, hitting the barriers with the front and rear wheels on the right side of the car, causing a red flag. While the damage initially seemed repairable, a driveshaft issue discovered on warm-up to the grid on race day forced him to withdraw, promoting Verstappen to the lead car for the start.

Verstappen seized his opportunity, taking the lead into Sainte Dévote and never looking back. In complete control of the race, Verstappen maintained a commanding pace to claim his first Monaco victory and, with it, the lead in the Drivers' Championship.

Sainz brought his Ferrari home in second, a result that signalled a clear step forward for the Scuderia after their struggles in 2020. Norris secured third in the McLaren, his car looking stunning in the one-off light blue and orange Gulf Oil livery that had turned heads all weekend. Pérez finished fourth in the second Red Bull, while fifth place went to Vettel, who finally had something to smile about after a miserable 2020. His Aston Martin debut season was beginning to show promise. On Lap 52, Ricciardo in the McLaren was lapped by his teammate Norris. It was a real fall from grace for the Aussie, who had won at Monaco only three years earlier.

Hamilton, starting from seventh after a disappointing qualifying, endured one of his most frustrating races in years. Stuck in traffic and battling tyre wear, he could only salvage seventh—well below his usual standards. Mercedes had an even bigger headache with Bottas, who retired on Lap 30 due to a wheel nut failure that left his tyre stuck on the car. Hamilton was understandably annoyed, but if there was any silver lining, it was that the race itself had barely any overtaking. In fact, across the entire Grand Prix, only one on-track pass was made—proof, if ever it was needed, that overtaking in Monaco remains near impossible.

### The Azerbaijan Grand Prix

The Azerbaijan Grand Prix in Baku, held on 6 June, was a race full of carnage and highly unpredictable. The high-speed street circuit, known for its drama, lived up to its reputation as it produced one of the most astonishing races of the season. Leclerc again showed that his one-lap pace in the Ferrari was a force to be reckoned with in qualifying, scoring another pole position. Hamilton lined up alongside, with Verstappen third on the grid. On race day, the top three played it safe into Turn 1, slotting into position without drama as they settled into the race.

On Lap 2, with DRS still inactive, Hamilton powered past Leclerc on the pit straight, taking the lead with ease. He looked in control at the front, managing the pace comfortably. However, just four laps later, Verstappen made his move on Leclerc and set his sights on Hamilton. The Red Bull looked beautifully balanced through the corners, lighter on its feet, turning in later, sharper, and putting the power down earlier—a clear threat as the chase began.

Mercedes brought Hamilton in several laps earlier than Verstappen, and Verstappen capitalised by putting in some blistering laps. His pit crew were just as quick, lifting the car, changing all four wheels, and dropping it back down in just 1.9 seconds. Verstappen's pace and the rapid pit stop put him into the lead. He appeared destined for victory, his pace unmatched, and he seemed to have the Championship momentum firmly in his grasp.

On Lap 31, Stroll, in his Aston Martin, suffered a blowout coming onto the main straight at over 200mph. The car was immediately pitched sideways into the concrete barriers, the front wing torn off, and most of the wheels battered by the impact. It was a terrifying incident. His car sprayed carbon fibre for hundreds of metres down the track. This would likely play a key part in Verstappen's own race further on. The Safety Car was deployed, and the cars bunched up until Lap 35 before the race restarted.

On Lap 46, disaster struck for Verstappen. In a near carbon copy of Stroll's earlier crash, and possibly caused by leftover debris, he blasted down the start-finish straight at over 200mph when his rear tyre suddenly gave way. The Red Bull snapped violently to the right and slammed into the barrier, his race ending in an instant. Frustration was evident as Verstappen clambered out of the wrecked car. He casually tossed his steering wheel over the nose before walking to the back of the Red Bull and giving it a solid kick with his left foot—an image that perfectly captured the fury of the moment.

The crash triggered a red flag, stopping the race and setting up a dramatic standing restart with just two laps to go—one final twist in a Grand Prix that had already delivered plenty of chaos. Now in prime position to reclaim the Championship lead, Hamilton lined up on the front row alongside Pérez. As the grid waited for the lights to go out, plumes of smoke poured from Hamilton's front brakes—a sign of the tension to come.

As the lights went out, Hamilton locked up into Turn 1 after accidentally engaging his brake magic setting, a feature used to heat the brakes. The error sent him careening off the track and to the back of the field. Frustrated, Hamilton apologised to his team over the radio, expressing his regret for the mistake.

Pérez capitalised on the chaos, taking a memorable victory for Red Bull. Behind him, Vettel delivered an inspired drive to finish second in the Aston Martin, with Gasly completing the podium in third in his AlphaTauri Honda. Despite his disappointment, Verstappen remained defiant, later reflecting that sometimes it was easy to hate the sport. He noted that up until that point, the day had been going perfectly—the car had been performing brilliantly, and he had been comfortably managing the race from the lead. He believed the victory would have been straightforward but acknowledged that in motorsport, there were never any guarantees.

Pundits reflected on the race's unpredictability and its implications for the Championship, highlighting how momentum in the title fight had swung one way, then the other, in minutes. Monaco and Baku demonstrated the ebb and flow of the 2021 season. Verstappen's triumph in Monaco was a psychological boost, but the chaos of Azerbaijan showed how quickly fortunes could change. For Hamilton, the frustration of these races only deepened his resolve to fight back. Both drivers left Baku knowing that the road to the title would be anything but straightforward.

**The French Grand Prix**

The French Grand Prix, held on 20 June, delivered one for the strategists. Starting from pole position, Verstappen made a rare error at Turn 2 on the opening lap, running wide and allowing Hamilton to snatch the lead. The wind had been strong, with gusts of up to 31mph (50km/h), causing the cars' balance to change lap by lap, and this had caught Verstappen out in the first corner.

Both teams engaged in a strategic chess match as the race unfolded. Red Bull opted for an aggressive two-stop strategy, pitting Verstappen on Lap 32 for medium tyres, while Mercedes gambled on keeping Hamilton out on a one-stop plan. The decision left Hamilton defending on aging tyres as Verstappen closed in with fresher rubber. On Lap 52 of 53, Verstappen made the decisive move, overtaking Hamilton at Turn 8 to secure a hard-fought victory, radioing his team with his famous "simply lovely" line.

After climbing out of his Red Bull at the end, Verstappen reflected on how hard they had to work for the win but acknowledged that it was very rewarding. He also anticipated that the rest of the season would be a close battle with Hamilton. Hamilton, meanwhile, accepted the challenge with grace, stating post-race that considering how difficult Friday had been, he was really happy with the result.

Before the Championship battle moved to Austria for the Styrian Grand Prix, the teams had to start thinking about a change to the regulations involving pit stops, which would come into effect in Hungary. Technical Directive TD22A was introduced to improve safety during pit stops by setting a minimum reaction time for wheel changes.

In the last few years, the teams had perfected ultra-fast pit stops, sometimes changing all four wheels in under two seconds, as demonstrated by Red Bull's 1.9-second stop in Baku. However, the FIA had become concerned that some teams were relying too much on automation rather than manual confirmation, which could lead to unsafe releases, including cross-threaded wheel nuts or wheels not being properly secured, as had happened with Bottas at Monaco. TD22A required mechanics to manually confirm certain steps of the wheel change before the car could be released. This meant a slight delay compared to previous methods, as teams could no longer depend solely on pre-set automated systems to signal when a wheel was fully attached.

The directive faced resistance from some teams, particularly Red Bull and some of their followers, who felt it was aimed at slowing down their consistently fast pit stops. It seemed they had short memories, as it had only been three years since the unfortunate Francesco Cigarini, a mechanic at Ferrari, had to undergo surgery after fracturing his shinbone and fibula in a botched pit stop, and since then, there had been more near misses.

Despite the controversy, the rule was enforced, and teams had to adjust their procedures accordingly. Red Bull adapted along with everyone else. Some Team Principals appreciated the change in the interests of safety, with Andreas Seidl of McLaren notably welcoming the change. Before Hungary, however, there were the Styrian, Austrian, and British Grands Prix to contend with.

**The Styrian Grand Prix**

On 27 June, race day, Verstappen made the most of his pole position, leading from start to finish in a dominant display. Red Bull hailed his performance as "flawless," a word that perfectly summed up his control of the weekend. With their strongest run of form since 2013, Red Bull were increasingly confident that Verstappen could challenge for the title.

While the gap to Verstappen appeared larger than it needed to be due to Hamilton making a late stop for fresh tyres to secure the fastest lap, Hamilton acknowledged the pace difference to his rival. He didn't dwell on it, but felt Red Bull were plainly faster. There was little he could do about it beyond continuing to do his best job each weekend, though he stressed that Mercedes needed to find performance from somewhere.

Wolff dampened the mood for Mercedes further when he told reporters that the team's focus was now on the 2022 car and the new regulations, and he did not see Mercedes bringing any further updates for the 2021 season. Hamilton, however, was pushing for more, stating after the race that they needed an upgrade of some sort, particularly after he had struggled to keep pace with Verstappen. There was an apparent disconnect between Wolff's objectives and Hamilton's. This divergence would resurface in the coming seasons.

Just as the teams battled on track, they also fought off it, sometimes questioning new developments from rivals or a sudden increase in performance. At the Styrian Grand Prix, Mercedes and some other teams raised concerns about Red Bull's straight-line speed, which had grown significantly since France after Honda introduced another power unit for the season. While a new engine was allowed, regulations prevented manufacturers from enhancing performance beyond the original homologated design.

Christian Horner listened to the criticism from Toto Wolff and hit back, pointing out that Mercedes had used a larger rear wing for the race, while Red Bull had opted for a much thinner one. He suggested that it was easy to understand why Red Bull had been quicker on the straights.

It was becoming obvious that as well as the fighting taking place at each venue, the teams would start to apply pressure at every conceivable level, including lobbying and appealing decisions or performance gains. It was set to become a fraught second half of the season. Mercedes had not experienced a four-race winless streak since 2014, so this was new territory for the team. Mercedes and Hamilton would indeed need to dig deep, and the seven-time World Champion woulnd't give up without a fight.

## The Austrian Grand Prix

Returning to the Red Bull Ring for the Austrian Grand Prix a week later, Verstappen delivered a perfect performance. Securing pole position, he led every lap, took the fastest lap bonus point, and claimed his third consecutive victory.

For Hamilton, it was a race of damage limitation. Struggling with floor damage from Lap 20 onward, he could only manage a fourth-place finish. Hamilton was candid in his assessment, admitting that Mercedes needed to find answers to Red Bull's dominance. He acknowledged that they were miles behind their rivals and that all hands were needed on deck. Red Bull had introduced multiple upgrades over the last few races, whereas Mercedes had not brought any.

Bottas had a good race, finishing second, while Norris claimed third in the McLaren. Norris was becoming a fixture on or around the podium, establishing himself as a force to be reckoned with.

As the teams left Austria, Verstappen led the standings with 182 points, while Hamilton sat second on 150 points. Hamilton needed to stem the tide.

## The British Grand Prix – The Copse Collision

The British Grand Prix at Silverstone is always a highlight of the Formula One calendar, combining high-speed corners and a passionate home crowd. In 2021, the race took on added significance due to the fierce Championship battle. It also marked the introduction of the Sprint Qualifying format, adding an extra layer of strategic complexity. The weekend ran from 16–18 July, and it was a lovely British summer weekend, with a maximum temperature of 27°C. Whilst it was warm around the circuit, it was about to become red hot on it.

In Saturday's Sprint Race, Hamilton, starting from pole, was out-dragged into Turn 1 by Verstappen, who snatched the lead immediately. On Lap 2, Hamilton got a far better exit from

Luffield into Woodcote and had the momentum to attack along the National Pits Straight into Copse. Sensing the danger, Verstappen darted from the outside to the middle of the track to block any move up the inside. Hamilton switched to the outside instead, and as both cars approached the apex, it was clear that unless one of them backed out, a huge crash was inevitable. This time, Hamilton chose to lift, avoiding contact. Verstappen, on the absolute limit, barely kept within track limits on the exit, his car bottoming out violently as it rode over the kerbs. It was a sign of just how committed they both were.

Verstappen took the Sprint victory, with Hamilton finishing right behind in second, and Bottas completing the top three. But for Hamilton, the lesson was clear—if he wanted to stop Verstappen's momentum, he would need to be far more aggressive. The Dutchman had shown time and again that he was willing to risk a collision rather than yield a position. Overnight, Hamilton reflected on what he would have to do in the Grand Prix.

On race day, Hamilton lined up second behind Verstappen, the near-miss from the Sprint still fresh in his mind. The pressure was immense—this was his home race. The grandstands, once empty due to Covid, were now packed with British fans, and he needed to make a statement. His father had always told him to do his talking on the track. Now was the time to speak.

The lights went out, and the fight was on. From the very first corners, neither Hamilton nor Verstappen was willing to give an inch. The battle built towards a crescendo as they went into Lap 2.

Verstappen and Hamilton were locked in a fierce fight as they powered through Woodcote, with Hamilton hugging a tighter line to maximise his exit onto the straight. The move gave him better momentum and a real chance to challenge Verstappen as they hurtled towards Copse—one of the fastest corners on the track—at blistering speed. It was a repeat of the Sprint Race, but this time, Verstappen held his normal racing line to the left, and spotting a gap, Hamilton went for the inside. But with both cars closing in at nearly 180 mph (290 km/h), the margin for error was razor-thin.

As they converged, space was at a premium. Hamilton understeered slightly, drifting out but staying well within track limits and leaving Verstappen room. Verstappen, expecting Hamilton to hug the apex and seemingly unaware of the slight understeer, turned in near to his usual racing line. With both cars rotating at different angles, their wheels made contact. Verstappen's car snapped sideways and spun violently into the barriers, smashing into the tyre wall with a brutal 51G impact.

The crash caused significant damage to the barriers and forced a red flag, bringing the race to a halt. Verstappen, though winded and visibly shaken, managed to climb out unaided before being taken to hospital for precautionary checks. It was a terrifying moment but not unexpected, given the determination of both drivers on the absolute limit.

Hamilton went on to win the race, despite receiving a ten-second penalty for the collision with Verstappen. The British crowd was jubilant. Second was Leclerc in the Ferrari, and third was Bottas.

The incident immediately ignited controversy, dividing opinions across the Formula One community. Some placed the blame firmly on Hamilton, arguing that he had been too aggressive, while others insisted Verstappen should have yielded for once rather than holding his line so stubbornly. As expected, fan reactions were completely dependent on allegiance, with social media descending into chaos.

Christian Horner was furious. In an interview with Sky Sports F1's Ted Kravitz, the Red Bull Team Principal made his feelings crystal clear, laying the blame squarely at Hamilton's feet. He stated that Hamilton should not have been making manoeuvres like that, calling it unacceptable. While he was grateful that Verstappen had not been injured, he hoped Hamilton was happy with himself. He emphasised that drivers simply do not stick a wheel up the inside at Copse, describing it as one of the fastest corners in the Championship, and argued that Hamilton had more than enough experience to know that the move was unacceptable.

Kravitz attempted to offer a counterpoint, suggesting that Mercedes and Hamilton might have had a different perspective on the incident. But Horner was not interested, cutting him off sharply. He dismissed the idea that there was any point in discussing Hamilton's view, insisting that anyone could analyse the footage and draw their own conclusions. He regarded the win as a hollow victory, his frustration obvious as he spoke with an edge of anger, appearing ready to walk away from the conversation altogether.

Damon Hill, who had first-hand experience of wheel-to-wheel contact with Michael Schumacher several times in the 1990s, was asked for his thoughts. He did not assign blame but shared his perspective based on experience. He remarked that a collision between the two had seemed inevitable at some point due to the aggressive nature of their racing. He stated that he had never seen Hamilton drive that aggressively before and struggled to recall a comparable moment, eventually suggesting that the closest example was his battle with Nico Rosberg in Barcelona. Hill speculated that Hamilton's full-on attack mode may have been influenced by what had happened in the Sprint Race, where he had lost pole position.

Hill went on to say that he had received numerous calls and messages from racing friends and others with strong opinions on the matter, but that there was no consensus. In his view, the debate was split 50/50, with no clear answer on whether Hamilton deserved a penalty or whether Verstappen should have been penalised instead. He noted that both drivers were incredibly uncompromising, and when two such determined racers went into a 180mph corner, an incident was bound to happen—and it did.

Hamilton's victory reignited his Championship hopes and reduced the points deficit to Verstappen. The win was met with mixed reactions; while the crowd celebrated, the paddock and fans online remained divided. Verstappen still led, on 185 points to Hamilton's 177.

The British Grand Prix was more than just a race; it was a flashpoint that defined the 2021 season. The incident at Copse Corner had ramifications for the drivers' relationship, the teams' strategies, and the Championship standings. Despite Hamilton winning multiple back-to-back titles, and having said in the past that he was prepared to back out against Verstappen as he lived to fight another day, he had set his stall out at Silverstone: there would be no more backing down.

This shifted the dynamic for the rest of the season, as Verstappen appeared to be equally determined regardless of the risks. No one was willing to give an inch, as both drivers knew that every point would matter. The gloves had come off.

**The Hungarian Grand Prix**

The Hungarian Grand Prix on 1 August began in hectic fashion under overcast skies and wet conditions. It was very warm and humid, with ambient temperatures ranging from 26°C to 31°C.

At the start, into Turn 1, Bottas misjudged his braking, triggering a multi-car collision that eliminated both Red Bull drivers. Stroll, in the Aston Martin, also arrived into Turn 1 far too quickly and speared straight into Leclerc, putting them both out of contention. With multiple cars stranded at the side of the track, the race was red-flagged.

Verstappen somehow managed to recover his car back to the pits once the red flag had been thrown and was able to take the restart. However, his car had suffered significant damage, and the handling was compromised for the rest of the race.

Upon the restart, a bizarre scene unfolded as Hamilton was the sole car on the grid, while all others filed into the pits to switch to slick tyres. In what was possibly the only race in Formula One history where this occurred, one car raced away from the five red lights all on its own while the rest of the field started from the pit lane. Hamilton needed to return as quickly as possible to pit for slick tyres.

This strategic misstep relegated Hamilton to the back once he pitted on the next lap. Despite the setback, Hamilton fought valiantly through the field to finish third on track, which became second after Vettel was disqualified for a fuel infringement. David Croft praised Hamilton's resilience, describing his performance as a recovery mission. Incredibly, Ocon in the Alpine won the race, while Sainz in the Ferrari bagged a net third after Vettel's disqualification.

Hamilton looked unwell on the podium, appearing fatigued and slightly unsteady. After the ceremony, he skipped the initial part of the post-race press conference to visit the doctor. Later, he admitted that he was still struggling with lingering effects from his previous COVID-19 infection, explaining that he was okay but had experienced significant dizziness, with everything becoming blurry on the podium. He reflected on the battle he had been facing all year to stay healthy after contracting the virus at the end of the previous season. He believed the effects of COVID-19 were still lingering, recalling how difficult it had been when he had the virus and how training had felt different since then. The level of fatigue, he noted, was unlike anything he had experienced before and remained a real challenge. His comments shed light on the long-term physical toll the virus had taken, even on an elite athlete at the peak of his career.

## The Belgian Grand Prix – Rain Stops Play

The Belgian Grand Prix, held on 29 August, was plagued by relentless rain that rendered the iconic Spa-Francorchamps circuit undriveable. After hours of delays, race control conducted two laps behind the Safety Car to satisfy the requirement for classification. Half points were awarded, and Max Verstappen was declared the winner, with George Russell achieving a remarkable second place for Williams and Hamilton finishing third. Verstappen, not having completed a single lap at racing speed, had now closed to within three points of Hamilton in the Drivers' Championship.

Hamilton was critical of how the event had been handled, arguing that the two laps behind the Safety Car had been purely a financial decision, ensuring that payments were still made. He expressed his disappointment for the fans, stating that they should receive refunds since they had not been able to watch the race they had paid for. He lamented that it was unfortunate they couldn't race the following day and noted how much he loved the track, making it even more frustrating that they had not been able to compete properly. However, in his view, there had not been a real race.

Hamilton's concerns prompted the FIA to respond constructively. Formula One president Stefano Domenicali dismissed the idea that there had been a commercial motivation behind the decision but emphasised that the fans were a priority and that Formula One would address the situation appropriately. A number of Team Principals also called on the FIA to revisit the rules regarding races affected by such extreme conditions.

## The Dutch Grand Prix

The Dutch Grand Prix returned to the Formula One calendar on 5 September 2021, for the first time since 1985. Held at Circuit Zandvoort under sunny skies and mild temperatures of 22°C, the atmosphere was electric. The circuit's orange-clad stands were filled with fervent support for local hero Verstappen, who was vying for a victory on home soil. The King of the Netherlands, Willem-Alexander—a former member of the International Olympic Committee and an avid sports fan—attended the race to cheer Verstappen on.

Starting from pole position, Verstappen led from the first corner and controlled the race. Hamilton, starting second, pushed hard to challenge him but struggled to match Red Bull's pace on the undulating and narrow Zandvoort layout. Late in the race, Hamilton pitted for fresh tyres to secure the fastest lap point, but Verstappen was unshaken, crossing the line to a deafening roar from the Dutch fans—the Orange Army.

Verstappen was ecstatic after the race, describing the victory as incredible. He acknowledged the high expectations coming into the weekend and admitted it was never easy to fulfil them, but he praised the crowd and expressed his happiness at winning at home. He reflected on the race itself, noting that it had been quite tough, with Hamilton putting on significant pressure and both Mercedes cars showing strong pace.

Hamilton discussed challenge he had faced and acknowledged the passionate Dutch fans. He described it as an amazing weekend, congratulating Verstappen on a great job. He stated that he had given absolutely everything in the race, pushing flat out, but ultimately, Red Bull had been too quick. Despite the result, he shared how much he had enjoyed his time in Holland and thanked the crowd for their support.

As the teams left Holland, the Championship was on a knife-edge: Verstappen was now on 224.5 points, with Hamilton close behind on 221.5.

**Monza – The contenders clash again**

A week later, the Championship fight moved to the high-speed Autodromo Nazionale Monza for the Italian Grand Prix on 12 September. Under warm and clear skies, with temperatures of 27°C, the stage was set for another showdown between Hamilton and Verstappen.

Bottas won the Sprint Race, with Verstappen finishing second and Ricciardo in the McLaren third, while Hamilton came in fifth.

The main race was set to be tight, with Verstappen claiming pole position, Ricciardo second, Norris third, and Hamilton in fourth. The McLarens would obviously be a thorn in Mercedes' side.

At the start of the main race, Ricciardo got a great launch from second on the grid, making a lightning-fast getaway and overtaking pole-sitter Verstappen to seize the lead into the first chicane. Hamilton also had a strong start, passing Norris into the first chicane and closing in on Verstappen as they came around the long right-hander of Curva Grande, accelerating up to 180mph (290km/h) with the cars heavy on fuel and bobbing as the suspension took the load. Hamilton started to close in, benefiting from the slipstream.

As they exited Curva Grande, Ricciardo moved right to take the normal racing line in preparation for the tight left-right chicane at Variante della Roggia, while Verstappen kept to the left to prevent Hamilton from diving down the inside.

Hamilton, carrying momentum, jinked right and went around the outside of Verstappen. As they braked for the left-hander, they were side by side. As they turned in, Verstappen allowed his Red Bull to drift outward, squeezing Hamilton, leaving him with little room. Their tyres made slight contact, sending up smoke. Hamilton was forced to take the escape road, bouncing over the sausage kerbs before rejoining the track. This dropped him to fourth behind Norris. Over the radio, Hamilton relayed to the team that Verstappen had pushed him wide, his voice measured but carrying an undertone of frustration. Pundits ultimately judged it as a racing incident.

As they exited the corner, Sainz in the Ferrari and Giovinazzi in the Alfa Romeo made contact, sending Giovinazzi spinning into the barriers and triggering a Virtual Safety Car.

When the race resumed, Hamilton maintained a steady pace in fourth, biding his time while nibbling away at Norris when possible. On Lap 23, Ricciardo and McLaren blinked first, bringing Ricciardo in for fresh tyres from the lead. Verstappen soon radioed his team to report that his tyres were finished, prompting Red Bull to call him in on the next lap. However, Red Bull endured a disastrous pit stop, taking eleven seconds, which dropped Verstappen to tenth. Hamilton now led the race but still needed to stop.

The race took a dramatic turn on Lap 26 when Hamilton exited the pit lane after a slow stop and found himself half a car length ahead of Verstappen heading into Monza's tight first chicane. Neither driver yielded, resulting in Verstappen's car launching over the top of Hamilton's Mercedes. The rear wheel of Verstappen's car struck Hamilton's helmet, highlighting the life-saving role of the Halo device. Both drivers retired from the race, leaving McLaren's Ricciardo to claim a stunning victory—his first since 2018—and McLaren's first one-two finish since 2012.

If not for the Halo, the crash could have been far worse for Hamilton. The device saved him twice in just a few seconds—first, when Verstappen's Red Bull landed on top of his Mercedes, its carbon fibre floor snapping in half as it struck the Halo beside his head. Then, as the Red Bull rolled further forward, Verstappen's right rear tyre passed directly over Hamilton's helmet before the cars came to a stop. Without the Halo, Hamilton's head would have taken the full force of the impact, likely leading to serious injury or worse. Even with the protection, his helmet was compressed and pushed forward inside the cockpit, straining his neck.

Verstappen climbed out of his car and walked away, glancing briefly twice into Hamilton's cockpit as he walked straight past without stopping to check on him. Hamilton remained sitting in his cockpit for a moment before slowly getting out, shaking his head. Later, Hamilton admitted that he was surprised by Verstappen's reaction and his decision not to stop to see if he was okay. He noted that drivers usually acknowledge each other after a crash, even in the heat of battle.

Afterwards, Hamilton was clear about how close a call it had been and said he felt very fortunate that day. He thanked God for the halo, which he believed had ultimately saved his life and protected his neck, saying it had been a big hit. While he planned to travel in the coming days, he expected to see a specialist to ensure he was fit for the next race, as his neck was getting tighter and tighter. He still bubbled with optimism, and while he understood the risks, he felt that experiencing an incident like that gave him a real shock and a deeper appreciation of life's fragility.

Toto Wolff was equally certain about the importance of the halo, stating that it had definitely saved Hamilton's life that day. He shuddered to think about how horrific the accident would have been without it.

Damon Hill, who had remained neutral regarding the Silverstone clash between the two title rivals, was far more direct this time. He suggested that, while he did not like accusing drivers of such things, it appeared to him that Verstappen had made a calculated decision to take Hamilton out.

Verstappen had his own take on the incident and thought they could have a good battle into Turn 1 and through Turn 2, but as soon as he was alongside Hamilton, he felt he had squeezed him further and further to the left. He believed that there was still enough space to make it into Turn 2 but ultimately felt Hamilton had run him out of road, which caused him to clip the sausage kerb and led to their collision.

When asked if he had spoken to Hamilton, Verstappen said he had not but would do so. He explained that he had walked away from the crash because he thought it was best to let emotions cool down in the heat of the moment. Christian Horner took a pragmatic view, calling it a racing incident and acknowledging that both drivers were fighting for the biggest prize in motorsport.

The Stewards, however, saw it differently, determining that Verstappen was at fault and awarding him a three-place grid penalty for the following race in Sochi.

**The Russian Grand Prix – Hamilton Reaches a Century**

The Championship fight resumed on 26 September at the Sochi Autodrom in Russia. The race, held under overcast skies with temperatures of 18°C, was defined by changing weather conditions that tested every driver's ability to adapt in a dramatic and unpredictable race that kept fans on the edge of their seats.

Norris secured his maiden pole position in a thrilling qualifying session, with Sainz alongside him on the front row. As the lights went out, Sainz managed to overtake Norris into the first corner, taking the early lead. However, Norris remained close and, by Lap 13, reclaimed the top spot with a clinical move.

Behind them, Hamilton, who was fourth on the grid, faced a challenging start, dropping positions after minor contact with other cars. Meanwhile, Verstappen, starting from the back of the grid due to an engine penalty, began a determined charge through the field.

As the race progressed, Norris maintained his lead, displaying maturity and control beyond his years. Hamilton steadily climbed back up the order and, with timely pit stops, positioned himself as a contender for the win, edging closer to Norris.

In the closing stages, the weather took a dramatic turn. Rain began to fall on Lap 47, and teams faced the tough decision of whether to switch to intermediate tyres or stay on slicks. Norris, aiming for his first victory, chose to stay out, hoping the rain would ease. At this stage, Hamilton was right behind Norris, while Verstappen sat in seventh, some 47 seconds adrift of the lead. Hamilton and Mercedes opted to pit for intermediates, a decision that proved pivotal. They ran for two laps as the rain intensified, and McLaren called Norris to ask if he wanted to switch to intermediates. His response was blunt, insisting that he did not.

By Lap 51 out of 53, the rain had intensified, and visibility was reduced as the spray came up. Norris was still hobbling around on his slicks, but Hamilton, having been eight seconds behind at the beginning of the lap, shot past as Norris slid off the circuit, his tyres offering zero grip. Verstappen, who had also pitted just after Hamilton, blasted through the field up to second.

Hamilton kept his cool and crossed the finish line to claim his historic 100th Grand Prix victory. Verstappen and Red Bull's strategic decisions had allowed them to secure an unexpected second place, with Sainz completing the podium in third. Hamilton, however, had dominated, winning by over 52 seconds from Verstappen. Norris, who had driven a stellar race, was heartbroken, finishing seventh after his gamble did not pay off. Despite the disappointment, his performance throughout the weekend solidified his reputation as a future star in Formula One.

While there may have been tension between Hamilton and Verstappen on the track, on the podium there was nothing but respect, with both drivers toasting each other for a job well done. The Championship battle between Hamilton and Verstappen remained as intense as ever, setting the stage for an exhilarating remainder of the season. Hamilton now led by two points. Bottas, in third, was nearly 90 points behind.

As the 2021 season entered its critical final third, the Championship fight between Hamilton and Verstappen reached fever pitch. With just a handful of races remaining, every point mattered, and each circuit brought fresh challenges and drama. The Turkish Grand Prix at Istanbul Park, the United States Grand Prix in Austin, and the Mexico City Grand Prix at high altitude pushed both drivers to their limits.

**Turkey**

The Turkish Grand Prix took place on 10 October at the Istanbul Park Circuit under grey skies and in damp conditions. A persistent drizzle throughout the race left the track slippery, challenging drivers to find the balance between aggression and caution.

Red Bull ran a special white livery paying tribute to their engine supplier, Honda, commemorating their partnership in what was originally scheduled to be Honda's home race weekend at Suzuka before its cancellation. The predominantly white design drew inspiration from Honda's first Formula One victory in 1965, adding a historical touch to the weekend.

Despite setting the fastest time in qualifying, Hamilton had to start from 11th due to a grid penalty for a new engine. He faced an uphill battle, while his teammate Bottas led the field from pole position. Hamilton carved his way through the field, making his way into third by Lap 51. However, Mercedes faced a tough decision as the intermediate tyres began to degrade, becoming virtually slick, and Peter Bonnington advised Hamilton that they should pit him.

Hamilton was reluctant and made it clear that he felt staying out was the better choice. However, Mercedes insisted, and they brought him in with just seven laps to go for new intermediates, dropping him from third to fifth. Frustrated, Hamilton immediately questioned the logic of the decision over the radio after leaving the pits, complaining about the graining on his tyres and reiterating that he had warned them.

Bottas won the race, and Verstappen finished a comfortable second. When asked about the most difficult aspect of the race given the challenging conditions, Verstappen wryly remarked that it had been staying awake.

Toto Wolff defended Mercedes' decision to pit Hamilton, stating that he believed it was the right call and that they would discuss it on the flight home. As the teams left Turkey,

Verstappen had retaken the lead in the title race and was now six points clear.

**Texas**

Two weeks later, on 24 October, the paddock travelled to Austin, Texas, for the United States Grand Prix at the Circuit of the Americas. The warm weather, with temperatures hovering around 28°C, created a stark contrast to the wet Turkish conditions, although on race day, heavy clouds loomed. The atmosphere crackled with tension as Verstappen and Hamilton prepared for another showdown.

Verstappen secured pole position in qualifying by two-tenths of a second, with Hamilton right alongside him. The top two in the Championship fight were separated by just yards on the grid. The tension mounted.

On race day, Hamilton got the jump at the start and was alongside Verstappen almost immediately. On the run down to Turn 1, Verstappen aggressively pushed Hamilton left, forcing him well beyond the track boundaries and over into the pit lane exit area. Hamilton kept his cool, overtaking Verstappen on the inside into Turn 1 as the crowd roared.

Red Bull, known for their aggressive strategies, pitted Verstappen very early on Lap 11, executing an undercut to regain track position. Mercedes kept Hamilton out three laps longer, hoping that fresher tyres in the final laps would allow him to chase Verstappen down. By Lap 16, Hamilton was six seconds down.

By Lap 30, Hamilton had closed to within a couple of seconds of Verstappen, prompting Red Bull to bring the Dutchman in early once again. Mercedes stretched Hamilton's stint to Lap 38 before pitting him, setting the stage for a late showdown. He had 18 laps to catch Verstappen, with his tyres eight laps fresher.

The closing stages delivered more drama. Hamilton, on fresher rubber, rapidly closed the gap to Verstappen. With just a few laps remaining, he was within striking distance but could not find a way past the Red Bull driver. Verstappen was under immense pressure, and in a preview of the tension that would later involve the two top teams and FIA Steward Michael Masi, Verstappen took to the radio, urging his team to ask Masi to clear the backmarkers out of the way.

Ironically, one of those backmarkers helped Verstappen secure victory by allowing him to gain DRS, which otherwise would have left him vulnerable to Hamilton's attack. Keeping his composure, Verstappen crossed the line 1.3 seconds ahead to claim victory and extend his lead in the Championship to 12 points.

**The Mexican Grand Prix**

On 7 November, the Championship moved to the Autódromo Hermanos Rodríguez in Mexico City, typically a happy hunting ground for Red Bull, as their car was usually well suited to the high-altitude environment. The weather was clear and mild, and a carnival atmosphere prevailed.

Despite Mercedes locking out the front row in qualifying, Verstappen seized the lead at the start with a breathtaking move around the outside of both Hamilton and Bottas into Turn 1, as Bottas played it safe to give his team leader room to manoeuvre. Unfortunately, it wasn't safe enough for Bottas, as he was hit from behind by Ricciardo in Turn 1, spinning his Mercedes around in a plume of tyre smoke. Ricciardo continued minus his front wing, whilst Bottas let out a string of Finnish expletives over the radio.

Pérez surged into third place in the other Red Bull, sending the Mexican crowd into ecstasy. Their celebrations were briefly put on hold when a Safety Car was deployed following a collision between Tsunoda and Ocon. At the restart, Verstappen controlled the race effortlessly, his superior pace and tyre management too much for the others.

Behind him, Hamilton found himself under relentless pressure from Pérez, who was determined to become the first Mexican driver to stand on the podium at his home race. For nearly twenty laps, he harried the Mercedes, forcing Hamilton to defend for all he was worth.

Verstappen eventually cruised to victory, with Hamilton holding on for second and Pérez securing third, sending the Mexican fans into wild celebrations. The atmosphere was superb as their home hero delivered a result they had long dreamed of.

After the race, Chris Medland of *Motorsport* captured the mood in an article titled *"Uncatchable? Verstappen takes control."* Yet, for all the talk of Verstappen's dominance, there remained one undeniable fly in the ointment—Hamilton.

**The Brazilian Grand Prix**

Interlagos, officially known as Autódromo José Carlos Pace, is renowned for its undulating layout and passionate fans. The 2021 event was no exception, with 181,000 spectators filling the stands over the weekend of the 14 November race, their energy palpable as they honoured the legacy of Ayrton Senna, a national hero. The weather remained consistently sunny, providing ideal conditions for both the drivers and crowd.

While Interlagos was a favourite among drivers, it was also one of the most physically demanding tracks on the calendar. Most Grand Prix circuits run clockwise, meaning drivers are conditioned to handle intense G-forces on one side of their necks. But Interlagos, one of the few anti-clockwise circuits, forced them to adjust their training to cope with the strain in the opposite direction. For Hamilton, still nursing neck fatigue after Verstappen's Red Bull had landed on his head at Monza, the challenge would be even greater. But he wasn't one to let pain get in the way of a fight.

After securing pole position in Friday's qualifying, Hamilton faced disqualification due to a technical infringement related to his car's DRS system. The Stewards explained the issue, outlining that with the DRS open, there must be a maximum gap of 85mm between the lower and upper elements of the rear wing. The FIA measured the gap by attempting to push a gauge with a maximum load of 10 Newtons between the upper and lower sections, simulating the force of air.

In Hamilton's case, the device passed through, indicating that under load at speed, the gap would be greater than 85mm, making it illegal. Historically, some cars had used 'bendy' front or rear wings that altered into a flatter profile as top speed increased, sometimes known as moveable aero or flexible wings, which was outlawed under Article 3.8 of the Technical Regulations. The 10 Newton test was designed to ensure that the elements of the rear wing did not bend beyond the 85mm limit when the Mercedes was at high speed.

To confirm that it was not an issue with the gauge itself, the Stewards performed the test multiple times using a second gauge and in front of key Mercedes team members. The wing still failed. As a result, the FIA deemed that the rear opening did not comply with the regulations, and Hamilton was forced to start from the back of the grid for the Sprint Race.

The drama didn't end there. Verstappen, suspicious that the Mercedes rear wing was flexing too much, decided to investigate for himself. After checking the movement of his own Red Bull's wing by hand, he then did the same to Hamilton's car. It was a costly move—touching a competitor's car is against the rules, and Verstappen was hit with a €50,000 fine.

Hamilton, however, was unfazed by his own penalty and made it clear that he would be on maximum attack for the Sprint Race. He wasn't bluffing. The Sprint Race in Brazil was a perfect display of determination.

Bottas, starting from pole, made full use of his soft tyres to beat Verstappen into Turn 1. Verstappen, running on mediums, couldn't match Bottas' early pace and had to settle into second.

But the real spectacle was unfolding further back. Starting from the back of the grid, Hamilton put on an overtaking clinic, slicing through the field with relentless aggression. In just 24 laps, he gained 15 positions, crossing the line in fifth—an incredible recovery drive. The pundits praised Hamilton's brilliance.

Yet his challenge wasn't over. A five-place grid penalty for an engine change meant he would start Sunday's race from tenth instead of fifth. Bottas took the Sprint victory, securing pole for the Grand Prix, with Verstappen second and Sainz third after an early tussle with Pérez.

Hamilton's charge through the field had already become the biggest talking point of the weekend. The scene was set for a thrilling Grand Prix on Sunday, with the title fight intensifying by the lap.

When the lights went out, Bottas got a sluggish getaway, allowing Verstappen to surge into the lead while Pérez also passed the Finn, making it a Red Bull one-two in the opening corners. Meanwhile, Hamilton was a man on a mission. He carved through the midfield in the opening laps, picking off cars with aggressive but calculated moves. By Lap 3, he was already up to fifth, around fourteen seconds off the lead car of Verstappen.

Hamilton was flying and, by Lap 5, had caught Bottas. Mercedes instructed the Finn to hold station at Turn 1 to let Hamilton through. As Hamilton went by, the Mercedes looked to be on the ragged edge, dancing between understeer and oversteer continually. He set off after Pérez, who still lay in second place. By Lap 18, he was on the Mexican's tail.

Pérez put up a fierce defence, moving around on the straights more than was allowed, but Hamilton was having none of it. He went around the outside into Turn 1 in a move identical to his pass on Bottas. Pérez, however, playing the perfect role as Red Bull's number two driver, repassed Hamilton on the long straight of Reta Oposta and into the double left-hander of Descida do Lago. Hamilton tucked in behind as the crowd, many of them Mexican fans, cheered wildly at the battle.

Lap 19 was almost a repeat of Lap 18 as Hamilton went around the outside of Turn 1 again. This time, however, he was able to turn in earlier, carrying more momentum onto Reta Oposta and making a break for it. Verstappen, still leading, was now the next target, but with a four-second gap, it was a tall order. There were still 51 laps to go.

By Lap 48, after all the pit stops had shaken out, Hamilton was on Verstappen's tail. As they approached Turn 1, Verstappen, anticipating a lunge up the inside, made a last-second move to block the line. This compromised his speed and entry into the apex of the Senna S. Hamilton took a wide entry for maximum exit speed, positioning himself for a run down the straight. As the Red Bull rolled out of the left-hand second part of the Senna S, Hamilton lined the Mercedes up in the slipstream, his now-legal rear wing wide open as DRS was activated.

Verstappen went defensive, staying to the inside all the way down Reta Oposta. His car porpoised slightly as it bounced over the deep bumps. The heat haze made the Red Bull appear as if it was emerging from a mirage in the desert. What did emerge a second later was Hamilton's Mercedes, which bolted to the outside of the track on entry into the double left-hand Descida do Lago. Verstappen made no effort to make the corner and instead drove Hamilton completely off the circuit, both cars running well wide and rejoining at high speed. Hamilton was fortunate that his Mercedes was not damaged as it clipped a grass run-off area on rejoining. The Stewards deemed no investigation was necessary.

The team games then started, and Red Bull radioed Michael Masi, the FIA Steward, saying, "Michael, that is all about 'let them race,'" meaning it was OK for one driver to run another completely off the circuit. This constant badgering by the teams was uncalled for and unprofessional, and would later have a disastrous effect on Hamilton's season. However, the

Stewards had clearly heard Red Bull and deemed no investigation was necessary.

In what was probably the funniest radio exchange of the entire season, Peter Bonnington radioed Hamilton with a healthy dose of dry British sarcasm, his voice slow and measured, "So, Lewis. Apparently, no investigation necessary for running you off track." Hamilton's response was just as deadpan: "Of course, man. Of course."

There was no anger in Hamilton's voice, just the quiet determination of someone who knew exactly where this was heading. *Rise above it, son. Do your talking on the track.*

For the next nine laps, Verstappen held firm, fending off Hamilton's relentless pursuit. The Mercedes would edge into DRS range now and then, but Verstappen had just enough in hand to keep him at bay. Hamilton bided his time, knowing the moment would come.

On Lap 58, with his battery fully charged and the Mercedes dialled up to full attack mode, Hamilton launched another attempt. He got a strong run out of the Senna S, but Verstappen was already on the defensive, weaving across the entire width of the track like a man trying to shake off a wasp—left, right, left again—earning himself a black-and-white flag in the process. As Verstappen moved right for a second time, Hamilton feinted to the outside, looking to set him up. But instead of fully committing, he tucked back in, saving his brakes and tyres for the next opportunity.

Lap 59 was a near carbon copy of Lap 48. Verstappen jinked left late into the Senna S, compromising his line. Hamilton, expecting this, went deeper into the corner to give himself the best possible exit. He planted his foot, the Mercedes snarling at full throttle as they hurtled onto the back straight. This time, he was right there.

As they entered the DRS zone, Hamilton pulled to the outside, the Mercedes at maximum revs, closing rapidly. Before they even reached the braking zone at Descida do Lago, he was ahead. He chopped across Verstappen's nose, slamming the door shut. There would be no second chance. The Brazilian crowd, longtime admirers of Hamilton, erupted in celebration. The roar from the grandstands drowned out the sound of the engines as their adopted hero finally took the lead.

In the Mercedes garage, the mechanics, still strapped into their fireproof suits and helmets, leapt up from their seats, clapping furiously. Behind them, Toto Wolff, shirt open at the collar, black Bose headphones on, and glasses perched on his nose, channelled every bit of pent-up frustration from the weekend. He pointed wildly at the camera watching him, his face contorted in a mix of joy and defiance, and let out an almighty, unfiltered celebration.

Peter Bonnington, in contrast, sat back, cool as ever, a huge grin across his face. He simply watched, knowing his driver had done what he always does best.

Hamilton took the victory, with Verstappen second and Bottas third for Mercedes. On his cooldown lap, he drove back to the pits with the *Bandeira do Brasil*—the Brazilian national flag—gripped in his right hand, arm raised high in triumph. The flag billowed behind him, a fitting tribute to the country that had embraced him as one of their own. Arriving at parc fermé, he climbed onto his car, waving to the roaring crowd, their cheers echoing around Interlagos.

On the podium, Hamilton looked at peace, a rare moment of stillness after an exhausting and emotional weekend. He lifted another *Bandeira do Brasil,* this time holding it high across his back, stretching it out with both hands. He gazed out at the fans and then up to the sky, perhaps searching for Ayrton. Afterwards, he described the win as one of the best of his career.

Wolff, who had been emotionally charged all weekend, feeling that Mercedes and Hamilton had been targeted, let rip after the podium. He expressed frustration over what he saw as multiple setbacks for the team, stating that they had received many blows over the weekend with decisions that could have gone either way but had ultimately gone against them. He admitted that he was angry and vowed to defend his team and drivers no matter what came next. While he had always been diplomatic in discussions, he declared that diplomacy had ended that day.

As they left Brazil, both titles were in the balance. Verstappen led Hamilton on 332.5 points to Hamilton's 318.5. Mercedes led the Constructors' standings on 521.5 points, with Red Bull close behind on 510.5 points. It was all to play for, and Hamilton looked to have the momentum.

## Qatar

A week later, on 21 November, Formula One debuted at the Losail International Circuit in Qatar. The desert setting provided clear skies, with ambient temperatures settling in the mid-20s°C for the evening race. Under the floodlights, the track shimmered, offering a visual spectacle as well as a fresh challenge for the drivers.

Hamilton dominated qualifying and took pole, finishing over half a second ahead of Verstappen. In contrast, Verstappen faced setbacks, receiving a five-place grid penalty for a yellow flag infringement, relegating him to seventh on the starting grid. This development intensified the anticipation for the race, as Verstappen's task to maintain his Championship lead became more daunting. The Stewards, rightly or wrongly depending on which driver or team one supported, were getting more and more involved in the destiny of the Championship.

As the lights went out, Hamilton made a flawless start, quickly establishing a lead. Verstappen, demonstrating his determination, surged through the field and was up to second place within the opening laps. Despite the Dutchman's efforts, Hamilton's pace was unmatched, and he maintained a comfortable gap, managing the race from the front.

Meanwhile, Bottas, who should have been taking points away from Verstappen, was struggling, languishing down in twelfth place with ten laps to go.

A standout performance came from Fernando Alonso. The seasoned Spaniard executed a calculated masterstroke borne out of all his experience, opting for a one-stop strategy that paid dividends. His skilful tyre management and consistent lap times earned him a well-deserved third place, marking his first podium finish since the 2014 Hungarian Grand Prix. The Alpine team was understandably delighted with their driver's result.

The race wasn't without its challenges. Several drivers, including Bottas, Russell, and Latifi, suffered front-left tyre failures, leading to retirements and raising further concerns about tyre durability on the abrasive Losail surface. These incidents prompted teams to reassess their strategies, emphasising the importance of tyre management in such demanding conditions.

Hamilton's victory in Qatar narrowed the gap to Verstappen in the Drivers' Championship standings, with just eight points now between them, setting the stage for a thrilling conclusion to the season. The Constructors' Championship also remained fiercely contested, with Mercedes and Red Bull Racing separated by only five points.

**Storm in Jeddah**

On 5 December, the Championship headed to Jeddah, Saudi Arabia, for the inaugural Saudi Arabian Grand Prix at the high-speed Corniche Circuit. The warm evening conditions, with temperatures in the high 20s°C, contrasted sharply with the tension that crackled through the paddock.

The circuit, a 6.174 km street track along the Red Sea, was introduced as one of the fastest circuits on the calendar, with average speeds exceeding 250 km/h. Its design, featuring numerous high-speed corners and limited run-off areas, combined with artificial lighting and a dusty surface, promised an exhilarating yet challenging experience for the drivers. Lined with unforgiving walls and blind corners, the circuit was unpredictable—and it delivered.

In the intense qualifying session, Hamilton secured pole position for Mercedes with a 1:27.511. Verstappen, pushing hard on his final flying lap, came across double waved yellows for Gasly, who was stuck at the side of the road with a puncture. Verstappen had claimed third place and was lucky not to be penalised, the Stewards considering a five-place grid drop.

The race started under the floodlights, with Hamilton maintaining his lead off the line. However, the event was soon marred by multiple incidents. On Lap 10, Mick Schumacher in the Haas went off at very high speed between Turn 21 and Turn 22, turning the car into a pile of scrap in an instant, the back end being completely destroyed. The accident would have been much worse but for the multiple layers of TechPro barrier.

Bottas backed Verstappen up under the yellow flags—not only unkind but also illegal—while Hamilton pitted for new tyres. Verstappen, quite understandably, vented over the radio. Two laps later, given the amount of damage caused by Schumacher's accident, the race was red-flagged, allowing Verstappen, who hadn't pitted, to inherit the lead after changing tyres during the stoppage. The subsequent standing restarts added to the chaos.

The first was a standing restart on Lap 15 from the grid, effectively turning the race into a new 35-lap sprint. Verstappen lined up on the new 'pole' with Hamilton alongside. The tension was as palpable as the heat rising off the racetrack, shimmering and distorting everything around it. Things seemed to go silent as the fifth red light was illuminated—the calm before the storm. Then, the five red lights went out.

Verstappen got a poor start, while Hamilton got away brilliantly. Well before the braking area, Hamilton was completely ahead as they approached the left-hand turn. Verstappen, not wanting to concede, tried to go around the outside of Hamilton from behind and locked his front wheels heavily, going off the track in the left-hand corner before cutting over the sausage kerbs, launching his Red Bull directly at Hamilton's Mercedes. Hamilton had to take evasive action to avoid a collision. Ocon in the Alpine saw the gap and jumped between the pair to take second place.

Before the teams could get on the radio to protest to Michael Masi and start an argument, Pérez was tagged further down the field while accelerating hard onto the straight. This spun him around, and several other cars were caught up in an accident. Nikita Mazepin, in the other Haas, failed to spot the slowing cars ahead as they tried to avoid Pérez and ran into the back of Russell at high speed. The impact lifted Russell's Williams into the air, with the back of his car striking the front of the Haas violently—the Halo once again saving a driver from serious injury. With another Haas in pieces, the race was red-flagged again.

Then followed a major controversy that further brought into doubt Michael Masi's competence. While the cars headed back to the grid under the red flag, Masi radioed the Red Bull pit, giving them the 'opportunity' to return the place to Hamilton. It was presented as an 'offer'. Normally, a driver would receive a penalty for gaining an advantage by overtaking off the track if they did not voluntarily hand the position back. The way this situation was handled, however, raised questions of favouritism.

The race restarted yet again on Lap 17 from the grid, with Hamilton on 'pole' alongside Ocon, and Verstappen in third. In a reversal of the earlier start, Verstappen was off the line in a flash and dived down the inside of Hamilton into Turn 1, forcing him into Ocon. The Mercedes and Alpine clashed, though not violently, while Verstappen quickly pulled away into the distance. Hamilton overtook Ocon on Lap 18 and set off after Verstappen.

The tension, already electric, now reached fever pitch, reminiscent of the classic Senna and Prost battles. Everyone held their breath, anticipating what would happen next. It took Hamilton another 18 laps, but by Lap 36, he got a good tow down the main straight. Verstappen, sensing the danger, weaved aggressively. Holding the inside line, Verstappen forced Hamilton to go around the outside. Hamilton's superior momentum meant he was ahead as they approached the braking zone, but Verstappen, in a mirror image of his earlier move, braked far too late. His car ran off the track and snapped sideways, narrowly avoiding a crash. Hamilton, seeing the danger once again, was forced to take the escape road to avoid a collision. Hamilton, usually a bastion of calm over the radio, called the move crazy.

Verstappen cut the chicane, gaining a significant advantage of several seconds, and shot off down the road without lifting or allowing Hamilton to gain or overtake him. A penalty seemed inevitable. The Red Bull team was evidently given another 'opportunity' to rectify the dangerous driving, and Gianpiero Lambiase radioed Verstappen on Lap 37, instructing him to give the position to Hamilton.

As they approached the marker boards for one of the left-handers, Verstappen slowed on the right side of the track and then moved gently left to where Hamilton was headed before appearing to brake again. Hamilton, unaware of what was happening, hit the back of the Red Bull, damaging his wing in the collision. Toto Wolff was out of his seat like a jack-in-a-box, ripping his headphones from his head in fury. The pundits attributed it to a misunderstanding, as Hamilton was unaware that Verstappen had been instructed to hand the position back.

There was further debate between the Stewards and the teams, and Verstappen was again asked to give the position back to Hamilton. He did this on Lap 42, just before the DRS zone, and immediately retook the position. The Stewards, evidently conscious of the multiple incidents, handed Verstappen a five-second time penalty for leaving the track on Lap 36.

Despite the damage to his front wing, Hamilton made his way past Verstappen on merit to win the race. Verstappen came home second, and Ocon, in another amazing result for Alpine, was on course for third but was overtaken on the line by Bottas.

In the post-race interviews, tensions were at an all-time high, and Hamilton made it clear that he was unhappy. He remarked that some drivers went over the limit and that the rules did not seem to apply. He stated that he had simply tried to do his talking on the track, keeping it within the white lines and racing the right way. When asked if he felt Verstappen drove over the limit or as if the rules did not apply to him, Hamilton, usually measured in his words, did not hold back. He stated outright that Verstappen was beyond the limit, adding that he had avoided collisions with him on many occasions. He said he did not mind being the one to back out, as it meant living to fight another day.

Christian Horner was critical of Michael Masi and the Stewards, stating that some of the decisions and behaviours had been highly unusual. He likened the negotiations and discussions with the Race Director to something akin to bargaining at a local market. It was an odd thing for Horner to say, given all the bartering seemed to benefit his team.

With Bottas coming in third, Mercedes now had a 28-point buffer in the Constructors' title.

### The Final Showdown

There was just one week to go. As the teams left Saudi Arabia, Verstappen and Hamilton were tied on 369.5 points. If both drivers failed to finish in Abu Dhabi, Verstappen would be crowned World Champion on account of having won more races, with nine to Hamilton's eight. It would be a winner-takes-all battle in the final race.

Hamilton and Verstappen arrived at Yas Marina Circuit after 21 thrilling races. The stage was set for an epic showdown under the floodlights, with the world watching to see who would claim the Championship. The battle between the two had been intense all year, leading to this final, decisive race with both drivers level on points—a scenario not seen since 1974.

The weather was calm and warm, with temperatures hovering around 25°C as the sun set over the picturesque Yas Marina. The tranquil skies belied the storm of tension that engulfed the paddock. Fans, pundits, and teams alike felt the weight of the moment as the two drivers prepared to battle for glory.

In the build-up to the race, emotions were running high. Speculation was rampant over whether Verstappen or Pérez would attempt to take Hamilton out of the race. The qualifying sessions were charged with tension. Verstappen secured pole position with a stunning lap time of 1:22.109, aided by a tow from Pérez. Hamilton claimed second on the grid, trailing by 0.371 seconds. Norris delivered an impressive performance, placing his McLaren in third. Notably, Verstappen opted to start the race on soft tyres, while Hamilton chose mediums, setting the stage for varied strategies.

As the lights went out, Hamilton, starting second, launched off the line brilliantly to overtake Verstappen into Turn 1. The Mercedes driver immediately began pulling away, showing superior race pace on the medium tyres.

All the cars came out of Turn 7 onto the very long back straight. From Hamilton backwards, the cars started to 'snake' across the track, each car gently weaving to try and break the tow and the slipstream of a following car. As they approached Turn 8, the cars reached 200mph.

The drivers hit the brakes at the 100-metre board marker. At this point, Verstappen was a good two lengths behind Hamilton. Verstappen moved left, sparks flying, and pointed his Red Bull at an angle up the inside of Hamilton. Hamilton tried to take the turn, but Verstappen, carrying a lot of momentum, came sailing up the inside. The two cars touched briefly, forcing Hamilton to take the escape road, cutting across and retaining the lead. A huge roar erupted from the crowd. Verstappen was immediately on the radio, demanding that Hamilton give the place back.

The Stewards reviewed the incident but decided that no further action was necessary, given that Verstappen had run Hamilton clean off the track—a call that infuriated Red Bull. As Verstappen had remained within track limits, unlike in other instances, it seemed reasonable that Hamilton would be asked to give the position back. However, the FIA had much more data than anyone watching.

By Lap 14, Hamilton was leading comfortably, stretching the gap to over six seconds. Mercedes' race engineer Peter Bonnington kept Hamilton updated, asking him to just manage the tyres. Verstappen pitted early on Lap 14, switching to hard tyres in an attempt to undercut Hamilton. Mercedes responded swiftly, bringing Hamilton in on Lap 15, and he rejoined ahead.

Pérez then came into the equation, holding Hamilton up for two laps to try and back him into Verstappen, who was closing from third. Some of Pérez's moves were questionable, prompting Hamilton to radio his team, saying that the driving was dangerous. Verstappen, who had been over three seconds adrift going into Lap 20, was now just 1.2 seconds behind Hamilton. Recognising Pérez's efforts, he praised his teammate, calling him a legend. Hamilton then dug deep and pulled away, heading for his eighth world title. Or so it seemed.

The race appeared to be heading towards a straightforward Hamilton victory as he comfortably extended his lead to over 12 seconds. That was until Lap 53, when Nicholas Latifi crashed in the final sector, bringing out the Safety Car. With just five laps remaining, the mood shifted dramatically. Red Bull seized the opportunity, pitting Verstappen for soft tyres, while Mercedes kept Hamilton out on his older hard tyres to maintain track position, expecting the race to end under the Safety Car.

As the laps ticked down under the Safety Car, controversy erupted. Initially, race director Michael Masi instructed that lapped cars would not be allowed to un-lap themselves, a move that seemed to seal the race for Hamilton. Various radio calls took place at Red Bull. Gianpiero Lambiase radioed Verstappen to inform him of Masi's decision, to which Verstappen responded with frustration, sarcastically remarking that it was a typical decision and expressing no surprise.

The cars continued circulating behind the Safety Car, while Red Bull persistently pressured the FIA officials over the radio. Christian Horner, now evidently fully embracing the art of bargaining at the local market, was haranguing Masi, demanding to know why the lapped cars weren't being allowed to move out of the way.

Under Article 48.12 of the 2021 regulations, the race director had the authority to instruct that "*any cars that have been lapped by the leader will be required to pass the cars on the lead lap and the Safety Car,*" provided it was safe to do so. This rule allowed lapped cars to move to the back of the pack, ensuring a cleaner restart with all front-running cars grouped together. Crucially, the regulation also stated that once the final lapped car had overtaken the leader, the Safety Car would return to the pits "*at the end of the following lap,*" meaning the restart would typically take place one lap later.

It was clear that Red Bull wanted the race to resume immediately and, crucially, that they only wanted the lapped cars between Verstappen and Hamilton to be removed, rather than the full field of lapped runners, which was contrary to the regulations.

Under mounting pressure, Masi responded to Christian Horner's appeal, sounding flustered as he asked Horner to bear with him while he sorted out the situation. One lap later, Race Control announced that only five lapped cars—numbers 4, 14, 31, 16, and 5—would be allowed to overtake. These were the cars sitting between race leader Hamilton and second-placed Verstappen. It was an unprecedented decision in Formula One history. The race was now on Lap 57 of 58.

Before those five cars had even finished unlapping themselves, Race Control made another announcement: the Safety Car would be coming in immediately, rather than waiting for an additional lap as per the regulations. The race would restart on the final lap.

Confusion rippled through the paddock, fans, and commentators alike. But no one was more outraged than Toto Wolff. Livid, he got on the radio to Masi, his frustration boiling over as he protested that his decision was not right.

As the Safety Car peeled into the pits, the tension was unbearable. The entire season had come down to this—one final lap, one last showdown. Verstappen, armed with fresh soft tyres, wasted no time. He launched an attack into Turn 5, diving down the inside to snatch the lead from Hamilton. The Dutchman then weaved aggressively down the back straight, doing everything possible to break the tow and prevent Hamilton from mounting a counterattack. Hamilton fought back hard, pulling alongside Verstappen, but with DRS disabled for the first two laps after a Safety Car, he lacked the straight-line speed to make a move. Verstappen held firm, defending perfectly into Turn 9.

In the Mercedes garage, Toto Wolff was beside himself—furious. Pacing. Unable to contain his frustration. He snatched his headset and erupted over the radio to Michael Masi, exclaiming in disbelief and anger that the decision was completely unfair.

With the crowd on their feet, Verstappen powered out of the final corner and took the chequered flag to become Formula One World Champion for the first time. Overcome with emotion, he screamed his celebration over the radio, his voice breaking.

Christian Horner was immediately on the radio to congratulate his driver, his delight in stark contrast to the scene at Mercedes, where Wolff sat in stunned silence, his head in his hands. As he pulled into parc fermé, Verstappen climbed out, dropped to one knee by his rear tyre, helmet still on, head bowed, taking in the gravity of what had just happened.

Despite the controversy, Hamilton was gracious in defeat. He walked over to Verstappen and embraced him, giving him a firm pat on the back. Verstappen, clearly appreciating the moment, returned the gesture, and as they broke apart, they shared a mutual slap on the back—two warriors acknowledging the fight of a lifetime.

Hamilton addressed the moment, first congratulating Verstappen and his team. He talked about the season, saying that he believed the team had done an amazing job that year. He expressed pride in everyone back at the factory, recognising the hard work of all the men and women who had contributed throughout the season. He emphasised how proud he was to be part of the journey with them, adding that they had given everything in the final stretch and never gave up, which was the most important thing. He also noted that he had felt great in the car over the past couple of months, particularly at the end.

Despite the way things had ended, Hamilton still took a moment to acknowledge the ongoing global situation. He wished for everyone's safety during the pandemic and hoped they would have a good Christmas, adding that they would see what happened next year.

The events of Abu Dhabi sparked widespread debate in the motorsport world. Some believed what had happened was acceptable and added spectacle to the sport, while others were unhappy about how the rules had been massaged to help Red Bull.

The 2021 Abu Dhabi Grand Prix marked the end of a season that would go down in history as one of Formula One's most contentious and dramatic. Verstappen's victory cemented his place as a World Champion, while Hamilton's gracious response underscored his class. The fallout from the race would resonate through the off-season, but one thing was clear: the rivalry between these two titans had only just begun.

# History the Hard Way

The 2022 Formula One season heralded a revolutionary shift, the likes of which hadn't been seen in decades. It was a year marked by uncertainty as teams grappled with the most comprehensive overhaul of technical regulations in the history of the sport. The stakes were high, and the paddock whirred with speculation on who would adapt fastest and most effectively.

At the heart of the 2022 season's transformation were the cars themselves. Engineers and designers faced the monumental task of reimagining the Formula One car with a philosophy centred around ground effect aerodynamics—technology banned in the early 1980s for being too effective. Ground effect emphasised the use of floor tunnels, diffusers, and underbody aerodynamics over the previous high dependency on front and rear wings. This change was designed to reduce turbulent air and improve racing by allowing cars to follow each other more closely. The cars also featured simplified front and rear wings to smooth turbulent air, enabling a following car to get closer without losing its own aerodynamic performance.

One of the key changes which had a significant impact was the shift from 13-inch wheels with thick sidewall tyres—a design largely in use in Formula One for decades—to a new 18-inch wheel with a much shallower sidewall tyre, more resembling a road car. While the tyre diameter was increased, the overall diameter (wheel plus tyre) did become slightly larger. This change increased the overall diameter of the wheel and tyre combination by around 10 cm (approximately 4 inches). The sidewall of the tyre became stiffer and lower-profile, resulting in a smaller tyre bulge, reducing the amount of vertical deformation in the tyre. The philosophy behind this significant change was to more closely align the sport to road cars.

The wheel and tyre changes had a number of unintended consequences, including affecting driver vision in corners due to the increased diameter, but the key effect was the reduction in sidewall flexibility. Previously, on the 13-inch wheel and tyre combination, when a Formula One car hit a bump or kerb, the tyre wall would have a large amount of flex, in effect acting as its own form of suspension. The engineers could compensate for this with stiffer car suspension and be able to run very low ride heights. However, under the new rules, the suspension did much more of the work, and the tyres had far less flexibility. This meant that if a designer had made a car with an inherently stiff chassis and suspension that didn't 'flow' along the track with effective aerodynamics, it could be much harder on the drivers, with more violent vertical movements. The reduced sidewall flex meant the cars tended to pitch more dramatically, affecting visibility.

Car weight increased again, and the minimum weight of a car, in its unfuelled state, was now 798kg, including power unit. The 80kg driver allowance was retained. To put this into context, when Hamilton made his debut in 2007, the total car and driver weight limit was around 605 kg, or 1,334 lbs. This lighter weight made the cars more agile and responsive and much more kart-like. Braking distances were shorter, and the cars could decelerate more quickly, enabling drivers like Hamilton to brake later into corners. The handling was more nimble, with the cars reacting quickly to steering inputs and changing direction with ease, especially through tight corners and chicanes.

However, as Formula One progressed, so did the weight of the cars, driven by changes in technology, safety requirements, and power unit specifications. By the 2022 season, Hamilton found himself behind the wheel of a car that, while considerably heavier at 798 kg, also had a very different feel. The introduction of ground effect aerodynamics and new 18-inch tyres meant the cars were now more sensitive to changes in airflow, and the handling became far more unpredictable. Despite the added weight providing more mechanical grip, the shift in aerodynamics made the 2022 car notably more nervous, particularly in corners.

For Hamilton, this was a stark contrast to the machines he had driven in previous seasons. The car's increased sensitivity and the new tyre characteristics made it harder for him to extract consistent performance. The handling was less stable, and the car frequently felt like it was on the edge, especially when following other cars or battling for position. This was a sharp departure from the more predictable handling of his earlier cars, which he had learned to master and make the most of. In 2022, the nervousness of the car presented Hamilton with new challenges, demanding a different approach to racing, particularly in terms of tyre management, braking, and dealing with the car's aero balance.

The Mercedes W13, spearheaded by James Allison, was built under these most sweeping aerodynamic and wheel changes. The design philosophy for the W13 was rooted in maximising the benefits of the new ground effect regulations. Allison described the challenge as one of the toughest the team had faced in recent years and later criticised the regulation change philosophy. He pointed out that there were aspects of the regulations that did not serve the teams well, specifically questioning whether it was sensible to have cars that hugged the ground in the way these new designs did. He also expressed scepticism about the idea that good racing could be achieved solely by controlling wakes while ignoring tyres.

Mercedes' design aimed to create a car that could exploit the low-pressure area under the chassis to generate massive downforce through ground effects. However, balancing this with the new aerodynamic constraints proved tricky. Several teams suffered from 'porpoising'—aerodynamic oscillations that caused the car to bounce at high speeds, impacting performance and driver comfort—but in this regard, the

Mercedes seemed to be the most affected. It did not help that Allison had stepped into a more strategic position and was less hands-on.

Barge boards were also banned for 2022. These boards were vertical pieces of carbon fibre that were bolted to each side of a Formula One car in front of the side pod and below the driver cockpit. The purpose of the barge board was to 'clean up' the airflow and direct it through and around the side pod. These boards had been instrumental in previous designs but were outlawed in 2022 to reduce costs associated with complex interlinked aero, to lessen reliance on aerodynamics in some key areas of the car, and to reduce the 'dirty air' being thrown off the back of the car, allowing a following car to get closer. Some of the teams dealt with the absence of the barge board differently.

Red Bull focused on creating a side pod that had more sculpture to its shape, making it in effect its own piece of aero. Mercedes, on the other hand, attempted to eliminate the side pod altogether, leading to what was labelled by many as a 'no sidepod' or 'zero sidepod' design. The car looked striking, but it would be the start of a difficult period for Mercedes, compounded by the team's refusal to drop the no-sidepod design until midway through the following 2023 season. Mercedes also adopted a 'low rake' strategy and this, combined with the zero sidepod, would ultimately lead to a car that was problematic.

Analysts noted that Mercedes' issues were emblematic of the difficulties of pioneering new technologies in Formula One. Ted Kravitz of Sky Sports suggested that Mercedes might have been "too clever by half" with their zero-pod design, which appeared to be costing them both in handling and outright speed.

Throughout pre-season and the early races, Mercedes struggled to address the issue of porpoising—the violent bouncing of the car at high speeds. This made it difficult to handle, significantly affecting performance. The team's efforts to resolve the problem became a major storyline early in the season, as both Hamilton and Russell battled an unpredictable and aerodynamically unstable car.

Red Bull Racing's car, the RB18, designed by Adrian Newey, was one of the most eagerly anticipated of the season. Newey, who had been behind some of the most dominant cars in modern Formula One history, played a crucial role in shaping the RB18. His unparalleled ability to craft aerodynamically efficient machines was a key advantage in exploiting the new ground effect regulations.

Although Newey had not worked on a ground effect car since the 1980s, when he designed the March 881, his deep understanding of aerodynamics remained unmatched. His academic background—he had written his thesis on ground effect—provided him with an early foundation that he continued to build on through his work at McLaren and later at Red Bull. His approach to the RB18 was centred on maximising downforce through the car's floor and rear diffuser while minimising drag. The car featured a heavily reworked rear suspension, a more efficient floor, and front and rear wing designs that fully adhered to the new regulations.

Newey's ability to translate complex aerodynamic theories into a car that was both fast and stable would prove pivotal for Red Bull's success in the 2022 season. His innovations enabled the RB18 to become the benchmark car, particularly in race trim, giving Verstappen a machine capable of mounting a serious title challenge.

After several seasons of underperformance, Ferrari entered 2022 with a car that was much more competitive. The SF75, developed under the leadership of head of chassis engineering Enrico Cardile and technical director Simone Resta, benefited from a refined interpretation of the ground effect regulations.

Ferrari focused on achieving an optimal balance between aerodynamic efficiency and mechanical grip, making the SF75 one of the fastest cars in qualifying trim. Their powerful engine and well-designed chassis allowed Leclerc and Sainz to fight at the front of the grid from the very first races. However, Ferrari's race pace and reliability would become recurring issues. Despite securing multiple pole positions, the team failed to consistently convert them into victories due to strategic errors and mechanical failures.

McLaren, under the leadership of technical director James Key, adopted a more conservative approach to the 2022 regulations. Their MCL36 was designed with a focus on reliability and overall balance rather than outright aerodynamic innovation.

Early in the season, McLaren struggled with the car's rear stability, which affected performance on circuits requiring high-speed cornering. However, they were able to extract decent pace from their Mercedes power unit. While the car showed flashes of competitiveness—particularly at tracks that suited their aero package—consistency remained elusive as the season progressed.

In the week leading up to pre-season testing on 17 February 2022, the FIA announced that Michael Masi, the Formula One Race Director, had been removed from his position following the controversy surrounding the 2021 Abu Dhabi Grand Prix. Many in the motorsport media viewed this as an implicit admission by the FIA that the race's restart in Abu Dhabi had been mishandled.

Alongside Masi's removal, the FIA introduced new procedural changes, including banning direct communication between teams and the Race Director. Instead, all communication would now go through an intermediary to prevent undue influence during races. These decisions were overseen by the newly elected FIA President, Mohammed ben Sulayem, who had succeeded Jean Todt. His arrival was seen as a pivotal factor in Masi's departure, as he sought to restore credibility to the sport's governance.

For Toto Wolff and Lewis Hamilton, Masi's removal provided little solace. Wolff remained deeply frustrated over the events of Abu Dhabi, while Hamilton, who had effectively been denied an eighth World title, initially struggled to move past what he felt was a grave injustice. However, despite their lingering resentment, both managed to channel their frustration professionally, accepting the outcome and focusing on the new season ahead.

As the 2022 season unfolded, the controversy surrounding Abu Dhabi did not fade. Fans remained deeply divided, with many believing Hamilton had been "robbed" of the 2021 title. The increasing toxicity of online discussions and fan behaviour prompted the FIA to release a video in which drivers urged fans to stop the abusive conduct, both at races and across social media platforms, and in life in general.

Hamilton, always an advocate for respect in sport, responded to the situation by calling for greater accountability. He stated that fans should not allow those who engage in abuse to get away with it, reinforcing the message that passion should never cross the line into disrespect. His words carried weight, serving as a reminder that while Formula One thrives on intense rivalries, respect and integrity must always prevail. As someone who had been subject to bullying and racial abuse, he spoke both from experience and from the heart.

**Pre-Season Testing**

The 2022 Formula One pre-season testing kicked off in late February, with the first official test taking place at the Circuit de Barcelona-Catalunya from 23 to 25 February—a track that had become a staple for pre-season preparations.

In stark contrast to the sweltering heat of Bahrain where the second test would take place in March, Barcelona's weather proved to be a different challenge entirely. Early morning temperatures hovered between 10 to 15°C, making it more difficult for teams to assess tyre performance and car balance. The cooler conditions put a significant emphasis on car reliability, as teams worked to understand how their new machines would perform in less-than-ideal temperatures.

For Mercedes and the W13, it quickly became apparent that the car was struggling with porpoising—where it would oscillate and bounce due to aerodynamic instability. Technicians referred to this as the car 'stalling'. The ground effect worked by 'sucking' the car into the ground, creating a vacuum of air. This vacuum would then be broken, for example, by hitting a bump, braking, or the air under the car becoming uneven. When the seal was broken, the car would violently pogo up into the air, only to be sucked back down again immediately. This cycle could happen multiple times a second at high speed.

The team spent much of the Barcelona test grappling with the balance of the car, with Hamilton acknowledging that the new machine didn't feel right. The car's unpredictable behaviour prompted a lot of head-scratching within the team, and they would need to make swift adjustments as they headed to Bahrain for the second round of testing.

Driver movements added another layer of intrigue to the season for Mercedes as George Russell joined the team to partner Hamilton. Russell was a favourite of Wolff's and seen as a bold step into the future for the Silver Arrows. Bottas, meanwhile, took his talents to Alfa Romeo, bringing experience as the team was eager to climb the standings.

Red Bull was in a strong position from the outset. Adrian Newey's RB18 was an early standout, demonstrating stability and balance from the first lap. Red Bull's car, designed to take full advantage of the new ground effect regulations, appeared to be dialled in straight away. It had a 'high rake' design, which was fundamentally the way to go with ground effect, as this reduced the impacts of 'stalling' and porpoising. Verstappen, now driving with the Number 1 on his car to reflect his World

Championship status, appeared satisfied with how the car was performing in early testing, describing the initial runs as smooth and productive, with no major issues hindering progress.

Christian Horner remained cautiously optimistic, knowing that the real test would come once the teams headed to Bahrain for the final pre-season sessions. Adrian Newey had again designed a car that maximised new technical regulations. It helped that they had the same drivers in Verstappen and Pérez, so there was no bedding in required or changes for driver fitting.

Ferrari, too, looked strong in Barcelona. Their SF75 quickly caught attention for its balance between aerodynamic efficiency and mechanical grip. Charles Leclerc and Carlos Sainz both demonstrated impressive pace, putting in competitive laps, though reliability concerns began to surface. Ferrari, fresh from several years of underperformance, appeared to have a legitimate shot at being a frontrunner in the new season, though the team would need to iron out a few issues before the season opener in Bahrain.

McLaren, meanwhile, found themselves in a more conservative position. While their MCL36 showed potential, especially in high-speed corners, the car's rear stability and balance still left something to be desired. Lando Norris and Daniel Ricciardo struggled to find a perfect setup, with McLaren's early challenges hinting at a more difficult season ahead. The car was competitive enough in the right conditions, though McLaren's ultimate test would come when they tried to extract performance over longer distances in warmer weather.

After Barcelona, the teams made their way to Bahrain for the second and final round of pre-season testing from 10 to 12 March. The heat of Bahrain provided much more representative conditions for the season ahead, as teams could now assess tyre degradation and long-run performance.

For Mercedes, the W13's porpoising issue remained a significant challenge, and despite their best efforts, the car was still a handful for Hamilton and his new teammate, the 24-year-old George Russell.

In contrast, Red Bull's RB18 continued to impress in Bahrain. Verstappen and Pérez were both able to extract good performance from the car, and Red Bull looked like the team to beat heading into the season. The car was fast, stable, and well-balanced. Newey's expertise in aerodynamics had provided the team with a distinct advantage.

Ferrari showed flashes of competitiveness too, with Leclerc and Sainz continuing to look strong. However, there were still some lingering doubts about the team's ability to manage race strategy and maintain the reliability of the SF75 over a full race distance. While they were undeniably quick in qualifying trim, Ferrari's challenge would be converting that speed into race wins.

McLaren, despite ongoing issues with rear-end stability, managed to put in some decent laps in Bahrain, and Norris remained a consistent performer, though the team was still looking for the right balance between aerodynamics and mechanical grip.

Pre-season testing in 2022 was a rollercoaster for many teams, but the general consensus by the end of the Bahrain test was that Red Bull had emerged as the car to beat, with Ferrari looking like serious contenders. Mercedes, however, faced significant hurdles with the W13, and the team would have to adapt quickly if they were to keep up with their rivals. For Hamilton, the discomfort of porpoising was just the beginning of a season filled with challenges, but the real test would come when the lights went out in Bahrain for the season opener, with all teams hoping their work in testing would translate into race-day performance.

As the teams finished Bahrain testing, many of them were scrambling to rectify the porpoising issue. Teams like Mercedes, Alfa Romeo and AlphaTauri had a lot of work to do.

**Bahrain Grand Prix: The Season Opener**

The 2022 Formula One season kicked off under the hot, desert sun of Bahrain over the weekend of 18–20 March, at a venue that always promised drama. As the teams arrived, the excitement was palpable, but so too was the uncertainty. This was the first race of a completely new era, with the sport's sweeping technical changes leaving everyone wondering how the new cars would perform. The Bahrain International Circuit would provide the first real clues.

The weather in Bahrain was typically warm, with temperatures in the mid-20s, but as the evening approached and qualifying loomed, the air cooled slightly, offering drivers an ideal chance to push their cars to the limit. The conditions were perfect for what would be a thrilling opener to the season.

For the race weekend there were new upgrades, especially from the teams that had struggled in testing. Mercedes, still grappling with their W13, had brought some fresh updates to help address the porpoising issue that had plagued them and to try and improve the balance. Red Bull, by contrast, was confident their car was already in great shape, as were Ferrari. McLaren, still had work to do on their MCL36, particularly in fine-tuning rear-end stability, and brought a couple of small changes to the car.

As the practice sessions progressed, the pressure was on, and it quickly became clear that Verstappen was the man to beat. The reigning World Champion showed impressive pace from the start, his Red Bull handling beautifully around the Bahrain layout. Nevertheless, it was Charles Leclerc who stunned everyone with a blistering lap in qualifying, taking pole position for Ferrari with a 1:30.558, with Verstappen second, a tenth adrift, and Hamilton in fifth, some seven tenths down on Leclerc's pole time. Hamilton's new teammate Russell was down in ninth, a full second behind Hamilton. The cars looked significantly slower than the 2021 designs, as well as much larger, but the lap times overall were just one and a half seconds down on the previous season.

Qualifying had served as a reminder that 2022 would be filled with surprises. Ferrari had arrived with a car that seemed to deliver strong single-lap pace, while Red Bull, despite some technical issues during qualifying, had shown that their race pace could be strong. Hamilton, however, was still adjusting to the W13 and its balance issues, leaving Mercedes with plenty to work on ahead of the race.

Race day arrived and the tension rose as the sun began to set. As the lights went out, Leclerc made a perfect start from pole, holding off Verstappen. The two went wheel to wheel for a few laps, with Verstappen staying within the DRS one-second limit, but as the race progressed to Lap 10, Verstappen was almost three seconds adrift.

Further down the grid, Mercedes faced a tough start. Hamilton was struggling with the balance of his car, unable to keep up with the leaders. Russell wasn't faring much better, as both of them fought with the unpredictable quirks of the W13. Their difficulties were clear as they dropped down the order, but they knew the season was long, and the hunt for points was still very much alive. On the straights, Hamilton's bright yellow helmet, which had been redesigned for 2022, was bouncing violently up and down, a result of the W13's infamous porpoising. The movements were intense. Vicious. The yellow helmet glinted under the artificial light, reminiscent of his karting days when his helmet had carried a design inspired by his hero, Ayrton Senna.

The Mercedes, handling like a bucking bronco, struggled to maintain pace with the likes of the Red Bulls and Ferraris. Pérez and Sainz both found their way past Hamilton, who clung on as best he could, desperately trying to keep up.

As the laps wore on, Ferrari and Red Bull were pushing their strategies to the limit. The result was shaping up to come down to tyre management and potential late-race incidents. Leclerc and Verstappen were trading places at the front, neither willing to give an inch. The respect between the two was clear, their battle thrilling to watch. On Lap 17, after a careful buildup, Verstappen made his move, passing Leclerc and taking the lead. The two continued to swap positions in an intense, back-and-forth fight for supremacy.

By Lap 46, the tension increased when Pierre Gasly's AlphaTauri came to a halt at the side of the track, flames pouring from the back of the car. Gasly's stricken car prompted the officials to 'deploy' the Virtual Safety Car, bunching up the pack and giving Hamilton and Russell a chance to make up lost ground. Verstappen, meanwhile, was on the radio complaining about his steering feeling heavy.

Red Bull's reliability woes surfaced again in the final laps. Verstappen's car began to suffer power unit issues on Lap 54, causing him to lose pace and eventually retire from the race. With Verstappen out, Leclerc was in clear control, heading for a well-earned victory. Sainz followed closely in second, while Pérez, still in third, had to contend with Hamilton, whose car was bottoming out and sparking as he fought to stay in touch with the Red Bull.

As they started the last lap, Pérez reported a loss of power over the radio. Approaching Turn 1, his Red Bull spun out violently, the rear wheels locked solid due to a seized engine. Hamilton sailed past into third, with Russell not far behind.

Leclerc held his nerve and took the chequered flag, securing Ferrari's first win of the season, with Sainz in second. It was a stunning performance, and a message to the rest of the paddock that Ferrari was back. Behind them, Hamilton completed the podium in third, with Russell finishing fourth. Had it not been for Red Bull's reliability issues, Mercedes would have been looking at fifth and sixth places, a far cry from their dominant position in previous seasons. Under the new regulations, Mercedes had seemingly dropped to third in the pecking order.

Other teams were hurting. McLaren, on a resurgence in 2021 and challenging the top teams, stared into the abyss as Ricciardo and Norris came home 14th and 15th. Team Principal Andreas Seidl was blunt about McLaren's woes, describing the weekend as a deeply disappointing and painful experience for everyone involved, including the fans. He stressed that the team was analysing in detail why they were not competitive and working urgently to bring more performance to the car.

On the positive side, Haas, a team often caught up in incidents and struggling for consistency, achieved a brilliant result with Kevin Magnussen finishing in fifth place. The Ferrari power unit was clearly performing well, helping Magnussen secure a standout result.

For Mercedes and Hamilton, however, the signs were not promising. The W13, with its radical zero-sidepod design, looked completely different from anything else on the grid, and as the old adage went, if something didn't look right, it probably wasn't. The car's performance was far from ideal—it was bouncing relentlessly, making it difficult to handle, and that instability took a toll on the drivers. Both Hamilton and Russell found themselves constantly fighting the car, and the constant physical strain meant they were more fatigued than most of their rivals, affecting their overall performance.

The Bahrain Grand Prix marked a dramatic and unpredictable start to the season. Leclerc's victory was a clear indication that Ferrari was back in business, while Red Bull's technical struggles reminded everyone that no team could take success for granted. For Mercedes, it was a sobering reminder that the path to the front of the grid would be far from straightforward.

**The Formula One Circus Arrives in Jeddah**

A week later, the Formula One circus rolled into Jeddah for the second edition of the Saudi Arabian Grand Prix, held at the Jeddah Corniche Circuit. Built for sheer speed and lined with walls that left no margin for error, the street circuit had already proven its capacity for chaos in its inaugural race the previous year. The 2022 event, held under floodlights on 27 March, promised another spectacle—both in terms of high-speed heroics and, inevitably, controversy.

Hamilton and Mercedes were still licking their wounds from a lacklustre Bahrain opener. The team's radical new W13 car was still suffering from 'porpoising' and they had no time between events to come up with any significant remedy. Red Bull, meanwhile, were smarting from a double retirement in Bahrain, while Ferrari were rightfully buoyant.

Off-track, the build-up to the race was overshadowed by an alarming attack with drones and missiles by Yemen's Houthi rebels on the North Jeddah Bulk Plant Aramco oil facility just 10 miles from the circuit during Friday practice. A lengthy meeting between drivers and Formula One officials eventually led to an agreement to continue with the race weekend, though unease remained.

Jeddah's Corniche Circuit, a 6.1-kilometre ribbon of high-speed corners and narrow straights, held the title of the fastest street circuit on the calendar. With walls looming ominously close and an average lap speed exceeding 150 mph, it was a place where bravery and accuracy were rewarded, while misjudgement was swiftly punished.

As expected in Saudi Arabia, the weather was balmy, with temperatures hovering around 25°C for the evening sessions. The crowd—mainly a mix of local dignitaries, well-heeled spectators, and fans eager for high-speed drama—filled the grandstands, while the post-missile strike tension hung uneasily in the air. The atmosphere was surreal: half thrilling, half apprehensive.

Hamilton's struggles in practice were evident. The Mercedes was still a handful, and while George Russell managed to extract some performance from it, Hamilton seemed at odds with the car's balance. Come qualifying, things went from bad to worse. The Q1 session had its fair share of incidents, notably when Latifi in the Williams went off, bringing out the red flag and compromising several drivers who were on hot laps.

The seven-time World Champion suffered the indignity of an early exit in Q1, managing only 16th place—a stark confirmation of Mercedes' early-season struggles. It was the first time Hamilton had been eliminated on pure pace since Brazil 2017, an unwelcome footnote in his illustrious career. As he climbed out of his car, Q2 was already underway.

Five minutes into Q2 the session came to a violent halt when Mick Schumacher suffered one of the most terrifying crashes of the season. Entering the 170mph chicane at Turn 12, he took too much kerb, unsettling the car and sending it into an uncontrollable snap. In the blink of an eye, he slammed into the concrete barrier at near-top speed. The impact was catastrophic—the Haas was torn apart, with wheels sheared off despite the tethers and the rear section completely severed from the chassis.

For a tense few moments, there was concern that Schumacher had been knocked unconscious. He remained motionless in the cockpit, prompting immediate action from the marshals and medical team. By the time they reached him, he was responsive but unable to exit the car unaided. He was swiftly taken to hospital for further checks, where, miraculously, he was found to have escaped serious injury.

The severity of the crash was underscored by the fact that Haas lost all telemetry the moment Schumacher hit the wall. Usually, teams are able to communicate with their drivers or assess impact data, but this time, everything simply went dark. The Haas garage was tense as they waited for news. Back in the Mercedes garage, Hamilton was quick to show his concern, acknowledging the brutal speeds at that section of the track and hoping Schumacher was unharmed.

Schumacher's crash reignited safety concerns about the Jeddah circuit, particularly its mix of extreme speeds and unforgiving concrete barriers. Pérez, who would show his mettle in qualifying, did not mince words, describing the track as the most dangerous on the calendar and stating that the risks were well known.

Once the session resumed, the drivers refocused. Pérez delivered a masterclass, claiming his first-ever Formula One pole position—the first for a Mexican driver in Formula One history. The Ferraris of Leclerc and Sainz secured second and third, while Verstappen, for once, was overshadowed by his teammate, managing only fourth. Russell salvaged some pride for Mercedes, wrestling his difficult W13 to sixth on the grid. Hamilton, meanwhile, could only watch from the sidelines, contemplating just how far Mercedes had fallen.

Starting from an unfamiliar 15th place due to Mick Schumacher's crash-induced withdrawal, Hamilton needed a dose of the old magic. The opening laps were cautious—Jeddah's unforgiving nature meant weaving through the field was a measured rather than reckless task.

While Verstappen and Leclerc waged a thrilling DRS-fuelled battle at the front, Hamilton steadily climbed the order. However, any hopes of a top-five charge were scuppered when his strategy unravelled. Running long on hard tyres, he was caught out by the timing of a Virtual Safety Car, forcing Hamilton into a late stop that left him outside the points.

To make matters worse, his pit entry was blocked when he finally did come in, costing him yet more time. In a season where every position would be hard-fought, the frustration was palpable. He eventually crossed the line in 10th, salvaging a single point—small consolation for a man used to fighting at the sharp end.

Up front, Verstappen and Leclerc were again engaged in a relentless battle lap after lap towards the end of the race. Verstappen seemed to be more measured in all of his attacking and defensive moves, reflecting the confidence that came with being Champion. He narrowly edged Leclerc after a tactical game of DRS cat-and-mouse, taking his first victory of the year by half a second. Pérez, who had been unlucky with a poorly timed safety car, finished fourth behind Sainz. Russell was fifth. The gap between Hamilton and Russell was not reflected in their lap times, as there was just one-tenth of a second between them in their fastest laps.

For Hamilton, this was another reality check. The dominant Mercedes of previous years was a distant memory now, and the hard grind of development lay ahead. While his talent was undiminished, the tools at his disposal were clearly lacking. Meanwhile, Verstappen's victory confirmed that Red Bull were still in the fight, and Ferrari's resurgence was real.

Jeddah had delivered the drama expected of it—both on and off the track. But for Hamilton, it was a race to forget.

**Formula One's Long-Awaited Return to Melbourne**

Formula One's return to Melbourne was met with a mix of excitement, nostalgia, and a lingering sense of the surreal. The last time the sport had gathered at Albert Park in 2020, COVID-19 had shut down the event hours before the cars were due to take to the track. Two years later, the paddock was finally back in Australia, though some reminders of the pandemic remained. A few drivers and personnel still wore masks, and the memories of that strange, aborted weekend were not easily forgotten.

Melbourne itself was eager to make up for lost time. The Australian fans, starved of live Formula One action, packed the grandstands in record numbers. The city had always embraced its role as an early-season race, and this time was no different—crowds swarmed to Albert Park, lining the fences and basking in the autumn sunshine. The circuit had undergone some modifications since the last visit, with widened corners and a reprofiled layout designed to improve overtaking. The changes, combined with the new generation of ground-effect cars, promised an intriguing weekend.

Mercedes arrived still searching for answers. The porpoising issues that plagued the W13 in Bahrain and Saudi Arabia remained unresolved, and while Ferrari and Red Bull looked set to duel for the Championship, Hamilton was locked in a battle with the laws of aerodynamics. His podium in Bahrain had been a fortunate anomaly, and his single-point finish in Jeddah was a brutal reality check. The seven-time World Champion had been here before—fighting from behind in the early stages of a season—but this time, the road back to the front looked longer than ever.

Practice sessions hinted at another uphill struggle. The Ferrari of Leclerc looked supremely balanced, while Verstappen and Pérez were competitive in their Red Bulls. The Mercedes pair, meanwhile, spent most of their time wrestling an unruly car and making frantic setup changes. When qualifying arrived, it was no great surprise to see Hamilton unable to challenge the front-runners. He secured fifth on the grid, an improvement on his disastrous Jeddah outing, but still a world away from his usual place at the sharp end. Russell, continuing to make a strong case for himself in his first season with the team, lined up just behind in sixth.

At the front, Leclerc continued his one-lap dominance, taking pole position with a commanding lap. Verstappen settled for second, while Pérez and the ever-improving Lando Norris completed the second row.

Race day dawned bright and clear, a perfect Melbourne autumn afternoon. The atmosphere was one of enthusiasm, the grandstands packed with fans eager to see if local hero Daniel Ricciardo could deliver something special, despite McLaren's early-season struggles.

As the lights went out, Leclerc made a clean getaway, while Verstappen, despite his best efforts, found himself unable to challenge the Ferrari into Turn 1. Behind them, Hamilton made a strong start, jumping Pérez to slot into third. It was the sort of opening lap that suggested he could at least be a thorn in Red Bull's side, even if outright victory was beyond his reach.

The early laps settled into a rhythm, but Melbourne's reprofiled layout meant drivers were pushing harder than usual, and mistakes were inevitable. Sainz, hoping to fight back from a poor qualifying, made an uncharacteristic error on the second lap. Struggling for grip on hard tyres, he ran wide and lost control, beaching his Ferrari in the gravel. It was an embarrassing early exit for a driver who had ambitions of fighting for the Championship.

With the Safety Car deployed, strategies were reset. On the restart, Leclerc immediately reasserted his control, pulling away from Verstappen with apparent ease. Hamilton, meanwhile, was engaged in an entertaining scrap with Pérez, but the superior straight-line speed of the Red Bull eventually proved too much to resist. Russell, running a slightly different strategy, managed to get ahead of his teammate during the pit stops, a move that would later prove crucial.

The defining moment of the race came just past half-distance when Verstappen suddenly slowed with smoke trailing from the rear of his car. Another Red Bull reliability failure had struck, and the reigning World Champion was out. His frustration was evident as he climbed from the car, shaking his head, though he remained trackside long enough to direct the marshals with their extinguishers.

With Verstappen out, Leclerc's path to victory was clear. He controlled the remaining laps with the confidence of a man who knew he had the fastest car on the grid. Behind him, Pérez salvaged second for Red Bull, while Russell's strategy gamble and the luck of the pit stop timing with the VSC paid off, allowing him to claim his first podium as a Mercedes driver. Hamilton finished fourth, frustrated but pragmatic. Given the circumstances, it was a solid result, but it was clear that fighting for victories was still a distant prospect.

For Leclerc, it was a statement win. Ferrari had arrived in 2022 with a car capable of challenging for the title, and the Monegasque driver was seizing the opportunity. For Hamilton, the result reinforced the reality of the season—

Mercedes were adrift, and patience would be required. Albert Park had once been the scene of his triumphs, but this time, it served as another reminder of just how much work lay ahead.

If the opening three rounds of the 2022 season had hinted at trouble for Hamilton and Mercedes, the next five confirmed it. By the time the European leg of the calendar got underway, it was clear that the all-conquering Silver Arrows of the previous decade had been replaced by an unpredictable, porpoising riddle of a car. With Ferrari and Red Bull streaking ahead, Hamilton found himself in an unfamiliar position—scrapping for the lower reaches of the top ten while his young teammate, Russell, quietly established himself as the more consistent performer.

What followed between Imola and Baku was a bruising period, both figuratively and literally. Mercedes continued to wrestle with their aerodynamic gremlins, while Hamilton endured weekends that swung between unlucky and downright miserable.

### A Miserable Weekend in Imola

Formula One's return to Imola should have been a nostalgic trip to one of Hamilton's happiest hunting grounds. Instead, it turned into a damp and dispiriting affair. The first Sprint race of the season saw him qualify a lowly 13th, a stark confirmation of Mercedes' ongoing struggles. The sprint offered little respite—Hamilton failed to make progress, finishing outside the points.

Race day provided no redemption. Stuck in a frustrating DRS train behind Gasly's AlphaTauri, he spent much of the afternoon staring at the Frenchman's rear wing. Meanwhile, Russell was carving his way to a respectable fourth place, rubbing salt in the wound. Hamilton crossed the line in 13th, a lapped bystander as Verstappen cruised to victory.

Toto Wolff's radio message after the race summed up the situation, apologising for the car's poor performance and acknowledging that it was undriveable and undeserving of such a result. Hamilton, already seeing the writing on the wall this early in the season, admitted there was no hope of competing with Red Bull or Ferrari. While ruling himself out of the Championship fight, he remained determined to keep working hard and find a way to pull things back together.

### A Frustrating Weekend in Miami

Formula One's much-hyped debut in Miami brought American glitz and glamour to the calendar, but for Hamilton, it was another case of style over substance. The W13 remained a stubborn, bouncing enigma, and while Mercedes had brought updates, they did little to transform the car into a front-runner.

Hamilton started sixth and found himself locked in yet another midfield battle, scrapping for positions rather than podiums. A late-race Safety Car offered a glimmer of hope, but what should have been an opportunity quickly unravelled. Unsure of the positions around him, Hamilton sought guidance from the team on whether to pit. Peter Bonnington, his usually infallible race engineer, advised staying out—an unfortunate call given that Russell, opting to pit, would restart on fresher tyres and inevitably move ahead.

Hamilton's frustration was evident, both over the radio and in his post-race discussions. The car was already proving to be a nightmare, but now even Mercedes' renowned strategic sharpness seemed to be deserting them. It was yet another race where things had gone from promising to lacklustre, with Hamilton finishing a disappointing sixth.

### Signs of Progress in Barcelona

Barcelona had long been considered a crucial testing ground, and Mercedes arrived in Spain with renewed hope. Their upgrades did appear to reduce some of the porpoising, and for a brief moment, Hamilton reminded everyone of his brilliance.

After contact with Magnussen on the opening lap of the race, he dropped to the back of the field. What followed was a vintage Hamilton recovery drive. Despite losing significant time, he carved through the pack and at one stage looked set to finish fourth. Then, in a cruel twist, overheating issues forced him to back off. He crossed the line fifth, in what was at least a moral victory—proof that Mercedes were inching in the right direction.

Sainz made another unforced error on Lap 7, running off track before recovering, though not without consequence. He wasn't the only one struggling—just two laps later, Verstappen also had a brief off-track excursion, a rare misstep from the reigning Champion, but it did nothing to dampen his speed. The new-generation cars, designed under fresh regulations, were proving to be a handful, particularly when pushed to their limits.

Verstappen won again, capitalising on Leclerc's Lap 28 retirement. The Ferrari-Red Bull fight raged on, while Hamilton remained a distant observer. Russell, who had been caught by Hamilton until the issues arose, finished third but was still over half a minute down on the Red Bull.

## Another Tough Weekend in Monaco

Monaco, where Hamilton had often danced his way through the streets, turned into another slog. The W13, still lacking balance and grip, was wholly unsuited to the tight and twisting circuit. Hamilton was struggling to get the car turned into corners. A rain-delayed start and a series of blunders from Ferrari—who had locked out the front row—stole the headlines, but for Hamilton, it was another day spent in midfield obscurity. The Ferraris were running one-two comfortably until the pit stops, when their errors allowed Pérez through into the lead.

On Lap 27, Mick Schumacher destroyed another Haas, losing control through the swimming pool section and ripping the entire rear section of the car off, bringing out the Safety Car. Trapped behind Alpine's Fernando Alonso for a torturous number of laps in the damp weather, Hamilton voiced his frustrations over team radio but had no way past. By the time the chequered flag fell, he was eighth. Pérez won the race—his first ever Monaco win in Formula One—with Sainz second and Verstappen third. Leclerc finished fourth. It was a bad weekend for Ferrari, who should have comfortably won the race.

**Pain in Baku**

Baku, a circuit that had delivered chaos and triumph in equal measure over the years, provided something different for Hamilton—pain. The bouncing issue that had plagued Mercedes all season reached its most extreme level on the long, high-speed straights. Every lap, the car violently pounded the asphalt, and by the closing stages, Hamilton was physically struggling to hold onto the wheel.

Despite the discomfort, he battled through, finishing fourth—his best result since Australia. On the radio, Toto Wolff acknowledged the car's severe issues, openly admitting that it was difficult to drive and apologising for the strain it had put on Hamilton's back, while assuring him that the team would find solutions, Wolff vicariously describing Hamilton's car as a 'shit box'.

As Hamilton climbed out of the car, wincing and clutching his back, the images told the story. It was clear that whatever was going on with the Mercedes, it wasn't sustainable. In post-race interviews, he admitted he had been praying for the race to end. He also reflected on whether, given the amount of pain he was in, he would have been able to pass the mandated FIA extraction time—the minimum time drivers are given to exit the car.

Russell, once again, finished ahead, taking third in what was fast becoming an awkward subplot to Mercedes' wider struggles. But even Russell, despite his third place, was clearly having a torrid time with the bouncing, expressing relief when the race came to a close. He explained that the constant pounding of the car on the ground for an hour and a half was incredibly brutal, particularly on a circuit that wasn't normally so physical, and he was looking forward to a good night's sleep.

Verstappen and Red Bull seemed to have turned a corner with their gremlins, and Verstappen went on to win comfortably, with Pérez second. Ferrari, who had looked the strongest in the first four races, were now falling to pieces. Sainz retired on Lap 8, and Leclerc on Lap 20, with smoke pouring from the back of the stricken Ferrari.

Verstappen now led the Driver's Championship on 150 points, with Pérez in second on 129. Leclerc was third on 116 points. If Red Bull kept their reliability in order, Verstappen would be hard to peg back from here on.

Ahead of the Canadian Grand Prix, Hamilton revealed that he had started experiencing frequent headaches. He spoke openly to the media about his concerns, explaining that his body and head were being subjected to repeated 10g forces as he was bounced violently around the cockpit hundreds of times per lap. It was not just his own wellbeing that troubled him—he was concerned for the health of every driver enduring the same punishing conditions. Discussing the potential effects, he admitted he had certainly been experiencing more headaches in recent months.

A micro concussion, sometimes called a sub-concussive impact, does not meet the official diagnostic criteria for a full concussion, yet involves similar forces acting upon the brain. These repeated, lower-level impacts, though individually minor, can accumulate over time, leading to long-term neurological consequences. They are of particular concern in sports where continuous jolts or vibrations are part of the activity—motorsport being a prime example.

Scientific studies had already shown that even minor, repetitive head vibrations could have serious cumulative effects. For Hamilton, the immediate symptoms—headaches, fatigue, and back pain—were troubling enough, but the larger concern was what might lie ahead. If the problem remained unresolved, the risks would only increase, potentially affecting cognitive function and reaction times over the course of the season. Given the fine margins of Formula One, where a split-second decision can mean the difference between victory and disaster, the idea that a driver's ability to process key information and react instinctively might be compromised was deeply unsettling.

Research had also linked repeated concussions to cognitive impairment and mental health issues, a growing concern in high-performance sports. The British Medical Journal and the British Journal of Sports Medicine had published findings that were difficult to ignore: "Multiple concussions appear to be a risk factor for cognitive impairment and mental health problems in some individuals." If Hamilton was experiencing micro concussions, then his mental health could also be at risk—something he would later discuss more openly. While the micro-concussions were distinct from a 'regular' concussion, the symptoms were worrying.

In the immediate aftermath of such impacts, symptoms could include mood swings, irritability, and increased stress levels. Brain trauma, even at a mild level, disrupts the brain's ability to regulate emotions, making frustration and anxiety more pronounced. Fatigue—both physical and mental—was another likely consequence, as the brain requires additional energy to function properly after sustaining repeated trauma. Concentration lapses and "brain fog" are common effects, an alarming prospect for an elite athlete whose entire profession depended on rapid processing and reaction times.

The long-term risks were even more concerning. Repeated exposure to brain trauma, even at relatively low levels, had been linked to increased risks of depression, emotional instability, and neurodegenerative conditions such as chronic traumatic encephalopathy (CTE). While CTE was more commonly associated with sports like American football and boxing, where heavy blows to the head were routine, Formula One drivers were now facing similar concerns. Even disruptions to sleep patterns, caused by changes to melatonin production, could have a compounding effect—insomnia, poor rest, and increased mental fatigue would only add to the strain.

Hamilton's frustration throughout the 2022 season was easy to see, but his emotions may not have been attributed to competitive struggles alone. Mercedes' performance issues, the weight of expectations, and his natural desire to fight for wins were all factors, but there was another battle taking place—one with his own body. The effects of porpoising had been widely discussed as an engineering issue, but for Hamilton, they represented something more fundamental and personal. Repeated trauma to the brain and spine had the potential to shape his entire season, not just in terms of performance, but in his overall wellbeing. The energy he was having to expend just to endure a race weekend was significantly higher than in previous years. It was not just a question of how competitive Mercedes could be—it was whether the sport was doing enough to protect its drivers.

It was a dark and difficult period for Hamilton. Having endured the global pandemic like everyone else, now he was faced with repetitive injuries that could have serious long-term effects. While he rarely let his struggles show, this was a very real crisis, both physically and mentally.

Thankfully, after the Azerbaijan Grand Prix, the FIA recognised the scale of the problem. On 16 June 2022, they issued a formal statement acknowledging the safety concerns posed by porpoising and confirmed that steps would be taken to reduce the phenomenon.

*"Following the eighth round of this year's FIA Formula One World Championship, during which the phenomenon of*

*aerodynamic oscillations ("porpoising") of the new generation of Formula One cars, and the effect of this during and after the race on the physical condition of the drivers was once again visible, the FIA, as the governing body of the sport, has decided that, in the interests of safety, it is necessary to intervene to require that the teams make the necessary adjustments to reduce or to eliminate this phenomenon." (Source FIA)*

A technical directive was issued, ensuring that porpoising was now a formal area of focus for the FIA. They also consulted medical experts, who reinforced the need for urgent action. *"All of a driver's concentration needs to be focused on that task, and excessive fatigue or pain experienced by a driver could have significant consequences should it result in a loss of concentration." (Source FIA)*

It was a relief to see that safety was being prioritised. While some teams resisted the intervention, arguing that it was a competitive issue rather than a medical one, the FIA made it clear that driver wellbeing came first. The question, however, remained: was this response too late for those who had already suffered the effects of months of brutal bouncing?

From Imola to Baku, the season had become a test of endurance. Hamilton's once-dominant, title-winning machine had been replaced by an unpredictable and deeply flawed car that refused to behave, causing him both literal and figurative headaches. Meanwhile, Russell's consistency—five consecutive top-five finishes—only reinforced the reality that Hamilton was no longer fighting for victories, but for relevance. As the summer break approached, there was cautious optimism that Mercedes might finally get their unruly creation under control. But for Hamilton, the challenge was now something entirely different. This was no longer a battle of endurance alone.

If the early part of 2022 had been an exercise in frustration for Hamilton, the next five races at least offered something resembling progress. Mercedes had spent much of the season grappling with their uncooperative W13, watching Red Bull and Ferrari disappear into the distance, but as the summer approached, the worst of their porpoising nightmare seemed to be behind them. The car was still far from a race-winner, but it was, at last, more predictable. Hamilton, bruised from a painful Baku weekend, began to rediscover some of his old form—though podiums, rather than victories, remained the ceiling.

Montreal had always been a happy hunting ground for Hamilton, the scene of his first-ever Formula One win back in 2007. But as he arrived in 2022, it was less about nostalgia and more about damage control. The previous race in Baku had left him wincing in pain from the relentless bouncing, and Mercedes needed a circuit that would be kinder to their troublesome car.

On Friday 17 June, it seemed things had taken a turn for the worse as Hamilton continued to struggle with the car's bouncing around Montreal. After the second free practice session, he expressed his frustration over the radio, saying the car had become undriveable. Once out of the car, his frustration deepened, calling the situation a disaster. He explained that the car appeared to be getting worse with each adjustment, becoming more and more unhappy. He acknowledged that this was the car for the year, and they would have to tough it out, hoping to build a better car for the following season.

The Mercedes mechanics and engineers went away overnight hoping for a miracle—and they got one.

The high-speed straights of the Circuit Gilles Villeneuve still exposed the W13's deficiencies, but the worst of the bouncing was gone, and Hamilton finally had a machine he could work with. Qualifying in fourth, he ran a solid race, making the most of a well-timed Virtual Safety Car to secure his first podium since Bahrain. Third place felt almost like a win in a season where simply having a competitive car had become a luxury. It wasn't a turning point, but it was a sign that Mercedes wasn't done just yet. Russell, who had qualified in eighth, came home fourth. At the front, Verstappen held off a late challenge from Sainz to take his first victory in Canada, further tightening his grip on the Championship: he was looking unstoppable already.

### British Grand Prix

Two weeks later, Formula One arrived at Silverstone in early July. If there was anywhere Hamilton could summon a moment of brilliance, it was at the British Grand Prix. The home crowd, still unwavering in their support despite his lack of wins, cheered him on throughout the weekend. For the first time in 2022, Mercedes looked somewhat competitive. A fresh round of upgrades had made the W13 more manageable. Hamilton, enjoying the improved balance, was in the mix. He qualified fifth, with Russell in eighth. Sainz took pole for Ferrari, with Verstappen lining up alongside him on the front row.

The race was messy from the start. A horrifying first-lap crash involving Zhou Guanyu brought out the red flag almost immediately. As the field accelerated towards Copse, Russell, struggling on cold tyres after a slow getaway, moved left and clipped Gasly. The contact sent Russell into Zhou, who was launched into a terrifying roll. His Alfa Romeo skidded upside down across the gravel before flipping over the tyre barrier and into the catch fencing. Trapped in the wreckage as the car lay on its side against the barrier, Zhou was unable to escape. Russell, shaken from what he had seen at close range, immediately abandoned his own car and sprinted to the scene. Marshals and medics worked quickly to extract Zhou, and when he was finally freed, the relieved British crowd erupted in applause.

Once racing resumed, Hamilton found himself in genuine contention. For a few glorious laps, he even led, sending the Silverstone crowd into a frenzy. But the fairy tale was short-lived—Ferrari had the pace to pull away, and a late-race Safety Car left Hamilton vulnerable to Pérez's Red Bull, which moved up into second. What followed was a breathtaking four-lap duel between Hamilton and Leclerc as they fought for the final step of the podium, with the pair going wheel to wheel in a battle that had the British crowd on its feet. In the end, third place marked Hamilton's second consecutive podium, but unlike Canada, this one was achieved on pure performance rather than fortune. It was the strongest Mercedes had looked all season. At the front, Sainz claimed his first-ever Formula One victory, navigating the chaos and Ferrari's usual self-inflicted errors to finally get his name on the winner's board.

### A Reality Check in Austria – 10 July 2022

After the highs of Silverstone, Austria provided a bump back down to reality on 10 July. The Red Bull Ring had been a happy venue for Mercedes in their dominant years, but with Red Bull now holding the upper hand, this was Verstappen territory. To make matters worse, Hamilton, who had been close in Q1 and Q2, in the top three each session, crashed in Q3 qualifying. Russell also crashed in Q3, giving the team extra work overnight to repair the cars. The cars were now so heavy that any loss of traction and going sideways meant they were carried a long way into the barriers.

Hamilton recovered well in the Sprint race, climbing up the order to put himself in contention for solid points on Sunday. In the main race, he was once again consistent, keeping out of trouble while others faltered. Ferrari's reliability woes continued as Sainz's engine exploded spectacularly, with parts scattered across the track, the car being engulfed in flames as he scrambled to get out. Verstappen struggled with tyre wear, allowing Charles Leclerc to snatch victory.

For Hamilton, it was another podium—his third in a row—though by now it was clear that third place was the absolute best Mercedes could achieve if someone else had a bad day. The W13 was improving, but it still wasn't a match for the Ferrari or Red Bull over a full race distance, with Hamilton finishing forty seconds behind the leader. Russell in the sister Mercedes finished fourth.

**Mercedes' Progress in France**

By the time Formula One arrived in the south of France on 24 July, Mercedes had established themselves as the "best of the rest" behind Red Bull and Ferrari. The Paul Ricard circuit, with its long straights and sweeping corners, wasn't expected to be particularly well-suited to the W13, but another solid weekend awaited. The weather was absolutely glorious.

Hamilton, now comfortable with the car's limitations, qualified fourth and got himself into the mix early on. In the first third of the race, Verstappen gave Leclerc a really hard time, staying close behind the Ferrari. Red Bull pitted Verstappen on Lap 17 to try the undercut. This led to the biggest moment of the race when Leclerc, leading comfortably but trying to go flat out to negate Verstappen's undercut, crashed out—an unforced error that all but handed Verstappen another win.

Hamilton, ever the opportunist, kept it clean and brought the car home in second place, his best result of the season. Russell finished third after a feisty battle with Pérez, marking Mercedes' first double podium of the year.

The Championship fight was now becoming a one-horse race. Ferrari, having started the season as title favourites, had spent the past few races self-destructing. Verstappen, by contrast, was ruthlessly efficient, racking up win after win. As they left a wonderful summer's day behind, Verstappen was leading on 233 points, with Leclerc now in second on 170 points. There would be no way back for Ferrari now.

**Another Step Forward in Hungary**

The final race before the summer break brought another step forward for Mercedes on 31 July. Budapest's twisty Hungaroring was often likened to Monaco without the walls, and while it hadn't always been a happy venue for Hamilton, it at least minimised Mercedes' straight-line deficiencies.

Qualifying was messy, with a sudden drop in temperature catching many drivers out. Russell, in a surprise twist, put in a stunning lap to take his first-ever pole position, while Hamilton could only manage seventh after a DRS issue on his final run.

Come race day, the story was one of strategy. Ferrari once again found a way to snatch defeat from the jaws of victory, putting Leclerc on hard tyres in a baffling decision that saw him sink down the order. Hamilton, meanwhile, put in another of his well-executed Sunday performances, climbing through the field with strong race pace. A late charge saw him overtake Sainz for second place, securing his fifth consecutive podium.

Russell, despite leading the early laps, couldn't hold off Verstappen, who, despite having a spin in the middle of the race, still won yet again after starting from tenth—an ominous sign for anyone still hoping to stop him given the difficulties of overtaking in Hungary. Russell, despite starting six places ahead of Hamilton, finished behind his teammate, rounding off the podium in third.

From Canada to Hungary, Mercedes had slowly clawed their way back to respectability. The W13 was still far from a title-winning car, but at least it was more predictable, and Hamilton—after months of battling an unruly machine—was finally able to drive on instinct again.

Five podiums in a row were hardly the standards Hamilton was used to, but after the brutal start to the year, they were a welcome shift in momentum. Verstappen, however, was now running away with the Championship, and as the summer break commenced, one thing was clear—unless something extraordinary happened, 2022 would not be the year Hamilton added an eighth title to his collection. At last, for the first time all season, he was in the fight. But before the battle resumed, he needed to step back and find himself again.

With the factory in its 14-day mandatory summer shutdown, Hamilton took the opportunity to escape to Africa. It was more than just a break from the relentless demands of Formula One—it was a chance to reconnect with nature, something he had always cherished. The trip was deeply personal, a moment to pause and gain perspective after months of struggle. He shared glimpses of his journey on Instagram, posting photos alongside reflections on the experience. He spoke of gaining "a new perspective on life," calling it a life-changing reset—a rare moment of stillness amid the turbulence of a difficult season.

Refreshed, he returned to the second half of the campaign with renewed purpose. But no amount of soul-searching could change the reality of Mercedes' situation. The W13 was no longer the unpredictable, bouncing mess it had been at the start of the year, but it remained fundamentally flawed. The zero-sidepod concept was proving to be more of a liability than a breakthrough, and while progress had been made, Red Bull and Ferrari were still out of reach. As Verstappen tightened his grip on a second title, Hamilton found himself in unfamiliar territory—not fighting for Championships, but for pride, performance, and the fading hope that, somehow, a victory might still be possible before the season was over.

### A Disappointing Return in Belgium

The first race back after the summer break brought little reason for optimism. In late August, the teams arrived in Belgium. Spa had always been a circuit where straight-line speed mattered, and that was still Mercedes' Achilles' heel. Red Bull, on the other hand, arrived in Belgium looking almost untouchable. A grid penalty for Verstappen meant he started 14th, but it hardly mattered—within a handful of laps, he was already slicing through the field with alarming ease.

For Hamilton, the race lasted all of a few corners. Starting from fourth, he found himself alongside Alonso heading into Les

Combes on the opening lap. In a move Hamilton later admitted was his fault, he misjudged the space, squeezed Alonso too tightly, and was launched into the air as the two cars made contact. The Mercedes came crashing back down, landing heavily before limping a few corners further and grinding to a halt. His race was over, and the familiar frustration was all too evident as he walked back to the pits.

Alonso made a quip over the radio, saying, "This guy only knows how to drive and start in first." It was classic Alonso—razor-sharp and dripping with just the right amount of salt. It didn't affect Alonso's race as he came home a strong fifth.

Meanwhile, Verstappen was clinical, slicing through the field from 14th to first with such ease that it felt almost unfair. Second was Pérez, with Sainz in the Ferrari third. Russell came home in fourth, half a minute down on the leader.

### Verstappen's Honour Before the Dutch Grand Prix

On the eve of the 2022 Dutch Grand Prix, Verstappen received a distinguished honour, being appointed an Officer in the Order of Orange-Nassau. The royal decoration was presented by the Netherlands' Minister for Sport in a ceremony attended by Verstappen's family and close friends. Minister Helder commended Verstappen's dedication and perseverance, highlighting how his achievements had significantly elevated the Netherlands' profile in the motorsport world. Verstappen talked of his profound gratitude, acknowledging the unwavering support from his family, team, sponsors, and the passionate "Orange Army" of fans. He described the accolade as a tremendous honour and looked forward to performing at his home race in Zandvoort.

### Zandvoort: A Festival of Orange Smoke and Verstappen-Mania

Zandvoort had been one of the best atmospheres of the previous season, a festival of orange smoke and Verstappen-mania. This year was no different, with the crowd fully expecting their home hero to deliver.

In Free Practice 1, there was a light-hearted moment over the Red Bull team radio between Christian Horner and Verstappen, where Horner congratulated Verstappen on his national honour. He joked about not knowing whether to call him "Sir Max, Lord Max, or Super Max," and offered congratulations from the whole team.

Mercedes arrived at Zandvoort with genuine hope. The flowing nature of the circuit played to their car's strengths, and for the first time in months, Hamilton felt like he had a realistic shot at fighting at the front. Hamilton did well in qualifying with a strong fourth place, with Russell in sixth. Verstappen, just ahead of Leclerc, took pole.

In the race, Mercedes executed a clever strategy, keeping both drivers out on a one-stop plan while others committed to multiple stops. As the laps ticked by, Hamilton suddenly found himself leading the race, albeit with Verstappen closing in fast. Then, the race took a dramatic turn. A bizarre retirement for Yuki Tsunoda brought out the Virtual Safety Car, allowing Verstappen a free pit stop. When a later full Safety Car followed, Mercedes opted to leave Hamilton on older medium tyres while Russell and Verstappen pitted behind him for fresh softs. This decision would prove costly.

On the restart, Verstappen breezed past Hamilton immediately. Russell followed soon after, and Leclerc wasn't far behind. What had looked like a genuine chance for victory evaporated within a few corners. Furious over the radio, Hamilton lashed out at the team for the strategy call, unusually for him lamenting their decisions with strong language, before cooling down after the chequered flag. On the cool-down lap, he received an apology from Bono and then from Toto Wolff. Hamilton showed his true colours as he sportingly thanked his mechanics for their brilliant pit stops, a sentiment that was appreciated by the team. Fourth place was still a good showing, but that hardly mattered. The opportunity had been there, and it had slipped away.

### The Struggles at Monza

The Italian Grand Prix on 11 September at Monza was never expected to suit the Mercedes, and that proved to be the case. While he had qualified in fifth, again ahead of Russell, a penalty for Hamilton saw him drop to 19th at the start. Hamilton knew it would be a damage-limitation exercise. Fortunately, the W13 was at least stable enough to allow for a steady climb through the field.

Verstappen, meanwhile, was once again in a class of his own. Starting from seventh due to his own penalty, he took the lead with ease and never looked back. Ferrari's attempts to challenge him were optimistic at best, and when the race ended under a Safety Car after Ricciardo's retirement, the home fans were left frustrated by the anti-climactic finish, with Leclerc rolling in second. Russell came in third.

Hamilton, having quietly worked his way through the pack, finished fifth. It was another respectable recovery, but nothing more. Mercedes were still firmly in the role of bystanders while Red Bull and Ferrari fought at the front.

### Hope Fades in Singapore

Under the bright lights of Singapore on 2 October, there was at least hope that Mercedes might have a better showing. The twisty layout of Marina Bay reduced the straight-line speed deficit, and Hamilton had always performed well on street circuits. In tricky wet-dry conditions, he qualified third, hinting at the possibility of a stronger weekend.

Any optimism, however, quickly faded. The race was messy, defined by Safety Cars, crashes, and mistakes. Hamilton's came as he chased Sainz in the early stages. Sainz had nudged Hamilton off in Turn 2 at the start, and pushing hard to close the gap to Sainz, Hamilton locked up into Turn 7 and went straight into the barriers. While he managed to reverse out and continue, the damage was done—his podium hopes were over.

Further mistakes followed as he struggled to make progress, and a late clash with Verstappen only compounded his frustrations. He finished ninth, a disappointing end to what had initially looked like a promising weekend. Meanwhile, Pérez took an impressive victory, holding off Leclerc in the closing stages to claim Red Bull's first win in Singapore since 2013.

**A Chaotic Japanese Grand Prix**

As the teams arrived in Japan in early October, Verstappen could clinch the title, even though there were four races to go after this. The gap was a massive 104 points, and he just had to stroke the Red Bull home to a good result.

Suzuka, a favourite among drivers, played host to one of the most chaotic races of the year. Torrential rain at the start made conditions treacherous, leading to a first-lap crash for Sainz, and multiple drivers going off or spinning before rejoining. The race was red-flagged. What followed was a long, tense delay before racing finally resumed in wet conditions. Sainz seemed to be making a habit of crashing out in the first few laps.

For Hamilton, it was another frustrating afternoon. Stuck behind Ocon for much of the shortened race, he simply could not find a way past the Alpine. With visibility poor and overtaking opportunities limited, he had to settle for fifth place, with Russell coming home eighth. It was another weekend where Mercedes had the pace for more but lacked the straight-line speed to capitalise.

The bigger story was at the front. Verstappen dominated once again, crossing the line first, but confusion reigned as the race ended. A post-race penalty for Leclerc meant Verstappen was unexpectedly crowned World Champion in the most anticlimactic fashion, as even he was unsure if the title was officially his until the FIA confirmed it moments later.

From Belgium to Japan, the trend of the season remained unchanged. Mercedes had improved, but they were still not quick enough to fight for wins on merit. Hamilton had glimpses of competitiveness—particularly in Zandvoort—but more often than not, he found himself fighting in a no man's land between the front-runners and the midfield.

Meanwhile, Verstappen had put the title fight beyond any doubt, wrapping up his second Championship with four races to spare. For Hamilton, it was a campaign unlike any other he had faced. The days of fighting for the Championship were long gone. Now, the challenge was simply to extract whatever performance he could and hope that, before the season ended, there might still be one more shot at victory.

Ferrari, once seen as a real threat, had faded into inconsistency once more, leaving Mercedes as the only team capable of challenging Red Bull in the closing rounds—though even that was a long shot. With a final round of upgrades coming, there was cautious optimism that Mercedes might finally be in a position to win a race before the season ended. Hamilton, still without a victory, was more determined than ever to avoid his first-ever winless campaign.

As the season entered its final stretch, Mercedes still searched for their first victory of the year. While Verstappen had already wrapped up the Drivers' Championship in Japan, Red Bull arrived in Austin for the United States Grand Prix in late October with the chance to secure the Constructors' title. However, the weekend was overshadowed by the passing of Dietrich Mateschitz, Red Bull's co-founder and the driving force behind the team's rise in Formula One. His death, announced just before qualifying, cast a sombre tone over the paddock. For Red Bull, it turned their inevitable Constructors' title win into something far more personal.

**The Rise of Formula One in the U.S.**

Formula One, once an afterthought in the American sporting landscape, had now become a blockbuster attraction, with over 440,000 fans pouring into the Circuit of The Americas in Austin over the October weekend. The surge in popularity of Formula One in America didn't happen by accident. A mix of factors had transformed the sport from a niche European pastime into a full-blown spectacle, drawing record-breaking crowds like the 440,000 who had flocked to Austin.

The Netflix documentary series *Drive to Survive* played a huge role in Formula One's explosion in the U.S., bringing the drama, rivalries, and personalities of the sport to a whole new audience. What had once been seen as a technical, distant motorsport was now a soap opera on wheels, complete with heroes, villains, and plenty of off-track intrigue. The wider accessibility of Formula One through social media and streaming services had also made following the sport easier than ever, turning casual viewers into dedicated fans.

The presence of American sponsors, the Haas Formula One team, the growing number of U.S.-based races, and an increased focus on fan engagement had further cemented Formula One's status as a major event. But it wasn't just the sport itself—it was the drivers who were pulling people in.

Few had done more to bridge the gap between Formula One and mainstream culture than Hamilton. A global icon beyond just racing, Hamilton had long been at the forefront of expanding Formula One's reach. His impact on diversity, fashion, and activism had made him one of the most recognisable figures in sport, attracting fans who might never have otherwise paid attention to Formula One. In the U.S., where star power is everything, Hamilton was the sport's biggest crossover name.

His influence extended beyond just image. His long-standing battles with Verstappen, his presence in *Drive to Survive*, and his ability to thrive under pressure had made him a key figure in drawing American audiences into the sport. Even in a season where he wasn't fighting for the title, Hamilton remained one of Formula One's biggest attractions—someone fans wanted to see, whether he was winning or not.

The massive crowd at the Circuit of the Americas wasn't just there for the racing; they were there for the show. And Hamilton, no matter where he was on the grid, remained one of the sport's biggest headliners. The track's design, inspired by classic circuits like Silverstone, Suzuka, and Hockenheim, made it a favourite among drivers, while its setting in one of the most vibrant cities in the U.S. helped turn the event into a huge fan spectacle. By 2022, with Formula One's surging popularity in America, the event was attracting record crowds.

Austin had always been one of Hamilton's favourite circuits, and with Mercedes bringing another round of upgrades, there was genuine optimism that they might finally have a car capable of fighting for victory. He qualified fifth, just ahead of Russell, with encouraging signs that they were closing the gap.

Ferrari locked out the front row, with Sainz taking pole ahead of Leclerc, while the Red Bulls of Verstappen and Pérez slotted into third and fourth. The top six lined up in neat two-by-two formation, setting the stage for what promised to be a tightly contested race.

The action began immediately. As the lights went out, Russell had one thing on his mind—outbraking Hamilton into Turn 1. So focused was he on his teammate that he failed to notice the bright red Ferrari ahead of him. Locking up, he clattered into Sainz, spinning him around and effectively ending the Spaniard's race before it had even begun. Russell picked up a five-second penalty for his troubles, while Sainz, understandably furious, could do nothing but trudge back to the garage.

The drama didn't stop there. On Lap 22, Alonso, who had been vocal in criticising Hamilton's racing incident at Spa, found himself in an airborne moment of his own. Attempting to pass Stroll—his soon-to-be teammate—down the back straight at close to 180mph, Alonso clipped the Aston Martin's rear wheel. The Alpine's nose pitched skywards, and for a brief moment, it looked as though he might take flight. The car came crashing back down before veering into the barriers, yet somehow, Alonso managed to limp the car back to the pits, missing a few crucial pieces of bodywork.

Closer analysis showed that Stroll had made a last-second move to defend just as Alonso committed to the overtake, a fraction of a second too late to avoid contact. Both were fortunate to escape unscathed.

Hamilton found himself in the lead late in the race, giving the Texan crowd a brief flashback to his dominant days. However, Red Bull's superior straight-line speed made it almost inevitable that Verstappen would reel him in. With just a handful of laps remaining, the Dutchman, on fresher tyres, made his move, sweeping past the Mercedes and denying Hamilton what would have been a morale-boosting victory.

Second place was still Hamilton's best finish of the season, but it was another painful reminder of how far away Mercedes remained. Meanwhile, Red Bull sealed the Constructors' Championship, marking the official end of Mercedes' eight-year reign. On the cool-down lap, Verstappen dedicated the win fittingly and the Constructors' title to Mateschitz: "this one is for Dietrich."

**The Mexican Grand Prix**

Mexico City, with its high altitude, had often played to Red Bull's strengths in previous years. This time, though, it appeared to be another chance for Hamilton to fight at the front, as he qualified third.

The race, however, was a straightforward affair. Mercedes opted for a hard tyre strategy that never really worked, leaving Hamilton powerless to challenge Verstappen for the win. Once again, he found himself in second place, but never truly in contention. It was another solid drive, but the frustration was evident—Mercedes had improved enough to beat Perez on pace, but not Verstappen. The home favourite Pérez came home third, and Russell was fourth. The Ferrari duo rocked up in fifth and sixth. Verstappen cruised to victory, setting a new record for the most wins in a single season. Red Bull's dominance was now beyond doubt, while Hamilton was still left searching for his first win of the year.

**A Chance for Victory in Brazil**

If there was one race where Mercedes could realistically break their winless streak, it was Brazil. The team had a strong history at Interlagos, and this time, their car looked genuinely competitive.

The Sprint saw Russell claim victory, giving him pole for Sunday's main event—an arrangement where the Sprint race result would determine the main race grid for 2023—while Hamilton battled through to finish third, setting up the prospect of a Mercedes fight at the front in the race. It was an exciting prospect—finally, a race where they weren't just the best of the rest. Better news came as Sainz, who had finished second, received an engine penalty, putting both Mercedes on the front row, with the Red Bulls right behind.

In the Grand Prix, Russell led from the start, while Hamilton found himself in the middle of an early clash with Verstappen. Verstappen received a five-second penalty and had to pit for a new front wing, while Hamilton lost valuable time as he dropped down the order. He recovered well, charging through the field to move into second, but by then, Russell had built enough of a gap to hold on for the win.

Russell claimed his first-ever Formula One victory, delivering Mercedes' only win of the season. Hamilton crossed the line just a second behind, a strong recovery after dropping to the lower half of the field following his collision with Verstappen. It was Mercedes' first one-two finish since 2020—a rare bright spot in a challenging year. While Hamilton had missed out on the win, it was at least a satisfying result for the team, proving that their relentless development had finally paid off.

**A Frustrating End in Abu Dhabi**

Twelve months on from one of the most controversial races in Formula One history, Hamilton returned to Abu Dhabi under very different circumstances. There was no title on the line this time—just one final chance to avoid ending the season winless for the first time in his career.

Qualifying was unspectacular, with Hamilton lining up fifth on the grid with Russell just behind him. Verstappen was again on pole.

It was a tough race. While battling with Sainz early on, Hamilton's car suffered floor damage after bouncing heavily over a kerb, robbing him of any real pace. As he struggled with a worsening handling imbalance, his hopes of fighting for a podium faded. In a cruel final blow, his car suffered a hydraulic failure just a few laps from the finish, forcing him into retirement. It was a fittingly frustrating end to a season that had never quite gone his way.

Verstappen cruised to his 15th win of the season, capping off one of the most dominant campaigns in Formula One history. Hamilton, meanwhile, was left to reflect on a year unlike any other he had experienced. There had been no wins, no poles, and for the first time in his career, no realistic shot at the Championship.

The 2022 season had been a sobering one. The once-dominant Mercedes had spent the year chasing shadows, and Hamilton had been forced to fight in the midfield rather than for victories. Yet, despite the frustrations, his late-season performances proved that his fire had not faded. While a win had eluded him, a string of podiums showed that, with the right car beneath him, he was still more than capable of competing at the very top.

Statistically, it was Hamilton's worst season in Formula One, finishing sixth in the standings. For a driver whose median finishing position had been second, it was nothing short of a disaster. As Wolff had bluntly admitted during the year, the W13 was a dog. The question was whether Mercedes would simply give it a trim and a wash for 2023 or whether they'd find themselves showcasing a car with a pedigree.

If it had been a frustrating season for Hamilton, Mercedes had at least salvaged some pride by finishing third in the Constructors' Championship, behind Ferrari. But for a team that had won every title since 2014, third place was a fall from grace.

As Hamilton stepped away from the W13 for the final time, one thing was certain—this was a season that could not be repeated. If Mercedes took his advice and designed a radically different car for 2023, there was hope for redemption. But if Red Bull and Adrian Newey produced another dominant machine, Hamilton might find himself staring down yet another year of disappointment.

# Endurance and Frustration

The 2023 season had all the ingredients for another difficult year at Mercedes. The team was still recovering from a bruising 2022 campaign, where the new ground-effect aerodynamic regulations had exposed fundamental weaknesses in their car. The W13 had been plagued by porpoising, the violent bouncing that made high-speed driving a physical ordeal, leaving Mercedes unable to mount a serious challenge to Red Bull and Ferrari. Despite a strong end to the season in Brazil, there was little certainty that 2023 would bring a genuine turnaround.

As Hamilton prepared for the new season, there was an air of expectation, but also a fair amount of scepticism. The previous year had been a battle from start to finish, but there had been signs of progress in the closing rounds. Now, with fresh technical regulations designed to refine the ground-effect era, there was hope that Mercedes could reset and move forward. On paper, the team appeared determined to adapt and evolve, but beneath the surface, concerns remained over whether their development direction was the right one.

The reintroduction of ground-effect aerodynamics had successfully brought cars closer together on track, but it had also created an unintended side effect—porpoising. The issue had been a major talking point throughout 2022, with Hamilton among the most vocal critics, particularly after the brutal race in Baku. The bouncing had been so severe that he struggled to climb out of the car at the end of the race, while other drivers, including Russell and Ricciardo, had also spoken out about the physical strain it was causing.

In response, the FIA introduced revisions to the technical regulations for 2023, aiming to mitigate porpoising and improve driver safety. While these changes were welcomed in principle, they also had the potential to shake up the competitive order.

One of the most significant alterations was the adjustment to the car's floor design. The regulations now required the floor edges to be raised by 15 millimetres, a move intended to reduce the suction effect underneath the car and, in turn, limit the ground-effect downforce that contributed to porpoising.

On the surface, this seemed like a positive step for Hamilton and Mercedes. In reality, it was likely to hurt them more than most. Their W13 had been designed with a low-rake philosophy, meaning that when viewed from the side, the car sat almost parallel to the track. Red Bull, by contrast, had developed a high-rake concept, with the rear of the car significantly raised compared to the front. When stationary on a flat surface, the Red Bull looked as though it was tilting downhill.

Raising the floor edges for 2023 would likely penalise teams running a low-rake design far more than those with a high-rake concept. In other words, while this regulation was introduced to tackle porpoising across the board, the team it would least affect was Red Bull—the very outfit that had dominated 2022.

To improve oversight of porpoising, the FIA also introduced a requirement for teams to install additional sensors on their cars. These devices would provide real-time data on vertical oscillations, allowing the FIA to monitor and enforce acceptable limits throughout the season.

For Mercedes, the technical changes presented a fresh set of challenges. While porpoising might be reduced, the question remained whether the W14—built as an evolution of its flawed predecessor—would allow Hamilton and Russell to fight at the front. The first test of their progress was fast approaching.

The 2023 season's additional regulatory refinements aimed at improving safety, performance, and fairness across the grid. One of the most significant safety-driven modifications concerned the roll hoop design. Zhou Guanyu's dramatic crash at Silverstone in 2022 had exposed a major weakness when his Alfa Romeo's roll hoop collapsed upon impact, leaving the car to slide along the tarmac on its halo. In response, the FIA introduced stricter regulations for roll hoop construction, ensuring they could withstand greater forces. The revised design also required a rounded top to prevent the roll hoop from digging into the ground in the event of an accident. The changes, while seemingly minor, represented a crucial step in further strengthening driver protection.

Aerodynamics also saw refinements, largely in response to the porpoising issues that had plagued the grid the previous year. The diffuser throat height was increased, making cars less sensitive to changes in ride height, while the stiffness of the floor edges was improved to prevent excessive flexing that could lead to aerodynamic stalling. These adjustments were intended to stabilise the airflow under the cars, reducing the bouncing that had made certain circuits unbearable for drivers.

Another subtle yet important change was made to rear-view mirrors. The size of the mirrors was increased by 50%, a seemingly small tweak but one that would improve driver visibility and reduce blind spots—particularly useful in close-quarters racing and defensive battles.

Weight had been another topic of discussion, with an initial proposal to reduce the minimum car weight from 798kg to 796kg. However, this plan was later scrapped, with the 2023 cars retaining the same weight limit as the previous season. While teams were always searching for ways to shed unnecessary weight, the FIA opted for stability, knowing that drastic reductions could compromise structural integrity.

Fuel temperature regulations were also tightened for 2023, closing a potential loophole that had allowed teams to gain a density advantage by excessively cooling fuel before it entered the engine. Under the new rules, fuel could not be colder than either ten degrees below ambient temperature or a minimum of 10°C, whichever was higher. The update ensured that all teams were operating under the same conditions, removing any possibility of manipulation.

These rule changes were just another part of the ever-evolving landscape of Formula One. With safety and performance at the forefront, the teams would need to ensure they adapted quickly. The foundation for 2023 had been set—now, it was time to see who had made the best of it.

Even before the 2023 season had begun, troubling signs were emerging from Mercedes. While no single statement raised immediate alarm bells, a closer look at the team's broader messaging suggested a growing disconnect between the drivers and the technical leadership. It was subtle, but it was there. If the tone from Brackley was anything to go by, 2023 was already shaping up to be another season of frustration.

At the centre of the concern was Mike Elliott, Mercedes' technical director. Despite the W13 being widely regarded as a failure, Elliott remained insistent that there was a great deal of merit in the car. This was the same machine that had spent much of 2022 bouncing violently down the straights, would not turn into corners, and was generally unstable: a car even Toto Wolff had described as a 'dog'. Yet Elliott remained committed to the idea that Mercedes should continue with its concept into 2023, arguing that tearing everything up and starting over would only set the team back further.

For Hamilton, this was alarming. He had been clear throughout 2022 that the W13 was something they had to endure and that he hoped Mercedes would go in a different direction for 2023. Russell had also voiced his frustrations, calling for a more predictable car and summing up the W13's handling characteristics as an example of poor balance. Yet rather than responding to their drivers, Mercedes stuck to their guns.

The result was a compromise that pleased no one—a car built on the flawed foundations of its predecessor, with no clear direction on how to correct its fundamental weaknesses. Worse still, the W13 had been designed around a low-rake philosophy, meaning that persisting with the same concept risked locking the team into another year of struggle.

The decision to push ahead with the zero-sidepod concept raised a bigger question—where did Wolff stand in all of this? More concerning for Hamilton than Elliott's technical philosophy was the fact that Wolff had backed it. At the launch of the W14, Wolff defended the concept, insisting that the sidepod design was not the fundamental reason for their lack of performance. This was a bold statement, but also a worrying one. The team had spent all of 2022 insisting that progress was being made, yet they had finished a distant third, winning just one race all season. Russell had taken victory in Brazil, but that was an outlier rather than proof that Mercedes had turned a corner. Hamilton, meanwhile, had gone an entire season without a win for the first time in his career—something unthinkable just a year earlier.

Despite this, Wolff placed his faith in Elliott and the technical team, rather than listening to his seven-time World Champion. But would Niki Lauda have allowed this? It was difficult to imagine. Lauda was a pragmatist. He did not believe in being bold for the sake of it—he believed in winning. If something was not working, he would not have wasted time trying to tweak it; he would have scrapped it and started over. He was also the crucial bridge between Wolff and the drivers, ensuring that cockpit concerns were not lost in a sea of engineering theory. If Hamilton had told him the car was fundamentally flawed, Lauda would have backed him.

Without Lauda's influence, cracks were beginning to show. Mercedes had gone from a team that was willing to admit and correct its mistakes to one that seemed increasingly stubborn, convinced that persistence would pay off. The absence of his ruthless clarity had left them more hesitant, more risk-averse, and, ultimately, vulnerable to being left behind.

For Hamilton, the situation was becoming impossible to ignore. He had spent years insisting he wanted to finish his career at Mercedes. But now, for the first time, he had a golden opportunity to look elsewhere. The team had ignored him once. Why stay with a team that was not listening to one of the most successful drivers in history?

Hamilton had always trusted his instincts, believing in the importance of following gut feeling. And as he prepared for the new season with a car built on the back of an old failure, his instincts must surely have been telling him—perhaps now was the time to move on.

Wolff, once regarded as a clear-headed strategist, had struggled to move on from Abu Dhabi 2021. Throughout 2022, the bitterness remained—he had refused to attend the FIA's prize-giving gala in 2021 when Verstappen was crowned, repeatedly voiced his frustration over the outcome, and made it clear that the scars of that night had not faded. Now, in 2023, he was refusing to move on from the concept of a flawed design. In Lauda's absence, was a pattern beginning to emerge? When emotionally or technically challenged, was Wolff becoming more resistant to altering his perspective?

Back in December 2022, Ferrari had announced a pivotal leadership change, appointing Frédéric Vasseur as Team Principal and General Manager, effective from 9 January 2023. This move signalled a strategic shift for the Scuderia, aiming to revitalise their Championship aspirations after a series of underwhelming seasons.

Vasseur, a French engineer with over 25 years of motorsport experience, had previously led Alfa Romeo Racing since 2017. His tenure there was marked by maximising performance despite limited resources, showing his adeptness in team management and development. His earlier successes included co-founding ART Grand Prix, where he collaborated with emerging talents like Hamilton, guiding them to Championship victories in the GP2 Series.

Upon his appointment, Ferrari's CEO expressed confidence in Vasseur's capabilities, stating that throughout his career, he had successfully combined his technical strengths as a trained engineer with a consistent ability to bring out the best in his drivers and teams. This approach and his leadership were seen as essential to pushing Ferrari forward with renewed energy.

Vasseur himself acknowledged the weight of Ferrari's legacy and the challenges ahead, describing his appointment as an honour and highlighting his lifelong passion for motorsport. He saw Ferrari as the pinnacle of the racing world and was determined to lead the team forward.

His high-level objectives were clear: enhance strategic decision-making, improve reliability, and foster a cohesive team culture. Recognising the passionate Tifosi and the high expectations surrounding Ferrari, Vasseur was committed to steering the team back to the forefront of Formula One competition.

The motorsport community watched closely, eager to see how Vasseur's pragmatic approach and leadership would influence Ferrari's performance in the seasons to come. After a 2022 season that had promised much but ultimately fallen apart due to strategic missteps and reliability woes, Ferrari turned to Vasseur, a man with a reputation for no-nonsense leadership and a deep understanding of race team dynamics. His arrival was seen as an effort to bring stability and a winning mentality to Maranello.

Vasseur outlined the rationale behind his priorities aimed at putting the team back on a Championship trajectory. First and foremost, he planned to streamline and optimise Ferrari's strategic decision-making. Ferrari's 2022 season had been marked by questionable strategy calls, and Vasseur was adamant that a more coordinated and data-driven approach would improve race results.

Another critical goal for Vasseur was to enhance Ferrari's reliability. He emphasised the need for a car that was not only fast but also consistent and capable of completing races without mechanical issues. Vasseur was also vocal about improving the team's in-season development, ensuring that Ferrari could adapt quickly to the evolving demands of the season. In addition to his technical goals, he highlighted his commitment to building a cohesive team culture at Ferrari, focusing on unity and a shared vision. His comments reflected a collaborative management style aimed at bringing stability and confidence back to Maranello.

From the outside, it was just another team reshuffling its management. But for Hamilton, watching from the Mercedes garage, it must have seemed like something more. This was his old mentor, the man who had guided him to his GP2 title in 2006 and set him on the path to Formula One greatness. A person he connected with. At the same time, Hamilton was grappling with his own frustrations—ignored by Mercedes when he pushed for a fresh car concept, stuck in a team that seemed more focused on proving itself right than winning races.

There were clear parallels to 2012, when Hamilton had made the bold decision to leave McLaren for a struggling Mercedes team. At the time, many had questioned why he would walk away from a race-winning car to join a team that had only won a single Grand Prix. But Hamilton had sensed something—a shift, an opportunity, a chance to build something new. Was he now feeling that same pull, seeing history repeating itself, but this time in Ferrari red?

While Mercedes continued down a technical rabbit hole that had already failed them, Ferrari was reshaping itself. And, crucially, they were being led by someone Hamilton knew, trusted, and had won with before. For the first time in years, a future beyond Mercedes was no longer just an abstract thought. It was beginning to take shape. A new challenge. A fresh start. A new dawn. A red dawn.

There had been plenty of movement over the winter break, with several key driver changes reshaping the grid. Fernando Alonso had left Alpine to replace the retiring Sebastian Vettel at Aston Martin, while Alpine had brought in Pierre Gasly to fill the vacant seat alongside Esteban Ocon. Oscar Piastri, the 2021 Formula 2 Champion, had joined McLaren after a contract dispute with Alpine, marking the start of what he hoped would be a long and successful career in Formula One.

Elsewhere, Nyck de Vries had earned a full-time seat at AlphaTauri after an impressive stand-in drive for Williams the previous season, while Nico Hülkenberg made a return to the grid with Haas. Logan Sargeant, the highly rated American rookie, completed the line-up at Williams.

The big question was how the teams would respond to the regulatory tweaks for 2023. Red Bull, having dominated the latter stages of 2022, had opted for an evolutionary approach with the RB19, refining what was already a near-perfect car. Ferrari had focused on addressing their reliability issues while making subtle aerodynamic improvements, aiming to sustain a Championship challenge over the full season.

Mercedes, however, had taken the biggest gamble of all. Despite a troubled 2022 campaign, they had chosen to persist with the zero-sidepod concept, hoping that tweaks to the car's floor and aerodynamics would be enough to close the gap to Red Bull. Aston Martin, meanwhile, had raised eyebrows with a car that looked markedly different from its predecessor, leading some to speculate that they had made the biggest gains over the winter.

The 2023 Formula One season was fast approaching, and with only three days of pre-season testing scheduled, teams arrived in Bahrain knowing that every lap would count. This was their one and only chance to fine-tune their new cars before the opening race. For some, it was about refining an already strong package. For others, it was about damage limitation and hoping they had got their calculations right.

When testing got underway in Bahrain the pecking order began to take shape. Red Bull looked ominously strong, with Verstappen setting the fastest time on the opening day. Ferrari appeared solid, though not spectacular, while Aston Martin's pace had the paddock talking. It was Alfa Romeo, however, who produced the biggest surprise, with Zhou Guanyu topping the timesheets on day two—though fuel loads and testing programmes made direct comparisons difficult. The final day saw Pérez put Red Bull back at the top with an impressive lap, reinforcing the belief that the reigning Champions were still the team to beat. AlphaTauri, perhaps not the fastest, at least demonstrated strong reliability, completing more laps than any other team over the three days.

For Mercedes, the results were mixed. The W14 was undoubtedly an improvement on its predecessor, but it was far from a race-winning machine. The violent bouncing that had plagued them in 2022 had been tamed to an extent, but the car still lacked the outright pace of Red Bull and even looked vulnerable to Ferrari and Aston Martin. Hamilton was realistic in his assessment, acknowledging the progress made but warning that there was still a lot of work to do if they were to fight for wins.

Hamilton's own assessment reflected a mix of optimism and realism. Yet by the final day of testing, that cautious optimism had shifted. While Mercedes had successfully eliminated the violent porpoising that plagued them in 2022, deeper issues remained. Some of the balance limitations from the previous season were still present, and the team was working through them. Meanwhile, Russell's test had been disrupted by reliability issues, raising concerns that Mercedes might still be dealing with more than just a lack of outright speed.

While much of the focus was on Red Bull, Ferrari, and Mercedes, another team was catching the eye—Aston Martin.

Having spent much of 2022 in the midfield, they arrived in Bahrain looking far more competitive, with Alonso delivering some eye-catching runs. Pundits began speculating that Aston Martin might emerge as a dark horse, capable of challenging Mercedes and perhaps even Ferrari on occasion.

McLaren, on the other hand, had a far less encouraging test. Their car appeared difficult to drive, and Piastri, making his highly anticipated debut, was struggling with an uncooperative MCL60. Even Lando Norris, widely regarded as one of the most adaptable drivers on the grid, found himself spending more time managing the car than pushing it to its limits. It was clear that McLaren had a lot of work to do before the season opener.

As testing concluded, Toto Wolff was keen to stress that Mercedes still had more to show, hinting that there was performance to unlock and that the team had yet to reveal everything. Whether that was genuine confidence or a hopeful smokescreen remained to be seen. What was certain, however, was that Red Bull had set the benchmark, Ferrari looked strong, Mercedes still had unanswered questions, and Aston Martin might just have been the surprise of the winter.

Predictions among pundits varied. Some believed Mercedes would mount a strong recovery, pointing to their late-season form in 2022 as proof that progress had already been made. Others felt that Ferrari, now under Frédéric Vasseur's leadership, had a real shot at being Red Bull's closest challenger—if they could address the reliability and strategic blunders that had cost them in 2022.

### A Dominant Start for Red Bull in Bahrain

The 2023 Formula One season roared to life under the floodlights of the Bahrain International Circuit on 5 March. Verstappen, the reigning World Champion, picked up right where he left off, securing pole position and converting it into a commanding victory. His Red Bull teammate, Pérez, ensured a perfect start for the team by finishing second, marking a decisive one-two finish.

However, the spotlight was not solely on Red Bull. Alonso, now driving for Aston Martin, delivered when it mattered most, capitalising on the team's improved performance, and he clinched a remarkable third place and his first podium since 2014. This result signalled Aston Martin's emergence as a genuine contender in the Constructors' Championship.

Mercedes, on the other hand, faced a mixed weekend. Hamilton managed a respectable fifth-place finish, but it was evident that the team still grappled with lingering balance issues from the previous season, finishing 50 seconds off the lead. Team Principal Toto Wolff acknowledged the challenges ahead, emphasising the need for swift developments to bridge the gap to Red Bull. Russell came home seventh.

**Pérez Dominates in Saudi Arabia**

The Formula One circus then moved to the Jeddah Street Circuit for the Saudi Arabian Grand Prix. This time, it was Pérez who stole the show. Demonstrating his prowess on street circuits, he secured pole position and maintained his lead to take the chequered flag. Verstappen, starting from 15th due to a driveshaft failure in qualifying, showed his mettle by carving through the field to finish second, resulting in another one-two finish for Red Bull. After only the second race of the season, it looked to be all over for everyone else.

Alonso again had a strong race, rounding off the podium. The Aston Martin, at least in his hands, looked competitive. His teammate, Lance Stroll, failed to finish.

Mercedes showed signs of improvement. Russell finished fourth, narrowly missing out on a podium, while Hamilton secured fifth. The W14 exhibited better pace, but both drivers noted the need for further enhancements to challenge the Red Bulls consistently. Hamilton talked at length after the race about how his set-up choices had been a limiting factor over the weekend. He admitted to struggling with both qualifying and race balance, though he remained encouraged by the team's position ahead of the Ferraris.

**Chaos in Melbourne**

Albert Park on 2 April in Melbourne played host to the third round of the season, and for the first time in 2023, Mercedes had a glimmer of hope. Verstappen had secured pole position, but as the lights went out, it was Russell who seized the initiative. Launching off the front row, he dived down the inside of Verstappen into Turn 1, forcing the Red Bull wide. With Verstappen's exit compromised, he suddenly found himself under attack from all sides—Alonso, Sainz, and Hamilton all swarming in as they thundered down towards Turn 3.

Hamilton looked unstoppable and in a flash of instinct and precision he slipped ahead of Alonso and Sainz before lunging down the inside of Verstappen in a move straight out of the textbook. For a moment, the Red Bull was swallowed up in a sea of black, red, and green, but Verstappen, now a two-time World Champion with a car that was untouchable in race trim, did not panic. There was no erratic defending, no last-ditch desperation. He simply bided his time.

Then, the race descended into chaos. On the opening lap, Leclerc found himself beached in the gravel, triggering a Virtual Safety Car. Just a few laps later, Albon lost control coming out of Turn 6, sending his Williams spinning into the barriers, his car came to rest half on the track and half in the gravel, bringing out the Safety Car before race control made the call to red flag the race to clear the debris.

Russell, having pitted under yellow, found himself shuffled down the order, leaving Hamilton to lead the field on the restart. But any hope of a fairytale victory was short-lived. On Lap 12, Verstappen breezed past the Mercedes and disappeared into the distance, his Red Bull in a different league when it came to race pace. The Dutchman looked to have the race comfortably wrapped up, but fate had one more twist in store.

With just two laps to go, there was another red flag, setting up a dramatic standing restart. Verstappen held firm at the front, but behind him, the field erupted into complete carnage. In a desperate bid to make up positions, drivers lunged down the inside, braked too late, and left carbon fibre scattered across the track. Alonso was unceremoniously spun around by Sainz, while further back, Gasly ran wide before rejoining straight into the path of his teammate Ocon, sending both Alpines into the barriers. Another red flag followed, and after much deliberation, the race was restarted for a single lap under safety car conditions, effectively neutralising the order.

Verstappen took the victory, with Hamilton securing a hard-fought second place, his first podium of the season. Alonso, despite the earlier chaos, was classified third after the finishing order was reset to the previous lap.

For Mercedes, this was a good weekend. The raw pace of the W14 still was not enough to challenge Red Bull, but they had at least established themselves ahead of Ferrari and Aston Martin. In a season where every position in the Constructors' Championship mattered financially, that was a small but significant victory for the Brackley squad.

### Red Bull Unstoppable in Baku and Miami

The tight and twisty streets of Baku set the stage for the Azerbaijan Grand Prix on 30 April. Pérez reaffirmed his increasing strength on street circuits by taking the victory, closely followed by Verstappen. This result underscored Red Bull's dominance, particularly in low-speed, high-downforce conditions. Ferrari showed a glimpse of their potential, with Leclerc securing pole position and finishing third. Mercedes, meanwhile, had a subdued weekend, with both drivers finishing off the podium and expressing concerns over the car's performance in slow corners—it still showed a reluctance to turn in.

The Miami Grand Prix on 7 May was another dominant weekend for Red Bull. Verstappen bounced back from his Baku defeat, overtaking both Ferraris to claim victory. The event was a spectacle, with celebrities and fans thronging the venue, but on track, it was business as usual for Red Bull.

Mercedes showed signs of resurgence, with Russell finishing fourth and Hamilton sixth. The team had introduced several upgrades, which seemed to have a positive impact, but the gap to Red Bull remained significant, with Russell 33 seconds down and Hamilton 51 seconds adrift. Alonso once again delivered an impressive drive, securing another third-place finish.

The teams departed America for a brief respite before heading to the most prestigious race on the calendar—Monaco, scheduled for 28 May. As Hamilton left the States, he had plenty to ponder. The car was not performing, the team was not listening, and patience was wearing thin. But soon enough, Mercedes would have no choice but to listen.

On 22 May, Italian media began to circulate a bombshell story—Ferrari was interested in signing Hamilton. As the Monaco Grand Prix weekend approached, speculation intensified. With Hamilton's contract at Mercedes set to expire at the end of the year and negotiations for a renewal ongoing, reports emerged that Ferrari was preparing a substantial offer to lure him away.

The Italian newspaper *AutoSprint*, part of *Corriere dello Sport*, claimed Ferrari was ready to offer Hamilton a £40 million per year deal, with Ferrari President John Elkann personally leading the charge. It was a level of detail that suggested the rumours were not mere speculation, but something more concrete. The debate then shifted to what Ferrari's lineup would look like—if Hamilton arrived, who would make way? Leclerc or Sainz?

On 24 May, *AutoSprint* ran another story, this time focusing on Leclerc and the swirling rumours of Hamilton's arrival. It was perhaps the most revealing piece yet, and when viewed objectively, seemed to suggest that Leclerc was safe and that Sainz would be the one to go. Leclerc's response to the speculation was telling. He refused to comment directly, but acknowledged that it was a new experience in his career. His refusal to dismiss the reports only fuelled the fire.

But it was what he said later that all but confirmed the situation. Speaking about his relationship with Frédéric Vasseur, Leclerc emphasised their long-standing connection and the trust between them. He highlighted how rare it was to find genuine honesty in Formula One and praised Vasseur's clear vision for the competition. This sentiment, when read in context, strongly implied that Vasseur had reassured Leclerc about his position at Ferrari.

If this was not an admission that Leclerc's seat was secure, then it was difficult to interpret it as anything else. The real question now was not whether Hamilton had an offer—but whether he would take it.

Hamilton addressed the rumours directly. Speaking ahead of the Monaco Grand Prix, he reaffirmed his commitment to Mercedes and stated that he was close to finalising a new contract with the team. While dismissing the Ferrari links, he also acknowledged the challenges Mercedes had faced over the past two years. His comments, reported by *The Guardian*, suggested that while an approach had been made, his primary concern remained the team's performance.

Hamilton acknowledged that mistakes had been made in car development and that the team was still working through those issues. The way he framed his response raised questions—why reference Mercedes' missteps in the context of Ferrari's approach unless there was some level of dissatisfaction?

When asked about the speculation during a press conference at the Monaco Grand Prix, Hamilton remained composed. He said contract negotiations always brought speculation and urged people to rely only on his own statements rather than media reports.

Frédéric Vasseur was also asked about the rumours and denied them outright. Some pundits pointed out the irony of Ferrari's previous denials—most notably, when they dismissed speculation about Mattia Binotto's dismissal just weeks before it happened. Vasseur insisted it was simply that time of year—Formula One's famous 'silly season'—and that no offer had been made to Hamilton.

Leclerc, Ferrari's lead driver, also commented on the swirling rumours. When asked about the possibility of Hamilton joining the Scuderia, he diplomatically avoided the speculation, reaffirming his commitment to Ferrari and his respect for his current teammate. His measured response aimed to quell the media frenzy without adding fuel to the fire.

Despite the intense media buzz, both Hamilton and Leclerc maintained their focus on their respective teams, downplaying the rumours and concentrating on the season ahead.

Amidst the swirling rumours of Hamilton being courted by Ferrari, Mercedes arrived in Monaco with a raft of new developments for the W14. The team introduced significant upgrades, marking a departure from their previous 'zero-sidepod' design philosophy. The updated sidepods featured a wider and higher inlet, aimed at improving airflow to the floor edge and enhancing overall aerodynamic performance.

Additionally, Mercedes made changes to the front suspension, adjusting the top wishbone's inboard pick-up point to improve airflow into the sidepod area, thereby enhancing cooling and aerodynamic efficiency. Despite these modifications, the team maintained their low-rake chassis configuration, focusing on optimising other aerodynamic and mechanical aspects of the W14. However, given Monaco's high-downforce nature, there were questions over whether these upgrades would provide any immediate benefits.

**Verstappen Dominates in Monaco**

On 28 May, the legendary streets of Monaco played host to another masterclass from Verstappen, as he delivered a flawless performance on a street circuit. From securing pole position to controlling the race from start to finish, he was never truly threatened.

Alonso gave chase, but with overtaking all but impossible in Monaco and Red Bull's superior race pace, second place was the best he could manage. Still, it was a huge result for Aston Martin in the prestigious Monaco surroundings. Team owner Lawrence Stroll's decision to bring in Alonso was proving to be a masterstroke, with the Spaniard looking more invigorated than he had in years.

Ocon delivered a stellar performance for Alpine, clinching third and providing a much-needed boost for the team. Meanwhile, Mercedes endured another frustrating weekend. Hamilton finished fourth, with Russell just behind in fifth, both drivers once again calling for significant upgrades if they were to have any hope of challenging at the front.

Yet Monaco also highlighted a growing sense of inevitability within the Mercedes camp. The team had arrived with another set of updates, but it was becoming increasingly clear that they were simply applying superficial fixes to a flawed concept: it was lipstick on a pig. The core weaknesses of the W14 remained—poor balance, a narrow performance window, and an inability to extract pace over a single lap. Hamilton and Russell had been asking for changes for months, yet the updates they were receiving were more akin to temporary solutions rather than the fundamental redesign they needed.

Perhaps these upgrades would bear fruit on the high-speed circuits later in the season, but for now, Mercedes was still chasing Red Bull and increasingly watching Aston Martin outperform expectations. The frustration was beginning to show.

As the season progressed from Bahrain to Monaco, Red Bull's dominance was unmistakable. However, the resurgence of teams like Aston Martin and the intermittent challenges posed by Ferrari and Mercedes hinted at a season that, while heavily leaning towards Red Bull, promised that second, third, and fourth places were still wide open.

Mercedes was doing just enough to stay in the conversation. The challenge now was ensuring that their upgrades delivered—not just to remain best of the rest, but to convince Hamilton that his future still lay in black or silver, rather than Ferrari red.

As the Formula One paddock packed up and left Monaco, the Championship standings painted a familiar picture. Verstappen led the way with 144 points, with Pérez trailing on 105 and Alonso holding third with 93. In the Constructors' standings, Red Bull was in a different league on 249 points, while Aston Martin and Mercedes sat well behind on 120 and 119 points respectively. Ferrari, meanwhile, were struggling in fourth with just 90 points, their season so far littered with missed opportunities and self-inflicted wounds.

Frédéric Vasseur had inherited a talented but error-prone driver pairing in Leclerc and Sainz. Both had shown flashes of brilliance, but too often they had been let down by overdriving, desperation, or a simple lack of patience. Vasseur knew that rebuilding their confidence would be crucial—not just in the car, but in each other. He needed to steady the ship, encourage a more measured approach, and remind them that Championships are won through consistency rather than moments of heroism. His calm, pragmatic, and upbeat leadership style would be key in getting Ferrari back on track.

### Mercedes' Upgrades Begin to Deliver in Spain

Arriving at the Circuit de Barcelona-Catalunya in early June, Mercedes revealed their upgrade package for the W14, aiming to close the performance gap to Red Bull. The enhancements included a revised floor and aerodynamic tweaks designed to improve overall downforce and balance. Hamilton seemed optimistic, saying the car felt more predictable during practice sessions. Free Practice 1 was steady, but after adjustments for FP2, he reported that the car felt significantly improved.

In qualifying, Hamilton secured fifth on the grid, while teammate Russell faced challenges and started from 12th. Race day saw both drivers making impressive strides; Hamilton demonstrated his racecraft and finished in second place, securing his best result of the season to date. Russell complemented the team's performance by climbing to third, resulting in Mercedes' first double podium of the year.

Despite Verstappen's dominant victory, the upgrades signalled a positive trajectory for Mercedes. Hamilton was delighted, acknowledging that he had not expected to finish second and that the car had felt good to drive and under control throughout the race. While Red Bull remained untouchable, Mercedes had, on merit, beaten Pérez in the sister Red Bull, the Ferraris, and Alonso's Aston Martin. The signs were encouraging.

**Another Podium in Canada**

At the Circuit Gilles Villeneuve in Montreal, Mercedes aimed to build on their recent momentum. Qualifying saw Hamilton secure fourth on the grid, with Russell fifth. However, following a penalty for Hulkenberg, both Mercedes drivers moved up to third and fourth for the race. The race began with Hamilton making a strong start, overtaking Alonso to claim second place behind Verstappen. Russell, however, faced trouble; on Lap 12, he collided with the wall at Turn 9, causing significant damage. Despite rejoining after repairs, brake issues forced his retirement on Lap 53.

Hamilton maintained his position, finishing third and securing another podium, while Verstappen took the victory, marking Red Bull's 100th win in Formula One.

Aston Martin, which had clearly been the second-fastest team in the first quarter of the season, still looked strong but did not seem to be developing at the same pace as Mercedes or Ferrari. Alonso would need all his skill to keep Hamilton and Russell at bay as the season progressed.

**A Challenging Weekend in Austria**

The Red Bull Ring in early July presented a more difficult scenario for Mercedes. Hamilton qualified fifth, with Russell starting from 11th. The race was marked by numerous track limit violations, leading to several drivers, including Hamilton, receiving time penalties. Struggling with the car's handling, particularly in Turn 10, he accumulated multiple infractions, resulting in a ten-second penalty. He ultimately finished eighth. Six other drivers also received track limit penalties in what was a busy weekend for the Stewards.

Russell, meanwhile, managed to navigate the race with fewer issues, finishing seventh. Reflecting on the weekend, Hamilton admitted that the team had not expected to be as slow as they were, acknowledging that their lack of performance had been a surprise.

Toto Wolff was equally frustrated, as the team was clearly bewildered by their lack of pace in Austria. He described it as a bruising day for the team, noting that while there had been a positive upward trajectory in recent races, they simply had not found the pace they needed in Austria. Both drivers had struggled with the car since Free Practice 1, and the weekend had been a step backward.

**A Home Podium at Silverstone**

The British Grand Prix took place on 9 July at the Silverstone Circuit under partly cloudy skies, with a record-breaking attendance of 480,000 over the weekend. Verstappen secured pole position for Red Bull, but the local crowd had reason to hope as Norris lined up alongside him in the McLaren. Russell and Hamilton started sixth and seventh for Mercedes.

At the start, Norris made an electrifying move to take the lead, sending the British fans into rapturous celebrations. Piastri in the second McLaren applied pressure on Verstappen for several laps, but as had been the case for months, the Dutchman remained composed. On lap five, he made his move past Norris and into the lead, resuming control of the race.

Hamilton, having been pushed wide on Lap 1, recovered well and began working his way through the field. A well-timed Safety Car deployment, triggered by Magnussen's Haas coming to a halt on track, allowed him to gain further ground. He spent over ten laps putting Norris under pressure but found himself unable to pass the McLaren, which had impressive straight-line speed. Ultimately, he finished third, much to the delight of the home crowd.

For Mercedes, this result was a significant achievement and reflected the progress made with their recent upgrades. However, it also revealed another emerging threat—McLaren had now entered the fight at the front, adding another challenge for the Brackley-based squad.

**Hungary – A Lap of The Gods**

The Hungarian Grand Prix, held on 23 July, arrived with its usual unpredictability. The weekend had been marked by thundery showers disrupting Friday's sessions, but the forecast for race day looked promising.

The Hungaroring had always been a special place for Hamilton. With eight wins and eight pole positions to his name, it was arguably his strongest circuit. If there was anywhere he could break Red Bull's stranglehold on the season, it was here. Yet despite his deep connection with the track, Hamilton was still struggling with the W14. The fundamental flaw in the car—its cockpit position being too far forward—meant he never felt fully in sync with the rear, a confidence issue that no amount of upgrades could entirely fix.

But if there was one thing that had always set Hamilton apart, it was his adaptability—his ability to extract pace when it mattered most.

Qualifying was shaping up to be a classic Formula One shootout, with the top drivers pushing the limit on their final runs. Verstappen held provisional pole with a 1:16.612, Hamilton trailing by nearly two-tenths. As the clock hit zero and the chequered flag fell, the packed grandstands at the Hungaroring collectively held their breath.

Verstappen failed to improve, but Norris was still on a flying lap. With a stunning effort, he slotted his McLaren between Verstappen's provisional pole and Hamilton's then second place, setting a 1:16.694, and along with it dropping Hamilton in his Mercedes to a provisional third.

But one car was still on track—and in it the most successful driver in history, who was yet to complete his final lap.

Hamilton flowed through Turns 10, 11, and 12 with an elegance that looked almost effortless, his inputs impossibly smooth. The Hungaroring rewarded precision over aggression—Jenson Button and Damon Hill had mastered it in their time, and Hamilton had perfected it.

What had made Hamilton the greatest driver of all time was not just his raw speed but his ability to adjust his style to the demands of any track, in any conditions. He could be aggressive when required, but here, it was all about control.

Approaching Turn 13, the long left-hand hairpin before the final corner, Hamilton turned in just past the 50-metre board. The W14 had been unpredictable all year, but for once, it looked planted, perfectly in sync with its driver. Then, a heartbeat later, the Mercedes understeered slightly more than anticipated. Instinctively, Hamilton adjusted, adding a fraction more lock while lifting off the throttle, helping the car rotate. The front tyres hooked up, but the rears, already on the limit, protested by stepping out.

For most drivers, that would have been the lap gone—the momentum lost. But Hamilton, drawing on years of karting, racing, and an innate feel for grip, let the steering wheel breathe, unwinding just enough lock to stabilise the car without scrubbing too much speed, feathering the throttle. It was a masterclass in control—on the ragged edge but never over it.

Into the final corner, he took a slightly wider entry to maintain a constant radius, carrying every ounce of speed onto the straight. Foot pinned to the floor, the Mercedes strained for every last fraction of performance as it hurtled towards the line. Then came the timing refresh. *1:16.609*. He had done it. Pole position. By three-thousandths of a second.

It was a gap so small it was barely perceptible—the length of a pencil, half the width of a Formula One tyre. But it was enough. For the first time since 2021, Hamilton was back on pole. He knew instantly. As he crossed the line, he pounded his fists against his helmet, pure elation pouring out over the radio.

Even after all these years, all these pole positions, all these victories and titles, Hamilton's passion and hunger were as fierce as ever. He laughed, revelling in the perfection of the lap, before, as always, thanking the team. But his race engineer, Bono, knew the truth. Sometimes, it was not about the car. This was about the driver.

Wolff praised Hamilton's performance, but his words carried an unintended slight. His comment suggested that Hamilton could only deliver a pole position when given the right machinery—when, in reality, this lap had been more about the driver than the car. He acknowledged Hamilton's brilliance but framed it as dependent on having the right tools, stating that when given a competitive car, Hamilton could deliver. Russell had qualified in $18^{th}$, so this was hardly the case.

It was an odd takeaway from a session where Hamilton had wrung every last ounce of performance from a car that was not supposed to be on pole. The W14 remained flawed, still unpredictable, yet Hamilton had found a way to make it work when it mattered most. If anything, this was proof that his brilliance could transcend the machinery beneath him.

Hamilton knew that while securing pole was a triumph, race day would be a different challenge. Over a single lap, he could extract magic from the W14, but across a full Grand Prix distance, its weaknesses would inevitably be exposed.

As the lights went out in Hungary Verstappen wasted no time in asserting Red Bull's superiority, launching past Hamilton into Turn 1 and disappearing into the distance. From there, the Dutchman controlled the race with ease, never looking threatened as he cruised to another dominant victory. Norris came home second ahead of Pérez, a real show of force from the resurgent McLaren team, who were now regular contenders.

Hamilton battled hard but ultimately could not hold onto a podium, slipping to fourth by the chequered flag behind Pérez. Meanwhile, Russell, who had been left with a mountain to climb after a difficult qualifying session, produced a determined drive from 18th to finish sixth.

Mercedes' weekend had been a mixed bag. The W14 had shown real promise over one lap, but its race-day struggles remained. While the upgrades had delivered more outright pace, the car still lacked the consistency and balance needed to take the fight to Red Bull when it mattered most.

The fastest lap times painted a revealing picture of the sheer magnitude of the gap to Red Bull in race trim. Verstappen's best lap stood at *1:20.504*, while Hamilton's was *1:21.601*—over a second adrift. Russell, in third, was another half a second behind Hamilton.

The reality was clear. On Saturdays, Hamilton could still create magic. But on Sundays, Red Bull was untouchable.

### A Challenging Weekend at Spa

The Belgian Grand Prix took place a week later at the legendary Spa-Francorchamps circuit, a track where the weather is as much a factor as the racing itself. True to form, the weekend delivered a mix of sunshine and rain showers, keeping the teams on their toes.

Mercedes arrived in Belgium with a fresh set of upgrades aimed at improving straight-line speed—an essential trait for Spa's long, high-speed sections. The W14 sported revisions to the sidepods, rear wing, and floor, with the most striking change coming at the rear of the sidepods. Gone was the previous smooth, gradual slope; in its place was a far more aggressive, sharply ramped design that plunged downwards towards the rear suspension and wing, earning comparisons to the curve of a banana. It was a bold shift in aerodynamics, one that suggested Mercedes were still searching for the right formula to unlock their car's full potential.

In qualifying, Hamilton secured fourth on the grid but was promoted to third due to Verstappen's grid penalty. Russell, meanwhile, struggled for outright pace and lined up eighth, a full eight-tenths behind pole-sitter Leclerc. Verstappen had been fastest in qualifying but started sixth due to a gearbox change penalty, while Pérez joined Leclerc on the front row.

Race day remained dry, and as the lights went out, Hamilton found himself in the thick of the action. Into La Source, he was caught in a three-wide battle, elbows out as he fought to hold position. Ahead, Leclerc fended off a charging Pérez, while the pack thundered downhill towards Eau Rouge. Further back, Verstappen, unfazed as ever, began slicing through the field with the ease of a man completing his weekly shop at the supermarket, picking off cars one by one—just like at the supermarket, he was about to check out.

Hamilton held firm in fourth, keeping within reach of the podium places but never quite having the pace to challenge Leclerc ahead. Russell endured a scrappy race, losing ground early but recovering well to finish sixth. At the front, the result was inevitable. Verstappen breezed past Pérez and then

Leclerc, taking yet another commanding victory for Red Bull. Pérez finished second, with Leclerc completing the podium.

By this stage of the season, Red Bull had an iron grip on Formula One, winning every single race. It was becoming less of a competition and more of a procession, with no signs of their dominance fading. They sat comfortably at the top of the Constructors' standings with 503 points, reinforcing the gulf between them and the rest of the field. Behind them, the battle for best of the rest had shifted. Mercedes, after trailing Aston Martin in the early part of the season, had now overtaken them for second place with 247 points. Aston had slipped to third on 196, while Ferrari remained close behind in fourth with 191.

Ferrari team boss Frédéric Vasseur was still working to bring the Scuderia back into serious contention, tweaking the team's operations and trying to instil consistency. One of his more immediate tasks was managing the dynamic between his two drivers. He sat down with Leclerc and Sainz, urging them to work together rather than against each other to maximise results for the team. The message was clear—less aggression, fewer risks, and a focus on simply getting both cars to the finish in one piece.

### The Unpredictability of Zandvoort

The Dutch Grand Prix was held at the end of August at the Zandvoort Circuit, a track that posed a unique challenge with its fast, flowing layout and steeply banked corners. Overcast skies and intermittent rain only added to the difficulty, making setup decisions even more critical. Mercedes, still searching for the optimal balance in their unpredictable W14, focused on refining their suspension to better handle the banking, hoping to find more consistency through the sweeping turns.

Upgrades were a common theme in the paddock. Aston Martin arrived with a revised floor and diffuser, aiming to recapture some of the early-season momentum they had lost in recent races. Ferrari, meanwhile, chose to leave the SF-23 untouched, with Frédéric Vasseur instead directing his attention towards optimising the team's operations rather than the car itself.

McLaren continued its aggressive development push, taking further inspiration from Red Bull's aerodynamic philosophy—particularly in how the beam wing and rear wing worked together. The beam wing, a smaller wing element mounted low between the rear wheels, played a crucial role in how airflow exited the car. It helped generate additional downforce at the rear while also managing turbulence, improving overall efficiency. By refining its interaction with the rear wing, McLaren aimed to enhance straight-line speed without sacrificing cornering stability. In simple terms, this was an attempt to give the car more rear grip through the turns while reducing drag on the straights—something Red Bull had perfected.

And then there was Red Bull. Already in a league of their own, they still found room for improvement, introducing yet another set of upgrades. Their ruthless pursuit of performance, despite being comfortably ahead of the competition, showed why they remained so dominant. For the rest of the grid, the challenge was not just catching up—it was keeping up.

Hamilton qualified 13$^{th}$ and expressed cautious optimism about the car's balance. As the drivers lined up for the formation lap, conditions were slightly damp but dry enough for slick tyres. However, as the race began, rain started falling, then intensified, testing the drivers to their limits.

It seemed inevitable that the field would pit at the end of the first lap, but more than half stayed out. Alonso was making strong progress, climbing to second and following Verstappen into the pits on lap two. Hamilton, caught in the mid-pack and dealing with both rain and heavy spray, wanted to pit but was instructed to stay out. By lap three, he made his frustration clear, remarking over the radio that they should have stopped as conditions had become treacherous. His race engineer

Bono encouraged him to stay out, gambling that the rain might ease and the track would dry quickly—a questionable call, given that Russell, in the sister Mercedes, was losing 20 seconds per lap to Verstappen.

The conditions remained marginal. Those who had switched to intermediates in the opening laps soon found themselves back in the pits as the track started to dry by Lap 11. Hamilton, having not pitted earlier, gradually moved up the order as others stopped.

With ten laps remaining, the rain returned, triggering another chaotic round of pit stops. On lap 63, Pérez slid off in the worsening conditions, allowing Alonso to move into second. Two laps later, the rain intensified, forcing Verstappen to pit from the lead for full wet tyres. The pit lane was drenched, and with cars starting to slide off track, the Virtual Safety Car was deployed before the race was ultimately red-flagged.

On the restart, Verstappen maintained control, leading the pack away with five laps remaining. Despite Red Bull's superiority, the Dutchman still had to stay on track in treacherous conditions to seal the win. Hamilton had recovered well, making up six places to finish sixth. Russell, battling Norris, had minor contact with the McLaren, forcing him to retire but he was still classified 17th.

Verstappen delighted the home crowd with yet another victory, while Alonso and Gasly rounded off the podium. The win marked Verstappen's ninth consecutive Grand Prix triumph, an astonishing feat that underscored Red Bull's dominance.

**Ferrari Thrills at Monza**

The 2023 Italian Grand Prix took place on 3 September at the historic Monza Circuit, renowned for its high-speed straights and passionate tifosi. The weekend unfolded under clear skies, with warm temperatures providing ideal racing conditions. Mercedes made minor changes to their rear wing to reduce drag, hoping to be more competitive on Monza's long straights.

Sainz electrified the home crowd by securing pole position with a time of 1:20.294, narrowly edging out Verstappen. Leclerc placed his Ferrari third on the grid, while Russell qualified fourth. Hamilton, struggling with an unstable rear end that sapped his confidence, managed only eighth in qualifying.

At the start, Sainz held his nerve, fending off intense pressure from Verstappen. For the first 14 laps, the Spaniard defended valiantly, keeping the Red Bull at bay. On Lap 6, Verstappen attempted an overtake on the outside into Turn 1, a move reminiscent of his past battles with Hamilton. However, this time he thought better of it and backed out, much to the delight of the Italian fans.

However, on Lap 15, a slight lock-up into Turn 1 allowed Verstappen the opportunity he had been waiting for. Seizing the moment, he powered around the outside of Sainz at Curva Grande at 190mph, the cars separated by mere inches. Once ahead, Verstappen demonstrated Red Bull's superior race pace, gradually extending his lead. Pérez followed him through, demoting Sainz further.

Behind Verstappen and Pérez, Leclerc closed in and overtook Sainz. This was like a red rag to a Spanish bull, and Sainz fought back as if his life depended on it. Any prior discussions with Vasseur about teamwork were cast aside. The tifosi held their breath as the scarlet cars swapped places, at times making light contact and even running off track.

An accident seemed inevitable, particularly on the last lap when Leclerc locked both front wheels and looked certain to plough into the back of his teammate. At the last moment, he managed to avoid contact by taking the escape road, allowing Sainz to retain third place.

Mercedes had a relatively uneventful race. Russell maintained his starting position to finish fifth, while Hamilton, despite starting eighth, climbed to sixth. However, his race was not without incident; a collision with McLaren's Piastri resulted in front wing damage for the rookie and a five-second penalty for Hamilton. Fortunately, he had built enough of a gap to the cars behind, ensuring the penalty did not impact his finishing position. Hamilton later apologised to Piastri for the incident.

Further down the field, Williams' Alexander Albon demonstrated impressive pace, securing seventh place and adding valuable points for the team. Norris and Alonso finished eighth and ninth respectively, while Bottas brought his Alfa Romeo home in tenth, rounding out the points-paying positions.

The race was notable for its clean nature, with minimal incidents and no safety car deployments. Verstappen's victory marked his record-breaking tenth consecutive win, surpassing Sebastian Vettel's previous record of nine. Red Bull continued their dominant streak, having won every race so far in the season.

In the post-race interviews, Sainz expressed satisfaction with his podium finish but acknowledged the challenge of keeping the Red Bulls at bay. Hamilton reflected on his collision with Piastri, accepting responsibility and expressing relief that both cars were able to continue.

As the European leg of the season concluded, teams began preparations for the upcoming races in Asia, with the Championship battle heavily favouring Verstappen and Red Bull. Ahead of the first Asian race in Singapore, several drivers intensified their training, focusing on high-aerobic work while wearing multiple layers of clothing to simulate the extreme heat and fluid loss they would face.

**The Gruelling Singapore Grand Prix**

The 2023 Singapore Grand Prix, held on 17 September at the Marina Bay Street Circuit, set the stage for a gruelling night race under the glow of the city's skyline. Renowned for its tight, twisting layout and relentless humidity, the circuit is one of the most physically demanding on the calendar, pushing both drivers and machines to their absolute limits.

Singapore is always a punishing environment, but this year the conditions were particularly brutal. Temperatures during practice climbed to 32°C, while humidity levels hovered between 80-90%, turning the race into an endurance test as much as a contest of speed. Inside the cockpit, temperatures soared to nearly 50°C, creating a sauna-like effect that drained drivers over the 62-lap slog.

For taller drivers, fluid loss can reach extreme levels, with some shedding as much as four to five kilograms of body weight over the course of the race. Dehydration is a serious risk, and failing to prepare properly can be catastrophic, leading to dizziness, muscle fatigue, and a dangerous drop in concentration. In a race where precision is everything, even the slightest lapse could mean the difference between victory and disaster.

Sainz secured pole position with a time of 1:30.984, again highlighting Ferrari's strength on street circuits. Mercedes showed good pace, with Russell qualifying second and Hamilton fifth. Most notably, Red Bull's dominance wavered. Both Verstappen and Pérez struggled, starting from 11th and 13th respectively. Verstappen, usually so assured, described the car as "undriveable." For the first time in 2023, the paddock sensed that Red Bull might not have it all their own way.

At the start, Sainz maintained his lead, while Leclerc, starting on soft tyres, jumped ahead of Russell into second place. Hamilton briefly moved up but had to relinquish positions after running wide at Turn 1. An early incident saw Yuki Tsunoda retire due to contact, leading to a Safety Car deployment when Logan Sargeant crashed, scattering debris on the track.

Mercedes opted for a gamble during a Virtual Safety Car period caused by Ocon's retirement on Lap 42. Both Russell and Hamilton pitted for fresh medium tyres, aiming to capitalise on the closing laps. This decision set up a tense finish, with the Mercedes duo rapidly closing in on the leading pair of Sainz and Norris.

In a thrilling conclusion, Sainz cleverly managed his pace, ensuring that Norris remained within DRS range to help defend against the charging Mercedes pair. Hamilton, faster than Russell in fourth, was eager to get past his teammate to mount a challenge for the lead. However, Russell held firm, but in doing so he appeared to start overdriving the car in his bid to maintain position.

The punishing conditions had taken their toll, pushing drivers to their physical and mental limits. For Russell, the challenge proved one step too far. On the very last lap, in a desperate push for second place, he clipped the wall at Turn 10 and crashed out, throwing away what would have been a hard-earned podium finish. Hamilton inherited third place, finishing behind Sainz and Norris.

Russell reflected on the crash with frustration, admitting that he had seen Norris brush the wall moments earlier and, in an instant, found himself in the barriers. He was left bewildered as to how it had happened, citing possible frustration or loss of concentration in the heat of the battle. It was the kind of unforced error easy to make when fatigued and showed that under the brutal conditions of Singapore, even the sharpest drivers were vulnerable.

While dehydration was not cited as a direct cause, the sheer physical toll of the race was undeniable. Wrestling a Formula One car around Marina Bay's relentless corners in extreme heat and humidity had always made the Singapore Grand Prix one of the most punishing events on the calendar. The 2023 edition was no exception, and for Russell, it ended in heartbreak just moments from the finish line.

Perhaps even more astonishing than his crash was the sight of a podium without a Red Bull driver. For the first time all season, they had failed to win, failing even to finish in the top three. It was a rare misstep—but one they would not make again for the rest of the year.

After stepping out of the car, Hamilton climbed onto the podium once more. However, observant viewers noted an unusual scene—the customary Mercedes team presence during the post-race celebrations was noticeably reduced. This deviation from tradition sparked speculation among fans and commentators.

Mercedes later clarified that the absence was not intentional. The team explained that due to logistical challenges and the immediate need to attend to Russell's last-lap crash, many team members were occupied, leading to a reduced presence during the podium ceremony. They emphasised their unwavering support for Hamilton, highlighting that as many team members as feasible were present to celebrate his achievement. The team reiterated that the apparent lack of celebration was a result of unforeseen circumstances rather than any reflection of their sentiments.

After the ceremony, Ferrari team principal Frédéric Vasseur sought out Hamilton, placing a reassuring arm around his former driver in a moment that did not go unnoticed.

**Red Bull Secures the Title in Japan**

The 2023 Japanese Grand Prix, held on 24 September at the iconic Suzuka International Racing Course, was a pivotal event in the Formula One calendar. The race solidified Red Bull Racing's dominance in the Constructors' Championship.

Ferrari arrived in Japan with upgrades, recognising the need to close the gap to Mercedes in the battle for second place in the standings. However, it was Verstappen who once again asserted his authority. Starting from pole, he delivered a commanding performance, leading the majority of the race and securing victory with a twenty-second margin over his nearest rival. This win marked his 13th of the season and played a crucial role in Red Bull clinching their sixth Constructors' Championship title.

For Mercedes, the race presented several challenges. Hamilton, starting from seventh on the grid, found himself in a chaotic opening sequence. A tense moment saw the two Ferraris, Pérez, and Hamilton running four abreast down to Turn 1. In the melee, Hamilton was forced onto the grass at 160mph as Pérez, himself being squeezed by the Ferrari, unintentionally pushed him wide. Remarkably, Hamilton managed to keep control of his car and later recovered to finish fifth. However, his race was not without controversy, as he aggressively passed Russell at Spoon, pushing his teammate wide. Russell's frustration was evident over the radio.

Russell's race did not improve from there. Running a one-stop strategy, he struggled with tyre degradation in the final stages and had to settle for seventh.

McLaren had reason to celebrate, with Norris and rookie Piastri completing the podium in second and third respectively, marking McLaren's first double podium since the 2021 Italian Grand Prix.

With the Constructors' Championship sealed, Red Bull had now shifted their focus to ensuring Verstappen wrapped up the Drivers' Championship in dominant fashion. For the rest of the grid, the fight for second place—both in the Constructors' and Drivers' standings—was still very much alive.

During the podium celebrations, Christian Horner joined Verstappen to celebrate another dominant victory. It was a poignant moment for Horner, who had been instrumental in bringing Adrian Newey to Red Bull—a move that had paved the way for their sustained success.

Following the Japanese Grand Prix, Verstappen tightened his grip on the Drivers' Championship, extending his tally to 400 points. Pérez remained second with 223, while Hamilton held onto third with 190. Red Bull's latest victory propelled them to an unassailable 623 points, officially sealing the 2023 Constructors' Championship with several races to spare. The battle for second, however, remained fiercely contested. Ferrari had begun chipping away at Mercedes' advantage, closing the gap to just twenty points. Hamilton's consistency was proving crucial in keeping Mercedes ahead, particularly as Russell struggled to match his teammate's results.

## Qatar: A Title Decided Under Brutal Conditions

The 2023 Qatar Grand Prix, held at the Lusail International Circuit on 8 October was run in extreme conditions. It didn't stop Verstappen however, who secured his third consecutive World Drivers' Championship title over the weekend and dominated the race, leading every lap. The McLaren duo of Piastri and Norris completed the podium, further demonstrating the team's resurgence.

The race commenced with immediate turmoil for Mercedes. Russell started second, with Hamilton third. As the lights went out, Hamilton made an excellent start and pulled alongside Russell, who was boxed in behind Verstappen. Sensing Hamilton's momentum, Russell aggressively jinked left, nearly making contact. Hamilton, determined to hold his position, attempted to go around the outside. However, as both cars turned into the corner, Hamilton clipped Russell's front wing, sending himself spinning into the gravel with three wheels, bringing his race to an abrupt end.

Hamilton later accepted full responsibility for the collision, acknowledging his misjudgement and apologising to Russell and the team. Despite the setback, Russell staged an impressive recovery drive, climbing from the back of the field to finish fourth.

The event was complicated by extreme heat and humidity, pushing drivers to their physical limits. Several competitors struggled to cope, with Ocon reportedly vomiting in his helmet mid-race and Sargeant – radioing his team to say he didn't feel well - forced to retire due to severe dehydration, having battled flu-like symptoms earlier in the week. The gruelling conditions sparked discussions about driver safety and whether racing in such extreme weather was sustainable.

As the cars pulled into Parc Fermé, the extent of the physical toll became evident. Several drivers strained to climb out of their cars, including Albon and Stroll. Stroll, upon finally extracting himself, staggered around unsteadily before leaning on his rear tyre, visibly drained. He then realised there was an ambulance next to him and in a daze walked over to it, leaning into the window and getting immediate medical attention. Albon, also disoriented, was assisted by his mechanics before being taken for evaluation by the medical team.

The Qatar Grand Prix had not only crowned Verstappen as a three-time World Champion but also raised pressing questions about the physical demands placed on drivers in extreme conditions.

Several drivers spoke candidly about the dangers they had faced. *Autosport* spoke to Norris, who was blunt in his assessment, stating that the conditions had pushed safety limits too far. He acknowledged that while drivers were always prepared for challenges, this race had crossed the line, citing concerns about competitors ending up in the medical centre or even passing out.

Verstappen, who looked absolutely exhausted despite his dominant victory, echoed Norris' concerns, describing the race as "definitely way too hot." The intense humidity and relentless heat had pushed drivers to their physical limits, reigniting discussions about safety protocols in extreme conditions.

The drama did not end with the conditions. In the aftermath, Hamilton received a reprimand and a fine for crossing the track after his first-lap collision, reinforcing the FIA's strict enforcement of safety regulations.

**A Landmark Victory for Verstappen in Austin**

The United States Grand Prix, held on 22 October at the Circuit of the Americas in Austin, saw Verstappen secure his 50th career victory. Despite starting from sixth on the grid and struggling with brake issues throughout the race, he once again demonstrated his dominance, fending off late challenges to take the win.

Mercedes arrived in Texas with more upgrades, introducing a completely redesigned floor as they sought to defend second place in the Constructors' Championship against a resurgent Ferrari. The most noticeable change was at the rear, where the floor now sat higher, creating a steeper incline towards the rear wing. It was an unexpected shift towards a high-rake concept—something Mercedes had largely avoided in previous seasons. The update was designed to improve airflow management and overall downforce, and early signs suggested it was working.

In qualifying, Leclerc once again demonstrated his one-lap brilliance, securing pole position, with Norris lining up alongside him on the front row. Encouragingly for Hamilton, he placed third, just a tenth off pole, suggesting that Mercedes' upgrades were delivering results.

On race day, Norris got a strong launch and immediately took the lead from Leclerc, while Hamilton, showing much-improved pace, soon passed the Ferrari to slot into second. By Lap 6 he was in pursuit of Norris, looking every bit like a genuine contender for victory.

As the race unfolded, Mercedes opted for a bold strategy. Initially planning a one-stop, Hamilton was switched to a two-stop late on, taking on fresh medium tyres while most of the front-runners remained on hards. The move gave him a significant pace advantage, and he rapidly carved his way back through the field, closing in on Verstappen in the final laps. However, despite reducing the gap to just two seconds, he ultimately ran out of time before the chequered flag.

On pure performance, it was one of Mercedes' strongest races of the season. Hamilton had beaten both Ferraris, both McLarens, and even Pérez in the second Red Bull. Or so he thought. Russell, meanwhile, finished seventh—solid but unremarkable compared to his teammate.

Four hours after the race, the Stewards dropped a bombshell. During post-race scrutineering, both Hamilton's and Leclerc's cars were found to have excessive wear on the skid blocks, leading to their disqualification. This handed second place to Norris, with Sainz inheriting third. Russell was promoted to fifth, salvaging more points for Mercedes, while Sargeant benefitted from the reshuffled order to score his first Formula One point—becoming the first American to do so since 1993.

It was a brutal outcome for Hamilton, who had delivered one of his finest performances of the year, only to see it wiped from the results sheet. Mercedes had shown genuine progress, but the technical infringement meant that, on paper, the result counted for nothing. Some drivers commented after the race that had all the cars been checked they would probably all have been disqualified due to an inability to alter the cars after the Sprint Race, the bumpy nature of the circuit, and the wear underneath the cars.

### Verstappen Conquers Mexico

A week later, on 29 October, the Autódromo Hermanos Rodríguez hosted the Mexico City Grand Prix. Verstappen continued his dominant form, clinching his 16th victory of the season and matching Alain Prost's career tally of 51 wins. Starting from third on the grid, Verstappen swiftly took the lead and controlled the race from the front.

Hamilton delivered a commendable performance, finishing second after starting from sixth. His teammate secured sixth place, contributing valuable points to Mercedes' Constructors' Championship campaign. Leclerc, who had started from pole position, completed the podium in third.

The race was marked by disappointment for local hero Pérez, who collided with Leclerc on the opening lap and was forced to retire. The incident left the home crowd deflated, as their hopes of seeing a Mexican driver on the podium were dashed within moments of the race beginning.

As the teams departed Mexico, Red Bull remained untouchable at the top with 731 points, while Mercedes sat in second with 371, just 22 points ahead of a charging Ferrari on 349. McLaren, continuing their late-season resurgence, held fourth with 256. With Ferrari closing in, Mercedes could not afford any lapses if they wanted to hold onto the runner-up spot in the Constructors' Championship.

### Chaos at Interlagos

The São Paulo Grand Prix at Interlagos on 5 November saw Verstappen claim his 17th victory of the season, further extending his record-breaking dominance. Starting from pole, he led every lap with typical efficiency, once again stamping Red Bull's superiority over the field.

Elsewhere, chaos reigned. Before the race had even begun, Leclerc's Ferrari dramatically speared off into the barriers on the formation lap, an immediate disaster for Ferrari's fight with Mercedes in the Constructors' Championship. Leclerc reported a sudden loss of hydraulics, shutting down the engine and leaving him helpless as he spun out before the race had even started. Team boss Frédéric Vasseur confirmed the failure, acknowledging the costly setback and emphasising the need to prevent similar issues in the future. Ferrari had been in a good position, but this was a missed opportunity just as they were closing in on Mercedes.

As if that were not enough, the start itself was utter carnage. Before Verstappen had even navigated the Senna S, yellow flags were waving after a multi-car pile-up on the main straight. The Safety Car was deployed, but with debris scattered across the track, the race was quickly red-flagged.

When the race eventually resumed, Mercedes once again found themselves battling the inconsistencies of their W14. Hamilton initially looked promising, running in third, but tyre degradation and a lack of outright pace saw him slip back, eventually finishing eighth. Russell's race ended even earlier, as his power unit failed on lap 57, forcing him to retire. Despite multiple upgrades throughout the season, the car remained unpredictable and difficult to extract performance from.

After the race, Hamilton summed up the ongoing struggles, acknowledging the car's inconsistency throughout a lap. While slow on the straights, it was still unstable in the corners, making it difficult to find a balanced setup. This lack of consistency had been a recurring issue since the introduction of the W13 in 2022, a car Hamilton had repeatedly said was fundamentally flawed. Despite his calls for a fresh approach in 2023, Mercedes had persisted with their concept, hoping iterative changes would bring them back to the front. But with just two races left in the season, the same problems Hamilton had highlighted over a year ago remained, leaving the team stuck in a frustrating cycle.

The race once again underlined Red Bull's absolute control of the 2023 season, with Verstappen seemingly in a class of his own. Behind them, the fight for second in the Constructors' Championship remained wide open, with Ferrari closing to within 20 points of Mercedes with two races to go.

Further back, McLaren's resurgence showed no signs of slowing. Norris delivered yet another outstanding performance, bringing his car home in second place, while Alonso wrung every last ounce of performance out of his Aston Martin to claim the final podium spot. With Aston

Martin now locked in a battle with McLaren for fourth in the standings, the fight in the midfield was fierce.

The final two races of the 2023 Formula One season—the Las Vegas Grand Prix and the Abu Dhabi Grand Prix—provided thrilling conclusions to a year dominated by Red Bull Racing and Max Verstappen. While the Championship titles were already decided, the battles in both the Drivers' and Constructors' standings remained intense, keeping fans on the edge of their seats until the very end.

**A Spectacle in Las Vegas**

On 18 November, Formula One made its long-awaited return to Las Vegas, with the spectacle unfolding under the dazzling lights of the Strip. Verstappen, starting second on the grid, wasted no time lunging at pole-sitter Leclerc into turn one. The move forced Leclerc wide, but rather than giving the position back, Verstappen pressed on, earning himself a five-second time penalty. It proved to be little more than an inconvenience. Even after serving the penalty, he comfortably reclaimed the lead and controlled the race to take his 18th victory of the season.

Leclerc, despite his early frustrations, kept his composure and secured second place, while Pérez finished third, ensuring Red Bull locked out the top two spots in the Drivers' Championship for the first time in their history.

The race was eventful. Norris suffered a heavy crash on lap three, bringing his race—and his streak of finishes—to an abrupt end. Later, Russell found himself in the wars again, colliding with Verstappen and scattering debris across the circuit. A Safety Car was deployed, and Russell was handed a five-second penalty for causing the incident. He eventually recovered to eighth, just behind his Mercedes teammate, who brought his car home in seventh.

As the teams left Las Vegas, the battle for second in the Constructors' Championship had reached its climax. Mercedes held a slim lead with 392 points, but Ferrari were breathing down their necks on 388. Everything would be decided in Abu Dhabi. Meanwhile, the fight for fourth was also heating up, with McLaren on 284 points and Aston Martin still in contention with 273.

The Drivers' Championship, while long since wrapped up by Verstappen—who had obliterated the field—still had unfinished business behind him. Pérez, despite trailing his teammate by a staggering 276 points, had secured second place, while Hamilton's consistency throughout the year had sealed him third. The real intrigue lay just behind, with Norris, Sainz, and Leclerc all within a handful of points of each other in a tense scrap for fourth heading into the final race.

**Mercedes Clinches Second in Abu Dhabi**

The season finale at Yas Marina Circuit on 26 November brought a familiar sight—Verstappen once again stamping his authority on the field. Starting from pole, he saw off an early challenge from Leclerc before settling into his rhythm, controlling the race from lights to flag. It was his 19th win from 22 races, an astonishing record in what had been a year of near-total domination.

But while the Drivers' Championship had long been decided, the battle for second in the Constructors' was going down to the wire. Mercedes and Ferrari were locked in a tight scrap, and the tension in both garages was undeniable after qualifying. Leclerc had put his Ferrari on the front row alongside Verstappen, while Russell lined up fourth for Mercedes. Hamilton, meanwhile, endured a frustrating session, wrestling with the unpredictable W14 and only managing 11th. However, with Sainz struggling even more—qualifying a lowly 16th—Mercedes had reason to be cautiously optimistic.

On race day, Hamilton made immediate progress, climbing three places at the start to put himself back in the fight. His position fluctuated through the pit stop phases as he and Sainz traded places, but by lap 47, he made a decisive move on the Ferrari to secure ninth place.

Russell, despite losing a position at the start, drove a composed race and ultimately claimed a crucial podium in third. His result proved vital, sealing second place in the Constructors' Championship for Mercedes by just three points over Ferrari.

Hamilton acknowledged the team effort but felt the team was not where it needed to be yet. He praised the collective effort at Mercedes but was clear that their ultimate goal remained competing for Championships, not just securing second place. It was a hard-fought end to a season of mixed fortunes. Mercedes had done just enough to keep Ferrari at bay, but their ambitions were far greater than finishing best of the rest.

Throughout the 2023 season, Mercedes battled the inconsistencies of the W14. Hamilton, with his wealth of experience, often extracted performances that belied the car's limitations, securing multiple podiums and consistently finishing in point-scoring positions. Russell, in his second season with the team, showed flashes of brilliance, including a crucial podium in Abu Dhabi. However, a few retirements and on-track incidents affected his overall points tally.

As Mercedes turned their focus to 2024, the challenge remained the same - closing the gap to Red Bull and returning to Championship contention. Whether they could do it remained to be seen, but one thing was certain: finishing second would never be enough.

Hamilton and Russell had delivered contrasting performances. Hamilton secured third place in the Drivers' Championship with 234 points, while Russell finished eighth with 175. Hamilton achieved six podium finishes, including second places in Australia, Spain, and Mexico, and recorded four fastest laps. Russell, meanwhile, attained two podiums and one fastest lap over the course of the season.

Hamilton's consistent high finishes proved crucial in Mercedes' battle with Ferrari, ultimately securing second place in the Constructors' Championship by just three points. Given Ferrari's superior one-lap pace for much of the season, Hamilton had been the difference-maker. His relentless drive had not gone unnoticed within the Ferrari camp.

When reflecting on the standout moment of the year, Hamilton immediately pointed to his pole position in Hungary. It had been a rare moment of optimism, as the performance had briefly disrupted Red Bull's dominance, offering hope that continued effort could eventually close the gap.

The season had left its mark on Hamilton. Throughout 2022, he had urged Mercedes to abandon the flawed W13 concept and start fresh, but without the influence of Niki Lauda, his concerns had not been acted upon. Instead, he had been forced to battle with the W14—another compromised machine. The cockpit's position affected the feel for the rear end, the car retained an outdated low-rake philosophy, and its balance shifted unpredictably from one corner to the next. None of these characteristics allowed a driver—let alone a seven-time World Champion—to perform at their best.

By the end of the year, Hamilton was physically and emotionally drained, stretched to his limits after another season of wrestling a car that was incapable of winning. The relentless length of the calendar, coupled with external pressures, had made maintaining a positive mindset increasingly difficult.

Perhaps the most telling insight into his frustrations came when he reflected on how his concerns about the car's direction had been dismissed by the team. Hamilton warned the team that without any changes they would continue down the wrong path, only to be told they knew what they were doing and that he was wrong. It had been a defining moment, one that made it clear Mercedes was not listening. And when the time came to consider his future, that moment would undoubtedly influence his decision.

With the Formula One season complete, Hamilton shifted his focus to his passions outside racing. In early December, he made a striking appearance at the British Fashion Awards at the Royal Albert Hall in London, wearing a bold Wales Bonner outfit. His reputation as a trendsetter in fashion remained strong, as he continued to push boundaries and influence the industry with his distinctive style.

Beyond fashion, Hamilton remained deeply committed to his philanthropic efforts and advocacy for diversity and inclusion. He continued to support various charitable initiatives and used his platform to drive positive change, both within and beyond motorsport. While 2023 had been a physically and emotionally demanding year on track, off it, Hamilton remained as engaged and influential as ever.

Hamilton continued to lean on his external interests to maintain balance amidst his demanding schedule. But soon, life was set to become even more hectic.

# Still I Rise: The Mercedes Finale

As the 2024 season unfolded, changes were already reshaping the world of Formula One. The winter break had been anything but quiet, with several key developments influencing the competitive landscape before a single car had turned a wheel in anger.

One of the biggest stories came from Haas, where long-time team principal Guenther Steiner parted ways with the American outfit after a decade at the helm. Known for his charismatic presence, Steiner had become a fan favourite, but Haas opted for a new direction, promoting Ayao Komatsu, their Director of Engineering, to lead the team into the future.

Elsewhere, McLaren unveiled a striking new livery, blending their traditional papaya with anthracite and chrome—a design that paid homage to their past while incorporating modern branding influences. The team hoped this fresh look would be matched by strong on-track performance as they aimed to build on the momentum of the previous season.

Off the grid, the debate over Formula One's expansion continued. Andretti Autosport, backed by General Motors (GM), reignited its bid to enter the sport, pushing for a place on the grid by 2026. Having previously faced rejection, the team remained determined, but with existing teams, the FIA, and Liberty Media all engaged in political wrangling, the prospect of an 11th team remained uncertain. There was speculation that GM would need to take control of the process in order for things to move forward.

Meanwhile, preparations for the new season were in full swing. Mercedes, determined to put two difficult years behind them, hinted that the W15 represented a step forward. Early feedback from within the team was cautiously optimistic, with Hamilton describing aspects of their pre-season work as some of the strongest he had seen in recent years. There was hope that the mistakes of the W13 and W14 had finally been left behind. It was the calm before the storm.

From the outside, Mercedes had projected confidence heading into 2024. The W15, they claimed, was a step forward, a car designed to finally free them from the flawed concepts that had plagued them since 2022. Hamilton, always the professional, spoke positively about the team's preparation. But beneath the surface, tensions remained.

The frustrations that had simmered throughout 2023 had never truly gone away. Hamilton had spent much of the previous season battling a car that still carried the DNA of its predecessors—its cockpit positioned too far forward, its balance unpredictable, its weaknesses all too familiar. He had warned the team, urged them to abandon their concept and start fresh in 2022, but his concerns had been dismissed. The sentiment from within the team had been clear: they believed they knew best. It was a moment that had stuck with him.

On the other side of the paddock, Ferrari was evolving. Frédéric Vasseur had wasted no time in restructuring the Scuderia, making the kind of decisive moves that signalled a team determined to return to the front. His no-nonsense approach, honed during his years at Sauber and in junior formulas, was reshaping Maranello into a more efficient and less chaotic operation. The days of unforced errors and internal divisions appeared to be numbered.

Crucially, Vasseur and Hamilton already shared a strong relationship. The Frenchman had played a key role in Hamilton's early career, guiding him through junior formulas and into Formula One. There was a level of trust, a shared understanding—something Hamilton had once felt at Mercedes, but which had slowly eroded, particularly since the passing of Niki Lauda in 2019. Lauda had been more than just a Mercedes executive; he had been a mentor, an ally, and the key figure who had convinced Hamilton to leave McLaren for Mercedes. Without him, Hamilton no longer had the same advocate at the very top of the team, and the shift in dynamic had become increasingly evident.

As pre-season testing approached, Hamilton was weighing up his future. He had always maintained that he wanted to finish his career at Mercedes, but the events of the past two seasons had tested that resolve. The team had stopped listening. Ferrari, on the other hand, was listening. The pieces were falling into place, and before the first race of the season, Formula One was about to witness one of the biggest driver moves in history.

In early 2024, speculation about Hamilton's future intensified. Whispers of a potential move to Ferrari began circulating in mid-January, catching many by surprise. The first public indication of this seismic shift reportedly came through an unexpected channel—Carlos Sainz Sr., father of then-Ferrari driver Carlos Sainz Jr. According to insiders, Sainz Sr. had informed Mercedes team principal Toto Wolff about Hamilton's impending switch to Ferrari two weeks before the official announcement.

The timing of the leak raised questions, with some suggesting that Wolff himself may have strategically disclosed the information. A former driver speculated that the leak had been an attempt to pre-empt Ferrari's announcement, disrupting their narrative and gaining a psychological advantage. The theory was that by bringing the news to light prematurely, Mercedes could control the narrative, position themselves as proactive rather than reactive, manage sponsor expectations, and possibly unsettle Ferrari's internal dynamics.

The official confirmation of Hamilton's move to Ferrari came on 1 February 2024, marking the end of an era at Mercedes and the beginning of a new chapter for both the driver and the Italian team.

For Mercedes, the announcement was more than a change in personnel—it marked the departure of the driver who had been instrumental in delivering six Drivers' Championships and playing a central role in their record-breaking run of eight consecutive Constructors' titles. Losing Hamilton wasn't just about lap times and podiums; it was the loss of a leader, a symbol of resilience, and the driving force behind an era of unprecedented dominance.

As the dust settled, the focus shifted to what lay ahead. Hamilton would now embark on a new challenge at Ferrari, a team that had spent years searching for the final piece of the puzzle in their quest for a title. Meanwhile, Mercedes faced an uncertain future—one without the driver who had defined their most successful era.

The 2024 season had barely begun, but Formula One had already been shaken to its core.

Toto Wolff, the man who had helped build Mercedes into a dominant force, now faced one of the most significant challenges of his tenure. While he maintained a diplomatic front in public, his comments in the aftermath of Hamilton's departure hinted at something deeper—whether it was frustration, disbelief, or even a sense of betrayal. He admitted that he had only learned of Hamilton's decision shortly before it was made public, suggesting that discussions with Ferrari had been kept highly confidential. It was an unusual situation for Wolff, who had always been in control, shaping storylines and playing the long game. Now, for the first time in his Mercedes tenure, he had been blindsided.

Reports suggested that rather than allowing Ferrari to unveil their move on their own terms, Mercedes had forced the story out first, prompting Ferrari to accelerate their announcement. If true, this was a typical strategic move—an attempt to disrupt Ferrari's momentum and ensure Mercedes dictated at least part of the story.

But beyond the political manoeuvring, one undeniable truth remained: Hamilton had chosen to leave. And it wasn't just about Ferrari offering him a fresh challenge—it was also about what he was leaving behind. The trust and alignment that had once defined the Hamilton-Mercedes partnership had eroded. Hamilton had spent much of 2022 and 2023 urging the team to abandon their flawed car concept, only to be ignored. The team had insisted that they knew best, dismissing his concerns. Now, he had given his answer.

The emotional weight of losing Hamilton was likely compounded by everything Wolff had endured since 2021. The controversial Abu Dhabi finale had left deep scars, and for much of 2022, Wolff had struggled to move on, visibly frustrated as Mercedes failed to recover. But through it all, Hamilton had remained loyal. He had put faith in the team, trusted their process, and believed they would return to winning ways. Now, two years later, he had reached his breaking point.

Hamilton had always admired Ferrari—the history, the legacy, the passion of the tifosi. Over the years, he had spoken fondly of the team but had remained unwaveringly committed to Mercedes. Even when speculation of Ferrari's interest had surfaced in the past, he had stayed put, trusting that Mercedes would always provide the best opportunity to win.

If anything, Ferrari's allure had been something he had resisted rather than actively pursued. It had always been a dream, but not necessarily the plan. He had built something special at Mercedes, a partnership that had redefined dominance in Formula One. His long-standing loyalty had been rooted in trust—the belief that Mercedes would listen, adapt, and continue to deliver.

But loyalty has its limits. Mercedes had tested those limits by ignoring him. They had dismissed his concerns, persisted with a failing concept, and expected him to simply fall in line. This wasn't about money, prestige, or even Ferrari's mystique—it was about respect. For the first time, Hamilton had felt unheard at Mercedes, and that, more than anything, made the decision to leave easier.

In the end, it was Mercedes that had pushed him toward Ferrari. Not deliberately, not maliciously, but through their own stubbornness. The dream of driving in Ferrari red had always been there, lingering in the background. But it was Mercedes' refusal to change that finally turned it into reality.

Wolff now faced a new challenge. For the first time since taking charge at Mercedes, the team would enter a season without Lewis Hamilton in twelve months' time. The unshakeable fortress he had built was beginning to show cracks. The man who had delivered so much success was finally walking away, and Mercedes had no one to blame but themselves.

Hamilton spoke with excitement and emotion about his decision to join Ferrari, reflecting on both his long journey with Mercedes and the new chapter ahead. He described himself as incredibly fortunate, acknowledging that after everything he had achieved with Mercedes, he now had the opportunity to fulfil another childhood dream.

He recognised the deep connection he had with Mercedes, a partnership that had spanned 26 years, from his junior career to his record-breaking success in Formula One. Reflecting on their achievements, he expressed pride in what they had built together and appreciation for the dedication of those he had worked alongside. He also spoke about Wolff's role, valuing both his leadership and their long-standing friendship. Their time together had delivered championships, shattered records, and cemented one of the most successful driver-team partnerships in the sport's history.

There was also a heartfelt nod to Niki Lauda, the man who had convinced him to move to Mercedes in the first place. Hamilton acknowledged the profound impact Lauda had on his career and admitted that he still missed his presence every day.

Hamilton's words reflected both gratitude for the past and anticipation for the future—a driver ready to embark on one of the most significant moves in Formula One history.

Frédéric Vasseur outlined the reasoning behind Ferrari's decision to bring Hamilton to Maranello and the impact his arrival would have on the team. According to him, convincing Hamilton to join had not been a difficult task, as Ferrari's improving form in 2023 had played a significant role in the discussions. He suggested that Ferrari's performance, which had surpassed Mercedes in race victories that season, helped make the project an appealing one. The move, however, had likely been on Hamilton and Vasseur's minds for much longer, as they had discussed the possibility decades earlier when Hamilton was in the junior formula.

Vasseur also acknowledged that Mercedes had undergone a shift in dynamics toward the latter stages of Hamilton's time with the team and made it clear that Ferrari would need to integrate him in its own way. He emphasised the importance of creating the right working environment, rather than attempting to replicate what had been done at Mercedes, particularly as the atmosphere within the team had changed in recent years. His remarks hinted at a deeper understanding of why Hamilton had ultimately chosen to leave—a recognition that Mercedes, once a well-oiled machine, had not only lost some of its cohesion but had also stopped fully listening to its most successful driver. At Ferrari, the approach would be to build a new chapter, not to recreate an old one.

Many within the Formula One world shared their thoughts on Hamilton's move to Ferrari. Some saw it as a momentous shift for the sport, while others questioned how successful the transition would be.

One commentator described the move as a highly anticipated storyline, noting that the combination of Hamilton and Leclerc in Ferrari red would add a new dynamic to the grid. Others pointed out that Hamilton's unwavering loyalty to Mercedes in previous years made the decision even more significant.

However, not everyone viewed the move as a guaranteed success. Some former drivers warned that differences in driving style between Hamilton and Leclerc could pose challenges in car development and team dynamics. Others questioned whether Ferrari, despite making strides forward, would have the machinery to allow Hamilton to fight for another championship. While acknowledging Hamilton's immense ability, some argued that success at Ferrari would still be dependent on the competitiveness of the car, overlooking the fact that Hamilton had frequently outperformed expectations and beaten world-class teammates in equal machinery.

As news of Hamilton's move to Ferrari spread, discussions emerged over whether he would still be performing at his peak when he joined the team at 40 years old in 2025. Felipe Massa, who raced for Ferrari from 2006 to 2013, acknowledged Hamilton's immense talent and stated that if he were making the decision as a team boss, he would have no hesitation in signing him. However, he also suggested that age could be a factor worth considering, questioning whether Hamilton would be able to sustain the same level of performance over the coming years.

Massa's concerns weren't entirely without merit. Formula One is a physically demanding sport, and no driver can completely escape the effects of aging. Reflexes slow, recovery times lengthen, and adapting to new machinery becomes more challenging. Massa pointed to Michael Schumacher's return to Formula One in 2010 as a cautionary tale—Schumacher, despite his legendary status, struggled to match Nico Rosberg at Mercedes and never added to his record 91 wins.

However, concerns about Hamilton's age did not take into account the differences in his circumstances. While some drivers had struggled later in their careers, Hamilton had maintained peak physical fitness and had remained at the sharp end of the grid throughout his time in the sport. Unlike Schumacher, who had taken a three-year break from racing before his return, Hamilton had continuously competed at the highest level, securing podiums and delivering strong performances even as Red Bull dominated in 2023 and 2024.

Massa's perspective may have been influenced by his own experiences in elite motorsport. While he rightly acknowledged the challenges of aging in Formula One, his outlook was shaped by the serious head injury he suffered in 2009, when the spring from Barrichello's Brawn struck his helmet at high speed during qualifying for the Hungarian Grand Prix. His return to racing in 2010 was a remarkable achievement, but research has indicated that those who experience significant concussions or traumatic brain injuries often face longer recovery times, increased fatigue, and reduced exercise tolerance compared to those without such injuries. While Massa remained a fit and competitive driver, the impact of his recovery may have led to a more cautious view on how age affects performance at the highest level.

Hamilton, by contrast, had maintained peak physical fitness throughout his career and had not taken a multi-year break from the sport, as seen with some former champions. He had remained at the sharp end of the grid well into his late 30s, continuing to claim podiums and battle at the front. In 2023 he had been Mercedes' most consistent performer, securing third place in the Drivers' Championship in a season where Red Bull's dominance made race victories nearly impossible, and carrying the team to second in the Constructors'. Teammate Russell meanwhile, had languished in eighth.

Schumacher's struggles in his comeback were not solely due to age. By the time he returned, Formula One had undergone significant technical changes—refuelling had been banned, Bridgestone had been replaced by Pirelli, and the high-downforce machines of the 2000s had been replaced by more delicate, tyre-sensitive cars that required a different driving approach. Schumacher, who had always thrived with a strong front end and aggressive turn-in, found that the characteristics of the new era did not suit his natural style.

Even so, his final season in 2012 painted a closer picture than results alone suggested. In races where both Mercedes cars finished, Schumacher had a 7-3 advantage over Nico Rosberg. In qualifying, Rosberg edged him 11-9, but Schumacher was often within a tenth of a second. Had he been in a stronger car, free of reliability issues, his comeback might have been judged very differently.

This is where Hamilton's situation is entirely different. While Massa's concerns about aging in motorsport are understandable, they do not fully consider Hamilton's sustained level of performance, his continued race-winning ability, and the fact that, unlike Schumacher, he is not returning from an extended absence. Instead, he is moving to a team that has spent years restructuring under Frédéric Vasseur, positioning itself for future success.

If anything, Massa's comments—though well-intentioned—highlight how Ferrari, Mercedes, and even the sport itself may be underestimating Hamilton. As history has shown, when people doubt him, he tends to prove them wrong.

But while Ferrari was the future, Hamilton remained a Mercedes driver for the 2024 season. A competitor to his core, there was no intention of simply seeing out his final year. He would give everything, pushing to make his last campaign with the Silver Arrows count. Before stepping into Ferrari red, there was still unfinished business in Mercedes black.

## Team Updates for 2024

As the 2024 Formula One season approached, teams revealed their latest challengers, with discussions about Hamilton's move still dominating the paddock. The February car launches provided the first insights into the design philosophies and technical innovations that teams hoped would deliver a competitive edge.

Ferrari launched the SF-24 on February 13, 2024, unveiling a car designed with a greater focus on aerodynamic efficiency and power unit performance. Modifications to the front wing and nose aimed to optimise airflow, while rear suspension updates were introduced to improve tyre management and traction. These enhancements reflected Ferrari's determination to mount a serious challenge for both the Drivers' and Constructors' Championships.

The SF-24 also debuted a slight livery change, incorporating subtle yellow and white accents to break from the traditional all-red design. Charles Leclerc and Carlos Sainz entered their third season together, though Sainz now faced an uncertain future following the announcement of Hamilton's arrival in 2025.

Mercedes introduced the W15 E Performance on February 14, 2024, at Silverstone, marking a decisive shift after two difficult seasons. After securing second place in the 2023 Constructors' Championship, the team opted for a substantial overhaul rather than an incremental update. The W15 retained its striking black livery, primarily bare carbon fibre to minimise weight, but the most crucial changes lay beneath the surface.

One of the most significant updates was a complete revision of the front suspension, transitioning from a pull-rod to a push-rod configuration to improve handling and stability. The sidepods were also reshaped, continuing the departure from the zero-sidepod concept that had hindered Mercedes in previous seasons. However, perhaps the most crucial alteration was the repositioning of the cockpit. After repeated concerns raised by Hamilton throughout 2022 and 2023, the team finally moved the driving position roughly 10cm further back, allowing for better control over the car's rear—a fundamental issue that had previously prevented him from pushing with confidence.

Hamilton acknowledged that the previous car's unpredictability had limited his ability to extract its full potential. With the W15 incorporating key changes he had requested for over a year, he expressed optimism that both he and George Russell could take full advantage. He highlighted that comfort and stability in the car were essential for maximising performance, adding that a more predictable machine would allow the drivers to extract both their own potential and that of the car itself.

Whether these changes would be enough to challenge Red Bull remained uncertain, but for the first time in years, Mercedes had fully acknowledged—and acted upon—some of Hamilton's concerns.

McLaren had made a significant investment in late 2023 with the introduction of a state-of-the-art wind tunnel at their Woking headquarters. This upgrade marked a crucial step forward, as the team had previously relied on Toyota's wind tunnel in Germany, which often introduced logistical delays and inconsistencies between simulation data and on-track performance. The new facility allowed McLaren to develop their first fully in-house car under the current regulations, addressing previous limitations in correlation.

On February 14, 2024, McLaren revealed the MCL38 at their headquarters. The car featured a striking black and papaya orange livery, with multicoloured wheel inserts reflecting their partnership with Google.

Technically, the MCL38 focused on aerodynamic refinement and weight reduction. Key developments included a revised floor and diffuser to optimise ground effect, along with a slimmer rear end to enhance airflow to the rear wing. These upgrades were aimed at building on the team's strong momentum from the previous season and closing the gap to the front-runners.

At the launch, Lando Norris shared insights into his preparations for testing, explaining that he had spent the past few weeks back at the MTC, putting in significant work on the simulator with his engineering team to ensure they were fully prepared ahead of the following week.

Norris remained the team leader alongside Oscar Piastri, who had delivered an impressive rookie season in 2023 and was eager to build on his strong performances. Encouragingly for McLaren, early testing results suggested that their new wind tunnel was delivering accurate and reliable real-world data, reinforcing their optimism for the season ahead.

Red Bull unveiled the RB20 on February 15, 2024. Building on the dominance of its predecessor, the RB20 featured subtle but significant aerodynamic refinements. The team focused on refining airflow management around the sidepods and rear wing, aiming to enhance downforce and overall stability. The livery remained consistent with Red Bull's signature colours, symbolising continuity and confidence in their design evolution. Max Verstappen and Sergio Pérez continued their partnership for a fourth season, with Verstappen firmly established as the team's leading driver.

Formerly known as AlphaTauri, the rebranded Visa Cash App RB team unveiled their VCARB 01 in early February 2024 during a launch event in Las Vegas. The car bore similarities to Red Bull Racing's previous models, incorporating a pull-rod front suspension and redesigned sidepods to enhance aerodynamic performance. Despite criticisms suggesting it was a replica of Red Bull's earlier cars, Team Principal Laurent Mekies emphasized that the VCARB 01 was a distinct entity, with shared components not necessarily translating to performance parity.

The rebranded team retained Daniel Ricciardo and Yuki Tsunoda, with both drivers vying for potential future promotion to Red Bull.

Aston Martin kept faith in their driver lineup, with Fernando Alonso and Lance Stroll continuing for another season. While Alonso had delivered standout performances, Stroll faced increasing scrutiny over his.

Elsewhere on the grid, the pairings remained the same at Alpine, Kick Sauber, Haas and Williams. At Williams James

Vowles continued to restructure the team, hoping to take another step forward.

### Pre-Season Testing

Pre-season testing for the 2024 Formula One season took place at the Bahrain International Circuit in Sakhir from 21st to 23rd February. Teams and drivers gathered under clear skies and warm temperatures, eager to assess their new machinery ahead of the season opener.

Mercedes entered the test with their W15 E Performance, aiming to address the challenges faced in the previous season. Throughout the three days, the team focused on reliability and data collection, completing long stints.

While they didn't top the timesheets, both Hamilton and Russell expressed some optimism. Hamilton felt Mercedes had taken a useful step in the right direction, noting that the new car was clearly an improvement and much nicer to drive. While there was still progress to be made, he saw it as a good foundation to build on.

Russell was also positive about the test and the new car, saying they had a strong footing to work from, with plenty of laps completed and significant data to analyse. It had been a productive first day.

Ferrari's SF-24 had evolutionary changes aimed at building upon their previous successes. The team demonstrated strong pace in testing, with Carlos Sainz setting the fastest time on the second day and Charles Leclerc leading on the final day. This performance indicated that Ferrari had made strides in both speed and consistency. Leclerc expressed confidence in the team's progress and their preparations for the upcoming season.

Red Bull's RB20 continued the team's tradition of strong performance. Verstappen led the opening day of testing, setting a benchmark that others struggled to match. Despite their dominant display, the team remained cautious, with Verstappen stressing the importance of understanding the car's behaviour under various conditions. The RB20's reliability and pace suggested that Red Bull would once again be a formidable contender.

McLaren faced a challenging test session. Lando Norris managed to secure the second-fastest time on the first day, but he was over a second behind Verstappen, with the team acknowledging a significant gap to the Red Bull of the Dutchman. CEO Zak Brown noted that while Red Bull appeared to be in a league of their own, McLaren was focused on closing the gap to Ferrari and other competitors. Reliability issues and setup challenges indicated that there was considerable work ahead for the Woking-based outfit.

The testing period was relatively smooth, with teams completing extensive mileage. However, a few incidents occurred. On the final day, a drain cover issue led to Pérez's Red Bull sustaining some damage, causing a brief halt in proceedings. Additionally, Williams experienced a stoppage on track, highlighting that even minor issues could impact testing programmes.

Daniel Ricciardo found himself near the bottom of the timesheets on the final day of testing in the RB. Once the golden boy of Red Bull, having soundly beaten Vettel, and the only teammate to have genuinely challenged Verstappen over multiple seasons, the Australian now seemed a shadow of his former self. The raw speed and fearless overtaking that once defined him appeared to have faded, raising questions about whether he could rediscover his past form in 2024.

As pre-season testing concluded, teams left Bahrain with valuable data and insights. While lap times in testing are not always indicative of true performance, the sessions provided a glimpse into the competitive order. Red Bull and Ferrari appeared strong, Mercedes showed potential improvements, and McLaren faced challenges to overcome. The stage was set for an exciting season opener, with fans eagerly anticipating how the changes would pan out.

The 2024 Formula Oneturn season commenced with two thrilling races in the Middle East, beginning under the floodlights of Bahrain and swiftly moving to the high-speed streets of Saudi Arabia.

**Bahrain Grand Prix**

The Bahrain International Circuit in Sakhir hosted the season opener on Saturday, 2nd March 2024, marking the 20th anniversary of the Grand Prix. Notably, the race was held on a Saturday to ensure a week's gap before the subsequent Saudi Arabian Grand Prix, which had been adjusted to avoid coinciding with the start of Ramadan. The event attracted a record attendance of 100,000 spectators, eager to witness the dawn of a new racing year.

In the lead-up to the race several teams introduced significant updates. Mercedes focused on engine cooling and Energy Recovery System (ERS) enhancements, aiming to rectify issues from the previous season. Ferrari introduced new aerodynamic parts, while McLaren debuted a revised suspension system to improve tyre management.

Qualifying sessions saw reigning World Champion Verstappen in his Red Bull secure pole position with a lap time of 1:29.179. He was closely followed by Ferrari's Charles Leclerc and Mercedes' George Russell, setting the stage for a fight at the front.

Lewis Hamilton admitted his qualifying performance had been below his usual standards, but he remained optimistic about the race and the season in general, believing the W15E was a material improvement over previous seasons.

As the sun set, the race commenced under clear skies. Verstappen demonstrated his dominance by leading every lap, clinching victory and recording the fastest lap. His teammate,

Pérez took second place, ensuring a strong start for Red Bull. Ferrari's Carlos Sainz Jr. completed the podium, finishing only a few seconds behind Pérez, hinting at the Scuderia's potential for the season. Verstappen, however, had been well clear at the front, finishing with a commanding 22-second margin over his teammate. Charles Leclerc managed a commendable fourth place despite grappling with brake temperature discrepancies throughout the race.

The Mercedes pair of Russell and Hamilton were the best part of 45-50 seconds adrift in fifth and seventh at the flag, struggling with engine cooling and ERS battery issues, leaving the team with plenty of work to do at Brackley.

McLaren's Lando Norris and rookie Oscar Piastri impressed by securing sixth and eighth places. Remarkably, all 20 cars completed the race, marking the first season opener in Formula One history without any retirements.

**Saudi Arabian Grand Prix**

A few days later, on Wednesday, the Formula One circus arrived in Jeddah for the Saudi Arabian Grand Prix, gearing up for the race, which would be held a day earlier than usual on Saturday, 9th March, in respect of the start of Ramadan. The Jeddah Corniche Circuit, with its high-speed layout and unforgiving walls, promised another ding-dong battle.

The drama began days before a single lap had even been turned. Ferrari's scheduled media duties on Wednesday were thrown into disarray when Carlos Sainz, feeling unwell, withdrew at the last minute and returned to the team hotel. As the first two free practice sessions got underway on Thursday, Sainz attempted to push through, but by the end of the day, he admitted it had been one of the toughest days he had ever experienced in a Formula One car. The discomfort only worsened overnight, and by Friday morning, it became clear that something was seriously wrong. Doctors diagnosed him with appendicitis, and he was immediately sent to hospital for surgery.

With just hours to go before the final practice session, Ferrari team principal Frédéric Vasseur made a call that would change one young driver's career. Oliver Bearman, a member of the Ferrari Driver Academy and a competitor in Formula 2, was told at around 2pm that he would be making his Formula One debut that afternoon. The British teenager had driven a Formula One car before, having taken part in a couple of free practice sessions with Haas in 2023, but being thrown into a grand prix weekend with no preparation was another level entirely.

Bearman took to the track in Free Practice 3 and delivered an assured performance, setting a 1:29.306 to finish the session in tenth place—a highly respectable effort given the challenge of adapting to an Formula One car on one of the sport's most demanding circuits.

Meanwhile, several teams had brought even more upgrades following the season opener in Bahrain. Aston Martin introduced further aerodynamic refinements in a bid to close the gap to the front-runners, while Williams continued their work on optimising power unit performance.

As the Jeddah floodlights illuminated the circuit, qualifying began with a familiar result—Max Verstappen continuing his dominance, securing pole position with a time of 1:27.472. Charles Leclerc once again demonstrated his one-lap prowess, lining up alongside him on the front row, while the upgraded Aston Martin proved its worth, with Fernando Alonso claiming fourth next to Sergio Pérez.

For Ferrari, it had already been a weekend of disruption, yet Oliver Bearman continued to handle the pressure superbly. On his Formula One qualifying debut, the 18-year-old impressed, narrowly missing out on Q3 by less than a tenth of a second to take 11th on the grid. It was evidence to his competitive mindset that he was frustrated not to have progressed further.

Mercedes, meanwhile, found themselves firmly in no man's land. Hamilton and Russell qualified seventh and eighth, both around a second adrift of Verstappen's pole time. It was an ominous sign of the challenges ahead, with Red Bull seemingly in a different league once again.

When the lights went out on race day, Verstappen made a clean getaway, while behind him, Pérez and Leclerc went wheel-to-wheel for several corners before the Ferrari driver asserted himself into second place. Further back, Russell and Hamilton settled into a long evening in seventh and eighth, while Bearman held his starting position, calmly getting a feel for race conditions in the opening laps.

The race's first major incident came on Lap 6 when Lance Stroll misjudged Turn 22, clipping the inside barrier with his left front wheel. The Aston Martin was flung across the track, hitting the outside wall before coming to a halt. Bearman, running just behind Yuki Tsunoda's in the RB, kept his composure and moved up into the points-paying positions in tenth.

With Stroll's car stranded and the Canadian facing a long walk back, the Safety Car was deployed. The field scrambled into the pits, triggering a flurry of tactical decisions as teams looked to capitalise on the neutralised race conditions.

As the race unfolded, Verstappen never looked in danger, expertly managing his tyres and pace to secure his second consecutive win of the season. Perez followed his teammate home for a Red Bull 1-2, ensuring Red Bull's stronghold in the early championship battle remained intact. Leclerc chased hard but ultimately had to settle for third, further proving Ferrari's improvements over the winter.

Mercedes, despite showing marginal improvement in race trim, still found themselves lacking the pace to challenge the frontrunners. Hamilton and Russell finished sixth and ninth, a reality check for the Brackley team. McLaren continued their solid start to the season, with both Norris and Piastri finishing in the points, further confirming their upward trajectory.

For Bearman, it was a debut to be proud of. Holding his nerve and bringing the Ferrari home in seventh place, he became the third-youngest points scorer in Formula One history. It was a drive that earned him respect up and down the paddock, and if nothing else, he had ensured that his name would be in discussions for a full-time seat in the future.

With two races completed, Red Bull's dominance remained unchallenged. However, Ferrari and McLaren had begun to show glimpses of real speed and were looking more threatening in the Constructors' standings. Meanwhile, Mercedes found themselves stuck in limbo—too far off the frontrunners to compete for wins, but still ahead of the midfield. Behind them, the fight for best of the rest was intensifying, with Aston Martin looking like the strongest contender.

The season was still in its infancy, but clear patterns were already emerging. Among them was a recurring frustration for Hamilton. The same fundamental issues that had plagued the W13 in 2022 had persisted into 2024, and despite repeated concerns from the seven-time champion, the team had yet to find the breakthrough needed to return to the front.

**Australian Grand Prix (24th March 2024)**

The 2024 Australian Grand Prix, held at Melbourne's Albert Park Circuit, shook up the competitive order and proved to be a difficult weekend for Hamilton and Mercedes.

The weekend began with Red Bull's Verstappen securing pole position, once again demonstrating the team's continued dominance. Sainz, having only just recovered from surgery to remove his appendix, qualified his Ferrari in second. Hamilton faced significant issues with the Mercedes, which struggled with consistency, resulting in him starting from 11th on the grid.

As the race commenced, Verstappen maintained his lead but was passed by Sainz on Lap 2, the Red Bull seemingly not at its best. By Lap 3, Verstappen began to encounter brake issues, leading to a dramatic retirement on Lap 4 as his right rear wheel started to smoke before catching fire. Limping back to the pits, he approached the pit lane speed limit marker just as the right rear disc appeared to explode, firing a plume of dust horizontally towards the wall. It was the first time Red Bull had encountered reliability concerns in two years, and it opened a window of opportunity for their rivals. This unexpected turn allowed Leclerc to move into second behind his teammate.

On Lap 17, Hamilton could be seen slowing down at the far side of the circuit before radioing the pits to report an engine failure. The response from Mercedes was brief and to the point. Hamilton ensured he did not impede any following cars before pulling up adjacent to a gap in the wall next to a marshals' post so his car could be cleared quickly. Despite this, a short Virtual Safety Car (VSC) was deployed to remove the stricken W15E.

Mercedes' troubles deepened in the closing moments of the race when Russell, chasing down Fernando Alonso, pushed too hard under braking. As he closed in on the Aston Martin through a right-hander, he suffered a snap of oversteer after initially understeering into the corner. Overcorrecting, the Mercedes lurched violently towards the grass on the outside, sending Russell straight into the barriers.

The impact tore the left front wheel from the suspension, catapulting the car back onto the circuit as it bounced across the tarmac. The damaged wheel, still attached by its safety tether, flailed wildly. As the wrecked Mercedes skidded onto the racing line, the front-left lodged beneath the chassis, momentarily threatening to tip the car over. With Russell momentarily stranded, side-on to the oncoming traffic and unable to see what was approaching, it was a heart-stopping moment.

The VSC was immediately deployed, neutralising the race in its final moments. For Russell, it was another costly last-lap mistake—an all-too-familiar pattern that Mercedes could ill afford.

Ferrari delivered a commanding performance throughout the race, securing a one-two finish with Sainz taking victory ahead of Leclerc. The result was particularly significant for Sainz, given his surgery. Leclerc's second-place finish, combined with the fastest lap, highlighted Ferrari's competitive pace throughout the weekend.

The result was also an early indicator - especially given Mercedes' struggles—that Hamilton's decision to join Ferrari in 2025 was looking increasingly astute. Beyond that, it signalled a shift away from Red Bull's absolute dominance for the first time in two years. Chinks in their armour were beginning to show, and it would not be long before the reasons behind them became clear.

It was a weekend to forget for Hamilton, who made no secret of his frustrations following qualifying. He spoke candidly about the car's unpredictability, with the balance shifting from one session to the next without any clear explanation. What frustrated him most was that the Mercedes felt entirely different in qualifying compared to practice, despite the lower fuel load, when conventional wisdom suggested it should have been even quicker.

Once again, it was the same story he had been telling for three years—a car that was inconsistent and failed to behave as expected. The lack of predictability made it impossible to extract consistent performance, and for Hamilton, that was the biggest hurdle. If the team could at least create a car that responded in a way that made sense, he believed they could start to close the gap. But until then, they remained stuck in a cycle of frustration.

## Japanese Grand Prix (7th April 2024)

Returning to Suzuka, Verstappen once again asserted his dominance, securing pole position with teammate Pérez locking out the front row for Red Bull.

The start was clean, with Norris settling into third behind the Red Bulls. However, the race was quickly thrown into chaos as Ricciardo ran wide at high speed heading into Turn 4, collecting Alex Albon and sending both cars heavily into the barriers. With significant damage to the crash structures, the Safety Car was deployed before race control swiftly escalated it to a red flag to allow for repairs.

At the restart, Verstappen comfortably retained the lead, followed by Pérez and Norris, while Sainz slotted into fourth for Ferrari. The race unfolded in a relatively straightforward fashion until Lap 26, when Leclerc, under pressure from Pérez, ran wide and gifted the position to the Red Bull. From there, Red Bull cruised to yet another dominant one-two finish, with Ferrari securing third and fourth.

For Mercedes, it was another uninspiring afternoon. Russell and Hamilton finished seventh and ninth, far adrift of the leaders, leaving little doubt that their struggles were set to continue. For Hamilton, the prospect of another long, frustrating campaign with an unpredictable car loomed.

## Adrian Newey Departs Red Bull

On 25th April, news broke that Adrian Newey—arguably the greatest designer in Formula One history—was set to leave Red Bull. His departure followed controversial allegations against Red Bull Team Principal Christian Horner, who strongly denied claims of inappropriate behaviour. Reports suggested that Newey had become increasingly unsettled by the internal turmoil, with tensions rising not just over the allegations but also amid a wider power struggle within Red Bull's senior management.

Speculation over Newey's next move dominated discussions in the paddock, with every top team linked to the design genius. Horner, keen to downplay the impact of his exit, insisted that Red Bull remained focused and unaffected. Yet history suggested otherwise. Losing the man responsible for shaping their dominant cars was a seismic blow, and behind the scenes, there were signs that Red Bull's once-unshakable stability was beginning to fracture.

With the lengthy garden leave processes in Formula One, Newey was unlikely to join another team immediately—assuming the 65-year-old even wanted to continue working. The late Eddie Jordan, well known for his forthright opinions and close ties to Newey, was uncharacteristically silent. For once, people would have to wait and see what developed.

As the drama played out, Verstappen remained undeterred. Just as ruthless in managing off-track distractions as he was in cutting through traffic on race day, he refused to be drawn into the speculation, keeping his sights firmly on his only objective—winning. But with growing unrest at Red Bull, even he must have wondered whether this was the beginning of a much larger storm.

### Chinese Grand Prix

After a five-year absence, Formula One returned to the Shanghai International Circuit in late April, with fans eager to see local hero Zhou Guanyu compete in his home race for the first time. The weather was mild, with temperatures around 19°C, providing ideal conditions for racing.

Verstappen secured pole position for Red Bull with a time of 1:33.660, with teammate Sergio Pérez joining him on the front row. Fernando Alonso impressed for Aston Martin, qualifying third. Mercedes' struggles continued, as George Russell managed only eighth, while Lewis Hamilton suffered a shock Q1 elimination, leaving him to start 18th on the grid.

At lights out, Verstappen maintained his lead, while Lando Norris made a strong start from fourth, quickly moving up to challenge Alonso for third. Hamilton, starting from the back, began a determined charge through the field.

The race's first major incident came on Lap 19 when Valtteri Bottas' Sauber suffered an engine failure, bringing out the VSC. Several drivers, including Norris, took advantage of the opportunity to pit for fresh tyres.

Shortly after the VSC period ended, a collision between Daniel Ricciardo and Lance Stroll triggered a full Safety Car, shuffling the order as some drivers gained from the timing of their pit stops.

As the race resumed, Verstappen retained the lead, with Norris in close pursuit. Hamilton continued his recovery drive, hustling the Mercedes into the points-paying positions.

In the closing stages, Verstappen extended his advantage to take his 58th career victory. Norris finished second, securing his 15th career podium, while Pérez completed the podium in third. Hamilton's impressive fightback from 18th culminated in a ninth-place finish, salvaging valuable points for Mercedes.

**2024 Miami Grand Prix: Miami International Autodrome (5th May 2024)**

The Miami International Autodrome hosted the sixth round of the 2024 Formula One season, drawing a record attendance of 275,000 fans over the weekend. The warm and humid conditions, with temperatures around 27°C, set the stage for an exciting race. As a Sprint weekend, the shorter race took place on Saturday.

McLaren introduced extensive upgrades to their MCL38, revising the front wing, front suspension, floor, brake ducts, sidepod inlets, bodywork, and rear suspension. The team aimed to break into the top three consistently, but the Sprint format made the decision a risky one—if the upgrades failed to deliver, they would have no chance of reverting to a previous setup for the main race. However, with consistently accurate data from their new wind tunnel, McLaren felt the gamble was worth taking. Zak Brown acknowledged the risk but remained confident, emphasising that in Formula One, calculated risks were essential for performance gains.

Verstappen continued his dominance, taking pole position. Leclerc once again proved to be the quickest of the rest, just over a tenth behind, followed closely by Sainz. The gap to Red Bull was narrowing.

McLaren's Norris and Piastri qualified fifth and sixth respectively, just three-tenths off pole, with both drivers believing that their race pace would be even stronger. The upgrades appeared to be more effective on a heavier fuel load.

Mercedes, however, continued to struggle. Russell and Hamilton lined up seventh and eighth, with the car's inconsistent balance remaining a major issue for both drivers.

At the start, Verstappen held his lead, but chaos unfolded behind him. Pérez locked up heavily, narrowly avoiding contact with both Ferraris and nearly collecting his teammate. This allowed Piastri to leap from sixth to third, while Norris lost ground as he took evasive action. Hamilton, caught up in the melee, dropped outside the top ten before quickly recovering to eighth by Lap 4, moving two places ahead of Russell.

As the race approached the one-third mark, teams began their pit stops between Laps 20 and 27. Norris, having been pushed back by Pérez at the start, extended his stint on medium tyres to gain clear air and improve his track position.

The dynamics of the race shifted dramatically on Lap 28 when Kevin Magnussen's Haas collided with Logan Sargeant's Williams, sending Sargeant into the barriers and bringing out the Safety Car. Norris, who was due to pit imminently, seized the opportunity to make a 'free' pit stop under caution on Lap 30, rejoining the race in the lead on fresh hard tyres.

Racing resumed on Lap 32, with Norris defending brilliantly against Verstappen. Further back, an aggressive move by Sainz on Piastri resulted in front wing damage for the Australian, dropping him out of the points. Sainz was handed a five-second penalty for the incident.

Norris showed composure and skill beyond his years, holding off Verstappen to secure his first Formula One victory after 110 races. Verstappen settled for second, struggling with balance issues, while Leclerc completed the podium in third. Hamilton recovered well to finish sixth, with Russell in eighth, both securing valuable points for Mercedes.

Zak Brown was ecstatic, embracing anyone wearing McLaren's papaya colours. After crossing the finish line, a jubilant Norris sprinted into the arms of his team, who were waiting next to parc fermé, celebrating a well-earned and long-awaited victory.

**2024 Emilia Romagna Grand Prix Race Report (19th May)**

The 2024 Emilia Romagna Grand Prix, held at the historic Autodromo Internazionale Enzo e Dino Ferrari in Imola, delivered another closely fought battle between Verstappen and Norris.

In the lead-up to the race weekend, several Formula One teams introduced key upgrades. McLaren implemented further aerodynamic developments tailored specifically for Imola, significantly enhancing their performance. Meanwhile, Mercedes rolled out a second wave of upgrades following their initial efforts in Miami. These adjustments included modifications to the rear wing, floor, floor fences, and brake ducts—an important step in their bid to close the gap to front-runners like McLaren.

Andrew Shovlin of Mercedes acknowledged ongoing challenges with the car's consistency across different sessions, noting that it was still behaving unpredictably. Until the team could resolve these fundamental issues, the effectiveness of any updates would remain limited.

Former Formula One designer Gary Anderson was critical of Mercedes' approach, suggesting that the changes indicated a lack of understanding within the team regarding how to extract performance from the current generation of cars—a situation that did not bode well for Lewis Hamilton's prospects.

Red Bull's Max Verstappen continued his streak of pole positions, setting the fastest time in qualifying. McLaren's Lando Norris and Oscar Piastri also delivered strong performances, though Piastri suffered a setback with a three-place grid penalty for impeding another driver. This reshuffled the starting order and placed Norris in a more advantageous second position for the race start.

Race day saw typical Imola weather, with sunny intervals, light winds, and a slight chance of showers. Verstappen led from the start, but the McLaren drivers, particularly Norris, remained close contenders throughout the race.

With margins tighter than ever, teams were under pressure to execute their pit stops flawlessly. Norris pitted for hard tyres on Lap 22, aiming to undercut his competitors, while Piastri followed a lap later, both gaining crucial positions. Norris, in particular, mounted a serious challenge to Verstappen's lead, closing the gap to under two seconds in the final laps.

With five laps remaining, Norris was on the limit, wrestling with oversteer in several corners. He worked furiously at the controls on his steering wheel, adjusting brake bias, differential settings, and other parameters in an effort to extract every last fraction of performance. He closed to within a second on the final lap, but Verstappen held on to secure victory. Leclerc completed the podium in third for Ferrari.

Hamilton once again delivered a stronger race performance than in qualifying, jumping ahead of Russell to finish sixth. Russell crossed the line 12 seconds behind his teammate in seventh.

Toto Wolff acknowledged a slight improvement within the team, though progress remained modest and incremental. He also noted that rival teams were making significant strides in performance, implying that despite Mercedes' efforts, they were not advancing quickly enough.

Shovlin echoed Wolff's assessment, admitting that there was still considerable work to be done at Brackley. Without substantial changes, the team risked remaining fourth among the top contenders. Amidst these challenges, Hamilton's decision to move to Ferrari appeared increasingly justified with each passing week.

**Monaco Grand Prix (26th May 2024)**

The Monaco Grand Prix was particularly poignant for Lewis Hamilton, as it marked the 30th anniversary of Ayrton Senna's death. McLaren, a team both Senna and Hamilton famously drove for, paid tribute with a special livery. The car's design echoed Senna's iconic helmet colours, with the rear third in green and the front two-thirds in yellow, divided by a blue stripe along the nose cone—reflecting the Brazilian flag and Senna's personal branding. Dominating the blue stripe was the iconic Senna "S," proudly displayed on the nose.

Qualifying took place on Saturday, 25th May, with Leclerc securing pole position for Ferrari, virtually guaranteeing him victory given Monaco's notoriously processional nature.

The opening lap saw immediate drama. Sainz made contact with Piastri at the first corner, suffering a puncture later in the lap.

Greater chaos followed when Kevin Magnussen attempted an audacious overtake on Pérez while climbing the hill from Sainte Devote through Beau Rivage towards Massenet. As Pérez took the normal racing line, Magnussen tried to squeeze between the Red Bull and the barrier, slamming into Pérez's side at over 150mph. The impact sent Pérez spinning violently into the barriers with such force that, despite the FIA safety tethers, one of his front wheels detached and bounced up the track. His Red Bull then rebounded backwards, striking Nico Hülkenberg's Haas as he attempted to avoid the wreckage. The second impact was just as severe, ripping off Pérez's rear wheel and wrecking Hülkenberg's race.

As his car came to a halt, Hülkenberg could be heard expressing frustration over the radio, noting that the incident had been unnecessary. The Haas pit wall was visibly unimpressed.

With the track blocked by three cars and carbon fibre debris strewn across the circuit, the race was immediately red-flagged.

Just seconds later as the red flag was being deployed, Alpine suffered its own disaster when Esteban Ocon attempted a risky move on teammate Pierre Gasly at Portier. Running wide at the apex, Ocon left Gasly no room, clipping Gasly's front wheel with his rear and launching his own car into the air before it crashed back down. Gasly, clearly frustrated, was vocal on the radio as his team informed him of the red flag. Both Alpine drivers limped back to the pits, but for Ocon, the race was over. In just 30 seconds, two Haas cars, a Red Bull, and an Alpine had been eliminated.

One positive outcome of the red flag was that Sainz was able to recover his Ferrari for the restart.

At the restart, Leclerc kept his cool and controlled the race, securing an emotional victory in his home Grand Prix. Ferrari and McLaren had another strong weekend, with Sainz finishing third behind Piastri, while Norris took fourth. Russell, running Mercedes' newly designed front wing, finished fifth, while Hamilton, still using the older specification, came home in seventh—having graciously allowed the team to give the new upgrades to Russell first.

**Canadian Grand Prix (9th June 2024)**

As the teams left Europe for Canada, Mercedes introduced further technical upgrades to their W15E in an effort to close the gap to Red Bull, Ferrari, and McLaren.

One of the most significant updates was a new front wing design, the same first tested on Russell's car in Monaco. Encouraged by its performance, Mercedes equipped both Russell and Hamilton with the updated wing for the Canadian Grand Prix, expecting even greater benefits on the Circuit Gilles Villeneuve, where long straights and varied cornering speeds would put the design to the test.

The team also introduced larger front brake duct inlets to improve cooling, a crucial factor in Montreal's heavy-braking zones. This modification aimed to maintain optimal brake temperatures, ensuring consistent performance and reducing the risk of overheating.

Additionally, Mercedes realigned the front suspension to improve airflow to the floor, enhancing aerodynamic efficiency and downforce. If all three upgrades worked together effectively, Hamilton hoped they would provide a much-needed step forward. He wouldn't have to wait long to find out.

The Circuit Gilles Villeneuve provided another gripping race weekend. Mercedes had a strong start in qualifying, with Russell, having had a full race in Monaco to adapt to the new front wing, securing pole position. Incredibly, Verstappen set an identical lap time of 1:12.000, but because he recorded it after Russell, he was classified second. Hamilton, still adjusting to the upgrades, was less than three-tenths behind his teammate but had to settle for seventh on the grid.

The race began in wet conditions, with most cars starting on intermediates while a few gambled on full wets. By Lap 8, the sun emerged, and the track started to dry.

On Lap 21, following a series of pit stops, Norris made a bold move on Russell just before the main straight. His McLaren twitched as it hit a damp patch, sending up a spray of water, but he had significantly more grip on the drying racing line, allowing him to sweep around the outside. Russell, making the strange decision to defend on the wetter part of the track, could do little to prevent the pass.

Four laps later, Logan Sargeant lost control and hit the barriers, bringing out the Safety Car.

Although a well-timed Safety Car had played to Norris' advantage in Miami, this time it worked against him. Having been in the lead, he emerged third after the pit stops had shaken out. He fought his way back up to second, securing yet another strong result, but there was little doubt that, without the intervention, he likely would have taken victory on merit.

While Verstappen continued his winning streak, Mercedes had reason to be encouraged. Russell converted his pole position into a third-place finish, marking a return to the podium. Hamilton secured fourth, though he was frustrated with his own performance.

Hamilton was candid in his post-race reflections, admitting that he had made too many mistakes, and that the car had been capable of winning. However, he saw the weekend as a step forward and remained determined to keep pushing.

**Spanish Grand Prix**

The 2024 Spanish Grand Prix, held at the Circuit de Barcelona-Catalunya on 23 June delivered another close battle under clear skies, with temperatures hovering around 25°C.

Norris clinched pole position with a lap of 1:11.383, edging out Verstappen by a narrow margin. Mercedes showed signs of resurgence, with Hamilton qualifying third and Russell fourth. The Ferraris of Leclerc and Sainz followed in fifth and sixth, setting the stage for a competitive race.

At lights out, Verstappen got the better start. Sensing the threat, Norris moved right towards the pit wall, squeezing Verstappen slightly too much. The Red Bull was forced onto the grass, losing traction and snapping sideways at over 150mph, yet Verstappen somehow avoided a major accident. Dried mud was thrown into the air as the Dutchman fought to keep control.

As Norris and Verstappen scrapped, Russell seized the opportunity. Tucking in behind Norris, he used the slipstream before making a decisive late move to the left, going three-wide into Turn 1. Russell braked late and swept around the outside into the lead. Norris, boxed in between Russell and Verstappen, had to back out, allowing Verstappen into second. By Lap 3 Verstappen had reeled in Russell and he took the lead.

Further back, Hamilton engaged in a hard-fought battle with Sainz. After a fierce wheel-to-wheel contest into Turn 1, Hamilton emerged ahead, leaving Sainz frustrated. The Ferrari driver took to the radio, demanding the position be handed back, but by then, Hamilton had already pulled away.

As the race unfolded, Verstappen maintained a commanding lead, while Norris, after adjusting his pit stop strategy, rejoined in second and steadily closed the gap.

Hamilton, locked in a straight fight with Russell, finally made his move on Lap 52. As Russell once again defended the inside line—his trademark move—Hamilton swept around the outside, the two Mercedes running inches apart before Hamilton secured third. He then managed his tyres to the flag, marking his first podium of the season.

The final standings saw Verstappen take victory, Norris finish second, and Hamilton complete the podium in third. It was a strong result for Mercedes, proving they could now beat Ferrari on merit.

After the race, Hamilton reflected on his overtakes against Sainz and Russell, noting that all of them had been extremely close but fair. He emphasised that while the battles had been on the limit, space was left where needed, making for exciting yet respectful racing.

**Austrian Grand Prix (30th June 2024)**

At the Red Bull Ring, Verstappen continued his dominance in qualifying, securing yet another pole position.

On race day both Mercedes looked competitive once again, engaging in early tussles with Ferrari and McLaren. However, as the race progressed, Norris applied relentless pressure on Verstappen at the front of the race. On Lap 52, the Red Bull driver locked up into a right-hander, running slightly wide and allowing Norris to close in. By Lap 55, Norris was challenging for the lead.

Over several laps, Norris attempted to pass Verstappen, but the Red Bull driver was seen moving under braking—something explicitly against the rules. After the second incident, Norris took to the radio, frustrated at the aggressive defending, warning that if Verstappen continued, a collision was inevitable. Norris' words turned out to be prophetic.

On Lap 63, Norris got a strong run out of Turn 1 and made another move under braking into Turn 2. Verstappen ran wide, completely off the circuit, in an attempt to maintain his momentum and hold position. Norris demanded over the radio that the Red Bull driver be instructed to give the place back. Verstappen, however, refused.

A lap later, the scenario repeated itself—only this time, Norris had had enough. Anticipating Verstappen's defensive tactics, he opted to go around the outside. Verstappen initially defended towards the middle of the track before suddenly moving back towards the racing line, colliding with Norris. Both cars ran wide, Verstappen picking up a left-rear puncture and Norris sustaining front-wing damage. As Verstappen crawled back to the pits, Norris also limped in with a puncture and damage of his own.

Running third, Russell was 15 seconds behind when the drama unfolded. Sensing an opportunity, Toto Wolff came over the radio, urging him on: "George, you can win this. You can win this, George!" Russell, fully focused, simply responded: "Just let me f*****g drive."

As Verstappen and Norris hobbled towards the pits, Russell stormed past both of them to take the lead. With the race turned on its head, Russell controlled the final laps and secured a remarkable victory—Mercedes' first of the season. Hamilton finished fourth, celebrating the team's success.

While Verstappen remained one of the sport's elite, his aggressive racing tactics had been a growing concern for years. Stretching the boundaries of what was permissible, he frequently teetered on the edge of regulatory limits. The events in Austria, however, marked a turning point. With increasing frustration among his rivals and the stewards finally stepping in, it was clear that Verstappen's approach could no longer go unchecked. The rest of the grid was no longer willing to back down.

**British Grand Prix (7th July 2024)**

The British Grand Prix delivered yet another classic, packed with drama and emotion. Mercedes continued their resurgence, with Russell securing pole position and Hamilton lining up beside him in second, marking a long-awaited front-row lockout for the team. The British fans were purring in anticipation as their home heroes prepared for battle. Overhead, the clouds loomed, the weather unpredictable. The shifting skies stood in stark contrast to the motionless grid, where the cars sat poised, engines throbbing, awaiting the lights.

The Mercedes pair held their positions on the opening lap while Verstappen, once again engaged in battle with Norris, pulling off a daring move around the outside to take third place. However, on Lap 15, Norris got a strong exit from Becketts and retook the position. The British crowd exploded as their home drivers filled the top three spots.

On Lap 17, Piastri also found a way past Verstappen, just as the first drops of rain began to fall. Fans hurriedly reached for waterproofs and umbrellas as the track conditions started to change.

By Lap 18, Hamilton, renowned for his skill in wet conditions, closed in on Russell and made his move to take the lead. The Silverstone crowd roared in appreciation. As the rain intensified, the drivers remained on slick tyres, pushing the limits to maintain heat and grip.

At the start of Lap 19, both Hamilton and Russell ran wide at Turn 1 as their tyres struggled for traction. They quickly regained control, but Norris, whose McLaren was working well in the damp, seized the opportunity. He passed Russell into second and, just a lap later on Lap 20, overtook Hamilton to take the lead.

What followed was a breathtaking battle between Hamilton, Russell, and Piastri. The three drivers went wheel-to-wheel through multiple corners, each fighting to keep control in the treacherous conditions. By the time they reached Stowe, Piastri had surged into second, making it a McLaren 1-2, with Mercedes running third and fourth.

After running on slicks for around ten laps in the wet, most teams opted to pit for intermediate tyres. Verstappen was among the first to switch, followed soon after by other key drivers.

On Lap 34, Mercedes' hopes took a hit as Russell was told to retire the car due to a water leak, with the team keen to preserve the power unit. By Lap 35, the sun reappeared, prompting Hamilton to radio the team, putting them on alert for a potential switch back to slicks. On Lap 39, he became one of the first to make the change, followed closely by Verstappen.

Norris, sensing the shift in conditions, immediately asked for a pit stop but was forced to stay out one extra lap. When he finally pitted on Lap 40, a slight overshoot of his pit box cost him precious seconds. As he exited the pit lane, Hamilton swept past into the lead. A few laps later, Verstappen also overtook Norris to take second place.

Hamilton crossed the line on Lap 52 to take the chequered flag, securing his ninth career victory at Silverstone. The British crowd celebrated their hero, as Bono, Hamilton's race engineer, shouted his signature phrase: "Get in there, Lewis!" before adding, "You're the man!"

Hamilton pumped his fists in triumph, clearly overwhelmed with emotion. On the cool-down lap, his voice cracked as he radioed the team thanking them and telling them what it meant to him. He thanked all the fans, telling them how much he loved them.

As he pulled into parc fermé, Hamilton was greeted by his father. Keeping his helmet on, they embraced, Hamilton's shoulders rising and falling as he sobbed. The emotion of the moment was clear—a release of tension after a difficult few years. Later, in an interview, he dedicated the win to the fans, saying the feeling of the win was indescribable.

Although McLaren had shown superior pace in the mixed conditions, Hamilton's strategic decision to pit early proved pivotal. His victory was not just a personal achievement but a triumph for his team, a tribute to his father, and a moment of pure exhilaration for the thousands of fans in attendance.

**Hungarian Grand Prix (21st July 2024)**

The Hungarian Grand Prix delivered another race filled with incident and controversy.

McLaren locked out the front row, with Piastri leading Norris into Turn 1. Piastri refused to yield, forcing Norris wide onto the very edge of the track. As the McLarens fought, Verstappen attempted an audacious move, running completely off-track in an attempt to overtake Norris.

Norris immediately took to the radio, demanding that Verstappen be forced to return the position. His race engineer assured him that they were in contact with the FIA.

Verstappen, however, insisted he had been ahead at the apex. By Lap 4, his engineer, Gianpiero Lambiase, advised him that the incident was under investigation and suggested he give the place back to avoid a penalty. Reluctantly, Verstappen complied, allowing Norris through at the start of the lap.

Hamilton, running inside the top five, was the first to pit on Lap 17 for hard tyres, attempting an undercut strategy.

On Lap 35, Verstappen caught Hamilton at the end of the pit straight. Both drivers braked late into Turn 1, and on the exit, Verstappen got a better drive. They ran side by side down the hill into Turn 2—a long, sweeping left-hander. Verstappen tried to go around the outside but ran wide, later complaining that his brake bias was making turn-in difficult.

By Lap 41, Hamilton and Leclerc pitted together. The McLarens followed suit on laps 47 and 48, with Norris pitting first in an attempt to cover Verstappen. Piastri, pitting a lap later, managed to rejoin in second place.

Verstappen made his final stop on Lap 50, rejoining in fifth behind Leclerc. Meanwhile, Hamilton had moved up into third.

Closing in on Hamilton down the main straight, Verstappen attempted a late lunge from several car lengths back into Turn 1. Locking up both front tyres, he misjudged the move, making wheel-to-wheel contact with Hamilton. The Red Bull bounced into the air and ran off into the runoff area, while Hamilton carried on unscathed.

Despite his earlier pit stops, Norris retained the lead, with Piastri running second. On Lap 67, Norris slowed and allowed Piastri to retake the lead.

Two laps later, Oscar Piastri crossed the line to take his maiden Formula One victory, followed by Norris in second. Hamilton completed the podium in third, while Verstappen, having been outmanoeuvred on strategy, finished down in fifth.

In his post-race interview, Verstappen refused to take responsibility for the collision with Hamilton. When asked about it, Hamilton took a measured approach, describing it as a racing incident. He acknowledged that Verstappen had been much quicker into the corner, but ultimately, the Dutchman's lock-up had sealed his fate.

Reflecting on Mercedes' progress, Hamilton's smile said it all. He acknowledged that while the McLarens and Red Bulls still had the edge, the team was making real strides. His message was clear: Mercedes was back in the fight. It was a moment of optimism for Hamilton and a reminder to the rest of the grid that he was not done yet.

**Belgian Grand Prix – The Stewards Weigh in**

Verstappen secured pole position at the Belgian Grand Prix on Saturday, 27th July, but a penalty forced him to start from 11th, promoting Charles Leclerc to pole, with Pérez alongside him in second and Hamilton starting third.

At the start, the leading trio held position, but Hamilton wasted little time in making his move. He first battled past Pérez before overtaking Leclerc on Lap 3 to take the lead.

By the middle of the race, Hamilton's rear tyres were showing signs of degradation. Russell, who had climbed to fourth, radioed the team on Lap 26, suggesting they consider a one-stop strategy, his Mercedes seemingly much kinder to the tyres than Hamilton's. A minute later, Hamilton, who was leading, made his second pit stop.

Behind them, the McLarens and Ferraris were locked in a fierce battle for the final podium position.

Russell stayed out and Hamilton, with his fresh tyres, had a lot of time to make up to try and catch his teammate. With two laps to go, Hamilton was in striking distance, just six tenths of a second behind. But despite his fresher tyre advantage, he seemed unable to capitalise. Oddly, Russell's Mercedes, despite being on significantly older tyres, seemed to have better traction out of the tighter corners such as La Source. As a result, Hamilton was unable to get close enough down to Eau Rouge and up along the Kemmel Straight to challenge, always seemingly just a few tenths of a second too far adrift.

In a tense finish, Russell held off Hamilton by half a second to take victory, with Piastri finishing just behind them in third. Even more bizarre than Russell's pace was Toto Wolff's expression. As the winning Mercedes crossed the line, Wolff appeared downcast.

The podium celebrations began, and Mercedes were quite rightly proud of their 1-2 victory. However, a few hours later, Russell was disqualified from the event. His Mercedes had been weighed by the Stewards and was found to be 1.5kg under the 798kg minimum weight. A 1.5kg difference around Spa would equate to around a 0.35-second per lap difference, enough to have possibly kept Hamilton at arm's length coming out of La Source.

So, a few hours later, Hamilton had inherited another victory. It was a fitting end to a great weekend.

As the teams entered the mid-season summer break, the first half of 2024 had produced seven different winners, highlighting the close competition.

Mercedes had made up some ground and going into the second half of the season they were now more competitive, but they still had ground to make up in the points. Red Bull, McLaren, and Ferrari had emerged as the strongest forces, with Norris and Verstappen set for a championship showdown. Under Frédéric Vasseur's leadership, Ferrari was making strides and pushing McLaren hard.

A month later, at Verstappen's home race in the Netherlands, Norris took victory, with Verstappen finishing second and Leclerc third. Mercedes struggled, with both cars finishing down in seventh and eighth. The teams then moved on to Italy.

**Italian Grand Prix: Hamilton's Future Home**

The Formula One paddock arrived in Monza on 30th August for a weekend of hard racing. For Hamilton, the occasion carried extra significance—12 months from now, he would be returning to the Temple of Speed in Ferrari red. How would his future team perform in front of their passionate tifosi?

Qualifying was fiercely competitive, with the top six separated by less than three-tenths of a second. McLaren locked out the front row with Norris on pole, while Russell secured third, and the Ferraris of Leclerc and Sainz were just behind in fourth and fifth. Hamilton was sixth.

The race day dawned on 1 September warm but with clouds lingering, as teams prepared for possible mid-afternoon rain. As the cars formed up on the grid, the papaya McLarens stood out against the hazy sky. The tifosi in the grandstands were in full voice, urging Ferrari on to victory. Many also had an eye on Hamilton—how would he fare against Russell on this circuit where he would soon be racing in red?

The lights went out, and the front two McLarens jostled for position as they charged toward Turn 1. Sensing the slipstream advantage, Russell attempted a move but drifted too far onto the grass, forcing him to take the escape road and rejoin behind Verstappen.

Further ahead, Piastri had the momentum through Curva Grande and attacked Norris into the Variante della Roggia chicane. Norris defended hard, placing his car in the middle of the track, but Piastri refused to back down, sweeping around the outside in a breathtaking move. Norris had to compromise his exit, which allowed Leclerc a chance to pounce.

As they exited the chicane, Leclerc used his extra momentum to challenge Norris. The McLaren driver tried to defend by moving right, forcing Leclerc onto the grass. But with the tifosi roaring him on, Leclerc refused to lift, keeping his foot planted and surging past, dust and debris shooting skywards, as they entered Lesmo 1. The Italian fans went ballistic.

Leclerc settled in behind the lead car of Piastri, either struggling to match his pace or simply waiting for his moment.

Running fifth in the leading Mercedes, Hamilton was just a few seconds behind Sainz. He pitted on Lap 16, exiting just behind Leclerc. As he flashed past Ferrari's pit crew in their red overalls, it was a glimpse of the future—soon, it would be his car pulling into that box.

On Lap 39, McLaren made a puzzling decision, calling Piastri in for new hard tyres despite him leading comfortably. The move proved costly, handing Leclerc the lead with Sainz moving into second. The tifosi, 335,000 strong over the weekend, held their breath—could Ferrari hold on?

While Piastri fought back and overtook Sainz on Lap 45, Hamilton remained in a solid fifth place, 13 seconds behind Norris. The Ferraris and McLarens were in a league of their own, while Mercedes had emerged as the best of the rest. Red Bull, meanwhile, was languishing further down the order.

A few laps later Norris overtook Sainz, putting McLaren in pursuit of Leclerc. But the Ferrari driver held his nerve, keeping both McLarens at bay.

As Leclerc crossed the line, he moved symbolically toward the pit wall, greeted by his ecstatic team hanging over the fence. The tifosi erupted, celebrating a famous home victory.

Leclerc had put everything into the race, a quality the Italian fans admired most in their drivers. It was also why they were so eager to welcome Hamilton—his relentless fighting spirit had already won them over.

Hamilton crossed the line in fifth, finishing just behind the man he would replace at Ferrari in a few months' time. Russell followed in seventh. While not in the podium fight, Hamilton had demonstrated his potential to the tifosi—a sign of intent for what lay ahead.

Sainz's fourth-place finish was a disappointment for Ferrari, given how close they were to McLaren in the Constructors' standings. Every point mattered now.

The battle for the championship continued to rage over the next four races in Azerbaijan, Singapore, the United States, and Mexico. McLaren, Ferrari, and Red Bull all traded victories, but crucially, Red Bull was no longer dominant. Despite Verstappen's efforts, his championship lead was beginning to slip. Was Adrian Newey's impending departure being felt?

Like Hamilton, Verstappen was a fighter. But Norris was relentless, chipping away at the points gap slowly but surely. The growing tension led to speculation that the title battle could go down to the final race of the season. Then came Brazil.

**Brazilian Grand Prix (3rd November 2024)**

Before the race, Hamilton, an honorary Brazilian citizen since 2022, was given the distinction of driving Ayrton Senna's legendary McLaren MP4/5B—the car Senna had used to win the 1990 World Championship.

Wearing a commemorative Senna helmet, Hamilton set off from the pits in the rain, waving to the Brazilian fans. The wail of the 3.5 litre V10 echoed around the Autódromo José Carlos Pace as thousands of voices chanted, "Senna, Senna, Senna."

After two laps, Hamilton stopped on the main straight, climbed out, and crouched beside the car, his hands resting on its bodywork in a moment of reflection. Speaking afterwards he described the experience as deeply emotional. He spoke with fondness of watching Senna race as a child, and saying the opportunity to drive his hero's car the greatest honour of his career. Talking of his connection to Brazil, he described the weekend as one of the highlights of his life.

Heading into the Brazil race, expectations were high that Norris could close the championship gap to Verstappen. That belief was reinforced when Verstappen had a poor qualifying session and, after penalties, started 17th on the grid.

Norris secured pole, with Russell alongside him in second. Ocon, in a surprise performance for Alpine, qualified fourth.

At the start, most of the cars got away cleanly in the slippery conditions, but Pérez spun his Red Bull, dropping to the back of the field. Meanwhile, Verstappen made up six places on the opening lap, moving into 11th, just behind Hamilton.

By mid-race, the rain had intensified, leading to varying pit stop strategies. On Lap 31, as conditions worsened, the Safety Car was deployed. One lap later, Franco Colapinto crashed into the barriers while still under Safety Car conditions, heavily damaging his Williams and triggering a red flag.

Several drivers, including Verstappen and Gasly, had gained an advantage by pitting at the perfect moment before the red flag. When racing resumed, Verstappen delivered a demonstration in wet-weather driving, carving his way to the front.

By the chequered flag, he had won by 19 seconds, a dominant display that all but ended Norris' title hopes. Both Alpines finished on the podium, with Ocon second and Gasly third. Norris, who had led much of the race, could only manage sixth.

After the race, Verstappen acknowledged the significance of the victory, admitting he had not expected to win from so far back. However, his performance had secured crucial points, moving him ever closer to his fourth consecutive World Championship.

For Hamilton, São Paulo was a weekend of frustration. Despite moments of early pace, he struggled in the difficult conditions and finished tenth. Afterwards he admitted it had been a tough day, with the team unable to find the pace needed.

As the season neared its conclusion, Verstappen had reasserted his authority, edging closer to another title. Meanwhile, Hamilton remained focused on finishing the season strongly, knowing his final races with Mercedes were now fast approaching.

**Las Vegas – Verstappen bags his fourth**

Formula One's return to the entertainment capital of the world did not disappoint. Against the neon-lit backdrop of the Las Vegas Strip Circuit, the race delivered a spectacle. For Russell and Hamilton, it was a night of dominance. For Max Verstappen, it was the night he secured his fourth World Championship, further cementing his legacy in the sport.

The anticipation leading up to the Las Vegas Grand Prix was huge. Held under floodlights, with temperatures around 21°C and clear skies. Fans lined the streets, eager to witness Formula One's return to Las Vegas. The circuit, a mix of fast straights and tight corners, promised both high-speed action and slow speed technical challenges.

Speaking ahead of the race, Hamilton talked of the significance of the venue, describing it as an iconic location and expressing excitement about racing in front of such an enthusiastic crowd.

Starting from pole position, Russell controlled the race from the outset. His performance highlighted Mercedes' late-season resurgence, with the car appearing to thrive in slightly cooler, low-grip conditions. Managing his tyres effectively and maintaining a composed approach, he led from start to finish to secure his second victory of the season.

After crossing the line, Russell was euphoric and credited the team for their execution over the weekend, praising the car's performance. Having initially planned to fly home after the race, he instead opted to celebrate his win in Las Vegas.

Hamilton, meanwhile, produced an outstanding recovery drive from 10th on the grid to finish second, securing a one-two finish for Mercedes. Finishing just over seven seconds behind at the chequered flag, it was one of his strongest performances of the season. He acknowledged the team's progress, describing it as the culmination of their hard work throughout the year and commending Russell's drive.

Verstappen qualified fifth and maintained that position to the end—a result that secured his fourth consecutive World Championship. His consistency throughout the season had placed him in an unassailable position, and while he missed out on the podium in Las Vegas, he left the circuit as the undisputed champion. As the paddock started to pack up, Verstappen was seen wandering around, drinking beer and in a great mood.

In contrast, Pérez endured a difficult weekend, qualifying 16th and finishing 10th. His struggles throughout the season had left questions hanging over his future at Red Bull, and speculation was mounting that his time with the team was nearing its end. Red Bull were well known for being brutal about driver selection and Perez's days were looking numbered.

The focus now shifted to the final two races in Qatar and Abu Dhabi, where teams would look to end the year on a high.

**Qatar Grand Prix**

The 2024 Qatar Grand Prix, held at the Lusail International Circuit on 1 December, provided a tense race under the desert floodlights. With temperatures around 25°C and clear skies, conditions were ideal for another mix-up.

Heading into the Grand Prix, McLaren led the Constructors' Championship with 608 points, holding a 24-point advantage over Ferrari, who were on 584. Red Bull Racing sat third with 555 points.

McLaren's driver pairing of Lando Norris and Oscar Piastri continued to impress, particularly during the Sprint weekend, where Norris allowed Piastri to pass in a clear demonstration of teamwork. Speaking about it afterwards, Norris emphasised that collaboration remained their greatest strength.

In the Sprint race, Russell secured third place, while Hamilton finished sixth, setting up an intriguing battle for the main event.

Qualifying saw George Russell take pole position after being aided by a one-place grid penalty for Max Verstappen, who was penalised for unnecessary slowing during the session. The decision sparked debate, with Russell describing Verstappen's actions as dangerous and avoidable, though acknowledging that no one's lap had been ruined as a result.

McLaren's Norris and Piastri qualified third and fourth, positioning the team well, while Ferrari's Leclerc and Sainz lined up fifth and seventh. Splitting the Ferraris was Hamilton in sixth, with the Mercedes team now pressing both McLaren and Ferrari on outright pace if the conditions were cool enough.

At the start, Verstappen made a strong getaway, leapfrogging Russell into Turn 1 before defending against Norris through Turn 2.

Hamilton appeared to mistime the start, moving slightly before the lights went out. Recognising his mistake, he tried to stop the car, compromising his launch. He was immediately placed under investigation by the Stewards.

Further back, the low-grip track caught out several drivers. Hulkenberg and Ocon were forced out of the race after contact, while Stroll hit Albon, sending the Williams driver tumbling down the order and earning himself a penalty.

On Lap 30, an unusual incident highlighted Verstappen's championship-winning mindset.

Albon, whose Williams was already carrying damage from his earlier collision, had his wing mirror and assembly detach and fly into the middle of the track near the pit exit. Recognising the potential danger, the Stewards put out waved yellow flags on the start-finish straight, which also included flashing yellow lights.

Verstappen, leading the race, spotted the yellow light near the pit wall and instinctively checked his mirrors to gauge Norris' distance behind. He marginally reduced his speed, aware of the regulations that you must be shown to have lifted off when passing a yellow flag area. Norris, however, kept full throttle and Verstappen could see this marginal gain in his mirror. Sensing an opportunity, Verstappen immediately radioed his team to question whether Norris had lifted—a calculated move to ensure the Stewards reviewed the situation. Moments later, a Kick Sauber hit the stray mirror at full speed, shattering it into pieces.

Seconds later, Hamilton, who had been running ahead of Russell and making progress, suffered a puncture from the debris, sending sparks flying from his front left tyre. Carlos Sainz encountered the same fate, limping back to the pits as Ferrari's Constructors' hopes took another hit.

With debris scattered across the track, the Stewards deployed the Safety Car, ordering all cars to follow it through the pit lane while marshals worked to clear the circuit.

Hamilton, having to limp back to the pits while others were still at full racing speed, dropped to 16th. As he exited the pit lane, he inadvertently exceeded the speed limit while warming his brakes and was handed a drive-through penalty. Had an average-speed detection system been in place, he may have avoided it, but under the regulations, a breach was a breach. It was one of those days.

As the field prepared for the restart, Pérez spun his Red Bull while warming his tyres, dropping to the back. The Mexican's struggles had become a recurring theme. Since May's Miami Grand Prix, he had contributed little to Red Bull's Constructors' efforts. With Verstappen leading and Pérez once again playing no role in the title fight, questions over his future grew even louder.

Ferrari then received some unexpected, good news. After reviewing the footage, the Stewards ruled that Norris had failed to lift under yellow flags and handed him a 10-second penalty, dropping him out of the points.

Verstappen went on to win the race, with Leclerc finishing second and Piastri taking third.

Hamilton, having lost ground due to the puncture and subsequent penalty, finished 12th, out of the points. It was a frustrating result, especially as Russell—who had been behind him earlier in the race—secured fourth.

After the race, Hamilton reflected on what had been a missed opportunity. Despite his initial error at the start, he had shown strong pace before the debris incident derailed his race. However, he acknowledged that, once again, the Mercedes was proving difficult to handle, particularly in cornering.

Hamilton's ability to take both victories and setbacks in his stride had been a key part of his career. While the race had not gone in his favour, he remained focused on the bigger picture, drawing on his resilience to keep pushing forward.

At Red Bull, the contrast between their two drivers had never been clearer. Verstappen had once again demonstrated why he was champion, using both his speed and sharp race awareness to take another victory. Meanwhile, Pérez's latest setback only added to the growing speculation that Red Bull would soon be looking for a replacement.

As the teams packed up, only one race remained - Abu Dhabi.

## Abu Dhabi – Still I Rise

The Abu Dhabi weekend of 6-8 December had a multitude of battles to play for. For some, it was an end-of-year opportunity to show their mettle and advertise their capabilities, perhaps for a new contract with another team. Liam Lawson and Yuki Tsunoda, in particular, were in the frame for promotion to the main Red Bull seat to replace Perez, who was likely to leave after a dismal season.

The Constructors' Championship was on the line. McLaren looked like the favourites to take it, being 21 points ahead of Ferrari, but, as had been shown year after year, Formula One could spring surprises. Would the papaya cars be able to hold out for just one more weekend and reward the efforts of Zak Brown and everyone at the McLaren Technology Centre? With Piastri and Norris in the cars and Andrea Stella leading the team, they deserved the chance.

Equally, Frederic Vasseur had worked wonders at Ferrari. The team, which had languished in sixth in 2020, had worked its way back into the top three since and was now on the cusp of taking the manufacturer crown. Vasseur had laid the foundations in 2023, and this was the fruit of his, and everyone's, labours at Maranello. Leclerc, once too error-prone but ridiculously quick, had tempered his approach under Vasseur and become a more complete package, bringing consistency to his racing. Sainz had always been quick but had been outshone by Leclerc the last two years. The Scuderia needed to bring the title back to Maranello. Second place in the Drivers' Championship was up for grabs. Leclerc had a strong end to the season and was now just eight points behind Norris, so that was all to play for.

And in addition to all of this, Sir Lewis Hamilton was about to step into his W15E Mercedes to race in anger for the last time. Hamilton had given absolutely everything to Mercedes since joining in 2013, and the results spoke for themselves: six Drivers' Championships, eight Constructors' Championships, 84 race wins, 78 pole positions, 55 fastest laps, and 153 podiums. In 246 races, Hamilton had been on the podium more than 62% of the time. Including his time at McLaren, where he used Mercedes power, he had started 356 races and had 202 podium finishes – a ratio of 56.7%. To put that into context, Hamilton's idol Senna had been on the podium in 50% of races, Schumacher 50%, and Verstappen, who had been in the dominant Red Bull, had been on the podium 54%.

Hamilton's results spoke for themselves. His results 'did the talking on the track,' just as his dad had told him to. Hamilton was a legend, but Mercedes had helped him become one. There was no question that, in becoming the greatest Formula One driver that has ever lived, Hamilton was thankful to Mercedes, and he showed it every time he raced their car: 'Thanks, guys,' 'I'd like to thank everyone back in the factory.' These were phrases he said often, not because he had to, but because he meant it. He was grateful. Grateful to everyone who worked at the factory. Grateful to the team that went to the races with him. Grateful to Bono. To Toto, and to Niki Lauda. Hamilton knew that success was a team game. Equally, Mercedes knew Hamilton was a pivotal part of that.

But for all the incredible statistics, the amazing results, the highs, and the success, there were the lows. Hamilton endured two years with a difficult Mercedes that refused to perform: he was battered to bits by his own car with relentless porpoising. On top of this, despite his pleas to change the design philosophy, Mercedes simply hadn't listened. So, he was breaking up with his long-time partner, and, as everyone knows, breaking up is hard to do, especially when it goes on for a year.

Hamilton, a seven-time world champion, still thought of Mercedes in his last season. Despite him resolutely outperforming Russell in 2023, the press in some areas, and even some drivers-turned-pundits, questioned if he still had what it took to deliver. The facts were in black and white in

2023 on the lap times each weekend compared to his teammate. In 2024, Hamilton had the decency to let Russell take the new parts first so he could gain an advantage in some races. While the team had publicly said Hamilton would not be disadvantaged, this would be unlikely to achieve: any employee leaving a company, no matter how senior or junior, faces a shift in dynamics once their move is announced. Understandably, Mercedes' focus fell on Russell – that is just the nature of business. Hamilton knew this, but it's fair to say it would have hurt during the season.

As Hamilton slid on his helmet and gloves for his last qualifying session with Mercedes, everything he had been through was in his hands. In his feet. In the feel of the steering wheel. In his ears, with Bono's voice guiding him. There was only one thing on his mind: get a good qualifying and end on a high. As the old Formula One saying goes: if you can't win, the only true benchmark is whether you can beat your teammate. Could Hamilton do it one last time?

His hopes of reaching Q3 were dashed when Kevin Magnussen in the Haas drove over a bollard, which flew into Hamilton's path and lodged under the Mercedes, blocking airflow and destroying his downforce. He was out of Q1 and would start in 16th place.

Russell, with no bollards to contend with, sailed into Q3 and qualified 7th. Surely, coming from 16th to beat Russell was too much to ask?

Some had said he was 'over the hill,' 'too old,' or wasn't giving 100%. But this was Lewis Hamilton—the greatest Formula One driver ever. He had to beat the bollard and the baggage thrown his way. 'Still I Rise.' Wolff, watching from the garage, could only bow his head in frustration.

Elsewhere, McLaren looked strong, with Norris and Piastri locking out the front row. It was a big moment for McLaren, a team that hadn't won the Constructors' title in 27 years. Zak Brown was punching the air.

Ferrari, however, was struggling. Leclerc's fastest Q2 time was deleted for going outside track limits, dropping him down the order. His hopes of second place in the Drivers' Championship were slipping away.

The final race. The cars lined up. The grandstands glowed in the soft light of the evening sunset, with fans in summer clothes, enjoying the 26-degree heat and the end-of-season atmosphere.

For Hamilton, this was it. His last time racing with Mercedes. How much of a gap could he close to Russell?

His dad's voice came to him softly: "Do your talking on the track." "Rise above it, son."

The lights went out, and Verstappen seemed to find another gear, his Red Bull surging forward. But, as they approached Turn 1, he made contact with Piastri's McLaren, sending him spinning and to the back of the field. Zak Brown's blood pressure must have been through the roof. Verstappen quickly received a ten-second penalty.

Norris got away cleanly, putting his head down. Sainz set off in pursuit, but within half a lap, Norris had bolted.

Hamilton had chosen hard tyres, while most were on mediums. By Lap 7, he was up to 12th. Russell, still in fourth on mediums, was ahead. Hamilton kept pushing.

By Lap 10, Leclerc had pushed the Ferrari into sixth. Things were now looking tricky for McLaren, with Sainz in second and Piastri still stuck in 17th.

By mid-race, Hamilton had moved to fifth, just behind Russell. Now just eight seconds behind his teammate, could he catch him?

Surely someone as 'over the hill' as Hamilton couldn't do it? Surely the critics were right—he was no longer fast enough.

But Hamilton kept going, wringing every bit of performance from the Mercedes, the car dancing and glinting under the lights.

Bottas, in his last-ever Formula One race, gave Magnussen a nudge on Lap 31. The two collided, locking wheels. Bottas retired immediately with broken suspension. Magnussen limped to the end of the race.

Not long after Bottas's crash, Hamilton made his final pit stop. The hard tyres came off, the medium tyres went on. As the pit stops shook out, Hamilton rejoined 18 seconds behind Russell—18 seconds to make up in 22 laps.

With ten laps to go, it was all to play for. McLaren's Norris was in the lead, with Sainz five seconds back in second. Leclerc was third. Russell held fourth in the Mercedes, but Hamilton was pushing his medium tyres to the limit and closing in.

With four laps to go, Hamilton was just under four seconds behind Russell.

The laps counted down. One more to go. Hamilton's final lap for Mercedes in Formula One.

Russell was still in fourth, but Hamilton—his medium tyres at their limit after 17 flat-out laps—was relentlessly closing in.

Hamilton placed the Mercedes right on the edge, pushing the car to its absolute limit. Ahead, beyond view, another battle was being decided. Norris appeared to be holding his nerve at the front. His teammate, Piastri, had clawed his way to tenth—the final points-paying position. If McLaren held on for just half a lap more, they would reclaim the Constructors' World Championship for the first time in 27 years.

Entering the final lap, Hamilton was within DRS range. Could he pass? Hamilton had a 'shelf life,' Toto Wolff had said. *A shelf life.* Maybe, but not yet.

Rise above it, son.

Norris crossed the line, clinching victory, and McLaren were crowned Constructors' Champions. Zak Brown leapt in delight, shouting, cheering, and hugging everyone within reach. The McLaren garage erupted. Two battles were decided simultaneously: McLaren had ended a 27-year drought to reclaim the Constructors' title, and Norris secured second place in the World Drivers' Championship.

Only one fight remained—Hamilton versus Russell.

Exiting Turn 5, Hamilton got a superb exit and hammered down the straight. The Mercedes strained every sinew. As Hamilton closed on Russell at 200mph, the car began to bounce—a harsh reminder of three years of physical and emotional suffering. *We don't need to change the car; we know what we're doing.*

Hamilton rapidly closed in within the DRS zone as they approached Turn 6. Russell knew exactly where Hamilton was and moved slightly to the inside, revealing his hand. The unspoken message was clear: *"I know you're here, Lewis, but you won't do it—there are only nine corners left."*

Hamilton rolled off the brakes, letting the Mercedes breathe to the outside of Turn 6 to get maximum traction on the exit, which would set him up for the long back straight. Russell, while not taking a particularly tight line into Turn 6, had compromised his exit. The golden rule of motor racing - or rule number one - has always been 'carry as much speed down the next straight as possible,' and Russell had just broken it.

As Norris crossed the line, fireworks exploded, but Hamilton still had one rocket of his own to launch.

As they entered Turn 9, a long left-hand hairpin, Russell made his customary defensive move when under pressure. He moved to the middle of the track to block the inside line. A rookie error. Hamilton braked as late as his car would allow on the outside. As they entered the last fifty metres before the corner, sparks flew off Russell's Mercedes as his car bottomed out. Bottoming out—losing braking effectiveness—another mistake.

For Hamilton, it all slowed down. Time went into slow motion, going backwards.

His karting titles wheeled into focus: *1995 Cadet Kart, 1996 MSA Kartmasters, 1997 Super One Yamaha, 1999 Italian and European, and the 2000 World Cup.*

Hamilton came off the brakes, turned in, fed in more throttle, easing the Mercedes wider towards the wall and the marbles. Could a driver with a 'shelf life' pass around the outside, on marbles?

*Formula Renault Champion, 2003. Formula 3 Champion, 2005. GP2 Champion, 2006.*

As both Mercedes clipped the left-hand apex, Hamilton was inches from Russell, both cars starting to drift wide. A collision seemed inevitable.

*Seven Formula One World Championships.*

Hamilton pinned the throttle, the car breathed, just like it had on pole in Hungary, just like it had on every lap of every circuit for 29 years. He corrected a minor bit of oversteer and shot past Russell.

*"Do your talking on the track."*

Not bad for someone over the hill, past his best, not giving 100% and no longer good enough.

Frédéric Vasseur clearly knew what he was doing when he signed Hamilton to Ferrari, that was for certain.

Hamilton crossed the finish line in fourth place. He guided the Mercedes towards the pit wall, acknowledging the team that had been his family for 12 unforgettable years. Russell rolled home behind him. In fifth.

**McLaren**

Zak Brown was understandably proud of his team and praised everyone for their incredible work. The sign of a true leader is to take none of the credit and give it to those who work for you. But the truth was, Brown had steered the McLaren ship off the rocks.

As captain of the papaya boat, he had navigated through some dangerous waters. In 2015, the team lost some major sponsors, and revenue took a hit. Brown had joined at the end of 2016 when the team was struggling, the ship was sinking. He brought in new sponsors, made key staff changes, made some hard decisions, and kept the boat on an even keel.

Then the iceberg arrived in the form of Covid-19 in 2020, and the team was just months away from going under. Brown stuck with it, using his commercial expertise and experience to form new relationships and secure new partners to back the company. While there was no question he had two incredible drivers in Norris and Piastri, a genius leader in Andrea Stella, and a superb bunch of staff and investors, Brown had been the one at the helm, steering them into blue waters. He rightly deserved to enjoy the moment and be happy.

As the teams left Abu Dhabi, Hamilton said goodbye not only to Mercedes and Toto Wolff and all his mechanics and colleagues, but also to Peter Bonnington, 'Bono'. Bonnington had been there for Hamilton since the beginning, every step of the way.

Bonnington had been promoted by Mercedes in August to head of race engineering, perhaps in an attempt to retain him. Who knew? It was natural for people to ask if Hamilton was going to take Bonnington with him to Ferrari. Hamilton's response, as you would expect, was that he just wanted what was best for Bono and his family, whether this meant being with him or without him. It was typical Hamilton – he cared about others and wanted what was best for them. No self-serving, no narcissism, no selfishness: he was generous and caring to a fault.

And this is what makes Hamilton who he is. Much like Senna before him, he is an unbelievable athlete, incredibly gifted, but also very complex and deeply caring. Senna used to go out of his way to check on fellow drivers in distress, always seeking them out after an incident to ensure they were okay. Hamilton has shown time and again how much he cares about others, and this was no more evident when he saw Hubert's crash at Spa unfold on live television, spontaneously reacting and hoping Hubert was okay. That response, and his reaction, in the heat of the moment, could not be faked.

People need to remember that Hamilton is more than just a figure in the spotlight. He is a human being, like everyone else. What sets him apart is his genuine concern for others, a trait not always seen in the world of elite athletes. The world could do with more of the care and generosity Hamilton shows.

As Hamilton signed off from Mercedes, he could look to the future and Maranello.

But why would he go there? What is the legend that is Ferrari?

# The Legacy of Ferrari – A Journey Through Time

The history of Scuderia Ferrari is a tapestry woven with passion, innovation, triumphs, and the indomitable spirit of competition. Founded by Enzo Ferrari, the name has become synonymous with excellence in motorsport and automotive engineering. The conception of Ferrari, its key figures, and the legendary drivers who have etched their names into the annals of racing history is a story of folklore.

**The Birth of a Legend: Enzo Ferrari and the Conception of Scuderia Ferrari**

*Early Beginnings*

Enzo Anselmo Giuseppe Maria Ferrari was born on 18 February 1898, in Modena, Italy. From a young age, Enzo was captivated by the world of automobiles and racing. His passion was ignited when his father took him to watch a race in Bologna, sparking a lifelong dedication to motorsport.

After serving in World War I, Enzo pursued a career in racing, joining the Costruzioni Meccaniche Nazionali (CMN) team in 1919. He later became a works driver for Alfa Romeo, where he achieved considerable success. However, Enzo's ambitions extended beyond driving; he aspired to build and lead his own team.

*Founding Scuderia Ferrari*

In 1929, Enzo Ferrari established Scuderia Ferrari in Modena, initially as a racing division for Alfa Romeo. The term "Scuderia" translates to "stable," reflecting the team's origins in supporting gentleman drivers with their racing pursuits. Under Enzo's leadership, Scuderia Ferrari became Alfa

Romeo's official racing team, managing the factory racing cars and nurturing driving talent.

By 1933, financial strains led Alfa Romeo to withdraw its official support, leaving Scuderia Ferrari to operate independently. Despite limited resources, the team continued to compete, demonstrating Enzo's resourcefulness and determination.

*The Prancing Horse Emblem*

The iconic Cavallino Rampante, or "Prancing Horse," became Ferrari's emblem through a chance encounter. In 1923, Enzo met Countess Paolina Baracca, the mother of Italian World War I flying ace Francesco Baracca. She suggested that Enzo adopt her son's emblem of the prancing horse for good luck. Enzo embraced the symbol, adding a yellow background to represent Modena, and thus, the emblem became synonymous with Ferrari.

*Transition to Manufacturing*

World War II interrupted racing activities, and in 1939, Enzo severed ties with Alfa Romeo due to contractual obligations that prevented him from racing under his name for four years. He founded Auto Avio Costruzioni, producing machine tools and aircraft components.

During 1942 Ferrari began the process of moving the company that bore his name from Modena to Maranello in response to concerns about the expanding war in Italy. Maranello became Ferrari’s base and the location where its cars were built.

In 1947, Enzo unveiled the first car bearing his name, the Ferrari 125 S. Powered by a 1.5-litre V12 engine, the 125 S marked Ferrari's official entry into automobile manufacturing and racing under its own banner. It was a sports car design, and the car debuted at the Piacenza Circuit, and although it retired due to a fuel pump issue, it won the Rome Grand Prix nine days later. A year later, to fund his racing programme, Ferrari began producing and selling road cars, marking the start of Ferrari's commercial success.

In the 1950s Ferrari sports cars became one of the most dominant forces in the industry. At the same time, their Formula One legacy started to take off. However, as with many other drivers, from other teams, some of the great Ferrari legends were killed in the 1950s in accidents, the decade being a particularly dangerous era in motorsport: Ferrari drivers such as the great Alberto Ascari and Peter Collins lost their lives during this difficult period.

The 1960s marked a turning point for Ferrari as it solidified its position in Formula One, winning two Constructors' Championships, while continuing to dominate the sports car market.

In 1969, in an effort to expand the business Ferrari sold a 50% share to Fiat (this stake was expanded even further in the late 1980s when Fiat owned 90% of the company).

In 1971 work started on the construction of a test track on farmland owned by Ferrari at the Maranello site next to the town of Fiorano Modenese: the circuit ultimately being named Fiorano. Ferrari became the only Formula One manufacturer to have its own test track. The circuit was short, but it was designed to replicate some of the more challenging aspects of corners from existing circuits such as Monaco, Zandvoort and Nürburgring. The different left and right corners, and use of inclines and cambers helped Ferrari design both racing and road cars that had effective aerodynamics. Traction, a significant factor in any racing car, as well as mechanical grip. would also be tested with some tighter corners designed at the circuit.

The Ferrari Formula One team did well in the late 1970s and early 1980s, largely as a result of one of their best ever engineers and some famous drivers, winning six titles. However, after that, Ferrari went into a decline, not winning another Constructors' title until 1999.

Like any racing organisation, key people, whether they be managers or drivers, played significant roles in Ferrari's legacy.

## Key Figures in Ferrari's History

*Enzo Ferrari: The Founder*

Enzo Ferrari's vision and uncompromising drive for excellence laid the foundation for Ferrari's legacy. Known for his charismatic yet enigmatic personality, Enzo was deeply involved in every aspect of his team. His philosophy centred around the belief that the engine was the soul of the car, famously stating, "Aerodynamics are for people who can't build engines."

Enzo's management style was both revered and criticised. He demanded absolute commitment from his team and drivers, fostering a culture of intense competition even within the team. This approach often led to internal rivalries but also propelled the team to extraordinary heights. His results began to speak for themselves, as he enticed renowned specialists to become part of the Ferrari team. Ferrari passed away in 1988, aged 90.

*Luigi Chinetti: The Ambassador*

Luigi Chinetti was instrumental in introducing Ferrari to the international stage, particularly in the United States. Chinetti, who was born in Italy, emigrated to America in World War II was a skilled mechanic at an early age. He was also a skilled driver. Chinetti won Ferrari's first victory at the 24 Hours of Le Mans in 1949. Recognising the potential market, he became the official importer of Ferraris to North America, establishing the brand's presence among American enthusiasts and contributing significantly to its commercial success. Chinetti passed away in 1994, aged 93.

*Mauro Forghieri: The Engineer*

Born in Modena in 1935, Forghieri joined Ferrari in 1960 after graduating with a degree in mechanical engineering. His talent quickly became apparent.

As Ferrari's chief engineer from the early 1960s to the late 1980s, Mauro Forghieri played a pivotal role in the team's technological advancements. He was responsible for designing some of the most successful Ferraris, including the 312 series. Forghieri's innovations in aerodynamics, chassis design, and engine development were crucial in maintaining Ferrari's competitiveness during a period of intense rivalry in Formula One. At a time when the racing drivers were the focus of the sport, Forghieri's achievements were often overlooked, but the numbers tell their own story.

Forghieri had some incredible innovations that transformed the sport, including what was believed to be the development of the first rear-mounted wing on a Formula One car, as well as implementing transverse gearboxes in the Ferrari 312T in 1975 (the 'T' meaning transverse). Under his technical leadership, Ferrari won the Constructors' Championship in 1964, 1975, 1976, and 1977, and Drivers' Championships with John Surtees, Niki Lauda, and Jody Scheckter.

Beyond Formula One, Forghieri also designed successful sports cars, contributing to Ferrari's victories in endurance racing. His engineering prowess and innovative designs cemented Ferrari's reputation for technological excellence for over a decade, giving them an international reputation. Forghieri passed away in late 2022 at the age of 87.

*John Barnard: the innovator*

Barnard brought modern carbon fibre composite construction to Formula One and designed the first semi-automatic gearbox used by Ferrari. Nigel Mansell would go on to comment about how ingenious the semi-automatic gearbox breakthrough was.

*Luca di Montezemolo: The Modernizer*

Luca Cordero di Montezemolo played a critical role in revitalising Ferrari during the 1990s and early 2000s. His legend and positive influence on modern day Ferrari cannot be understated: he was pivotal in turning Ferrari around.

Montezemolo dabbled in motor racing in some Fiat and Lancia cars before moving into management. He first joined Ferrari in 1973 as Enzo Ferrari's assistant and then became team manager. He oversaw Niki Lauda's first World Championship in 1975.

In 1976 Montezemolo was promoted within the FIAT group outside of Ferrari and the race team. His career blossomed and he diverged into some interesting sporting arenas such as the America's Cup yacht race and was also on the Committee for the Football World Cup which was held in Italy in 1990.

After Ferrari had been through a lean patch, struggling both commercially and on the track – its last Championship victory being in 1979, something needed to be done. In 1991 he was asked to return as Chairman and CEO. Using his considerable business acumen and breadth of experience, Montezemolo initiated a comprehensive restructuring, focusing on innovation, quality, and brand strength. He invested in both the racing team and the road car division. It wasn't long before his vision for change became a reality.

Montezemolo was instrumental in recruiting key personnel to Ferrari, including Jean Todt as Team Principal, Ross Brawn as Technical Director, Rory Byrne as Chief Designer, and convincing Michael Schumacher to join as lead driver. This became the Ferrari dream team of the early 2000s. Montezemolo's success came full circle when he was elected as Chairman of the FIAT Group in 2004.

Under Montezemolo's leadership, Ferrari experienced a renaissance, winning six consecutive Constructors'

Championships from 1999 to 2004 and re-establishing itself as a dominant force.

*Rory Byrne: The Designer*

Possibly the most under-recognised genius in modern Formula One, Rory Byrne was a key part of Ferrari's resurgence in the late 1990s and into the 2000s.

Rory Byrne's journey from a modest background in South Africa to becoming one of the most successful designers in Formula One history is a story of ingenuity, dedication, and quiet excellence. His role at Ferrari during their golden era from 1997 to 2006 was pivotal, contributing to an unprecedented streak of Championships that solidified the team's legacy in the sport.

Born in 1944, in Pretoria, South Africa, Rory Byrne displayed an early aptitude for science and engineering. He graduated from the University of the Witwatersrand with a degree in applied mathematics and physics, initially embarking on a career as a chemist. However, his passion for motorsport soon led him to pursue a different path.

Byrne began his involvement in racing by designing and building his own Formula Ford car in the early 1970s. His talents caught the attention of Ted Toleman, leading to a position as a designer for the Toleman Formula One team in 1981.

At Toleman, Byrne's engineering prowess started to shine. He was responsible for designing the TG184, the car in which Ayrton Senna famously finished second in the wet 1984 Monaco Grand Prix.

When Toleman was acquired by Benetton Formula in 1986, Byrne continued as the chief designer. His innovative work on aerodynamics and chassis design helped Benetton become increasingly competitive.

Under his technical direction, the Benetton B186 to B195 models saw significant improvements. The culmination of this

period was the 1994 and 1995 seasons when Michael Schumacher won back-to-back World Championships driving Byrne-designed cars.
In late 1996, following Schumacher's move to Ferrari, Rory Byrne was persuaded to join the Italian team, reuniting with Schumacher and Technical Director Ross Brawn.

Byrne took on the role of Chief Designer at Ferrari, facing the formidable task of ending the team's long Championship drought. Ferrari had not won a Constructors' Championship since 1983 or a Drivers' Championship since 1979.

Byrne's impact at Ferrari was immediate and profound. His design philosophy focused on creating cars with exceptional aerodynamics, balance, and reliability. In 1998, the Ferrari F300 marked a significant step forward. Byrne introduced a narrower car design to adapt to new regulations, which resulted in improved performance. Ferrari narrowly missed out on the Championship that year.

The Ferrari F1-2000 was the car that ended Ferrari's 21-year wait for a Drivers' Championship. Byrne's design emphasised aerodynamic efficiency and mechanical grip. Michael Schumacher praised the car's balance and responsiveness.

The Ferrari F2002 was regarded as one of the best Formula One cars ever built. The F2002 dominated the 2002 season with 15 wins out of 17 races. This was at a time when the average finishing rate for a Grand Prix, when there were no restrictions on the number of engines in use, was around a 60-65%. Contrast that with 2022 when Formula One cars had an 85-90% finish rate, and it's easy to see why the F2002 was considered one of the greats. Ross Brawn has spoken fondly of how the work Byrne had done was transformative, citing innovation in aerodynamics and weight distribution.

The Ferrari F2004 was another masterpiece and secured both the Drivers' and Constructors' Championships with ease.

Byrne was known for being methodical and collaborative. He prioritised close communication with drivers and engineers to fine-tune every aspect of the car. Those who worked with him commented on his calm and considered approach to every aspect of his craft and how Byrne would shun the spotlight.

His legacy continues to inspire engineers and designers, reminding the motorsport world that innovation, dedication, and collaboration are the cornerstones of greatness. Byrne stands alongside legends like Forghieri and Barnard, not just as a great designer but as an architect of an era. His contributions transcended car design; they fostered a culture of excellence and teamwork that became the hallmark of Ferrari's success. Like Hamilton, Byrne firmly believed success in Formula One was about the team and not individuals.

Despite going into 'retirement' in 2009, aged 65, Byrne has been called back on occasion to help Ferrari when they have been in a downward spiral. Notably, after Ferrari's slump to sixth in 2020, he came back to help with the 2022, 2023, and 2024 cars, which helped Ferrari secure second, third, and second respectively in each season. Not bad going for a man in his late 70s.

## Great Drivers Who Shaped Ferrari's Legacy

When we think of Ferrari, as well as their beautiful cars, we also think of 'the greats'—those drivers whose names are synonymous with the brand, with the vision, and with the passion.

*Alberto Ascari (1950–1953)*

Alberto Ascari was Ferrari's first superstar driver, securing back-to-back Formula One World Championships in 1952 and 1953. He dominated the 1952 season and became the youngest ever world champion at the age of 34. Known for his smooth driving style and relentless consistency, Ascari gave Ferrari its initial taste of championship success.

His partnership with Ferrari set the standard for future driver-team relationships within the Scuderia. Ascari left Ferrari in 1954 to drive for Alfa Romeo. Sadly, while testing a Ferrari 750 sports car in Monza, Ascari was killed on a high-speed corner. This corner was later renamed the Variante Ascari, a name still in use today.

*Juan Manuel Fangio (1956)*

The Argentine maestro, Juan Manuel Fangio, joined Ferrari in 1956 and secured his fourth World Championship with the team. Fangio's time at Ferrari was brief but impactful. His meticulous approach to racing and ability to extract performance from any car reinforced Ferrari's reputation for excellence.

Fangio's championship with Ferrari solidified the team's dominance during the era. He became what is considered one of the greatest Formula One drivers of all time, winning five world championships with four different teams. Fangio was one of the earliest drivers to associate fitness with performance: he did not look athletic, but he would train hard for endurance events, so he was at his best.

Ayrton Senna, one of Lewis Hamilton's idols, said of Fangio, "Fangio is a myth, a legend. The best driver there ever was." Senna repeated a similar view over and over in various interviews over many years. Murray Walker, the famous commentator, once said: "Senna often spoke of Fangio with profound respect. He saw in Fangio a pure embodiment of racing spirit, something that transcended time."

Fangio's move from Mercedes to Ferrari in 1956 is a distant echo of what will come for Hamilton in 2025. Fangio's move, and the adoration of Senna, who he met in 1990, cannot be understated in the context of Hamilton wanting to race for Ferrari. Fangio made it to a relatively old age, dying at 84.

*Phil Hill (1958–1962)*

Phil Hill became the first American Formula One World Champion while driving for Ferrari in 1961. His victory was bittersweet, overshadowed by the tragic death of his teammate Wolfgang von Trips at the Italian Grand Prix.

Hill's technical understanding of cars and dedication to racing contributed to Ferrari's engineering developments during his tenure.

Hill retired shortly after winning the championship, citing personal reasons. The terrible accident earlier in the season of his teammate Wolfgang von Trips was a contributing factor to his decision.

*John Surtees (1963–1966)*

John Surtees holds the unique distinction of being the only person to win World Championships on both two and four wheels. Surtees won four 500cc World Championships in motorcycle racing in 1956, 1958, 1959, and 1960 for MV Agusta. He joined Ferrari in 1963 and secured the Formula One World Championship in 1964.

His background in motorcycle racing brought a different perspective to car handling and setup, influencing Ferrari's approach to vehicle dynamics. Surtees went on to be an ambassador for motorsport and received royal recognition in the UK, being awarded the MBE and OBE.

Interestingly, in a distant echo of Surtees' racing heritage with MV Agusta and Ferrari, Hamilton's favourite motorbike is his own MV Agusta F4 LH44. Built in 2017 in collaboration with MV Agusta, only 44 units were produced.

*Niki Lauda (1974–1977)*

Niki Lauda's tenure at Ferrari marked a transformative period. After joining the team in 1974, he worked closely with engineers to improve the car's performance, leading to World Championships in 1975 and 1977. Lauda's analytical approach and feedback were key in advancing Ferrari's technical capabilities. His rivalry with McLaren's James Hunt in 1976, particularly after his near-fatal crash at the Nürburgring, became one of the most dramatic stories in motorsport history.

Lauda was instrumental in persuading Lewis Hamilton to move to Mercedes and praised Hamilton's abilities many times. One of Lauda's greatest praises for Hamilton was: "I've raced against some of the best—Prost, Senna—but Lewis is on that same level. He has a unique gift, and he's continuously pushing the boundaries."

Lauda would also go on to comment over the years on how focused Hamilton was, and how dedicated he was, with an incredible ability to stay calm under pressure. Lauda would be greatly missed by Hamilton after he sadly passed away in May 2019 at the age of 70.

*Gilles Villeneuve (1977–1982)*

Gilles Villeneuve was a driver whose fearless style and charismatic personality endeared him to fans and Enzo Ferrari alike. Although he never won a World Championship, Villeneuve's performances were legendary.

His battles on the track, such as the famous duel with René Arnoux at the 1979 French Grand Prix, showcased his extraordinary skill and determination. Villeneuve was killed during qualifying in an accident involving Jochen Mass at the 1982 Belgian Grand Prix.

The Circuit Gilles Villeneuve in Montreal bears his name. It's perhaps fitting that the most successful Formula One driver to have ever driven this track is Hamilton.

*Michael Schumacher (1996–2006)*

Jean Todt was lured to Ferrari in 1993 by Luca di Montezemolo, and Todt made it his key objective to lure Ross

Brawn and Michael Schumacher to the Ferrari team. This resulted in an era of success at Ferrari that was unprecedented.

When Michael Schumacher joined Scuderia Ferrari in 1996, he embarked on one of the most remarkable chapters in Formula One history. The German driver, already a two-time World Champion with Benetton, accepted the challenge of returning the iconic Italian team to its former glory. Over the next decade, Schumacher and Ferrari forged a partnership that would dominate the sport, capturing five consecutive Drivers' Championships from 2000 to 2004 and redefining what it meant to achieve excellence in Formula One during that era.

Schumacher's decision to leave Benetton for Ferrari was met with both excitement and scepticism. Ferrari had not won a Drivers' Championship since 1979, and the team was struggling with reliability and competitiveness.

While specific quotes are scarce, Martin Brundle noted that Schumacher's move was bold and carried significant risk, as Ferrari had not been a championship-winning team for many years. He recognised that Ferrari had the resources and heritage to return to the top but stressed that it would require substantial effort and time.

In an interview with *BBC Sport* in (1996), Murray Walker said: "Michael's move to Ferrari is one of the most exciting developments in recent Formula One history. He's taking on a monumental challenge, but if anyone can bring success back to Ferrari, it's him."

In his debut season with Ferrari, Schumacher faced technical difficulties but managed to secure three victories. His win at the 1996 Spanish Grand Prix in torrential rain is often cited as one of his greatest drives.

The late 1990s saw Schumacher narrowly miss out on championships due to a combination of mechanical failures and fierce competition. In 1997, Schumacher was disqualified from the championship after a controversial collision with Jacques Villeneuve at the European Grand Prix.

In 1998, a puncture ended his title hopes at the Japanese Grand Prix.

In 1999, a broken leg from a crash at Silverstone sidelined Schumacher for six races.

In 2000, Schumacher clinched his third World Championship and Ferrari's first Drivers' title in 21 years. Further titles followed in 2001, 2002, 2003, and 2004.

By 2005, changes in regulations and emerging competition began to challenge Ferrari's dominance, and in 2006, Schumacher announced he would retire at the end of the season—only to return later at Mercedes before handing over his seat to Hamilton.

*Kimi Räikkönen (2007–2009, 2014–2018)*

Kimi Räikkönen secured the World Championship for Ferrari in 2007, the team's last Drivers' title to date. Known as "The Iceman" for his cool demeanour, Räikkönen's raw speed and racecraft delivered crucial victories. His return to Ferrari in 2014 added experience to the team during a period of transition.

*Fernando Alonso (2010–2014)*

Fernando Alonso joined Ferrari with two World Championships already to his name. During his time with the team, he came close to securing additional titles, finishing as runner-up three times. Alonso's relentless driving and ability to outperform the car's limitations demonstrated his exceptional talent and dedication.

*Sebastian Vettel (2015–2020)*

Sebastian Vettel, a four-time World Champion, aimed to emulate his hero Michael Schumacher's success at Ferrari.

While championships eluded him, Vettel secured numerous victories and played a significant role in re-establishing Ferrari as a championship contender. His professionalism and experience were valuable assets to the team.

*Charles Leclerc (2019–Present)*

Charles Leclerc represents Ferrari's future. Graduating from the Ferrari Driver Academy, he quickly showcased his potential with victories and pole positions. Leclerc's blend of one-lap speed, maturity, and connection with the team evokes memories of past Ferrari legends. Under Vasseur's guidance, he is maturing into a complete driver.

**Ferrari's Enduring Legacy**

Ferrari's history is rich with triumphs and tribulations, embodying the very essence of motorsport. The team is driven by passion and innovation and is regarded as a symbol of excellence worldwide.

*Le Mans and Sports Car Racing*

Beyond Formula One, Ferrari has a storied history in sports car racing, particularly at the 24 Hours of Le Mans. Throughout the 1950s and 1960s, Ferrari dominated the event, with legendary cars like the 250 Testa Rossa and 250 GTO. Drivers such as Mike Hawthorn, Luigi Chinetti, and Phil Hill contributed to Ferrari's legacy at Le Mans, cementing its reputation across multiple disciplines.

*Technological Innovation*

Ferrari's commitment to technological advancement has led to numerous innovations in automotive engineering. From pioneering aerodynamic designs to advancements in engine technology, the team's developments have often transcended the racetrack, influencing the production of road cars.

*Ferrari Road Cars*

Ferrari's road cars are a direct reflection of its racing heritage. Models like the 250 GTO, F40, Enzo, and LaFerrari represent the pinnacle of automotive engineering and design. The blend of performance, style, and exclusivity makes Ferrari road cars coveted by enthusiasts and collectors worldwide. In 2023, a Ferrari 250 GTO—the holy grail of classic Ferrari road cars—sold for $51.7 million at RM Sotheby's.

*Ferrari's Cultural Impact*

Ferrari transcends motorsport, symbolising Italian excellence and luxury. The brand's iconic status is celebrated in popular culture, art, and fashion. The Ferrari red, the prancing horse emblem, and the roar of its engines evoke emotion and admiration beyond the realm of racing fans.

Ferrari's history is defined by ambition, innovation, and an unyielding passion for racing. From its founding by Enzo Ferrari to the present day, Scuderia Ferrari has been moulded by visionary leaders, exceptional engineers, and remarkable drivers. But it is the tifosi—Ferrari's legendary fans—who truly bring the story to life, with their unmatched passion, enthusiasm, and unwavering devotion to the team.

With 18 years in Formula One, Lewis Hamilton has a deep understanding of Ferrari's legacy and its influence on both his career and the sport's evolution. The Ferrari legend continues to inspire new generations of fans and drivers. Hamilton's move to the team promises to benefit not only Ferrari and the tifosi, but also the sport as a whole—and perhaps most significantly, it offers new opportunities for Hamilton himself.

# Red Dawn

Throughout his illustrious career, Lewis Hamilton has consistently relied on his gut instincts when making important decisions and key career moves. Time and again, his intuitive judgments have proven to be spot-on, guiding him to unparalleled success in Formula One.

Now, Hamilton stands at the threshold of a new era—a Red Dawn—where he can write a new chapter in his legacy, solidifying his place alongside all-time greats such as Ascari, Fangio, Senna, Prost, Schumacher, and Lauda.

The Ferrari Formula One cars of 2024 were fast and reliable, capable of pushing McLaren to the very last race of the season in the battle for the Constructors' Championship. Under the stewardship of Frederic Vasseur, Hamilton's mentor and close friend, Ferrari has undergone a remarkable transformation. Incremental changes made over recent years have eradicated most of the unforced errors that once plagued the team, creating a cohesive and strong outfit. The cars are faster, more reliable, and finely tuned, with meticulous attention given to every detail.

Charles Leclerc, Hamilton's new teammate, has flourished under Vasseur's guidance, maturing into a complete driver. Together, Hamilton and Leclerc form a formidable partnership, poised to lead Ferrari's charge for the Constructors' Championship. With all essential elements in place—competitive machinery, astute leadership, and supreme driving talent—Hamilton is poised to write another historic chapter, securing his legacy alongside the legends who preceded him.

Hamilton epitomises the very essence of what Ferrari fans value in their drivers: unparalleled speed, charisma, modesty, and an unyielding fighting spirit. This spirit echoes the legendary Nigel Mansell, affectionately dubbed 'Il Leone'—

Italian for 'The Lion'—by the passionate tifosi. Mansell was celebrated for his fearless and aggressive driving style, coupled with unwavering determination and bravery on the track. He would never give up, just as Hamilton refused to relent on the final lap of his final race for Mercedes in Abu Dhabi in 2024, overcoming Russell in the process. This resilience is precisely what the tifosi crave—a driver who pushes to the absolute limit, every second of every lap.

Hamilton embodies Mansell's lion-like qualities in abundance. Whether engaging in battles with Max Verstappen at Silverstone or competing against Fernando Alonso in his rookie season at McLaren, Hamilton consistently displays his tenacity. His capacity to push beyond perceived limits, maintain composure under pressure, and never surrender mirrors the fighting spirit deeply admired by the tifosi. With every race, Hamilton displays extraordinary talent and is poised to continue the enduring legacy of Ferrari's most cherished champions, carving his own place among the pantheon of motorsport greats.

Having been part of the dominant Mercedes team for years, Hamilton understands what it takes to build and maintain a winning culture. At Ferrari, he will bring a fresh perspective—one deeply rooted in technical expertise and the necessity of seamless collaboration. Having witnessed Mercedes' rise to dominance through meticulous attention to detail, Hamilton recognises the importance of ensuring that every element of a team—from engineering departments to drivers—works in harmony. His insights will prove invaluable as Ferrari seeks to reclaim its place at the pinnacle of the sport.

Hamilton's driving philosophy revolves around fine-tuning the car to his precise preferences, working closely with engineers to unlock maximum potential. Whether optimising cockpit position, adjusting spring and damper settings, or refining details as minor as steering wheel configuration, Hamilton consistently seeks perfection. At Ferrari, these skills will be essential—not just relying on raw talent but maximising every fraction of performance from the machinery. His meticulous approach to both racecraft and car setup promises to provide Ferrari with the crucial edge it needs to consistently challenge at the highest level.

Hamilton's leadership qualities make him the perfect fit for Ferrari. He has repeatedly demonstrated his ability to inspire and guide others, whether mentoring teammates at Mercedes or pushing his team to develop championship-winning cars. In Leclerc, Ferrari possesses a talented young driver who will benefit immensely from Hamilton's guidance. Together, they have the potential to form a powerful partnership, with Hamilton's vast experience complementing Leclerc's raw speed and immense promise.

Hamilton's leadership extends beyond driving skill; it encompasses mentality. He brings a calm and focused approach to every race, helping to steady the team during intense moments. Just as Schumacher's presence once transformed Ferrari into a dominant force, Hamilton's arrival could similarly elevate the entire organisation, bringing them closer to championship glory.

For Hamilton, joining Ferrari is more than merely a professional choice—it's a deeply personal journey connecting him directly with the team's legacy and its passionate supporters. Ferrari has always symbolised excellence in motorsport, and for a driver like Hamilton—who has achieved everything in Formula One—joining Ferrari represents the ultimate step in securing his place in racing history. His connection to Ferrari runs deep, having long admired the team, its rich heritage, and the profound way it resonates with fans worldwide.

Hamilton is not only an exceptionally gifted driver but also a role model who epitomises the values Ferrari fans cherish: hard work, humility, and determination. Despite his remarkable success, Hamilton has always remained grounded, openly acknowledging personal struggles and setbacks. His resilience under pressure, ability to bounce back from adversity, and unwavering dedication to his craft make him an ideal match for Ferrari. The tifosi have always revered drivers who combine humility with tenacity—qualities Hamilton embodies with ease.

Much like Federer in tennis or Messi in football, Hamilton represents the true spirit of sportsmanship. He has overcome significant personal challenges, from enduring bullying in his school years to facing the intense pressures of top-tier Formula One racing. Importantly, Hamilton has never hesitated to openly share these experiences, showing that true greatness transcends talent alone—it's defined by character.

Ferrari's resurgence is inevitable with a driver of Hamilton's calibre leading the charge. His vast experience and strong leadership provide exactly what Ferrari requires to reclaim its place at the pinnacle of motorsport. The essential elements—competitive machinery, strategic guidance from Vasseur, and a driver pairing that promises speed, consistency, and stability—are all firmly in place. With Hamilton leading the team, Ferrari can rediscover its dominance, allowing the tifosi to once again revel in the glory of success.

As the sun rises on the new 2025 season, Hamilton is a man transformed. The stresses, doubts, and negative emotions of 2024 have been left behind. Yet, a steep hill still lies ahead—a learning curve to conquer.

No one should doubt Lewis Hamilton in 2025. Just ask George Russell, who having started sixth in his final race alongside Hamilton, was passed by him on the last lap—around the outside—after Hamilton had started back in 16th place.

With the regulations remaining unchanged for 2025 ahead of the major overhaul in 2026, McLaren is undoubtedly the team to beat. Having invested heavily in a state-of-the-art, full-size wind tunnel in recent years, McLaren will present a significant challenge for Hamilton, Ferrari, and the rest of the grid as they challenge for supremacy. With Piastri and Norris in formidable form—and set to only improve—the competition will be fierce.

While Red Bull has lost Adrian Newey, they still have Max Verstappen. Verstappen's talent remains undeniable, and he will continue to compete at the sharp end. Liam Lawson, confirmed as Verstappen's new teammate, is relatively untested and unlikely to contribute significantly during the season's opening months. Nevertheless, the team that once dominated Formula One now seems to be fading. Verstappen will undoubtedly win races, but his era of dominance appears to have reached its conclusion.

Mercedes, having eventually listened to Hamilton, now has a more competitive car. Their design philosophy shifted significantly in the latter half of 2024, with those concepts carrying over into the new season. As a result, Mercedes will be regular contenders within the top six, and both Russell and Antonelli could pick up race victories.

Realistically, Ferrari will not have the strongest car in 2025 unless there is an unexpected regulatory change (such as adjustments to side pods, wing dimensions, or wing flexibility), putting rival teams on the back foot. Such shake-ups have often occurred in Formula One history, so it remains to be seen whether any changes are forthcoming this year. Towards the end of 2024, several front-running teams appeared to exploit overly flexible front and rear wings to their advantage—hopefully, the FIA will step in to ensure a level playing field.

Under Vasseur's leadership, Ferrari has become a formidable outfit. The cars look sharper and more refined than ever, the team now operates as one cohesive unit, and Hamilton, dressed in Ferrari red, completes the picture perfectly. Leclerc's pace and their strong working relationship make this partnership one to watch.

Will Hamilton win? The question shouldn't be whether he'll win, but how many times. He will undoubtedly take victories with Ferrari in 2025. If the team maintains reliability and Hamilton and Leclerc continue building their impressive synergy, there's every reason to believe they can mount a serious title challenge.

What are the risks? The most significant one is Hamilton's relationship with his new engineer. Adjusting to Ferrari in 2025 will take time: a new language, different working methods, and an entirely distinct culture. In comparison to Schumacher, Hamilton finds himself at a disadvantage, as Schumacher greatly benefited from Ross Brawn bridging the technical and cultural differences within the team. Brawn served as the ideal link, seamlessly aligning Schumacher's working style with Ferrari's engineering approach.

For Hamilton to thrive, he ideally needs an engineer who instinctively understands his personal communication style—someone who is direct, concise, and decisive, particularly during high-pressure moments at 200mph. Historically, Ferrari's trackside communications have sometimes overwhelmed drivers with information, as seen with Sainz and Leclerc, impacting their focus during critical race situations.

Additionally, personal compatibility under pressure is crucial. When pivotal decisions arise, especially in challenging conditions such as wet races, Hamilton benefits most from someone who naturally shares his intuitive approach. This is not about nationality; it's about mutual understanding and aligned working methods. Even Bono, who shared an almost telepathic level of communication with Hamilton, didn't always get every call perfect. If Bono occasionally found it challenging, even with their strong personal rapport, it highlights just how important compatibility—rather than nationality alone—is for Hamilton's success at Ferrari.

The second key risk is technical. Can Ferrari avoid tripping over itself, both in adhering to the regulations and ensuring reliability? There will undoubtedly be races where the car fails to finish or doesn't pass scrutineering, but the key will be to minimise these issues.

Hamilton is unlikely to be fully integrated into the new car until Miami in May. The modern era punishes new entrants and those who switch teams due to the limited testing opportunities, meaning it will take Hamilton time to get to grips with both the technical aspects of the car and the softer skills: understanding the team, his colleagues, and how everything fits together. Despite this, there is every chance he will secure a few wins before then. McLaren, however, will be his biggest challenge.

His best opportunities will come once he fully understands the car and competes at circuits where he traditionally excels—and where Ferrari is expected to perform strongly. Tracks like China, Bahrain, Canada, Hungary, Monaco, Britain, Italy, and perhaps the United States could offer Hamilton significant chances. Of course, Charles Leclerc will also be a formidable teammate, and together, they form a partnership with the potential to push Ferrari back to the top.

Hamilton undoubtedly possesses the talent and determination needed to succeed at Ferrari. However, Vasseur must carefully consider pairing Hamilton with an engineer who complements his communication style. Vasseur has already indicated that Hamilton will not be joining a 'Mercedes-style' team but must instead adapt to Ferrari's unique way of working. This adjustment could present one of the biggest challenges. Modern Formula One cars are complex enough, and Hamilton's dyslexia adds an extra layer to his communication needs. Clear, concise, and intuitive dialogue with his engineer will be crucial.

Despite these challenges, Ferrari is on the rise. With Vasseur's leadership, the team has taken significant strides, and the car is set to be more competitive than ever. If Hamilton and Leclerc can continue to develop their synergy, there's every reason to believe they can fight for race wins and the championship.

One thing remains certain: Hamilton always rises above challenges, no matter how difficult, and with the right support, he is poised to add another legendary chapter to his career at Ferrari.

# Bibliography

Al Jazeera
Alpine F1
AP News
Aruani Grid
Aston Martin F1
Autosport
Autosprint.corrieredelosport.com
Autoweek
BBC Sports
BBC Top Gear
BenzWorld
Bleacher Report
British Medical Journal
British Vogue
Business Insider
Car Throttle
Channel 4
Checkeredflag.co.uk
China.org.cn
CNN
CNN Sports
ConceptCarz
Crash.net
Daily Mail
Daily Times UK
Dailymotion
ESPN
ESPN India
Essentially Sports
Euro News
Express UK
F1 Fansite

F1 Racing Magazine
F1 Technical
F1 World
F1-Fansite.com
F1i.Com
Facebook
Ferrari.com
FIA
FIA Karting
Firstpost
Firstsportz.com
Formula One TM
Formula Scout
Formulapedia
Fox Sports
Geo TV
GP Blog
GP Today.net
GQ
Grandprix.com
Grandprix247.com
HAAS F1
Harper's Bazaar
Herald Sun Australia
Honda News EU
Instagram
ITV F1 Sport
ITV Sport
ITV X
Jordan Times
Kart Racing League
LBC UK
MaxVerstappen.com
McLaren
McLaren Racing Heritage
McLaren.com

Dan Lynch

Men's Health
Mercedes AMG F1
Mercedes AMG Petronas Formula One Team
Mercedes Benz Italy
Mercedes-Benz Archive
Motorsport 101
Motorsport Magazine
Motorsport Week
Movistar
NBC Sports Network
New Wave Magazine
News.com.au
Pirelli.com
Pit Pass
Planet F1
PMW Magazine
Pulse NG
Racecar Engineering
Racefans
Racer.com
Racing News 365
Red Bull
Reuters
RN365
Road and Track
Rye House Kart Circuit
Sauber-Group.com
SB Nation
SBS Australia
Side Podcast
SilverArrows.net
Sky Sports
Sky Sports F1
SkySports.com
South China Morning Post
Sport 360
Sports Illustrated

SucceedFeed
Sydney Morning Herald
talkSPORT
The 42
The Guardian
The Independent
The Race
The Sports Rush
The Sun
The Telegraph
The Telegraph of India
The Times
The Week
Theformula1girl.com
Time Magazine
Times of India
TNT Sports
Twitter
Vanity Fair
Verstappen.com
Visa Cash App RB Formula One Team
Waltham Forest Dyslexia Association
Wikipedia
WilliamsF1
Wired.co.uk
X
YouTube

# Acknowledgements

I would like to express my heartfelt thanks to my wife for her unwavering support during the writing of this book. Your constant encouragement and belief in me kept me going through long days and late nights. To my friends, thank you for always being there to lift my spirits and for your patience as I navigated the ups and downs of writing. Particular thanks go to Mick, Alex, Jamie, and Kay.

A special thank you to my editor, R.D.A. Wild, for invaluable guidance and for pushing me to bring out the best in this manuscript. Your expertise was instrumental in shaping this book.

I also want to extend my gratitude to the many people in the motorsport world who took the time to share their stories, wisdom, and experiences with me. Your input was essential in making this biography as authentic and comprehensive as possible.

Notable thanks also go to the Association of Racing Driver Schools, where I first gained my competition licence back in the 1990s and learned how to race, to Three Sisters Circuit – Wigan, where I experienced my first ZIP Kart in 1989, and to Croft Motor Racing Circuit. Thanks also to Dr. Alec Laraway for his insights into acquired brain injuries in sports, RRadar for their helpful advice, and Tim Sugden Motorsport.

I am especially grateful to Claire Williams, Williams Racing, and Red Bull for their extraordinary kindness in 2004. During a difficult time, they went above and beyond to take a terminally ill 10-year-old child and their family through their factories, providing them with an unforgettable day of generosity and care. Your compassion is something I will never forget.

Extra special thanks go to Daniele Paglino for the incredible photography. Your work truly brings the book to life. Also, a big thank you to Taka Suzuki for the equally brilliant photos. Thank you both for your contributions.

Lastly, I want to thank my readers—your support means everything. I hope this book meets your expectations and gives you the same joy and inspiration I experienced while writing it.

# Dedication

This book is dedicated to the brave men and women of motorsport who have lost their lives in pursuit of their passion. From the fast tracks of Formula One to the rally stages and the IndyCar circuits, their courage, determination, and love for the sport continue to inspire and resonate with every fan and participant.

Their sacrifices have shaped the sport we know today, and they are never forgotten.
A special tribute is given to the drivers, crew members, marshals, and all those whose names may not be remembered by all, but whose contributions and ultimate sacrifices are forever etched in the history of motorsport.

While it is impossible to list every individual, we honour their memory and remain grateful for their dedication to the sport. Their legacy lives on in every race, every lap, and every moment on the track.

**David Ferrer**

**Jules Bianchi**

**Susan Cameron**

**Ayrton Senna**

**Robert Foote**

**Roland Ratzenberger**

**Henry Surtees**

**Dan Wheldon**

**Paolo Gislimberti**

**Justin Wilson**

**Craig Breen**

**Michael Park**

**Elio de Angelis**

**Henri Toivonen**

# About the Author

Dan Lynch has motorsport in his blood. From an early age, he was surrounded by motorbikes and rally cars. In the 1980s, he raced a number of ZIP Karts on local tracks in the northwest of England. In the 1990s, he gained his British ARDS Competition licence and was on track for a career in touring cars in the UK, until a serious head injury forced him to step back from racing.

Once recovered, Dan shifted to a career that revolved around writing and investigative work, which took him to various parts of the world, experiencing life through different lenses.

His motorsport roots have never faded, and he has attended numerous Grand Prix in Europe and overseas, notably at Lewis Hamilton's debut in Australia in 2007, where he was cheering him on to the podium. Dan has followed Hamilton's career ever since.

Dan now lives in rural Lancashire, UK, where he enjoys running and walking. He is still passionate about engines and anything mechanical. Outside of motorsport, his main passions are his family and his pet cat.

A portion of the proceeds from this book will be donated to Headway, the brain injury charity, in recognition of the challenges faced by motorsport figures and others who have suffered head injuries, including drivers such as Jules Bianchi, Felipe Massa, Mika Häkkinen, and Fernando Alonso.

Printed in Dunstable, United Kingdom

72577985R10389